ROTH FAMILY FOUNDATION

Music in America Imprint

Michael P. Roth
and Sukey Garcetti
have endowed this
imprint to honor the
memory of their parents,
Julia and Harry Roth,
whose deep love of music
they wish to share
with others.

The publisher gratefully acknowledges the generous support of the Joseph Kerman Endowment of the American Musicological Society, funded in part by the National Endowment for the Humanities and the Andrew W. Mellon Foundation.

Nostalgia for the Future

CALIFORNIA STUDIES IN 20TH-CENTURY MUSIC

Richard Taruskin, General Editor

1. *Revealing Masks: Exotic Influences and Ritualized Performance in Modernist Music Theater*, by W. Anthony Sheppard
2. *Russian Opera and the Symbolist Movement*, by Simon Morrison
3. *German Modernism: Music and the Arts*, by Walter Frisch
4. *New Music, New Allies: American Experimental Music in West Germany from the Zero Hour to Reunification*, by Amy Beal
5. *Bartók, Hungary, and the Renewal of Tradition: Case Studies in the Intersection of Modernity and Nationality*, by David E. Schneider
6. *Classic Chic: Music, Fashion, and Modernism*, by Mary E. Davis
7. *Music Divided: Bartók's Legacy in Cold War Culture*, by Danielle Fosler-Lussier
8. *Jewish Identities: Nationalism, Racism, and Utopianism in Twentieth-Century Art Music*, by Klára Móricz
9. *Brecht at the Opera*, by Joy H. Calico
10. *Beautiful Monsters: Imagining the Classic in Musical Media*, by Michael Long
11. *Experimentalism Otherwise: The New York Avant-Garde and Its Limits*, by Benjamin Piekut
12. *Music and the Elusive Revolution: Cultural Politics and Political Culture in France, 1968–1981*, by Eric Drott
13. *Music and Politics in San Francisco: From the 1906 Quake to the Second World War*, by Leta E. Miller
14. *Frontier Figures: American Music and the Mythology of the American West*, by Beth E. Levy
15. *In Search of a Concrete Music*, by Pierre Schaeffer, translated by Christine North and John Dack
16. *The Musical Legacy of Wartime France*, by Leslie A. Sprout
17. *Arnold Schoenberg's* A Survivor from Warsaw *in Postwar Europe*, by Joy H. Calico
18. *Music in America's Cold War Diplomacy*, by Danielle Fosler-Lussier
19. *Making New Music in Cold War Poland: The Warsaw Autumn Festival, 1956–1968*, by Lisa Jakelski
20. *Treatise on Musical Objects: An Essay across Disciplines*, by Pierre Schaeffer, translated by Christine North and John Dack
21. *Nostalgia for the Future: Luigi Nono's Selected Writings and Interviews*, edited by Angela Ida De Benedictis and Veniero Rizzardi
22. *The* Doctor Faustus *Dossier: Arnold Schoenberg, Thomas Mann, and Their Contemporaries, 1930–1951*, edited by E. Randol Schoenberg, with an introduction by Adrian Daub

Nostalgia for the Future

Luigi Nono's Selected Writings and Interviews

EDITED BY
Angela Ida De Benedictis
and Veniero Rizzardi

UNIVERSITY OF CALIFORNIA PRESS

Translated by John O'Donnell

University of California Press, one of the most distinguished university presses in the United States, enriches lives around the world by advancing scholarship in the humanities, social sciences, and natural sciences. Its activities are supported by the UC Press Foundation and by philanthropic contributions from individuals and institutions. For more information, visit www.ucpress.edu.

University of California Press
Oakland, California

© 2018 by The Regents of the University of California

Library of Congress Cataloging-in-Publication Data

Names: Nono, Luigi, author. | De Benedictis, Angela Ida, editor. | Rizzardi, Veniero, editor.
Title: Nostalgia for the future : Luigi Nono's selected writings and interviews / edited by Angela Ida De Benedictis and Veniero Rizzardi.
Description: Oakland, California : University of California Press, [2018] | Series: California Studies in 20th-Century Music ; 21 | Includes bibliographical references and index. |
Identifiers: LCCN 2017053883 (print) | LCCN 2017056877 (ebook) | ISBN 9780520965027 () |
ISBN 9780520291195 (cloth : alk. paper) |
ISBN 9780520291201 (pbk. : alk. paper)
Subjects: LCSH: Nono, Luigi—Criticism and interpretation. | Music—20th century—History and criticism.
Classification: LCC ML410.N667 (ebook) | LCC ML410. N667 A25 2018 (print) | DDC 780.92—dc23
LC record available at https://lccn.loc.gov/2017053883

Manufactured in the United States of America

25 24 23 22 21 20 19 18
10 9 8 7 6 5 4 3 2 1

Contents

Preface ix

Introduction 1
OVERTURE. Clarifications (1956) 23

EXCURSUS I. An Autobiography of the Author
Recounted by Enzo Restagno (1987) 27

PART ONE. MUSICAL ANALYSIS
AND COMPOSITION 123

  1. Luigi Dallapiccola and the *Sex Carmina Alcaei* (ca. 1948) 125
  2. On the Development of Serial Technique (1956) 127
  3. The Development of Serial Technique (1957) 133
  4. Text—Music—Song (1960) 153
  5. [About *Il canto sospeso*] (1976) 179

EXCURSUS II. A Letter from Los Angeles (1965) 185

PART TWO. MUSIC ONSTAGE: FROM A
"THEATER OF IDEAS" TO THE "TRAGEDY
OF LISTENING"   *191*

   1. Some Clarifications on *Intolleranza 1960* (1962)   *193*
   2. Possibility and Necessity of a New Music Theater (1962)   *209*
   3. Play and Truth in the New Music Theater (1962)   *224*
   4. *Die Ermittlung*: A Musical and Theatrical Experience
      with Weiss and Piscator [Music and Theater] (1966)   *229*
   5. Toward *Prometeo:* Journal Fragments (1984)   *235*

Excursus III. Interview with Renato Garavaglia
(ca. 1979–80)   *247*

PART THREE. "CONSCIENCE, FEELINGS,
COLLECTIVE REALITY"   *263*

   1. Historical Presence of Music Today (1959)   *265*
   2. Music and Resistance (1963)   *273*
   3. Replies to Seven Questions by Martine Cadieu (1966)   *277*
   4. Music and Power (1969)   *287*
   5. In the Sierra and in the Parliament (1971)   *298*

Excursus IV. Technology to Discover a Universe of Sounds:
Interview with Walter Prati and Roberto Masotti (1983)   *311*

PART FOUR. PORTRAITS AND DEDICATIONS   *319*

   1. Josef Svoboda (1968)   *321*
   2. Remembering Two Musicians (1973)   *325*
   3. Victor Jara's Song (1974)   *328*
   4. Preface to Arnold Schoenberg's *Harmonielehre* (1977)   *332*
   5. Bartók the Composer (1981)   *338*
   6. For Helmut (1983)   *345*
   7. For Marino Zuccheri (1986)   *349*

Excursus V. Interview with Michelangelo Zurletti (1987)   *359*

PART FIVE. THE "POSSIBLE INFINITIES" 365
1. Error as a Necessity (1983) 367
2. Other Possibilities for Listening (1985) 370
3. Lecture at the Chartreuse in Villeneuve-les-Avignon (1989) 385

EXCURSUS VI. "Proust" Questionnaire (1986) 391

Notes 395
Bibliographic Notes and Comments to the Texts 451
Chronology of Nono's Works 471
General Index 479
Index of Luigi Nono's Works 489

Preface

> Dearest Nuria:
> Style can be merely external;
> Idea must be internal.
> I wish when you face such
> problems you might be guided
> by this discrimination, which
> was important to your father.
> —Arnold Schoenberg, June 1950

> Inscription by my father on the copy of *Style and Idea,* which he gave me when he received the first copies from the publisher (Philosophical Library, New York, 1950).

Rereading this inscription in the first American publication of Arnold Schoenberg's writings, I am reminded of the ideals which my husband, Luigi Nono, shared with my father, although they had never met.

This book is the first English language edition of Luigi Nono's writings, in interviews and in articles on a variety of topics. These writings provide access to information about so many aspects of his life, which include relationships with other major figures of the period, as well as insights into his works, which, I am certain, will inspire new performances of his music.

In his writings Nono usually expressed his ideas and/or told of his experiences—personal and musical—in as simple and comprehensible language as possible, even when the topic was complex. There was no attempt at writing "elegant" prose, no endeavor for stylistic ornamentation. The important thing is communication. Often his writings and his letters are telegraphic, saying what is necessary, leaving out embellishments and superfluous words, sometimes not using capital letters and punctuation marks! Some of the articles—clearly explained in the notes—were written for publication; others, like the interviews, took a printed form according to the interviewer's selective interest and the more or less limited space for publication. Again, some articles were written in reaction to situations or statements concerning other persons, experiences, or current events.

I would like to thank Angela Ida De Benedictis and Veniero Rizzardi for their conscientious scholarly work in selecting and commenting on the articles in this volume. They have already shown their excellence in editing the Italian edition of Luigi Nono's writings and are among the very first scholars who did research at the Luigi Nono Archive, founded in Venice in 1993, three years after Nono's death.

It is my sincere wish that this book will encourage interest in Luigi Nono's thought and music, and that it will contribute to the growth of an informed and enthusiastic audience for his work.

Nuria Schoenberg Nono

Introduction

The career of Luigi Nono (1924–90) constitutes a creative arc that spans almost the entire second half of the twentieth century, from his public emergence in 1950 to the threshold of the 1990s. Even at three decades' distance from his death, any attempt at a systematic interpretation of this forty-year journey remains premature. The research conducted in recent years, based mainly on archival materials, has certainly shone new light on various artistic and biographical aspects of his career. At the same time, the fruitful multiplicity of interpretations that lie at the heart of these various studies and endeavors has revealed what a complex matter it is to try to achieve a unitary vision of Nono's multifarious body of compositional and aesthetic thought, one that was nourished constantly by an acute awareness of his historical moment.

This multiplicity, intrinsic to Nono's biography as both artist and human being, is revealed in the texts collected here. The topics covered range from his apprenticeships with Gian Francesco Malipiero and Bruno Maderna to the final works of the Darmstadt period; from the development of a complex musical language, the result of an idiosyncratic treatment of the serial technique that he first adopted in the early 1950s, to the difficulties of presenting in notated form the sound utopias (the "mobile sound") of his last creative decade; from the gradual evolving of his ideas concerning the relationship with the verbal text to the definition of a new vocality and a new *stile rappresentativo;* from the various applications of his experiences with electroacoustics, initially through the medium of magnetic tape and later up to his use of live electronics; from the primary need to *communicate* to an inward reflection on the need for a *listening* that was qualitatively different from the usual kind; from an internationalist political commitment to the utopia of "*infiniti possibili.*"[1] These, and still many other aspects, reveal how difficult and futile it would be to seek to sketch in an all-encompassing way a perspective that—to use a favorite metaphor of Nono's—might be better compared to an archipelago whose individual islands one can map out, but without being able to establish predetermined routes between them. The texts and interviews collected here aim to offer readers a compass with which to orient themselves within this multifaceted creative itinerary, whose concept of continuity consists in its sum of differences and transformations.

As with many composers of his generation—Luciano Berio, Pierre Boulez, Karlheinz Stockhausen among them—for Nono the practice of composing was a path marked by continuous conquests and innovations, in his case often arising from a unique way of reinterpreting tradition. Throughout his creative itinerary, it remains possible to trace the thread of a constant development running through and beyond the different "turning points," which sometimes appear as abrupt bursts and are often interpreted as such with excessive emphasis by critics and musicologists. Behind each of these turns, it is in fact possible to perceive a *fil rouge*—that of elements constantly reelaborated to serve a visionary idea of sound. In 1987, this is how Nono retrospectively summarized this attitude:

> My works proceed at irregular intervals, that they group themselves in threes or fours. This discontinuity, this change, is even more evident after a theatrical composition. . . . I could say, as Schoenberg did, that at the conclusion of each work I wish more than ever to breathe the air of other planets. When people ask me if I have changed my mind, changed direction, and so on, I say yes. I hope to change every morning when I wake up, to continually seek something different. Concepts such as continuity and consistency are to me incredibly banal; you have continuity in spite of yourself, with it often working against you. In spite of all the violence of the various upheavals. (see 74–75)

Each of Nono's works presents itself, upon closer examination, as the application of a previous intuition, as a unity in which one can recognize, at one and the same time, past and future techniques and compositional elements. Always, for Nono, the evolution toward new "routes," opened up by a fresh intuition, coincides with revolutions (or crises), at times violent ones. His is a veritable creative vortex, and recognizable at its center is always the will to redefine the power of the meaning of *sound,* through its manipulation and its possible transformations.

In the end, what really seems to unite four decades of incessant research into sound is the strong desire, like that encountered in Rilke's Orphic landscape, to erect for listeners and present to them with each work a multiform and surprising "temple for them in their hearing."[2]

Born on January 29, 1924, in Venice, Nono received the first input for his artistic and cultural development from his family: his paternal grandfather, Luigi Nono, was a well-known painter in the late nineteenth-century Venetian tradition, and his great uncle Urbano was a sculptor; while his maternal grandmother, a descendant of the ancient Venetian family Priuli Bon, played the piano and sang, including the lieder of her own day (among her music Nono was astonished to find an early edition of Hugo Wolf's *Italienische Lieder,* and *Montezuma* by Sacchini). Both his mother and his father, an engineer by profession, were amateur pianists who enjoyed playing some of the major classics (including *Boris Godunov,* by Modest Mussorgsky, recalled by the composer as one of the first works he heard as a child).[3] In this fertile and privileged domestic environment one can recognize the roots of what was to become a hallmark of Nono's artistic universe, namely the idea and practice of music as an art without frontiers which can be inspired by, and grounded in, a whole range of artistic and scientific manifestations (painting, architecture, literature, poetry, philosophy, etc.) from all of history.

When he was about twelve Nono began to learn the piano with a friend of his mother, Signora Alessandri, who taught privately.[4] He had already begun to attend performances at La Fenice and the International Contemporary Music Festival of the Venice Biennale, and to make regular visits to St. Mark's Basilica, drawn by its unique acoustics (which would prove so important in his untiring exploration of space as a compositional element). In 1941, when he was seventeen years old, his father succeeded in presenting him to one of the leading musical figures of the day, Gian Francesco Malipiero, a composer who played a key role in his early years of training.[5]

Nono's education and musical apprenticeship took place during the crucial years of the Second World War and its immediate aftermath, in a family and intellectual milieu which were solidly middle class while being fundamentally hostile to Fascism. For health reasons, he was exempted from military service and did not play an active part either in the war or in the Italian Resistance movement. Nonetheless, during the war years Nono made a point of frequenting young Venetian socialists and exponents of the local underground opposition, pursuing political and cultural ideals that were at odds with the regime. In an Italian cultural climate characterized by a very limited presence of the avant-garde experiences that had emerged in Europe since the onset of the twentieth century, Malipiero's teaching involved above all the study of Monteverdi and the great Italian Renaissance tradition (featuring polyphony and the madrigal), the theoretical treatises by Zarlino, Gaffurio, and Vicentino, and the discovery of the music of Arnold Schoenberg, Anton Webern, Luigi Dallapiccola, Igor Stravinsky, and Béla Bartók (artists that Malipiero had personally met but was not well acquainted with). In 1946, thanks once again to Malipiero, Nono met the young Venetian composer and conductor Bruno Maderna, just four years older than himself, who had made his mark as a child prodigy.

It was with Maderna that Nono perfected his fundamental musical apprenticeship, coming eventually to question everything he had accomplished or learned up to that point. Before then, as Nono himself recalled on a couple of occasions, he had composed a work influenced by his long discussions with Malipiero on the music of the fifteenth and sixteenth centuries and modeled on the sacred representations, *La discesa di Cristo agli inferi* (Christ's Descent into the Underworld): in it, he later said, "I believed in a completely naive way that I was using the language of Monteverdi."[6] This first compositional essay, unfortunately lost, is almost contemporaneous with his first meeting with Dallapiccola, one of the composers he most admired and a touchstone for many others of his generation (it is no coincidence that the earliest known text by Nono, "Luigi Dallapiccola and the *Sex Carmina Alcaei*," is devoted to his music). The spark that set off that decisive change of direction, after some eight years of musical studies he came to regard as "quite 'useless' and at the very least insufficient" (254), appears to have been Dallapiccola's comments about the score of *La discesa di Cristo agli inferi*, which Nono had sent him at the suggestion of Malipiero: "'I saw your score'—Dallapiccola said—'and I understand that here in your heart you have a lot to express, only you need to study a lot more to be able to express it.' This gave me the impulse to start my musical studies all over again, and I then began my apprenticeship with Maderna" (255).

This encounter made an indelible mark on both Nono's musical and personal development, and to the end of his life he referred to Bruno Maderna as his first great mentor. In the course of lengthy days spent either in Maderna's home or in the Marciana Library in Venice, Nono applied himself to an in-depth study of the music of the fifteenth and sixteenth centuries, covering *ars antiqua* and French *ars nova,* the Franco-Flemish school and Italian polyphony, in a continuous confrontation of theory and practice. In the years around 1950, analysis of the ancient music stimulated a comparative study of the various compositional processes that characterized the history of music. Once an understanding of a musical technique had been achieved, the goal was to discover its *function* in relation to the historical juncture, seeking out new possible transformations or applications in the music of later ages, down to the present.[7] For Nono, the relationship between the state of the material, its elaboration, and the period of production took on a fundamental importance: he became—and remained—convinced that artistic language has to develop alongside the major political and social movements of the age, so that it represents one possibility (or means) of intervening in these events.

It is with these new understandings that, in 1950, Nono approached his first orchestral composition, *Variazioni canoniche sulla serie dell'op. 41 di Arnold Schönberg*—Schoenberg's opus 41 being the *Ode to Napoleon Buonaparte,* a work declaimed to Byron's poetic invective against tyranny—that "was the result of my first studies of the enigmatic canons, but ... also an ideological choice" (**255**). In 1950, he made his debut with this composition at the Internationale Ferienkurse für Neue Musik in Darmstadt, the main gathering at which the young musicians of the postwar avant-garde could meet and exchange ideas; he landed up there thanks to a recommendation from Hermann Scherchen, whom he and Maderna had met in 1948 during an orchestral conducting course in Venice. Over the next five years the two young composers enjoyed a fruitful relationship with the elderly conductor, who became a spiritual guide in both cultural and personal matters. By frequenting Scherchen and hearing his performances and recollections, Nono gained firsthand knowledge of the conductor's experiences in Germany from 1912 onward, including the first performances of his beloved Schoenberg and Webern, and also German social and cultural life prior to the advent of Nazism.

Nono went back to Darmstadt each year for ten years, from 1957 as a teacher, and the experience was of crucial importance in his artistic, personal, and political evolution. It enabled him not only to gain further knowledge of serial music, and in particular the works of Schoenberg—whose daughter, Nuria, he married in 1955—but also to get to know Edgard Varèse, who was among the admirers of *Variazioni canoniche* at its controversial first performance, and whose visionary music played a crucial role in the evolution of Nono's sound world. Also at Darmstadt he established important relationships—nurtured in some cases by mutual admiration, in others by constructive dissent—with a number of musicians from Europe and beyond, including Karlheinz Stockhausen, Pierre Boulez, Henri Pousseur, John Cage, and Hans Werner Henze. Above all, Darmstadt was the venue for the first performance of some of his most significant compositions of the 1950s: the *Variazioni canoniche* were followed by *Polifonica-Monodia-Ritmica* (1951), *Epitaffio per Federico García Lorca I: España en el corazón* (1951–52), *La victoire de Guernica* (1954), *Incontri* (1955), *Cori di Didone* (1958), and *Composizione per orchestra n. 2—Diario polacco '58* (1959).

These works revealed Nono as one of the leading exponents of the European avant-garde and the serial technique, alongside Stockhausen and Boulez. Nonetheless, in 1959 he explicitly distanced himself from these two composers and from the milieu of the *Ferienkurse*. In a lecture entitled "Historical Presence of Music Today" (1959), he took issue with what he himself had dubbed the "Darmstadt school," denouncing instances of incoherence and contradiction. After years in which valid stimuli had gone hand in hand with constructive clashes, this lecture marked a first rupture with the milieu and some of its representatives. The split reflected firstly the incipient academicism according to which Nono saw certain examples of serialism degenerating into "formulas," and secondly experiences based on chance and indeterminacy—those involving both a group of composers among whom Nono explicitly named John Cage and, especially, (unnamed) younger musicians who had, in his opinion, been fascinated by the poetics of indeterminacy.[8] In both cases Nono denounced the practitioners for shunning history and refusing to take a clear, responsible stance on the artistic issues of the present. His central argument consisted in reaffirming the need for composers always to bear in mind that the material with which they work is historically determined and thus to avoid the temptation of predicating their experiments on a pure contemplation of the sound material as such.

The split was made definitive when Nono gave another lecture in 1960 entitled "Text—Music—Song," in which he explicitly attacked Stockhausen. Ten years later, and still this controversy had not yet died down and indeed, Nono took it up again, thus indicating his detachment from the musical avant-garde in an even more explicit manner, trying to expose the political mystification concealed behind the various radicalisms, merely superficial in his view, of the new music of the 1960s.⁹

Another aspect of the speech-manifesto "Historical Presence of Music Today" is the alarmed denunciation of an American "colonial" aggression that harbored the ability to do significant damage to European culture. However, although Cage and Joseph Schillinger were then his two main polemical targets, the documents reveal that in reality Nono at the time had fruitful and long-lasting relationships with several North American artists he had met in Darmstadt, as well as with Varèse and with Cage himself. In 1954, he formed important friendships with Gunther Schuller, who would soon organize the first performance of a Nono work on the American continent,¹⁰ and a few years later Earle Brown, who, as producer of the Time/Mainstream record label, would be among the first to promote the dissemination of Nono's music on disc, as well as that of Berio and Maderna. Beyond the 1959 controversy, Nono would always show a keen interest in the new experiences arising on the other side of the Atlantic, and he would become an enthusiastic supporter of the experimental proclivities expressed by the ONCE group, for whom, in 1964, he promoted a pioneering collective performance at the XXVII International Festival of Contemporary Music of the Venice Biennale.¹¹ One should also not omit to mention his direct collaboration with the Living Theatre in the preparation of *A floresta é jovem e cheja de vida* of 1965–66.

Throughout the 1950s, another important experience for Nono was the exploration of twentieth-century political and cultural events outside Italy, from the Soviet Revolution to the culture of the Weimar Republic, covering the Russian and German historical avant-garde and the innovations in the domain of theater spearheaded by Vsevolod Meyerhold, Vladimir Mayakovsky, and Erwin Piscator. The stimuli he received from these sources were combined with his enthusiasm for the teachings of Antonio Gramsci, the philosophy of Jean-Paul Sartre, and for poetry that grappled with the issues of the day, notably that of Federico García Lorca, Pablo Neruda, Paul Éluard, Cesare Pavese, and also that of Giuseppe Ungaretti. The texts of the vocal works he composed during the 1950s were primarily by these authors, while the masterpiece dating from midway through the decade, *Il canto sospeso* (1955–56), was based on letters by European resistance fighters. With this work Nono improves a peculiar technique of fragmentation in which the text is enunciated in its vocalic or phonetic components either successively in the individual parts or simultaneously as a sound bloc or aggregate.

As can be seen from a number of his theoretical texts written during the 1950s, Nono became increasingly convinced of music's communicative capacity and of the imperative to express the multifaceted contradictions of his time in his art. In selecting texts he opted for political themes arising out of events of the present or immediate past. This transpires clearly in *Intolleranza 1960* (1960–61), the first work to give tangible form to the ideas concerning a "new music theater" he had developed during the previous decade. And the trend reached its apogee in the first half of the 1970s with the second *azione scenica*, *Al gran sole carico d'amore* (1972–74, revised 1977).[12]

During the 1960s and 1970s political commitment, social conflict, and denunciation, and the treatment of individual psychology always in relation to the collective drama—all elements which characterize *Intolleranza 1960*—became constants of Nono's production as the concept of *engagement* took on for him the value of a "moral imperative" (Jean-Paul Sartre) to match the aesthetic imperative. The relationship between art and the present became ever more interwoven and profound: each work, whether achieved or merely planned, was conceived as a means of participating actively in a broader process of transformation of the social reality. In both his artistic and human biography the concept of engagement has been (and indeed continues to be) one of the most complex and fiercely debated issues, which can easily be misrepresented. Nono was a member of the Italian Communist Party from 1952 and of its Central Committee from March 1975. But he never betrayed the ideal of the committed artist, even when, in the latter phases of his life, his denunciations took on less direct forms, moving away from the reality of an explicit commitment vis-à-vis current political issues and heading toward other sources of inspiration, more specifically mythical thought. But in his most intensely political phase during the years 1960–70,[13] artistic milestones often coincided with biographical highpoints, for example, the various journeys he made in Eastern bloc countries starting in 1958, to the Soviet Union in 1963 and again in the 1970s, to the United States in 1965 and 1979, and to Latin America from 1967 onward, first to Argentina, then to Chile, Peru, and Cuba. This was the time when he measured himself against the theory and practice of international Marxism, participating in workers' movements during the 1960s and the students' revolt in 1968. For him, political militancy—made explicit in his ethical, social, and artistic choices—was inseparable from his activity as a musician continually in search of new sound worlds. Composing, making, and disseminating music represented a dialectic synthesis of art and life which he saw as the only means for a composer to "attain full self-realization" (274). But in the context of his whole career, the concept of engagement also applies to the "responsible" conception of research implicit in each new work and in the construction of an innovatory musical language whose revolutionary aspect lies *in* the resulting sound world. This means putting into perspective, if not actually rejecting out of hand, the notion of an alleged unpolitical phase for Nono in the 1980s: art experienced as responsibility and *subjective* commitment (associating the author, performer, and listener) is a constant which characterizes his whole artistic trajectory and is not confined to political content, whether overt or latent.

In the mid-1970s, after *Al gran sole carico d'amore,* Nono underwent a profound creative crisis.[14] Previous attributes such as the performer's prime function in the creative process or the role of technologies, were complemented by a new impulse toward the interiorization of the musical message and the concept of commitment. With the onset of the 1980s the chief characteristics of Nono's style—starting from the string quartet *Fragmente-Stille, an Diotima,* 1979–80—are silence, pauses, the juxtaposition of fragments in which *pianissimi* verging on the imperceptible alternate with explosions of sound, and the structural value of space. Although these elements have prompted some critics and commentators to speak of either a "turning-point" or abrupt caesuras in his artistic development,[15] there can be no doubt that the germ of all these elements was already present (and indeed exploited) in a number of works going back to the 1950s. In *Polifonica-Monodia-Ritmica,* for example, there are silences and sonorities verging on the inaudible, just as the chiaroscuro use of dynamics and the lacerated sonorities typical of some works dating from the 1980s are to be found in *Due espressioni per orchestra* (1953), *Il canto sospeso, La terra e la compagna* (1957), and *Cori di Didone.* Contrary to interpretations of technique or style dictated by sequential decades, one can recognize a continuous development running right through Nono's creative career, involving the unremitting elaboration of elements that go to nurture a sound world with a rich potential for imagery, at times verging on utopia.

The changes in the world political and social scene and the awareness of the progressive loss of a collective subject and the illusory nature of social revolution are visible in the texts that Nono selected for his compositions during the 1980s, clearly influenced by his friendship with the philosopher Massimo Cacciari: Friedrich Hölderlin, Rainer Maria Rilke, Robert Musil, the Hebrew mystics, Walter Benjamin, Edmond Jabès,

Giordano Bruno, Friedrich Nietzsche, Greek tragedy, and mythology. These new literary stimuli were complemented by the technical resources offered by live electronics, which Nono was able to explore at the Experimental Studio of the Heinrich Strobel Foundation, in Freiburg, Germany. He began to use this brand-new electronic laboratory in 1980, after about twenty years of experiments carried out at the Studio di Fonologia of RAI in Milan.

The philosophy underlying the creations of his last decade is characterized by his progressing through "attempts" or "choices" and his use of constant transformations of sound events in performance. This mode of proceeding by way of modeling the sound in real time and allowing it to be enriched by new possibilities thrown up as reactions to technical hitches, can be clearly seen in the genesis of *Prometeo*, constructed out of at least four preliminary works: *Io, frammento dal Prometeo* (1981), *Das atmende Klarsein, Quando stanno morendo. Diario polacco n. 2*, and *Guai ai gelidi mostri*. Although *Prometeo* features among Nono's works for the theater, the scenic or narrative element has actually been completely stripped away: all the action is in the sound, viewed as a mobile entity deprived of any visual apparatus and projected into a resonant space consisting of a wooden arklike structure specifically designed by Renzo Piano for the deconsecrated church of San Lorenzo in Venice for the first performance in 1984. Ideally *Prometeo* can be seen as the culmination of all the dramaturgical experiments carried out in the wake of *Intolleranza 1960*, subsumed in a sound world in which *sight* gradually cedes to pure *listening* (see "Toward *Prometeo*").

The search for *unprecedented* sound realities and what Nono refers to repeatedly as *"mobile* sound" is the basis of Nono's late work, characterized by an awareness, almost utopian, of the impossibility and at the same time the transience inherent in a search, whether on an artistic or a human level, that is always projected toward an infinite "beyond": "I think that the transformation taking place in our time is making intuition, intelligence, and the capacity of expressing such transformation into the new necessity of life: openness, studies, highly risky experiments, renouncing security and all guarantees, and even *purposes*. We have to know that we may fall at any moment, but we must always seek, nevertheless, seek the unknown" (384).

Perhaps the time of Nono's death, in 1990, is also the beginning of the end of that historical season in which all so-called avant-gardes were seen as playing an active role in social and cultural progress more generally. According to such a perspective, a composer could acquire the status and prestige of a leader on the musical scene. Nono had this role right from the beginning, and he shared it with few other composers of his generation. This was so much the case that in the specialist journalism of the 1950s, the image very soon crystalized of a hegemonic triad on the new European music scene, which, other than Nono, included Pierre Boulez and Karlheinz Stockhausen. While the reality was much more complex and multifaceted than this journalistic image suggests, there is no doubt that these three composers were united not only in the special quality of their respective musical outputs but also in a radical attitude and a subjective conviction, publicly expressed, of the *necessity* of their own work in relation to the historical horizon of the progress of musical language.

It was therefore consistent with this conviction that the composer would offer some kind of theory. Nono soon began to set his ideas down in writing, and his first texts, aimed mainly at technical considerations, have an objective importance in the context of the compositional theories of the time. However, while artists like Boulez and Stockhausen methodically pursued a formalization of their thought that, for some time, offered technical elucidations that correlated precisely with their own musical output (or sometimes, even, that of others), within a short time Nono abandoned this direction. Already from the early 1960s, compositional theory and the purely technical questions addressed in "The Development of Serial Technique" (1957) or in "Text—Music—Song" (1960) gave way to other issues. What now preoccupied him was an intensive critical engagement aimed at examining the social role of the composer and addressing the problem of communication, albeit without making compromises at the level of technical-compositional innovation. Whenever these issues arise forcefully in his literary output, Nono finds himself turning to new expressive means, finally discovering, with *Intolleranza 1960*, a theatrical format adapted to the dramaturgy hitherto only implicit in his music. From that moment on—alongside the trajectory of Nono the composer, as briefly mentioned—the output of this *scriptor de musica* often takes the form of polemical or directly political statements, a form that persisted for some time and was apparently abandoned only in the last years of his life, when new ideas of a seemingly more interior nature appear to take precedence over open commitment.

The reader will find timely echoes of all this in this volume, which gathers together for the first time Nono's writings translated into English. It is the hope of the editors that it might provide the premise for a growth and a renewal in studies of his work, which up to now have flourished mostly in continental Europe. Recent signs of a promising increase in studies on Nono in English-speaking countries have, moreover, helped to highlight the lack (and the necessity) of a publication like this one.[16]

That a volume such as this sees the light of day only in 2018 should not, however, be taken to indicate that Anglo-Saxon music scholarship has been lagging behind. Even in Europe, knowledge of Nono's theoretical ideas has spread in a far from uniform fashion and not without obvious inconsistencies (on the linguistic and chronological level). Until the beginning of 2000, and more than ten years after his death, a collection of this type was not even available to the Italian public. Paradoxically, his most important theoretical writings of the 1950s (among them "The Development of Serial Technique") had until that date not even appeared in Italian.[17]

During Nono's lifetime, only one volume had been published, in German in 1975. This was a selection of writings published up to that point, many translated specially from the Italian originals, which appeared alongside a series of studies and commentaries by critics and musicologists close to him.[18] That first collection was conceived on the basis of criteria that inevitably reflected a specific phase in the reception of Nono's work. His profile, in 1975, was typically that of the politically committed artist who had his roots in a period of research—the 1950s—that had not yet been relegated to history, and toward which it was still legitimate to take a militant stance or, on the contrary, to adopt a distant position that allowed one to dismiss that recent past with an often excessive polemical verve. Only a year later, in 1976, Nono was urged by his friend the musicologist Massimo Mila to begin work on what would have been the first collection of his writings in Italian.[19] Nono welcomed the invitation and appreciated the opportunity that such a project presented. However, at the same time he felt for various reasons the clear need to adopt for the Italian edition a different approach from the German one. Unable to arrive at considered decisions in a manner not governed by haste, he thus decided to postpone the publication:

> Seeing it [the volume in German], I do not think it can be translated into Italian as it is.
>
> It has texts that are repetitive, short, and in some cases useless (perhaps for Germany it is fine in its entirety in view of their deafness, their ill-informed opinions or their a priori thinking). . . .

So:

I do not consider valid for Italy the republication of the book as it is.
It should be revised, edited down in parts, updated in others. . . .
So for now: let's suspend it altogether.[20]

After other unsuccessful attempts, Nono's initial interest in the edition project gradually began to wane, until it was finally set aside. In fact, for the first collection that took account of his entire career, one had to wait until 1993, the year in which the first posthumous edition of his writings came out, in a French translation.[21] The system was modeled by the editor on the collection published in Germany eighteen years previously, and many translations were made drawing not on the originals in Italian but on versions already subject to an initial translation into German.

In 1993, at the behest of Nuria Schoenberg Nono, the Luigi Nono Archive was established in Venice. This new accessibility of the author's legacy marked a decisive turning point for research into Nono's music and thought. It was thanks to having access to this extensive documentation and the composer's original materials that, as a result of several years of research, we managed in 2001 to collect almost all of Nono's Italian writings and conversations from the period between 1948 and 1989.[22] In editing the first edition of Nono's writings and interviews in Italian, we decided to follow a fundamental philological criterion, that is, to faithfully restore the author's original words, which had often been undermined in the various Italian or foreign publications by cuts, arbitrary editorial interventions, and translations that were at times approximate, and not always so merely by reason of Nono's idiosyncratic and sometimes impervious style. To this end, accurate checks were carried out, not only on all available print sources, but on the typewritten drafts (and in some cases, the manuscripts) that it was Nono's habit to preserve. This resulted in two volumes of writings and interviews (making a total of about twelve hundred pages), which contained almost everything Nono had published along with several unpublished items. All these appeared in a form as close as possible to the final "intentions of the author," as documented or at least able to be presumed.[23]

Having thus established a version of Nono's theoretical texts and his writings on his works, based on his original words, we came back six years later to compile those texts we considered the most significant into a more easily accessible edition, one that would be capable of wider dissemination.[24] With the new 2007 collection, we intended to offer a volume of readings destined not only for specialists but for those wider audiences potentially interested in the ideas of one of the greatest composers of the twentieth century. This collection included only a selection of theoretical writings and lectures; the talks and interviews, meanwhile, which in 2001 had occupied the entire second volume, were completely excluded. Also excluded were the notes on individual works—today available on the website of the Luigi Nono Archive.[25]

Although the selection required difficult as well as inevitable compromises,[26] it resulted in an edition that gave preference to those statements in which Nono had objectively offered a more articulate exposition of his ideas. To these was then added a scrupulous selection of texts that would complete (and restore) as comprehensive an image as possible of the multiplicity of Nono's thought. Furthermore, by grouping texts according to thematic areas, the aim was to provide an effective alternative to the purely chronological arrangement that had been chosen for the two volumes published in 2001.

This anthology edition is the inspiration for the present volume, which—for reasons that will be mentioned later—preserves the same title: *Nostalgia for the Future*. Despite the substantial affinity, there are nonetheless fundamental differences between the two editions, which make the present volume, specially conceived for a wider, international audience, new and exclusive. First, there is the considerable expansion of content that is due to the presence of a selection of interviews and other texts, here called "Excursus" (I–VI), placed as intermezzos or thematic introductions between the various sections of the collection. Among them—almost a book within a book—is the long autobiographical interview collated and organized by the critic Enzo Restagno in 1987, three years before Nono's death. It is placed at the beginning of the volume as an introductory compendium (and retrospective) of the most important events of the composer's life and work.

The grouping of the texts in the volume into thematic areas has a sound justification. It is guided by our intention to offer a valid illustration of the different focuses of interest in Nono's thought, and the changes that can be objectively noted within each over time. The chronological arrangement of the writings in these individual sections therefore follows as a logical consequence from this choice.

In the first section, entitled "Musical Analysis and Composition," are found the reflections, dating from circa 1948 to 1960, concerned with musical technique, many of them aimed at the international community of composers and referring to the Darmstadt courses; to these it was decided to add just one later text, written in 1976 (on *Il canto sospeso*), which, though preferring an approach that is more historical-documentary than analytical, presents a firsthand testimony regarding one of the most important compositions of the 1950s.

The second section, "Music Onstage: From a 'Theater of Ideas' to the 'Tragedy of Listening,'" is devoted to the renewal of music theater, a problem present in Nono's thinking since the early 1950s, and which came to the forefront following his experience with *Intolleranza 1960* (a period during which he wrote a group of texts dedicated to the subject). The realization of a "theater of ideas" and a "theater of situations," inspired by Sartre, dominates a long phase that embraces the central years of Nono's activity, approximately between 1960 and 1977. Thus, perceptible differences appear, in both the conceptual system and the form of expression, between the thoughts expressed in the 1980s in "Toward *Prometeo*" and Nono's earlier writings. These are indicative of the profound metamorphosis that his thoughts on musical dramaturgy underwent during those years.

Under the title "'Conscience, Feelings, Collective Reality,'" taken from a motto of Nono, one finds the most characteristic expressions of the "political" composer of the 1960s and 1970s. These pages begin by focusing the urgency of grounding the work of composition in an understanding of the historical emergence of social configurations, and represent the logical development of the program announced in 1959 with "Historical Presence of Music Today." This, in fact, is the prelude to the passionate resumption of the Sartrian question "Why write?" (formulated for the first time in "Text—Music—Song" of 1960), which, at the turn of a decade, is transformed into a harsh and thorough polemic against contemporary European avant-garde music (see "Music and Power," 1969). During those years, his orientation toward a politically focused musical production was sharpened and radicalized. It was aligned both with an agenda derived from a "progressive" reading of national culture (see "Music and Resistance," 1963) and with that of the international workers' movement. The five texts assembled, therefore, testify to Nono the political militant, not only in his role as a musician, but also as a political observer. A good example is provided by "In the Sierra and in the Parliament" (1971), a militant reportage of a trip to the countries of South America. In all, one can find traces of the rather complex relationship that Nono had with the Italian Communist Party, in which he was actively involved from 1952 onward.

The fourth section, "Portraits and Dedications," is devoted to backward glances into the past and to persons who featured in different ways in Nono's biography as both man and artist. Mirroring the progress of a journey, of an artistic and emotional awareness gradually attained, or of an ever more living "presence" of the past, it is no coincidence that they focus especially on Nono's last two decades, the 1970s and 1980s. Here too, in contrast to the Italian edition, we preferred to give space to personalities closer to American and extra-European cultures, rather than to those with closer links to the Italian political or artistic scene.

The fifth and final section, "The 'Possible Infinities,'" attests to the doubts and anxieties of Nono's last decade. It brings together his most radically questioning reflections, which go hand in hand with a poetic approach very different from that adopted in the past. It is marked by the productive uncertainties and the utopian openness that are typical of his last, but earnest, creative phase.

In a play of concentric circles, the five sections are embedded among the six "Excurses," of which the last ("'Proust' Questionnaire") is placed, as if closing the circle, as a literal *pendant* to the short text ("Clarifications") placed at the beginning as an "Overture" to the entire book. These two texts were in fact written thirty years apart from each other—the first in 1956, the second in 1986—and in their character as autobiographical sketches, they can be seen (playing with the title of a well-known composition of the 1980s) as a true *prae-ludium* and *post-ludium* to the entire collection.

It is precisely in the "'Proust' Questionnaire" that, to the question "The main trait of your character?" Nono responds: "Nostalgia for the future." No title could have summed up better that yearning toward a new and different knowledge and reality of sound, one that remains projected toward the future, and that particular propulsive *spleen* that accompanied Nono throughout his entire creative itinerary.

The texts reproduced in the present edition were translated from the definitive versions established for the 2001 and 2007 editions.[27] For a detailed illustration of the at times highly complex methods and issues involved in the heuristic and philological research that went into reconstructing the original forms of Nono's texts, we refer the more curious reader to a further explanatory article,[28] and also to the preface and the critical and bibliographical footnotes of the two collections in Italian.[29] The most pertinent information on the relevant sources and the history of the individual texts is nevertheless summarized here in a special section, "Bibliographic Notes and Comments to the Texts," which acts as a documentary appendix. As a rule, the first edition and the subsequent reprints and/or known translations are given here. The title of each text is provided in the original language (even if different from Italian) near the information regarding the first printed editions; only rarely, and in cases of multiple or spurious versions, are reprints and/or translations taken into account. The title should be assumed to be unchanged unless otherwise indicated. For interviews, the editorial title, if any, is given.

Editorial footnotes, explanations and contextual comments regarding individual texts are cued with superscript Arabic numerals and displayed at the end of the book. Any original footnotes (whether originating with the author or the text's publisher) are, on the other hand, placed at the foot of the page, with superscript Roman numerals; occasionally these may contain additional editorial comments placed in square brackets. Bibliographic references – here updated for the Anglo-American reader – contained within editorial footnotes occasionally include supplementary information about editions present in Nono's rich personal library, preserved at the archive in Venice. Mentioning the existence of an annotated copy is tantamount to providing a concrete testimony of Nono's interests and the reading he pursued alongside his activity as a composer.

The volume is rounded off with "Chronology of Nono's Works," a reference tool offered to enable the reader to retrace the composer's creative arc, especially in terms of the dating or the instrumental forces of works cited in the volume.

Unlike in the Italian editions, it was decided to overlook certain purely philological peculiarities. The texts are reproduced in their entirety; any indications of discrepancies or substantial variants with other sources are noted, if deemed important to the history of the text, in the "Bibliographic Notes and Comments to the Texts" or, exceptionally, in the editorial footnotes.[30]

Certain general choices implicated in the translation process involved the notion of presumed "faithfulness" to the register of the author's language. In the 2001 and 2007 editions, we made a priority of returning to Nono's original words, previously often distorted or "domesticated" in the editing of the various printed editions. In preparing this English edition, however, we considered the need to preserve as far as possible the utility and comprehensibility of the texts to be of paramount importance. The problems related to translating these texts into other languages are indeed particular ones that go far beyond the difficulties inherent in the usual dichotomy of "translation vs. betrayal." The difficulties, indeed, are related primarily to the altogether personal idiosyncrasies of Nono's writing.

Those scholars who have already set themselves the challenge of reading the texts in the original language will know that Nono's writing, even in Italian, often demands a painstaking hermeneutical effort. When delivering a piece of writing for publication, Nono would almost always submit a text whose stylistic and orthographical characteristics were ill-adapted to commonly accepted conventions. His style—in grammar, spelling, and syntax—is not easily reconciled with the conventional rules of his mother tongue, nor to the criteria of *bella scrittura*. Not infrequently, his personal syntax, certain writer's quirks (such as his constant use of the lower case),[31] or even the use of an entirely personal vocabulary, such as neologisms or substantivized verbs or adjectives, increases the risk of linguistic error. This state of affairs is not, moreover, attributable simply to the carelessness or alleged irresponsibility of those publishers of Nono's texts or interviews, even if, in their print editions, the originals were often inundated by corrections that tended to level the text and bring its readability back within the confines of recognized linguistic conventions.[32] The "utopia" often invoked by Nono in his later years to define his sound horizon was already, from the 1950s, firmly established in his way of phrasing and expressing himself on paper.

So, in translating Nono's peculiar manner of expression, most of the choices used here aim at the intelligibility of the text. On an orthographic level, for example, it was decided to follow English writing conventions in the use of initial capitalization and punctuation.[33] The formatting of the texts has been normalized in comparison with the originals. In only one case ("For Helmut"), the graphic layout of the text has been retained in a way that is faithful to the original, due to the importance of the manner of the text's spatial unfolding on the page. Even on the level of syntax, certain adaptations have been deemed appropriate to safeguard the intelligibility of the English idiom. The interlinguistic accommodation necessitated in the act of translation (faithful in meaning, free in adaptation) does not render these texts simple to read, nor does it amend them of their roughness or of the originality of formulation characteristic of Nono's style. Only in rare cases, and to leave intact the liveliness of his turn of phrase, have we opted for a literal translation of individual terms, typical of the composer's vocabulary: among these, words that Nono modified from technical languages, such as the frequent metaphorical use of the term *formant* (borrowed from acoustics). A number of these were carefully weighed up before being adopted in the English version. An example is the recurring term *sound bands,* which translates a phrase *(fasce sonore,* literally: "sound belts"), much used in the jargon of Italian composers to indicate multi-stratified, shifting, and continuous sound textures, but not firmly established in writing on music, especially in the English language.[34] Other words characteristic of Nono's vocabulary are sometimes placed in square brackets in the original language after the translation. In this way, we desired not so much, or not only, to highlight the difficulty of translating them, but to insert them in a specific context that indicates to the reader those points at which, even in his mother tongue, the flow of Nono's thoughts could no longer be contained within conventional linguistic or syntactic schemes. What is characteristic, in this regard, is the frequent use of substantivized verbs, attaining in the case of the term *pensari,* often present in the texts of Nono's last decade, the status of a true linguistic coinage. This term is born from the nominalization of the verb *to think* (It. *pensare*), but sometimes in the plural (*pensari*), and is often associated with adjectives that underline its vastness ("other *pensari,*" "infinite *pensari,*" etc.). This choice of Nono's is entirely poetic: *pensari* is an almost nonexistent word in the Italian lexicon, which can, and in a certain sense must, be watered down into the more conventional "ways of thinking" (the translation preferred here). But it is in the conciseness and vividness of such a nominalization, deliberately used in an arbitrary fashion, that Nono adds greater weight to the plurality of his thought, and it was therefore our wish to leave a trace of these grammatical stress points and to show some recognition of them.

Worthy of mention in itself is the translation of the terms *serial/series,* which are not always used in a manner consistent either with twelve-tone music or with the music properly termed serial (in which the concept of series is extended to all parameters). In this regard, we have preferred as far as possible to disambiguate the two meanings (fundamental in certain texts of the first section): whenever the Italian term *seriale/serie* relates to the dimension of pitch, as in the music of Schoenberg and Webern, it is always translated as *(twelve) tone/tone row;* on the other hand, whenever the Italian term refers to the more properly serial-multiparametric usage typical of the 1950s, the English *serial/series* is used. Indeed, in the text that is most significant in this regard, "The Development of Serial Technique" of 1957, Nono almost always places the adjective *serial* in quotation marks. Unique to this essay is also the observance of a usage on which Nono explicitly insisted,[35] that is the use of German to indicate certain forms and procedures of twelve-tone music (e.g., *Krebs, Umkehrung, Spiegel*): for consistency, they have not been translated into English here. The same choice has been made regarding other terms or concepts used systematically by Nono in a language other than Italian,[36] whereas certain general or place names that are well known in their English forms are for that reason translated into English, regardless of how Nono used to cite them in his originals.

Nono's habit of not providing in full the forenames of persons mentioned, tending rather to give initials only, has been respected here. Forenames have been added only in ambiguous cases, whereas they are given in full in the index of names. It should also be noted that we have chosen to retain the facsimile reproduction of manuscripts in the music examples of "Toward *Prometeo*" and the original examples of "On the Development of Serial Technique" (from 1956, partly taken from printed editions of the time); all other examples have been recreated *ex novo*.

Finally, due mention should be made of the long "Autobiography of the Author Recounted by Enzo Restagno," whose peculiar stylistic register and readable smoothness reflect the kind of origin that urges caution. As the text's title reveals, the one "recounting" Nono's memory streams and recollections is the interviewer, Enzo Restagno, who has subjected Nono's answers to a wholesale editorial restructuring, one that was admittedly arbitrary and which cannot unfortunately be documented today due to the loss of the original tapes of the interview.[37]

This edition would not have been possible without the support, determination and enthusiastic involvement of those who accompanied us in the individual phases of its gestation, first of all Nuria Schoenberg Nono, also for her passionate and competent assistance to the editorial work, provided together with Roberta Reeder; then: Luca Formenton, Mary Francis, Raina Polivka, and also Cindy Fulton, Aimee Goggins, Zuha Khan, John O'Donnell, Kim Robinson. With a special thank you to Andrew Frisardi for his brilliant copyediting.

Heartfelt thanks also go out to friends and colleagues who, at different times and in different ways, helped us with advice, suggestions, or by simply giving us their patient attention: Joseph H. Auner, Giovanni Cestino, Alvin Curran, Fabrizio Della Seta, Frederic Rzewski, Anne Shreffler, Alvise Vidolin, Claudia Vincis.

Special thanks are also addressed to those who, daily, have rewarded the various stages of this long journey with love, serenity and smiles, often making it lighter: our families, our loves.

Angela Ida De Benedictis
Veniero Rizzardi

OVERTURE

Clarifications

1956

Any *setting in stone* of aesthetic principles and axioms is futile, as indeed is the school of intellectual games played out in the *categorizing* of styles,[1] because the continuous development of human affairs, in being translated into art, regains the evolutionary and revolutionary vitality intrinsic to it.

Social-man[2] introduces ever new elements of progress into life's motion, which either complement those already existing, whose functions are not yet exhausted, or determine their immediate change, giving rise to new relationships.

Evolution and revolution, two strictly logical phases: thanks to their driving forces, and especially the even violent force of the latter, whose violence is nothing if not the expansion of human capacity, human continuity is realized.

[And] life is realized in a form so alive that the present is already the past in the future.

In a similar manner, but subject each time to concrete analysis amid the diversity of his concrete situation, poet-man proceeds among spaces among sounds among colors.

He gives form to the present turned toward the future.

He creates tradition, he does not vegetate within it in some academic fashion.

His means are those of his time, reaching him through the elaboration of history, critically understood by him and adapted to new requirements, not by jumping backward in history to borrow from particular periods of the past.

He acts based on the extent to which he experiences the forward thrust of his own epoch.[i]

It is that social-man and poet-man are two manifestations of the same reality: what resides in both, as a primal impulse, is the development of an objective consciousness of the external world in which they live, and to which they give shape by transforming it.

Subjective participation, of course, but on the basis of existing reality: the historical reality of society within its natural environment.

Because in light of this relationship, human action can truly assume its function in life.

Because inherent in this relationship is the potential capacity of humankind to give life a shape that is fuller and more pregnant in as much as the combination of movement and progress, in its totality, is deeper and more direct.

Because in the warmth of life, joyful for its beauty, one works far from empty artifices and visionary mists.

And Antonio Machado reminds and admonishes:

> it is not logic that sings in poetry
> but life,
> even if it is not life that gives structure to poetry,
> but logic.[3]

---

i. How distant, and not as regards time, now seems the condition of those who create art "far from strife and talk" and " . . . high propped/on a pillow of blue cloud," as Li Po wrote during a particularly tumultuous period of the Tang dynasty. And how close, and not as regards time, that about which Vladimir Mayakovsky wrote: "I am a witness of the '150,000,000.'"

[The preceding text, accompanied by a letter dated January 10, 1956, was sent to Luciano Berio for publication in his new journal *Incontri Musicali*. In the first issue of the journal, which came out in December 1956, Nono's contribution was, however, not published. Reproduced here, given its documentary and autobiographical importance, is the letter to Berio that accompanied Nono's manuscript. For the textual history of the latter, see "Bibliographic Notes and Comments to the Texts," in the book's back matter.]

Dear Luciano

Thank you for your letter and your request.

To you the editor, and to the journal, I wish a *healthy* and *transparent* life and action, especially in light of the medieval reactionary and mafia-like Italian situation.

As regards the theme you suggested, I'll tell you right away that it does not feel right for me (the others can do as they like), to write about my work and my experiences; indeed I find it rather ridiculous when someone writes analyses, outlines, formulas, and similar things in journals, just after they have finished a new work.

Inter nos any technical discussion, any exchange of analyses, experiences, etc.; but as for putting them in print, I don't agree.

I send you these "clarifications."

That in essence contain notes that should or will address the individual issues generalized here.

We'll be coming to Milan in a few days. So, that's all for now. Stay well.

Gigi.

EXCURSUS I

An Autobiography of the Author Recounted by Enzo Restagno

1987

I would like to begin our conversation, which should form the basis of an autobiography, specifically with music. When and under what circumstances did your life begin to be affected by music?

My meeting with Bruno Maderna back in '46 was undoubtedly a fundamental and determining event.

At that time, however, you were already twenty-two years old.

Yes, I was twenty-two, but I had already been following the work of Gian Francesco Malipiero, of whom I have many fond memories. Even during the war years, Malipiero was able to keep open a channel of information focused above all on the sixteenth and seventeenth centuries, not only Monteverdi but also the theorists. I still remember him showing us the composition treatises of Zarlino, Vicentino, Gaffurio, and Doni. In the last years of the war Venice was a strange cultural environment, a type of refuge that attracted people such as Massimo Bontempelli and Arturo Martini, the sculptor. On one occasion, Martini gave me a special type of clay that was used for making metal stamps, exactly like those German ones that could be used to falsify documents very well. I also remember Professor Arcangelo Vespignani, a socialist, who was a professor of radiology and a great man of culture and ideas. In 1946, I told Malipiero that I wanted to study Hindemith's *Unterweisung im Tonsatz,* and he informed me that a young musician had just arrived in Venice who possessed this treatise.[1] It was Bruno

Maderna, whose great generosity I would like to recall right away, but also—what for me was truly fundamental—his absolutely different way of living music. He did not teach recipes, he did not hand out catalogues of methods, above all he avoided teaching his own ideas or an aesthetic. His fundamental concern was to teach musical thought, in particular about music in different, combined times, like the enigmatic canons of the Franco-Flemish Renaissance, for example. Following this procedure, one already had to know what the last one would be while writing the first; that is to say, one knew that the same sound read with different prolations would have had different durations, and thus different harmonic and melodic relationships. This was not the mentality of *Gradus ad Parnassum,* of setting note against note, two notes against one note, three notes against one note, in which we find an undoubtedly important, but very academicized, historical mechanism.

Do you remember the circumstances in which you met him for the first time?

Following Malipiero's instructions, I went to find him and I remember that I met him in the corridors of La Fenice during the Contemporary Music Festival, where the first concert was being held of what was then called *la giovane musica italiana* [the young Italian music], with compositions by Bucchi, Vlad, Zafred, Turchi, and Maderna.[2] So I started to visit him at his home and I recall that he wasn't doing very well. He had just arrived from Rome, where he had been studying very seriously with Alessandro Bustini.

The same teacher as Petrassi had.

Yes, and I still remember that on Bruno's piano there was a *Requiem* that then disappeared, a *Requiem* in which there were double fugues, mirror fugues, fugues and counterfugues.[3] He used to say that this *Requiem* was meant to be like a garland of flowers that floated along the river, and that the idea had come to him while reading Shakespeare's *Hamlet* at the point where Ophelia slowly disappears into the river. For Bruno, thinking about music meant studying together at the Marciana Library, studying the Coussemaker anthology, studying the various theorists starting with Hucbald of Saint-Amand and ending with the Venetians and Zarlino, always making continual comparisons between theory and practice.

And all this took place in the reading rooms of the Marciana under Bruno's guidance?

We spent entire months working together at the Marciana Library, and recalling that atmosphere it seems to me that it was the same as those of the great schools of painting in sixteenth-century Venice.

But what kind of instructions did Bruno give you. How did he develop your work in a concrete way?

Bruno would read one theorist, I would read another. Then we would exchange the information we had acquired and our thoughts about it. We then took the texts, for example, *Odhecaton* by Ottaviano Petrucci with its collection of two- and three-part chansons by the great Franco-Flemish masters are collected. We would transcribe them, comparing the practical aspect of the composition with the theoretical discussion contained in the various treatises. However, to give a more complete idea of our work, I would like to remind you that at the same time we were studying *The Dialogue Concerning the Two Chief World Systems* by Galileo Galilei, in which there appear three fundamental characters: Salviati, the Copernican, Sagredo, who posed the problems and the questions, and Simplicio, the conservative, thus the Ptolemaic. Other habitual reading for us was Zarlino's *Istitutioni harmoniche* and *Dimostrationi harmoniche*,[4] in which the debates which evolved in the semidarkness of St. Mark's Basilica among Zarlino, Francesco della Viola, who was a composer from Ferrara, Claudio Merulo and Adrian Willaert were reported. These discussions would then continue in the square.

Therefore, a dialectical journey that developed as it passed from the shadow into the light.

Yes, but it did not involve a dialectic. What developed in those dialogues was rather a journey, whose aim was to provide information that was made available to the reader. The reader would then relate to it to his own culture, his own needs, his own instinct, his own feelings, trying to find a logical thread. The texts neither dictated rules nor decreed anything.

Something like the serenity of a Platonic dialogue where one puts forward information and allows it to grow and develop. Now, however, I would like to ask you for a clarification of the general environment. Through the teaching of Bruno that you have described, by different means you discovered a reality about your city, a reality of which you had only a rather vague idea. Malipiero had already shown you something similar, as you told me, but now it was a matter of taking hold of a reality into which you were born but, of which, deep down, you were ignorant. I would like to ask you now to reconstruct this landscape a bit, that of the Venice in which you were born, as a physical and cultural reality. Because you were living more or less unconsciously in that reality until your studies with Bruno aroused in you a new awareness. From that moment all of the invisible veils of history began to be lifted, revealing each time diverse and unsuspected realities. How did this unveiling of Venetian reality come about? What was it like, the Venice of 1924, where you were born?*

To start with, I have to tell you that this unveiling continues even today. In fact I would say that I feel as if I have been uncovering, knowing, listening, seeing, and feeling Venice more than ever in these recent years. Above all through the experience that I have gained in the seven years that I have been with the Freiburg Experimental Studio, an experience which, by revealing to me other acoustic spectra, has given me other capabilities of seeing and hearing. On the other hand, I can tell you very little about Venice in 1924. The house in which I was born is on the Zattere, and my grandfather, who like me was called Luigi, was a painter. He was part of that Venetian school at the end of the nineteenth century which also included Giacomo Favretto, Guglielmo Ciardi, and Lino Selvatico. That was the world that invented the Biennale.

And what did your father do?

He was an engineer. He lived by projecting himself totally into his father's world, a world that he tried to preserve in every way because he worshiped it and considered it to be unique.

Up until this point an interest in the figurative arts has been revealed, but what place did music have in your home and in your family?

Many years later, much to my surprise, in a crate I found a copy of the *Italienische Lieder* by Hugo Wolf, one of the first editions.

Who read and played this music?

My grandmother. Through my father and mother I found out that my grandmother read and sang the modern music of that period. To think that even then in Venice they were singing Hugo Wolf is quite astounding, but just think that along with the Wolf's score I also found a very beautiful nineteenth-century edition of *Montezuma* by Sacchini.

My grandmother came from the Priuli Bon family, an old Venetian family. But my mother and father were also dedicated to music. I remember—my recollections start from when I was seven or eight years old—my father and mother at the piano playing and singing *Boris Godunov* by Mussorgsky.

Who played the piano?
My mother, but my father as well.

In the mists of these recollections, are you able to see some of the images that that music evoked in you?
Of course. I began to hear the name of Mussorgsky, I began to hear a kind of music that I did not know and that later, at a distance of ten years, I heard for the first time at La Fenice.

So that is probably the first music that you heard.
Mussorgsky, yes, but there were also records that my father collected in large quantities. There were Beethoven symphonies conducted by Toscanini with the NBC Orchestra and many Wagner records. A very strange thing happened to me then—I was twelve or thirteen years old—an impression truly of something unknown which I was unable to identify, namely the *Adagietto* of Mahler's *Fifth* conducted by Mengelberg. At that time, however, I read some advice by Schumann that stated, "If you pass a church and hear an organ, go in and listen."[5] I decided to put that into practice and so I often found myself in St. Mark's Basilica listening to the organ. I was often disappointed because the kind of music that I heard was of no interest to me. However the proto of St. Mark's (the proto is the architect responsible for the Basilica, one of the old offices of the Venetian Republic) was the architect Luigi Marangoni, whose second marriage was to my widowed grandmother. I asked him if there was an archive in St. Mark's, and so I established contact with the choir director, a Monsignor who was a mediocre musician,[6] under whose direction the chapel choir performed many masses composed at the end of the nineteenth century. It was in this way that I got hold of my first score, and I remember that it was the *Missa Papae Marcelli* by Palestrina in an eighteenth-century edition. Anyway, I had developed the habit of attending St. Mark's Basilica, mostly on Sunday, not really to listen to the choir as much as to the special acoustics of the church.

And how old were you when this happened?
Fourteen or fifteen years old.

So during that period you were going to high school in Venice?
Yes, in Venice.

And which high school?
"Marco Polo," which was a very rigorous school for both the professions and the humanities. At that same time there were various attempts to begin piano lessons, but I stopped right away because the practice was incredibly irritating to me, tedious in a way that I could not put up with.

What did you enjoy studying in high school?
I loved physics the best. I absolutely couldn't bear Latin, but then I also began to love Greek, because I had an extraordinary teacher, Francesco Rossi.

So physics and Greek. These are the things that in a way led you toward ancient classics.
As with Latin, I had little interest in Italian because of the hostility I had toward Dante, toward this world that was very difficult to understand and very difficult to memorize. With Greek, on the other hand, there were continual discoveries and continual insights because there was an extraordinary teacher, a famous Venetian Greek scholar who had disconcerting charm in the true sense of the word. Also the physics professor was an atypical person, old, very serious, who did the experiments while joking with us with a *bonhomie* and a kindness that in those days was very rare because those were the times when school was very "black shirt,"[7] authoritarian.

In 1942, you finished high school and passed your exams. Those were the war years. You were eighteen years old and, therefore, you were capable of reflecting upon the social and political realities that surrounded you. You spoke before of school as being "black shirt." What memories do you have of those times, and of the war years, when you finished high school?
Those high school years were, in a certain sense, lucky for me. This was because of Giovanni and Luigi Vespignani, the two sons of that radiologist who was already a socialist in 1942. We were very good friends, and still are today, even though we see one another only rarely. But at that time in the Vespignani home one breathed an air of opposition and resistance, an air of freedom in a cultural and political sense,

and naturally not without risks. Meetings like those I have mentioned took place there, with the sculptor Arturo Martini, who provided the clay to create the counterfeit stamps. It was there that I used to meet Bontempelli, who at that time had distanced himself from fascism and was completely absorbed in his magic imagination, real and unreal. In addition to the Vespignani home, there was another place in Venice that had a great attraction for me. It was Carlo Cardazzo's art gallery "Il Cavallino," which is now in Milan in Via Manzoni and is called "Il Naviglio." Carlo Cardazzo was a man of remarkable and high culture, who published Cocteau, Verlaine, and Malipiero's monograph on Stravinsky.[8] In his art gallery he mounted exhibitions that were surprising for us because they had nothing to do with the fascist rhetoric of that time.

During that period, when you were still a high school student, what were you reading?
My father had a remarkable library, which always intrigued me. I remember that during fascism I found the first Italian translations of the Russian poets and writers of the first years after the revolution: the Serapion Brothers,[9] Lunts, Yesenin. Moreover, Einaudi had already begun its project to deprovincialize Italian culture, translating the Americans as well as the Russians.

You were also reading the Americans then?
Yes, that was the great advance made by *Il Politecnico*.[10] There was Pavese, there was Gogol circulating in the first translations.

You read these things, you read Gogol?
Yes, I read Gogol, I read Rilke who both had an incredible attraction for me because that world was so far away and mysterious.

It was in these same years that your meeting with Malipiero also took place, who in Venice was a bit of a guru in the musical community. When and how did that meeting come about?
This also happened thanks to my father, who one day told me, "Look, I spoke with Malipiero. He is expecting you."

But when you met him, you knew almost nothing about music. You had tried many times to study the piano, and every time you had failed; you loved music, but you weren't even an amateur. You had only the slightest rudiments. Did you know how to read music?

Barely. In the 1940s in Padua, from the publisher Zanibon, I had obtained the *Practical Manual of Harmony*, by Rimsky-Korsakov.[11] I remember that I wanted to understand the difference between the major and minor triad, and the fourth and the sixth, and I played them on the piano in order to understand what the difference was.

So at twenty years old you went to meet Malipiero knowing little or nothing, having only the desire to develop a closer acquaintance with music.

Yes, but I found myself in a bizarre position between great attractions and repulsions: the Cardazzo exhibitions at the "Cavallino" had induced me to reject all nineteenth-century painting, and then I had listened to Monteverdi's *Orfeo* at the Vespignani home, where there were also drawings by Giorgio Morandi, and drawings and paintings by Massimo Campigli and Mario Sironi. In this state, full of desire, nostalgia, and curiosity, I introduced myself to Malipiero, who was, as you said, a music guru. However, from then on, I began to understand that in Venice Malipiero had been treated badly.

What do you mean by that?

In Venice he was a little bit like a monarch, and, as such he had his court. At the Conservatory, when he came down from his Director's rooms, there was the court of teachers who would be waiting for him, and there they would have their first meeting with their monarch, who would say witty and bizarre things, thus arousing laughter from his courtiers. I said that he was treated badly because the greater Malipiero was in a way blocked out by readings and interpretations that never went beyond the surface.

Therefore, according to you, a deeper and more attentive interpretation could today reveal unknown depths in Malipiero's music.

In my opinion, yes. The only one who tried to do it was Hermann Scherchen who died in Florence while conducting the *Orfeo* triptych [in 1966].[12] In those years of cultural closed-mindedness, Malipiero spoke to me of Schoenberg, Webern, his meetings with Bartók, and of the early music composers. It was thanks to him that I first got my hands on scores by Monteverdi and the Gabrielis. With him one would feel as though one were being led by the hand through a labyrinth of thoughts and knowledge drawn from extremely varied cultures. I remember, for example, that it was he who introduced me to Dallapiccola.

Did he introduce you personally or only to his music?
Personally. From 1946 I began to feel a great attraction to the music of Dallapiccola, but I was already a little more trained because Malipiero had made me study with one of his students. At that time I was then a type of external-internal student of the Conservatory. I took the fourth-year and seventh-year exams.[13]

Who was this student? We would like to know his name.
Raffaele Cumar. Along with the study of counterpoint, which I was really interested in, above all in its more complex forms, I continued my ritual meetings with Malipiero. I knew that when he left the Conservatory around one-thirty, he had the habit of going for a walk and so I would go and wait for him. We would walk and converse, and from him I heard for the first time about Schoenberg and Webern. It was then practically impossible to listen to the music of the Viennese, and having just read Herbert Fleischer's book on contemporary music,[14] I felt very attracted to those composers.

And Malipiero, what did he tell you about Schoenberg?
Well, many different things: you know, Malipiero's conversation was very erratic. Sometimes he spoke to me about Schoenberg as a guest in his house, at the villa in Asolo, but in all those observations, even those that were impromptu, there was always the greatest respect. He also spoke to me about Berg. He gave me a lot of details that I was later able to verify through reading the letters that Malipiero had exchanged with the two Viennese musicians, a vast and enormously interesting correspondence, which are perfectly cataloged and preserved in the archive at the Fondazione Cini. Through my meetings with Malipiero I discovered the illustrious centuries of Venetian culture, the fifteenth century, the sixteenth century, the seventeenth century, but an interesting incident caused this discovery to become interwoven with another. When I was eighteen years old I met Emilio Vedova for the first time, and with him I began a long "journey," at times very slow, and at times fast and sometimes it became even subversive in the true sense of the word. Vedova lived in a studio-warehouse in San Vio.[15] At the age of sixteen he had made splendid drawings of the great Venetian architecture through which he performed his own unveiling of historical reality, following the classic path of the complete autodidact.

The Vespignani home, the Cardazzo art gallery, the acoustics of St. Mark's, the walks with Malipiero, Vedova's drawings, the discovery of cultures that were so close at hand as to be invisible: these are, as you yourself have described, restlessness and nostalgia, immersions in a mysterious past that almost become the omens of your future challenges. Alongside these precious moments is also everyday life, for example, going to school, and not to the school of a "Maestro," but to the more mundane one of the University of Padua, to study law.

In fact I did those studies mostly to absolve myself of a family obligation. But secretly I would have preferred to study physics or engineering, fields of study toward which an old passion for Jules Verne directed me. Captain Nemo, submarines, or mines exerted a great fascination on me. By then, however, I had begun to study music and, therefore, I willingly agreed to study law. I have good memories of those years of study at the University of Padua because there was a very stimulating intellectual environment: just imagine, I studied philosophy of law with Norberto Bobbio. I would have liked to write my graduate thesis with him. I went and proposed one on Berdyaev, but he refused. He asked me why I had made that choice, but evidently my reasons were not sufficiently convincing for him. Berdyaev, alongside other Russian works translated into Italian, fascinated me enormously: for me they were voices from afar, expressions of a different reality.

You have already told me of other occasions when distant things have fascinated you, things that came from Russia, from Rilke's Prague, the depths of the sea, Captain Nemo. I would like to ask you if, in practice, this fascination with distant things had an impact on your life. Did you travel, did you go elsewhere or did you never leave Venice?

You know, there are two ways to travel: the journeys that one does with one's feet and those that one does with one's mind. At that time, my means of travel was the latter.

You never left Venice?

I made my first trip when I graduated, in 1946.[16] The classic journey after the degree.

Where did you go?

To Assisi. Giotto and St. Francis were my objectives. Then I went to Rome to get to know Ungaretti. I had written to him some time before asking his permission to set his *Poema della solitudine* to music.[17] This is how I first met the poet who I had been reading and admiring for so long and it was a very important meeting. You know, thinking about the encounters in my life, I think I have been privileged to have had such good fortune. Not only because I happened to meet extraordinary people, but because those meetings always involved something unexpected, but at the same time I always had the impression that they had been written down in advance somewhere.

Not only people but also places and objects seem to have come to you by way of unforeseen paths that, nevertheless, coincided with desires, expectations, anxieties; even sometimes with a vague nostalgia. This is something that recurs, and I don't mean as a leitmotif, but as an important way of interpreting your life today, of remembering it. It almost seems that you believe in it, that you ascribe a certain importance to it. What is chance for you?

It could be that chance is something that is already written without one knowing it. It could be something like what happened to me five days ago. I was in the Freiburg Studio doing my experiments and my studies, when who should enter but Gidon Kremer, who had come looking for me. To tell the truth, I had tried to find him before, but had failed to do so, and exactly the same thing had happened to him. At that moment, however, he came into the studio where I was working. We had never met before, and all of a sudden we spent five hours together talking. It was like a meeting of thousands of years because the words, the silences, the gesture of a hand, the glances expressed an infinite eloquence, which might just as well have arisen from a very old familiarity.

Do we want to recall these thousands of years in a few minutes?

Private things, never told to anyone, feelings, problems, inner disasters, everything flowed as though we had always known one another. It was almost like a contest to see who could ask the most intimate and direct questions. Maybe I was predisposed for such a meeting because a few days previously I had participated in an international forum organized by Mikhail Gorbachev's government.[18]

In the meetings between Sakharov and the many scientists, between the Californian physician who flew in to help the victims of Chernobyl, the industrialists, the representatives of high finance, the artists and the intellectuals, an atmosphere was created that was vibrant and even overwhelming. There was almost a physical sensation that something absolutely new was happening. All this happened with a generosity that was able to break down all barriers, all ideological tenets, all restrictions, even religious ones. That atmosphere, which was so fervid and in which the various feelings, the various instincts and the various explanations were blown sky-high, reminds me of a phrase of Nicola Vicentino, who says, in his *Ancient Music Adapted to Modern Practice,* "You will recognize many cases in which reason is not a friend to sense, and sense is not receptive to reason."[19] He was referring to the problem of chromaticism, which at that time was being opposed by the Church, but for me his argument contained a fundamental concept, that new problems need to be addressed in another way, creating a different mental *habitus*. There is a line of thought that goes from Faust to Breuer and Wittgenstein, which goes something like this: where science can no longer explain, there life begins.

Ancient Music Adapted to Modern Practice?

In Moscow something similar happened. One experienced one of those great moments of physical, moral, sentimental, and historical disorientation in which one felt the new pressure from all directions. You know, in those moments I thought that what was being put at stake was not only our lives and our world, but much more. I thought that other worlds were called into question, other planetary systems and so I called to mind the great lesson of Giordano Bruno with his infinite universes, which today's astronomy is discovering from the observatories of Pasadena in California, identifying completely new galaxies and extraordinary rainbows billions of light years away. That desire for change was supported by such an acute awareness of the problems afflicting the present that it acquired universal vibrations. The eternal battle between the conservatives and the innovators creates difficulty, tensions, and hopes that are difficult to imagine. I heard about the great Russian events from the periods of Peter the Great, Alexander II, and now Gorbachev. But in those discussions there was a typically Dostoevskian mixture of hope and pessimism. Daily life is black, difficult, and very hard, and one can say with Hölderlin that the gods are dead and that the present time is miserable; the new gods have yet to be born.[20] These contradictions, this pessimism, but also this enthusiasm create a different condition. Basically, for us in the West, real life is much more advanced than political reality, which tends to preserve the status quo. In Moscow today, I think that things are exactly the opposite. This is because the innovators are in power, while the resistance and the opposition—Gorbachev has said this openly many times—are widespread within the party, but above all among those who have lived up until now according to a methodology which is not that of the seventy years of the revolution. This deep desire for change can take on diverse expressions, depending upon the countries in which it occurs, but in substance it overrules ideologies. In my opinion, it is the great historical force in today's world (this is why I spoke before of Giordano Bruno's planetary suggestions). It is the force of things, problems, our feelings, and it springs from today's technology. The use of information technology and of the mass media is governed by a "know-how" that is absolutely outdated. And instruction, from elementary school to the university, remains humanist. It is a real disaster. No effort at all is undertaken to prepare for what one can easily foresee, that is, for a different development of the future.

This terrible conflict in which you recognize the great historical force in the world of today derives from an extremely deep and widespread awareness of the present contrast between technology and mindset. The difficulty of forging an adequate mental attitude toward technology is, in the first place, an educational problem and at the same time a political responsibility. Therefore, let us again return to speaking a little about that unsurpassed genius of teaching that Bruno Maderna was. Our discussion stopped in 1946, during the time of those first meetings and your first studies together of the old treatises at the Marciana Library.

Bruno's life at that time was very difficult. In practical terms he was just about making ends meet by writing soundtracks for fourth-rate films. During that period he was conducting only a little, but his great generosity, the generosity typical of men who define an era, was not diminished by this. His teaching did not consist of one or two hours of lessons; it meant practically living together.

We remained shut up in the attic to study, copy, and write music for hours on end, then we went out to walk and eat. Bruno, I, and the other students (Gastone Fabris and Renzo Dall'Oglio, who are nowadays working in the management of the RAI) went to the Lido together to swim with our girlfriends. We got totally plastered and had the most euphoric escapades. We moved with great ease from the most rigorous discipline of our studies to this incredibly entertaining atmosphere, and in every circumstance the same desire to participate in life affirmed itself in us.

You spoke of courses, students, but where and how did these take place?

At Bruno's house.

But then it was something that was absolutely private, from which Bruno gained nothing materially.

That's correct. Bruno never wanted a cent.

He spent, in other words, he spent much of his time training those boys who he believed in.

Certainly, certainly. It was like one of those painting workshops of the Renaissance, but the quality of Bruno's instruction would be revolutionary even today. The essence of that instruction consisted in what could be defined as comparative study. For example, one would take an element of composition such as rhythm or duration, and would examine how the various composers had thought of it and used it in various periods. From the *isorhythmic* motets by Guillaume de Machaut or from John Dunstable one would leap forward to the compositional techniques of the Flemish Masses, in which it was the *tenor* (which could be a secular song or a Gregorian chant) that provided the basic compositional elements, which could be intervals or rhythm, as in the case of the *Missa Di dadi* by Josquin Desprez.

What does "Missa Di dadi" mean exactly?

You are aware that the *tenor* has a particular song: in the six pieces of the mass the durations are varied according to the roll of dice. If, for example, a six comes up, a value is six times the doubled note value; if it is one, it is doubled once.[21]

So it is an augmentation technique from one to six, but stochastically, to quote Xenakis.

Exactly. However, the extraordinary thing is that I am discovering that the various techniques, the varied conceptual perspectives of the Flemish in music, painting, and literature are closely linked to Jewish thought. In the Talmud, you find a concept presented, but underneath it, along with the scripture the oral traditions with diverse opinions on that theme are recorded.

The concept, in other words, does not become fixed once and for all, but is made dynamic through all its variants throughout the various ages. The continuous mutation of the rhythmic values that is revealed in the *Missa Di dadi* continued to be produced in other music of other periods. I was able to recognize its reflection in the *Fantasy in C* [op. 17] by Schumann, and in the variations by Beethoven, Brahms, and Schoenberg. At other times our study focused on song. We would start with

Francesco Landini and his rhetoric about song, come to consider the *tenor* of *L'Homme armé* in *Odhecaton* or of the Ockeghem masses, and then we would proceed up to the lieder by Schubert, Schumann, Wolf, Webern, and Dallapiccola.

Another fundamental lesson that was taught in our school was the way of thinking about music in time. To think about it, not at the moment in which it takes place, but in various different moments. It was about overcoming the idea of the progression of time understood as a process moving from left to right. According to this more fluid and elastic perspective, in the course of a composition, after fifteen minutes, for example, you discover a relationship with something that happened seven minutes earlier and so forth in an unceasing network of references that advance, return, intersect, and superimpose themselves, building bridges all of a sudden in various directions.

This is basically about the discovery of the potentiality implicit in the material, and that can be noticed only in the course of the composition's development.

Yes, certainly, and it follows that a unique time does not exist, and one can see the same thing very well in literature. For example, Robert Walser in *The Walk* goes out of the house to buy bread. He meets some people, sees some friends, listens to a song, and watches the cat. All these kinds of things happen, but he doesn't buy the bread. It is not true therefore that, between two points, there is a straight line that joins them. Quite often the lines start out but do not arrive at that point.

Then it would be necessary to replace straight lines with hieroglyphics that do not go anywhere in relation to the set objective.

Just so, and Bruno's teaching ended up by questioning the very idea of planning. A fundamental contribution to that discussion was provided by our study of enigmatic canons. It was a study but it was also a bit of a game. Bruno and I went along for a while, exchanging enigmatic canons. He would write one without giving the solution, and then he'd pass it to me so I could solve it, and I would do the same thing.

You were therefore aware that through this enigmatic canon game something like a contemporary ideology of composition was being created?

Yes. Already at that time I had, and continue to have, a great love for Dallapiccola's musical thought, which is very often based on canons. Moreover, Aldo Clementi works exclusively on canons in an absolutely brilliant and innovative manner. Therefore, it is not by accident that my first piece is entitled *Variazioni canoniche sulla serie dell'op. 41 di Arnold Schönberg*, opus 41 being the *Ode to Napoleon Buonaparte*.

Therefore, the term canonical *in this case is due directly to the experience with the enigmatic canons that you had with Bruno Maderna.*

Exactly. It is not like a Frescobaldi-like canon or a Renaissance canon. What it involves is rather certain elements that are composed in a canonical manner.

That are arranged in a circle.

Yes, that are arranged in a circle, but not necessarily. Therefore, it is not about the interval, or the duration, or the timbre. There are certain elements that even today, when looking at the score, I can't remember, but I know that they were a particular kind of canon. Fundamentally, what I am doing today in Freiburg with this tool that is called a *Halaphon* is something similar.[22] You render a sound more dynamic in space by projecting it through various loudspeakers at contrasting speeds. This sound can then be extended, moving around in a single direction and in multiple directions. You can then make the same sound move by means of four other movements in space. For example, this can be done with different dynamics, with different tempi, accelerating and slowing down, or even in leaps. With just a single element, a single acoustic signal, you can create various dynamics in space, naturally depending upon the spaces you have available. The resulting listening experience is extremely complex, but the more extraordinary thing is that you do not need four different signals; a single signal is enough. This is again an illustration of the Talmudic concept whereby a theme is considered in various ways. Musil states, "There are six possibilities; the one chosen is not always the best one." Many times I am asked: "Why does C sharp come after C?" I don't know. After C there could be an eighth-tone or any other sound. These are the mysteries of composition and Bruno knew how to introduce them to me in an incomparable manner. Bruno also helped me to approach these types of secrets by studying Webern. I remember that we successively compared Webern to Schubert, Schumann, Wolf, Heinrich Isaac, and Haydn. The comparison with Schubert focused essentially on the melody because often in Webern one single sound is like an entire melody by Schubert. The sound quality, its mode of attack, its development, and its decreasing contain a whole melodic arc, in a highly concentrated synthesis. Therefore, it is not a matter of one or another single sound becoming fixed like a stone in a mosaic. This conception of sound, as you know, was Maderna's great quality as a conductor.

Yes, and, moreover, in the preface to Webern's Six Bagatelles op. 9, Schoenberg hints at the same concept by talking about a novel in a sigh.[23] *And the Webern-Schumann comparison? This seems less obvious to me. I would be happy if you could explain it a bit.*

Schumann has a way of fragmenting material that I find extraordinary.

Melodic material?

Harmonic and also melodic. In the *Fantasy in C*, but also in the large Sonatas, Schumann proceeds by means of fragments that fit together one after another. There isn't any thematic development, nothing progressive. There are harmonic, rhythmic or melodic fragments that become completely broken down by other fragments. There is the fragment that fragments itself. Think of the thought process and the invention of Edmond Jabès, the great poet who lives in Paris. Think of Hölderlin and the relation between yesterday, today and tomorrow: the yesterday that lives in the today that anticipates the tomorrow, the tomorrow that lives in the yesterday, in the past, the rediscovery in ourselves of that which was, the relationship with tradition that isn't such because so often it is betrayal. No, rather I think of an authentic past that lives buried in us and which suddenly jumps out and which we then discover is from two thousand years ago, carried along by the currents of history, by great waves of culture.

All this, in a certain sense, would be overshadowed in Schumann's compositional technique, which makes the fragments interact with one another?

Exactly. Those same things that I also find in Webern. The Wolf-Webern binomial resembles that of Schubert-Webern, except that the same type of relationship is revealed through another technique, which is much more closely related. It concerns a contiguity that recalls that between Mahler and Schoenberg, and between Berg and Webern. The instrumentation of Mahler's *Ninth* is again found in *Wozzeck*, in *Lulu*, and in the *Three Pieces for Orchestra* [op. 6].

Yes, and I believe one could also add that the first measures of Mahler's Ninth, with their fragmentation of the material, also remind one very much of Webern. The next binomial, the one formed by Webern and Heinrich Isaac, seems too transparent to me. It is known that Webern graduated with a dissertation that was actually on Isaac. I would like you, instead, to discuss the Webern-Haydn comparison a little.

Yes, certainly. The Webern-Isaac comparison is clear for the reasons that you mentioned, but one must not forget that all of Webern's choral output is based on canons. The comparison with Haydn is clearer if one takes into consideration Webern's quartet,[24] in which a construction of the beats within the rhythms and the refrains is found that reminds one of Haydn's quartets.

Webern was often accused of rhythmic impoverishment, but it is precisely in those pulsations within an apparently simple meter, that the recollection of Haydn suddenly explodes in one's memory. I tell you these things because it was precisely on this basis that the conflict regarding the interpretation of Webern flared up at Darmstadt.[25] On one side there was Bruno and I who thought in this way, and on the other side there was Pousseur and Stockhausen, who did their statistical analyses of Webern's *Concerto for Nine Instruments* [op. 24].

You talked about a clash. How big was that clash?

It was a clash between differing analyses and interpretations that then reached the point of the absolute dominance of a vision of Webern that was abstract and purely mathematical. The difference was between Webern being understood as a purely acoustic phenomenon, and our conception of Webern's musical thinking, that is, of its connections, of its contexts and of its derivations. So we get to the clash of 1959, which was erroneously understood as my attack on John Cage, when in reality it was an attack on the academism that was developing in Europe, in Darmstadt in particular.[26]

Borio found, I no longer remembered it, a letter of mine from 1958, thus before the clash, in which is indicated the fact that Steinecke had appointed Wörner and me to edit the *Darmstädter Beiträge*. I had proposed to dedicate the second volume to Cage because I had understood that we were dealing with a problem that needed to be faced.[27] From that point my total isolation caused by my denunciation of their inability to deal analytically with Cage and his world, reducing it to a formula that was easy to copy. The Darmstadt circle was unable to penetrate, and was, therefore, responsible for misunderstanding, the significance of Cage and of his proposals. I remember that when I finished giving my lecture ["Historical Presence of Music Today"], Stockhausen was very violent toward me because he felt personally attacked and he was right. In fact, I stated clearly that John Cage represented a culture emanating from California, a culture that demonstrated in its painting and in its music clear relationships with the East, think of Tobey, Rothko, and the other schools of that country that have relationships with certain mentalities and thoughts, and with Chinese, Buddhist, Indian, and Zen practices.

Let us put aside for the moment these phantoms of Zen and these controversies of long ago, often arising, as you have explained, from misunderstandings. Speaking of Bruno's teachings, you previously touched on the name of Bellini, that Bellini whose scores I see lying around everywhere here in your study, even on the carpets. What does it mean, this resurgence today of your interest in Bellini, and what did this music mean for you many years ago when you discovered it while reading it with Bruno Maderna? The enigma and the miracle of the Bellinian melody reported with overwhelming clarity by Wagner—what is it to you?

Also Schopenhauer spoke of Bellini and above all of the vocal writing in *Norma*,[28] whose musical purity he identified as one of the greatest models of the necessity of pure listening, in contrast to the habit already then much in vogue and prevalent today of seeing music instead of listening to it. Above all, I think that in Bellini's vocal writing there aren't those differences among the recitatives, arias, cabalettas, and so on, even though they are marked in the score. It is all about one voice that manifests itself in a varied manner, according to the various mysteries of *musica practica, musica mundana, musica coelestis, musica imaginalis*. In this voice it is not well known, at least as far as I am concerned, where the physicality of the vibrations and the acoustics truly begin and where instead there emanates a musical thought, much more explicit, than the undulatory vibrations. It reminds me of Giorgio Agamben's statement, taken from his book *Stanzas*: ". . . giving a body to the incorporeal and rendering the corporeal incorporeal. . . . To shape the maximum reality seizing on the maximum unreality."[29] One of the reasons Bellini's vocal writing still upsets me is precisely this: I can never tell where the corporeal is and where the spiritual is, where the physicality is and where, on the other hand, the thought. There is a passage in Henri Corbin's book *Spiritual Body and Celestial Earth* in which all this seems to me to be wonderfully explained: "there are sounds . . . perfectly perceptible by the active Imagination, which are not conditioned by vibrations of the air; they constitute the archetype-Image of sound [sound as it exists in the pure state of *mundus imaginalis*] . . . that presupposes the integration of physics as such into psycho-spiritual activity, their conjunction in an intermediate world rising above the dualism of matter and spirit, of senses and intellect."[30] Bellini, Catania, Sicily. Answering a question of mine on sounds in the high register, Sciarrino said, "When thoughts make sounds, they sound very high." Sicily, with the varied mixtures of Greek, Arabic, Spanish, and the very ancient Egyptian or Hebrew cultures; wisdom from which emanates music; the infinity of Sicilian panoramas with songs that suddenly come and go like winds bringing the sounds of a Jew's Harp or of other ancient songs: all this is what I hear in Bellini. In Bellini, a contemporary of Rossini and Donizetti, I really perceive another culture. In his scores I am struck by the use of fermatas. There are fermatas that interrupt words, interrupt the rhetoric of the song, inject silences in which other sounds resonate, other voices vibrate. Other physical or imaginary undulations come to life, creating within that monody an opening that allows it suddenly to rise up. In Bellini, the orchestra performs its function of accompanying the singing in a nonuniform fashion: first preceding it, then falling silent, and the song rises alone. I think what can be observed in this phenomenon is the reflection of a very ancient concept, even Greek, of singing as a privileged moment in music, a reflection, if you will, of the conflict between Apollo and Marsyas. I believe this kind of mythical antagonism between voice and instruments in Bellini's scores should be investigated, and also the meaning of the silences. For example, in the prelude to *Norma,* fermatas block the sound of the orchestra. The empty measures, which are not usually observed, introduce sudden silences that are not empty but constitute a silence dense with other sounds gushing from the memory, from the ear, from a sudden gathering of surrounding acoustical signals. Scriabin said that "even silence is sound. There are musical works that are based on silence,"[31] and Varèse, for his part, observed that "Debussy and Strauss both had a wonderful sense of using silence and the suspense and intensity latent in the musical pause."[32]

You mentioned before Wagner's admiration for Bellini and this brings to mind one of the most prodigious musical silences. I think, the third act of *Tristan* is a continuous silence that every so often comes to rest on a fragment that is the B-flat minor chord with which the act begins and to which it occasionally returns. Although there are voices and instruments, I think this chord that returns every so often is like a limit that says: now begins a silence.

It is these extraordinary silences of Wagner, the farewells, the continuous *Lebewohl,* that burst forth from that absence of sound. They operate exactly as Scriabin and Varèse said, or as Bellini did, for example, in the prelude to *Il pirata,* where the dramatic, highly explosive moment of the storm is given by the pauses, the silences, the empty measures. The same thing is found in Verdi's *Otello.* Here too, the storm does not arise so much from loud sounds, but rather from the silences that scream, that shriek, that rage. As Wittgenstein observed, there is an *Unklangbar* which is much more violent than what is actually said.[33]

These observations that you have made on the musical use of silence resulted as a direct and indirect consequence from a situation that the new music underwent in Darmstadt in 1959, when your positions with regard to the music of the past and traditional music were clarified. Fundamentally, the key to the scandal was a certain way of understanding and analyzing Webern's music. But in 1959 we are already quite well advanced in your output. I think we should go back a moment to those early days which, as you mentioned previously in passing, are given to Variazioni canoniche. *How did you get to appear on the music scene as a composer? We had reached 1946, your meeting with Bruno Maderna and your studies with him. Then within four years your professional training had arrived at the point that you felt you were ready for your debut. How did these things happen? How did the circumstances arise to allow your appearance on the new music scene?*

The reasons or the components are various, but fundamental—as you say—was the rigorous study I did with Bruno Maderna. Four years of comparative studies jumping between various histories, between different periods, and also among non-European cultures. Studies of theoretical texts, practical texts, experimental texts, and especially on the mode of thought of the enigmatic canons. Then a very important incident took place in 1948. It was my meeting with Hermann Scherchen, who was in Venice that year at the invitation of the Biennale, teaching an international orchestral conducting course which lasted one month. Once again it was Malipiero, who guided our steps, Bruno's and mine, suggesting that we attend that course. It was he who introduced us to Scherchen. That meeting meant very much to me. I started following him around when he gave concerts. I often stayed with him in Zurich or Rapallo, and it was a continual learning experience during which he told me of all the musical experiences that he had had since 1912 in Berlin. The premieres of Schoenberg and Webern, of Stravinsky, of Bartók, the cultural life at the time of the Weimar Republic, of Berlin before Nazism and above all the research on the transformation of sound which took place when it was broadcast on the radio. Bruno went to Darmstadt for the first time in 1949, and on that occasion a piece of his for two pianos was performed. I do not know if it still exists.[34] The following year he and Scherchen saw a score of mine and told me, "Send it to Darmstadt and we'll see." So it was that I came to Darmstadt on the basis of Maderna and Scherchen's introduction. I had the first performance of my *Variazioni canoniche,* which provoked an incredible scandal. There is a tape recording of that concert in which you hear Scherchen's voice addressing the clamorous audience, saying, "Schwein[e]bande" ("bunch of pigs"). The really important thing related to the premiere is the fact that the professor of composition in 1950 at the Darmstadt Ferienkurse was Edgard Varèse. I did not know who he was. I had never heard of him. The day after the performance I went to his class and he asked me for the score. He analyzed it for hours and later, instead of giving me advice, he posed problems to me. He made me realize the problems that the score raised, in this way informing me of what I had done in certain places without realizing it. As you can see, it always comes back to that famous mystery of composition. Darmstadt was thus a brilliant invention on the part of Wolfgang Steinecke, Mayor Ludwig Metzger, who was of the Social Democratic Party, Karl Amadeus Hartmann, Scherchen, who, for the first time after the war, gave a group of young people the opportunity to meet. Stockhausen, Boulez, Maderna, Berio, Henze, Clementi, Evangelisti, Klebe, and other composers were the first to arrive. Then came the interpreters of Schoenberg: Kolisch, Steuermann, Leibowitz, Fortner, Strobel, Stuckenschmidt, Horkheimer, and Adorno. It was a unique opportunity: discussions, disagreements, and commonalities formed the very fertile basis of the Ferienkurse. Within a few years we ourselves became consultants, thanks to Steinecke's great intelligence. Boulez, Stockhausen, Bruno, and I were invited several times to spend a few days in Darmstadt to develop proposals and projects. An invaluable tool was created when Bruno founded the instrumental group made up of performers who later became very famous, such as Gazzelloni, the Kontarsky brothers, and the percussionist Caskel.[35] Under Bruno's direction, this chamber group brought to life the premieres of numerous works of music by the young composers of that time. Meanwhile, unleashed within me was Varèse's great lesson that I had begun to understand as a composer the day after our first meeting. This lesson of Varèse, which I hold to be fundamental, was completely ignored until a few years ago because I was regarded schematically: either the legacy of Schoenberg or Webern. In *Il canto sospeso* there is a section for wind instruments alone and percussion in which, I think Varèse's influence is very strong.[36] It is an influence that lasts to this day. In fact I continue to study his scores, discovering in them unique comparisons between Scriabin and Schoenberg, which I find very interesting. The famous combination of the interval of the fifth and the tritone, which Scriabin uses in his Sonatas, is also a typical chord of Schoenberg and Varèse. The octaves that Varèse uses, those superimposed octaves reminiscent of the beginning of Mahler's First Symphony where they determine the spaces, those sudden openings, today come back to me very clearly.

In those years, which were dominated by the Viennese legacy, Varèse was definitely out of fashion, and was considered to be something of an outsider. With very few exceptions, young composers were looking in other directions. Among these exceptions are you and Iannis Xenakis, who was also close to Varèse in the collaboration on the construction of the Philips Pavilion for the 1958 Brussels Expo. The Varèsian conception of music as an acoustic reality that corresponded to the intelligence contained within things, the perception of the dazzling musical potential in the currents of rivers, in the sandstorms of the desert, in the enchantment or the structure of the cathedral in Tournus seems like a metaphor for Einstein's equation of matter and energy. Varèse argued that music must release the energy contained in the hard core of physicality. However, this seems to me to take music composition in a specific direction, which is that of freedom, that freedom that in those years seemed to have slipped dramatically through the fingers of the musical avant-garde of Darmstadt. You knew Varèse during those years, and little by little you got in touch with him and with his music. What attractions, what things—which were missing from other models of modernity that you knew and you practiced through the lessons of Bruno and Scherchen—did you find in his music?

Besides Xenakis and I, in those years Bruno was particularly close to Varèse: he had become one of the conductors who was most devoted to and inspired by his music.[37] I remember very well seeing Bruno engaged in deciphering his scores with the composer beside him. It was a beautiful and friendly musical relationship in which I also shared.

You spoke of Varèse and freedom: I felt an attraction toward him, but by a strange destiny those fascinations intertwined with other insights and other knowledge. Just at that time, I slowly began to understand the great importance of Schoenberg through a deeper knowledge of the Jewish thought of the medieval Andalusian poet Yehudah Halevi translated by Rosenzweig, Benjamin's great teacher. Through reading his work and that of Martin Buber I turned to the great themes of the Torah. I then read Arab treatises, such as those by Safi-ad-din of the thirteenth century, in which certain problems are anticipated which Zarlino then addresses. The relationship between music and nature, so intense in the works of Varèse, is also particularly developed in *Neue Hall- und Ton- Kunst* by Athanasius Kircher, where a relationship-union among art, music, and nature is explicitly described and illustrated.[38] Echoes, resonances, water, and not only the famous four elements (water, air, earth, fire), and water assumes a great importance as, for example, in the work of the painter Grünewald, who was a hydraulic engineer. I am reminded of the Elector of Heidelberg's great garden, with its statues and water which, warmed by the sun, produces sounds. Those magnificent architectures with magic and mystery that hovers everywhere, the esoteric thought, the cohort of the alchemists and the strange characters who crowded the court of Rudolf II in Prague: all are places through which Giordano Bruno passed and in which he was active. And I am telling you all these things to enable you to understand how I realized that Schoenberg should be understood in another way. The idea of the twelve-tone series is, in fact, not a mechanical conception that is exhausted in the four possible forms of the series. It is a way of thinking that constantly challenges itself and seeks other possibilities, exactly as was the case in the Flemish period. Varèse had and still has great importance on a conceptual level and on that of compositional thought. Where he will always remain as an absolute innovator, however, at least in the European area, is in the use of percussion.

In the archives of the Havana Philharmonic in Cuba I found the letters that were exchanged between Varèse and Amadeo Roldán. Roldán was a musician associated with the New Corporation, to which Varèse, Antheil, Cowell, Ruggles, and Malipiero had also belonged.[39] He had made a thorough study of Yoruba percussion, which is that African musical culture that had been imported to Cuba by the Spanish with the slaves. Percussion, as you know, is at the center of interest of eminent scholars such as the Cuban musicologist Fernando Ortiz or Simha Arom, who is especially interested in the music of the Pygmies. Varèse, through Roldán, came into contact with this culture, in which the concept of percussion is infinitely more complex and subtle than we are used to here. Varèse knew of these drum orchestras in which the skins of two opposite parts of the drum are tuned differently from each other. These are drums that one strikes with the fingers, with the fingernails, with the palm, doing scales with one hand and simply striking with the other. The last time I visited Varèse in New York, he showed me the new drums that he had received from Africa.[40] It is no accident, I believe, that Varèse's *Ionisation* was premiered in 1931, in fact, in Havana. At the same time that such reductive statistical analyses of Schoenberg and Webern's works were being put forward, Varèse was perceived as moving toward other cultures, opening up other spaces, and in this way he was isolated in the position of an outsider.

And yet Varèse's example is certainly not unique: I am reminded of Marius Schneider's famous essay on the drum.[41] *Even Schneider, however, is regarded with some suspicion because his writings emphasize the ritualistic aspects of making music, in some way, creating a bifurcation in our musical culture: on the one hand, there is the impulse toward rationality, statistical analysis, structure, and series; on the other, there is an irrational horizon where there are ritualistic and magical aspects, aspects which, it should be noted, are not at all alien to our culture.*

I agree. You put your finger on what I, perhaps exaggerating a little, call the catastrophe of Western European culture.

The different horizons pointed out by Varèse were revealed to you just as by dissociating yourself from the dominant European culture, you discovered a different and infinitely richer way of interpreting Schoenberg's music. Speaking of Schoenberg, I would like to delve into a private aspect. You married Nuria, Schoenberg's daughter. How did you meet her? And in what way has this family connection helped you understand new aspects of that musician who for years was at the center of your interests?

I have already told you that at the beginning of the 1950s I was very close to Scherchen. I often followed him during his concert tours in a kind of permanent apprenticeship. In 1953 Dr. Herbert Hübner, who was the director of "Das neue Werk" in Hamburg and who had often invited Maderna as conductor and me as composer, asked me who, in my opinion, could make a full score of Schoenberg's *Moses und Aron* from the microfilm of the condensed score. I suggested Scherchen, who had already conducted *The Dance around the Golden Calf* with extraordinary success in Darmstadt, and he immediately accepted. So

Scherchen reconstructed the score, which was performed in Hamburg in 1954 with Hans Rosbaud as conductor.[42]

Naturally I went to Hamburg to attend that extraordinary event, and there I met Nuria, who had come from America with her mother, Gertrud. In 1955 Nuria came to Darmstadt because her uncle was there, the great violinist Rudolf Kolisch, founder and leader of the famous Kolisch Quartet. In that same year Nuria and I were married.

If I remember correctly, the first time I went to the Schoenberg house in Los Angeles was in 1964.[43] What made the deepest impression on me was his study. It was really a piece of Vienna from the 1920s transported there like an island. His hand was present everywhere. There were tables built by him, books bound by him, scores by Brahms and Beethoven studded with his annotations, photocopies of scores by Berg and Webern dedicated to him, and entire boxes of correspondence with the letters collected in sets: Schoenberg-Kandinsky, Schoenberg-Berg, Schoenberg-Webern, and many others not yet filed away. I happened to find there the first edition of Busoni's *New Aesthetic* with all of Schoenberg's glosses written on pieces of paper glued to the printed sheets: practically a conversation at a distance between the two musicians, which appropriately was later reproduced here in Germany in a printed edition.[44]

I noticed that the classics of philosophy were missing from Schoenberg's library. Not even the shadow of a book from the period between Marx and Adorno. But this, they explained, was due to reasons of prudence with respect to FBI "visits" during the McCarthy period, which were extremely frequent in the homes of Schoenberg, Eisler, Brecht, Klemperer, Feuchtwanger, Thomas Mann, and all other German emigrant intellectuals who had given birth in America to that community they called "the new Weimar."[45]

Schoenberg died with a seventy-dollar-per-month pension, and there are letters from the Guggenheim Foundation which refused him any form of a subsidy. But it was not just the material hardships. The difficult plight of the exile, the Jew in exile, who experiences the contrast between the culture of his devastated country and a form of foreign culture, revealed before my eyes an inner scenario that was shocking, a terrible tragedy. From that point on, little by little, I began to understand the great violence of certain of Schoenberg's expressions, a violence triggered by the contrast between different cultural stratifications.

All this, however, was not immediately obvious to me. There were smokescreens erected around Schoenberg, especially by his German prophets. The book of letters edited by Erwin Stein is an obvious example. The very act of choosing the letters limits, excludes and censors.[46] Two letters, recently discovered thanks to his grandson E. Randol Schoenberg (the son of one of the Nuria's brothers) and addressed respectively to Einstein and to the rabbi of Los Angeles, spoke of the Jewish element in the Flemish school, a matter that had previously never been raised. By a curious coincidence, two years ago I found a Kabbalistic text in Granada, the *Sefer Yetzirah,* which contains an analysis of phonetics based on numbers.[47] There are three mother letters, seven double letters, weak and strong, and twelve simple letters. God's name is unpronounceable because when the first temple was destroyed by the Assyrian-Babylonians, vocalization was lost. In this book it is written that only when the temple will be rebuilt, God's name may be pronounced. In the analysis of the Hebrew alphabet, of the guttural, palatal, lingual, dental, and labial consonants, there is a technique midway between inhaling and exhaling that is found in Schoenberg's music: in *Sprechgesang,* in the choruses, in *De profundis,* and all this naturally derives from other cultures, in comparison with which you can see how reductive current interpretations are.

From the Schoenberg study in Los Angeles, we have now returned, through the recently discovered letters, to the Jewish element illustrated by the Kabbalistic treatise of ancient Granada, a city located at the confluence of Arab, Christian and Jewish cultures. Let's follow this seemingly capricious itinerary and let's stay a little while in Granada, where for a moment I would like to try to tie together some of the things you've said so far.
    The Jewish culture in Schoenberg, the game of consonants in his choral works as a distant refraction of the analyses of the alphabet conducted in the Sefer Yetzirah, a very ancient stratification of culture in the mysterious charm of Bellinian melodies, a music that arises from the mists of time. From this dark and distant background, according to García Lorca, the folk song arises. Your Epitaffi per Federico García Lorca *date from between 1951 and 1953. Do we want to try to tie up this plot which was apparently woven by chance?*
    In 1948, when Scherchen was giving his conducting course, a group of thirty Brazilians arrived in Venice who had come from a school in Brazil that was founded and directed by Koellreuter, a German composer and conductor who had left Germany after 1933. Among these Brazilians was a very talented pianist and composer whose name was Eunice Catunda. She was half-Indian from Mato Grosso, and Scherchen

encouraged a kind of partnership between her, Bruno Maderna, and me. These were the years of the Popular Front, with their violent climate of disruption, and Catunda was a communist. Bruno and I would sign up in 1952, but even at that time we participated in the activities of the party. With Catunda there was, therefore, a profound affinity of viewpoints. From her we also garnered our first information about the rhythms of Mato Grosso, in a certain way anticipating the lesson that we would learn from Varèse. The most extraordinary thing that we experienced together, however, was the discovery of García Lorca, who Catunda already knew well. Scherchen invited us to compose some vocal pieces: Bruno chose those Greek lyrics in Quasimodo's translation, Catunda chose García Lorca, and I took a bit of one and a bit of the other.[48] What most attracted our attention was not so much the gypsy aspect of Lorca, but rather the metaphysical and surreal ones. It was a voice that put us into contact with other worlds.

So we found ourselves engaged in the study of Lorca, of the rhythms of Mato Grosso and Andalusia. Bruno had a book that contained a special study of gypsy rhythms, not gypsy in the folkloric sense but the Arabic gypsy rhythms of the Muezzin, whose songs use quarter and eighth tones. Thus was born the first *Epitaffio [España en el corazón]*, and it is notable that this work, as well as *Polifonica-Monodia-Ritmica*, is based on a Brazilian song. Everyone said that this latest work was based on Webern, but it is actually based on a song for Jemanja, who in Brazil is the goddess of the sea. It is a ceremonial song that the natives of Brazil chant while throwing wreaths dedicated to the goddess into the sea. It was actually Catunda who taught it to us. I took this material and used it both from the rhythmic and the intervallic point of view in *Polifonica-Monodia-Ritmica*.[49] I also derived *Epitaffio per García Lorca* [no. 1] from the same material, adding the rhythm and sounds of the *Bandiera rossa* in the second part. When the premiere took place in Darmstadt in 1952, Bruno, who always knew what was going on, told me that he was worried. If they had noticed that melody, entrusted in the second part to four tuned cymbals, it would have been a problem. Just imagine! In 1952, right in the midst of the Cold War, with the communists put on the index! The second *Epitaffio* was for Severino Gazzelloni's arrival at Darmstadt. I had received a commission for him from Strobel, that peculiar character who only loved music by Hindemith, but who also had the intelligence to support those composers whose music, while he did not care for it personally, he thought might be important. It was my first commission, and for Severino I came up with

Y su sangre ya viene cantando, also based on the superimposition of Andalusian rhythms. In these types of stimuli I also recognize Varèse's lesson that was slowly growing inside me. In the superimposed Andalusian gypsy rhythms I in fact discovered relationships with African rhythms and even with certain modes of singing. The use of speech in this work also has an undeniable connection with the discovery of *A Survivor from Warsaw,* which was revealed to us by Scherchen at the 1948 Venice Biennale.

So in your early works, timidly at first with Variazioni canoniche *and then more decisively with* Polifonica-Monodia-Ritmica *and* Epitaffio per García Lorca, *those phantoms are beginning to take shape and are being hybridized a little on the basis of your understanding of the New Music, leading it in other directions. These phantoms are those of Varèse, the rhythms of Afro-Cuban music, the Brazilian songs that Catunda had taught you, the Andalusian gypsy rhythms, and Lorca's poetry with its surreal visions, but it concerns materials that are essentially rhythmic in a strictly musical sense. The horizontal element, that aspect which is properly melodic, never appears, although the music of the Andalusian gypsies could have suggested this to you.*

The reason is simple. At that time I was still under the influence of those studies that Scherchen had made me do using three or four notes. If you take the pieces of *Epitaffio,* you will see that they are based on four or five notes and have nothing to do with a twelve-tone series. These four or five notes might come from the *Bandiera rossa,* from that song of Catunda, or, in the final song of the *Guardia civil,*[50] simply from the notes of the six strings of the guitar.

The use of melodic materials was therefore very frugal, very limited, and perfectly consistent with the analytical spirit of the New Music, filtered through your studies undertaken with Scherchen and Maderna.

Already in 1948, writing his two *Studi su Kafka,*[51] Maderna had made use of a minimum of material, a minimum of intervals, seeking so many possibilities of relationship and combination with the famous "magic squares."

The triptych marked your first encounter with García Lorca. The relationship would last until the next year, 1954, when you wrote, commissioned by Tatjana Gsovsky, the ballet Der rote Mantel, *adapted from* Don Perlimplín. *In that same year, however, there is* also La victoire de

Guernica, *a work that was inspired by Picasso's famous painting and which uses Paul Éluard's poetry. How did you set yourself on this path?*

One cannot say that it's really a path; it's an intersection of various circumstances: in 1952 I went to Paris with Scherchen and I met Boulez for the first time. He had just finished *Structures I*. Scherchen introduced me to Pierre Schaeffer and his studio of *musique concrète*.[52] In those days I also encountered Paul Éluard, not personally but through his poems. By now you already know of my curiosity about texts which I don't know, this sort of mysterious attraction, at that time it was toward Éluard as well as Apollinaire. Musically, I was feeling the need for a break with the schematic approach with which some were reducing Darmstadt. So I used other preexisting materials: *La victoire de Guernica*, its notes-intervals-rhythms, are based on the *Internationale*, but nowhere is it cited. What is obvious here is the extension of Bruno's lesson, the study of the Flemish masses where the *tenor* is the generator of material. Evident most of all is the mathematical musical thought implicit in the enigmatic canons, which I had studied for so long with Bruno. In *Guernica* I used only the intervals of the *Internationale*, just like Josquin, exemplary among others, who used the intervals or durational values of the *tenor* to invent the other parts of the mass. When Scherchen saw the score, which was dedicated to him, he told me, "Gigi, this is the right road, continue on it. You will have many difficulties because everyone will be against you." In fact *La victoire de Guernica* is one of many occasions when there really was a crossfire around me.

A crossfire, I agree, but even then your name was present in the most important events of the New Music. As discussed, you were a young star of the music scene in those years. I would like to ask you then: let's try a bit to think back to those years, try to remember how you were, what your intentions were, your desires. Let's try to reconstruct your musical world of that time. You told me about the teaching of Maderna and Scherchen, of Schoenberg, of your reluctance to bend to any form of dogmatism, of the attraction to Varèse, of your Flemish favorites. But you know better than I that for a talented young composer, the fundamental problem is to have clear ideas about what he wants to do, which aspects of musical language to concentrate on, to understand which new developments are fertile and which are eroded. Well then, thinking back today to the successful beginner you were then, not even thirty years old, what areas did you consider to be fertile, how did you think about building your projects?

Even then I proceeded, I worked in cycles: starting from the first composition one can observe that often with every three compositions something happens that breaks a cycle for other attempts and leads toward other research. The starting point was the great fascination that emanated from the creative conceptions of a particular culture, that of Russia. Especially that of the early decades of this century, before Stalin, from Khlebnikov to Mayakovsky, Tatlin, Malevich, Blok, Vertov, and Eisenstein.

It was, therefore, an encounter with the great, inimitable season of Russian culture that was to be swept away by Stalin and wonderfully recounted to us by Ripellino, who was to appear later at your side as a collaborator.
Yes, indeed, in 1960.

However, you already knew him. When did you meet him for the first time?
In the 1940s and 1950s:[53] translations by Ettore Lo Gatto, also published in other languages, catalogs and books on the Cubo-Futurists, on the Russian Suprematists, then Ripellino's book on Meyerhold's theater published by Einaudi.[54] I wrote to him asking for other suggestions to deepen my knowledge of that era. A classic relationship, if you will, from student to teacher, or between a young man who is searching and one who possesses a whole library, and not just in his head. Ripellino replied. And so began our collaboration. There then followed several meetings in Rome. He gave me a tremendous number of documents on the extraordinary creativity of the Russian avant-garde. In those same years and even before, Emilio Vedova fascinated me, speaking about the Russian Constructivists and Futurists, Tintoretto, the German Expressionists. And so began my profound friendship with Emilio. While traveling in Germany with Bruno and Scherchen, I became aware of the explosive culture of the Weimar Republic. I was very impressed by the great political theater of Piscator and Toller. I was passionate about the use of total space along with the great unrealized project of Meyerhold's theater, Gropius's plan for Piscator's theater, within which the audience, scenery, action, spaces, technical inventions, and texts would be constantly moving, never static or frontal as was traditional practice. In those years I also spent time with Alberto Burri. I admired him very much, as I still do.

Listen, I would like to ask you a question that is a bit indiscreet. You told me that you got in touch with Ripellino after reading his book. You did not know him and you wrote to him with the curiosity and humility of one who, wanting to know more, turns to one who knows much more. You told me that you had done the same thing a few years earlier with Ungaretti, so we are talking about a habit. If you read a book that you really like and the author is living, do you still write to them?

Yes.

Could you tell me of some other cases where you wrote letters to the authors of books that you found interesting?

I not only write to writers and scholars, but to people I "happen to meet." Recently right here in Berlin, I saw in a few exhibitions the paintings of a young German artist, Anselm Kiefer, mistakenly associated with groups of banal German painters of today such as the "New Savages" [*Neue Wilde*]. I found his phone number and I called him to tell him that his pictures had really impressed me and that I wanted to get to know him. We are going to meet.

Today, however, you can make those kind of contacts more easily because you show up with the business card of the famous composer, but once was it perhaps more difficult.

Maybe it was more difficult but today I still have an open "curiosity." And I often receive letters from composers, students, and young people. They ask to meet me and show me their work.

And you always answer yes?

Always. One of the many things I learned from Bruno and Scherchen is always to open more doors, always build more bridges. Schoenberg had already taught in an extraordinary way that one can learn many things from young people and students. I try to listen more and more to what others say, to understand how their research differs from what I think.

Can we go back for a moment to the cyclical process of your works which you spoke about earlier? You said that after every two or three works, a disruption and a profound rethinking take place. What were the challenges that were then on the horizon?

After *Variazioni canoniche* and *Polifonica-Monodia-Ritmica* there were the three compositions on Lorca and then *La victoire de Guernica*, which put everything violently into question.

To those who do not understand anything at all about music, how would you describe this turning point?
After *Guernica* I composed *Canti per 13*, purely for instruments.

But at the same time there is also Liebeslied.
Yes, *Liebeslied* is music that I would define as "occasional," intimate, born of the encounter with an extraordinary woman, music written for Nuria. Often meetings of various kinds are provocative and "occasional." In *Canti per 13* I wanted to try to make another attempt to use instruments only and deal with technique, language in itself, in a different way. Kraus said that thoughts are developed with language,[55] and in this sense I am speaking about continuous study between language and thoughts. At times the language of music induces me to a kind of distortion of the text. The text, besides inspiring me, is also acoustic material. It must, it can also become pure music. At other times it is, on the other hand, the text which imposes itself on the musical language. With *Guernica*, the two elements are in conflict with each other, as often happens. Afterward, I immediately felt the need for additional studies.

But in La victoire de Guernica *this conflict is resolved in favor of which of those two elements?*
It may seem strange, but I don't know how to answer you. I can never be sure about these things. In the music for Lorca I studied and put into practice mainly the superimposition of varied Spanish rhythms. It is precisely these which form the language of that time for me.

So Lorca's text served rather to allude to the horizon that was behind Lorca? The horizon of Andalusian music?
Of course, the text was an inducement to other knowledge, studies, research. In the case of *Guernica*, there is Éluard's text with its civic passion; there is the great theme of the painting by Picasso; but there are also other circumstances at work here. We were in 1954, in the midst of the Cold War, the memories of the Spanish Civil War resuscitating other possible tragedies. In that atmosphere of great civic and political tension in 1954, there was also my trip to Turin, the great love for Pavese, the meeting with Giulio Einaudi, with Massimo Mila, Giulio Bollati, Italo Calvino, with the Turin of *l'Ordine Nuovo* [the New Order] of Gramsci, Gobetti, and the Rosellis.

And how did it come about this encounter with the city and that environment to which, I think, you are still very much attached?

For me, this Turin is politically and historically a fundamental culture, a different city. A little while ago in Paris, Boulez told me things that were absolutely right about this city's efficiency, organization, respect, and love of culture. When I went there for the first time in 1954, I had been registered with the Italian Communist Party for two years. The discovery of Gramsci's *l'Ordine Nuovo*, Vittorini's *Il Politecnico* and the culture that had been put in motion by Giulio Einaudi threw open the doors to another yesterday, another today, another tomorrow. I was struck by the soul of that Turin—democratic and aristocratic, very open-minded and profoundly innovative. The need to renew, as you already know, is my ruling passion. These were also the early days of Giangiacomo Feltrinelli.

All this happened then in 1954 with Guernica, *but the abrupt change of direction occurs immediately after with* Canti per 13, *where, with a peremptory gesture, the temptations of the text are removed and pure music takes the stage. Why did you call it "Canti" when it is purely instrumental music?*

Because, thinking about the way in which I had read Webern with Bruno, for me at that time an isolated sound was a song, an entire lied.

Therefore, a single sound sings, just as in Webern the individual notes sing?

That's exactly right. The title is *Canti per 13* because the instruments sing and the conductor sings with them. This music also reveals my way of understanding the series: I do not use the total chromatic scale, but two segments, one with seven intervals, the other with five. The composition is divided into two movements: in the first I attempt a horizontal construction, just like a song. In the second, on the other hand, I again take up the study of Spanish rhythms, a dance.

Again the influence of Lorca then.

Yes, but at the same time there were also memories of the Renaissance music, of Giovanni Gabrieli. Often at the end of his compositions the rhythm goes from quadruple to triple time (indicated by prolations, of course), thus creating a transition from song to a final—often alleluiatic—dance.

You have often spoken of your intolerance toward a strict application of the serial technique which you avoided, putting Scherchen's teachings into practice. Now I would like to ask you something. Leaving aside the issue of whether you are using the full series or fragments of it, the serial technique being understood as a more rigorous control of materials, did you think of it then as a historical necessity?

You speak of using the series with reservations, I speak instead of using the series with free fantasy. Bruno and I were perfectly convinced of this necessity. From an analysis of Schoenberg's works, for example the *Variations* op. 31, it appears that the use of the series never follows the numerical ordering schematized by Leibowitz and so many other cadastral surveyors of music.[56] Letters from performers, such as Kolisch and Steuermann, questioned Schoenberg on possible "serial" errors in his scores that did not follow the aforementioned schematic ordering. Schoenberg's reply explains his free fantasy: more or less (I can't recall exactly) he said: "It is possible for you to calculate at one moment a given note in the series, but at that moment I heard other compositional fantasies."[57]

In this breaking of the rigidity of the serial technique there is a particular attitude that I want you to explain to me. I would like to ask how we can apply this in contrast to a composer like Bartók, who I know in those years was at the center of your attention. He once said that he would never use the serial technique. We know, however, that his compositions are often prepared with a structural rigor capable of drawing tremendous results from a given material, even a minimal amount of it.

Decisive, in my opinion, is the moment in the Rilkean sense, *Augenblick,* or the moment when something unexpected happens, and it is here that we come to the great lesson of Bartók, whose works Bruno and I studied with great admiration, in the years 1947, 1948 and 1949. Besides, even Varèse says you must constantly break the preexisting rules, and that you must be disrespectful toward tradition, and make experiments.

We've spoken of the protagonists of twentieth-century music, of Varèse, the Vienna school, Bartók, but a certain name has not been mentioned: that of Stravinsky. What does that mean, a total deafness on your part toward Stravinsky?

A total deafness, no, but in the years that we have been talking about, Stravinsky was trying to use even the twelve-tone system like new clothes. In my opinion he failed miserably with this "fashion" of his. I met Strawinsky in Venice a few times and remember him with great respect. But respect is one thing, another is criticism and instinctive reaction. I admired *Les noces* rather than *The Rite of Spring*. It may seem strange to you, but that's how it is.

To tell the truth, it does not seem strange to me at all. Composers usually prefer Les noces, *I read somewhere recently, that Ravel also considered* Les noces *Stravinsky's masterpiece.*[58]

I did not know that, but you must not forget that when Messiaen and Boulez arrived at Darmstadt, their analysis of *The Rite of Spring* became a kind of sacred text. *Les noces,* instead, was considered as being at a different level, not unlike the one on which Bartók's works were placed.

Speaking of Bartók, I remember very well having heard in those years (I think from Adorno) that one could not listen to music any more vulgar than his. It seemed to me then and it seems to me now quite possible to hear in that banality an echo of Bartók's tragic life, exiled in his homeland like the young Lukács. No one talks about it much but it is another shocking story: at the Lukács Institute of Budapest there are thousands of archived papers that have not yet been studied. Every year two or three volumes of hitherto unreleased letters are published. Recently the diary that Lukács wrote in 1911 has been translated into Italian and published, edited by Massimo Cacciari.[59] A really tragic diary, in which one feels how the condition of exile in one's own country, together with other afflictions, had become unbearable. The only "solution" appeared to be suicide (so it was for his friends). In these pages, Lukács dramatically attempts to explain why he did not commit suicide. These anxieties that darken and upset one's thoughts, that torment the soul, that frighten and often severely depress, testify at certain points in history, such as the one I mentioned and such as others today, to something desperate and relentless: the possibility, the attempts to live. Woe to fake optimism, to wretched positivity.

Yes, but in spite of everything I still do not understand why, since you are so fascinated by these ruptures of thought, by this tragic anxiety that still impels forward those who are searching for something, that you could feel so distant from Stravinsky's intellectual travails. I can understand that the serial Stravinsky, as Dallapiccola said, could look to you basically like a clever sleight of hand. But, however, the torment that afflicts him after the outstanding success of The Rite of Spring, *and that leads him to a kind of relentless self-restraint—up to the point of arriving at the sublime frugality* of Les noces, *to continue on toward neoclassical asceticism, whose smoothness is like a veil under which tragic ghosts stir—is this not a worthy example of those which you call disorientations of thought, capable of making one abandon one's own certainties?*

Maybe, but, you know, I am extremely passionate, and also often partisan, and very much so. At that time I felt a tremendous love for those a cappella choruses, beautiful like all his choruses, in which Schoenberg joked about Stravinsky, presenting him disguised as Bach with a wig.

We can say then that you perceived Stravinsky through Schoenberg's musical description.

Yes, certainly.

But the personal meetings, where and when did they take place? In Venice, I suppose.

Yes, we met in Venice. Stravinsky was in Venice for the occasion of *Canticum sacrum* and of *Monumento a Gesualdo*.[60] We had lunch together and Nuria was with me as well.

Did he know that Nuria was Schoenberg's daughter?

Yes, of course, they had met previously in Los Angeles. Nicolas Nabokov, his very good friend, was also with us. I was seated right next to Stravinsky, we were talking constantly, eating very little but drinking a lot. The conversation, which was extremely interesting for me, concerned the concept of tempo. On the relationship between a music in which tempo is based on the pulsation of the blood, which had to be a kind of common denominator as practiced by Stravinsky, and music, instead, in which a nonunitary tempo could be created through the superimposition of other tempos, of other components, a tempo thus freed from naturalistic and folkloristic physicality, with references to various spaces, levels, and acoustic spectra.

What kind of interest did he seem to have toward the music of younger composers? To judge from the conversations with Robert Craft, where he speaks about Stockhausen's works, he seemed rather well informed.

Not much, I think. Of my work, he only knew *Il canto sospeso* and he was fixated on only two or three composers.

Where had he heard Il canto sospeso?

He hadn't heard it, but he knew the score. This conversation, now that I've remembered it, brings to mind my meeting with Shostakovich. I was in Moscow, engaged in one of many attempts to get Yuri Lyubimov, the brilliant director of the Taganka Theater, to direct *Al gran sole carico d'amore*. I wanted to meet Shostakovich again. Since he was not feeling well, we all met at his dacha, Lyubimov, Volkov, Yulia Dobrovolskaya, and I. There we spent six hours talking about Webern, Boulez, Cage, Stockhausen, and young Russian musicians, with a lot of vodka. Suddenly he got up and took me to his piano. There on the piano unfinished, was the score of the Sonata for Viola and Piano. It was like a secret signal, a goodbye that he was giving us. He died six months later.

You said that Volkov was with you on that visit; what do you think of the arguments put forward in his much discussed book on Shostakovich?[61]

I accept them, knowing that Shostakovich's tragedy is much more profound. It seems to me that to listen to his symphonies—except the last—is to hear the great tragedy of a musician who lives and writes of emptiness (Stalin-Zhdanov). I think they are symphonies written like film music (of which Shostakovich has written so much, typical of the ill-fated "socialist realism." This impression, on the other hand, disappears when listening to his chamber music, especially the last quartets, the lyrics of Michelangelo and the Jewish songs, in which I sense a formidable interiority closed within itself as within a fortress.

I would now like to go back to your music, to Incontri *in particular, which follows* Canti per 13 *and which is again an instrumental work.*

In this music I use the chromatic totality, that is to say, all of the intervals.

It would, therefore, be an Allintervallreihe *as in Berg's* Lyrische Suite?

Yes, but it did not involve a series, but rather a process, a catalog of intervals which in *Incontri* are continuously altered through a process that already at that time I called positive and negative. The positive was the duration and the negative was the pause equal to that duration. The idea was to create a game of shifting note values in which the attacks and the ending of the notes disrupted any possible serial mechanization. It was a lot of fun for me to see how those elements, which could be systematic and systematizing, became completely distorted. Nothing to do with an alleged pointillism. Many lieder (echoes-presences-absences) were also in this music. In *Incontri* I also used the mirror procedure in an openly schematic manner because I was very much interested in retrograde projection. So often this is present not only in the music but also in the paintings of the Flemish, in certain of the breaks in perspective of Tintoretto, Pollock, Vedova, and Burri. This is not so much about pure technique as it is one of those ideas about different, simultaneous, nonunitary perspectives, which continue in waves throughout history. From the musical point of view I was interested in trying different ways of working with the attacks, the endings, the qualities of sounds in different superimpositions, intermittent also, which transform otherwise banal successions. The same problems, a game of varied compositional thought, if you will, are also present in *Il canto sospeso*. But here the text functions like other phonetic-acoustic material beyond the initial semantic stimulus. Only afterward, in the Milan electronic studio and even more so in the Freiburg live electronics studio, I realized what I had been hoping to achieve in certain of the choral parts of *Il canto sospeso*. Often I used a forte dynamic for the soprano and a piano dynamic for the bass, with the result that one practically eliminated the other. I remember a long, difficult discussion with Ligeti in Venice on this point. But, as I told you before, only much later did I realize that underlying this problem was my urgent need for a spatial approach. At that time, I would have needed the forte to be on one side of the hall, and the piano on the other, so that they could be combined and heard perfectly. Also from this point of view, *Il canto sospeso* still contains hidden compositional "mysteries," which even to this day are not analyzed or analyzable.

In answer to the endless problems that this work has caused, and I refer to the now historic articles by Stockhausen and Mila,[62] one could perhaps find truly new arguments, but now I would like to ask you: how does it make you feel to speak about this work that the public considers to be your masterpiece? I ask because sometimes there is a slight reluctance on the part of authors to accept this super-qualification being saddled upon one of their works. You know very well, in fact, that for many people you are the composer of Il canto sospeso.

Yes, I know and it is quite disconcerting. So many times I have thought that for many people, it is as if I had died after it, and that, therefore, I had not done anything further. Too bad for them. The superficial effect of *Il canto sospeso* was perhaps determined, at least in part, from a reading that was typically ideological. Not so much from listening to the music. The texts, those fragments of letters, might have encouraged "ideological convenience," "analytical incapability." Mario Bortolotto and Massimo Mila *listened*. Many years later I read analytical studies on *Il canto sospeso*, especially here in Germany. The well-known essay *La linea Nono* by Massimo Mila constitutes a contribution to listening-reading-analysis of the rarest kind in Italian criticism and marked the beginning of a profound friendship.[63]

I am convinced that compositional "mysteries" still persist because of too much journalistic deafness, performance difficulties, and some are just true mysteries.

In the second, purely orchestral episode of *Il canto sospeso* [no. 4], a cluster opens slowly with all twelve notes, superimposed with and without percussion instruments, thus creating a true *Klangfeld* (sound field). In the eighth episode, after the farewell to the mother, the music for the wind instruments and timpani is composed using the principle of the alternation of positive and negative, which I spoke of earlier: agglomerations of sounds which come together and then disband. A laceration of thought, music, and feelings that I feel is very close to Varèse. There are choral parts that bring to mind very distant choruses, echoes, intuitions, of which I can now say—after the experience of *Diario polacco n. 2*, *Prometeo*, and *Risonanze erranti*—that they are "suspended" choruses awaiting *Caminantes . . . Ayacucho*, 1987, performed in April in Munich with live electronics.

The revelation, therefore, of certain hidden signals in this work arrived almost thirty years later, when you got hold of new instruments that allowed you to mobilize the sound sources in space and to obtain what in Il canto sospeso *is still in its virtual state. Overall, however, I think that in this way it has turned out well for you because after all you have been identified with a work that is important in your own output. Think of the resentment of Ravel, who continued to be considered the composer of* Pavane pour une infante défunte, *or of Bartók, who had to go as far as prohibiting the performance of an early quintet by him, to which they continued to affix his image even after he had written his masterpieces.*

You speak of *Il canto sospeso*, and you define it as a celebrated work, maybe so. It is rarely performed, only tape recordings of it exist. For years, letters have continued to come to me from different countries all over the world asking me to tell them the name of the record company and what the record number is, and I have to respond: sorry, but it is not available on record.[64] Interesting "mythology!"

Il canto sospeso, *however, also represents the beginning of a new triadic cycle. In fact, it opens the series of your great choral works:* La terra e la compagna, Cori di Didone *and* Sarà dolce tacere. *These choral works are considered, along with* Il canto sospeso, *one of the most original contributions that you have made to contemporary music. In its use of the choruses in its way of using the voices, it seems to me to come directly out of the legacy of the studies done during your time with Bruno Maderna, that long and daily practice with the scores of the masters of classical polyphony.*

It is especially difficult for me to talk about these choruses because each of these compositions has a very special inspiration, very intimate, that touches not so much the secrets of composition as the secrets of life. At that time I loved Pavese, Ungaretti, and Machado very much.

Sarà dolce tacere is dedicated to Bruno Maderna for his fortieth birthday. The dedication is to Bruno and Pavese, who speaks of life, grapes, wine, of the quiet of the countryside, where at a certain point "it will be sweet to grow quiet." This silence of nature that makes one listen to sounds, the voices that nature produces, often abused and forgotten.

Cori di Didone is dedicated to Wolfgang and Hella Steinecke in gratitude for all they did for music in Europe of the postwar period; it also incorporates another dedication to painters and poets who committed suicide: Mayakovsky, Yesenin, Gorky, and Pollock. Ungaretti: I still have his voice in my ears; he had a particular way of pronouncing consonants, he made them long, whereas he pronounced vowels in a sliding fashion. A strange phonetic heightening of the more anticharacteristic aspects of the Italian language ensued. From all this came a desperate tragedy that I find again in his poetry and in the laceration and Dido's tragedy.

["Ha venido." Canciones] Para Silvia, on a text by Machado, was written for the first birthday of Silvia, my first daughter. Machado speaks of spring which has finally arrived, of something new and alleluiatic that is born because it was written that it would be born, but no one knows how or when. In *La terra e la compagna,* on the other hand, I followed another criterion with regard to the text. Two poems by Pavese: I made interpolations between them in order to combine them into a third. You already know that texts have a great importance for me; I use them like provocations, an illumination. Therefore, even these

texts by Pavese have their own particular history, both from the point of view of the use of intervals, as well as on the general level of the composition, timbres, and tension. In *Para Silvia* I used a technique of continual instinctive choice between possible intervals, unserialized. From time to time I chose one of the possibilities, not to the exclusion of others, but feeling and unveiling the others. The result is a continuous opening up of various combinations that were unforeseen and, for me, surprising. A continuous chasing, revealing by unveiling.

In *Cori di Didone,* the vibrations of the cymbals and the voices meld together, especially with the vibrations of the consonants. Ungaretti's voice had been a tremendous musical lesson for me. I had already been in the electronic studios, Schaeffer's Studio of *musique concrète* in Paris, Stockhausen's in Cologne and, naturally, the one in Milan, but at that time I did not sense the urgency of those means. It seems to me that *Cori di Didone* already presages other possibilities. The oscillations of the differently tuned cymbals actually work like frequency generators, and with the voices, seem sometimes able to be modulated with the ring modulator, filtered, added, and subtracted. *Sarà dolce tacere,* with its eight voices (four against four), recalls Andrea and Giovanni Gabrieli, whom I studied a lot, namely with Bruno.

The problem of the spatial mobility of the voices is also present in *Para Silvia:* the seven sopranos are positioned on the podium spaced apart from one another so that the sounds move, chase each other, and recombine in space as though coming from acoustic sources, from different loudspeakers placed far apart from one another. *Sarà dolce tacere* brings to mind St. Mark's two choir stalls.

For me it is very interesting that you say that in the choral works there were potentialities that would be expressed many years later with the help of electroacoustic instruments. But you've also said that there were here and there, especially in Cori di Didone, *more or less conscious forerunners of instruments that could add to those traditional ones. When we get to the 1960s—and our recollections have now reached this point—the magnetic tape also appears in your repertory. Before we talk about this new tool, which from this point on will quite regularly accompany your compositions of the 1960s, I would like us to linger for a moment on a work from 1959,* Diario polacco. *It is here, in fact, that a rather interesting connection is produced between ideological commitment and technological inclination, putting together motivations that are usually opposed to one another. By what mysterious threads is this fabric woven?*

Here, too, I am struggling to give you a clear answer; precisely because a whole part of my work has been ambiguously or poorly understood. And why can't I? I would rather not say certain things from where I am standing today. I will, therefore, try to control myself to the utmost so as not to say things that I believe today, but that at that time I didn't say.

What circumspection! After all, this is a good opportunity to make things clear: we must take advantage of it!

Certainly. Ultimately at a certain moment *La victoire de Guernica* represented a loss of control, and I have tended to use these words to mean a kind of falling in love. They are moments when you lose, fortunately, your sense of continuity and balance. You lose control and discover something different, very different: that to me is falling in love. *La victoire de Guernica* was a loss of control that was born as a reaction against what was happening in Darmstadt: always more sterile repetitive formulas, supreme exaltation of the unifying "rational." This type of intolerance of mine is already perceptible in the *Epitaffi* for García Lorca. But it is possible that it is more evident in *Diario polacco n. 1*. This was my first trip to a socialist country and in Poland of that time, after the Stalinist lock-down, they were experiencing the Władysław Gomułka years (1958). The Warsaw Autumn Festival opened up at that time to contemporary music. It led to so many new acquaintances and disputes.

Then I met Josef Patkowski, and this encounter was destined to lead to a very important friendship. He was creating an electronic music studio in Warsaw. I also met Lutosławski, whom I admire very much. That festival, with its spirit of openness, was a surprise to all Poles, for the entire Eastern world, for so many. Naturally, also for me. The possibility, in practice, of overcoming limits and breaking out of rigid, authoritarian molds (in this case it was a Stalinist government), the violent sensations I experienced at Auschwitz, caused me a real upheaval. The contrast between a past full of various atrocities and a present in which sudden hopes were unfolding: they were like notes from diaries, fragments of feelings, upheavals, passions that I continued to collect, to live. I found myself putting together, composing fragments of so many diaries with a technique or way of thinking that I used much later in my quartet *Fragmente-Stille, an Diotima*, not so much adding, but subtracting, from diaries indeed.

Just a year later, in 1960, with Omaggio a Emilio Vedova, *your first electronic work was created. This time you no longer went into the electronic studio as a visitor, but with the intention of really using that equipment. How did the transition come about, from a visitor's curiosity to an operational commitment?*

In a completely spontaneous manner. Already on other occasions I had gone into the Milan studio, above all when Bruno was working there. One day I stopped by to try it out, to study, especially with Marino Zuccheri.[65] I wanted to know how the studio worked and what one could dream up. At the same time, at his own expense, in his home in Gravesano, Scherchen had set up a special electronic studio to study new problems of musical diffusion with nonmechanical radio technology. He also published a journal, the *Gravesaner Blätter*, organized courses, and invited physicists, acoustic engineers, and musicians. He often invited me, too, and in those meetings I got to know, among others, Iannis Xenakis, with whom at that time I had a very great friendship. At Gravesano, Scherchen had invented a rotating loudspeaker, a loudspeaker made up of many loudspeakers: a kind of prism that rotated in various ways while projecting sounds. It involved an idea that was then underestimated, but which was on the other hand full of great insights because it overcame the principle of a fixed sound source, causing superimpositions and reverberations that combined with one another. So for a certain period I studied both at Milan and at Gravesano.

In the meetings that you had with him, had Varèse ever spoken to you about electronic music? For him, as you know, it was almost an obsession.

Yes, he had spoken to me about it, I believe, in 1958.

1958 is the year of Poème électronique, *composed to acoustically furnish the Philips Pavilion of the Brussels Expo. But in your previous meetings, what did he tell you about that electronic music which he was almost unique in believing in?*

He was always complaining to me about the inadequacy of the electronic instruments in relation to his intuition. And he spoke to me of the instruments invented by the Futurists.

Luigi Russolo's intonarumori?

Yes, and he told me of his Italian descent on his father's side.

Indeed. His father was from Pinerolo and Varèse spent a few years of his childhood in Turin, where he received his first music lessons from Bolzoni.

I was fascinated by his great intuitive and creative imagination, and of how it was held back and restricted by the limitations of the technological tools that he then had available. This is revealed *in Poème électronique* of 1958. With *Déserts,* Varèse succeeded in creating an authentic masterpiece, which is unfortunately threatened today by the bad state of preservation of the tape.

In addition to the examples of Varèse, when you composed Omaggio a [Emilio] Vedova, *there already existed other electronic compositions, among them a masterpiece such as* Gesang der Jünglinge, *by Stockhausen. Did you know this work well?*

But of course. For ten years Stockhausen and I had had an extraordinary friendship. Many letters, we'd meet at Darmstadt, we went on beautiful trips together, he, I, Nuria and Doris. The rapport that I had with him was unique. On the one hand I felt a great respect for the musical nature, instinct, and ability of Boulez and Maderna; on the other, I was fascinated by the scientific-rational radicalism that spurred Stockhausen on, which led him to continuous experimentation with materials that were often not just materials but had already turned into ideas. I sensed in him a different musical nature, of which the *Gesang der Jünglinge* is one of the most brilliant expressions. But one must not forget that there already existed *Musica su due dimensioni,* realized with true intuition and foresight by Maderna, with Severino Gazzelloni, first the 1952 version then the 1958 one.[66] At that time there was a Professor Meyer-Eppler who was teaching physics at the University of Bonn. He was the one who taught us the rudiments of acoustic physics. Maderna, Stockhausen, and I attended some of his lessons (Stockhausen attended them for a long time); he also taught information theory. From 1952 onward, Professor Meyer-Eppler also held regular courses at the Darmstadt Ferienkurse.

One year after the electronic debut of Omaggio a Emilio Vedova, *your friend Ripellino enters the scene with* Intolleranza 1960. *A scenic action in two acts based on an idea of Ripellino with texts by Ripellino himself, Brecht, Césaire,[67] Mayakovsky, Éluard, Sartre, and so on. What is Ripellino's idea, from which arises this very explosive work, in which those theatrical obsessions that you had nurtured, meditating on the experiences of Meyerhold and Piscator come to light?*

It all began with my enthusiasm for the theater of Meyerhold and Piscator. Mario Labroca, who at that time was the director of the

Biennale invited me to write an "opera" in three months.[68] It was a unique opportunity. I turned to Ripellino with the greatest insistence, asking him to write a text for me for a spatial theater like those of Meyerhold and Piscator. Ripellino accepted. He sent me the text as he wrote it. Every four or five days I received pages from him; I read them and remained perplexed. I could not recognize a creative capacity in them that measured up to what his books were able marvelously to evoke. I was forced to invent a collage of various texts, almost by improvisation. The phrase "on an idea of Ripellino" in the title was to acknowledge my gratitude to him for having contributed to my enthusiasm. Ripellino did not take it very well, and he felt betrayed. So what can you do, these are classic incidents that happen between composer and librettist, assuming that the word *librettist* makes sense in such a context.

An antecedent: my first journey to Prague in 1958. There I saw the famous *laterna magika* for the first time and met the architect that invented it,[69] Josef Svoboda, and the director Radok. When Labroca suggested I write *Intolleranza 1960*, I asked him immediately to invite Svoboda and Radok because I wanted to use the *laterna magika* technique, which consisted of simultaneous projections, some in color and some not, from various projectors on moving curtains, in different forms. In Prague there was also an encounter-confrontation at the Union of Composers; my music had been rejected in the name of socialist realism. No doubt because of that dispute, when the request for Svoboda's and Radok's collaboration arrived from Venice, the reply of the ministry of Prague was negative. I decided to turn to Palmiro Togliatti and wrote him a letter in which I told him everything: my idea-proposal and Prague's rejection. I continued to work happily because Bruno was to conduct the premiere with the orchestra of the BBC of London. After about a month, I got a phone call in Venice from the Ministry of Culture in Prague. They said they would send Svoboda to Venice, not with Radok, but with the director Kašlík.[70] The path of *Intolleranza 1960* had various obstacles and difficulties. Professor Siciliani, then president of the Biennale, tried to censor the text. Svoboda had already prepared a plan for his picture-projections without having seen or heard anything yet. His slides, which reproduced fragments of monuments, gardens, and palaces of Prague, besides being unconnected to what I had written, ended up provoking difficult discussions.

At this point, Emilio Vedova entered resolutely onto the scene. I had invited him to collaborate with me. Within three days he created and prepared colored plates, real fragments of splendid paintings, to be used in the projectors instead of slides. It wasn't easy, that's for sure. The result was a theatrical scenic-action, beyond and different from the experiences of Meyerhold and Piscator. Vedova's colored plates were projected onto Svoboda's moving surfaces, surfaces of round, oval, square, and rectangular shapes, moving from right to left, left to right, and top to bottom, creating visual paths that occupied the entire space of the theater. Sound sources were also placed throughout the La Fenice theater, in collaboration with Marino Zuccheri and the Milan studio, with tapes recorded on four channels.

The idea of a theater acoustically and visually moving in space thus came from the truly unprecedented fervor of the Russian avant-garde, which had achieved the union of revolution and progress in the most astonishing way. Recalling these things, Ripellino rightly speaks of a unique season, and he speaks of it with an endless nostalgia. It seems to me that your enthusiasm for these projects, which are as bold as utopias, is really the key to understanding your work and the thought that gives birth to it and nourishes it. Continuing on this trajectory, in which the story of an elective affinity discovered and experienced many years later is revealed more and more, I would like to discuss a work produced some years after Intolleranza 1960. *I am thinking about your collaboration with Peter Weiss, the author of that* Investigation [Die Ermittlung], *for which you wrote incidental music based on the use of magnetic tape. The piece, also quite well known through concerts, significantly carries the title* Ricorda cosa ti hanno fatto in Auschwitz [Remember What They Did to You in Auschwitz].[71] *I think that the meeting and the collaboration with a playwright of the stature of Peter Weiss is worth recalling.*

It was Erwin who brought about the meeting between Weiss and me. I had already met Piscator right after his return to Germany after a concert at Radio Hamburg in 1954, in which Bruno had also performed my music.[72] I suddenly found myself in the presence of one of the figures who had most inspired my imagination. I asked him, among other things, how I could finally read his book *Das politische Theater*, which had been publicly burned by the Nazis and was, therefore, unavailable. Piscator let me have it. Peter Weiss had just written *The Investigation* based on records of the Frankfurt trial against the Nazis responsible for the massacres of Auschwitz.[73] The premiere was set to take place in Berlin at the Volksbühne, with none other than Piscator as the director, who suggested to Weiss that he ask me to compose the incidental music for *The Investigation*. It was autumn, Weiss had come to the sea near Jesolo like a typical solitary Nordic intellectual. I met him on the beach with his wife, Gunilla Palmastierna, a sculptress who worked with him as a set designer.

But you already knew his works?

Yes, I had seen *Marat-Sade* and I had already obtained all of his books.[74] Many other meetings followed that first one on the seashore, also in the RAI Studio di Fonologia in Milan, where Weiss came with Piscator to listen to the various magnetic tape compositions. In Berlin, in the Volksbühne, there were numerous loudspeakers placed all around (right, left, onstage, on the ceiling) and, something very unique, a loudspeaker also in a space under the floor of the hall right under the audience. Using dynamics up to the maximum level and frequencies in the lower registers, the floor itself trembled, and the public who were on it trembled as well. The result was an acoustic-musical opportunity for emotional involvement greater than anyone could imagine. Very low frequencies, violent, continuous dynamics that were propagated, not as if they came from the depths of the earth, but as if the earth itself were generating them.

I have many very cherished memories from *The Investigation*. This was one of those rare events that gives rise to a common feeling of passions, purposes, and perspectives. Weiss, Piscator and I had become friends, and here in Berlin we often met at Piscator's home, for evenings-nights that were unending and unforgettable. Piscator conveyed to me his memories, still alive and vivid, of those years of the 1920s and 1930s in the Weimar period. They constitute one of my fundamental reference points. We spoke, we discussed, we "utopiasized," and we did some incredible drinking. Scherchen, Schoenberg, Piscator: three giants of that great culture of the splendid, tragic Berlin of the Weimar Republic.

With the incidental music for Peter Weiss's The Investigation, *we have arrived at 1965. However, in following your theatrical passion, we have neglected the works that followed* Intolleranza 1960, *among which there are a couple,* Canti di vita e d'amore *and* Canciones a Guiomar, *which seem to me to spring from a rather different inspiration.*

I have already told you that my works proceed at irregular intervals, that they group themselves in threes or fours. This discontinuity, this change, is even more evident after a theatrical composition. After *Intolleranza 1960* there was a change with *Canti di vita e d'amore* and with *Canciones a Guiomar,* and after *Al gran sole carico d'amore* came ..... *sofferte onde serene...* and the Quartet. I could say, as Schoenberg did, that at the conclusion of each work I wish more than ever to breathe the air of other planets.[75] When people ask me if I have changed my mind, changed direction, and so on, I say yes. I hope to change every morning when I wake up, to continually seek something different. Concepts such as continuity and consistency are to me incredibly banal; you have continuity in spite of yourself, with it often working against you. In spite of all the violence of the various upheavals. For me they are also the silences and the pianissimos of *Polifonica-Monodia-Ritmica*, the a cappella choruses of *Il canto sospeso* and the Quartet, or the fermatas and empty measures of Bellini (Prelude to *Norma* or to *Il pirata*, poorly performed as they tend to be), the pianissimos of Verdi's *Requiem* or of Mussorgsky or Webern, the articulation signs with which Wagner accompanies Wotan's singing in the scene of his farewell to Brünnhilde, who is not separate from him but a part of himself that he must punish.

After each composition I feel terribly anxious. I question everything; I even have long periods of depression.

And how did this feeling of rupture come about in the aftermath of Intolleranza 1960? *How did this impulse translate into those two new works?*

It was my sudden falling in love with the poetry of Antonio Machado, Günther Anders's warning on Hiroshima, and my love for Pavese. A falling in love that had otherwise already begun, with *España en el corazón*.

But what do you mean, "falling in love?" I understand that this is not about a person; sometimes it can be that also, but that's not the issue. The "falling in love" that you are talking about produces experiences, phantoms, and utopias. It is a "falling in love" that continually "falls in love" with other possibilities, other visions, a kind of passionate approach to one's own utopias.

Yes. Utopias that become obsolete or collapse completely. The disorientations and upheavals that arise from other incidents of "falling in love:" I maintain a certain optimism precisely because of these continuous doubts, uncertainties, and illuminations.

That time, however, Machado's text produced a serene "falling in love," a somewhat filtered and smiling passion rather than the infernal atmosphere of Intolleranza 1960.

Maybe you're right: *Guiomar* is also an element for me. Physically and spiritually, it's essential. Water, the sea. Machado's text in *Guiomar* is a text all about the sea, and this element accompanies my music, my life. In *Cori di Didone*, for example, where it reaches the point of seeming like an echo of Ungaretti's voice and it spreads through the oscillations of the cymbals, the prolonged-undulating sounds of the chorus. Perhaps, at times, so obvious, I almost get confused, I get lost.

I do not think that the presence of the sea should make a musician uncomfortable. If it did Debussy would have had to blush continuously.

Right, Debussy: I really love *La mer*. Or that famous B-flat minor chord at the beginning of the third act of *Tristan:* it's the sea, the sea that continues with very long waves and, in between, there is silence, Tristan's silence, Isolde's silence.

But I'm talking with you about it for this very reason because it involves an enormously stimulating element for musicians. Debussy was literally obsessed, and not only in La mer: *the marine element penetrates and breathes in almost every one of his scores and becomes the eternal and enigmatic testimony to life itself.*

Your words remind me of something. Last year in August, when the weather was at its hottest, when everyone fled to the sea, to the south, I chose a different sea. I went to the northern part of Greenland, with a small ship carrying a few solitary passengers. For ten days we sailed among huge icebergs, right near the great glacier that extends from the North Pole, which is the mother of all the icebergs. The nights were almost as bright as the day, and when the few passengers went to sleep I finally was able to remain in silence in front of the sea, its colors, and the North Star. That sea that was so special was neither cold nor dark, but a continuous transformation of indescribable colors filtered through the clouds, among the icebergs. That spectacular scene had nothing to do with what you read in books: white, dark, gray, and dark-blue phantoms were moving, slowly becoming light emerald green, of a rare topaz. Another unforgettable thing: the sounds, the most violent explosions one hears when icebergs separate from, break off, glaciers. It may have been pure chance, but I had brought the score of *Arcana* by Varèse with me, to study it once again, and I thus happened to hear this score in the midst of the violence of nature. My travel diaries are also the scores that accompany me: Thomas Tallis, Striggio, de Victoria, Varèse,

Kurtág, Lachenmann, Schnittke, and many others, new and old, for me they become like diaries, discoveries, fragments.

Yesterday in a German journal I read an interview with you, asking you the same questions that Marcel Proust had been asked in a famous interview.[76] *When asked about your favorite painter, you included in your answer, among many others, the English Turner. While you were telling me about your trip amid the sea and the ice, I thought precisely of Turner and your fondness for him. Reminiscences and analogies fluctuate continually: the predilection for the sea, the lights, and explosive sounds in those dazzling silences populated by icebergs, the sea that penetrates Debussy's music through the favorite images, also for him, of Turner. The clouds on the horizon, the threatening silences, the specter of shipwrecks, and even more the late work of Turner, with its swirls of light that absorb and dissolve forms in mysterious spirals. Is this not the work of Turner that attracts you the most, the one closest to the formulation of a musical thought?*

I often go with my daughter Bastiana to "listen again" to him at the Tate Gallery in London. Especially the wonders of the late Turners. You're right, it is precisely the vortices of light, but not vortices that you feel you might be sucked into; on the contrary, you feel yourself becoming a vortex. For me it is something similar to those endless abyssal and celestial vortices that *love* you in the high mountains. It was Mila who spoke to me, advising me to go to the Himalayas to feel them and love them, those vortices, not the blowing of the wind but a swirl of colors and sounds that blend into each other. They are silent vortices from which sound springs with an unheard of and an unhearable violence. I think of the apse of St. Francis in Arezzo with Piero della Francesca's frescoes. Turn your head and you're swept up in the vortex of those spaces, colors, silences, and voices. I think of the Scrovegni Chapel, the Tintorettos of the School of St. Rocco, the Friedrichs at Charlottenburg in Berlin, the icons of the Rublev Museum in Moscow, the Van Goghs in Amsterdam, the Tiepolos of Würzburg and of St. Mark's Basilica. I keep going back to listen to the various internal and external sounds that vibrate in that space: the sound of footsteps, bells, boats, and voices, different at noon or in the evening, during the liturgical ceremonies or during the passage of the crowds of tourists. You feel as if you are in the depths of the sea, and beyond the seven heavens, in a continuously variable dimension, totally unexpected. And your feet are on the ground. Or up in the air?

I'd like to try to summarize the sequences of our digressions: from the marine element present in Antonio Machado's poetry and echoed in your Canciones a Guiomar *we went to the Arctic seas with their icebergs. This then led to the marine influences and vortices of light of the late Turner paintings because the marine element with its mobility is the opposite of that static quality that crystallizes forms, and the vortex of light and sounds is precisely the place where all staticity disintegrates. I said digressions, pleasure of conversation, perhaps, but I think that through this itinerary of influences, when you evoke the inside of St. Mark's Basilica and a marine abyss teeming with sounds, at the same time the path of your music is being revealed, and the future reader, finding the trace of this conversation on this page, will probably have a key with which to penetrate the edifice of your latest music.*

Basically, however, all these considerations derive from a couple of your pieces from the 1960s, Canti di vita e d'amore *and* Canciones a Guiomar, *which seem to be inserted like a different parenthesis after the experience of* Intolleranza 1960. *Different because, immediately afterward,* La fabbrica illuminata, *a work of a totally different inspiration, appears in your catalog. If I continue to read your catalog, beyond what I just mentioned, I find* Ricorda cosa ti hanno fatto in Auschwitz, *based on the incidental music for* The Investigation *by Peter Weiss,* A floresta é jovem e cheja de vida, Per Bastiana—Tai-Yang Cheng, Contrappunto dialettico alla mente, Musica-Manifesto n. 1, Y entonces comprendió *and a series of other works without those breaks after every three that you mentioned before. Probably the period had lengthened this time, but what interests me most is the fact that these works, which are characterized by the presence of magnetic tape, strongly manifest that union to which I have already referred between ideological commitment and technology. May we try to revisit in more depth that political engagement tag that was put on your work after* Intolleranza 1960?

I had, and I continue to experience, various human moments, different musical possibilities, different experiments, technological studies, and acoustics. They challenged me then and they challenge me now and they open me up. If anything, it has made possible a greater desire for political motivation, a greater distinction, be it analytical or emotional, between yesterday, today, and tomorrow. A civil commitment, mindful both of the Greek sense of the word, as well as that of Hasidic joy, or that of the eternal wanderer. A registered Communist Party member from time to time I adopt different ideas, controversies, and positions, in various different attempts to participate in the ongoing discovery of life. In *Crowds and Power*, Canetti writes about civil responsibility for those who work in the world of culture, namely of the choices and taking positions that are not made once and for all. Through the various raging waves of life, the political-human moment of innovation sometimes appears more charged and explicit, at other times more tense, implying, "With whom to be alone?" the cancellation of the dichotomy "external-internal," "social-private," "extrovert-intimate," for other spaces, nature, feelings, constantly in tension or even in rupture. Thus I think a certain way of listening seems possible, for example *Non consumiamo Marx:*[77] 1968 had just exploded all over Europe, and there were a hundred or a hundred and fifty of us students and workers against the Venice Biennale facing five thousand police who had militarily occupied the city. Before, in 1967, my first trip to Latin America. I traveled for three months with Nuria, Silvia, and Bastiana from Argentina to Uruguay, from Chile to Peru, from Mexico to Venezuela, and finally also to Cuba.

That, then, was the occasion of the first meeting with Fidel Castro?
Yes.

So let's talk a little about this figure for whom you feel so much admiration!
Yes, but not now. I want to offer a better response to your question on political engagement. There is nothing to hide or retract. But to change and to transform, yes, a lot. If anything, it is necessary to better understand that alternation of moments of which I spoke earlier. Sometimes the purely political moment came into the foreground (see *La victoire de Guernica* with Éluard's text and the theme of the civil war), at other times, instead, it is technology, experimentation, and risk that intrigue me more. In other cases, and these were and remain for me the most stimulating, the two elements come into conflict with each other, not into synthesis. Others should feel the need to correct, to innovate, starting with themselves. I should point out that this alternation, sometimes an intriguing interweaving of different moments, has always been part of a way of thinking, of an attempt to live that continues to call me into question, often to put me in jeopardy with no safety net.

I know and I accept the things that you are telling me. But there is something that I would like to define better because what you said is true and has been said and experienced in a very vibrant way, but it runs the risk of being misunderstood. Your life as a man and a musician is one and the same thing. One can feel this from the way you describe them, but this rhapsody of falling in love, this living on the edge of passion, of falling in love first with one thing and then with another, delimits, so to speak, the positive side of existence. But there are deeper and darker currents to which I would now like to draw your attention. You have spoken so far of the things that you love; I would like you now to speak of those that you hate, and so I'll ask you a terse question: what are for you, oppression, violence, and injustice? Let's talk a little about these targets of your hatred that trigger resentments of a proverbial intensity. Let's approach this dark side of existence, this dark illness seeping into existence with subtle appearances, with alluring garb, perhaps, and under the guise of common sense.

What you say, and what you ask me could be one of the most tragic things that I feel. You're right, let's leave aside for a moment the enormous tragedies that are plain for all to see, in order to consider the modest, everyday face of the tragic. For me this "everyday" (dear, tragic Hölderlin, in his rebellion against the "everyday"!) looks a bit like a game that is often perverse: you find yourself faced with or overwhelmed by an attempt to cram you into pigeonholes that have already been reduced to a system by mythologies, markets, classifications, determined by certain powers with an almost absurd authoritarianism for a presumed order that is totally arbitrary. History is full of predetermined circles, of appeals to order, that resonate like perverse refrains: "Order reigns in Prague," "Order reigns in Warsaw," "Order reigns in . . . " or "Watch out for the risks you take," or then "Too bad for you, you don't want to understand." But history is also full of attempts to force, to break the so-called rules of the game until there are rebellions, revolts, new paths, even "everyday" loneliness, despite the possible daily marginalization, accusations that are breathless self-defenses of privileges or likewise preconceived rules, cunning misrepresentations resulting in alibi conceded and accepted by the subjugated-accomplice. I instinctively rage against this "everyday," taking all possible risks, against those who (and how many there are!) manipulate the mass-media newspapers and the various institutions in favor of a false mass culture (Zhdanov would be happy!), a leveler of values, including moral ones, a total offense and a polluting violence toward the new other intelligence, new other knowledge, new other unknowns, a new other quality of life.

Since the Middle Ages, and certainly before and elsewhere, the most classic way to get rid of those who thought differently was to banish them, accuse them of witchcraft, heresy, or madness.

Think of that mad text, the extraordinary joy of that great German work of literature of the fifteenth century, *Narrenschiff,* the ship of fools.[78] The ship wanders about on the Rhine, rejected at all the landings because it is crowded by the "authorities" with free thinkers, some considered to be insane, and thus bearers of disorder, even carriers of the plague. The *Narrenschiff* was pursued by various means: how many Pontormos were forced onto it! How many Schumanns! How many Hölderlins! How many Gramscis! How many Giordano Brunos! How many Rosa Luxemburgs! How many Rudi Dutschkes! How many Ulrike Meinhofs! How many Antonin Artauds! How many Andrey Tarkovskys! In recent times it has also taken the form of psychiatric hospitals. And always, whether the abuse of power is mild and cunning or violent, there is at the origin that sort of centralizing octopus that wants to grab everything with its tentacles and reduce it all sadly, to the unity, of a single mass will. It is this very abuse of power—political, financial, economic, cultural, fideistic, ideological, unidirectional, worse if disguised as cunning permissiveness—that triggers my deepest instincts of rebellion and against which I will never tire of fighting. It is perhaps difficult to understand how intertwined human violence is with what is musical. *A floresta, Y entonces comprendió, Non consumiamo Marx,* or *La fabbrica illuminata* are works in which traditional language does not work anymore. Instead what takes over is a completely different way of using the electronic material and even that material recorded directly from the factory, in that case Italsider of Genoa. The fusion of electronic material and natural material is analyzed and composed so as to make it impossible to distinguish where one begins and the other ends. In *Non consumiamo Marx* various recordings, various types of materials have other possible alchemies. The demonstration in the St. Mark's Square, the clashes with the police, the songs, the shouting in the streets, the speaker's voice that tells the story, the inclusion of the slogans from the French May protests spoken by Edmonda Aldini, all this is resolved in a technique-form-language which seems to me a latent form of the Bach cantata. I say this not without being irritated because it is only years later that I recognize, in those operations, almost a form of unconscious distortion of the data of an ancient culture that I carried inside me. A similar case is found in the way Schoenberg and Walter Benjamin treat the Petrarchan sonnet form. But in my case it involved materials which required and contained other principles of combination-composition.

Among other things, a special relationship exists between *Non consumiamo Marx* and *Un volto, e del mare* on a text by Cesare Pavese.[79] In the Studio di Fonologia in Milan I tried many times to superimpose the two parts with Marino Zuccheri. I wanted to superimpose and interweave two different types of falling in love, that is, two conceptions, two materials, two techniques, two different uses of instruments, voices, and feelings, so as to induce a kind of ambiguity between titles and texts, and sounds and songs. This conflicting combinatorics of music is almost like the conflict of feelings that I experienced. Technological innovation causes, touches, and even shakes the reality of feelings and vice versa: "Thoughts are born of language."

It may seem strange to you to hear me talk so much about feelings, but I have no doubt about it. I feel deeply that there are feelings in music, sensory and psychic moments, intellectual, instinctive, rational and irrational. I sense, however, that all these moments fit together, combine, perforate, creating disorientations in me that break and split apart on different levels time, space, body and spirit, the real and the magical. Yes, like the Latin American prismatic magic of spirit and nature, which still lives in Gabriel García Marquez. I think of the real magic of the generous soul of Cuba, of Fidel Castro and of "Che" Guevara, of the forests where the Yoruba rituals still exist, the Afro-Cuban percussion, and the continued presence of guerrillas who were killed, of the "26th of July," the movement that liberated the island. There is earth so red (reminiscent of Pavese),[80] a lot of indescribable green (Lorca: "Verde que te quiero verde"),[81] endless decision, the joy of living, continually flinging open skies, lands, human waters, feelings, loves; all of this in spite of serious difficulties. Also this is the Cuba of Fidel Castro, whom you asked me about.

Listen, before we follow the magical paths of Latin American nature, I would like to pause for a moment on the strange relationship with old forms that was foreshadowed in your electronic works. You said that in La fabbrica illuminata *and, to a certain extent, also in* Non consumiamo Marx, *the old form of the Bach cantata remained immanent, almost floating in the subconscious. This shadow looms in a more explicit way in* Contrappunto dialettico alla mente, *even in the title. Even then, therefore, you were aware of this type of relationship.*

Certainly, and it was an inextricable interpenetration of old and new components. There is the anxiety of the unknown, of the unfamiliar, research and experimentation: analyses, other technical-human qualities of new sounds, endless studies of infinite spaces, and so on. And continuous study of the Venetian school, of the great Spanish polyphonic school, almost unknown, of many other cultures, even those very distant. And today's technological innovation. This possibility of interpenetration between the memory of the old and the game of the differences is brilliantly composed in *Contrappunto bestiale alla mente* by Banchieri. But "bestial," or the genetic adjectivization, is changed to "dialectical," but not in the sense of a scholastic dialectic of thesis and antithesis. The elements that interpenetrate—in this case the texts, sounds, voices—are multiple, in continuous transformation, in continuous conflict.

But how does your Contrappunto dialettico *work in practice?*
An element of contrast results from the use of two voices with different characteristics, those of Liliana Poli and Kadigia Bove, used in very different ways, singing, whispering, laughing, and so on, but allowing the more personal characteristics of each one to be unleashed. At the Studio di Fonologia in Milan, with Marino Zuccheri, we tried hard to combine these elements and weave them together with the voices of the chorus [of RAI Milan] of Nino Antonellini. Often the texts which were sung-spoken were filtered in their harmonic spectrum, subtracting frequency bands, using only part of them. Zuccheri and I then noted a fairly unique fact (which would later also arise during the work at the Freiburg studio with Peter Haller and Rudi Strauss), namely, that the material itself contained, expressed, and suggested certain compositional principles. It is the materials, the signals themselves that propose, that require various duration times of listening and different possibilities of combination and spatial projection. It is possible that one memory of mine might help me in this apparent disorder of possibilities, not to bring order but to help me understand other ways or practices differently.

You have just spoken of chaos. I think that among your works, A floresta *is the one most steeped in a kind of sonorous chaos. This is the work that is sonically the most violent you've ever written, and it also involves that sonorous assault against the word already spoken about. How did the sonorous hurricane of* Floresta *come about?*

It was a true stroke of luck: the friendship of Giovanni Pirelli and the opportunity to work with the Living Theatre, which just at that time was exploding in Italy. Exiled from the United States, it had found lively support in Italy, especially in the red cities of Emilia. We had met in Venice during a Biennale and immediately decided to work together. We spent a week in the electronic studio of the Milan RAI. The Living was really explosively violent. One of their most violent expressions, which I used in *Floresta,* was the "reading of the dollar." They only read the numbers in the series, the name of the bank, and a few other things you can read on an American banknote, but the different ways of saying the numbers, screaming them, whispering them, the sound of footsteps, the racing between the recording studios, the improvised and interrupted singing, constituted a kind of varied magnetic fields that increased their range more and more.

A kind of human Halaphon, *then?*

Yes, and it was a decisive motivation for the composition of *Floresta.* I felt the urgency of the experiences I had had during a three-month trip to Latin America. I had seen every sort of violence.

Do you want to talk about some of those experiences?

In 1967 in Chile I took a bus trip from Santiago to Coronel, where there are large coal mines. A hard journey, twelve hours. I did it with Victor Jara, the great Chilean singer and guitarist. In 1973, Pinochet's police amused themselves by smashing his hands, his fingers, before they murdered him, together with thousands of Chileans in the Santiago stadium. His name and his songs still resonate in Latin America and in many countries. At Coronel we spent a whole day with the workers, the miners, who were extraordinary for their struggle and for their hospitality. I met Isidoro [Carrillo], the great leader of Chilean mining trade-unionism, who was later murdered by Pinochet:[82] Coronel, with its nearly impossible living conditions, on the Pacific Ocean almost at the latitude of Easter Island, with its struggles and clashes against the Chilean army and police, exemplary in the tragic history of Chile.

Also in 1967 I was invited to Lima to lecture at the University of San Marcos. I was well aware of the opposition, which also included armed guerrillas, against the military dictatorship in the area of Ayacucho. I was also aware of dissent, to the point of violent resistance, which had spread among intellectuals, chiefly among the students and professors of the University of San Marcos. I also knew of the horrible repression by the Civil

Guard of General Belaúnde Terry's dictatorial regime, of guerrillas thrown out of military helicopters that flew over the forests or who were suffocated with plastic bags. When I started my first lesson at the University of San Marcos, I said that I intended to address real Peruvian culture, exemplifying it in the political prisoners who were detained in El Frontón, one of Peru's most tragic prisons, exemplifying it in the guerrillas massacred by the Civil Guard and those still alive and fighting. Amazement and enthusiasm on the part of students and professors. Inevitably, the next day, not only was the course suspended, but the Civil Guard showed up at the hotel and took me to the prison at El Sexto, where I spent a day and night with the interrogations and threats of angry colonels, and the Civil Guard asking me to recant what I had said. But what I had told them had been the subject of news reports in the public domain, in Europe, and I was quoting *Le Monde* and *l'Unità*. There was an immediate intervention on the Italian side, and the next day I was expelled from Peru. I was with Nuria, Silvia, and Bastiana. I was lucky, as you can see, but the memory of those meetings with the Coronel miners, that night in jail—punctuated by the characteristic greetings of the prisoners, who immediately knew of the Italian communist musician who had publicly sided with them—the spectacle of oppression that accompanied me everywhere, even in other Latin American countries, aroused in me the most violent reactions and feelings which I felt the need to express in some way.

And therefore all those experiences, those trips, those encounters with the people you've recalled constitute the background of some of the works created in those years. Perhaps it is not wrong to understand those scores as a kind of diary, a fragmented diary, made of partial annotations, I would almost say aphorisms on this type of experience, but which are interwoven with memories of culture, with other passions that are, perhaps, more serene, intellectual passions that take us back to the tables of the Marciana, to the books browsed and studied with Bruno. From the interweaving of these themes those works are derived in which sonic violence, technological commitment, and constructive knowledge mingle with metal plates with explosive amplifications, with the documentary character of the scores.

Returning for a moment to Cuba, did you have the opportunity sometimes to meet with the writer Alejo Carpentier?

Yes, many times, in Venice, in Rome, in Paris, and also in Havana. He was an extraordinary person of rare culture, a great friend of Varèse. In his writings and in long interviews on Cuban television, through his personal experiences he was able to document an entire epoch, from the Paris of Picasso, Duchamp, Kandinsky, Éluard, and René Char to the war in Spain, to the Cuban revolution, through Apollinaire, Miró, Stravinsky and Varèse, Boulez, Amadeo Roldán and Caturla, two Cuban composers still unknown in Europe.

Carpentier was a good connoisseur of music, almost a musicologist, correct?

He had extraordinary musical antennae that allowed him to enter into words and into sounds with equal depth. It is through him that the great fascination and love for Cuba and for the Caribbean area has become part of me, with everything tragic and bright that this reality contains. He was attracted not only by music in general, but especially by the mystery of music, which he felt in a somewhat different way from ours, in a way that was fertilized by a sense of the magic of the tropics, of a land inhabited by strange phantoms. He had the desire to trace the origins of that act of magic that is music, and this desire made him something between an ethnomusicologist and a magician.

Having this type of curiosity and sensibility, I suppose he was very attracted to your music. Did he know it?

Yes, yes, he knew it and we spoke of it, or rather I would say that we spoke of it without speaking of it. It was the reciprocal knowledge of our thoughts that allowed us to communicate without too many words. What we have said about Alejo Carpentier is just as true today for Gabriel García Marquez. Last November in Havana I asked him whether in his novel *Chronicle of a Death Foretold* the recurrence of certain phrases, like real leitmotifs, derived from some musical presupposition. He answered yes and said that while he was writing the book he was constantly listening to two piano concertos by Bartók.[83] That Varèse filters through the words of Carpentier and Bartók through those of Marquez is really exciting to me. I discover that, in fact, the events stored in my memory are increasingly losing their immobility, and suddenly I can hear with different ears and with other thoughts that which I had believed to be already fixed and settled. To listen to Bartók in another way after the conversations with Marquez is a subject that could hold my attention indefinitely.

But this time I would like to be zealous and even a little pedantic. I would like to ask you how things went with Y entonces comprendió? *Why did it provoke arguments?*

At the root of the discussions which you are alluding to is the case of Carlos Franqui. I met him in Havana in 1968 at a cultural conference for Latin Americans and Europeans. He had taken part in the Cuban Revolution led by Fidel Castro. He was the director of Radio Rebelde in the Sierra Maestra. After the victory, he was in charge of the historical archive of the revolution, and there were internal episodes of ideological conflict. His was criticized as a microfaction. Later he came to Rome in an official capacity, and there we met again. In Milan he had prepared a portfolio for a Milanese publisher. It contained reproductions of several painters such as Miró, Vedova, Lam, and so on, and for each illustration he had written a poem also inspired by Cuba.[84] I liked them—some say they are ugly—and I decided to pick some of them as texts for a new work. And so was born *Y entonces comprendió*, a composition that I dedicated to all the Sierra Maestras of the world. My tribute to the Cuban revolution, however, was destined to provoke dissent because in the meantime Carlos Franqui had somewhat distanced himself from his Cuban comrades. So I found myself in an embarrassing situation: *Y entonces comprendió* was a composition, which I really cared about, so I did not withdraw the piece, which was then recorded by Deutsche Grammophon.[85]

In this work, how were the voices treated with respect to the tape?
I continued with the technique of mixing the live voices with those modified and transformed on the tape. Having placed speakers throughout the hall I was able to obtain continuous transitions and transformations between those live sound sources and those modified. As you see, it involved a technique that I was then doing a lot of work on in the Milan studio and that would be fully implemented only much later, thanks to the live electronics of the Freiburg studio.

You have repeatedly described to me the techniques used in these compositions which involved voices and magnetic tape. I would now like to try to penetrate a little deeper to tell you how these things are perceived by the listener. The impression experienced when listening to this interweaving of voices, natural or modified by tape, is that a kind of echo exists between the two sources: a voice is heard and then the same voice again, transformed. The space between the one and the other is a mysterious zone, and not only because that is where the transformations take place. This transformed reprise has always seemed to me to be something that had to do with time. Whenever the pure and simple voice appears in these works, you realize that you find yourself in the presence of a givenness, and when the same voice returns modified by the tape, you realize that it is less corporeal, as if it involves a ghost from the past. So it is as if that givenness, which was anchored in the present, immediately raises that anchor from its corporeality to sail toward a mysterious dimension where past and future, remembrance and prediction are equivalent.

What you say is true and remarkably perceptive in terms of listening. In the performances in which the tape is fixed once and for all (but then requires a new modulation according to the space of the hall), the relationship with the live part can define this relationship between present and past. You can modulate, produce a better or worse mix, leave some things out, but there is always a relationship between something that is live and real and something that has already happened. In this lies the profound difference of live electronics: everything happens simultaneously, in real time, as they say, as is happening now between the two of us as we speak, and as you were able to hear in *Prometeo* and in my other recent works. The very moment when things happen is also when the planned, but not preconditioned, selections and transformations occur. Even if the program is stored on the computer, the manner of the transformation of the spatial diffusion, of the dynamic-timbral articulation, always remains in our hands, at the mixing desk, the true center for listening and directing, for the production of everything.

I would like to try to say all this in a somewhat more metaphorical way. We could say, for example, that the real-time processing that you've just described can practically introject the music into a mental space. It often happens when listening to music, any music, far or near in time, good or bad—it does not matter—that our imagination travels far away, almost as if those sounds were the opportunity to create incredible refractions, unpredictable associative links. I remember a remark of Lévi-Strauss that I have always liked very much. He observed that when a piece of music is performed, one often speaks about the ensemble. It is said that the performers are one, two, four, or fifteen, or a hundred plus the conductor, but in the ensemble a key component is never mentioned, and that is the heartbeat and the nerves of the listener. And this beating is unpredictable, imaginative, and extraordinarily creative. The subjective component, the existential value of making music vibrates in him. In this soundbox, inaccessible to objective auscultation, music obtains its supreme results. It seems to me that live electronics, with its immediate and impromptu variants, is not just a metaphor, but a kind of objective revelation of imaginative and unpredictable paths of subjective sensibility and at the same time the synthesis of acoustic reality and of its subjective shadow. I think that the history of live electronics could also be told in this way, with the intention of showing which fundamental human qualities these machines possess and their use. Naturally this is just an idea. What do you think?

Not only do I agree, but strangely enough you make me want to share an experience I had at the Freiburg studio with Roberto Fabbriciani, the extraordinary musician and inventor of the modern language of flutes.

Among various experiments, using the computerized analyzer known as the Sonoscop, we once tried to see how many levels of *piano* he could produce with his bass flute. We calculated with the utmost precision and we got to ten *p*. When we arrived at the limit of silence, we heard the strangest pulsing through the microphone, like a very distant drum, yet very much alive. We wondered what it could be. We checked if there were resonances produced by timpani and bass drums that were in the studio. Suddenly we discovered that the microphone in front of which Fabbriciani was playing pianissimo, was also capturing his heartbeat in his breath. I therefore fully agree with you when you say that these machines amplify human possibilities, offering us, for example, even the possibility of hearing a heartbeat along with a sound that is pianissimo. This and other discoveries at the Freiburg studio occurred by chance (as Wittgenstein teaches us!), followed closely, however, by new technologies that are now being fully developed and continue to surprise us, continue to force to study, transform, to expand our knowledge and our listening every time we carry out a performance in different spaces. The same technology today also allows us to better understand the Venetian school and the great Spanish polyphonic tradition for multiple choirs, those compositions for forty voices or those for eight organs and four choirs that were performed at Escurial during the time of Philip II.

Why can we understand that music better today?

Because with the digital electronic instruments that are available, with the analyzers in particular, from time to time we carry out trials and acoustic analyses in space to better study the diffusion of the acoustic signals that vibrate continuously, that combine, making the different available spaces resonate differently. That is to say: the sound-space-listening relationship, beyond that of the traditional hall with a single frontal sound source.

This is very clear; but what continues to intrigue me is the idea of live electronics as a probe lowered into the inner spaces of the listener. You've spoken of the experience of how Fabbriciani's heartbeat was picked up by the microphone along with his breath, and it is as if the live electronics had cracked a wall and made it possible to catch sight of what lies beyond, in that interior space occupied not only by the heartbeat but by a varied collection of things. From a certain point in time in his career, Stockhausen began to be very attracted to this sort of thing. He made some comments on the relationship between musical reality and the subjective reality of the listener that I think are very interesting. He argues that when an interpreter is performing a musical piece, if he plays it very well, what comes out is not only the acoustic waves that emanate from his instrument but actual radiations.[86] *If the listener is receptive, he will allow these radiations to pass through him and will assume the state of a transistor, otherwise he becomes shielded from and impervious to the radiations and, therefore, not receptive.*

Our efforts in the face of musical reality must, therefore, be to achieve the condition of a transistor. Of course it is a metaphor, but it is confirmed in each of us, because we all know those more or less rare, but always extraordinary, moments in which we feel that our receptivity has suddenly increased. The Stockhausenian metaphor of the transistor seems to me, however, also to allude to the superior complexity of the phenomenon of reception. The tools we have available to seek such knowledge are as yet inadequate to the task. With regard to this perspective, I said before that I think that live electronics have created the first crack in a wall beyond which lies a whole universe.

Stockhausen says interesting things. However, I would like to add more. He says that the receptive listener is like a transistor, and this could very well be. However, in my opinion, with live electronics the listener is required to carry out a task that is still more active. The live electronics system sends acoustic signals into the hall, but these wandering sounds, varied in quality, transformed and composed, must also be connected to one another by the listener, not simply to pass through him. The composition will not be given to you, dropped from Sirius. But you yourself become situated within the compositional possibilities, spatial combinatorics in constant motion, often purposely confused—at least for me—so that a process is triggered which goes far beyond the function of a transistor. In fact, it calls into question your ability to fuse together relationships even to a point not conceived of by the composer. It is the space that makes the sound.

To better understand the complexity of this phenomenon, I would refer to the experiences of Alexander Kluge, the great master of German cinema and mass-media experimentation. In one of his books Kluge presents a description of the Battle of Stalingrad through three or four hundred fragments of interviews, memoirs, and other extremely varied statements.[87] He does not describe, does not solve, does not synthesize, does not formulate judgments, but he limits himself to supplying x-number of pieces of information on a single subject that cover an extremely varied and conflictual range. Through this outpouring of information, the reader finds himself drawn into many vortices of different feelings and understanding and he feels connected to so many seismographs that simultaneously transcribe his perceptions-reactions-connections. It is the reader who must or is able to glean varied reflections on that decisive battle.

If I'm not mistaken, your enthusiasm for Kluge's technique stems from the fact that it renounces definition, and he renounces it because he is aware of the fact that every definition is inevitably reductive, limiting. Kluge chooses instead to be more respectful of reality, and then, instead of defining, he prefers to provide information through a sum of data which, in a certain sense, is roughly speaking the mimesis of the immeasurable complexity of the event.

The experience which I referred you to concerns narration. But Kluge also made me listen to an extraordinary experiment that he carried out in the field of music. In his studio in Munich he showed me a videotape of a film he had made of Wagner's *Siegfried* at the Frankfurt Opera, conducted by Michael Gielen.[88] He had placed one microphone in the middle of the hall, a second *directional* microphone to the right in the orchestra pit, where the woodwinds and basses are usually placed, and a third on the left, where the strings and the other wind instruments are located. On the other hand, he excluded direct microphones from the stage and the singing. While showing me his film on videotape, he opened up the central channel located in the audience, and then you could hear the prelude to *Siegfried* as we are used to hearing to it; he then slowly closed this microphone and opened up the one positioned on the right. Then for the first time in my life I really felt those compositional microcosms which Nietzsche said Wagner's music is made of.

Selecting and opening up the other microphones, he continued this operation from which, a Wagner emerged that was completely new for me. His music was in no way diminished by the distribution of the different sound sources, indeed it was revealed in the most intimate folds of composition with an extraordinary inventiveness of dissected details which were then "drowned" in the whole. And for the ear the result is continuous surprise and the keenest attention, no longer the ritual abandonment to a worn-out mythology.

It is like a spotlight that illuminates an object intermittently, moving from one area of the object to another. This analytical vision in motion, which is so typical of our time, brings to mind the most recent music that has been produced in France for some time and is called "spectral music," thanks to its new understanding of the acoustic spectrum. In my opinion, the ones who do it very well are composers such as Hugues Dufourt or Gérard Grisey, who assume that starting from today with the new knowledge of the acoustic spectrum a new era has begun; it is as if we had just invented a microscope for looking inside music.

The composers you mentioned almost reinvent the wheel. Think of the analyses, discussions, and research of the 1950s in Darmstadt!

Pursuing a different line is a young composer who has made very thorough studies, after Venice with Vidolin and after IRCAM with Boulez, then at MIT in Boston, and who I think has an extraordinarily new scientific and humanistic intelligence. I am talking about Marco Stroppa. He has long maintained that the acoustic spectrum which we are accustomed to, including so-called tape music, is already obsolete, and we must break away from it to get to the point of composing sounds with sounds. Compared to the purely mechanical capitulation to today's technology, with its sterile and all-too-limited results, this thinking seems to me really provided with an innovative intelligence. In fact, what is important is that the composer returns to composing after having assimilated the lessons of the new technology. The use of technology is neither mandatory nor exclusive, but its study and experimentation is because only then will one be able to transform musical thought, the principles of composition, listening and composition itself. Another point of view that I find very interesting is that of Claudio Ambrosini, who alluding to today's technology speaks of invisible acoustics. Sometimes I jokingly say that Ambrosini's cultural formation occurred in the wake of the alchemists of Rudolf II's Prague: invisible acoustics or sounds that one hears but does not see within the mechanics of composition: basically you hear "the Philosopher's Stone" or the infinite colors-sounds-echoes-spaces, specific to Venice.

The suggestion of the interweaving of past and present in your tape compositions dragged me into this huge digression: we spoke a lot of the techniques of live electronics, but these are the most recent, the ones you do today at the Freiburg studio. I would like to go back for a moment, however, to those works from which we started because there is one in which I think all the elements of which we have already spoken appear with greater intensity. I am talking about Como una ola de fuerza y luz.

In Santiago, Chile, in the years before Allende, I had met Luciano Cruz, one of the best loved leaders of the MIR (Movement of the Revolutionary Left). I met him again when I returned to Chile after the victory of the Popular Alliance and the election of President Allende. Luciano was very well known. A little later I learned of his death, which was sudden and quite mysterious, apparently due to the inhalation of fumes from a heater in his house. I had established a very close relationship with him. The news of his death reached me while I was working at the request of Maurizio Pollini and Claudio Abbado, and affected me deeply. It was actually the news of his death that clarified the reasons for my inspiration. As you see I have no reluctance in using the term inspiration. In this way, on a text by Huasi—an Argentine poet who lived and worked in Santiago, who is also active in the Latin American struggle—*Como una ola de fuerza y luz* for soprano, piano, orchestra, and magnetic tape was born. I did not want this music to be limited to problems of innovation of language nor even to the exaltation of Maurizio Pollini's musicality, which I find very fascinating. I wanted my music to be like a space that opens and closes, something like a life that extends and closes again, something like a programmatic metaphor, but free. I thought of using only half the piano, that is, from the center of the keyboard down, and in the Studio di Fonologia in Milan, with Marino Zuccheri, I moved the sound material of the piano even further downward in order to double the bass regions. What was thus created was an acoustic game of rebounds, echoes, beats, and pulsations between the piano played live by Pollini and that doubling toward the bass on the magnetic tape. The soprano's voice also underwent transformations on tape. Furthermore, I had placed five loudspeakers behind the orchestra in order to obtain a kind of spatial illusion of unlimited depth, of the type one can have in the great Baroque basilicas. In this way I obtained an alternation of bursts, violence and silences, which were diffused horizontally in space with the effect of coming closer and moving further away.

As you have just told me, Como una ola de fuerza y luz *is a kind of epitaph for the death of Luciano Cruz. The term epitaph, sometimes explicitly and sometimes not, occurs quite often in your music.* Cori di Didone *is a compilation of musical moments dedicated to poets and painters who died tragically, and Dido is the emblem of violent death by suicide. There are the* Epitaffi per García Lorca, *the farewells to life by the martyrs of* Il canto sospeso. *With the background of this tragic landscape of suicides of poets, murdered friends, and victims of the fury of history, I would like to ask you what death is for you. Canetti, whom you have quoted, says that death is the most terrible insult to humanity, and I remember, as one of the most moving things I've ever heard, his idea of the interrupted lament on death. Canetti says that our lament for the someone's death should last indefinitely. If continued indefinitely, perhaps, it could give us back those whom death has taken from us, but at some point we stop lamenting. I think that if Canetti had listened to your music he would have been very sensitive to these epitaphs, these laments for lost friends, which do not go in search of consolation but, resonating, ask only to last.*

Your words make me think of the great Jewish lamentations of the seventeenth and eighteenth centuries, after the pogroms in Poland and Ukraine. They resounded in my memory for years until they were suddenly revealed to me by the great poet Edmond Jabès in Paris. These songs not only express lament, but also feelings of hope, gratitude, and memory. This multiplicity of feelings, seemingly contradictory, is expressed through the infinitesimal oscillations of the song, as demonstrated by the studies of Idelsohn, the great German musicologist who has collected, in a monumental work, Jewish songs from various sources.[89] Through Jabès' explanations and Idelsohn's studies, I seem to catch a glimpse of an answer to your question and to Canetti's affirmation. I feel that perhaps death navigates between times and spaces that open up in a different way. For me, death is not something that ends, but something that transforms. A spiritual force is transformed and becomes something else, wandering in other spaces with other memories, anticipating or bringing with itself new feelings. It was not by chance that my *Epitaffi per [Federico] García Lorca* were connected to a special study of dance rhythms. In Granada I learned that, on the anniversary of Lorca's death, the gypsies meet and dance in the place where the poet was shot. And you can also find similar accounts in the Hasidic tales collected by Martin Buber.[90] They are all accounts that concur with Jabès' interpretation. In the infinite variety of inflections of singing there coexist various moments of lamentation, hope, love, despair, absence, oblivion, need, and waiting, they resonate together and exist together. And also the difference between the great Hebrew singing, ritual and otherwise, mobile in its microintervals, and the Christian-Gregorian, static in the pitch of the sounds. In other words: the profound difference between the culture of "listening" and that of "belief."

And so, through this simultaneity of feelings, music—the lament in particular—and the place in which life and death meet and mingle, join together like two streams. Therefore, Canetti is right when he says that if continued indefinitely, the lament could give life back again.

Certainly, because the lament, in the sense of the simultaneity of the various feelings, expresses the inseparability of death and life.

The chronological sequence now takes us up to a work of great commitment. Between 1972 and 1975 you were busy composing Al gran sole carico d'amore. *Again the theater, therefore, and with a willingness to completely redefine the ideology of performance that refers directly to* Intolleranza 1960, *but at a distance of fifteen years. In the meantime, however, things had changed more than a little, and with the new work the director Lyubimov enters the scene. In him we can see the continuation into the present of that brilliant boldness that characterized the Russian avant-garde of the early years of the century. How did you meet this unusual person?*

Wladimiro Dorigo, this curious and very intelligent globetrotter, was the first to tell me about him. At that time he was director of the Theater Festival of the Biennale and always returned from his travels with valuable information for its activities. Around 1970 he had been to Moscow and, on his return to Venice, he told me he had seen a theater and a director who, in his opinion, would be of interest to me, namely Yuri Lyubimov. A few years passed and Paolo Grassi asked me to write a work for La Scala. This is how the discussions began with him and Claudio Abbado, who was then the chief conductor. Paolo Grassi brought an element of formidable practical organization into the discussion. We also began to speak about the stage direction. I remembered Dorigo's suggestion, and I mentioned Lyubimov even though I had never seen anything by him, not even photographs of any of his work. I continued thinking about and working on this new project when I received a telegram from Grassi from Moscow. He had seen the Taganka theater and was now convinced that Lyubimov was the director for me. It was then that the real difficulties began. Lyubimov was completely unknown in the West and in Russia worked almost only in Moscow at the Taganka theater, a theater of six hundred seats, officially not very important, but in intellectual and international circles incredibly well known. I went to Moscow and met Lyubimov in his theater.[91] In his office, which I had entered with all my sketches, I was struck by the walls all covered with signatures of visitors from around the world: among. Among them I saw those of Willy Brandt, Giancarlo Pajetta, and Enrico Berlinguer. I also learned that the Taganka was a theater with a strange practice: Lyubimov worked under the control of constant critical censorship, extremely deaf and myopic. Despite this he was able to invent a completely new theater, based primarily on the collaboration of literary scholars, historians, young composers (whose lives were far from happy because of the typically bureaucratic Stalinist authoritarianism of the general secretary of the Union of Soviet Composers) and a group of young actors and actresses, including the extraordinary Volodya Vysotsky. Volodya was an actor, singer, poet and author of songs that were harsh, critical, passionate, and violent, and which were circulating all over the Soviet Union through audio cassettes. He was very famous, and when he died, still young, destroyed by alcohol, work, and a bad heart, his funeral, despite not having been officially announced, blocked Moscow because entire columns of Muscovites wanted to go to the Taganka to give him a final farewell.

I was more and more convinced of Lyubimov's exceptional talent and, therefore, of the need for his collaboration to realize my work, but the bureaucratic difficulties proved to be enormous. I had numerous discussions with the minister of culture, the famous Yekaterina Furtseva. I requested Lyubimov's collaboration and this refined woman, very intelligent, but also inflexible, continued to propose other names. Seeing the futility of my pleadings and those of Paolo Grassi, I turned to Enrico Berlinguer, with whom I had a profound bond of esteem and affection. I explained my whole project to him and asked him if he thought he could help in any way.[92]

It is thus fate that in order to be produced, your theatrical works required the intervention of the secretary of the Italian Communist Party, Palmiro Togliatti, for Intolleranza 1960 *and Enrico Berlinguer for* Al gran sole carico d'amore!

It's true. But just think that in 1960 at the time of *Intolleranza 1960*, socialist realism was in full force, and dodecaphony was considered a scandal! In the East, pseudo-criticisms circulated around me which agreed to recognize the very serious humanitarian ideas that I put forward, but also, unfortunately, that they were at the service of a bourgeois and imperialist language. Certainly the 1970s were different, but many difficulties persisted.

Berlinguer's intervention and Paolo Grassi's continuing insistence were crucial in breaking the deadlock. Lyubimov finally came to Milan with his brilliant set designer David Borovsky. There then began very intense and impassioned discussions in which Claudio Abbado and the unforgettable Paolo Grassi also took part. It was just because of these discussions that the shape of the work became ever more precisely defined, and together we came up with the text and especially the staging solutions. Lyubimov and Borovsky had begun a detailed reconnaissance of the technical facilities of La Scala and the Lirico. Paolo Grassi had made both theaters available, and the final choice fell on the Lirico, whose characteristics were better suited to the staging techniques of the Taganka, based essentially on lighting effects. In this sense, the Taganka had ingeniously known how to make a virtue of necessity. It was basically a poor theater, and was thus forced to make up for the scarcity of its budget with lighting techniques. I remember seeing a *Hamlet* put on by them that was a huge success. It was later imitated to some degree everywhere throughout the West. Practically, the only scenic element consisted of a wall of fabric in motion. Sometimes it stood as a wall, sometimes, instead, it was death advancing, sweeping away the corpses. Sometimes it became a table and chairs. There was nothing more, but this unique mobile element ingeniously structured the stage space.

At the Lirico we decided to set up the first part of the production mainly on the vertical dimension and the second on the horizontal, using the bare stage just as it was. It was precisely from these elementary starting points that both the directorial and the stage conception were developed as well as the very concept of the text and even that of the music.

This means that basically the theatrical idea, what is traditionally called the libretto, was largely suggested by the possibilities of the theatrical technology.

Certainly, and there was the constant participation of the four of us, Lyubimov, Borovsky, Claudio Abbado, and I, to which Marino

Zuccheri was also added for the part pertaining to the use of space with the loudspeakers in the hall. From that collaboration, new possibilities sprang forth for the use of space, for the use of the chorus situated in another hall. The large La Scala chorus was connected to the loudspeakers distributed throughout the space while the small communard chorus was virtually strapped to those five planks of wood that moved vertically and horizontally. I remember that when it came to experimenting for the first time with these movable planks, there was a moment of confusion on the part of the chorus members who thought that it was too difficult to sing in that position. Then Lyubimov, Abbado, and I had ourselves strapped to the planks and then lifted up. I tell you, frankly, that when I came down I had to admit that it was not easy. But the problem was resolved satisfactorily when Paolo Grassi bought computer equipment which regulated the movement of the planks with maximum precision, and by the generous participation of the chorus. The problems that arose, "so many," were addressed and resolved with a solidarity and a feeling of affectionate participation that came from all the collaborators: chorus, orchestra, technicians, workers, costume department. To have created a climate like that I think was mainly due to Lyubimov and Borovsky, who practically managed to re-create the atmosphere of the Taganka within the Lirico, with the generous, intelligent collaboration of Paolo Grassi.

Here is the basic idea of the entire work: the continuity of the female presence in life, in struggle, in love; yesterday, today, tomorrow, superimposed, anticipated, and fragmented, passing from the Cuban Revolution to the Soviet one of 1917, from the Russian Revolution of 1905 to the Commune, to the Resistance. The second part of the work is largely based on *The Mother,* by Gorky, but according to Brecht and Lyubimov's versions. The character of the Mother encompasses the following women: the Cubans Haydée Santamaría and Celia Sánchez of the assault on Moncada, Deola—the woman of the Turin slums created by Pavese—and the communard Louise Michel. Onstage a kind of cage confronted the multiple identities of the female character. The cage was closing by the action of soldiers of Thiers, Batista, of Tsarist and Nazi soldiers in a continuous game of superimpositions, visual and gestural, of styles and uniforms.

We managed to create *Al gran sole carico d'amore* in the midst of all kinds of difficulties because, in addition to the problems that were more specifically theatrical, there were also ones of ambience. In certain Milan newspapers at that time there was a violent campaign that accused us of wanting to transform the Lirico into a kind of Winter Palace. They wrote no end of nonsense, with the only result being the strengthening of the climate of cooperation of all those who were working in the theater. All were very interested, I would say liberated, in doing something that was not restricted to the staging of the usual repertory works.

With this work, stemming from such a close collaboration between the composer, director, and set designer—raised in some cases almost to the rank of coauthors—it was to be feared that it might remain inextricably linked to the theatrical set-up that saw its birth, that it might not be transferable elsewhere, with other directors, and yet, this was not so. Al gran sole carico d'amore also had a good run in other locations and in other productions. After the Lirico in Milan, where did it go?

The work was presented [in 1978] in Frankfurt conducted by Michael Gielen and directed by Jürg Flimm, and they came up with a completely different production and dramaturgy. Different again was the staging in Lyon [in 1982], which was presented in a factory, in two large rooms, with the audience moving along with the singers, who were moved by mechanical means. The lighting system, the placing of the loudspeakers and all the movements overseen by the director Lavelli had an effectiveness of their own.

Al gran sole carico d'amore was a work of enormous commitment that in the mid-1970s burned up years of experience. The research on the mobility of sound in space, the experience of the magnetic tape, the political commitment, a new concept of theater that went along the path indicated many years previously by the Russian avant-garde, all of these elements, I would say your whole history as a composer, came together in the great synthesis of Al gran sole carico d'amore. *You told me, however, that, after theatrical works come turning points, sudden changes of direction in your output are dictated by the desire to explore other roads. The turning point at that time was provided by . . . . .sofferte onde serene. . . for piano and tape, a composition written for your friend Maurizio Pollini.*

Yes, that's true, but all the experiences that you have mentioned and that gave life to *Al gran sole carico d'amore* constitute a rhapsody of my occasions for "falling in love." From time to time I had literally fallen in love with the great tradition of Russian theater up to the Taganka, with the possibility of giving space to sound, with the opening up of other frontiers for sound with electronic means, with the great themes of freedom and oppression. These passions were behind this work. Afterward I felt the need for other occasions for falling in love.

Those who then attempted to consign me to a phase of intimacy and retreat into myself were quite deaf and inflexible. *Al gran sole,* with the complexity of its themes, still appears to me like a wave that had become huge, almost a tidal wave. After that complexity, I felt the need to start again from the beginning, to get back to studying, commencing precisely with the most obligatory and binding instrument that exists, the piano. I felt very attracted by Maurizio Pollini's technique, not only by his extraordinary way of playing, but by certain nuances of his touch which in concert halls are not perceptible. With the help of microphones, these elusive and extraordinary details could be amplified and projected in a completely new dimension. It's interesting that in doing things of this type on Pollini's sound, some old Venetian memories came to me: the classical resonances of the school of St. Mark's and of the lagoon ideally reverberating in the lights and colors of the city. To obtain these magical effects I sometimes made use of the cut of the attack, the sound that thus arose had a kind of resonance without time.

This means perceiving a sound that does not have a before and an after, a sound where past and present come together in a single dimension.

Yes, it's like listening to the wind. You hear something that passes but do not hear the beginning, do not hear the end, and perceive a continuity of absences, presences, and indefinable essences. We worked three days in the studio with Maurizio Pollini. Maurizio was the first to be surprised by the results obtained in the takes done by that great master Marino Zuccheri. Unlike in *Como una ola,* here I used the whole piano keyboard. With the sounds composed on tape, I was able to achieve an ambiguous effect that energizes the performance. Sometimes certain piano sonorities, actually composed on tape, are like echoes of the same pitch played live, creating various resonances between tape and piano. In reality what is involved are the infinitesimal variants that are produced during certain moments of the running of the tape or minimal differences in pitch that create curious microintervallic relationships between the same pitch recorded on tape and the same pitch of the piano resonating in different spaces and times. Of course, this confusion between the piano and itself as recorded-composed on tape, from impromptu observation, here becomes something intentional, an ambiguity scrupulously pursued.

In our conversation we mentioned Luigi Dallapiccola almost in passing. If we continue now in the examination of your work, we see in 1979 the reappearance, and this time peremptorily, of the musician whom Malipiero had called your attention to many years ago. The work in question is called Con Luigi Dallapiccola.

In 1948, when Scherchen came to Venice to give his conducting course, he asked all the students what the music or the composer was that most attracted them. I replied that it was Dallapiccola, a few of whose scores I already possessed at the time. I had begun to study them in parallel with those of Schoenberg and Webern. There were the *Canti di prigionia*, which I had heard at the Biennale of 1946 or 1947.[93] Scherchen then made me do a study of *Liriche greche,* which I analyzed only in relation to the vocal part.[94] I transcribed all the songs one after another as if they were a very long monody and then began to study the intervals, phrasing, relationship with the text, and durations, making an analysis similar to those made with Bruno of other musicians and which I still do today. From this study arose my boundless admiration for Dallapiccola, an admiration that also applies to the moral and human aspects of this person, whom I consider fundamental for Italian culture and with whom I find myself as if in the presence of the great masters of the Renaissance. Certainly, Scherchen made a remarkable contribution to my knowledge of Dallapiccola. I remember *Canti di liberazione* conducted by him in Florence, the premiere of *Il prigioniero,* and many meetings with him and with the Maestro.

And when did you meet for the first time?

In Venice, in 1946 or 1947, I saw Malipiero walking on St. Mark's Square with Dallapiccola, and I went to greet him with the intention of taking advantage of that classic Venetian encounter. Other meetings followed. We wrote to one another, and I went to Florence to meet with him, talk to him, and especially listen to his erudite digressions in which he jumped from one thought to another, every time revealing to me things I had never heard before.[95] From him, from *Canti di prigionia* and from *Il prigioniero,* came my great love for heretics and the persecuted.

Through his words I discovered a living testimony of that Central European civilization for which I felt an inexhaustible passion. I remember his visits to Asolo during the last years of Malipiero's life. He would telephone and then come to Venice, where he would stop over for two or three days and where we would meet with Scherchen and Maderna, with whom Dallapiccola shared a mutual admiration. They were wonderful, unforgettable meetings. After his death I felt cruelly hit by the sudden and unforgiving silence that had fallen upon his music. I decided to offer a testimony of my dedication to him and to the continuous presence in me of this great man. That is why I called the work *Con Luigi Dallapiccola*. It is a composition for percussion instruments alone, among which are those that Dallapiccola used in the Girolamo Savonarola chorus.[96] My whole work is based on three notes, F-E-C-sharp, those of the word "Fratello" [Brother] in *Il prigioniero*. This reduction of material, already begun with . . . . .*sofferte onde serene*. . ., as you can see, continued in a drastic fashion. But I wanted to tell you that in the ambit of my friendship with Luigi Dallapiccola was also the figure of Sylvano Bussotti. I respect him, I admire him, and I have a deep affection for him. Always, whenever we get together, the memory of Dallapiccola comes back. Sylvano tells me of the long walks and conversations he had with the Maestro through the streets of Florence, more real and unforgettable than any lesson.

In this work, dedicated to the memory of Dallapiccola, electronic technology plays a significant role: the composition is, in fact for six performers of percussion instruments, four pick-ups, three ring modulators and three frequency generators. What relationship is established between the percussion and the electronic equipment?

The pick-ups are contact microphones that are used very often by rock groups. Their main characteristic is that they immediately capture the vibration emitted by the instrument without it first passing through the air. In this way, you only have to touch the instrument—in the case of *Con Luigi Dallapiccola* we are talking about metal plates—so that the vibration is picked up at its root and then immediately amplified. The ring modulators, in combination with the frequency generators, instead act in a different way: you have on the one hand the vibration of the instrument, and on the other a frequency produced by the generator. The intervening ring modulator gives you a different sound spectrum in which you have the subtraction and the summation of the two acoustic signals.

The practical result is, therefore, a kind of continuous transformation of the timbre.

Yes, applying it to the metal plates which reproduce the three notes of "Fratello" in *Il prigioniero*, this process generates an energized undulation in space. Therefore, you hear the simple spectrum of the original sound that through the ring modulator becomes a complex sound and in my view, not only involves an acoustic amplification, but something like a sign of the memory that is propagated and amplified in space.

Speaking of Dallapiccola, you told me about the letters that the two of you exchanged. In the course of our conversation, you have often spoken of letters exchanged with all types of people. In what kind of condition is your correspondence with people such as Dallapiccola, Ungaretti, Maderna, Scherchen, Stockhausen, Karl Amadeus Hartmann, Wolfgang Steinecke, and Paul Dessau?

It is simply part of the chaotic material that I have in my home, but it is likely that other composers, Boulez, for example, would have a much larger and much more orderly archive.[97] Regarding the letters of composers, I would point out to you a case of enormous interest that is the object of scandalous neglect. At the Fondazione Cini is the bequest of Malipiero, which, in addition to the splendid essays, contains his correspondence. I went to see it and noticed that the letters had already been assembled and classified by Malipiero himself. Of course, we are talking about a collection of correspondence that is of enormous interest. His correspondents include Schoenberg, Berg, Bartók, Varèse, Antheil, and other American musicians. Furthermore, the correspondence with Dallapiccola is of an extraordinary breadth and interest. Thirty years of musical life are reflected in those documents from the point of view of those very acute, very tough and very critical minds. So when I think about that huge wealth of information, moods, feelings, and criticism, it seems impossible to me that it has not yet occurred to anyone to publish them.

Perhaps you have chosen the right place to launch an appeal, and it may well be that some young musicologist finds a valuable suggestion in your words for a dissertation.

I would be very happy, also because it would help to overcome that all too exclusively Venetian and localized interpretation of Malipiero, projecting his work onto an international scene.

And if we now speak a little about your quartet, of this work that, in spite of its complexity, within six or seven years has had an incredible number of performances and a recording on disc, and especially in Germany has been able to inspire, a veritable wave of musicological essays.

Rather than define the quartet Fragmente-Stille, an Diotima *as one of those works that mark a turning point,*[98] *I would say that it is a composition that contains a host of problems that were happily resolved. Rather than a turning point, the quartet seems to me more like a prelude. It is, in fact, a work in which the spiritual questions and the great problems that will begin later on with your work at the Freiburg studio are concentrated. And I find it striking that this overture, which opens onto a horizon of sonority dominated by electroacoustic experiences, is performed by one of the most classic ensembles in the history of music, that of the string quartet.*

It is probably true that this work marks a turning point, in the sense that the past anticipates the future, and the future memorizes today and the past. I have recently been taught a lot about this interpenetration of the temporal planes by the thought of the great poet Edmond Jabès. But on the road to the quartet there is also another great figure. For years I read and studied Hölderlin, in the new and extraordinary *Frankfurter Ausgabe*, an edition that reproduces the original manuscripts in facsimile.[99] There you can follow the development of Hölderlin's poetic thought: over an initial line others are superimposed, written with different inks and even sometimes using Greek or other ideas in French. Above a word there can be found another two, three, four, or five, like a process of elaboration that advances through the accumulation of various types of materials, various types of thoughts, and various possibilities assigned to words that are extremely remote. Sometimes Hölderlin makes a selection amongst these materials, and sometimes he doesn't. The thought remains open without coming to a conclusion. For me this second hypothesis is essential, and it is what makes the *Frankfurter Ausgabe* something completely different from any one of so many philological publications that aim to demonstrate how the path of sketches and variations is destined to arrive at a single solution. The key issue is that principle of openness toward the multiplicity of meanings and possibilities. But a concept that for me is very profound and topical in Hölderlin's poetry is that in which the gods of yesterday are dead and today is a very dark and ominous time, and the new gods have not yet been born (and yet, who are the gods?).

This is true, but Hölderlin's thoughts on this subject should be somewhat corrected. He has this affirmation regarding the gods of yesterday, those of Greece, that have disappeared. They are not dead, they've disappeared, and the world is thus plunged into darkness, a darkness in which one can-

not make out the divine presences. However, Hölderlin also speaks of a privileged moment, that of the "evening theophany,"[100] *in which the gods, who are now invisible, can be glimpsed only by poets. In this way the poet comes to be the mediator between a reality that has disappeared and a reality that is yet to come. It seems to me that this thought of Hölderlin is supremely musical, and I say this, thinking about those empty places, those long pauses in your music in which resonate the memory of what once was, but at the same time the emptiness is pregnant with what is going to happen. These large pauses, with their white spaces ploughing through the page, seem to me, therefore, very similar to the evening theophanies, the ambiguous moments caught between light and darkness in which the imagination has the task of springing into action.*

It's true, you've corrected and supplemented this in a way that is very precise. It is not about disappearance and not even about absence in the physical sense. The absence is there because there is no word that is capable of expressing that reality. Here you can see the analogy with Jewish thought, according to which God's name is unpronounceable because his vocalization disappeared with the destruction of the first temple.

This is the great musical teaching that I have drawn from the thinking of Hölderlin and Jabès. You are correct to speak of silences, but those of my music have nothing to do with those of Cage, which are meant as a provocation or à la Zen. I can think, for example, of that famous piano piece by Cage entitled 4'33", in which the pianist sits motionless at the keyboard in front of the audience which is becoming increasingly intolerant, producing sounds. In my quartet there are silences with which silent and unpronounced fragments taken from Hölderlin's texts are associated and intended for the inner ears of the performers. These silences, in which what we have already heard is added in our ear to anticipations and expectations of what is still missing, are moments of suspense in the true sense of the word. From *Il canto sospeso* onward, this is a feeling that keeps nagging at me, the suspension from, to, or through something, a classic Rilkean *Augenblick* [instant] that derives, anticipates, and dreams.

Were these extreme works of Hölderlin, then, what inspired your Quartet, precisely through their own unique graphic form?

Yes, a true inspiration, an enormous inspiration.

While you were talking about these things I was thinking about the graphic aspect in which I seem to see an unusual element, but also a link with certain currents of contemporary thought. Hölderlin was and continues to be in a preeminent position in inspiring musicians. It would indeed be good and useful to write a book on Hölderlin and musicians.[101] *Many have approached him and have set his poetry to music, but not you. You have approached his poetry, attracted, in this case, by the intersecting, superimposed, and sometimes broken lines that he wrote on the blank page. In that graphic process you traced thoughts, concepts, and methods of composition, inspiration, and a poetics. I find it interesting that the same thing happened with the verses of Mallarmé, which, like those of Hölderlin, have often provided direct nourishment to musicians. How can we forget the superb results of Debussy or Ravel? But suddenly Mallarmé's texts also began to manifest a different influence through their graphic form. You understand very well I am alluding to the idea of* Livre, *which is poetics and philosophy at the same time. The idea of* Livre, *whether it is declared or not, is a very fertile influence on contemporary music, one that can be examined on the pages of Boulez's or Bussotti's music. First Mallarmé and now also Hölderlin, both have become inspiration to musicians through the latent philosophy revealed in graphic form in* Livre *or in the pages reproduced in the* Frankfurter Ausgabe. *In this, your attention to the graphic aspect and its metaphysical projections, I seem to recognize a typically modern sign, a type of attention that has passed through the ideological filter of* The Gutenberg Galaxy *by McLuhan.*

You've mentioned Karl Kraus several times. He is able to overcome the unbearable dichotomy of form and content with his comments on style. But now, with attention to the graphic aspect, we are at a higher stage of evolution, we are at a true point of textual metaphysics, at an absolutely musical way of addressing semantics, in which the graphic element appears as a pure metaphor of the phoneme. Janáček spoke of listening to the music hidden in words, the infallible vibration capable of revealing even what wishes to remain hidden in the depths of the soul. The graphic form of these Hölderlin poems seems to me at this point to be the secret phoneme of the written word, and your quartet probably has a lot to do with all of that.

Certainly. However, there's more. I also felt a very strong attraction to Hölderlin's life, especially the last part of it spent in the tower at Tübingen. I read a lot on the issue of Hölderlin's insanity, even the clinical literature, and I share the opinion of those scholars who rule out the idea of his insanity. His last poems seem extraordinarily lucid and innovative. If anything, it is his solitude that intrigues me. It makes me think of those Cistercian monks who in certain historical periods spent their lives locked up in a cell solely preoccupied with handing down the past to posterity while living in a present, a daily life that was difficult or tragic. Their condition was, as you said before, pregnant with the future, and it is this that I am excited about. In fact, I find it extraordinary to preserve in a difficult present a capacity for creation, of invention directed toward something, or a time, which can be utopian and visionary. You mentioned Mallarmé's *Livre,* and you made me remember one of Jabès' most extraordinary collections which is entitled *Le livre des questions:*[102] a continual asking of questions, a continual series of problems that is exactly the opposite of every enunciation, declaration, and definition. Endless restlessness. Following Hölderlin's thought, I have moved forward and I continue to move forward, entering many labyrinths of doubt, uncertainties, risking silence, a silence that has nothing to do with death but that requires other presences, other words, other sound spectra, other skies. For me, this is Hölderlin's great fascination. Crucial for me in this venture was the collaboration with Walter Levin, the first violinist of the LaSalle Quartet. We worked together for at least two years. Just think that Levin and his colleagues had asked me for a quartet already at Darmstadt, in the '50s. During a workshop that we held in Bonn on the occasion of the Quartet's premiere, Levin said that the composition of this music had taken twenty-five years.[103] In a certain sense it's true. The quartet form is one of the most traditional and also one of the most difficult to think about today. As I told you, the work done with Levin and the other members of the quartet was decisive. It was a work that shifted constantly from the technical level to the spiritual and human one. How much new knowledge, and wonders, of the Jewish culture! It was a continuous succession of problems, attempts, proposals and counter-proposals on the sound quality, the bowing techniques, and the extension of the instruments' traditional possibilities. As you can see, I continued with the working method that I had used with Lyubimov, Abbado, Borovsky, and, originally, with the singers in the electronic studio.

After all this is nothing new. Think of Bellini, Verdi, and Wagner, who wrote their works for the particular qualities of voices-singers in a relationship of mutual inspiration. Think about the relationship between Brahms and Joachim, Monteverdi, Willaert, and Bach, who composed expressly for and with their choruses, creating a close collaboration between composer and performer. Working in this way, the LaSalle four and I not only found solutions to individual problems, but through long discussions and experiments, we tried to understand how it was possible to maintain tension through the inaudible, and we discovered how often the inaudible can be extremely more tense than the audible.

The Quartet is, therefore, the door through which we enter the last phase of your output, the one that for a few years now has been unfolding at the Freiburg studio. When were your first contacts with the studio?

During a trip to Los Angeles I wanted to meet John Chowning and the group of composers who worked and still work at the large computer center at Stanford University. I have great respect for Chowning. His compositions made with the computer seem to me to have been really successful, totally freed from any type of memory and conceived with a genuinely innovative scientific and human mentality. I spoke with him at length about the possibility of a period of study at Stanford because by now the Studio di Fonologia in Milan was really inadequate and the RAI management had totally lost interest in it and had provided it with neither support nor the necessary upgrades.[104] During these conversations with Chowning we happened to mention the "delay," an instrument that has the ability to delay the sounds that have been played or programmed even by many seconds, thus giving you a way of constructing interesting and varied superimpositions: anticipations, delays, memories, even transformations of time. Then I found out that there was such an instrument at Freiburg, and this provided the opportunity for my first visit to the studio. Once I got there, Hans Peter Haller, director of the studio and professor of experimental music and acoustics at the University of Basel, showed me all the other instruments as well. Immediately I asked if I could stay for a period of study. And so began a period that is still going on.

In the early 1980s I passed through a difficult period, even physically. That stay turned out to be very healthy for me and still is. The studio is a short distance outside Freiburg, right at the edge of the Black Forest. I found a magnificent place to stay, eleven hundred meters above sea level, in an old hotel made entirely of wood and completely isolated,[105] from where there was a view of the forest almost as far as Colmar. I often made excursions: to Colmar, with the wonderful Grünewald altarpiece at Isenheim, to Strasbourg, to the enchanted and enchanting Black Forest, and a little throughout the whole of southern Germany, discovering German and French painters of the Middle Ages, the great Baroque architecture, and the Neckar with all its history. The air that I breathe is good for me, as are those open spaces which, because of the wind and the clouds, change continually. In winter the snow reaches a height of two to three meters: snowstorms, true blizzards, are unleashed with white, so much white, that rages and overwhelms you from all directions.

The Freiburg studio, the new live electronics technology, the programming of the various computers, the continuous discovery-study of space, the analyses with the Sonoscop absorbed me completely and little by little drew me out of the distraught condition into which I had sunk.

Assisted by the profound knowledge of Professor Haller, Rudi Strauss, and Bernd Noll, in that studio I began an overwhelming experience that also led me to an expansion of the capacity of perception. One proceeds by way of ongoing research and continuous technical errors that are immediately put to good use because they are considered as breaking with what is already known and the standards that are already established. Following Wittgenstein's concept according to which science proceeds through errors, many times we found that errors suddenly open up other possibilities. These involved technical errors which were always possible, and the sometimes strange reactions of the instruments. From this type of experience arose other possibilities for listening,[106] other possibilities for the transformation of musical ideas and other knowledge necessary for composition based, in particular, on taking space into account as a fundamental element of the project, of the attempted composition. As you see, once again and in another way I find myself studying the old school of St. Mark's and the Spanish school, in which music was composed as a function of particular spaces.

What you've just told me took place in the early 1980s. During those same years musical life registered some quite unusual phenomena. On the one hand the old avant-garde definitely entered into a crisis. On the other hand young composers came to the fore, bearers of trends that proclaimed a desire to break with the past in the name of a "New Simplicity," or at least of a more communicative language. With respect to these new requirements, these sometimes unrealistic proclamations, nevertheless rooted in the historical moment, your position seems somewhat eccentric, even isolated. I'd like to know your views of these new voices, the motives behind them, the polemics and the latest deviations.

It was precisely in thinking about these things that after a few meetings Italo Gomez, Franco Donatoni and I decided to launch the "Opera prima" project at La Fenice in Venice.[107] We did not want to redo Darmstadt in Venice, but simply to offer young composers an opportunity and a meeting place where they could perform their music, make comparisons, exchange information and impressions. Then, especially among the students of the Milan Conservatory, the polemics with certain teachers were the order of the day in the name of that concept of "neosimplicity" that in my view belongs to a type of musical sociologism that can be traced back to the more tragic banalities formulated by Zhdanov in the Soviet Union during the Stalinist period.

With Gomez and Donatoni and then with Bussotti, Sciarrino, Clementi, and Manzoni we thought it would be useful to create a space where the young people could compare themselves not only with each other, but also with us. Unfortunately already by the second year the disputes, not only among the young people, but especially among ourselves, wrecked everything. The clashes were violent, exasperatingly ridiculous and banal. Of course, the wrecking of "Opera prima" in Venice did not exhaust the problem. The overall picture of compositional trends is complex and multi-faceted, but it is not just to do with trends. In my opinion a decisive influence is exerted by the current type of music market. The mass media have a decisive influence on the dissemination or nondissemination of new music. Institutions strictly maintain their policies, mostly encouraging composition on the basis of traditional forms. For economic reasons, often the rehearsals for a concert are reduced to a few, sometimes just one and this also applies to the so-called best orchestras in the world. In this way you get a striking mediocrity of performance quality, one that does not allow the performers the chance to mature nor to study new scores. Think by contrast of the musical working practices of Erich Kleiber, Scherchen, Klemperer, Bruno Walter, Furtwängler, De Sabata; think of the rehearsals in which Giulini, Carlos Kleiber, Boulez, and Abbado apply themselves! This general consumer conformity, this mercantile haste, ends up fostering the feeling of routine in the performers and the artistic directors. It makes them resistant to any effort or risk that breaks away from this schematic approach and these repetitive habits. At the time of Darmstadt, we took an incredibly aggressive stance against all these things. What made any kind of conformism intolerable was the discovery of *musique concrète*, electronic music, new theories, and new types of composition, anxious to discover the unknown. For years there has been an opposite tendency, a tendency to repeat expedient habits, also retrieving certain names from the past (I'm not thinking of Ravel and Debussy, who are also often invoked), a sort of provincial academicism of the past.

For example?

Today there is a certain superficiality not only in the performance but also in the understanding of Puccini, and the same goes for Verdi and

Bellini. There is something pejorative in the way of thinking about composers like Mascagni, Zandonai, and Pizzetti, in the "Menotticizing" even more of Prokofiev,[108] the banalization of Bruckner or Mahler, in the name of a putative facility of language, communication, comprehensibility for the masses. But ignorance of the past, with all its rich otherness, is widespread.

Notwithstanding human know-how, the disgraceful presumption spreads to the point of denying the dramatic responsibility to innovate, take risks in inventing today for another tomorrow, be it real or visionary or utopian. It is the wind of restoration that is making itself felt, and which tends to flatten things out.

Yes, but the situation is now quite clear. That tendency which when it first emerged was so imperious and aggressive is now somewhat reproportioned, also because different and important participants who are following other roads have imposed themselves into that youthful scene. I'd like you to indicate some of the more promising composers, and not only in Italy, but especially in those countries about which we don't have a great deal of information, but who are able to express new realities.

You are right in saying that things have settled down, but this came about because, instead of assuming an adversarial attitude right to the bitter end, many of us have made sure that the opportunity to prove oneself was given to everyone, to be heard, reflect, collapse, or go on. Certainly new and interesting names have arisen: from "Opera prima" came Gilberto Cappelli, and then there are the already-mentioned Marco Stroppa and Claudio Ambrosini, composers such as Federico Incardona and Fabio Vacchi, and others even younger. They have very different personalities, are beset by different concerns and problems and have opportunities before them that will be up to them to develop.

I remember that period in the Soviet Union in which official musical life was dominated and blocked by the bureaucratized models of Moscow. During the first visit that I made to that country many years ago [in 1963] with Luigi Pestalozza, we went almost clandestinely to the homes of young composers such as Denisov and Schnittke, who could not set foot in the Union of Composers. By now that generation has broken through after long and very tenacious work. I want particularly to mention a very talented musician, Sofia Gubaidulina, who until a few years ago was totally suppressed. With a tenacity and a spiritual force typical of Russians who are often compelled to resist in order to survive the adversities of everyday life, she continued to work and is today receiving her much deserved recognition. One of her compositions for large orchestra, *Stimmen ... verstummen ...* , received great acclaim from musicians, audiences, and critics last year at the Berlin festival.[109] In this music, one does not feel at all the presence of the models of Prokofiev and Shostakovich, but rather a relationship with Scriabin's visionary genius and with those different currents of Russian music that are expressed through such composers as Ogolovets and Vishnegradsky.

In addition to that of Gubaidulina, you told me the names of Denisov and Schnittke, composers who are now over fifty. I would now like to ask you if you know any Soviet composer of the next generation who seems to you to be furnished with an interesting personality, to merit an international reputation.

In my opinion, the musical life of the Baltic Republics, Georgia, and Armenia is very interesting. There composers live and work who are almost completely unknown in the West, who definitely have an original talent which is often inspired by the great idealistic tradition of Solovyov, Rozanov, and Florensky. Among these I know and admire Artemyev,[110] who often collaborates with the director Elem Klimov, the dynamic and innovative secretary of the Union of Soviet Filmmakers. Like Gubaidulina, he also uses quarter-tones, ancient modes, and Orthodox chants, combining these elements in a conception that differs totally from what can be called the classical school of Moscow and of Leningrad. Artemyev composes with quarter-tones, sound bands [*fasce sonore*] that are continuously moving with changing harmonic spectra, especially making use of string instruments. Mark Pekarsky, a musician in his thirties, from Moscow, is doing extraordinary things with percussion instruments, which he masters with a completely new technique. It seems to me that it is not by chance that new musicians live and work in the Baltic Republics, in the Vilnius area, where a strongly visionary musician and painter like Čiurlionis has left such deep traces.

And how do you see the condition of today's music in Germany?

Here the situation is quite curious. We move from Helmut Lachenmann, who is a musician with a capacity for prismatic, timbral, and temporal invention to subject the sound material to transformations so rapidly that, at first, it is difficult to perceive (hence, its fascination!), to Wolfgang Rihm, who is entirely different. Recently I read the score of *Hamletmaschine,* the new work that he wrote on the text by Heiner

Müller, the great German playwright. It seems to me that in his musical production, as exuberant as it has been up to now, this work represents a really new point. Other interesting personalities are, I think, Spahlinger, up to now unknown in Italy, and Wolfgang Motz, but there are also other very young composers who represent opposing and restless tendencies. Some of them come to see me in Berlin to show me their works. I would not want to conclude my limited tour of the horizon without mentioning Budapest, the city where György Kurtág lives, works and teaches. He is a very great musical personality in whom I feel the vibration of the great Jewish presence of Budapest and Prague. Speaking of him, I think of the young Lukács, of Kafka, of the painter Lajos Kassák, and of all those great cultures that arose in peripheral areas of the Austro-Hungarian Empire, modeling themselves on the concept of opposition to the metropolis, to Vienna. These are cultures that expressed themselves in absolutely original and autonomous ways in architecture, literature, philosophy, and music. I find all these things in the personality of Kurtág, who is not only the mirror in which those many cultures are reflected, but the continuation of the spiritual condition of those who considered themselves exiles in their own homeland, such as Endre Ady, László Moholy-Nagy, Béla Bartók, and the young Lukács himself.

There is another country where for some time musical life seems to have been set in motion again, driven by a lively desire for renewal. I am thinking of Spain, where the voices of Luis De Pablo and of Cristóbal Halffter, the only ones who in the past were able to pierce in the lead curtain of repression, are now no longer alone.

I have been to Barcelona several times and I also taught seminars at the Miró Foundation. I've been to Granada, Toledo, Córdoba, Madrid, and Sitges, a little town near Barcelona, where summer courses are held. My impression is that the past is really very burdensome there. I would say that the condition of fragmentation and isolation still weighs heavily. In Granada, but also in other universities and other musical environments, I really feel the weight of isolation. In the Institute of Hispanic Musicology in Barcelona, directed by Father Josep Maria Llorens i Cisteró—a man of great intelligence, who fights against economic and financial difficulties—they are publishing the great Spanish polyphonic school. My feeling is that they sense they are close to discovering something, that they sense the need for information, that they are awaiting from themselves the moment when they will be able to overcome a certain condition. For example, the overcoming of a restrictive interpretation of García

Lorca, traditionally regarded as the poet of the gypsies, of the *cante jondo,* and not also as the metaphysical, surrealistic Lorca, associated with the great French poetic currents. A similar limit is noticed in the slightly provincial way of understanding De Falla, whose international dimension is not given adequate consideration, that of the De Falla who goes to Paris and Vienna and is a friend of Stravinsky, Gian Francesco Malipiero, Bartók, and Schoenberg. I think, therefore, that with the exception of certain names, the Francoist past still weighs heavy in Spain, with its isolation and its fragmentation, and that the need is therefore greater than ever to establish relationships that look beyond, that would build informative bridges.

I would now like to go back to your music and ask you something about one of your recent works. In 1983 you composed Guai ai gelidi mostri. *What do you mean by a title of this kind? I, too, can imagine what it is, but I'd like you to tell me.*

This is one of those compositions for which the friendship, participation, and the wonderful inventiveness of Massimo Cacciari has been a determining factor. It is a work born of the set of problems and the endless questions and upheavals that his thought provokes. The title is taken from a text by Nietzsche,[111] a tirade against the State or against the cold monsters that try to freeze, block, and immobilize everything with a violence and a monstrosity typical of power. It deals with a very current idea also dealt with by Canetti. The text of this violent invective also incorporates Rosenzweig's words extracted from his essay *In tyrannos!* The idea is, therefore, the need to oppose the monstrous violence of the State with a rediscovery and an affirmation of a life that is continually to be freed from any form of coercion in the reality of today and tomorrow. Musically, certain techniques of live electronics have been used. The tempos are composed on various levels: the three strings have a tempo totally distinct from that of the other instruments. Two contraltos intervene occasionally with words taken from the text that is not entirely sung. They intervene with the technique of *phasing,* that is, the sound is modulated, moved upward or downward by the Publison by a difference of one, two or three Hz. Suddenly the sound is energized, it is amplified according to both its spectrum and its energy, as if the two voices were becoming two choruses, gaining a presence that is something quite different with respect to the other spectra and the other instruments, to sing certain particularly significant words taken from the texts chosen by Massimo Cacciari.

Depending on the performance, Guai ai gelidi mostri *lasts forty or fifty minutes.* Diario polacco n. 2 *lasts about forty and with* Omaggio a György Kurtág *we are at thirty-five and with* Prometeo *over two hours. This type of music is often on the threshold of audibility, almost elusive, and the listeners must not only strain their ear but also their intelligence. I would like to ask you a very simple question: how do you reconcile a type of music at the threshold of comprehensibility with these durations?*

Well, when it comes to length, then even Beethoven's Ninth and Mahler's symphonies are no joke.

Yes, but in those compositions the sound events are not whispered; indeed, they possess an overtness that is quite monumental.

You're right, the problem of the duration must be addressed seriously. A first reason lies in the material, in the sonic-acoustic substance of today, as well as in electronic music, in the possibilities to invent with the computer. The material that is used requires different time lengths [*tempi di durata*] in order to develop, combine, wander, and arrange in and with the space, until the space itself sounds, sings, and expands. It involves a time, various speeds of diffusion in space, dynamization, spatial perception completely different from that required for a traditional orchestra, a single acoustic source which in principle is "monodirectional." The music of the eighteenth and nineteenth centuries, except for that of Bruckner (the reverberation of the hall in St. Florian, which lasts many seconds, makes Bruckner's long harmonic fields sound different from the normal "leveling" concert halls),[112] was conceived for a performance and mode of perception that is, in fact, unidirectional and with the typical reverberations of the nineteenth-century hall. Halls of this kind continue to be built today, and it affects programming.

Purcell composed differently for Westminster Abbey (stone, marble, and glass) and for the Chapel Royal (tapestries, carpets). The so-called acoustic sound checks of a large orchestra on tour are ridiculous, precisely because of this perceptive, analytical, and acoustic ignorance.

According to the different experiments that we have made at the Freiburg studio, the material we use—including transformations and varied diffusions in a space that is always different—in order to be able to move in space and have it perceived as such requires more and different times.[113] Physics, psychology, acoustics, emotions, and conditioning, all together.

The difficulty to which you referred, the perceptibility of music on the threshold of audibility, actually exists, but it is possible to expand both our inventive and perceptive abilities. Let me tell you of an experiment performed with the help of Roberto Fabbriciani and Ciro Scarponi. On certain occasions I made an agreement with them that, on my invitation to perform pianissimo during the introductory talk at the concert, they would act as though they were playing but without producing any sound. I then asked the audience what they had heard. Some would respond that they had heard an almost inaudible pianissimo, but that they had still heard something. Hence you can become aware of the extent to which our physical and psychic receptivity is conditioned, and is capable of modification: certainly more capable than we are at accustomed to using it.

With highly differentiated scales of dynamics (remember Verdi's five to six *p!*),[114] our perception is also greatly differentiated. Initially this occurs with difficulty, as often happens, but then it increases, and we are able to hear much more and more varied things.

If you find yourself confronted with Richard Strauss's *ff*, you tend to put up with them, just like the many-decibel acoustic violence of our daily urban life.

But if you find yourself immersed in an unprecedented variety of dynamics up to ten *p* as in a forest cut through by sudden violence (and which could then only be a single *p!*), the tension you feel will reveal other times and ways of listening, which would be more limited with other, less varied material.

But I would also like to tell you how I came to these convictions through daily experiences and reflections. In many walks, moments of pausing and listening, in the Black Forest or in Berlin or Venice, I always ask myself what I am listening to. In the Black Forest I listen to sounds that are almost imperceptible, through which I discover another wider capacity of listening, another acoustic environment. Thus, in the city, listening to the marginalized, pianissimo sounds, compared to the acoustic violence of traffic, for example, or that of TVs blaring out of the windows. We live, that is to say, in a greater dynamic articulation. I have had particular acoustic experiences during my stay here in Berlin. During the first few months I felt that something was not working, whether it was every time I listened to a record, or whether I was out in the Berlin air. I thought that the record or the needle was worn out. Then, suddenly, I was aware that the low and dark noise that I was attributing to wear and tear came from the elevated train and penetrated into the house through the foundation, transmitting through the walls an acoustic spectrum that was, in fact, very low. I, on the other hand, was accustomed in Venice to perceiving spectra that were higher in frequency due to the reverberations, to the echoes among the bells and to the other sounds and their transmission on the water. In Berlin, in the neighborhood where I live, the sound of bells is instead totally absent. The bell towers are in another part of town, and the diversity of the environmental harmonic spectrum at first caused me great uneasiness. When I realized all these things, I began to ask myself if what we hear now is really what we are able to hear, or if we can hear still other and very different things as well. I believe this is a question to which there is no definitive answer.

I would now like to try to come to Prometeo *which, not unlike your other theatrical works, has the character of a compendium and a synthesis of long and troubled past experiences. For years at the Venice Biennale and elsewhere I listened to your compositions which were presented as fragments of* Prometeo. *They were fragments that were a bit mysterious because they did not allow us to perceive any outline of a general project, nor, above all, could one deduce, from those excerpta, any staged conception. Only when* Prometeo *came out in its entirety for the first time at the Venice Biennale was it possible to understand from your statements that the work intentionally dispensed with any staging plan in order to take shape as a drama contained completely in the world of sounds, in other words, as a "tragedy of listening," exactly as you have defined it.*

At the basis of *Prometeo* are long conversations with Massimo Cacciari. We started from Aeschylus's *Prometheus*, but through those conversations everything continuously evolved. Under no circumstances did we intend to present once more a reading of *Prometeo* connected to mythology, and we were not even interested in the image of a progressive Prometheus. Our points of reference were Nietzsche and Benjamin, through whom we encountered a Prometheus-*Wanderer* continuously striving in search of new "laws" with which to discard the previous ones, in a word, Promethean continuity without end. Cacciari's original idea was to conceive of the "opera" as an archipelago made up of many islands.[115] Therefore no scenes but islands, so that the so-called path of the "opera" would be configured like a wandering navigation among these islands. From this arose the initial projects that at that time concerned the visual level. We had talked with Renzo Piano about the possibility of having islands suspended in space and various stalls for the choruses. The navigation between them could have been created also by projecting on the walls and on the audience a kind of luminous, colored route, such as the colored navigation maps of the fifteenth and sixteenth centuries.

How did the choice of Renzo Piano come about for the construction of the shell in which Prometeo *was set?*

It just happened to me, as had happened before with Lyubimov. We had never met, although I was familiar with Beaubourg and his other constructions. So, following a kind of radar, I called him and asked him if he thought he could take part in inventing something that would be between the resonating chamber and the outer container, designed to have space for many choruses, four orchestras, vocal and instrumental soloists and the islands, with the possibility of placing microphones and loudspeakers at various points, above and below, far and wide: in other words, a space generating space [*spazio spaziante*].

I knew the church of St. Lorenzo well and I went there many times to study it. Once there were restoration works going on. Two workers, at a considerable distance and height, were speaking normally without straining their voices, almost whispering. One could hear them very well at every point in the church. I then asked Piano to build something that would multiply these possibilities.

The initial idea was also to have a visual part, and in that sense Massimo and I were very interested in the relationship between sound and color. I began to study, or tried to study, Runge and Goethe's color theories and the various color theories of the Russians of the twentieth century, the experiences of the Bauhaus and Kandinsky, the relations between Khlebnikov, Malevich, and Milyutin, the use of colors and the chorus in Schoenberg's *Die glückliche Hand* [The Hand of Fate] and the relationship between color and sound in Scriabin's scores, like *Prometheus* and *The Poem of Ecstasy,* always with the intention of finding a relationship between color and sound that would not be mechanical. There were also many meetings and discussions between Cacciari, Emilio Vedova, and me dedicated to the examination of the various possibilities. Here in Germany, near Stuttgart, with a technician of the Freiburg studio, I visited certain industrial firms that produce different types of projectors: projectors that were self-propelled, moving up and down and able to rotate 180 degrees, whose movements could be programed by computer. With Vedova we thought of sheets of glass and a type of undulating projection, in movement. Vedova showed us some beautiful slides that he had prepared in a glass factory in Murano for the Universal Exposition in Montreal.[116] The results were remarkable, but at some point I started to feel a kind of antivisual syndrome which not only distanced me from any visual project, but made all the different experiences I had had at the Freiburg studio explode within me. Suddenly I was completely taken by the necessity of listening itself, of issues involved and the enormous tensions that it could provoke. I realized that with a single instrument, whether it was Schiaffini's tuba, Fabbriciani's flute, Susanne Otto's voice, Ciro Scarponi's clarinet, or Scodanibbio's double bass, with various transformations in real time, with the use of the Halaphon, that is, with the possibility to simultaneously dynamize four or five different spatial paths, what I call acoustic dramaturgy was audible, feasible and capable of being created. And so the visual projects that had been developed in collaboration with Vedova were abandoned. Massimo came up with "tragedy of listening" as a subtitle to Prometeo.

The experience of Prometeo *is very recent, but already this "tragedy of listening" reveals a strong attractiveness: after the Venetian premiere in the St. Lorenzo church, the work was taken up by La Scala, which presented it in the Ansaldo factory. Next August it will be presented by the Alte Oper in Frankfurt and in September at the Festival d'Automne in Paris.*

Yes, and I would add that in 1988 a performance of Prometeo is foreseen at the large Berliner Philharmonie.

In Frankfurt, on the premises of the Alte Oper, in Paris at the Palais Chaillot, and in Berlin at the Philharmonie: in your opinion, which of these places are the most suitable for hosting Prometeo*?*

At the Palais Chaillot I very much hope Piano's structure will be reused. Uncluttered and open, the space of the Palais Chaillot is extraordinary, of a size to finally allow the use of Piano's structure as a unified whole. In Venice, in St. Lorenzo, because the altar in the center bisects the space, it was necessary to break up the structure, even from the point of view of acoustics, creating a hall A and a hall B, putting everything in parallel. Instead at Ansaldo everything worked in the horizontal dimension, although it was broken up because of the columns and the differing heights in the hall in the factory. The space of the Philharmonie in Berlin, on the other hand, is absolutely extraordinary. The architect Hans Scharoun devised it in the 1950s, designing it with a type of articulation that adapts wonderfully to the various spatial needs of contemporary music. But, as you know, the hall is occupied permanently by Karajan with the Berlin Philharmonic Orchestra, and, therefore, it is designated for traditional symphonic use. Last year I listened to *Gesang der Jünglinge* finally performed at the Philharmonie. This masterpiece by Stockhausen resonated there in a totally new way.

Before Prometeo *resonates in the perfectly congenial acoustic space of the Berliner Philharmonie, your music will have to deal with another famous hall, the new and very grandiose Gasteig of Munich, where the premiere of your new work will take place at the end of April. It is only just over a month until the performance, and the score is already finished. Therefore, we can speak concretely. What is the title of the new score?*
It is *Caminantes . . . Ayacucho.*

What does it mean?
In Toledo on the wall of a cloister of 1300 I read an inscription: "Caminantes no hay caminos hay que caminar."[117]

I'll try to translate: "Oh you who walk, who go, there are no paths, no roads are shown, but you have to walk, go." It seems to me that the sense is clear.
Certainly.
It's the Wanderer of Nietzsche, of the continuous search, of Cacciari's *Prometeo*. It's the sea on which he goes inventing, discovering the route.

The meaning is very clear and perfectly consistent with everything that you have said up to now, but "Ayacucho," what does that mean?
I am thinking about three compositions: *Caminantes* is the first one, and then there's a name that locates it. *No hay caminos* will be the second one, and *Hay que caminar* the third one.[118] In *Caminantes . . . Ayacucho* the text is by Giordano Bruno, a Latin sonnet *Ai principi de l'Universo* from *De la causa, principio et uno* (1584) that I shall now read to you in translation:
"That the tenebrous Earth which, from the beginning, has cleaved to the wavy expanse of the waters, may leave its seat and fly towards the heavenly orbs, I beg you, O Sun. And you, wandering stars, behold me as I proceed towards the twofold heaven, since it is you who have

opened this path to me. May your movements open before me, as I rush through the spaces, the doors of sleep: that which miserly time has kept long hidden, may it be allowed me to draw into the light out of the dense gloom. What prevents you, O suffering spirit, from hastening to give birth to your truth, though you bequeath in to an unworthy age? Though the flow of shadows submerges the Earth, you, my Olympus, make shine your peak in the clear heavens."[119]

It's really the boundlessness of the continuum, the continuity of the infinite universes of Giordano Bruno, a *caminante* [walker] whom I love very much. *Caminantes . . . Ayacucho* is the first part of the triptych. The other two will be based on the other two parts of the Toledo inscription. Next to the words in my title, there is a name, Ayacucho. It is an area in southern Peru that is in perpetual revolt. The Spanish were never able to penetrate it and today it is inhabited by peasants kept in the most miserable conditions. It is almost isolated from the rest of the country, but in contact with students and professors of the University of San Marcos in Lima and with all those who represent the most advanced and aware of the social protest, even to the point of armed struggle.

What ensemble is required by the score of Caminantes . . . Ayacucho?

Two choruses—one is that of the Bavarian Radio, the other is that of Freiburg, with which I have been working for eight years—and two soloists, the contralto Susanne Otto and the flutist Fabbriciani, with the Munich Philharmonic, an orchestra wonderfully nurtured by Sergiu Celibidache. The Gasteig has a large triangular hall with a capacity of twenty-five hundred people. To the right and left are types of choir lofts at various heights, built for acoustic reasons, and there I have placed some instrumentalists so that there is a spatial arrangement in which you have three choir lofts on the right, three on the left, the organ high up in the center, the strings in the center, and on the sides the wind instruments and the percussion. One chorus at the back, the other subdivided on the right and on the left.

Will there also be electronic instruments?

Yes, the live electronics of Freiburg. Unlike what I have done up to now, the loudspeakers (as sound sources) will no longer be arranged around the audience, but in positions totally in front, up above, down below, in the back, on the right, on the left. The orchestra will be conducted by Maestro Kakhidze, artistic director of the Opera and the Philharmonic Orchestra of Tbilisi, Georgia. The fact that he is coming to

Munich for this premiere is unprecedented, one of the many signs of that new situation which is causing great change, and, unfortunately, stiff resistance, in the Soviet Union, in the Eastern countries, in the world.

This will, therefore, be the first panel of a triptych, and the other two?

For the second, with another title from the Toledo inscription, the premiere is scheduled for November 1987 in Tokyo. For the third, other times and other expectations.

Regarding this inscription read on the Toledo wall, a curious coincidence reminds me of Dallapiccola, who in going around America read writings that reminded him of St. Augustine and other signs of his destiny.[120] *On this inscription, which summarizes the anxiety that for years has driven your work forward and has brought together the past and the future, according to a criterion of interpenetration of which your latest music has unveiled the mysterious depths, our conversation can come to an end.*

Berlin, March 1987

PART ONE

Musical Analysis and Composition

I

Luigi Dallapiccola and the *Sex Carmina Alcaei*

ca. 1948

In Dallapiccola, the dodecaphonic way of thinking took shape gradually, as the progressive attainment of a spirit that bore witness to a truly total musical conception. This conception had already been introduced by the Franco-Flemish. It was taken up again and greatly developed by J. S. Bach in exemplary fashion in *The Art of Fugue*.

L. Dallapiccola displays a contrapuntal nature of the utmost soundness, which leads him to construct music truly imbued with a sense of architecture. That sense, in its developed form, impresses upon his most recent music an organic and logical impulse that finds its resolution in the dodecaphonic vision. He first grapples with the twelve-tone technique in *Canti di prigionia* (1938–41), but not in an all-embracing manner. In *Congedo di Girolamo Savonarola* (1941), he bases the whole composition, for chorus and percussion, on two series and a quotation (the Gregorian *Dies irae*). But both the chorus and the instruments have free passages, not derived from series, albeit forced into the formal severity of canons in prime, inversion, and retrograde form. With the cycle of *Liriche greche,* on the other hand, Dallapiccola attains a superior result with a stricter dodecaphonic approach.

The *Sex carmina Alcaei* are dedicated to the memory of Anton Webern. The significance of the dedication goes beyond the simple act of devotion and tribute to a friend. It expresses his admiration and indebtedness to the teaching of the maestro and to the composer who was "newest among the new."[1]

The polyphonic and instrumental technique demonstrates the extent to which Dallapiccola had set great store by Webern's message. The *Sex carmina Alcaei* are based on a single twelve-tone row,[2] in which a manifest weight is given to the chromatic character that will go on to form the unifying principle of the whole work. Also the frequent use of semitones will help create that atmosphere based on archetypal expressive tension that very often characterizes Dallapiccola's music. The intervals of the row indicate that it has been conceived with regard to the specific poetic quality of the text (see, for example, the frequent use of intervals such as the min. 3rd, the min. 2nd, the Maj. 6th and the Maj. 3rd).

From the original row, Dallapiccola derives the other three basic forms: inversion, retrograde, and retrograde inversion. He keeps within the boundary that Schoenberg specified as marking the natural dimensions of any series. While in *Congedo di Savonarola,* having divided the row into three fragments, he shifted them around, producing continuous changes in the original series, in *Sex carmina Alcaei* he no longer uses this method. In this case, rather, he follows the succession of the intervals as they are presented in the original twelve-tone row. The only difference is in their varied rhythmic interpretation, this being done to emphasize the text. In *Expositio,* the voice introduces the original row,[3] then the retrograde in a varied rhythm.[4] The retrograde inversion, always in a varied rhythm, appears at the beginning of the third fragment.[5] In the second fragment, the original row is given to the voice, again in a varied rhythm,[6] while the instruments enter in perpetual canon with the inversion of the row; the augmented canon passes alternately from the piano to the harp.

In the fourth fragment, the voice has the retrograde row,[7] in a varied rhythm. The instruments follow the voice with a prime canon, except the oboe and cello that have the canon by inversion. In the remaining fragments, too,[8] the formal construction is based on the various forms of the canon. The row, applied almost always in its complete form, passes among the various instruments in a fragmented manner, according to a timbral logic. In this way, Dallapiccola minimizes the idea of linear phrasing and volume of sound, thus paying a further tribute to Webern. A particular effect of timbre and mass results from a sum of the fragmentary movements of each instrument. If Dallapiccola remains tied to the four forms of the series, this does not prevent him from illuminating any section, for reasons that are specific and related to expressiveness, by entrusting fragments or sometimes isolated notes (doubled or not) to other instruments, this too according to a principle of dodecaphonic logic.

On the Development of Serial Technique

1956

SOME CHARACTERISTIC TWELVE-TONE ROWS

1. Arnold Schoenberg:
   a) *Serenade* op. 24, fourth movement.

This row consists of the following 11 intervals:

3 minor seconds (D-E♭, B-C, C-C♯)

3 major seconds (E-D, G♯-F♯, F-G)

2 minor thirds (F♯-A, G-B♭)

2 major thirds (E♭-B, A-F)

1 perfect fourth (C♯-G♯)

At the base of the row there is, therefore, a calculated principle of choice regarding the intervals used. Such a principle must be present in each row. The individuality of the row is dependent upon it.

Also in this row there is that clear thematic significance that Schoenberg requires in every row.

The row does not yet manifest the organization of fixed intervals (both from the melodic and harmonic points of view) that excludes the use of "relative" intervals.

The instruments play the row twice in its original form (measures 1–5). Then follows the voice which repeats the row another thirteen times (measures 6–69).

b) Variations for Orchestra op. 31.

This row is extremely important and constitutes the basis for all further development of the serial technique. It is the basis of the first twelve-tone work for orchestra composed by Schoenberg.[1]

On the Development of Serial Technique | 129

He constructs the theme of these variations with the four fundamental forms of the twelve-tone technique: original, retrograde inversion of the row, retrograde of the row, inversion of the row.

The row incorporates a permutation of the intervals that make up B-A-C-H (E-F♯-E♭-F).

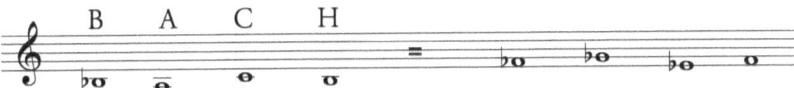

Therefore, it contains a thematic-formal element independent of and pre-existing to the row itself! The four fundamental forms constituting the theme are varied according to Schoenberg's typical methods.

2. Anton Webern: *Symphony* op. 21.

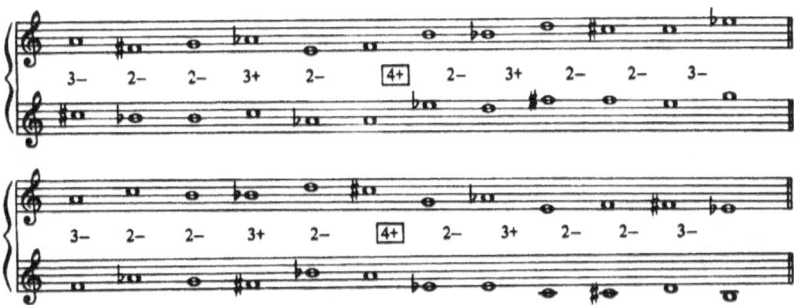

This row is composed of two parts connected by an interval of a tritone (1–6 and 7–12). Its second half (7–12) is the retrograde of the first half:

1–6	7–12
3–/2–/2–/3+/2–	2–/3+/2–/2–/3–

This way of constructing a twelve-tone row is typical of Webern.

The four fundamental forms are reduced here to two, because the retrograde of the original becomes at the same time a transposition of the original, and the retrograde of the inversion in turn becomes a transposition of the inversion.

The organizational structure of this row acquires a particular force by virtue of the simultaneity and succession of its projections.

3. Pierre Boulez: *Structures, premier livre* (for two pianos, four hands).

On the Development of Serial Technique | 131

Duration values (1 = ♪)

12 11 9 10 3 6 7 1 2 8 5 4 (piano I)
 5 8 6 4 3 9 2 1 7 11 10 12 (piano II)

Here the first seven measures contain not only the twelve-tone row but also the twelve duration values.

The piano I plays the original series, the piano II at the same time plays the inversion of the same row.

The series of twelve duration values corresponds to the arithmetic progression from 1 to 12, in an ascending line rising up to 12, where 1 = ♪ (hence 1–12 = ♪—𝅗𝅥.).

It is logical that the serial technique could not be limited to the relationship between the tones (intervals and precise pitch), but had to be extended also to their duration (rhythm).

4. Karlheinz Stockhausen: *Klavierstück I.*[2]

This row is based on the natural chromatic scale: C-D♭-D-E♭-E-F // G♭-G-A♭-A-B♭-B, divided in two perfect fourths:

C-F   G♭-B
(C-D♭-D-E♭-E-F)   and   (G♭-G-A♭-A-B♭-B)

Within both sections a certain number of permutations is performed (thirty-six for each) between the notes that constitute them (C-Db-D-Eb-E-F and Gb-G-Ab-A-Bb-B): the chosen interval order occurs every time according to the form of a twelve-tone row divided into two sections.

5. Luigi Nono: *Il canto sospeso*.

This row uses all eleven intervals, from the minor second up to the major seventh. Here there is no longer a need for the four fundamental forms of the twelve-tone row. This is because the choice of the pitches is variously organized also with regard to durations, dynamics, and register, although it is the fundamental row fixed in its intervals.[3]

3

The Development of Serial Technique

1957

The "serial" concept has developed extensively from Schoenberg's time to the present day, as each constituent element of music has been taken into account and postulated anew in a manner consistent with the "serial" principle.[1] And the concept of "series," its initial thematic-dodecaphonic properties now historically exhausted, has extended its properties to the overall structure of the composition, in all its components: pitch—rhythm—dynamics—timbre—form, and, recently, to the very time itself in which the composition unfolds, coordinating the individual characteristics of each factor in relation to the function of the whole.[2]

From the initial "serial" phase to the present day there is only *logical historical development,* no breaks, only the time necessary for becoming aware of time itself—that is, history—and for its fulfillment. The precise terms that characterize its initial stage come from Schoenberg's writings. "The method of 'composing with twelve tones related only to each other' grew out of [the] necessity . . . for a new procedure in musical construction seemed fitted to replace those structural differentiations provided formerly by tonal harmonies. . . . This method consists primarily of the constant and exclusive set of twelve different tones" (from "Composition with Twelve Tones").[3]

"The first conception of a series always takes place in the form of a thematic character" (from the letter of February 5, 1951, to Josef Rufer).[4]

> "It will not often happen that one obtains a perfect series which is fit for use as the first immediate composition. A little working-over afterward is usually necessary. But the character of the piece is already present in the first form of the series" (from a letter of April 8, 1950, to Josef Rufer).[5]

That is, the "serial" conception is related to the successive order of twelve tones, as a unity of thematic material to be developed, and the use of the four fundamental forms of the series and their transpositions multiplies this thematic property.

The structure of the twenty-four measures of the "Thema" of the Variations for Orchestra op. 31, analyzed later, reveals Schoenberg's "serial" concept in the most complete and precise manner.

In Webern's letter of May 3, 1941, in which he explains his Variations op. 30 to the critic Willi Reich, it is possible to find the formulation of those new musical interests that would come to characterize what may be called the second stage in the development of the "serial" technique:

> Now everything that occurs in the piece is based on the two ideas given in the first and second bars (double bass and oboe!). But it's reduced still more, since the second shape (oboe) is itself retrograde; the second two notes are the cancrizan of the first two, but rhythmically augmented. They are followed, on the trombone, by a repetition of the first shape (double-bass), but in diminution! And in cancrizan as to motives and intervals. That's how my row is constructed—it's contained in these thrice four notes. But the succession of motives takes part in this cancrizan, though with the use of augmentation and diminution! These two kinds of variation now lead almost exclusively to the various variation ideas; that's to say motivic variation happens, if at all, only within these limits.... And that's how it goes on throughout the whole piece, whose twelve notes, that's to say the row, contain its entire content in embryo. In miniature![6]

The "serial" constructive function no longer develops in relation to the thematic characteristic of the "series," and the rhythmic-melodic-harmonic-timbral structure of the Variations op. 30 follows on closely from that of the twelve-tone "series." The four fundamental forms are reduced to two due to the symmetrical property and the ambivalence which are characteristic of Webern's "series" (an analysis of the new structural function of the basic "series" of opus 30 will be shown later).

The third stage is in full development: the "serial" principle encroaches on each element of the music, in such a way that the resulting reciprocity among the elements is rigorous. The twelve tones of the chromatic scale are organized in "series" of permutations in their own right, or in a reciprocal relationship between permutations and a fixed order in respect of other elements.

And the tone is then analyzed, studied for the first time in its original spectrum so as to render possible its direct *composition* (electronic music). This new logical and consequent phase of study, is defining a new musical conception of creation and of realization that will be our future.

Later the characteristics of this third stage will be identified and analyzed in compositions by Boulez, Maderna, Nono, and Stockhausen.[7]

THE "SERIAL" CONCEPTION OF A. SCHOENBERG IN THE "THEMA" OF THE VARIATIONS FOR ORCHESTRA, OP. 31

The Original "series" is exposed here in measures 34–38 by the cellos:

B♭-E-F♯-E♭-F-A-D-C♯-G-G♯-B-C

It is subdivided into two segments, each of six tones, by the interval of a 4th A-D (the interval of the 5th being equivalent to that of the 4th).

The first segment consists of the following intervals:

tritone—Maj. 2nd—min. 3rd—Maj. 2nd—Maj. 3rd

The second segment consists of the following intervals:

min. 2nd—tritone—min. 2nd—min. 3rd—min. 2nd

The intervals of tritone and min. 3rd are common to both.

These two intervals and the one that divides the series into two segments (the 4th) have a particular importance because of their common characteristic in determining the degrees of transposition of the series and the relationship between two (or among four) series when they are used simultaneously in superimposition.

Examples:

a) In Variation I the two parts in counterpoint with the "Thema," a true *cantus firmus* (bars 58–69: first part given to the woodwinds + violins I and II/second part to the brass + violas and cellos) are each formed by two series superimposed in parallel and related by the min. 3rd interval (and the equivalent Maj. 6th/min. 3rd above the octave), while the degree of transposition of the series, with respect to the four fundamental forms, is determined by the intervals of the tritone and the min. 3rd.

The four series constituting the two parts in counterpoint are related to one another (initial tone of the series) by unison, min. 3rd, tritone, and perfect 4th.

Bar 64: the first part (woodwinds + violins I and II) is constituted by the parallel superimposition at the Maj. 6th, of two *Krebs* series,[8] one of which one is transposed by a tritone (onto F♯ from C), and the second by min. 3rd (onto A from C).

The second part (brass + violas and cellos) is also created by means of the parallel superimposition, at the Maj. 6th and the min. 3rd, of two *Krebs-Umkehrung* series, one of which is transposed at the tritone (onto B from F), the second at the min. 3rd (onto D from F).

The series transposed by the same degree in the two voices is related by the perfect 4th.

b) In Variation II: the two voices in counterpoint, with a *Spiegel-*canonical procedure on a prime canon of the theme, a true *cantus firmus* (violin—oboe), are each built from series that are related by min. 3rd and tritone. The series are transposed by a min. 3rd and a tritone respectively.

Bar 87: the first voice (cello + bass clarinet) consists of the *Krebs* transposed by a min. 3rd (onto E♭ from C); the second voice (bassoon + flute) consisting of the *Krebs-Umkehrung*, also transposed by a min. 3rd (onto A♭ from F). The two series are related to each other by perfect 4th (E♭-A♭).

Bar 98: the first voice (cello + bassoon I) consists of the *Umkehrung* transposed by tritone (onto C♯ from G); the second (clarinet I + English horn) consists of the Original transposed by a tritone (onto E from B♭). The two series are related to each other by a min. 3rd (C♯-E).

The four series that make up each of the two voices that carry the theme in prime canon are related to each other at the min. 3rd.

bar 83: initial notes of both *Umkehrung* series: E-C♯

bar 88: initial notes of both *Krebs* series: A-C

bar 94: initial notes of both *Krebs-Umkehrung* series: D-B

bar 100: initial notes of both original series: G-B♭

The transpositions are by min. 3rd and tritone.

c) In Variation III the series are related to each other at the tritone (except bars 113–114, where the relation is at the Maj. 3rd) while the transpositions are by min. 3rd and tritone.

The function of these intervals (min. 3rd/4th/tritone) in determining the transpositions (and superimpositions) of the series is already evident in the organization of the "Thema," in which the four fundamental forms of the series (+ the repetition of the transposed Original, bars 52–57) occur, as melodic projection, in bars 34–57:

bar 39: the *Krebs-Umkehrung* is related by a 4th to both the initial tone of the Original (F with respect to B♭) and its final tone (F with respect to C);

bar 46: the *Krebs* is not transposed with respect to the Original, but is related by a 4th with both the initial and the final tone of the preceding *Krebs-Umkehrung* (C with respect to F/C with respect to G: 5th inversion of 4th);

bar 51: the *Umkehrung* is related to the Original by a min. 3rd (G with respect to B♭) and by a 4th with respect to the initial tone of the previous *Krebs* (G with respect to C) and a min. 3rd with respect to the final one (G with respect to B♭).

The tritone determines the relationship between the *Umkehrung* (G in bar 51) and the repetition of the Original (C♯ in bar 52); this in turn is transposed by a min. 3rd (to C♯ from B♭):

Original (bars 34–38):	B♭-E-F♯-E♭-F-A-D-C♯-G-G♯-B-C
Krebs-Umkehrung (bars 39–45):	F-F♯-A-B♭-E-E♭-A♭-C-D-B-C♯-G
Krebs (bars 46–50):	C-B-G♯-G-C♯-D-A-F-E♭-F♯-E-B♭
Umkehrung (bars 51–57):	G-C♯-B-D-C-A♭-E♭-E-B♭-A-F♯-F
Original (bars 52–57):	C♯-G-A-F♯-A♭-C-F-E-B♭-B-D-E♭
(transposed by min. 3rd)	

The tritone interval determines the transposition in the Original series of B-A-C-H [B♭-A-C-B],[9] which occurs in a new order:

Original series: B♭ E F♯ E♭ F A D etc.

```
              ———————— tritone ————————
       B           C           A           H
     [ B♭          C           A           B ]
```

Variation II is based on this element, the transposition of B-A-C-H and its new order.

Variation V is based on the intervening intervals in B-A-C-H: min. 2nd / Maj. 2nd / min. 3rd (and their equivalents).

```
                    B     A     C     H
      min. 2nd      L_____J     L_____J
         "
                          L_____J
      Maj. 2nd      L_____J
         "
                                L_____J
      min. 3rd      L_____J
```

The "Thema" bars 34–57, is divided formally into *A* and *B*, each with twelve measures:

A   34–45
B   46–57

They are subdivided in their turn:

```
                    ┌─────────── 12 ───────────┐
                    ┌─────────┐    ┌──────────┐
        A           5 bars    +    7 bars
                    34–38     +    39–45
        B           5 bars    +    7 bars
                    46–50     +    51–57
```

Exactly symmetrical.

This formal scheme is based on serial construction, in melodic and harmonic projection:

A   melodic projection   Original (bars 34–38)   + *Krebs-Umkehr.* (bars 39–45)
    harmonic projection *Umkehr.* (bars 34–38)   + *Krebs* (bars 39–45)

B   melodic projection   *Krebs* (bars 46–50)   + *Umkehr.* (bars 51–57)
    harmonic projection *Krebs-Umkehr.* (bars 46–50) + Original (bars 51–57)

That is, both *A* and *B* are made up of the four fundamental forms of the series.

In *A* and *B* each subdivision in 5 and 7 bars consists of one form of the series in parallel with its *Spiegel:* the matching parallel will remain unchanged in all variations.

```
        Original       and     Krebs-Umkehrung
           |                          |
        Umkehrung      and     Krebs
```

The Development of Serial Technique | 139

Each is built on a fundamental form of the series, and they remain unchanged in every variation.

Each form of the series that has a melodic projection in *A* assumes a harmonic projection in *B*, just as each form of the series that has a harmonic projection in *A* assumes a melodic projection in *B*. In fact, *B* is the *Krebs-Umkehrung* of *A*.

This structure of the "Thema" is fundamental to the whole composition.

The pattern of 24 bars, divided into 12 + 12, subdivided into 5 + 7, remains fixed for each variation, except:

Variation IV has the same pattern doubled, that is, twice 10 + 14.

Variation VI has 36 bars, divided into 18 + 18. What is the basic pattern in both *A* and *B*, determined by the four fundamental forms of the series, is here subjected to permutation by the new compositional technique, which develops by developing the concept of variation itself.

In its melodic projection, the "Thema" is made up of motifs, each with a well-defined number of tones:

A   Original (bars 34–38):

| B♭ E F♯ E♭ F | A D C♯ G | G♯ B C |
| 5 | 4 | 3 |

Krebs-Umkehrung (bars 39–45):

F F♯ A	B♭ E + E♭ A♭	C D B C♯ G
3	2 2	5
	4	

B   *Krebs* (bars 46–50):

| C B G♯ G C♯ D | A F E♭ F♯ E B♭ |
| 6 | 6 |

Umkehrung (bars 51–57):

G C♯ B D C	A♭ E♭ + E B♭	A F♯ F
5	2 2	3
	4	

There are constant motifs with five tones/with four tones (and subdivided into 2 + 2)/with three tones in the Original, in the *Krebs-Umkeh-*

rung (here also *Krebs* in terms of the order of succession of the motifs), and in the *Umkehrung*, while in the *Krebs* there are two motifs, each with six tones.

This same pattern remains unchanged even in the harmonic projection of the "Thema":

<table>
<tr><td colspan="3" align="center">*Umkehrung*
bars 34–38</td><td colspan="3" align="center">*Krebs*
bars 39–45</td></tr>
<tr>
<td>5 | D
B
G
C#
C |</td>
<td>4 | Eb
Ab
E
Bb |</td>
<td>3 | F
A
F# |</td>
<td>3 | B
G#
C |</td>
<td>4 | D
A
C#
G |</td>
<td>5 | E
F#
Eb
F
Bb |</td>
</tr>
</table>

<table>
<tr><td colspan="3" align="center">*Krebs-Umkehrung*
bars 46–50</td><td colspan="3" align="center">*Original*
bars 51–57</td></tr>
<tr>
<td>3 | F
A
F# |</td>
<td>3 | Eb
Bb
E |</td>
<td>6 | G
B
C#
Ab
C
D |</td>
<td>5 | E
Eb
F#
Bb
F |</td>
<td>4 | D
A
G
C# |</td>
<td>3 | C
G#
B |</td>
</tr>
</table>

The unity, a characteristic feature of the serial conception, between the melodic projection and the harmonic projection of the series is here strongly affirmed: the same pattern applies to the subdivision of the tones in both projections.

The scheme by which the tones are subdivided into melodic motifs results in the following rhythmic pattern:

A   (bars 34–38)

    (bars 39–45)

B   (bars 46–50)

    (bars 51–57)

Each group of five/four/three tones always keeps the same rhythm, with minor modifications:

the five-tone motif appears respectively as:

bars 34–35: 𝄽 ♪ ♩. ♪ | ♩ ♩ ‖

bars 43–45: 𝄽 ♪ ♩. ♪ | ♩ ♩. ♪ | ♩.

bars 51–52: 𝄽 ♪ ♩. ♪ | ♩ ♩ ‖

The four-tone motif appears respectively as:

bar 36: 𝄽 ♪ ♫ ♩ ‖

bars 41–42: 𝄽 ♩ ♩ | 𝄽 ♪ ♩ ‖

bars 53–54: 𝄽 ♩ ♩ | 𝄽 ♪ ♩ ‖

The rhythmic values of the first motif (bar 36) are exactly doubled in the tones that follow, with the insertion of a rest 𝄽 (negative value) with respect to the corresponding ♪ (positive value) of the ♩..

The three-note motif appears respectively as:

bars 37–38: ♩. ♪ | ♩ ♩ ‖

bars 39–40: ♩. ♪ | ♩. ‖

bars 55–56–57: ♩. ♪ | ♩. | ♩. ‖

Therefore the scheme for subdividing tones into melodic motifs has its counterpart in the rhythmic scheme.

THE STRUCTURE OF THE SERIES OF THE VARIATIONS OP. 30 BY A. WEBERN AND ITS PROPERTIES

In the first four measures the Original series is exposed, subdivided into three motifs:

a)	(doublebasses)	A B♭ D♭ C		min. 2nd	min. 3rd	min. 2nd
b)	(oboe)	B D E♭ F♯		min. 3rd	min. 2nd	min. 3rd
c)	(trombone)	F E G A♭		min. 2nd	min. 3rd	min. 2nd

Only two intervals are used: the min. 2nd and the min. 3rd, the min. 2nd also being the interval between each subdivision. In this series one encounters the typical Webern characteristic of ambivalence that is, in relation to the order of the intervals, the *Krebs-Umkehrung* is equivalent to the Original and the *Krebs* is equivalent to the *Umkehrung*. If one considers the series as being divided into two six-tone motifs, one will find that the second motif is the *Krebs-Umkehrung* of the first.

The subdivision into three motifs and the ambivalence of the series is crucial here for the compositional technique.

In the whole composition the subdivision of the three motifs remains clear, each motif containing four tones both used in the melodic and the harmonic projection.

a) In its melodic projection the four-tone motif is varied by the introduction of rests according to the total range of possible sum combinations among 1 1 1 1 (= 4) and, therefore: 1 1 2/1 3/3 1/2 2/1 2 1

Examples	
bars 43–46: motif c) is subdivided in the tuba into	1 1 2
bars 74–75: motif a) is subdivided in the flute into	1 2 1
bars 32–34: motif b) is subdivided in the trombone into	1 3
bars 38–39: motif a) is subdivided in the cellos into	3 1
bars 45–47: motif a) is subdivided in the tuba and the trombone into	2 2
bars 144–45: motif c) is subdivided in violins I into	1 1 1 1

The Development of Serial Technique | 143

These are also new motifs of six tones subdivided into 5 1/1 1 4.

These consist of two motifs, each of four tones, usually c) and a), in which owing to the principle of ambivalence, the last two tones of the previous motif are also the first two tones of the subsequent one, that is, the two central tones of the six-tone motif are ambivalent.

Examples:

bars 27–31: the clarinet has a six-tone motif subdivided into 1 1 4, constructed like this:

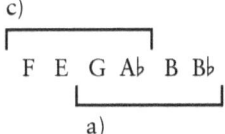

The central tones G and A♭ have ambivalence in these two motifs:

motif c) F E G A♭

motif a) G A♭ B B♭

bars 35–38: violins I have a six-tone motif, subdivided into 5 1, constructed like this:

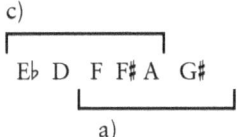

[The central tones F and F♯ are ambivalent]:

motif c) E♭ D F F♯

motif a) F F♯ A G♯

In Variation III the subdivision of the two four-note motifs, which is timbral as well (divided among several instruments) is based on the ambivalence of a single tone: the last of the previous one is also the first of the subsequent (which thus results in melodic groups of seven tones).

Example:

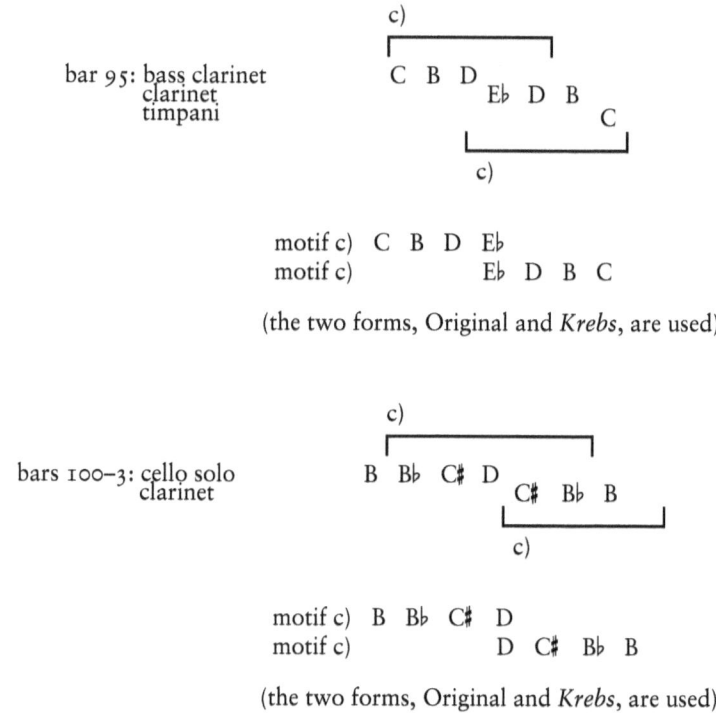

(the two forms, Original and *Krebs*, are used)

For the most part, the unity of the motif in its subdivisions is maintained in the timbre: it is therefore clear the unifying function of the timbre (cited examples).

The various subdivisions of the motifs regulate and distinguish the melodic process in the six variations.

The ambivalence of two tones is the principle behind Variations I/IV/VI. That of one tone is the principle behind Variation III.

b) A parallel procedure of applying ambivalence of tones occurs in the harmonic projection: this method is always based on motifs of four tones, on harmonic groups of four tones, except in bars 158/160/161/168/169/170/171, where the groups have three tones.

That is to say that a motif of four tones in harmonic projection is common to two series at the same time if this potentiality built into the structure of the series is exploited in a consistent manner:

bars 21–30 (Var. I) the melodic projection of the Original series and the harmonic projection of the Krebs are superimposed in a parallel fashion:

melodic projection, motif:

a) A-B-D♭ C // b) B-D-E♭-F♯ // c) F-E-G-A♭

harmonic projection, motif:

c) A♭-G-E-F // b) F♯-E♭-D-B // a) C-D♭-B♭-A

The motif b) is here in harmonic projection.[10]

Note the timbral consequences:
melodic projection, motif:
a) strings (solo violin)   b) woodwinds   c) woodwinds
harmonic projection, motif:
c) brass   b) woodwinds   a) strings (violas + cellos)

This procedure is systematic in Variation I, always in relation to motif b).

In Variation II there is a further development of such a procedure in relation to motifs c) and a). Motif c), the last segment of the Original, is simultaneously also motif a), the first segment of the subsequently transposed Original.

146 | Musical Analysis and Composition

Bars 56–63

Original series (transposed up by a min. 2nd):

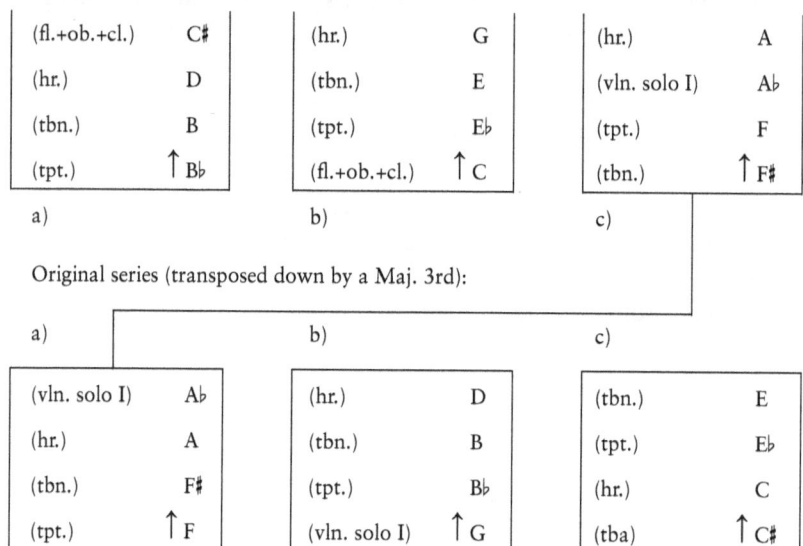

Original series (transposed down by a Maj. 3rd):

Motif c) and the subsequent a) are simultaneous.[11]

The same for the *Krebs*.

Bars 56–63:

Krebs series (transposed down by a min. 2nd):

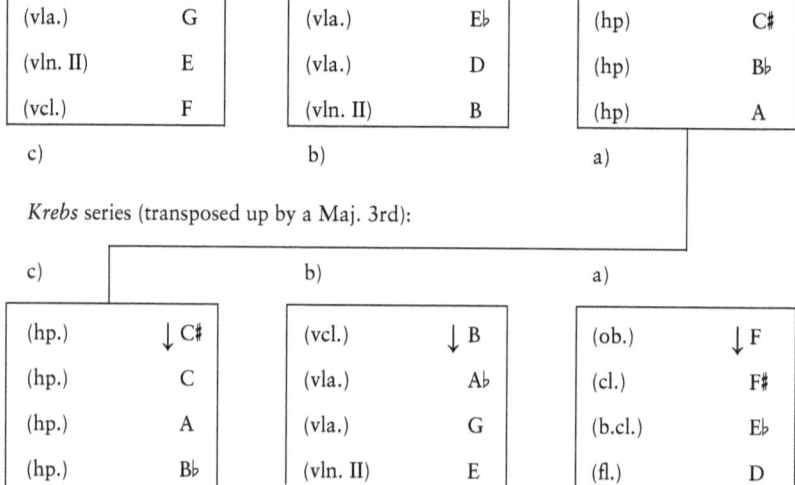

Krebs series (transposed up by a Maj. 3rd):

Motif a) and the subsequent c) are simultaneous.[12]

Note the precise correspondence among the transposition intervals of the series.

The principle of simultaneous ambivalence is fundamentally necessary to Webern's conception, and its application in this composition is rigorously logical.

At this stage it is possible to establish more clearly the intervallic structural function of the series in its three motifs: indeed superimposing them clearly shows the precise nature of the ambivalence between the melodic and harmonic patterns:

motif a)	min. 2nd	min. 3rd	min. 2nd	
motif b)	min. 3rd	min. 2nd	min. 3rd	
motif c)	min. 2nd	min. 3rd	min. 2nd	

The rhythmic structure is consistent with that of the series:

Three rhythmic motifs for the three motifs into which the series is subdivided:

a) ♩ ♩ ♪♩   b) ♫. ♬ ♬.   c) ♬ ♬

Just as in the series, treated as two motifs of six tones each, motif II is the *Krebs-Umkehrung*, of motif I, so, also in the rhythmic series, treated as two motifs of six note-values each, motif II is the *Krebs-Umkehrung* of motif I.

The rhythmic *Krebs-Umkehrung* is augmented by doubling the note values with respect to the shorter values and is diminished by half with respect to the longer ones.

I)	min. 2nd	min. 3rd	min. 2nd	min. 2nd	min. 3rd
	A	B♭	C♯	C	B	D

♩ ♩ ♪♩ ♬.

II)	min. 3rd	min. 2nd	min. 2nd	min. 3rd	min. 2nd
	E♭	F♯	F	E	G	A♭

♫. ♬ ♬

These three rhythmic motifs form the material for the whole composition. They remain clearly distinguishable across their variants as regards augmentation-diminution and the insertion of rests, corresponding to the three motifs into which the series is subdivided.

< Some of the current methods of serial composition can be deduced from the analysis of more recent compositions. They are the result of the historical evolution of music, conditioned by the musical and human needs of our time. Not only that, but they are also conditioned by more recent research, and are, above all, the result of utilizing the broadest possibilities available to us now for the use of individual musical elements in accordance with their particular nature. All this has helped to extend the scope of music, seeing that there are individuals capable of achieving this extension.

Everyone takes part in this development according to their nature and culture, and on the basis of their personal experience. Therefore, a multiplicity of clearly distinguishable forms of musical expression correspond to common principles of composition. Indeed, the nature and culture of the individual are not at all dissolved in this common evolution, but rather serve in large measure to determine its characteristics.

We shall now consider the musical output (especially the most recent) of those composers who could perhaps be called the "Darmstadt School"—an output that might be compared to that produced in the field of the figurative arts, by the Bauhaus in Weimar and Dessau in its time.

From the moment when the twelve-tone series was no longer being developed in its thematic function, but only in its "serial" function, the use of the four fundamental forms and their transpositions—so important for the thematic concept of the series—no longer appears necessary. The use of two series (typical of Webern) or eventually just a single series is all that is needed to deduce the order of the intervals and afterward the entire compositional structure: in this way the Original series remains unchanged or is subjected to permutation. The entire composition is, therefore, based on a single series. The permutation is carried out either internally within the series (in which case each note, depending on the nature of the series, appears only once), or the notes are permutated on a wider scale, generated by a multiplication of the series (by twelve or a multiple of twelve). ($12 \times 12 = 144$). Of course in this case each note of the basic series appears at least twelve times, but not necessarily every time according to the Original form of the series. In the first case the Original series is thus preserved; in the second it is projected across a much broader scope.[13]

The permutation procedure results in *sound material,* thanks to which and to other musical elements (each of which is preformed in its own fashion, more or less according to serial laws) the composer "creates" his music.[14]

The use of successive permutations of the twelve notes within the series is especially characteristic of the composition technique of Bruno Maderna, used for the first time in 1950 in *Due studi per il "Processo" di Kafka*.[15]

The organization of musical elements on the basis of the serial principle is determined from one instance to the next, in complete freedom, by the creative idea, both in relation to the individual elements and from the point of view of their mutual relationships.

In the first of the *Structures pour deux pianos à quatre mains* by Pierre Boulez,[16] the forty-eight twelve-tone series (the four basic forms and their transpositions) correspond to forty-eight series of duration (the durations form an arithmetic series from one to twelve, whose initial factor is a semi-quaver (16th note) and whose last factor is a dotted-quarter note). The two series (I = original, II = inversion) are superimposed in the two pianos, as, indeed, are the two series of durational values (bars 1–64).

Bars 1–64:

In the first piano twelve series are used (original and transposed), of which the first six are:	The corresponding rhythmic series:
E♭ D A A♭ G F♯ E C♯ C B♭ F B	12 11 9 10 3 6 7 1 2 8 4 5
E E♭ B♭ A G♯ G F D C♯ B F♯ C	11 12 6 7 1 9 10 3 4 5 2 8
A A♭ E♭ D C♯ C B♭ G F♯ E B F	9 6 8 12 10 5 11 7 1 2 3 4
B♭ A E E♭ D C♯ B A♭ G F C F♯	10 7 12 3 4 11 1 2 8 9 5 6
B B♭ F E E♭ D C A A♭ F♯ C♯ G	3 1 10 4 5 7 2 8 9 12 6 11
C B F♯ F E E♭ C♯ B♭ A G D G♯	6 9 5 11 7 8 12 10 3 4 1 2
In the second piano twelve series are used (inversion and transposed), of which the first six are:	The corresponding rhythmic series:
E♭ E A B♭ B C D F F♯ A♭ C♯ G	5 8 6 4 3 9 2 1 7 11 10 12
D E♭ A♭ A B♭ B C♯ E F G C F♯	8 5 9 2 1 6 4 3 10 12 7 11
A B♭ E♭ E F F♯ G♯ B C D G C♯	6 9 11 5 4 12 8 2 1 7 3 10
A♭ A D E♭ E F G B♭ B C♯ F♯ C	4 2 5 3 10 8 1 7 11 6 12 9
G G♯ C♯ D E♭ E F♯ A B♭ C F B	3 1 4 10 12 2 7 11 6 5 9 8
F♯ G C C♯ D E♭ F A♭ A B E B♭	9 6 12 8 2 11 5 4 3 10 1 7

The sequence of transpositions of the original is regulated by the sequence of the notes of the inversion. The sequence of transpositions of the inversion follows the sequence of notes of the original. When they are superimposed the following two-note combinations remain constant:

E♭ D A A♭ G F♯ E C♯ C B♭ F B
E♭ E A B♭ B C D F F♯ A♭ C♯ G

A similar thing happens when the two series of durational values are superimposed:

12 11 9 10 3 6 7 1 2 8 4 5
5 8 6 4 3 9 2 1 7 11 10 12

In the String Quartet in two movements by Bruno Maderna of 1955, the relationships between the different pitch registers, the dynamics and the attacks are determined in a specific way. The entire material originates from successive permutations of the basic series and is fixed in terms of pitch and duration. But the registers and the dynamics are determined each time by the attacks (*pizzicato—al ponte—con l'arco—col legno—battuto*). A characteristic feature of this composition is that the second movement is a variation of the retrograde of the first: the durations, registers, and dynamics are changed. The duration is varied by means of the insertion of rests between the notes and by the rhythmic subdivision of longer note values. In this work these two procedures (insertion of rests and the rhythmic subdivision) represent a new element of composition.

In Karlheinz Stockhausen's *Komposition Nr. 2 für Sinustöne* of 1953,[17] the duration of a tone is in inverse relation to its pitch: the relationships 12/5, 4/5, 8/5, 5/12, 5/4 (representing the intervals of the harmonics: descending min. 10th, ascending Maj. 3rd, descending min. 6th, ascending min. 10th, descending Maj. 3rd) also determine the degree of transposition of each structure (the structures are vertically or horizontally grouped from one up to six sequences; sequences = horizontal groups of tones formed from tone mixtures [*Tongemische*]; tone mixtures = vertical groups of notes) according to the following series: 12/5 4/5 8/5 5/8 5/4 5/12 (plus five permutations of this series).

In my *Incontri* for twenty-four instruments of 1955, the single basic series remains constantly unchanged, while the duration series and that of the dynamics are subjected to permutations in such a way that each note of the series differs each time with regard to duration and dynamics. The order of the duration series also determines the division into measures, and this in turn determines the pitch density.

In Karlheinz Stockhausen's *Zeitmasse* (1956), serial organization is applied to the multidimensional essence of time. The composition is determined by a combination of five different kinds of time-measures:

1. Twelve metronomically measured tempi between basic and doubled tempo [MM60 to 120], within a "time-octave," so to speak.

2. The measurement *as fast as possible*. This measurement can produce very different results, depending on the instrument and on the note figuration which must be played as fast as possible. For example, there are some note groups which the instrumentalist will play at the fastest possible tempo, but which will appear to be quite slow since within a group the longer values are far more numerous than the shorter and shortest values, so that the average velocity is *slow*.

3. The measurement *as slow as possible* applies to group of notes which the player has to execute in one breath. The player's breath will last more or less time depending on whether a group consists mainly of short or long, high or low, soft or loud notes. Therefore, the length of the player's breath determines the speed of the group: the shorter the breath, the quicker the group, and vice versa. Whenever an instrumentalist uses this type of measurement, all the other players adjust to this tempo. It sometimes occurs that an instrumentalist playing *as slowly as possible*—using the longest possible breath—actually has to play as fast as possible in order to be able to execute the given notes in one breath.

4. The measurement *fast-decelerate* applies to groups of notes which begin extremely fast and should end at a tempo four times slower.

5. The reverse applies to the measurement *slow-accelerate*. The ways of combining these measurements, both consecutively and simultaneously, are many.

(See the information provided by the composer in the program for the third "Musik der Zeit" concert of Westdeutsche Rundfunk, Cologne, January 1957.)[18]

We have consciously restricted ourselves here to technical and compositional aspects, leaving aside the aesthetic aspects. This demarcation has been clearly evident and in this instance also necessary, in order to allow a closer examination of the serial method in some of its contemporary lines of development. But it is also clear that the musical and human consequences that result from any technical method must also be taken into account.

But just as it was necessary to demonstrate the technical-compositional problems that have arisen in our time, so it is necessary—to avoid those academic discussions based on preconceived opinions—to study individual compositions separately, inasmuch as they reveal, each in their own way, our musical reality, however different they are in their own nature and their artistic result.>

4

Text—Music—Song

1960

I

In 1912 Arnold Schoenberg wrote regarding the relationship with text:

> A few years ago I was deeply ashamed when I discovered in several Schubert songs, well-known to me, that I had absolutely no idea what was going on in the poems on which they were based. But when I had read the poems it became clear to me that I had gained absolutely nothing for the understanding of the songs thereby, since the poems did not make it necessary for me to change my conception of the musical interpretation in the slightest degree. On the contrary, it appeared that, without knowing the poem, I had grasped the content, the real content, perhaps even more profoundly than if I had clung to the surface of the mere thoughts expressed in words. For me, even more decisive than this experience was the fact that, inspired by the sound of the first words of the text, I had composed many of my songs straight to the end without troubling myself in the slightest about the continuation of the poetic events, without even grasping them in the ecstasy of composing, and that only days later I thought of looking back to see just what was the real poetic content of my song. It then turned out, to my greatest astonishment, that I had never done greater justice to the poet than when, guided by my first direct contact with the sound of the beginning, I divined everything that obviously had to follow this first sound with inevitability.[i]

---

i. Arnold Schönberg, "Das Verhältnis zum Text," in *Der blaue Reiter*, ed. Wassily Kandinsky and Franz Marc (Munich: Piper, 1912), 30ff.; new ed., Klaus Lankheit (Munich: Piper, 1965), 65 ff. [In English: "The Relationship to the Text," in *Style and Idea* (New York: Philosophical Library, 1950), 4].

These reflections by Arnold Schoenberg are crucial to the historical delineation of a necessary stage in the development of the relationship between text and music. As far as this genius is concerned, whom we can consider as the culmination of our century, this stage encompasses the defining characteristics of the creative-musical conception that immediately preceded and has conditioned the present stage. Indeed, in a sense, these reflections serve as the starting point for a few general historical observations on the text-music relationship.

First, a few words on the autonomy of Schubert's lieder in relation to the poetic text. This autonomy is obvious when the composer's creative intuition and the structural necessity of the text are in close interdependence, since in this case the two structural elements, namely sound and word, interpenetrating one another, and the one not being subordinate to the other, form a new and autonomous whole. This reciprocal interpenetration is achieved in different historical periods and in various ways, depending on how the two elements, sound and word, are considered in their specific structure, that is, especially in how the word is considered, both in its given phonetic-semantic element, and in its translation, the musical invention applied to it, by analogy to rhetoric, diction, the emotion of the reciter, the folksong, or normal speech. Each of these analogical relationships has contributed to the characterization of the text-music relationship in the four successive stages that have led up to the current one. Specifically, these stages reveal a gradual development from an idealistic-formal conception, according to which man used to refer back to a superior model of theological-scholastic origin, up to the naturalistic conception of the nineteenth century, in which man lives and moves, especially among his own kind, with a greater understanding of his environment. One acquires a consciousness of the importance of the spoken language and studies it in its internal structure and in its relationship to song (see Verdi, Mussorgsky, Janáček), up to Schoenberg's conception, in which the legacy of historical tradition unites with a fundamental renewal of the text-music relationship. Here also, Schoenberg's contribution and role appear decisive, something that cannot be said of anyone else to this extent. To better understand this capacity for autonomy—and not only in the case of Schubert's Lieder—in relation to the poetic text, one must also consider the issue of the music's "representativity," namely, how the *ars dicendi,* musical rhetoric, developed. A study of the musical rhetoric of our century would be important, on the one hand, to analyze our current *ars dicendi,* and on the other, to shed light on the way it is hindered and encumbered by the past. Above all, a study of the melodic formulations of our century in comparison to those of the past would also clarify where the expression of our time has been fully realized and where only apparently so, in as much as it has been constrained by formulas, rhetorical modes, and procedures of the past that are connected to a different compositional and structural conception. A topic for a study of this kind might be the relationship between Webern's notion of melody based on motifs of two, three, or four tones and its consequence, in the melodic formulation, of the monotonous return of some fixed melodic patterns, which, in spite of their serial and intervallic function, can be traced back to certain formulas of song of the past. The same thing can also be noted in Webern's instrumental music, not only his text-related music.

In my view, regarding the issue of "representativity" in music, two studies, among others, are important, *Die Bildlichkeit der wortgebundenen Musik Johann Sebastian Bachs* [The Figurativeness of Vocal Music by J. S. Bach], by Professor Arnold Schmitz,[ii] and *Das Verhältnis von Wort und Ton in der Geschichte der Musik* [The Relationship Between Word and Tone in the History of Music], by Professor Joseph Müller-Blattau.[iii] During the Renaissance the scholastic trivium united the study of music, grammar, and rhetoric into a single synthetic study,[1] and this study had important consequences, especially in the Franco-Flemish school. Arnold Schmitz wrote about the composers of that time, "Wishing to reproduce the literal sense of the text faithfully with their own means and to express it in a manner that was comprehensible to the emotions, they based themselves on rhetoric. By analogy to the rhetorical figures they made use of musical figures, either homonymous with, or equivalent in meaning to, other figures, and they used them to amplify the meaning of the word and express emotions."[iv] The German theorist Joachim Burmeister codified this musical practice in three of his works—*Hypomnematum musicae poeticae, Musica autoschediastikè*, and *Musica poetica*[2]—and, as we are informed by Professor Müller-Blattau in the essay mentioned,[v] added an analysis of a

---

 ii. Mainz: B. Schott's Söhne, 1950 ("Neue Studien zur Musikwissenschaft," 1) [annotated copy held in the ALN].
 iii. Stuttgart: J. B. Metzlersche Verlagsbuchhandlung, 1952 [annotated copy held in the ALN].
 iv. Arnold Schmitz, *Die Bildlichkeit der wortgebundenen Musik Johann Sebastian Bachs* [see note ii], 21.
 v. Joseph Müller-Blattau, *Das Verhältnis von Wort und Ton in der Geschichte der Musik* [see note iii], 25 ff.

motet by Orlando di Lasso, which is based on the study of those musical figures.

At that time the relationship between text and music was based on an analogy between a potentially figurative musical symbolism and the semantic element of the word, which, however, was codified by means of a rhetorical figure. A motet by Dufay, a mass by Josquin, a madrigal by Gesualdo show the variety and diversity of this analogical relationship and its autonomy in relation to the text, when the text became music according to musical principles. According to the conception of the time, the content of the text became the meaning of the music. I will make a few observations later about the intelligibility of the word used, and if such intelligibility is possible or not, if it is necessary or not. With Claudio Monteverdi the new *prattica* of monody initiated by the Florentine Camerata, began a new phase. Musical rhetoric expanded and developed its own structural elements. There was no longer an analogy with formal rhetoric, but an imitation of the art of oratory with particular attention to diction and the emotional aspect of the text. In this way with Monteverdi's *recitar cantando*, the wonderful adventure of musical theater began. And especially in the final volumes of his madrigals, Monteverdi invented the use of different styles of musical rhetoric: *Madrigali guerrieri et amorosi, in stile rappresentativo*—here I would love to mention *Lettera amorosa* ("*Se i languidi miei sguardi*") *in stile recitativo, espressivo, concitato.*³ Arnold Schmitz wrote regarding this, "And as ancient rhetoric spoke of a δεινότης [eloquence], to define the power of oratory and the mastery of all rhetorical styles, so one could apply this definition also to Monteverdi. The musical rhetoric of the seventeenth and eighteenth centuries up to Bach and Handel is based on his art."[vi] In Monteverdi, a wealth and variety of human feelings correspond to this richness and variety of styles. The interest of the composer was, therefore, expanding and also turning to worldly feelings and passions. At about the same period in Italy, Galileo Galilei acted in a similar way with regard to the use of Latin as the official language of treatises and thus limited to a specialized caste, when he subscribed to the practice of using the vernacular for the widest possible reading public. The practice of musical rhetoric did not stop with the nineteenth century, but instead received a new impetus with the discovery and the stylistic contribution first of the folksong, and then of common speech. Johann Abraham

---

vi. Arnold Schmitz, *Die Bildlichkeit der wortgebundenen Musik Johann Sebastian Bachs*, 24.

Peter Schulz, an author of lieder and theoretician, wrote about the particular features of the folksong, "Only through a clear similarity of the musical tone with that of the poetic, by means of a melody which, as it proceeds, neither rises above nor falls beneath the natural flow of the text, and adheres to the declamation and the meter of the words as clothing does to the body; only in this way can a song take on a character that is unaffected, artless, familiar, in a word: the folk tone."[vii] Only if we stick to the principle set out in the essay by Müller-Blattau is it possible to justify the judgment of a renowned German on a composer of lieder, "The originality of his compositions is never, as far as I can judge, a musical idea, but the radical reproduction of my poetic intentions," wrote Goethe on the lieder of Carl Friedrich Zelter.[viii]

If on the one hand, as in the case just mentioned, the influence of the folk song could be considered a reproduction, in which the naturalistic conception of the reproduction had attained its highest degree of outward simplicity, on the other hand it enriched authentic musical invention with new constructive features, as was demonstrated by virtually the entire corpus of music from the first half of the nineteenth century. This was achieved to such an extent that even in purely instrumental music the melodic-formal formulation can often withstand the application of a text. I have often had occasion to note this, listening to Hermann Scherchen's orchestral rehearsals, during which, in order to clarify the musical meaning and the structural function of a melody to the performers, especially in Romantic symphonies, this brilliant musician used to interpret the melody with a suitable text. Not only that: but instrumental music could also support a programmatic explanation in the way that Wagner did—to echo Schoenberg's observation—when he wanted to give the average person a mediated idea of what he, as a musician, had intuited directly. This he used to do with Beethoven's symphonies. Beethoven developed the text-music relationship in the Ninth Symphony, finally considering the need to understand the text as such: as a formative element that does not exhaust itself in its musical, symbolical, affective, and emotional transposition. In this way the text becomes a true sound event in itself, but one that asserts itself in both the composition and the listening process as a precise semantic element in its formulation and meaning.

vii. Johann Abraham Peter Schulz, "Vorrede," in *Lieder im Volkston bei dem Klavier zu singen* (Berlin: [Georg Jakob Decker], 1785), vol. II.

viii. Johann Wolfgang von Goethe, letter to A. W. Schlegel of June 18, 1798 [in J. Müller-Blattau, *Das Verhältnis von Wort und Ton in der Geschichte der Musik*, 31].

Let us return to Schoenberg's considerations set out at the beginning on the autonomy of Schubert's lieder from the text regarding their comprehension. We have seen how what he said might correspond historically to the truth. But it is necessary, however, to raise a fundamental objection, namely: for the conception and complete understanding of a piece of music with text, is it possible to leave out of consideration the intelligibility of the text itself, in its phonetic and semantic presence? I do not think it is possible, despite and beyond any "musicalization" of the text itself, inasmuch as a word has characteristics and qualities that mark it as a particular structural and formative element of a musical composition, characteristics and qualities that cannot be eliminated. On the contrary, they contribute considerably to the enrichment of a musical structure, even if they involve complex relationships within this structure. Tomorrow I shall analyze this point in a few musical compositions.[4]

It is natural that reading or listening to music with text from any era whatsoever cannot ignore the presence of the text itself unless one confines oneself superficially to the vague suggestion that it is emotional or not, culinary or not, exotic or not, and a suggestion that disappears at the moment when the music starts. Whatever devotees of purism might dream of, a word cannot be stripped of its constituent elements. As Merleau-Ponty states in his *Phenomenology of Perception,* "there is no quality of sensation so bare that it is not penetrated with significance."[5] Based on Schoenberg's consideration of Schubert mentioned above, even if it were possible at first glance to deduce that Schoenberg had no interest in the meaning and intelligibility of a text, all of Schoenberg's works with text demonstrate in a masterly way, and one unique in this century, the fundamental importance he attributed to this question and the originality with which he resolved it. In his commitment, Schoenberg also reveals the greatness of Beethoven's legacy. The compositional conception of the fourth movement of the Ninth Symphony clearly indicates the urgency that Beethoven attached to the intelligibility of the words of Schiller's ode, not only in their musical setting, but also as literary text and precisely for their profound human significance. Because of its particular fullness of human significance, it is a wonderful example of how a text can solicit and provoke the idea of a new kind of expression in the composer, rather than a simple process of craftsmanship. "Maximum simplicity and comprehensibility of the melody," two requirements that according to Schulz are indispensable to the style derived from the folksong,[6] can be found in Beethoven's melodic formulation of "Freude schöner Götterfunken." From his sketchbooks we can see how hard Beethoven worked to achieve this natural simplicity. The successive presentation of this melody reveals Beethoven's requirement that it be intelligible in both its constituent elements, namely sound and word. At measure 92 (*allegro assai*) this melody appears for the first time in the cellos and double basses in octaves. At measure 241 the melody reappears in a second presentation, in a first timbral extension (the baritone joins the cellos in unison) and a constituent one: the presence of the text. At measure 257 finally a further extension of timbre and constituent elements: cellos, double basses, and chorus in octaves. In that way the listener is not hampered in the intelligibility of the new element, namely the text, on account of the nonnewness of the other element: the sound. Another application of this principle: between measures 655 (*allegro energico, sempre ben marcato*) and 730 there is the only use of contrapuntal elaboration in several parts in which each part is differentiated from the others in terms of both the melodic line and the text. The simultaneous use of several different texts here is perhaps reminiscent of fourteenth-century motets and the "confusion" of texts deriving from the contrapuntal structure is perhaps reminiscent of Renaissance polyphony. But the conception and the result differ profoundly from it precisely on account of the new requirements concerning the text and its intelligibility. In fact, the two melodic lines "Freude schöner Götterfunken" and "Seid umschlungen Millionen," previously heard by themselves, are now superimposed contrapuntally with rhythmic variants. In this way the intelligibility of this contrapuntal superimposition, a new acoustic element, is left undisturbed in the listening process because of the nonnewness of the two parts. Furthermore, the words are also clearly intelligible, despite the simultaneity of the two superimposed texts. This process cannot be interpreted in a formal manner as a gradual development, but is rather explained in close connection with the needs of the text.[7] During an era when neoclassical and *ancien régime*-style reactionary composers were reproposing models and conceptions of the past, even the distant past, in a highly formalistic manner, Arnold Schoenberg brought historical innovations to the text-music relationship, developing the role of quantitative metric accentuation in an original manner. In contrast to naturalism in the use of rhythmic speech, patterned by quantitative accentuation—which was the *busillis* of the, more or less psalmodizing, neoclassical composers—Schoenberg invented *Sprechgesang*. As Alban Berg wrote in his essay entitled "Die Stimme in der Oper" (Voice in Opera; 1929):

This manner of treating the voice safeguards, unlike recitative, all the prerogatives of absolute musical construction. It is proved that it represents one of the best means for assuring comprehensibility (as speech in opera must, now and then, be comprehensible); and also that it has enriched opera . . . with a most valuable artistic means, drawn from the purest sources of music. United with song—and it makes a welcome complement to song, an attractive contrast with sound—this sort of melodically, rhythmically, dynamically fixed spoken word can naturally participate in every other form of dramatic music. . . . These possibilities also show to what degree the opera, like no other musical form, is predestined to place itself in service to the human voice, to help it to safeguard its rights, those rights that have almost been lost in the music drama of recent decades, when opera music has often represented—to cite a remark of Schoenberg's—"nothing more than a symphony for large orchestra with vocal accompaniment."[ix]

If Alban Berg, on the basis of his own musical interests, relates the use of this new expressive medium especially to opera, Schoenberg applies it in almost all the musical forms used by him with a text. On each occasion the text is also clearly comprehensible in its semantic-literary component. Concerning this in his preface to *Pierrot lunaire,* Schoenberg specifies, "In no way should one strive for realistic, natural speech. Quite on the contrary, the difference between ordinary speaking and the kind of speaking involved in a musical form should become obvious."[8] *Sprechgesang* is used by Schoenberg monodically in *Pierrot lunaire* or contrapuntally combined with singing, as in *Moses und Aron,* where the use of one or the other method is determined by the relationship with the text. In the opera *Moses und Aron, Sprechgesang* and singing are in counterpoint with one another and contribute to characterize not only the difference but also the complementary function of the two protagonists. In the first scene of the opera the chorus, made up of six soloists, sing in counterpoint, using the same literary text as the speaking chorus, representing the "Voice from the Burning Bush." The different writing and the diverse function and spatial arrangement of the two choruses—one singing in the orchestra and the other reciting "from behind the scene, separated aurally . . . and broadcast over a loudspeaker so that it is only in the concert hall that they become unified"[9]— enhance the expressive possibilities of the text, expanding its timbral

ix. Alban Berg, "Die Stimme in der Oper," in *Gesang: Jahrbuch 1929 der Universal Edition* [349–50 (the volume was published as nos. 9–10 of *Musikblätter des Anbruch,* November–December 1928); English trans.: *Voice in Opera,* in *Modernism and Music: An Anthology of Sources,* ed. Daniel Albright (Chicago: University of Chicago Press, 2004), 44. In the passage quoted Nono does not show the *omissis*].

realization in the dual projection of singing and speech. As a result of this there is also a greater opportunity to understand the text. What must be emphasized here is the renewal of the technique and the function of the double chorus: not a game with the sound space, but the expressive fullness of a text now attained within the space by means of a double and differentiated sound projection.

At the end of this lesson let us listen to *A Survivor from Warsaw* by Schoenberg. *Sprechgesang* and singing are used here in the succession of dramatic narrative and prayer-appeal within the text. This masterpiece, in terms of its creative necessity, its text-music and music-listener relationships is the aesthetic-musical manifesto of our era. In a completely authentic way Schoenberg's creative necessity attests to that which Jean-Paul Sartre writes in his fundamental essay *What Is Literature?* on the problem "Why write?":[10]

> And if I am given this world with its injustices, it is not so that I might contemplate them coldly, but that I might animate them with my indignation, that I might disclose them and create them with their nature as injustices, that is, as abuses to be suppressed. Thus, the writer's universe will only reveal itself in all its depth to the examination, the admiration, and the indignation of the reader; and the generous love is a promise to maintain, and the generous indignation is a promise to change, and the admiration a promise to imitate; although literature is one thing and morality a quite different one, at the heart of the aesthetic imperative we discern the moral imperative. For, since the one who writes recognizes, by the very fact that he takes the trouble to write, the freedom of his readers, and since the one who reads, by the mere fact of his opening the book, recognizes the freedom of the writer, the work of art, from whichever side you approach it, is an act of confidence in the freedom of men. And since readers, like the author, recognize this freedom only to demand that it manifest itself, the work can be defined as an imaginary presentation of the world insofar as it demands human freedom.[x]

Moreover we can verify in Schoenberg what Arnold Schmitz detects in Bach, namely that "in his music with text, by means of musical figures, representative and rich in feelings, Bach refers not only to the sense of certain words or certain strophes, but also to the sense of the entire text," "even a sense that might be completely different from that of the text set to music." And again: "Bach's rhetoric is particularly powerful

---

x. Jean-Paul Sartre, "Qu'est ce-que la littérature?" in *Situations II* (Paris: Gallimard, 1948). [English trans.: *What Is Literature?* trans. Bernard Frechtman (New York: Philosophical Library, 1949), now in *What Is Literature? and Other Essays*, intro. Steven Ungar (Cambridge, MA: Harvard University Press, 1988), 67.]

because of its *docere* as well as its *movere*."ˣⁱ And if someone rejects the *docere* and *movere* of Schoenberg, and in particular in *Survivor from Warsaw*, the nineteen-year-old student Giacomo Ulivi addresses him, too, in his last letter before being shot by the fascists in Modena in 1944: "Do not say you no longer want to know. Think that all this happened because you no longer wanted to know."[11]

II

Our treatment of the relationship between text or spoken language and music was preceded by one according to which the composer treated the word almost solely as a vehicle of its semantics; therefore, the relationship between the phonetic structure of a word or phrase and its semantic content, even if recognized and taken into account, was customarily ascribed to the typical compositional features of the latter. Today a different compositional technique has developed in different ways in the domain of the relationship between phonetic and semantic material.[12]

At the beginning of *La terra e la compagna* I put two texts together simultaneously. From the dual relationship of their semantic contents, a new expressive unity was derived, along with its form. In this way, a functional differentiation arose between the meanings of the texts and their musical composition. One of the two texts, sung by sopranos, contraltos, and basses, expresses a secular symbolism between woman and nature. At the center of the other, sung by tenors, stands the figure of woman as beloved. The simultaneity of the two texts creates a unifying relationship between woman-nature and woman-beloved that is of greater significance. Corresponding to this is the simultaneity and superimposition of two compositional principles that are distinguished from one another by the more articulated projection of sound fields of the first text in comparison to the linear projection of the second, as well as in terms of the different structure of the duration and dynamic values. The combination of the two texts (music) leads in this way to a substantial expansion of their semantic contents (texts). In these latter there occurs, therefore, at the same time, a function of technical and expressive complementarity. The relationship thus created, reciprocal and highly significant, achieves the complex unity of the musical structure.

---

xi. Arnold Schmitz, *Die Bildlichkeit der wortgebundenen Musik Johann Sebastian Bach*, 86.

These examples show how there is a unifying line running through the two texts, not limited to the specific characteristics of their original formulation, as would not have been possible to think of in the era of polyphony and counterpoint:[13]

$$\begin{bmatrix} \text{First text:} & \begin{matrix} S \\ A \\ B \end{matrix} \Big\} & \text{Terra rossa terra nera. Tu vieni dal} \\ \text{Second text:} & T & \hspace{4em} \textit{Tu sei} \end{bmatrix}$$

$$\begin{bmatrix} \begin{matrix} S \\ A \\ B \end{matrix} \Big\} & \text{mare da verde riarso} & \hspace{3em} \text{dove sono parole} \\ T & \text{come una terra che nessuno ha mai detto} & \text{so-} \hspace{2em} \text{-le} \end{bmatrix}$$

$$\begin{bmatrix} \begin{matrix} S \\ A \\ B \end{matrix} \Big\} & \text{antiche e fatica sanguigna e gerani tra i sassi —} \\ T & \hspace{3em} \text{fati–} \end{bmatrix}$$

$$\begin{bmatrix} \begin{matrix} S \\ A \\ B \end{matrix} \Big\} & \text{non sai quanto porti di mare parole e fatica, tu ricca come} \\ T & \text{non sai quanto} \hspace{1em} \text{-ti} \hspace{1em} \text{mare} \hspace{2em} \text{fatica} \hspace{2em} \text{-a} \end{bmatrix}$$

$$\begin{bmatrix} \begin{matrix} S \\ A \\ B \end{matrix} \Big\} & \text{la brulla campagna,} \hspace{3em} \text{Tu dura e dolcissima} \\ T & \hspace{2em} \textit{Tu non attendi nulla se non la parola} \end{bmatrix}$$

$$\begin{bmatrix} \begin{matrix} S \\ A \\ B \end{matrix} \Big\} & \text{parola} \hspace{6em} \text{(etc.)} \\ T & \hspace{2em} \textit{che sgorgherà dal fondo} \end{bmatrix}$$

Just as contrapuntal and harmonic elements no longer have a function in music in which simple melodic and harmonic linearity has been developed in all directions through a new multidimensionality of relationships, so, also for the text in the composition there has opened up a world of new possibilities of combination of its semantic and phonetic elements. This multidimensional wealth of expressive-phonetic possibilities in singing, of the kind presented to us today, has been foreshadowed several times previously in the course of the development of music history, naturally always related to the compositional procedures of the specific era. As a first notable example—simple, despite their complexity—one should recall the motets of the thirteenth century, in which several completely independent texts set to music were superimposed, often in different languages.

The superimposition of different content created a semantic "confusion" (texts) or else a global idea resulted from this diversity (music + texts). Their simultaneity gave the composition a high degree of articulation, though with destructive "mechanical" consequences, owing to the absence of relationships between them (texts). One text would call into question the intelligibility of the other.

With the practice of multivoiced polyphony and the complexity of superimposition of texts resulting from it, more effective ways of creating relationships between words or syllables (music) were also being produced, beyond those of linear song (text). To the extent that one could measure the total complexity in relation to the number of voices being conducted independently—with their plasticity of rhythm and register—and in homophonic sections, the possibilities of composing relationships between the phonetic elements of the sung text became richer. One cannot say that a totally conscious compositional use was instantly made of these phonetic relationships, of text as both signifying material and as phonetic material that became music. It is clear, however, that the gradations between a phonetic "confusion" created by the polyphonic structure and the text rendered extremely clear by the use of homophonic-homorhythmic voices depended essentially on the degree of polyphonic complexity, and it is certain that the effectiveness of its extreme degrees had not escaped, or was not a matter of indifference to the compositional consciousness of that era. In this regard we will later examine an example by Gesualdo da Venosa more closely.

The clarity with which the parts are coordinated in Bach's polyphonic music, also with regard to the rhythmic structure of the text, as a consequence creates superimposed constellations of syllables—sound fields—that cannot be ignored, even and especially if in this way new phonetic aggregates are not formed, but instead the original words are reconstructed across different parts. The first two examples from Bach's Mass in B minor, show complementary superimpositions of the two pairs of syllables *ele-* and *-ison* in different degrees of density.[14]

The multidimensionality of the text's translation into music did not destroy the intelligibility of the text that was already known to the listener, but increased this new intelligibility and made it relevant to its time in a logical way through the composition itself. (Relationship between acoustic material and text, and their musical invention.)

The composition's complex form in several parts and the simultaneous clarity of the text transformed into music are closely connected to the clarity of the polyphonic structure and its harmonic *ductus*. The third example shows the cadential effect of a ordinary declamation of the text in relation to the harmonic cadence:

Only the bass text-part proceeds with the harmonic cadence. The other voices have anticipated the cadence itself. With the syllables or vowels superimposed on the harmonic cadence, its cadential characteristic, of resolution, gets shifted from the latter to the place where the formal structural continuity requires it. Here the phenomenon of the different functions of text superimposition has a practical result that is formal, musical, and complete. The incompleteness of the cadence (music) is directly related to the phonetic effectiveness of a differentiated use of syllables (text) on the chord that resolves to the tonic. A formal musical consequence arises immediately from the varied projection of the phonetic elements. Another example, also taken from Bach's Mass in B minor, shows the same principle once again. The syllables and initial vowels of the parts that enter sequentially in the canon are also combined with the text of the earlier parts, intensifying parts of the whole word:

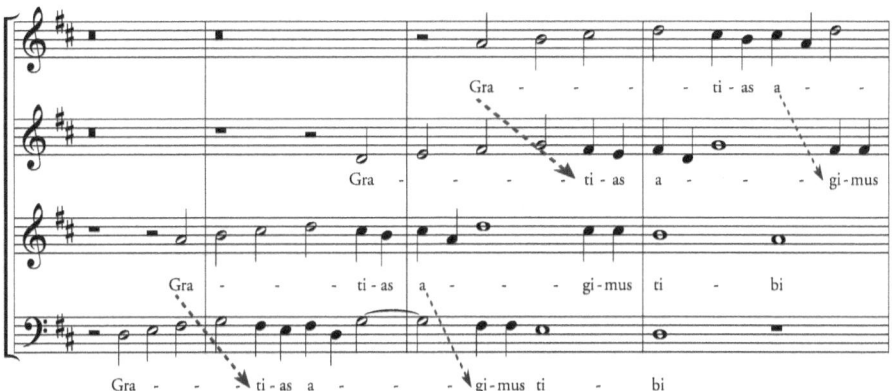

In Mozart's *Requiem* the *Requiem aeternam* theme, known to the listener from the opening, is accompanied when it returns later by a new countersubject, in which the words *Dona, dona eis* are sung, words that in their turn converge on the accusative form: *Dona eis requiem:*

The resulting vertical or horizontal "confusion" of syllables (music) does not offer a clear semantic correspondence with the phonetic material (text). Instead it produces a mechanical superimposition of the texts corresponding to the formal superimposition of theme and countersubject. In a similar way the words *Kyrie eleison* and *Christe eleison* are combined, but here, differently, with a minimum of phonetic "confusion," what is produced musically, in accordance with the overall theological sense, is a subdivision of the resulting text. The superimposition of texts in Mozart has a double aspect: on the one hand it indicates a certain affinity with text superimposition in the ancient French motets, on the other hand it opens up the new possibility of putting together different words and phrases at the same time that share a single semantic basis. Yesterday we saw how this principle of elaboration would later also be developed in Beethoven.[15] The reason, among others, why operas have not been more closely analyzed in this context is that the phenomenon of several texts sung simultaneously in theater must be considered in relation to the scenic-dramatic events, whereas here one must take into account very different aspects.

In the third piece of my *Canto sospeso* there is an example of how a new text is produced by interpolation from the musically distinct superimposition of three different texts. Unlike the example from *La terra e la compagna* shown at the beginning, here a new text is created, but not in the sense of a symbiosis of different semantic contents. Rather the superposition of the three texts, in which analogous situations are communicated, namely the moment that precedes the execution of the victims themselves, has given rise to a new text in which what is common to the three situations is formulated with increased intensity:[16]

Soprano	Mi portano a Kessarianì				*a*		
Alto		*o*	*o*	*a a ì*		*a*	Oggi
Tenor				*a a ì*	M'impiccheranno		

Soprano	*i*	*i e a*		insieme ad altri sette		
Alto	ci fucileranno			*e*	*e*		*e*
Tenor						perché sono	

Soprano	*a*	*i*			*a*	*a*	
Alto	a moriamo da uomini per la pa - -					tria	(etc.)
Tenor	patriota				*a a a*	*a*	

The musically increased intensity of the semantic content of a text, as it results here from the interpolation of several interrelated texts, was obtained in a radically different manner in a work created about 350 years ago, namely by means of the decomposition of a single word into various new syllabic constellations. At the end of the motet *O magnum mysterium,* by Giovanni Gabrieli, through the polyphonic superimposition of eight voices, numerous combinations of syllables are formed from the word *Alleluja,* which exalt the jubilant Alleluia in an exclamatory way and in all directions. By means of the phonetic "confusion" of the vowels of the word *Alleluja,* it renders the semantic content of the original word musically perceptible with an increased intensity:[xii]

---

xii. Giovanni Gabrieli, *Opera omnia,* ed. Denis Arnold, vol. I: *Motetta* (Rome: American Institute of Musicology, 1956), 10–17. This motet is also contained in Alfred Einstein, *Beispielsammlung zur älteren Musikgeschichte* (Leipzig: Teubner, 1927), no. 11, 21–25.

170 | Musical Analysis and Composition

This analysis poses another problem, that of the direct use of phonetic material in musical composition. The multiple superimpositions of words and combinations of syllables noted here in the *Alleluja* example create a kind of acoustic phonetic field in which the original semantics of words is increased through the richness of the phonetic constellations of the material, precisely in the musical semantics. The phonetic material thus created actively contributes to the composition's semantic aspect. One might ask whether there some logical relationship exists between the phonetic structure of a word and its meaning. In his essay "Sprache als Information" [Language as Information], Karl Friedrich von Weizsäcker still maintains the view according to which "the word is not simply its meaning, but independently of its meaning it has a body, a sound form; it is also something different from what it signifies."[17] But even scientific research has not contented itself with a mere dualism of meaning and phonetic structure, and Merleau-Ponty's study *Phenomenology of Perception* affirmed that there can be no quality or structure without meaning.[xiii]

The indissolubility of phonetic material from its semantic significance, despite their apparent autonomy in a musical setting, is for me a reality that requires the deliberate compositional inclusion of vowels and consonants in the creative process. In the second part of *La terra e la compagna*, whose text by Pavese is dedicated to the partisan resistance,[18] vowels were extracted from the sung syllables as simple phonetic material, but in another acoustic and expressive dimension different from that of the original syllables. A voice either anticipates the vowel of the sung syllables or prolongs it, for example:

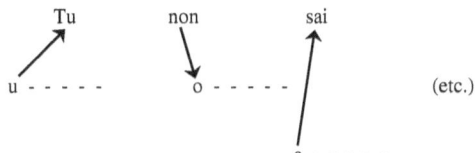

In this way in the composition, the semantic aspect receives a new expressive-structural dimension precisely through the use of autonomous and consequential musical means. In this method the treatment of vowels and consonants in *Cori di Didone* represents a step forward. Here the text and its expressivity has been recreated by means of the acoustic material of its consonants and vowels in harmonic fields and has been set to music in the sense of an absolute, even though autonomous, musical interpenetration of its semantic and phonetic totality.[19]

---

xiii. Maurice Merleau-Ponty, *Phénoménologie de la perception* (Paris: Gallimard, 1945; German ed., Berlin: De Gruyter, 1966) [but see the editors' backnotes for this chapter, note 5].

Now, an analysis of a part of the twentieth madrigal from Gesualdo's fourth book[xiv] will show us how composers have consciously or unconsciously made use of phonetic structures, bearing in mind, of course, the preponderance of vowels.

xiv. Carlo Gesualdo da Venosa, *Sämtliche Madrigale für fünf Stimmen*, ed. Wilhelm Weismann, vol. IV: *Viertes Buch* (Hamburg: Ugrino, 1958), 69–74.

Text—Music—Song | 173

In the first eight opening measures of this madrigal the words *Il sol, qual or più splende* [The sun, which shines more than gold] are translated into characteristic rhythmic-motivic cells. With numerous contrapuntally superimposed repetitions, what is presented to the listener is an incredible richness of sound fields, of decisive musical effectiveness, based on vowels. These phonetic sound fields are in direct relationship with the musical expression that results from the mutual interpenetration of all the material and intellectual aspects. In "direct relationship" means that this expression is not necessarily attained through the mediation of the comprehensibility of the words, but in such a way that the element of comprehensibility—not simply abolished, of course—is developed, in being transferred to music, according to different degrees of complexity, by using phonetic sound fields or linear procedures.

The clear exposition of the rhythmic-motivic elements connected to the text effectively guarantees gradations of comprehensibility without diminishing the independent effectiveness of the phonetic elements in the composition. Whether consciously or unconsciously a quasi-*continuum* has been created here between simple phonetic sound and the semantic musical result of a word or phrase perceived as a whole. Let us observe, in this example,[20] how the three rhythmic-motivic cells characterize the text in different ways: the first cell consists rhythmically of a quarter-note and a half-note (*Il sol*); the second consists of three eighth-notes (*qual or più*); the third has two half-notes (*splende*). These cells have characteristics so different that their superimposition not only does not compromise the phonetic effectiveness of individual words and syllables, but instead provides the possibility of creating musically meaningful relationships among the vowels. Of the three cells, the second has the fastest-moving structure. Besides the phonetic plasticity of the sequence of vowels and consonants of *qual or più,* the natural predominance of the smallest rhythmic values prevents the text, even when superimposed onto other cells, from falling beneath a certain level of comprehensibility (music-text). It is only the canonical arrangement of this cell with itself (measures 7 and 8) that, owing to an increased multiplicity of the phonetic relationships, apparently creates a further weakening of the original phrase's plasticity and, therefore, its comprehensibility. Instead, it intensifies it. The moment of semantic comprehension (text) is inversely proportional to the multiplicity of the phonetic relationships (music). As for the other two cells, the characteristic of the syllabic sequence of *Il sol* and its rhythmic emphasis is proportionately strong enough when combined with the others or with itself to be able to form phonetic sound fields from the cell, without the musical effectiveness of the text itself becoming entirely lost. In this way the superimposition of this cell upon itself right at the very beginning of the madrigal, creates a multivalent and purely phonetic relationship of syllables, without, on the other hand, destroying the semantic result.

The third cell *splende* has the lesser prominence from the point of view of its musical articulation. In compensation, the word *splende,* with its double presence of the vowel *e* and its consonants, represents a strong phonetic fact in comparison with the others, one which constitutes a constant element across the numerous changes in the other constellations of vowels. The semantic core of this cell, which as a verb has more weight than the others, has passed from the very limited measure of comprehensibility of the other words to clear musical semantics. The phonetic relationships of its sound structure have become musically very clear, even where the syllables are completely incomprehensible. The moment of splendor is exalted musically in the repetition of the vowels. It is interesting to note how the immediate comprehensibility of the text in itself decreases as the importance of the semantic musical content increases. In the simple superimposition of all three cells, the syllables *qual* or *più* have the greatest chance of being immediately understood musically; their semantic value (text) is, on the other hand, minimal. The syllables *il sol,* whose overall intelligibility is already quite "disturbed" by the introduction of eighth-note values, are basically the first to receive clear semantic value. The greater semantic content, however, resides in *splende;* in any case, compositionally it is transported almost completely from verbal immediacy to musical immediacy.[21] In the sixth measure, as well as a minimum of polyphony, here there is the simplest use of the phonetic relationship in the form of the ordinary homophony of the syllables *il sol,* which renders their semantic content maximally effective (text). In contrast to this, just two measures later, there is a maximum of complexity in terms of polyphony and vowels. The phonetic "confusion" makes access to the semantic level of the text impossible. Much more effective is the gradual convergence of all the superimposed voices in the phonetic emphasis on *splende*. The semantic concept of splendor thus acquires a penetrating musical effectiveness through the manner of its contrapuntal combination. The whole composition, moreover, can be seen as an example of a compositional gradation resulting from the differentiated use of phonetic materials in terms of their semantics (text).

The musical composition as a multidimensional whole formed by constellations of words and phonemes here called for various repetitions of the text. In this regard several issues are raised: what happens if the text flows from beginning to end and is used without repetition? Does the special modification to which a text is musically subjected condemn the syllables, once set to music, to incomprehensibility of their semantic content? But must one understand the text as transformed into music or the text as formulated literally? Does the phonetic structure of a text have another purpose apart from the function of making its semantic dimension comprehensible? How can it be possible in music to utilize the phonetic material of a given text with a precise meaning, if during the "breakdown" of its structure, its semantic effectiveness is destroyed? But is everything not reassembled according to musical-acoustic principles? Why not even derive the phonetic elements directly from the alphabet?

In order to respond to this complex of questions, since they arise particularly with regard to my work, I must first of all clarify certain misunderstandings that have arisen from the publication of a superficial analysis of the second piece of *Il canto sospeso*.[22] The text of this a cappella chorus was set to music from beginning to end. The smallest unit which is disassembled and reassembled is the *word*, not the syllable. Through the successive distribution of the words in different registers the enunciation of the text was preserved in its linear unity, almost as in a chorale; however, at the same time it was also loosened to create new possibilities of relationship among the structural characteristics of the sung words, so that, through the composed musical structure, a word can be adjusted according to its semantic content in relation to the semantic contents of the whole text, namely, compared to the musical expression taken as a whole. On the basis of this principle of the fusion of the musical and semantic content of the sung word, one can understand the further "breakdown" into syllables, as can be observed in the last piece of *Il canto sospeso*, as well as the further "fragmentation" of the word into vowels and consonants in my later works. For this reason a purely phonetic analysis of the vocal structure of the second piece of *Il canto sospeso*, as was attempted by Stockhausen, where it is a question of the compositional structure of an expression related to specific human subject matter, is revealed here as a totally senseless undertaking. This type of analysis can be valid for music that preoccupies itself exclusively with constellations of purely phonetic material. It was on such a basis that Stockhausen, with his one-sided analysis and subjective observation of the material of this chorus, demonstrated in the essay *Sprache und Musik,* became embroiled in questions that led him to the arbitrary and simplistic observation that the material obsolescence of compositional products occurs in relation to the *arbitrary* psychological state of mind of their composer. I quote from Stockhausen's essay:

In certain pieces in the *Canto,* Nono composed the text as if to withdraw it from the public eye where it has no place. . . . The texts are not delivered, but rather concealed in such a regardlessly strict and dense musical form that they are hardly comprehensible when performed. Why, then, texts at all, and why these texts? Here is an explanation. When setting certain parts of the letters about which one should be particularly ashamed that they had to be written, the musician assumes the attitude only of the composer who had previously selected the letters: he does not interpret, he does not comment. He rather reduces speech to its sounds and makes music with them. Permutations of vowel-sounds, *a, ä, e, i, o, u;* serial structure. Should he not have chosen sounds in the first place, rather than texts so rich in meaning? . . . Let us consider the entire composition. Some sections (II, VI, IX) go so far as to break up the sense; others (V, VII) quote, even clarify the text. . . . We can therefore keep to the idea, just mentioned, that the composer consciously "expelled" the meaning from certain parts of the text.[xv]

Here, I want to oppose my point of view to Stockhausen's opinion: the message of those letters of people condemned to death is carved in my heart as it is in the hearts of all those who see in these letters documents of love, of conscious choice and responsibility toward life, and as an example of the spirit of sacrifice and resistance against Nazism, that monster of irrationalism, which attempted to destroy reason. Has one learned nothing from the passion of Christ but shame? And does this latest passion of millions who were not gods but people have nothing to teach us other than to feel ashamed? Is this what they died for? It is not for me to judge here who it is that should really feel ashamed. The spiritual testament of these letters became the expression of my composition. And all my later choral compositions should be understood in terms of this relationship between the word as a phonetic-semantic whole and music as an expression composed from the word. It is absolutely absurd to want to deduce from the analytical treatment of the structure of the text that its semantic content has thus been expunged. The question of why a particular text and not another has been chosen for a particular composition is no more intelligent than the question of why, in order to utter the word *stupid,* one uses the specific letters *s-t-u-p-i-d.*

xv. Karlheinz Stockhausen, "Musik und Sprache," in *Darmstädter Beiträge zur Neuen Musik,* no. 1 (1958): 66 ff. [Now in Stockhausen, *Texte zu eigenen Werken, zur Kunst Anderer, Aktuelles, Band II (1952–1962)* (Cologne: DuMont Schauberg, 1964), 157–66, esp. 158. The trans. (by Ruth Koenig) given here is taken from "Music and Speech," which appeared in the English edition of *Die Reihe* 6 (1964): 40–64, esp. 48–49, slightly modified by the editors for the sake of a better correspondence to the original German formulation.]

The principle of the fragmentation of the text as developed in *Cori di Didone* right to the point of its subdivision into individual consonants and vowels, did not deprive the text of its meaning, but rather created a musical expression from the text, understood as a phonetic-semantic structure. Composition with the phonetic elements of a text serves today, as in earlier times, to transpose its semantic meaning into the musical language of the composer.[23]

5

[About *Il canto sospeso*]

1976

Since 1947, Schoenberg's *A Survivor from Warsaw* (based on the testimony of someone who escaped the Nazi destruction of the Warsaw ghetto) began to shake up public, concert halls, and the orchestras themselves with an artfully expressed violence that transcended purely aesthetic enjoyment in order to deepen the knowledge of reality (or of a symbolic moment) and therefore reflection and struggle, despite the novelty of the language used, the twelve-tone system. In 1948, Dallapiccola's *Il prigioniero* claimed world attention (inquisition-freedom) also with a new kind of language. In 1953, with the Tenth Symphony, Shostakovich continued his intelligent and risky odyssey in the rough sea of "socialist realism," which tended to restrict the composer's behavior to a simplistic, accommodating relationship to the people's understanding, based on traditional premises understood in a populist and dogmatic way with the dichotomy: "socialist-realist" music healthy and good, Western imperialist bourgeois music decadent in its entirety. In 1954, with *Déserts* (orchestra and magnetic tape) Edgard Varèse continued his innovation of musical means and his inspired and brilliant humane project. In 1953, Bruno Maderna wrote *Cantata da camera—quattro lettere—per Kranichstein*.[1] This cantata is still unknown in Italy, not least because of that obstinate failure to consider the great and wide-ranging importance of this musician in the life and development of Italian music and his contribution abroad. Maderna was, in fact, expelled from official Italian musical life, which, sadly only just before his tragic end, finally accepted that it ought to recognize him by appointing him conductor of the orchestra of RAI in Milan. The small book by Massimo Mila, *Maderna musicista europeo,* should mark the beginning of a fair revaluation of this great musician.[2] In his cantata, continuing his search for expressive language and for current subject matter, Maderna brought together a letter from an industrialist, one from Kafka to Milena, one from Gramsci to his companion, and one from a partisan before he was shot by a fascist firing squad. (In 1952 Maderna and I joined the PCI during the highly charged and boorish Scelba's repression. Comrade Lizzero,[3] then secretary of the Venetian Federation, spoke to us about our common intention, while the controversy of "socialist realism" was raging, to continue as musicians in the study, analysis, and research of new technical means, specifically at that time the twelve-tone method. In the presence of comrades Manlio Dazzi and Mario Baratto, he told us: "Continue your struggle, if you think it just. Confront each other!" If we consider today what has been developing for years among the young Soviet, Hungarian, East German, Bulgarian, Romanian, and Cuban composers—always wanting to access information directly and not submit passively to what the Western press intentionally mystifies—the great political and cultural intelligence of those comrades in charge in 1952 becomes clearly apparent!)

In 1955, the Greek Xenakis (sentenced to death by Greek fascists for having participated in Markos's struggle)[4] composed *Metastasis,* developing his musical project in an original way,[5] combined with his knowledge of stochastic science. And Dallapiccola composed *Canti di liberazione.* In 1956, Messiaen composed *Oiseaux exotiques* in a pagan-Catholic-naturalistic mixture with forms arising out of Indian ritual rhythmic structures; Stockhausen composed *Gesang der Jünglinge,* based on a biblical text with electronic music; I composed *Il canto sospeso,* Stravinsky composed *Canticum sacrum* based on a text of St. Mark, using the twelve-tone technique in a sterile fashion.[6]

All this is meant to give, albeit in an outline format, an idea of the problems and developments in European music at that time. With the Darmstadt Ferienkurse, the center for meeting and discussion for young people after the bloody Nazi nightmare; and during which, from the beginning, the differences manifested themselves (leveled at art by German critics who were nationally and aesthetically partisan). The study, the analysis of musical language with new methods, extending right up to electronics, and the already conflicting positions on the use of compositional principles, on social function. Music that disappears into itself in the moment of its appearance, music as an end in itself, ornamental music, especially French, a game of sounds and phonemes or based on ancient sacred texts, music engaged in varied attempts to understand the current state either of technical means or of the meanings of communication; also music's intervention, as such, in life, in the daily struggle, an ideal, a party decision, constantly to be verified, to be questioned, to be substantiated and never to be imposed a priori and in an authoritarian manner. (Despite the international music market, which operates in a different way.) These were the years of the great rediscovery of Antonio Gramsci's writings, of the brutal Scelba's repression, the antifascist front,[7] the continuous presence of the Resistance in the discussion. In those years the book *Lettere di condannati a morte della Resistenza europea* was published,[8] edited by Piero Malvezzi and Giovanni Pirelli (my very dear friend). Years of great ferment, struggles, political and cultural controversies. Perhaps more keenly felt and experienced by us in Italy. And they required rigor in terms of preparation, of innovative and open-minded study, of analysis of what was real, as opposed to the models or dogmatism that were certainly then in operation, of choices and confrontations that were often difficult. Perhaps music, because of the false acceptance of the traditional and the convenient, enjoyed a kind of suspension of attention in a way, however, since the West German musical organizations began a slow and ever more focused ostracism toward music considered to be "leftist."[9]

ON *IL CANTO SOSPESO*

I would like to reiterate the futility and vanity of the term *pointillism* coined by illustrious German aesthetes, true musical parasites,[10] and which is passively taken up by many who are unable to really reflect upon and study music.

Pointillism, which would result in giving attention to "points," "sounds" isolated in themselves, monads appearing and resolving of their own accord, rather than and as opposed to the relationships (in this case intervals, not only in vertical and horizontal projections, melody-harmony) that structure them by diversifying them and becoming diversified, additionally in relation to other compositional parameters (reflection on the consequences of the transformation of relations of production). From this arose an artificial and distorted analysis of the twelve-tone music and serialism, with consequences evident today in a deadlock in both the study and practice of acoustic material as a phenomenon with particular characteristics (and not ascribed a priori) with the potential to form new compositional principles (not idealistically imposed from above).

Text-composition relationship. This question is still debated: should the text be understood as such, literally, or does the text in its structural and semantic formants also serve as material, a stimulus, an object of study material to retransform by means of musical language? In the history of music, not only European, we find these two practices occurring over centuries. Moreover: text being used either purely phonetically, in terms of the technique by which the sound is emitted, or merely as a literary citation to be understood as such (the other side of the same coin)?

On the basis of ongoing studies, even outside Europe (physical structure of the vocal organ, linguistic, ritual, communication, use, function, composition, etc.), I am pursuing research and the attempt (to be understood in the Brechtian sense) to make the text become music and communicate as music. To be composed, and not simply to be applied. Here is the other question that arose, especially in respect to the choruses of *Il canto sospeso* with their misunderstood syllabic fragmentation of words. Stockhausen declared that the more shameful the incident described in the text (execution by firing squad) the more I covered, hid, and destroyed the text by reason of some inexplicable form of false modesty.[11] An analysis that openly declares a mentality, a behavior, a nonovercoming of (almost a complicity with) the incident itself. This is very far, totally removed from what I was trying to do. (It was the object of a dispute between the two of us during the Ferienkurse of 1958, I think.)[12]

Studying the Franco-Flemish and the Andalusian gypsy songs,[13] two examples among many (and Bruno Maderna was also a great promoter of these studies), what inspired me very much and still does is their different way of using vowels and consonants at various levels of register (above and beyond those studied by Julius Stockhausen in his *Gesangsmethode* of 1886–87),[14] but composed in relation to their acoustic emission (and their formants) and to the structure of the harmonic field, in the service of greater clarity, of greater musical flexibility and significance. Then, in my experiments in the electronic studio of Milan, aided by the great knowledge and musicality of the technician, Marino Zuccheri (a technician in the way that Joachim was to Brahms—relatively speaking!), I continue this practice, even in the new spatial possibilities, with further acoustic sources and now with contact microphones, with other possibilities both to experiment and to yield a wider range of flexible, compositional possibilities.[15]

It is certain that the particular practice in the choruses of *Il canto sospeso* (subsequently developed in *Cori di Didone, La terra e la compagna, Canciones para Silvia,* up to my recent compositions), the use of the structure of a word requires a development in the chorus's own way of learning: because of laziness or habits, sufficient attention is often not paid to the need in these choral works to study the varied construction of the word itself. This habitual ease continues because (with few exceptions) people do not read what is indicated in the score.

EXCURSUS II

A Letter from Los Angeles

1965

Dearest friends

After one week spent entirely in the theater at Boston, from nine in the morning to midnight, with guns always pointed to stop stupidity and attempts at falsification and make everything work according to our ideas (Bruno and I),[i] we are now in Los Angeles at the home of Nuria's mother.[ii]

So far the United States for me was the Boston theater (an example of nonorganization and nonpractical experience lacking in inventive intelligence. Private enterprise based solely on the dollar and its sanctity: time and stage solutions blocked in this sense). A brief meeting at Harvard University with some students, which I was told they're Marxists, and have organized a demonstration for Vietnam against the government here: of 8,000 students, only 150 have demonstrated in the midst of the people's insults.[1] Harvard University is a private one, and therefore limited and selected admissions, and amazing percentages. Roughly: one Jew for five hundred students and the same also for the Negroes. Tuition for the first year a million lire.[2] And now here in Los Angeles: Schoenberg Studio room is a small Mitteleuropean world transplanted here; perhaps—my interpretation—defense on his part,

---

i. Bruno Maderna, who conducted *Intolleranza 1960* in Boston [see this chapter in "Bibliographic Notes and Comments to the Texts"].

ii. Nuria Schoenberg, daughter of the composer and wife of Luigi Nono ["Nuria's mother" was Gertrud Kolisch].

where to find himself and live (he composed in this small room, full of books and furniture from the Vienna of the Jugendstil, reminds me at once of the tradition of the studio-rooms of Beethoven at Heilingestadt, of Schubert, of Mozart: a very great strength and culture which still exists and participates in this room).

And last night a car tour through Hollywood: striking by construction, lights, publicity, and I would say oppressing power, just as Los Angeles: but what hides behind all this? Or who wants and uses and crushes others with such a power? Yesterday too it was clear to me: while touring Hollywood among the lights, and so on, striking in the midst of such a display of self-assurance and so on, a small sign barely visible (a luminous newsboard giving the news on luminous screens), announcing "Heavy Bombers Landing at Saigon Ready to Bomb North Viet Nam." You cannot look at or be impressed by such a life without reconnecting to what such a life is conditioned, to the reason why it is even a result (in this sense I believe that those who in Italy interpret pop art as a recovery of the real object, without relating it to the system which produces it and needs it, are seeing but one of its aspects. For me, as a result of this limited experience, there is the precise confirmation that this economic system is a destructive one, and therefore to be destroyed).

Boston Theater: they were expecting to stage *Intolleranza 1960* in four days, considering that because of the business of the denied visa the common working plan had gone astray and everything was put off to my possible arrival.[3] As soon as I got there and saw the stage direction, refuse everything. Long conversations with clashes and I explain the sense and meaning and how it must be staged. Svoboda had been here ten days without being able to work (projectors with the wrong plates and glasses so that instead of nine projectors he could use only four: you can understand that then his stage idea was left in half). But then he worked like a madman and managed to save the situation somewhat. He even helped with the direction. Lights and projections only in the last three days to see and test: so that the choice of both projections to use and their place always in chaos with continuous clashes. The texts had been translated but two days before the performance they are projected and I find that both Mayakovsky and Brecht are falsified: and I exploded against everybody, with the theater full of orchestra men, critics (it was considered the dress rehearsal!!!), technical people. Either they find the right translation or I prohibit the performance. As an example of their *quickness:* I had to tell them to look at once at Harvard

University library (ten minutes by car) for the translations: they could not or would not think of it. Another clash: texts almost always translated and projected, only the demonstration slogans no.[4] Only "Down with discrimination" because here it comes in handy. Svoboda has added in the projection of the slogans also "Cuba yes, yenki no." Only before the premiere Caldwell accepts.[iii] A beastly thing here: I asked for a change, they gave me assurance and then nothing. Forced to ask for it and scream several times, till yes. Understand here the need for gang organization: pointed guns, if they agree all right otherwise shoot!!! Bruno has been magnificent once again: he imposed everything with his experience and assurance; the orchestra good (not more) quick in reading but technically not perfect (five double bass were missing!!!! and violins violas and cellos were not all that necessary). Then, with Bruno's assurance, everything went all right: Bruno has held up the stage and all the rest with his bull-like musical and human power. Without him it would have been impossible!!! Stage trials of singers only a dress rehearsal!!! Also for this continuous clashes between me, Bruno, and them: "no method in work, only improvisation—what kind of society is yours—financial difficulties: and your wealth? for wars only???" and so on. All this: the clashes at Venice for *Intolleranza* were polite by contrast.[5] Twice I really thought of dropping everything. Bruno always convinced me, but also the sympathy expressed to me by many in the orchestra (some fifty of them signed a protest against the denial of the visa) and by others who work in the theater, and in part also by young people in the University.

Another story: for one month my text and that by Luigi had been here:[iv] no translation had been done and they were almost lost. I managed to find a very nice and leftist English translator. Translation done two days before the premiere and taken to Caldwell: she asked me to cut off "capitalist exploitation" and "the bourgeoisie": of course I refuse but then it's too late for printing, so nothing printed!!!!! Another violent quarrel. There was one very hour, truly enough to exhaust a charge and a will. Perhaps this is method they use here to make it impossible to think and to act or to react. Crazy. Only pointed guns and shoot, one should. Another clash: at what should have been dress

---

iii. Sarah Caldwell, director of the Boston Opera and stage director of *Intolleranza 1960*.

iv. Luigi Pestalozza, our musical critic, who wrote the presentation of *Intolleranza 1960* for the Boston Opera program.

rehearsal. Result: the premiere is postponed two days so we can rehearse day and night. At last the performance, all sold out: good in the whole but not up to standard as a premiere and even as a dress rehearsal. 60 per cent. After first part, the public somewhat lost and uncertain, at the end applause and cries for and against, for a long time. Before the theater a picket with signs by Polish refugees "comrade Nono go back to Moscow, stay behind the iron curtain; Senator Kennedy *Intolleranza* is red propaganda by those who want to destroy the USA." Together they hand out anticommunist and Nazi and racist material. Many came to see Bruno and me during intermission and after, upset and enthusiastic thanking for what we had showed and the necessary and importance message given the situation. Only three composers have shown up: Kirchner, director of Harvard's music department, very kind and in agreement, and two from New York. They tell me: the others did not come because they were afraid of compromising themselves: what a frightful situation!!!!! I feel somewhat isolated. No meeting with musical people. Some interviews including *Times* and *Newsweek*.[6] It seems that Finkelstein,[7] too, was there but he didn't show up either! During the interviews arguments on culture and politics of course they disagreed. One newspaper correspondent told me: "the US is farther to the right than Europe, only the Universities here are rather to the left, farther left than the present government."

What is one to say? Contradiction between public people and government? And why does not this public act in some way against the government? Or perhaps still intimidation from McCarthy's days? Or lack of habit to think? Only to vegetate? And happy in the present mass media of this place?

I do not know. Certainly these are questions which arise to understand something here. I could understand only in the cooperation with the theater the frightful situation here and yesterday at Hollywood through the bombers announcement. Otherwise, here, one feels cut off from the world. Or that the world is this. I believe the system has done much here to eliminate man's ability to be an intelligent person. At best types like they have in New York, but all too often integrated rebels. The Harvard students I met were extremely pessimistic. Rather theoretical Trotskyists, they too seemed to me comfortably integrated. Their question: "why doesn't the Central Committee of the PCI make a revolution? What is it waiting for?" and purely abstract criticisms without a knowledge of the situation. It was easy for me to ask them, after so many criticisms for us, what are they doing, what are they organizing, circulation of papers, and so on. Nothing. Because it's difficult, they answer. A demonstration from time to time.

Certainly, it is impossible to understand at once here. Something, yes. And it's something frightful, at least what I have understood. On the other hand I have seen here at Los Angeles the State University, free from restrictions and impressive as an institution and in operation: but what comes out of it? How come almost everybody here integrated and quiet???? This is too hard to understand.

California and Los Angeles and S. Monica somewhat like the Cote d'Azur. A great Lido or an enormous Viareggio.

Another observation: Jim Dine, Claes Oldenburg, Kenneth Noland, and other pop-artists are short in imagination as compared to the imagination of advertising here everywhere, and to the overlapping of advertising objects: sometimes often most beautiful, always however to be taken in the structural context in which they are. Cage himself: the noises, sounds and silences you hear here are much more fantastic and *invented* than his stories.

Certainly, the average apparent standard of living is impressive. Shops, consumer foods, buildings, but what is underneath??? And what does it conceal??? And on what is based???? An absolutely intolerable fact is the continuing oppressive presence of the capitalistic mentality here: in the hotels, in some of the people, everywhere, you feel it, you see it, you submit to it. And you feel limited, very small, almost crushed.

And then continuously Vietnam is present to me and Congo and Cuba and Venezuela and the whole real life here they are trying to crush. Perhaps truly here "do not think, you, that he already thinks for you, he the government." "You vegetate and live in peace."

I am waiting for a cable to go to Cuba.

I truly want it very much.

Here for me it is very depressing and worse.

Another difficult test of resistance.

I understand how necessary it is for all of us to know directly everything, and check and understand. Afterward you are clear and concrete and less abstract and theoretical. But it is a very hard test.

One should resist, shoot, or commit suicide—moral, mental, or physical.

I embrace you all together with Nuria, with Silvia, and with Bastiana,

Gigi

Los Angeles, February 25, 1965

PART TWO

Music Onstage

*From a "Theater of Ideas" to the
"Tragedy of Listening"*

I

Some Clarifications on *Intolleranza 1960*

1962

Mario Labroca's request in October 1960 for a music theater work to be presented the following year at the International Festival of Contemporary Music of the Venice Biennale, provided the final "stimulus" for my decision to compose *Intolleranza 1960*.[1]

In fact, for years I have been studying the possibility of a theatrical-musical composition. I have studied the issues practically, regarding the use of voices (various compositions for chorus and soloists), the relationship between the semantics and phonetics of a text and its technical and musical expression, and the drafting of a text (various meetings with writers and poets such as Alfred Andersch and Italo Calvino), and theoretically, through the analytical and critical information of what had already been achieved in music theater especially during this century.

In no way do I think of a beginning—such is the theater of *Intolleranza 1960* for me—as a state of tabula rasa or from a sudden "flash of divine inspiration." The ballet *Il mantello rosso*, written in 1954, relates music and choreography.[2]

Having begun in early December 1960, I finished the score on March 7 the following year.

The theatrical-musical concept developed from a reciprocal relationship between the need for content, its ideological structure, and today's technical-linguistic possibilities: certain human situations in which intolerance and an awakening of conscience and an opposition toward it, manifesting themselves in various ways, are the two real protagonists. For example, the technical possibilities of the *laterna magika,* developed in Prague by Alfred Radok, Josef Svoboda, and Václav Kašlík,[3] whose multidimensional visual possibilities, both in the unity of an event and in the simultaneity of several events, allow a polyvalent radiation in the conception and drafting of a text.

I deliberately chose certain human situations that occurred in and before 1960.

The contrast and the conflict within these situations is ideological, and not to be reduced to subtle psychologisms of neurotic or literary kind, nor to "socialist realist" schemes. Their linking is related to different phases of a conflict and to an awakening of a specific kind of human awareness rather than to pragmatically existential moments, to more or less "colored" methods of combination, or random juxtapositions. The two ideas, intolerance and the opposition to it, are not embodied in two characters, but in the varied ways in which they manifest themselves in an unfolding sequence—capitalist exploitation, Fascism, and colonialism on the one hand; on the other, a migrant miner who rebels, and people who oppose and struggle against colonialism. In revealing new aspects and continually integrating them, these ideas contribute to creating two situations, the two real protagonists, in a way that is multifaceted, in the prism created by their conflicting roles. Some examples:

In scene I: on the one hand a presence implicit and evoked—the looming shadow of a mine and its disasters experienced by the chorus of miners; and on the other an active and direct presence—an emigrant miner who as a consequence decides to change his condition of life;

In scene III: a clear confrontation, physical and ideological, between the two protagonists. An attempt at a Fascist restoration represented indirectly on the stage—a demonstration, therefore, with unequivocal slogans—and the police intervention, its *longa manus*—now represented directly, and the demonstrators, the chorus, the shouts, the written texts;

In scene IV: interrogation and the beginning of the torture, both represented explicitly and directly. While scene III is dominated visually and acoustically by the demonstrators, hence by the opposition to the principle of intolerance, in scene IV it is torture, the age-old weapon of intolerance, that dominates.

The relationship between the two protagonists develops both within every scene and in their succession.

From this relationship a third protagonist arises and takes shape: an emigrant, the awakening of human conscience.

This result of this dialectic brings together both a specifically theatrical-musical factor and a part of the audience: certainly not of the bourgeoisie, which "wants a representation of itself which is subjective. That is to say, it wants produced in the theater an image of man according to its own ideology and not man seeking through this sort of world of individuals who see one another, of groups which form judgments about one another, because then, the bourgeoisie would be contested" (J.-P. Sartre).[4]

Corresponding to the prismatic, self-contained model of the two protagonists is the third protagonist, the emigrant-conscience, a continual overlapping between his individual presence and a collective reality—a collective situation synthesized in him with an individual situation related to that—and not a rigid separation like that of the schematic, ideological division of "mass-man" (Toller) or the formal musical division soloist-chorus. In the development of the theatrical-musical action, the delineation of certain characters and certain voices (a woman, the presence of erotic blackmail that turns into persecution; Alleg's voice;[5] a tortured person, Julius Fučík's voice;[6] Sartre's voice; an Algerian; his companion) should not be understood as sudden intrusions, but as stages focusing in a different way on the varied articulation of the dialectical presence of the three protagonists.

The genesis of a work of mine is always to be sought in a human "provocation": an event, an experience, a text of our lives provokes my instincts and my conscience to give testimony as a musician-man.[7]

Various "provocations" behind *Intolleranza 1960*:

a) mining disasters, the most tragic being that of Marcinelles in Belgium,[8] caused by the criminal negligence of a class for which the lives of others are instruments to be exploited: scene I.

In this scene, the mine is the initial motif of the oppression, which also symbolically contains the subsequent varied projections of it: scenes III, IV, V, VI of Part 1 and scene III of Part 2—direct intolerance of class—and scene IV of Part 2—indirect oppression through neglect by a class that seeks to exonerate itself by invoking the "natural" causes of mining disasters and floods.

b) the great demonstrations by the people in July 1960 that blocked an attempt to restore Fascism in Italy:[9] scene III.

c) the Algerians' struggle for their freedom, and the neo-Nazi systems of torture set up by the French *paras* in an attempt to crush the movement: scene IV, V, VI, VII.

d) various manifestations of racial intolerance and the neo-Nazi resurgences in 1960: scene III of Part 2.

e) the Po River flood and the Polesine tragedy:[10] the final scene IV.

For the text montage I used:

a) "materials for an opera" by A. M. Ripellino;
b) inserts from poems:

Ripellino, *Vivere è stare svegli*,[11] for the opening chorus

Éluard, *La libertà*,[12] for scene VI "in a concentration camp", with a chorus of prisoners

Mayakovsky, *La nostra marcia*,[13] for the chorus of revolt of Algerians and the emigrants at the end of the first part

Brecht, *A coloro che verranno*,[14] for the final chorus;

c) firsthand documentary material:

for scene III "Great mass demonstration" five slogans among the most popular of this century: "Nie wieder!" a German post–World War I antiwar slogan; "No pasaran!" of the struggle against Franco; "Morte al fascismo e libertà ai popoli!" of the Communist partisans; "Down with discrimination!" against racism; "La sale guerre" against the colonialist French-Indochina War;[15]

the Nazi interrogation undergone by Julius Fučík, reported in his book *Scritto sotto la forca*,[16] and those of Algerians carried out by the Paris police, reported in *La cancrena,* for scene IV, "In a police station, interrogation of some of the arrested";[17]

from *La tortura,* by Henri Alleg for the "voice of Alleg,"[18] at the end of scene IV;

from the introductory essay by J.-P. Sartre to *La tortura* for the "voice of Sartre," at the end of scene V "Torture";

certain expressions of the Parisian police reported in *La cancrena* for "the paras drag a tortured person" in scene VI;

phrases of Julius Fučík, after being tortured, reported in his book, for the "tortured person—voice of J. Fučík" in scene VI.

The ideological theme of these materials neither involves nor imposes per se any theatrical-musical validity, but rather informs the artistic conscience in its present commitment, a commitment that comes to fruition in working on these materials and in the technical-expressive result.

Scenes III, IV, and VI merge situations that are distant in time:

1) various movements of anti-fascist struggle—the five slogans—that were subsequently developed between the first and the second world wars;

2) Nazi police practices and those of the paras against the Algerians.

In scene III the character of the demonstration is heightened by the content and rhythm of each slogan, adding them all together.

In scenes IV and VI—as examples of situation 2)—the continuity of a method is displayed. And, in opposition, the song of "a person being tortured (by the Nazis)—voice of J. Fučík" is joined and dissolves into Éluard's *La libertà,* sung by the prisoners, the Algerian, and the emigrant.

Ideological motives within the text and in the staged conception as well.

I refer to what I said earlier about a polyvalent prismatic irradiation of a text in relation to a multidimensional use of the stage space, also by the use of the *laterna magika.*

For example, in scene III the following is possible:

a) unified singing and action of the demonstrators: the chorus sings and acts on the stage—I can physically see who and what I hear;

b) separate singing and action: the singing recorded on tape is projected throughout the hall through loudspeakers located in various places, thus expanding the use of the auditory space throughout the theater using multiple sources rather than a single and central perspective localized in the orchestra and on the stage.

Corresponding action carried out by extras and mimes who, compared to a chorus, are unrestricted in their movements.

In this case there is greater freedom of rendition in both the visual and audible dimensions—I do not see who but what I hear (arriving then at simultaneous receptivity: I do not see what I hear, and I do not hear what I see).

The visual element can be realized generically—a demonstration—or set in motion somehow according to the five slogans variously "composed" in the chorus and orchestra;

c) on the stage various fixed or mobile projection screens, enabling a multidimensional use of the visual space corresponding, but in a more limited way, given the present structure of theaters, to the expanded use of the auditory space: use of the *laterna magika*.

It is possible in this case to expand the stage both visually and conceptually by:

projecting into all the space, on various screens, details of the demonstration taken during rehearsals and captured on slides or in short film clips;

projecting supplementary elements of the demonstration: its earlier individual and collective phases, words, texts, slogans; instead of the five slogans,

projecting diverse documentation of struggle movements that generated those slogans over time, revised and reinvented both formally and materially, as is always the case when literary material is brought into a text-music relationship.

One example among many: the poster to "nie wieder Krieg!" by Käthe Kollwitz (1924),[19] photographs by Robert Capa on the Spanish war,[20] moments of the partisan struggle, and of various instances of racism, and of the French-Indochina situation, on their own or alternated with material from the opposing side, that is, the various moments of intolerance, themselves alone or alternated with plastic-pictorial projections superimposed onto them, such as, for example, those very beautiful ones created by Emilio Vedova for the Venetian performance.

It is clear that in this way one can achieve more wide-ranging possibilities of stage composition, simultaneous or successive, separated into several layers or superimposed, through the various combinations between live and recorded action.

Thus, between polytextual conception, musical and stage composition, there exists a relationship not of mechanical transposition, but of interaction and functional invention, each in respect of own formative elements.

Also in the conception of scenes III, IV, and VI of Part 1 of *Intolleranza 1960* I began to see the possibilities for music theater, which is now open to necessary developments.

(Regarding this I refer to my "Notes Toward a Current Music Theater," already published in issue 4 of *Rassegna Musicale* 1961; and to "Possibility and Necessity of a New Music Theater," in the forthcoming issue of *il Verri*.)[21]

Each scene is differentiated in its compositional-formal technique, which characterizes each time the diversity of the human-musical situation.

The result of this is the articulation of the relationship between Part 1 and Part 2.

In the voices and instruments and in their various combinations, the differentiation results from the diversity of compositional relationships that structure them.

What is fundamental for me is the critical consciousness and inventiveness in the specification of an existing relationship today, whether it be, among others, above all the intervallic relationship between two tones or between groups of tones, within those groups of tones or within continuous bands of sound.

Whether in the greatest complexity or in the monodic simplicity of sound material, just as it is not possible to ignore the sound phenomenon as an object in itself or abandon its constitution to chance, even more so it is not possible to somehow ignore or abandon to chance the relationship, that by connecting two sound objects in various ways, structures them.

And this goes not only for its direct and immediate occurrence but also, and especially today, for its indirect realization in a polyvalent, multidirectional, and multitemporal irradiation, a realization, namely, not exhausting itself in the immediate and seemingly final moment.

(It is possible to derive an analogy of an ideological nature from this, especially today in a time of "ideological disarmament" of various kinds, a convenient Trojan horse for a specific political-cultural position.)

The differentiation or integration among the solo voices is accomplished as a consequence of a precise technique in the vocal writing.

An example: the relationship between tenor and contralto—leaving aside the corresponding characterization in the instrumental musical texture to which it belongs, and being limited to the analysis of a single compositional element—is developed by the varied use of four basic intervals: minor second, major second, perfect fourth, and tritone.

When the expression of the woman is aggressive and blackmailing, in her dealings with the emigrant, the contralto's vocal writing is articulated, differentiated from that of the tenor, exclusively by a minor second (and major seventh and minor ninth) and tritone intervals.

Scene II, bars 208 to 211, "Resta! Resta! Resta!" [Stay! Stay! Stay!]:[22]

Bars 273–80, "Maledetto emigrante!" [Damn emigrant!]:

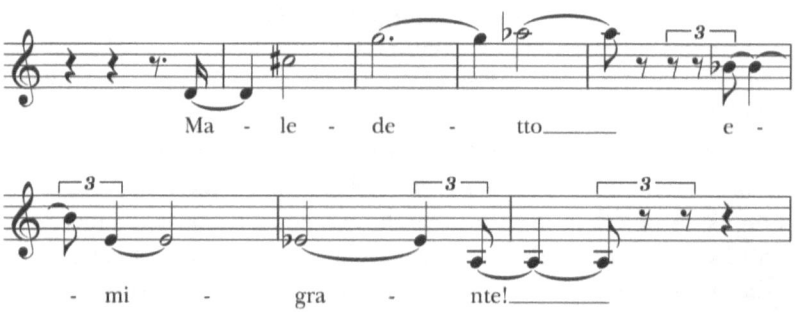

Scene IV, "Una donna qui come aguzzina" [A woman here as tormentor], bars 480–81, "[Cacciategli in corpo torrenti di scariche] elettriche!" [Unload currents of electric shocks into his body]:

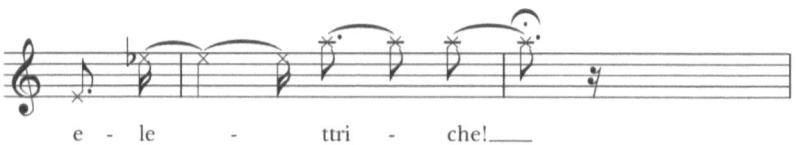

There is a moment of integration between the tenor and the contralto, when their active and reactive relationship is reflected in their common experience, of the darkness of the mine, in both the text and the vocal writing.

Tenor, scene I, bars 94–97, "[Sono stanco] di questo lavoro nelle tenebre" [I'm tired of this work in darkness]:

Contralto, scene II, bars 229 to 237, "Nella miniera i miei occhi ti facevano luce" [In the mine my eyes made you light]:

Here the contralto part is articulated by the four basic intervals that characterize the tenor.

In the contralto, there is, therefore, an individuation of the singing already limited to a single compositional element.

In the tenor the individuation also occurs through the varied reprise of "Il desiderio di tornare nella mia terra" [The desire to return to my country], bars 74–82, scene I:

The insertion of the minor third, the interval characterizing the soprano part, is also an anticipation, in his desire, for the companion he will meet later.

Scene IV, bars 463–67, "Sono di passaggio, torno al mio paese" [I'm passing by, I'm going back to my hometown]:

Scene IV, Part 2, bars 363–69, "Sul declivio dei sogni c'è la mia terra" [On the slope of dreams there's my country]:

Another example of the structural use, in the tenor, of two intervals: fourth and tritone begin the line "Da anni mi divora il desiderio" [For years the desire has been consuming me] (bars 67–70, scene I), return in "Il desiderio di tornare alla mia terra" (bars 749–52, scene VII), and they conclude, intensified in the repetition-exchange between soprano and tenor, with the oscillation also on the minor second "Qui bisogna restare e qui mutare" [Here we have to stay, and here we have to change] bars 499–503, scene IV, Part 2:

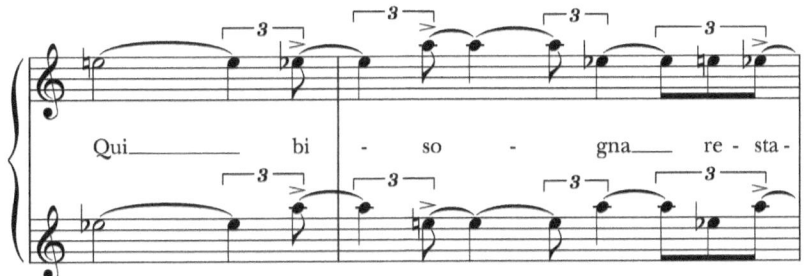

then taken up again, bars 509–13, by two flutes and two trumpets as a "memento."

All the choruses are recorded on tape and projected in various ways throughout the hall by four groups of loudspeakers.[23]

With the expanded use of the sound space, one intervenes to emphasize and intensify the different meanings in the various functions of the chorus.

This compositional element is added to others to differentiate the numerous choruses of *Intolleranza 1960*.

Three examples:

1) the opening chorus, bars 1–39, moves around the hall—dark and with projections of parts of the text—through the four groups of loudspeakers in succession:

I, bars 1–15, S. divided up to five parts, A. up to three parts,

II, bars 15–24, A.T.B. united or divided into two parts,

III, bars 22 (superimposed on the last three bars of the previous chorus)–31, S.A.T.B. united or divided into two parts,

IV, bars 27 (superimposed on the last five bars of the previous chorus)–39, S. united, A.B. united or divided into four parts, T. united or divided into three parts.

2) The chorus of miners, S.A.T.B. united or divided into two parts, bars 109 to 132 of scene I, begins—group I of loudspeakers—from the scene where the dialogue takes place between the emigrant ("La mia vita è sospesa all'uncino del bisogno" [My life is suspended on need's hook]) and the miners ("Tu giungesti qui emigrante con qualche speranza" [You came here, emigrant, with some hope]). It is also developed in group II ("I giovani del tuo paese sono costretti a lasciarlo" [The young people of your country are forced to emigrate]) being extended to all four groups ("Là non c'è lavoro" [There is no work there]).

The relationship is between the conceptual intensification in the text and its realization in the sound space.

3) The chorus of revolt—bars 764 to 790 to the end of the first Part—S.A.T.B. no longer subdivided, begins behind the audience, in group III of loudspeakers, while from the back of the stage a mass of Algerians and emigrants begins to advance: the audience is caught between two centers of revolt, visual and aural. Bars 764–70, "Battete sulle piazze il calpestio delle rivolte!" [Beat the squares with the tramp of rebels]: the chorus invades the entire hall, from all four groups of loudspeakers together, as the mass reaches the proscenium. Measures 772–90:

> In alto catene di teste superbe!
> Con la piena di un nuovo diluvio
> laveremo le città dei mondi!
> Battete sulle piazze il calpestio delle rivolte![24]
>
> [Higher, rangers of haughty heads!
> We'll wash the world
> with a second deluge!
> Beat the squares with the tramp of rebels!]

The compositional techniques in bars 40–67 (orchestra only), and 349–418 (scene III orchestra and chorus)—just two examples among others—is developed both with single continuous sound band and sound blocks.

With this particular compositional technique, the rhythmic structure is no longer limited to a quantitative metric function of pulsation, but extends to the possibility of construction derived from the function of various compositional elements: among others, the timbre, the attack of the sound, the harmonic groups, dynamic vibrations, and registers.

This technique of rhythmic interaction has been developing in my work since *Incontri* for twenty-four instruments (1955). It is not based on statistics or chance, and above all, it strongly contrasts with that stasis misinterpreted as a legacy of nineteenth-century naturalism: the nature of tempo based solely on rhythmic pulsations, so that fast tempos mean active vitality = cascades of sounds à la Liszt; slow tempos mean static contemplation = rhythmic stasis.

In the instrumental opening, bars 40–67, the major seventh

delimits a sound band shared by all the instruments, basses excluded. The twelve tones contained in this sound band are continually combined with each other and varied in time in different ways: differences in the individual or combined timbres; differentiation of the harmonic groups by means of varied intervallic relationships; through unified or contrasted dynamics; through differences in the attack and end of sound, also through the intervention of percussion instruments in varying combinations of eight side drums without snares, eight suspended cymbals, four bass drums, four tam-tams of different pitch; differentiations of performance technique, various trills, *flatterzunge*, accentuations, *arco* at the bridge, sliding from the bridge to the fingerboard, pizzicato.

The result is a prospective *continuum* of tensions structured within the unity of a sound band, for a specific musical expression and related to the dramatic action that will follow.

Scene III adopts a different approach.

As an example I will limit myself to bars 349–72 of this scene.

Four blocks occur one after the other, differentiated:

a) In their make-up from a single tone to harmonic groups of several tones that are either transformed, or fixed, or developed in different registers.

1) Bars 349–56, in their transformations:

2) Bars 357–62, a single tone:

3) Bars 363–69, as the sound block develops:

4) Bars 370–72, three tones separated by minor seconds:

b) In timbre, including the singing and shouting of the chorus.

c) In dynamics:

1) and 2) varied by simultaneous crescendos, from *p* to *fff*; by simultaneous diminuendos, from *fff* to *p*; and by simultaneous *fff*,

3) unidirectional: crescendo from *p* to *fff*,

4) repetition of *fff-p* crescendo to *fff* in the instruments using the varied durations within the basic unit:

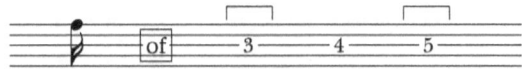

Some Clarifications on *Intolleranza 1960* | 207

while the chorus continues to sing and shout *fff*.

d) In the relationship of duration and dynamics in the sounds.

Durations are subdivided and varied in the basic unit; but in 1), 2), and 4) by the superimposition of their inversion also in dynamics, especially between chorus and instrumental unison, the sound acquires a vibrant plasticity:

bars 349–50:

Whereas in 3) this does not occur.

This differentiation is put in relation to the various uses of the five slogans:

In 1) the harmonic groups are transformed in the succession of the four slogans

349–50	351–52	353–54	355–56
S. NO PASARAN!	LIBERTÀ AI POPOLI!		NIE WIEDER!
A. NO PASARAN!	LIBERTÀ AI POPOLI!		NIE WIEDER!
T. NO PASARAN!	FREEDOM!	LA SALE GUERRE	
B. MORTE	AL FASCISMO		NIE WIEDER!

In 2) one slogan matched to one tone, the whole chorus: DOWN WITH DISCRIMINATION!

In 3) only orchestra, from a minimum to a maximum.

In 4) one slogan matched to one three-tone harmonic group, the whole chorus: NO PASARAN!

A formal technical-expressive differentiation is therefore precisely developed between the single, continuous sound band of the opening and the varied successive blocks in scene III.

Although, due to a misunderstanding, in the German edition the year was eliminated,[25] the definitive title remains: *Intolleranza 1960*.

It is dedicated to Arnold Schoenberg.[26]

2

Possibility and Necessity of a New Music Theater

1962

In this communication I will mainly touch on with the following points:

1. the possibility of a music theater as a theater of ideas;
2. the evolution of the theatrical conception;
3. an assessment of those genuinely new elements in the music theater of the twentieth century;
4. the formulation of a new theatrical experience today.

It is natural that the issue of music theater arises again today, although with conflicting terms and intentions.

The issue should be proposed again because of the complex consequences of the prospect of a formative encounter with the new creative linguistic-expressive methods of today's individual art forms, and in the relationship established between their conception and their social validity.

For an encounter, that is, in which music, painting, poetry, and stage dynamism, in their current state, contribute not to a synthesis of the arts—which, characterized by a uniform combination, would establish a simple correspondence between sound, color, and movement—but to a new freedom for the creative imagination. The interdependence continually reproposed among the various constituent elements of theater itself thus serves to shatter the univocal despotism of one constituent element over the others: music over text and staging.[1]

This collaboration, therefore, no longer involves a dependence of each element upon another: first text—then music—then direction, then stage and musical production (almost like a product prefabricated in its component parts and then assembled by stages), but a direct and simultaneous participation.

For this, by fostering the mutual interdependence among different technical and human individualities, a working collective produces continuous relationships and very significant choices, precisely for the interdependence of those singularities, of situations that in this way are liberated and enhanced.

Clearly quite alien to such situations would be the kind of leveling, almost the annulment of individuality, that Umbro Apollonio,[2] among others, seems to advocate, through some kind of misguided planning for an unspecified future civilization, even smuggling in a residue of theological thinking.

In the current conflict of terms and intentions—from *originales Theater* to *instrumentales Theater* to *happenings*[3]—it is necessary for me to try to clarify not only today's perspective, but also the line of derivation I have chosen and resolutely advocated in the maze of the various theatrical experiments of this century.

Because nothing comes about by chance or from a state of "tabula rasa."

And the new is not determined simply by self-proclamation nor mechanistically by technical updating.

This way of seeking and explicitly demonstrating in certain events of the past the successive stages of a development that is still underway responds to our need to know "where we come from" to be able to confront and act with critical awareness in the present situation.

If, instead, all too often this is childishly misrepresented by others as a "return," especially by those cunning people who easily label things, let them languish in their miserable mania.

I

"An avant-garde theater is one which, moving from the ideological assumptions that replaced the ancient sacred or mythological content, is inserted in a revolutionary situation and promotes it, assuming as a given the principle that revolution, as a process of transformation and growth, is the very principle of society's historical development, of the actualization of its destiny, of its own existence as a living organism."

Thus wrote Giulio Carlo Argan in his article "*Intolleranza 1960* e il teatro d'avanguardia" published in *Avanti!* on May 18, 1961. He clarifies his position: "Brecht yes, Ionesco no."

In fact, Argan writes: "In this sense Brecht's theater is certainly avant-garde, although full of traditional and folk motifs, while Ionesco's, although structurally very novel, is not avant-garde, played out as it is upon an ideological ambiguity that transforms the understanding between the actors and public into an amusing, intelligent, winking connivance, and so allows the bourgeoisie to accept without betrayal the deformed image of themselves that is being presented, with only implicit criticism."

This simple truth strikes the center of the discussion about the possibility or not, the topicality or not, the commitment of content or technical-formal speculation of a music theater, connecting everything to a single principle-relationship, that between a revolutionary ideology-situation and society as historically and progressively understood.

(It should be noted: ideology understood not as a remnant of idealism remote from living reality and often in contrast with it, thus tending to superimpose itself on real life to the point of suffocating it—Zhdanov-like, just so we understand—but a reacting consciousness that comes to life through actual contact with reality and that determines by determining itself; thus, not a veil that covers reality, but an instrument of truth.)

Why and on what grounds would one, on the one hand, want to base the lack of prospects for a renewed musical theater, or to limit, on the other hand, its innovative capacity, above all in our time?

One answer, generic but essential, can be found, in the restoration of the *belle époque* which—to borrow the words of Italo Calvino[4]—has operated for years, in various and often ruthless ways, in narcissistic self-contemplation.

Two instances of this narcissism can be observed which, in their contrast, correspond to one another. On the one hand, there is that humanism which, weeping for "the emptiness of the soul," disdainfully rejects the supposed materiality of current techniques (the legacy of this is especially noticeable in Italy). On the other hand, there are those positions that would attribute only to science and technology the capacity to know the truth and which relegate all other human activities either to the realm of sentiment or to the status of problems devoid of cognitive meaning. Thus, a rupture is created between science and other fields that is as absolute and as dangerous as the dualism asserted by spiritualistic humanism. This rupture easily causes a complacency manifested in the use of techniques adopted as ends in themselves, beyond any possibility of a global vision of the world.

And this attitude fascinates the neophytes of a presumed objectivity with the song of praise of purely technical procedures. They think they are avoiding any ideological contamination, are revealed in reality as albeit unwitting accomplices and instruments of a very specific ideology: that of neocapitalism. Moreover, the nonexistence of the presumed "ideological neutrality" of essentially neopositivistic positions has now been conclusively demonstrated, and their clear and definite philosophical presuppositions identified. I refer on this point to *Filosofia e filosofia della scienza,* by Ludovico Geymonat.[5]

Opera is dead! some are proclaiming, and they want to put an end ipso facto to any new possibilities for the theater; meanwhile others are smuggling in restoration in neoclassicism, or neo-Dadaism, complacently titillating the socialites, completely devoid of that human tension and anarchist energy that characterized the Dadaists of 1916, and in neogeometricism of a false and nostalgic harmony. By updating these utterances, they try to shore up and prolong a biased cultural monopoly that has almost become sterile.

Yes, it is finished, a particular conception of music theater, but rather subsequent conceptions have been exhausted one by one, but not music theater in its continuity, in the development of its relationship with history and society.

Yes, a particular historical epoch has come to an end. Its concerns were also in the technical-structural language, form, meaning, and social function of traditional opera.

But for what mysterious reason should our time not also involve urgent needs, themes, and linguistic properties for our expression-testimony in music theater?

Should we think that our life takes place in an idyllic realm far away from conflicts of ideas, human tragedies, enthusiasms, loves, struggles, new presences, that one justifies going back to evasive, idyllic, medieval themes, to Noah's ark and other myths of extinct civilizations, to more or less disguised seventeenth-century Baroque-ism out of nostalgic reaction or a complicit subordination to certain conventions of a particular society?

Certainly the fascination of the *belle époque* is an easy and corrupting form of seduction. As such, it has nothing to do with an unbridled and constructive enthusiasm for a new music theater.

Ideas are of value, some maintain, only if solved into formal structures. What matters is, therefore, not ideas, but language, the "way of forming" them.[6]

These attitudes conceal an old and ambiguous distinction between the truth of content and the truth of form. In the reality of the work of art, it is, however, impossible to dissociate the formal moment from the idea expressed objectively in the form. As Galvano Della Volpe has pointed out, one cannot, in a Crocean manner, separate the image from the concept and the intellectual meaning of the image.[7]

Therefore, it is not a matter of opposing an emphasis on content to the various manifestations of formalism, but of affirming the objective inseparability of form and idea in overcoming any abstract opposition between art and truth.[8]

Thus: theater of ideas, struggle, closely linked to the arduous yet determined movement toward a new human and social condition of life.

A theater totally *engagé,* as much on the structural linguistic level as on the social level: from the musician, the writer, the painter, the director, down to the last electrician and stagehand, insofar as they are working and innovating in their respective linguistic element, aware of the new possibilities and technical necessities at their disposal and insofar as they are responsible for precise choices in the current human, cultural, and political situation.

Theater of situations, conceived by Sartre to both oppose and supersede psychological theater.[9]

Theater of consciousness, with a new social function: the audience is not limited to observe a "rite" passively, involved and entranced by it for mystical–religious, escapist–gastronomic, or emotional motives, but, faced with clear choices—the same ones that have made possible the expressive theatrical result—is impelled to become aware of and also actively to put into effect its own choices, not channeling them into aesthetic categories, posed and resolved abstractly, or through the momentary speculations of an overt game, but deciding those choices in connection with life.

II

Opera in its conception as it has come down to us from tradition, reveals among others the following formal characteristics:

a fixed and differentiated separation on two levels, that is, between the audience and the stage, as in a church between the faithful who attend and the celebrant who officiates;

opera's two dimensions, the visual and the aural, experienced in their primitive relationship, according to which "I see what I hear, and I hear what I see";

the scenic-visual element—form, light, color—static in a merely illustrative function of the situation being sung;

the relationship between singing and orchestra developing in a univocal manner, as between the spoken word and the soundtrack of a film, perhaps today's industrialized version of traditional opera;

a single central focal perspective for both the visual and acoustic element; as a result of which the possibility of utilizing the space-time relationship is blocked.

From these observations it is clear how much this particular conception of opera remains tied, across the centuries, to an ancient ritual origin, onto which the static Catholic perspective was superimposed during a certain era, when there was a lack of open debate, even of a heretical nature, between artists and the Catholic audience.

It is worth considering how the gap between audience and stage, which still exists in theaters, originated, not only through liturgical practice, but also from the time when in the late Middle Ages religious mysteries and mystery plays started to be performed on fixed stages erected in the squares, around which the audience would gather.

One piece of documentation among others: the engraving *Ecce homo* by Lucas van Leyden of 1510 clearly depicts this situation.[10]

In this way that social relationship was eliminated which, even in the performance of mystery plays, had been freely established outdoors between stage action, with very specific content, and the possibility for an audience that was not selected or discriminated against economically or by caste, as would happen and still happens in many countries, when the stage action is brought into enclosed spaces.

The single central focus, the separation of the audience and the stage onto two levels and the static nature of the stage itself, at that time had a theological and practical justification, namely that it corresponded to a specific social structure.

With the advent of new structures and the development of scientific-humanist thought in this century, the necessity for a music theater living in our culture is logical.

The beginnings have already taken place, but have as yet received little attention.

And it is difficult to understand why Ferruccio Busoni, whose travels and encounters should have given him more than one occasion to detect the signs of a new theatrical reality was still, as late as 1921, doing an injustice to his otherwise brilliant intuition by stating: "In order to follow on from old mystery plays, the opera should be made into a rare half-religious and elevating ceremony which is at the same time stimulating and entertaining, . . . , just as the Catholic Church . . . can make good use of music, costume, choreography and theatrical mysticism—often with the finest taste."[11]

III

Between 1910 and 1913 Arnold Schoenberg composed his "Drama mit Musik" *Die glückliche Hand,* which, performed in 1924 in Vienna and badly in Cologne in 1954, is still ignored with regard to its staging.

And it is the starting point of a modern conception of music theater.

Naturally, this is usually related to the great artistic renewal that developed in Munich toward 1912 around the *blaue Reiter* group; and in general one is limited above all to evaluating the text in a typically expressionist production.

Labels are easy to apply and can facilitate . . . interpretative laziness.

In reality, though, it neglects the dynamic relationship between the need for revolt, for the polemic regarding that cultural ambience and its stylistic-technical consequences upon which Schoenberg felt the necessity to draw.[12]

In this "drama," in fact, singing and mimed action alternate and also develop simultaneously, not one as an illustration of the other, but each characterizing various situations independently.

The pattern—I see what I hear, I hear what I see—thus starts to be broken, expanding the use of the visual and auditory dimensions.

An ambivalent element, the chorus on stage, has a double function: aural and purely visual, color-form. In this latter it functions no longer merely as a chorus-extra waiting for its turn to sing, but is integrated into the staging and transformed into form, color, light, with its autonomous and symbolic use of these elements clearly specified in the score.

The result: not a purely abstract game, as the ballet *Der gelbe Klang* [The Yellow Sound], written by Kandinsky in 1912, might perhaps be considered,[13] but an expressive dynamization of the text on the basis of relationships established in various ways between the scenic and musical components, relationships that are no longer used unidirectionally.[14]

In 1932 Schoenberg left *Moses und Aron,* an opera in three acts, unfinished at the end of Act II.

(In terms of the idea expressed in this opera, there is no schematically drawn contrast between thought and action—as many think—but rather the search for a social structure. In this case the reference is not exclusively to the Jewish people, but is rather a tragic testimony to Germany's desperate condition at almost exactly by that time—1932—overwhelmed by Nazism. Years later, Schoenberg composed Act III, the consequential tragedy of the finale of Act II: *A Survivor from Warsaw.*)

For this grandiose conception Schoenberg found himself compelled to consider and make use of a new spatial dimension of the sound element, hitherto centralized in the orchestra and on the stage.

In the first scene of Act I, Schoenberg specifies for the speaking chorus, in four and six parts, "Voice from the Burning Bush": "It might be feasible to separate the voices from each other off-stage . . . using telephones which will lead through loud-speakers into the hall where the voices will then coalesce."[15]

Already in the unfinished oratorio *Die Jakobsleiter* [Jacob's Ladder], Schoenberg had thought of using various sound sources in the hall.

In a note related to the final idea of the oratorio, dating from as early as 1921, he specified, "The choir and the soloist join in: at first mainly on the platform, then more and more from far off—offstage choirs located next to the offstage orchestras—so that, at the close, music is streaming into the great hall from all sides".[16] (By offstage choruses and orchestras—*Fernchöre* and *Fernorchester*—Schoenberg meant choruses and orchestral groups separated from the podium and connected by means of microphones to groups of loudspeakers located at various points in the hall.)

The centralized perspective of a single sound source—orchestra-stage—has thus been shattered by the possibility of using various sources located at different points around the hall-theater.

It is easy to see in this a current development of the sixteenth-century practice of *cori spezzati.*

(Incidentally, it would be highly desirable to study and research such a musical practice, using strict criteria to analyze the relationship that existed at the time between the musical conception and its realization by means of sound sources projected acoustically, as practiced not only in the cathedral of Treviso and in St. Mark's, but also no doubt in other places in Venice, both outdoors and indoors. Besides reconstructing such a relationship by deducing it from the music and from the acoustic particularities of certain types of architecture, this would necessarily involve documentation, possibly with research at the state archives in Venice.)[17]

The recent development of electroacoustics greatly increases the possibilities of realizing a spatial concept with several sound sources. On the one hand, this confirms the truth of the intuition behind what has already been conceived; on the other hand, it liberates the creative imagination still further for new forms of expression of the present day, notwithstanding those who lament "the emptiness of the soul" and for those who leave little room for humanity, identifying it with the "harmonious textural objectivity" of a tool that often leads to nothing.

Lulu, Alban Berg's masterpiece, and *Il prigioniero,* the focal work by Luigi Dallapiccola,[18] in which elements of a theater of situations are already present, constitute successive stages in the modern conception of theater leading up to the present day.

Almost at the same time other musicians gave life to a distinctive experience, important not so much for reasons of technical-musical language as for the modernity of their ideas and the struggle of their theater: Bertolt Brecht was the pivot of this experience. I am referring to Kurt Weill, especially his *Aufstieg und Fall der Stadt Mahagonny* (of '29), to the Hindemith of *Das badener Lehrstück vom Einverständnis* (of '29), Hans Eisler in *Die Massnahme* (of '30); Paul Dessau, *Die Ausnahme und die Regel* (of '30), *Das Verhör des Lukullus* (of '39), and *Herr Puntila und sein Knecht Matti* (of '60).

It was on these two lines that, in the first half of the century, music theater became emancipated from the traditional concept of opera, participating in those innovative moments of social and artistic structure that were crucial for the time.

An essentially static-theological conception of traditional European opera (single visual focus—single sound source—the liturgical relationship between audience and stage, all rigidly determined, as if derived from Newton's "celestial mechanics"), is replaced by a dynamic conception of changing relationships (greater richness of dimensions and elements for theatrical composition—consequent expansion of the active capacity of the audience—visual and sound sources dispersed, possibly throughout the hall—consequent liberalization of the space-time relationship, with no longer Newtonian but rather Einsteinian derivation).

To further illustrate these principles, one might recall certain productions that took place in European theater, especially during the first thirty years of this century, because after that in one country a tragic restoration raged in the form of "bureaucratic degeneration," while in others Nazi barbarism went mad.

In Moscow, Meyerhold thought of "giving life to a theater, not only in keeping with the revolution, like Vachtàngov's or Tairov's, but directly involved in political disputes," as A.M. Ripellino wrote in his extremely well documented book *Majakovskij e il teatro russo d'avanguardia*.[19]

"He then proclaimed theatrical October arguing for the need to reflect in every play the struggle and aspirations of the working class."

Could anyone dream of accusing Meyerhold of inert political propaganda?[20]

As opposed to the static constructions, true wings, of Tairov's theater, Meyerhold based his theater on the movement of the various elements, ultimately taking advantage of the three-dimensionality of the stage with machines and construction scaffolding, also self-propelled.

"The sense of theater was not in the proscenium, in the atmosphere, in the dialogue, in the lights, but in the movement: a motoric symbolism."[21]

This offers a clear parallel with the expressive dynamics of Schoenberg's *Die glückliche Hand*.

At the same time, the gap between the audience and the stage is eliminated, bringing the stage action among the audience and transforming the audience into an actor, whether inside the theater itself or outdoors.

Outdoors: theater of the masses that is in movement and not limited to a square or arena, a theater through which the audience itself, in passing through the large squares of Leningrad where the action of *The Storming of the Winter Palace* unfolds by stages,[22] is transformed into the human deluge of the great days of the revolution.

True avant-garde theater, because "in moving from ideological assumptions, which take the place of the sacred or mythological content—in this case the mystery play—it becomes part of a revolutionary situation."[23]

Inside the theater itself: that is, theater within theater.

Pirandello, an innovator perhaps not yet completely understood in Italy, and the great experience of Piscator's political theater in Berlin '33.[24]

Regarding the theater within the theater, in the three-act comedy *Puss in Boots,* written by Ludwig Tieck in the first decades of the nineteenth century,²⁵ the action takes place both on the stage and in the audience: here a few actors actually play the role of the audience, commenting on the stage action, even while it is underway, arguing with each other and disputing the meaning of this fairy tale. Even the intermission, then, with the characters' discussions and exchanges of ideas on what they have heard and seen, has already been composed and inserted by the author of the play.

This provides another demonstration of that phenomenon in art by which a particular trend emerges at a time, then disappears, only to return some time later to pose its particular issues once more in light of new developments determined by the needs of emerging social structures.

(As a recent example of the revival of elements already present or foreshadowed in the history of forms, perhaps one might take *Momente* by Stockhausen; here the moment of the conductor's entrance and the audience's applause is inserted into this composition and *performed* by the orchestra, thereby reproposing recovery of the time beyond that of the performance, comparable to that by Tieck.)

IV

And today?

I shall now refer now to a recent experience as an example of what I proposed at the start for a new music theater, in other words, instead of an a posteriori collaboration, a direct and simultaneous participation in the interdependence of different forms of technical-human individuality (musician-painter-poet-director).

In May this year, a group of Venetian friends and I decided to try somehow to demonstrate our solidarity with the Spanish people on an artistic level. At the time they were struggling against the Franco regime with major strikes.

The meetings that occurred gave rise to a work collective composed of a painter, a filmmaker, a writer-actor, a musician, and a few cultural organizers.²⁶

Due to lack of time, first of all it was decided to use preexisting visual and sound materials, rather than create them ourselves.

It was decided to do all of this outdoors.

In Campo St. Angelo in Venice four screens were to be set up with four projectors at four different nonsymmetrical points.

The visual element was differentiated by four types of materials:

1. twenty-five slides of Picasso's *Guernica*—the original and preparatory studies for it;
2. three documentaries on Spain, including one by Buñuel;
3. forty slides of photographs from the war of '36 to the most recent strikes of this year, and poetry;
4. color slides—red, yellow, purple—the colors of the militia flag—inscribed with the titles of the songs that we were going to use during the course of the evening.

In another four different points of the square, four groups of loudspeakers were to be set up, connected to four microphones.

The sound element would be differentiated in its material as follows:

a speaker, offering historical references at various intervals;

four voices alternating between the reading of poems related to Spain, and songs of the Civil War and the new Spanish resistance.

Thus for the four types of differentiation of each visual and acoustic element, and with the availability of four visual and sound sources arranged at different points in the space, two possible forms of realization were determined: each different kind of material presented from beginning to end, from the same source, or circulating throughout the space.

That is: the Picasso slides or the songs always restricted to the same screen or group of loudspeakers in a schematic way or disseminated successively and even simultaneously among the four sources.

In possibility 1, the time-space relationship would have remained blocked; as in theater, restricting each element to one focal point, while in possibility 2 this unilateral focus would have been disrupted.

For the composition as a whole, based on this choice of elements-materials (and I stress the term *composition*, distinguishing it from the preparation of the materials themselves), there are four different methods to choose from.

1. At the drawing board the director would determine the temporal and spatial succession and simultaneity between different visual and aural materials and between the two elements themselves in precise detail.

That is, one would decide whether at a given moment a picture by Robert Capa should be projected on screen no. 3 or on all four; or alone on only one screen while on the other three, successively or simultaneously, a Picasso slide, a photo of Antonio Machado, and a text by Jesus Lopez Pacheco should be projected.[27]

Besides this, one would determine the relationship with the sound element.

In this case, the implementation-realization would have been in the hands of technicians.

2. One would set up certain points of contact and connection, leaving others to be improvised directly at the performance, by the director, the painter, the writer, the musician, forced in this way, to be responsible for their own part and to react immediately to one another.

For example, while the Buñuel documentary, projected on one screen, would constitute the fixed reference point, other visual and sound materials would have to be decided by the moment, by the four collaborators, in relation to the documentary itself.

3. One would determine moments at which the various materials would begin and how long each visual and sound element would last, so that each of the four, acting interdependently, would present the materials in predetermined durations. Let me be clear: presentation of materials. In this case it is possible that unprecedented relationships-results may be created among the various materials; results that, had they depended upon the choice of a single individual rather than on the creative interaction among the four collaborators, might otherwise have been formed according to a one-dimensional perspective.

This is not about an autogenesis of the material itself, but rather an direct and simultaneous participation, acting and reacting, of the different technical-human individual qualities involved.

4. One would make use of the method illustrated in the previous point, but not consider it as a final result, as theorists of the open work today speculate, but rather as a preliminary and preparatory moment, that is, as a moment of study, research, and essentially of rehearsal; and then, choose the various technical-expressive results achieved, to put them in a particular form.

I personally consider this last method to be the one most authentic for the creative consciousness, if based on the collaboration of more people.

Compared to a closed theater, this outdoor realization would permit greater freedom in the spatial distribution of sound sources, but above all in the use of various visual sources.

Indeed, in a closed theater—at least as they still exist and continue to be conceived and built, disengaged from modern issues and without in any way taking into account even those suggestions made by Gropius, Molnár, Weininger, among others[28]—a certain spatial use of sound is possible thanks to the electroacoustic equipment available today, but the use of a variety of visual sources is very difficult if not impossible.

And this also applies to the audience, which is limited by its fixed location and therefore its vision is restricted.

On the other hand, to the audience of the outdoor theater, as described here, the Campo St. Angelo would have offered the following possibilities: elimination of the discrimination or the ritual that still exists, for example, at La Fenice.

It is clear, in fact, that this collective theater should be offered to the audience by public or private organizations. In fact, I do not see why the Biennale, by combining its events once a year or every two years, should not be able to act as the promoter of a group formed by a painter (or sculptor), a writer, a musician, and a director in order to create a new kind of outdoor theater.

In Campo St. Angelo there would have been no chairs or similar seating.

The audience would have been able to enter the performance, turn around, listen, watch, stay, or go, not restricted to one location or with a limited view, but active in its choice of what was presented successively and simultaneously.

If one thinks about the amount, variety, and complexity of sound and visual material that we, consciously or not, absorb psycho-physiologically every day, thus strengthening our receptive capacity, and hence our knowledge of reality, even in its simultaneity, it is astonishing that we have to ask ourselves why we are still being conditioned by habit (I see what I hear, I hear what I see), and the limit to a single visual and aural focus.

An example, not as banal as it seems: the possibility of following the commentary on a football game on the radio and a basketball game on television at the same time with no interference in the autonomy of the visual and aural dimensions of the two.

If *Intolleranza 1960* led me to collaborate on the Campo St. Angelo experience, this experience, in turn, has offered me new grounds for my belief in a new music theater still in the making. I forgot: the actual realization of the project in Campo St. Angelo was prohibited by the Venice police commissioner.

And this prohibition itself can be a purely political corroboration of the validity of that cultural experience, which we have not given up.

Music theater is still under way.

The decisive need is: to communicate.

New human situations are urgently calling for expression.

Even more so if our life risks becoming fetishized through an exaltation of technology, or settling back "peacefully" into a cynical, indifferent political apathy, one should meditate, even with regard to our own work, on what Jean-Paul Sartre has said:

> And if I am given this world with its injustices, it is not so that I might contemplate them coldly, but that I might disclose them and create them with their nature as injustices, that is, as abuses to be suppressed.
>
> This, the writer's universe will only reveal itself in all its depth to the examination, the admiration, and the indignation of the reader;
>
> and the generous love is a promise to maintain,
>
> and the generous indignation is a promise to change,
>
> and the admiration a promise to imitate;
>
> although literature is one thing and morality a quite different one, at the heart of the aesthetic imperative we discern the moral imperative.[29]

Play and Truth in the New Music Theater

1962

During the International Summer Courses for New Music in Darmstadt, prior to 1961, an *ipse dixit* wanted to confine out of history and the development of music all those, without exception, who might have thought or who were already thinking about music theater.

History and the development of music have in actual practice promptly overturned this dogmatic *Achtung: Banditen!*[1] even in the work of the person who issued it.

Indeed, in recent years, various and conflicting conceptions of the music-theater relationship have arisen. Among these: *La sentenza*, by Manzoni (1960); *Il muro [Anno Domini]*, by Macchi (1961); my *Intolleranza 1960* (1961); *Collage*, by Clementi (1961); *Elegie für junge Liebende*, by Henze (1961); at Cologne, *Ich: Musikalisches Theater;* Karlheinz Stockhausen (1962); and *Instrumentales Theater*, by Kagel (1962).[2]

This experience is currently being developed in new compositions still in progress. If on the one hand the experience of music theater has succeeded in broadening the scope of study and elaboration for a diverse group of composers under the age of forty, it has, on the other hand, clarified and revealed in a still more obvious way the differentiation and contrast among the various musical and human positions, currently being adopted. These positions had been contrasting and differentiated right from the beginning, going back to around 1950, and they can be seen in the individual contributions to the concrete actual development of musical language and expression, and not in inflated theoretical verbosity conditioned by uncritical formulas or partisan interests.

The two fundamental and formative elements of theater, the visual and the auditory, create various possibilities of both conception and realization for the musician, depending on how one considers, or fails to consider, the various relationships generated between them: music-text (semantic-phonetic)—stage composition—audience.

Each element should also be considered in itself, that is, in its own reality of style and reception, according to the various technical-human possibilities that are being developed in music today, including those of electronic music and *musique concrète*. The results—distinguishing or even opposing each other precisely in the use, limitation or cancellation of those relationships—testify to a choice and a cultural and human connection, overt or covert, with contemporary society.

While it is absolutely untrue that a cultural phenomenon cannot influence social reality, in this case, the presumed abstraction of the musical phenomenon, whether related to the theater or not, whether as an end in itself or as being exhausted at the moment of the gesture or the technical procedure, in actual fact harbors two positions: On the one hand, there is an ongoing subordination to that categorical dichotomy originating from idealist aesthetics—absolute music or not, pure music or not. On the other hand, in its haughty disdain for any ideological and political "contamination," it inserts itself perfectly and precisely by way of cultural-political correspondence into that "miraculous elation" of technology, today elevated to a system, which, fraught with a more or less tragic restoration, is determined by precise prerogatives in every field, the cultural included.

By means of a dubious and late transposition from the visual arts, today there is a desire to codify a music of gesture, an instrumental and "mobile" theater. The whole thing is carried out and exhausted in the process of performance, a process left largely to chance and the performers rather than the composers, whose functions the performers now fulfill (in painting, the gesture is imbued with and fixed in the painter's characteristic stamp). The task of randomly incorporating disconnected moments is now at the mercy of the performers or the audience itself (as in literature, the plaything *Composition no. 1* by Marc Saporta),[3] with the pretence of giving a visual aspect to everything, also attempting to communicate in that way with the audience (one sees the pauses because the performer who does not play at that moment gets up and walks off the "stage"). These cases are a part of that conception by which in the process of working or simply the process of its performance on stage, the various relationships connected with the genesis and the significance of a musical event are exhausted.

This conception, which is immediately presented as ideological, when it claims to verify an artistic fact only in light of the newness or not of the procedures it uses to grant it *motu proprio* the status of contemporaneity and, tendentiously, the coat of arms of the cultural left.

Following this line of reasoning, one would think of FIAT as an authentic organization of the left simply on the basis of its new and updated production procedures.[4] But what about the relationship between producers and employers, the product itself and its use and consequent consumption: why and for whose benefit are these things left unsaid or not considered? A similar ideological sleight of hand occurs because a disdain toward politics, by assuming an attitude of superiority, always ends up subordinating itself to a particular political structure, in this case, neocapitalism, transforming itself into its instrument and vehicle.

Today, in Italy, one is continually urged toward a kind of cultural integration, which, because of its equivocal readiness, quickly turns into capitulation: the illusion of the new frontiers of Kennedyism—in the words of Lelio Basso—leads to yet further absorption,[5] and one may end up assimilated within the *Corriere della Sera* never reaching one's destination.[6]

On the one hand, the relationship with the audience, the communication with it, its integration and participation no longer as a spectator within the stage action; on the other hand, the nostalgia for and awareness of our everyday life—"a theater that is not the imitation of life, but life itself," as we also read in the program notes by Judith Malina and Julian Beck about the "Living Theatre" of New York[7]—embraces various conceptual possibilities and proposes them as *conditio sine qua non* for those involved with music theater today.

Also as a result of the consideration of the audience relationship, that formative and fundamental quality of Marxist culture is currently emerging, human and social commitment, precisely in those musical circles in which it had encountered the greatest opposition. Of course, with different emphases: moralistic, existential, instinctive, and pragmatic. In any case, it is breaking apart any formal conceptual crystallization.

(And here it would be necessary to introduce a digression to clarify what we mean by human and social commitment in culture, above all in the various fluctuations of today, also to filter out the confusion caused by current neophytes, who tend to claim for themselves exclusivity, declaring it speciously. I reserve this for a future issue.)[8]

I think it would be interesting to clarify the relationship with the audience by considering various productions that have occurred in prose theater.

In the ritual of "primitive" peoples there is active and homogeneous participation by the group of people present rather than one section acting and another watching or is allowed to watch.

On contemporary secular rather than mystical-religious grounds, Jerzy Grotowski's psychodynamic theater—"Teatr-Laboratorium 13 Rzedów,"[9] in Opole, Poland—devises a way of involving the community so that the whole hall is the stage where the two groups, actors and audience, act reciprocally with each other.

In the children's fairy tale in three acts, *Puss in Boots,* in the first decades of the nineteenth century,[10] Ludwig Tieck developed the action both on the stage and in the audience: here a few actors actually play the role of the audience, commenting on the stage action, even while it is underway, intervening in it, discussing and arguing among themselves about the meaning of what is being seen and heard.

This latter kind of participation, both apparent and physical—are actors that act within the audience, but who at the same time enlarge the space of the action, eliminating the schematic dualism of stage-audience—has also continued to develop in our day from Pirandello to Jack Gelber in *The Apple* (1961), among others.[11]

In Moscow, after the Soviet Revolution, the theater of masses in movement began, in which the audience itself moves in the large squares of Leningrad, where the action of *The Storming of the Winter Palace* develops in sequence and is transformed into the human flood of the great days of the revolution.[12]

And in creating his "Theatrical October,"[13] Meyerhold proposed and realized new solutions regarding the relationship and participation of the audience: not through simple physical contact, but in inventive and brilliant enthusiasm for a new social structure.

And on this road Piscator on the one hand, and on the other hand, of fundamental significance, Brecht's epic theater and his non-Aristotelian conception.

In the relationship with the audience, these experiences, are illuminated by a specific human and social commitment.

At a certain moment of *Ich: Musikalisches Theater; Karlheinz Stockhausen,* the audience was attacked by the throwing of different vegetables from the stage.[14] Communication or vegetarian or symbolic aggression toward the audience?

In the manifestations of the Japanese *Gutai*,[15] since 1955 and in the American *happenings* initiated in New York in 1956 by the Kaprow group, the audience is often attacked symbolically or acoustically by something dangerous, as in *Car Crash* by Dine,[16] or physically, by the launching of smoke materials that would force it to evacuate, as in some theaters in Tokyo.

Expressive violence, or vain?

Vitalistic or nihilistic?

Or generated by human frustration?—as might have been the case in postwar Japan (and a relationship with the Dadaists of 1916 and the period after the First World War cannot be overlooked) or again by a kind of "individual anarchism rather than organized protest . . . in the impossibility of having sufficient ideological clarity and strength to put pressure on structures"? (Thus Furio Colombo writes about the characterization of the Living Theatre in *Nuovo teatro americano* published by Bompiani.)[17]

Undoubtedly also for its relationship with the audience and for its new function-participation, music theater needs halls built according to new criteria so as not to remain influenced by a theatrical structure that was itself historically and socially conditioned.

And there is already talk of a theater-hall-space that is variable not only according to the type of performance, but also variable during it.

The Finnish architect Reima Pietilä has understood this need.[18]

The conditioning by the structure of the contemporary theater calls for special solutions.

In this regard with reference to *Intolleranza 1960*, I draw attention to my essay "Some Clarifications on *Intolleranza 1960*," soon to be published in *La Rassegna Musicale*.[19]

After my first experience of music theater, I am even more convinced of the need for a theater of struggle, of ideas concerning a new human and social condition of life, of a theater totally committed on both a social and a structural-linguistic level, not associated with aesthetic categories abstractly posited and resolved, but directly related to our lives.

4

Die Ermittlung: A Musical and Theatrical Experience with Weiss and Piscator [Music and Theater]

1966

The music-theater relationship and the new technical possibilities that an electronic studio can also offer to it are matters that I discussed with Piscator and Peter Weiss in the meetings that followed their proposal to write the music for the staging of Weiss's new text *Die Ermittlung* [The Investigation], at the Freie Volksbühne in West Berlin,[1] of which Piscator is the artistic director and often stage director.

I was not interested in a solution involving incidental music as such, nor a functional one, nor even less sound effects. I did not deem those solutions—banal and conventional in themselves—in any way corresponded to the significant materials collected by Weiss about the origin, responsibility for, and the process of the destruction of humanity in a Nazi concentration camp—Auschwitz.

In the tradition of European theater (with the exception of that of B. Brecht, in which the musical component has a particular characteristic), music has an illustrative function—naturalistic or psychological; it is lowered onto the stage like a wing or like a backdrop, or to acoustically "confuse" the wait during scene changes.

This last convention is dictated by a technical necessity, the time actually required for the scene change. That necessity is eliminated once technical and staging concepts have developed in a reciprocal dialectic and have been modernized, as in Josef Svoboda's kinetic approach. Now, from Prague, where he is architect designer at the National Opera,

Svoboda is ingeniously revolutionizing the spatial and temporal dimension of theater.[2]

His staging of *Hamlet,* also put on in Brussels in February 1965,[3] aroused great interest for the kinetic quality of its stage realization, which had two consequences: a) abolition of scene changes in favor of a continuous transformation or spatial movement of the staging that worked in parallel with the action itself—that is, a new dimension and projection for the actor as well; and b) along with the elimination of the wait for scene changes, the creation of an unbroken theatrical timespan, which gives greater prominence to the entire constructive arc of the text, which, with this greater continuity, becomes more easily perceptible.

Just think of Verdi's *Il trovatore:* those dull and conventional directors and conductors impose various, long minutes of waiting for cumbersome and often oleographic scene changes. The formal arc of each act, brilliantly composed by Verdi, is constantly broken and massacred, the isolation of the various scenes resulting in just as many disconnected moments.

It is easy to see how, if instead of long minutes it were a matter of a few seconds at most (and Svoboda ensures this possibility), the result would be a more serious kind of listening, indeed, a more serious understanding of even an opera as popular as *Il trovatore,* provided one wants to understand it in its totality and not reduce it to a few disconnected arias or isolated moments.

(Reading the score or listening to records cannot in any way relieve opera houses, directors, and conductors of these responsibilities.)

In *Die Ermittlung* there are no changes of scene: the setting remains the same from beginning to end, static in its representation of a trial: accused-witnesses-prosecutor-defense-judge, as in the Frankfurt trial of some of the torturers from the Auschwitz concentration camp, and from which Weiss drew various documentary materials.[4]

The text is subdivided into eleven songs, each with a specific title, following a path inside the concentration camp, from the entrance to the crematorium ["The Song of the Camp," "The Song of the Possibility of Survival," "The Song of the Death of Lili Tofler," "The Song of the Black Wall," "The Song of Phenol," "The Song of Cyklon B," and so on].[5]

In this static stage representation, the only dynamic element is: the word. In the word is the conflict and the superimposition between present and past, between memory, testimony, and current reality, between the attempt to justify and to judge and the limit of class justice (both that of the German bourgeoisie and that of contemporary German capitalism) to condemn itself—the convictions at the trial were shamefully and naturally mild—the conflict between the will to know and analyze a past in order to overcome it and the will to forget it, reasserting the apparent economic prosperity of the Federal Republic of Germany today.

Individual moments, collective moments, moments of objective information, of subjective participation.

Hence, the great need to differentiate the spoken word, for the variety of situations in its forming of the spatial acoustic composition. The knowledge of new acoustic techniques, their use expanded throughout the whole space of a theater, and their focus and perspective no longer restricted to the stage, can contribute greatly today toward achieving a new acoustic-theatrical dimension for the word.

It is possible that the box-stage annuls the static nature of the visual element—the stylization of a trial—precisely because of a different use of the aural element, providing a new dimension for the spoken word, overcoming its naturalistic projection with new techniques of acoustic diffusion that are useful for effectively communicating its significant value.

The word is thus energized on various levels, as part of an acoustic differentiation related to characteristics, rational or instinctive, mediated or immediate, evocative or provocative, choral or individual, objective or subjective. Not, therefore, to create a simple play of form.

Just think of the range of visual levels on which Dreyer animates the static nature of the trial of Joan of Arc,[6] working brilliantly with the visual element, using the means he had available, the movie camera.

In the theater it is possible—I would say necessary—to work in a parallel way, with the means at our disposal today, whenever the aural dimension is privileged and chosen as the sole element of action and communication in relation to the almost total static nature of the visual dimension, as is the case in *Die Ermittlung*.

For this reason I offered, precisely as a musician, my collaboration to Piscator for the acoustic realization of the text.[7] In other words, so as to give life to the word in its dimensions of both sound and meaning, using various means and methods of acoustic projection—microphones, various connections to loudspeakers arranged around the hall—alternating passages that are spoken live, passages transmitted through loudspeakers, and tape-recorded passages which offer the possibility of acoustic elaboration, however minimal, to be realized in an electronic studio.

Using various spaces and modalities of sound for the voice serves to enhance the communicability of a text like *Die Ermittlung,* which because of the constant violence and shock inherent in the documentation often risks injuring the audience, especially when the spoken word is used exclusively and in a monotonously one-dimensional way.

People's receptive ability is today much more highly developed and quick than we think or want. It calls for a kind of communication that is in continuous development, transcending convention and habit, which also—as regards the aural element—engages the ear as an acoustic event addressed to our present-day psychological and rational reception.

It was in that sense that B. Brecht worked on his reelaboration of Shakespeare's *Coriolanus,* which I heard and saw in the theater of the Berliner Ensemble in East Berlin.[8] This version is exemplary, new and enlightening for the rhythm of its staging and its brilliant acoustic-visual dimension.

Though in agreement with my proposal, for reasons of time Piscator was unable to carry it out or even try it. But at the Rostock Volkstheater in East Germany, a fortuitous case of necessity concretely demonstrated the effectiveness and validity of the use of technical-acoustic means for *Die Ermittlung.* The defense lawyer for the torturers of Auschwitz was speaking with a microphone, his low, hoarse, and distant voice disseminated by loudspeakers, such that the sound quality gained an immediate expressive significance. During the intermission, Hanns Anselm Perten, artistic director of the theater and stage director of Weiss's text, explained to me that he had been forced into using the microphone because of the actor's sudden hoarseness, but in view of its theatrical effectiveness would keep it, considering it for use in other situations as well. Perten, who should be credited with the best staged version of *Die Ermittlung*—which also openly accused German industry (Krupp, Siemens, Farben) of complicity with the concentration camps—had distinguished the choral part of the text from the individual moments, using speaking choruses of all the witnesses, resulting in a considerable clarification and better grasp of the text, eliminating the tendency for the solo actor "to say everything" in favor of a choral mode of utterance deriving from the synagogue.

Finally Piscator saw the music-theater relationship correctly: that what neither the word nor the stage were able to express and represent, the music had to do.

The millions of dead in the concentration camps.

Choruses, then, in the context of a compositional, musical, autonomous solution, alternating with the "songs" of the text, which required a development time of their own compared with that of the stage, the other formative aspect of the constructive arc of this production of *Die Ermittlung*.

Piscator's theater in Berlin has a sound system that I would say is exceptional. Loudspeakers everywhere, connected with tape recorders in the control room, that is, the room in which the various devices for controlling lights, projecting slides, and film clips, and so on are situated. Loudspeakers on the stage, on the proscenium, on the right and left sides, on the ceiling and under the floor in the hall. A veritable festival of the use of all the acoustic space of the theater, providing the sound dimension with the richest variety of movement. This movement is determined a) for purely musical reasons, b) in relation to what happens on the stage, c) in relation to the audience, which is no longer located in front of, but at the center of it all.

(Precisely in view of the considerable possibilities offered by this system, I suggested its use even for the actors' voices.)

The choruses, at first coming from the loudspeakers on the stage, would run over the audience with various movements, or would spring up behind the audience and run over the stage and the actors, or remain concentrated on one side, or would move only with the loudspeakers on stage, or with those in the hall, and so on. Thus, a relationship would be established with the actors themselves: one of rupture, superimposition, continuity, conclusion, precisely with the use of the various loudspeakers in their succession and simultaneity, fixed or mobile, would also disrupt the acoustic static nature of the box-stage, ensuring the diffusion of the choruses throughout all the dimensions of the theater.

The choruses are recorded on tape, and therefore they were played from a tape recorder. I composed them at the (electronic) Studio di Fonologia of RAI in Milan. I used various acoustic materials, all recorded on tape: children's voices (the chorus of the Piccolo Teatro di Milano)—sounds and phonemes sung by the Polish soprano Stefania Woytowicz—prerecorded choral and instrumental parts—original material produced for the occasion in the same electronic studio.

After the preparation and choice of material came various kinds of processing using the studio's equipment. Naturally, this was a time of study, research, and experiment to allow the actual composition finally to get underway. These three stages do not always occur in succession, but often overlap one another. And this is one of the most exciting features of an electronic studio, also for the possibility of hearing the results immediately, and than controlling and immediately verifying what is being done.

As a development of my previous experience with *La fabbrica illuminata*, also composed and completed at the Milan Studio,[9] in these choruses for *Die Ermittlung*, composing with simple sounds and phonemes of the human voice, deprived of the semantic element of a literary text. I studied how one could achieve an expressive charge that was meaningful in another way, and perhaps still more so than the expression anchored to a literary text.

A long and much-debated question: the greater or lesser influence exerted by a preexisting literary text on the music, also in relation to the much-discussed "understanding" of a piece of music with text: Should the text be made intelligible such as it is, or should it itself become music?

Does a text give music a precise meaning a priori, and is it therefore essential and a "guide" to its understanding, or, and in addition, does it provide a particular type of acoustic material to be analyzed and used in the composition?

Therefore, considering its phonetic structure or using simple phonemes, is it possible in music to arrive at a kind of expression that is semantically precise?

As always in my work as a composer, also in this case, experimentation, research, and study are accompanied by a specific kind of responsiveness and a need for commitment and human participation.

5

Toward *Prometeo*: Journal Fragments

1984

At the live electronics Experimental Studio in Freiburg there is an analyzer in operation consisting of three units: Sonoscop—Analyzer—Microprocessor.[1]

The Sonoscop is the digital development of the Sonograph, which has been widely used (see, among other things, analytical graphs of various ancient Hebrew songs, detailed to the microtonal level, published in *Der Gesang Israels und seine Quellen* [The Singing of Israel and Its Sources], by Joel Walbe, Christians Verlag 1975).[2]

This instrument analyzes any signal received in three dimensions: pitch-tempo-intensity. Intensity can be analyzed up to sixteen gradations between: *fff* = black, *ppp* = light gray. Pitch is visible, in all the resultant harmonics, graded in this same way. Moreover, even those pitches produced by the smallest movements of the lips can be analyzed (flute, clarinet, tuba, and voice, for example), whose consequences are not usually "heard" in normal concert halls. They are very high harmonics or *eolien* sounds,[3] between 11 and 15 KHz. Only by means of adjustable amplification is their perception made both possible and astonishing.

Tempo can be analyzed in fractions of 2"1/2 up to 5".

The Sonoscop data are further processed by the microprocessor: amplitude—frequency—mobility, in short the analysis of the acoustic spectrum, is visible on thirty-three channels from 70 Hz to 15 KHz.

In this way the signal is analyzed, both in its initial state and as it is modified, up to its complex *microtonal* reality.

All this is then transcribed by a "teleprinter."

It is a fundamental tool, like so much current technology, for study, experimentation, and knowledge.

In the music schools it should be fundamental and part of "new didactics" for everyone.

For thousands of years microintervals and microtones have been used, not only in the East, but in the varied and widespread Jewish traditions, also in those of Greece, and in folksongs of certain parts of Europe.

In his ten-volume collection *Hebräisch-orientalischer Melodienschatz* (1923, B. Harz, Jerusalem Berlin Vienna),[4] A. Z. Idelsohn, recorded, analyzed, and studied Hebrew melodies and various practices, and clearly emphasized the very precise use of the lips, tongue, and teeth, in relation to the Jewish phonetic alphabet, for microintervals and microtones.

Let us rethink, or rather, *let us listen to* synagogue chants (and a new and different reconsideration becomes necessary of A. Schoenberg's vocal practice) and, further, to the great laments of the eighteenth century for the pogroms suffered by the Jews in Eastern Europe. Using the aforementioned Sonoscop, one can analyze, see, and *hear* everything exactly, every minimal effect that Idelsohn indicates.

The Sonoscop, in addition to opening up other cognitive possibilities for contemporary imaginative and creative performance, also contributes to freeing one from the rigid modal-tonal (and tempered) rails, often revealing what has not been studied, not been perceived in the voice or the instrument, right down to the level of microintervals and microtones.

The problem-question of acoustic perception continues today with other difficulties (obviously!) and with them, other ways to overcome them. It is basically a question of music education that is not only wide open and updated to today's technology, but innovative in a thought that is *also* musical.

Moreover, frequency generators, with the choice they offer, differentiated up to microintervals of 1 Hz, between 16 Hz and 15 KHz, extend this basic freedom in a quite different way, right up to Peppino Di Giugno's new $4x$ computer at IRCAM in Paris and the $4i$ processor of the CSC in Padua, part of the same $4i$ system and the one existing prototype.[5]

For millennia, microtones, microintervals (and chromaticism) have continued to be used in musical, and not just vocal, practice, in various different cultures.

Another consequence, another consideration, and another result: *mobile* sound. That is, not tied statically to a given intonation imposed according to scales chosen to the exclusion of others: thoughts, systems, and mindsets that excluded or denied other thoughts, other systems, and other mindsets.

The piano, for example, with its fixed arrangement of pitches. How many attempts and researches have been undertaken to broaden it: Vishnegradsky (b. 1893) built two pianos with two keyboards tuned in quarter tones (also remember Busoni and his third tones); Mordecai Sandberg (b. 1897) subdivided the chromatic scale up to an eighth tone; in 1941 Ogolovets, built a harmonium based on seventeen intervals[6] (the prepared piano by J. Cage has different motivations).

But hostility to the point of denial was continuous and lasting.

In the fourth dialogue of *Dimostrationi harmoniche* (1571), by G. Zarlino, we read that the Lacedaemonians expelled and banished the great musician Timotheus from the city because he was the inventor of chromaticism.[7]

Nicola Vicentino, a great composer as well as a theorist, in *Ancient Music Adapted to Modern Practice* (1555), book III, "Demonstration and Example of a Completely Chromatic Composition for Four Voices," wrote: "I present ... a cheerful little motet, which is completely chromatic. We sing it in church on the day of the Resurrection of Our Lord, thus showing every one that chromatic music can be sung in church with a full choir," and he adds: "There are many kinds of chromatic music—sad, cheerful, harsh, gentle."[8]

The motets are: *Alleluia-exultemus,* [and] *Hierusalem, convertere ad Dominum Deum tuum,* for five voices.[9]

However, after a dispute with the Portuguese Vicente Lusitano (as recalled in G. F. Malipiero's *L'armonioso labirinto,* 1946), Vicentino, was fined two *scudi* because "modern chants should be diatonic" and "it is not good to mix chromatic, enharmonic, and harmonic genres."[10]

Again: Vicentino, with the archicembalo he constructed, was even able hear quarter tones.

It is clear that even at that time chromatism was not limited to typical "logocentric expressions or ideas" (death-pain-anxiety), but rather opened up technical and creative possibilities other than those of the diatonic [genre].

And this, at a time long before J. S. Bach.

In 1562 the Council of Trent thought of "systematizing" everything.[11]

Gesualdo da Venosa wrote six books of amazing chromatic madrigals, which were published in 1613.

In 1611 he had written the very strict *Responsoria* for Holy Week, with diatonic rigor.

In England, John Ward (sixteenth to seventeenth centuries) and John Wilbye (1574–1638) continued to extol the use of chromaticism in their excellent music (which is little known, even today!).[12]

Microtone, microinterval, chromaticism, and *mobile sound* constituted a very fascinating and genuine component of culture, not purely of technical interest, of course, but a kind of thinking with deep and different roots.

This is a highly articulated and varied component which continues, and goes beyond to the gypsy songs of Andalusia, the Romanian Christmas carols (collected and studied by B. Bartók, above all for the sake of the quarter-tones), and Alois Hába, who composed in Prague with four- and sixth-tones and who published the treatise *Neue Harmonielehre des Diatonischen, Chromatischen, Viertel-, Drittel-, Sechstel-, und Zwölftel- Tonsystems*, Leipzig 1927.[13]

Freiburg, IRCAM, Stanford, and Padua, and all the existing studios, restricted by being neither subsidized nor encouraged (especially in Italy), represent *new means* of studying, *taking your time* (also to avoid falling for banal tricks), to learn and always study anew, in order to consider other possibilities, other eventualities (Musil), other than those usually chosen and given, other musical ways of thinking [*altri pensari*], other infinite spaces, à la Giordano Bruno.

In this studio the collaboration between the specialized technician and composer reaffirms the need for a continuous relationship between technician-performer and composer, Joachim-Brahms, between theory-practice and practice-theory, not separate and closed off from each others' expertise, but instead continuous surprises that lead to surprising and innovative possibilities, at times initially "follies" of thinking or technique which can reveal spaces, perhaps already revealed in other ways, *to listen* for new memories, for unheard moments, for multidimensional, atemporal time.

And the restlessness, the anxiety for the unknown (B. Bartók),[14] is accompanied by the need for a continuous, innovative, critical analysis of language (the great Viennese, not only in music) to enable us to pass through and be able to wander beyond the doors opened also by today's technology.

And new ideas will emerge even within technological language, along with other perceptions and unexpected listening: here is that restlessness, that anxiety for the unknown.

There are different possibilities for obtaining *mobile* sound: in the voice, in instruments. Different exhalation and inhalation techniques with breathing and the related control of its articulation, the perception and modulation of microintervals, the wide range of intensity and quality of the voice. (Verdi, like Mussorgsky, like Schoenberg, indicated the articulation of intensity and quality of the voice with exemplary precision, not just frequent *ppppp pppp* but also: with *a mezza voce, voce offuscata, filo di voce,* and so on.[15] Very different from the almost completely trivializing practice in performances!)

And new techniques: from exact multiphonics, and *not aleatory,* to the various clusters of harmonics obtained with the lips, through a lot of pressure, medium pressure, minimum pressure on the reed of the clarinet to the new relationships between the intensity *pppppp* and those registers of the tuba unknown up until now; the *mobile* bow continually rotating on itself with even minimal variants between bow hair-wood (completely changing the timbre, the sound quality). And the research continues on ahead: by experimenting and studying directly with the performer = technician (as in analog-digital-computer studies). (We have carried out continuous experiments, research, and studies during the past four years in Freiburg, and we continue to do so together: Haller and Strauss of the Experimental Studio, and Fabbriciani, Scarponi, Schiaffini, Scodanibbio, Manca di Nissa, and young students from the Freiburg Musikhochschule.)[16] *Mobile sound* in the voice and instruments and *mobile sound* for modification and transformation of the former with technological tools. And synthetic *mobile sounds*

240 | Music Onstage

programmed and controlled by computer, not necessarily to be recorded on tape, but to be produced in real time, with great flexibility of control and modification (the beginning of experiments and study in Padua with Alvise Vidolin, using the *4i*).

a) *Varianti* for solo violin, strings, and woodwinds (1957):
attacks of the same tone, variations in intensity, with the bowing technique to create minimal difference when passing from one to the next (example A);[17]

certainly, problematic to carry out (also for the necessary rehearsals), if the violas are sitting in rows or too close. Less problematic if the violas are spaced apart: there is a need for space, yet neutral, however.

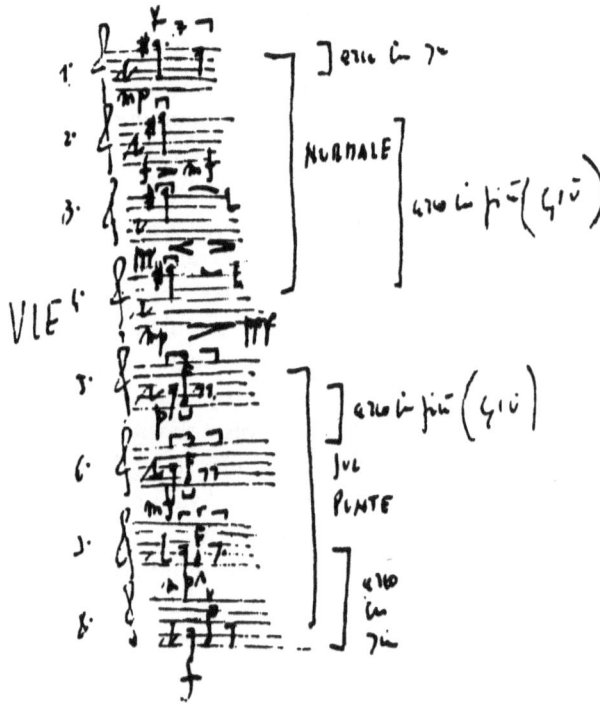

b) *Fragmente-Stille, an Diotima* for string quartet (1979–80):
the duration of the fermata, ca. 7″, and the different bowing technique, different intensity, completely aperiodic, contributes to make the sound

not fixed, not repeating in itself, but mobile, also in temporal terms, and in density—as a truly discontinuous signal (example B).[18]

Both the rehearsal time (the LaSalle Quartet rehearsed for about a year and a half, then we continued to work together, to modify, define, and redefine for at least three years), as well as the solo nature of the string quartet and its different arrangement from that of an orchestra, differentiates these two examples from example A, with more "precautions" required.

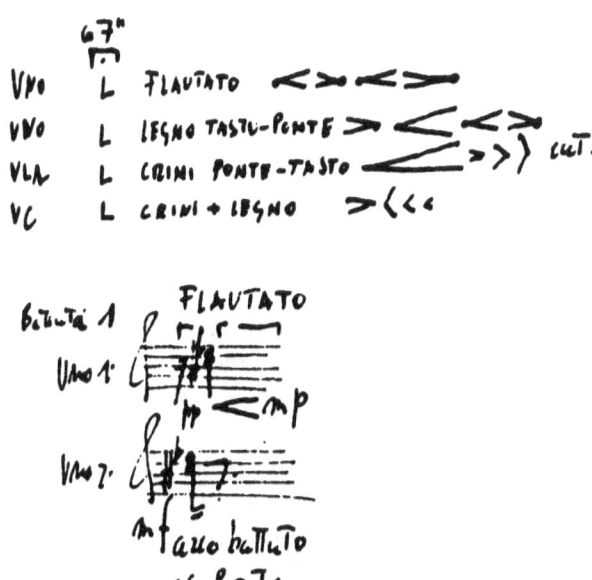

c) *Y entonces comprendió* for six female voices and magnetic tape (1970):

very often the six voices, differentiated by their vocal characteristics and quality, singers and actresses, discover the microintervals among themselves, the prescribed microtones, *they listen to each other* and "compose" on themselves (very important and rare), listening to themselves amplified in space (projected through loudspeakers arranged around the audience).

On the electronic-analog magnetic tape (composed in the studio of RAI in Milan with the performer-collaborator-technician Marino Zuccheri, who can never receive enough recognition for what he does),[19] the harmonic spectra or fields are constantly mobile (not only by beats, almost "distortions"), varied by microintervals for a calculated superimposition of up to 32 tracks (4–8-12–16–20–24–28–32), by means of amplitude modulator, dynamic modulator, frequency transposer.[20]

The diffusion in the hall with variously placed loudspeakers in relation to the six voices (each with a direct microphone) takes into account the space, still "uniform-rectangular," with different itinerant paths that "compose" the diversity of the signals-sounds. Active perception is complicated, of course, but it is "provoked" by the plurality of the sources and the multidimensionality of the acoustic diffusion.

d) *Das atmende Klarsein* for small chorus, bass flute, and live electronics—Freiburg studio (1981). Texts collected by M. Cacciari.

The programming of the live electronics involves both the chorus and the flute: sound purely natural-diffused-modified and transformed using the procedures of the Freiburg studio.

The Publison, an audio computer, transposes the given signal (here chorus and flute) at various intervals right down to microintervals, modulating the signal's onset or its beginning and its decay or its end. Thus the natural signal and the transposed signal are perfectly audible, in real time, and the difference between the initial and final modulation is what determines the signal's mobility in another way, whether in its intensity, its acoustical quality, or its timbre. The resultant harmonics are arranged according to the possibilities of transposition, multi-intervallic up to the microintervallic level offered by the audio computer.

Moreover the Halaphon, a spatial sound regulator, programs and modulates directional paths, circular, right-left and left-right, central and lateral intersections, in circular motion and with sudden intersections, sudden stops and sudden movements, very fast ↔ very slow at varying degrees, with intensities from − 0.50 dB to − 0.10 dB to − 0.05 dB.

Perception and listening can be made much more difficult, but in truth can greatly liberate the ears from almost "ritually" unidirectional, visualized and selective habits, compared to the very rich variety of acoustic life that constantly accompanies us. (Sometimes solitude is necessary, as J. W. Goethe during the din of the Roman carnival.)[21] Acoustic life naturally extends to silence, which can also be empty of air, empty of thoughts, empty of signals (why not?) and, *variously*, the opposite, that is, vibrant *for*, necessary *for*, modulating its vivacity, always of the silence, for signals, voices, memories, of the sudden moment, fantastic, the mad flash (why not?), that wander about seeking *other forms of listening.*

e) *Guai ai gelidi mostri* for two contraltos, flute, clarinet, tuba, viola, cello, double bass, and live electronics (1983). Texts collected by M. Cacciari.

The space is subdivided between the nine soloists (nine microphones, also closed) placed in an arc in front of the audience, and live electronics for eight "choir lofts" (loudspeakers are subdivided and grouped by the quality, the function, the modification, and the combinations of the nine soloists) arranged at different heights around and above the audience. Multiple sounds, noncontinuous, aperiodic, filtered, modified by the audio computer, delayed by the various depths of distances, the continuous sounds of the three strings that sometimes become distant choruses, voices, the two contraltos, central and above the audience, which often *blend* and become clarinet, flute, tuba, in especially pure registers. In short: the sound uncovers, articulates and *makes the space play* instead of spreading "linearly."

And the space articulates the diffusion and the directionality of the sound in different ways, becoming a creative component with respect to a single source.

The ritual of a synagogue, with differences between one rite and another.

Greek theaters and their fantastic acoustics, up to *pppppppppp* extremes, the Cappella Marciana in Venice and the musical thoughts that were invented constantly and moved on the fascinating paths of the Basilica,
the Thomaskirche in Leipzig, Bach's use of space, often forgotten,
choir lofts and organs and their placement in Catholic, Protestant, Norman, and Gothic churches, always at half-height, never on the floor (a current anti-acoustic concert practice),
marble, stone, tapestries,
mosaics, wood,
Tibetan monasteries, the Zagorsk monastery (*in real-time:* death-funeral songs, roaming alongside wedding or baptismal songs),
possibilities at the Philharmonie invented by Scharoun (1956) in Berlin and not used consistently,[22]
uniform rectangular and circular concert halls,
wood, stone, concrete,

various projects by Charles Nicolas Cochin II (1715–90), to W. Gropius (1927), Szymon Syrkus (1937), M. Barchin, and S. Vakhtàngov (1934–35).

Multiple considerations that derive from all these things: compositional thoughts, rituals, and not-rituals, differentiate. Sounds, various materials, architectural spaces inventing an *ars combinatoria*.

Not only memories, not only distant echoes, "non dire dell'ieri" [don't speak of yesterday] (W. Benjamin).[23] Today the continuous possibility of innovation.

Fabbriciani in the register ⸺ of the flute

Scarponi in the register ⸺ of the clarinet

Schiaffini in the register ⸺ of the tuba

are able to produce true sinusoidal wave sounds *without harmonics* (all analyzed in Freiburg with the Sonoscop).

Control, the exhaling inhaling of breath, extraordinary knowledge of the instrument. They obtain modulations of intensity from – 0.50 dB (virtually no sound) to *pppppppp pppppp pppp ppp p*: often the beginning or the "attack" of the sound cannot be heard, nor even where it comes from, that is, one is not aware where the performer is.

As true master innovators they use air, breath, tuned air, sound, microintervals, lips, tongue, and teeth: the results are true *mobile sounds* stemming from different textures, from very slow to very rapid exhalations and inhalations = aspirations, and the use of the microphone as another instrument to know how *to play,* and not simply for recording.

In the registers indicated above, with all three playing, what results is a spatial listening with no beginning and no direction.

Slow movement of the head (the two ears), from right to left and vice versa, is all that is needed to perceive not only the spatial mobility of "blown" sounds, their "nonorigin," but in the case of a single pitch, one notices a very strange mobile microintervallic diversity, even almost a memory of a "melody," almost a phasing effect.

It is the inaudible or the unheard that slowly or not does not fill the space, *but discovers it,* reveals it.

And it causes one suddenly, inadvertently, *to be inside the sound,* that is, *not to start* to perceive it, but to feel oneself part of the space, *resonating.*

Certainly different, but similar to what happens at the beginning of Mahler's First Symphony, with the A across several octaves and in harmonics. There is no beginning. One finds oneself suddenly in the enormous breathing space of an endless valley.

(D. Mitropoulos is rare-unique-among the rare who *listen to* this in his performance of Mahler's First.)[24]

Referring to *Prometeo,* Cacciari speaks of a "tragedy of listening."

Vedova speaks of theater, "spectacle," drama in itself.

Wandering, itinerant, programmed, and natural sounds, architecture, spaces, paths, continuous mobility, modification, and transformation, and purely *live.*

The performer listens to himself, and himself transformed, wandering in space, and he always acts upon himself in real time (as well as upon the other performers), he follows within and indeed interprets the articulation of space.

Of course, it is very complex. It requires another new perceptual ability, another participatory creative imagination besides a technical one.

New ways of thinking.

Time as single, unitary, unifying disappears.

The "rhythms" that are offered to our ears for listening are not mechanically and eternally linked to the pulse of the wrist; to the second as a unit of measure.

Different metrics coexist and multiply, they canceling each other.

Our life, intimate, internal, external, environmental, vibrates and pulses. It *listens differently to different acoustics:* continuous-discontinuous-perceptible-inaudible-depth of distances, of echoes, of memories, of nature, fragments, instants, subterranean, astral, fortuitous, aperiodic, endless.

Signals of very the rich life of acoustics inside and outside of us, which we can select by limiting it, and which we limit to become profoundly part of it, but to be able to discover it, to be able to marvel about the unknown, just perceived. Technology today can convey awe to our ears, our intelligence, our feelings, our knowledge, and, why not? to the possibility of nonetheless "not understanding."

Knowing how to listen.
    Even to silence.
    Very hard to listen, in the silence, to others, to the other.
    Other thoughts, other signals, other sonorities, other words, other languages.[25]

One listens and one tends sometimes to find oneself in others, to find one's own projections, habits, systems, and carisma validated or revalidated.
    One loves and one wants security, repetition, the nonconflicting familiar, the reassuring and the assurance.

Listening to music.
    Not *within one* possibility of listening.
    But with different probabilities of transformation in real time.
    The new "virtuoso" who listens to the silences together with their various acoustic modifications, whether programmed or not, but always *being aware of being able* to modulate live, has suggested the "tragedy of listening."
    Another possible perception from the inside in the "bowels" of the great wooden musical instrument, *and not a stage-set,* created by Renzo Piano.[26]

This wood, these stones-spaces of St. Lorenzo, infinite breaths.

EXCURSUS III

Interview with Renato Garavaglia

ca. 1979–80

Let's speak of your trip in the United States.
   Zubin Mehta, who had scheduled my composition *Per Bastiana—Tai-Yang Cheng* for the 1979 New York Philharmonic concerts at the Lincoln Center, asked me to attend the rehearsals. I gladly accepted this invitation, but I wanted to extend it to include other opportunities to study and to get to know the American musical world. I had already been to the United States in 1965, in Boston, for the performance of *Intolleranza 1960*,[1] but my trip at that time was limited only to this and a meeting with Varèse.[2] I spent an afternoon and an evening in his home: he was an extraordinary man.

Let's pause for a moment on your relationship with Varèse.
   The first time I went to Darmstadt, a mere "child," was in 1950, when there was a composition class being held by Edgar Varèse himself. I did not have the least idea who this composer was. During those days Hermann Scherchen was conducting a composition of mine, *Variazioni canoniche sulla serie dell'op. 41 di Arnold Schönberg*. After the performance, it was Varèse who came looking for me, holding my score. I knew immediately that this had to be someone important. In those days we had various conversations. But it was only after many years that I realized the importance of what Varèse had told me at the time, both about reading scores and the knowledge of modern and contemporary music.

When one speaks of Darmstadt, there is the official version, namely that Darmstadt is Schoenberg, Webern, and Berg. But the presence of Varèse, even if he was there only for a year, has been completely forgotten. Yet the mark that this musician left on all of us is indelible and only later, with the increasing knowledge of his works, did we realize the importance of that mark.

When you say "all of us" who do you mean?
Nineteen-fifty was the year I met Stockhausen and Goeyvaerts (a Belgian composer). In short, it was the opportunity for many young musicians from various countries not only to make contact with study and historical information, but also to meet with each other and discuss all the current problems of our day. Maderna was part of that group, a figure of enormous importance. Then came Henze, Berio, Pousseur, Boulez, and then in 1955 Manzoni, Evangelisti, and so on.

But what was Darmstadt, really?
It was Bruno Maderna who suggested I go to Darmstadt. It was a very lively center, initiated thanks to that city's social-democratic administration, which has supported the initiative since 1948. There was also a young German critic, Wolfgang Steinecke, who had the remarkable intelligence to understand that it was time to establish a knowledge of that musical historical past that Nazism had tried to erase. But it did not involve merely a recovery of the past. Darmstadt was a center where a group of musicians helped bring to life interests of various kinds among young people in the most open way possible. That is, all those young composers who were unable to find channels of information and performance had the opportunity to meet with one another, get to know each other, and exchange ideas. These were meetings open to the requirements of analytical study, open to new ideas, concerning both critical method and practical-compositional methodology.

In this sense, the contribution of Meyer-Eppler, the professor of physics at the University of Bonn, proved decisive. It was he who had introduced information theory in Europe and who had brought to Darmstadt this new method of seeking a knowledge of music through science. Meyer-Eppler then contributed significantly to the creation of the Electronic Music Studio at Cologne Radio. On the other hand, there was the presence of the Frankfurt school, Adorno and Horkheimer, the latter being the principal thinker but remaining always in the former's shadow. Adorno and Horkheimer brought an extremely advanced method of analysis to the Darmstadt seminars, and naturally, not only from a historical point of view. Third, there was the opportunity to get to know a whole range of composers (such as those of the Weimar Republic) who during the 1930s in Germany had represented (with Schoenberg, Berg, Webern, Weill, and Busoni) theoretical and practical innovation and who now in Darmstadt were the backbone of our meetings. Along with them came high-level performers who were starting to make a name for themselves, such as the LaSalle or the Juilliard Quartet. To all this must be added the experience brought to Darmstadt by composers such as Alois Hába, from Czechoslovakia, with his ideas for the use of quarter-tones, or by theorists like Professor Winckel,[3] an expert in acoustic physics at the Technical University of Berlin, with all his knowledge of the problems of musical language.

It was, therefore, not only a center for performance but for information, for the recovery of the past, examined in company with those who had been directly involved in the world of Schoenberg or Webern or Stravinsky or Hindemith. One read the scores of these greats with a continuous exchange of ideas among us young composers and those composers who were already well known. But it was not a training motivated by historicism: little by little as our capacity broadened for knowledge and for analytical, pedagogical, and scientific methodologies, we also established a continuous relationship with new technical ideas that broadened our speculative horizons even with regard to the past, which was no longer studied for its own sake as traditional musicology had taught us. It was the same method that, although only as novices, Maderna and I were then using to study Gramsci's ideas. In a composition from 1953 (unknown here in Italy) Maderna used four letters:[4] one from Kafka to Milena, one invented by Maderna himself and addressed to an industrialist, another from Gramsci to Julia, and the last one from a member of the Resistance. It was a very interesting and original score, which even then demonstrated Maderna's interests and the potential development of his work—not passive, but committed.

We youngsters were sending in our scores and these, although by unknown composers, were being proposed for performance by a group of musicians (not a jury). People like Scherchen, Hartmann, Steinecke, and others, who understood the usefulness for us young people of hearing our compositions performed. The main point, however, mind you, was not the festival. Those whose work was performed received a scholarship for a two weeks' stay with room and board.

Crucial for our training were the courses in the performance of modern and contemporary music. I remember the premiere of Stockhausen's first piano pieces. They alternated very young performers (including ourselves) with the greats such as Steuermann, Kolisch, and so on. They did not want the performances to be of an academic character, rather they were trying to break down the barriers so that the encounter with contemporary music would occur in the most direct way possible and sometimes also the most polemical.

What of all this is left today; could an experience like this be re-created?
Darmstadt has had a varied development which would benefit from more extensive analysis, especially in view of certain clichés with which Darmstadt is "sold."

The Biennale,[5] for example.
Addressing today's problems that are naturally very different from those of that time, I believe it would be possible, given the organizational structures that already exist, to set up a meeting center. But there must be a desire for new culture. I have a hard time seeing this either on the Italian scene or even perhaps on the international one. Let's see the problems we have today. I disagree with those young Germans who propose a return to simplicity and who consider Darmstadt to be an elitist and aristocratic experience. This is vulgar sociologism. It is the language of those who, despite not having been active during the period of '68 [*fatto il '68*], still adopt the thought-patterns of those years.[6]
Let's consider the teaching of music in its various fields: first, you have to give urgent information about what's happening in the music world and then very cautiously seek, not a synthesis, but rather an enhancement of everything that is already going on, valuing the various moments and various experiences without wanting to indicate a model.

Here could we raise again the idea of a permanent laboratory?
That term is now meaningless, and all that has been said is extremely generic. If by laboratory you mean research, a moment of experimental and critical knowledge but also of production, I believe that in a country like ours that suffers so much from humanistic culture, it is urgent that we accept the contribution of knowledge that comes from science. Here, then, we encounter the economic problem related to the technological development of the "machines" that "produce" sound. During my trip to the United States I went, for example, to Stanford, where

there is a research center for "artificial intelligence." I saw all the equipment they have for the study, use and testing of computer programming and I was overwhelmed. I saw what surpassed the "robot," the *musica ex machina*, and I saw and heard (thanks to director John Chowning) from the students themselves the progress they had made.[7] This is not only about manipulating instruments that are more or less advanced; it is a question of how it changes one's thinking: it is thought, human feelings that transform everything. This is an absolutely modern point of view, and there are very few here in Italy who think like this.

Therefore, a laboratory must first of all provide an opportunity for study; but then this also involves the problem of education in our country. Another thing that struck me at the University of Southern California is that the electronic studio is used not only by musicians but by all those who deal with communication (TV, film, video-tape, etc.). The language, whatever it may be, is then related to electronic instruments. Here immediately arises another way of thinking about music. In New York, Charles Dodge (a young man who is the director of the experimentation center of Brooklyn College) has been doing research on live voice transformation through computer programming for the past ten years.[8] Therefore, this involves scientific studies of a new type: a study of components, formants, up to programming. But it is not the machine that does this, that produces it, or, as they sometimes say, replaces the human brain, rather it is just the opposite: it is the human who uses the machine in a different way to discover new creative possibilities with unknown languages.

But all this requires great and lengthy study. All this advanced technology is no shortcut to young who should instead undertake a long and arduous study.

To get back to the laboratory, even the much-vaunted interdisciplinarity is proposed these days in a much too superficial way. It is not enough to just put together a film director, a theater director, and a musician to have interdisciplinarity. Instead, we must deal with the knowledge of linguistic techniques, and with the changes of thinking. Today one does not feel the need for so many products, for the new consumerism, even in music, but one needs above all to know how these new products are created and for whom they are intended. For the laboratory, therefore, it is not a question of re-creating another IRCAM, another Stanford, but one must have the intelligence to know how to tap into those experiences in order to carry forward the different studies. But to do this we need to invent new grammars, new behaviors, and new languages.

Let's move on to something else. Why precisely in Darmstadt, at a certain point, was there a great elevation of Webern over Schoenberg?

I risk being malicious here. Thinking back to that time, there may have been a racist attitude. Schoenberg has, however, such a complex of cultural formants that are much more difficult to analyze than those of Webern. The latter lends himself to an incredibly schematic analytical approach. I remember the statistical analysis of Webern's work done by Stockhausen.[9] It's easy to confine Webern within an "invented" rule, but not Schoenberg. One thing that in Europe has not yet been considered in the least is the formative significance of his Jewish thought. When I read the various critiques or studies on *Moses und Aron* and I see a typically European approach, or in the best of cases one that is illuministic, rationalistic, or idealistic (the contrasts between will and the action), I realize that there is an absolute inability to consider the way in which the formative elements of Schoenberg's culture are very different. When I speak of Jewish thought, I mean all Eastern thought (but not Zen or those types of things) with all its rational and imaginative components (for example Hasidism, with the big difference between the German Ashkenazy movement in 1200 and the Eastern one of 1700; the various diatribes that there have been between the orthodox and heretics, between the defenders of the Torah and the defenders of the Kabbalah, between the Spaniards and Italians).[10] These different mental processes that are now being studied also here by scholars such as Magris, Cacciari, and Gargani, help us to better understand certain historical moments.

Even in Darmstadt, then, there was a period of almost denigrating Schoenberg, but this was influenced by various reasons and incomprehension, not least by those that I mentioned earlier. Schoenberg is not reducible to Leibowitz's "series."[11] It is a lack of comprehension that even Varèse suffered from, made worse for him by the fact that he did not have a big publisher like Universal Edition behind him. European criticism of Varèse is limited, in general, and it has failed and still fails to overcome certain reductive analytical schemes. The great importance of a composer like Varèse lies not only in his having dealt with certain materials in a new way. For example, his relationship with folk music is absolutely unknown. In Cuba I found correspondence between Varèse and the Cuban composer Roldán, who had a great knowledge of Afro-Cuban rhythms and African instruments: a composition by Varèse's such as *Ionisation* must have taken into account Roldán's work *Cinco toques* of 1929 [*sic*] (four years earlier), for percussion instruments, in which even animal bones are used as instruments,[12] along with African instruments.

When I went to visit Varèse in New York in 1965, he showed me a number of African instruments that he had collected. Several subsequent studies have revealed that there are real orchestras made up of African percussion instruments. The Cuban musicologist Ortiz has shown that percussion instruments are not purely percussive but that there are differences in the timbre and in the pitch between one instrument and another, and from the way in which one strikes the same instrument with one's hand.[13] Now Varèse meant just that: a variety of intonations (not in the European sense), a variety in the quality of sound. Today (especially in American research studies) more attention is paid to the quality of sound than to the sound structures, to the forms. The duration is, therefore, no longer determined by the physical attack of the sound but is regarded as the moment of expansion of a dynamic harmonic spectrum. At the outset of the sound, then, time is no longer a decisive factor, but other compositional elements are instead. Varèse understood all this, but his "critics" have not done so yet. When, for example, one talks about the dynamic violence in Varèse, one slips easily into a kind of sociological interpretation, but if we are really going to analyze his grammar and his interests, what results is a very particular way of thinking that for me is of considerable help even in the study of composers of the past such as Gabrieli.

In my last composition, *Omaggio a Luigi Dallapiccola*,[14] for percussion instruments, Varèse's lesson prompted me to look for other things that were different from those achieved by him. It is not so much the challenge of the effect or the search for melody with the percussion; it is not so much the timbral use of the instruments or the search for a compositional logic; it is rather the study of the simultaneity of waves, of layers in which from time to time counterpoint occurs not between lines but instead relationships are established between waves that arise and others that disappear. Then, with the performers I really had to study to the utmost the sound quality, the type of material, the drumsticks, the way of producing the sound linked to the intrinsic dynamics of the sound produced.

You said earlier that you are studying Giovanni Gabrieli: why is that?

In my continuing studies, he is also among the many that interest me. I think that Gabrieli is an extremely multifaceted musician: there is

Giovanni the composer of the *Mottetti,* Giovanni the composer of sacred music for odd or even parts,[15] or multiple choirs, there is Giovanni who composes functional music for Venetian public life, Giovanni of the open air or the one who was performed in the chapel. Indeed, the multiplicity and complexity of his compositional art are extremely fascinating exactly from the point of view of acoustic research, of the search for a certain type of sound. In this regard, there are close links with Machaut's isorhythmic motets: the rhythmic component, the use of pitch, the use of the harmonic aspect, the organization and the exposition of the material. It is interesting to see how Gabrieli's imaginative contribution came about within various possibilities, within various choices of material, even the text, with its linguistic autonomy in relation to the musical material: there are no superimpositions, but rather a continuous imaginative exchange between the phonetic components of the texts and the acoustic components of the musical part.

In your studies are these composers constantly present?
Yes. All the Franco-Flemish school, the Notre Dame school, and so on, have always aroused the greatest interest in me. Already with Maderna we had fun "playing" with the enigmatic canons: we were studying the treatises of the period and then we'd start constructing all the possible musical solutions, in order to find the various voices on a given "enigma."

Let's return to the present day. Tell me a bit about your relationship with Bruno Maderna and your first studies with him.
Bruno had an extraordinary intelligence, eagerness for knowledge, analysis, and experimentation. When I began to study music with him, after eight years at the conservatory that were quite "useless" and at the very least insufficient, I really applied myself. It was comparative study: the various Franco-Flemish masses, the different ways of treating the tenor in relation to the other voices by the various composers of the same period, the development of "variations" from Beethoven to Schoenberg, the use of text and the human voice by various composers, Dallapiccola's choruses in relation to the solo parts, the pitches and timbres in Schoenberg. In short, the method was to discuss the matter more deeply without exhausting it by itself, not confining it in a museum, or within the historical grids of a specified period, but always opening our minds to the developments of a particular composer, a form, an era, a style, a technique of creating sounds and then making comparisons and analyzing

the differences. Not to find the influences or historical references, but to discover the procedural diversities; not to find formulas but to try to get back to the imaginative richness on a specific knowledge. The more scientific knowledge there is, the more the capacity for fantasy and inventiveness increases. With Bruno I completed a kind of basic training in methodology that has helped me increasingly to expand my fields of study. It is with this system of analysis that I approached my first scores of Schoenberg and Webern between 1945 and 1948, those that were available at that time.

It is no coincidence that my first work was the *Variazioni canoniche* on Schoenberg's *Ode to Napoleon* [op. 41]. It was the result of my first studies of the enigmatic canons, but it was also an ideological choice. Those were the years of great enthusiasm for Gramsci, the Soviet Revolution, the Weimar Republic, and so on. That time saw the relationship arise between the moment of ideals and the moment of linguistic innovation (which is the impulse that, for better or worse, continues to guide me). In other words, that was a moment in which the ideal level developed itself independently but in relation to the development of the musical language, with all the implications, even conflicting ones, that this entailed, and entails.

I remember when I used to visit Malipiero, influenced by the fascination he exerted on the island where I was living, and when he used to speak to me about the fifteenth and sixteenth centuries and of his relationships with Schoenberg, Stravinsky, and others, I wrote a composition along the lines of the sacred representations, *La discesa di Cristo agli inferi,* in which I believed in a completely naive way that I was using the language of Monteverdi. During that period I also met Dallapiccola. Malipiero told me to send my score to the SIMC (Società Italiana di Musica Contemporanea),[16] so I sent it and then I heard nothing more. Then one day Malipiero introduced me to Dallapiccola who said me, "I saw your score and I understand that here in your heart you have a lot to express, only you need to study a lot more to be able to express it." This gave me the impulse to start my musical studies all over again, and I then began my apprenticeship with Maderna. Then the *Variazioni canoniche [sulla serie dell'op. 41 di Arnold Schönberg]* allowed me go to Darmstadt.

Now I want you to tell me about another of your works: La fabbrica illuminata. *So much has already been written but I would like to hear about it from you.*

All those who have confined themselves merely to seizing the ideological moment whether leading to some form of exaltation of it on the one hand or rejection of it on the other, have understood very little of my work. Such an approach represents an extremely vulgar and fideistic manipulation of something much more complex. This way of approaching my production says nothing, adds nothing, and criticizes nothing. It is an analytical limitation to seek out the "red" in my entire musical thought. Only by starting from the music can one look for a serious relationship between the moment of ideals and the linguistic moment, and not vice versa. Unfortunately this type of "criticism" of my work is very frequent.

But let's come now to your question about *La fabbrica illuminata*.

I spent three days with the workers of Italsider of Genoa discussing my work with them, recording their words and the acoustic environment in which they worked. This was in 1964. It was not just a question of creating a work about a factory, but above all of seeing how that environment, that particular work environment, affected the private lives of the workers with all the problems of harmfulness it involved. So it was necessary to study the psycho-physical reactions of those workers rather than merely "photograph" them while they worked in the factory. Therefore it is not a work to be analyzed superficially, as has often been done.

When I let the Italsider workers listen to my work when they came in a delegation to the Venice Biennale,[17] there were some very interesting reactions. With them, with Rossana Rossanda, then in charge of culture at the PCI, with Sartre, Mila, and others, we discussed things in a Venetian bar until the morning after the concert. I remember it as a very special night of discussion, full of turmoil and of stimulation for future enterprises. The workers themselves made a criticism to me that was very much to the point, saying that the way I explained my music to them was not enough, and then they invited me to their association in Genoa to explain the whole thing better. They asked me to prepare better because they wanted to know the technical process of my work precisely. Those workers did not stop, therefore, at the fideistic, party-line, ideological element, but, showing very high cognitive intelligence not affected by a humanistic cultural bias, they were interested (rightly) in the technical data that for them was the only analytical and critical yardstick.

When I went to Genoa I had to make a considerable effort to communicate all the technical processes of composition (from voice to noise, from sounds to the electronic studio). It was much more difficult to talk to them than to give a nice musicology lesson at Darmstadt. But that meeting was very useful to me because I also learned so many things. Thus, it is important to note again that those workers were not interested in the "messages" of my work, but in the cultural and mental processes that had brought me to that work, my technical choices in the use of one particular kind of material rather than another. Very concrete questions therefore, but also very serious and deep, and not ideological hot air.

So now I'd like you to tell me exactly what these workers said to you, what they asked you, and what your answers were.
   First of all, the noises in the blast furnaces with the pouring of molten steel, with workers giving rapid orders in very loud and exasperated voices. I analyzed with them how such a moment that could be a purely naturalistic event, through both the processing in the electronic studio, and with other material developed later using the sounds of the human voice, did not have to emerge as a mere collage of sounds and noises (as many limit themselves to observing my work simplistically). The important thing was to analyze the relationship between the "natural" material recorded in the factory and the artificial, electrically generated material with all possible transformations implemented at various times. This was my intention, and this composition process is at the basis of this entire work. I have seen that this is the same work that they are doing in the United States with computers, although with more sophisticated methods: analysis of sound spectra, quantification, and synthesis. The relationship between the text drawn up by Giuliano Scabia, taken from the workers' words, employment contracts, and so on, and its semantic effect, the way it manifests itself within the composition. All this, however, conflicted with some of my thought patterns: persisting in my mind were some classic paradigms derived from certain habits of listening. What arose, was, therefore, a conflict between on the one hand a certain organization and the elaboration of the various sound materials I was using and on the other a compositional practice still consisting of two moments (those of form and content). It was necessary to overcome all these cultural limitations, and I must say that those workers gave me some very valuable assistance.

And now what are you composing? Tell me about your new work.
   I'm working on a string quartet, and then there's *Prometeo*.[18] *Al gran sole carico d'amore* was for me an experience of great reflection for

what it indicated that was new, for what was being organized within these innovations, and what problems it created that have not yet been understood. There is still a fideistic attitude by critics regarding *Al gran sole;* once again there are limits in reading music that make one stop at the surface, at the sanctioned ideological "message." Immediately after *Al gran sole* there was silence, an inexpressible silence, that is, I lacked the appropriate means to express myself. Starting at the same time was my friendship with Massimo Cacciari, whom I had actually known since 1965. I felt an urgent need to study—not only regarding my musical language but also my mental categories, and I restarted composing again with . . . . .*sofferte onde serene*. . ., a work that demanded a lot from me.

Two or three years ago Ronconi asked me to go to Prato to participate in his theatrical workshops with actors and students of the Laboratorio.[19] There I thought of *Prometeo* for the first time. I spoke about it with Massimo, who gave me a first draft of the text.

Why do a work specifically on Prometheus?

I have been thinking for a long time about Aeschylus. On the basis of conversations both with Massimo and with Francesco Dal Co, my horizon of interpretation regarding the figure of Prometheus and how the myth of Prometheus has been understood throughout different historical periods has broadened, especially in the relationship between laws and their transgression, for the sake of formulating them anew. Prometheus is not meant to be a rebel, a liberator, as in Schelling or also Schiller. I'm interested in the struggle between the foundation of principles for living and the continuous dynamic that leads to overcoming them, even in a continual relationship of conflict. This is to be developed through other texts both Greek (Presocratic and after) and certain Latin texts, sixteenth-century interpretations, Hölderlin (his relationship with Achilles and his idea of "the gods who are dead and the new gods who have not yet come"),[20] up to Benjamin. It is not, therefore, Prometheus as such at the center of the work, but rather all the issues that revolve around him.

So how will the work be structured?

Whereas in *Gran sole* there was an intersection of all the different moments, texts, and so on, here there are "islands," so to speak, in continual transformation. There are continuous trips between these "islands" that introduce new perspectives, new cognitive viewpoints.

There will not be a succession, a traditional development of the scenes, but a whole complex superimposition, with returns, utopian prospects that are recalled continually. For now I am not interested so much in the stage movement as I am in the use of the space in which the performance takes place and how space can bind together, arrange, and unbind the various moments and all the musical elements (voices, instruments, etc.). I think I will also make use of the text by means of computer programming. Thus, I'm interested in the use of the space in which all these moments inevitably meet, connect. This requires me to have a different focus on the perceptive capabilities, physical, intellectual, and emotional, a focus on the various relationships between text and music. Through long conversations with Cacciari, I have been able to broaden my methods of analysis, I have been able to catch a glimpse of new ways of thinking to increasingly embrace the multiplicity, to overcome certain schematic approaches, certain habits, certain obsolete categories.

What importance does writing an opera have today?
I think it is quite clear that in Italy there is a growing interest in the work of contemporary composers who (Italians especially) display a very fertile imagination and a wealth of very interesting ideas. I think, then, it's right to confront the question of musical theater according to the needs of today. Berio, Manzoni, Bussotti, Clementi himself, right up to Sciarrino, Carluccio, and others consider these new expressive possibilities to be very interesting.

Today, however, there is a tendency toward "open" works, that is, those continuously being remade, those that are constantly in process. Your own Al gran sole *has been subjected, in various performances from 1975 until today, to a similar transformation.*
When one makes a choice, it's not final. It does not cancel out other possibilities. There is a continuous need to clarify certain solutions, never being completely satisfied with the results obtained. Then, I have a violent need for self-criticism, for continuous evaluation both from others and from myself.

Let's go back to the very first question. The trip to the United States: tell me about your meetings with students and the organization of American musical life.
The United States presents a reality so broad and contradictory that a trip of a few days cannot give you a complete picture of the situation.

Therefore, I will make it clear immediately that I have seen and got to know only a small part of this reality. The meetings that I had (at universities: Columbia,[21] Yale, Montreal, Pittsburgh, Stanford, the Juilliard School in New York, the University of Southern California) were all very different and I have to talk about them very carefully. All in all, however, I received an impression of closed-mindedness. There is little in the way of an exchange of information between one university and another. Despite a remarkable capacity for specialist study, there is, nevertheless, an inability to establish relationships precisely because the approach to study is closed in on itself. Those students lack our capacity for critical study but there is a great wealth of analysis. At Yale, for example, during a conversation with students I was expressing *my* thoughts, asking for their opinions, but they responded instead by saying that polemic was not a method they used; they listen and then each one, at home, draws the necessary conclusions.

We must bear in mind that in American universities there is a continuous passing through intellectuals, European and others. I remained in Pittsburgh for two days, where I had a chance to listen to students' compositions, and I had a somewhat livelier rapport with them. Those were the days of the dramatic events in Iran.[22] On the twelve TV channels that I watched occasionally in New York there was a wealth of information on that situation, on oil, Islam, with very effective live *reportage,* including the opinions of scholars, politicians, and senators. There was practically a call for national mobilization against Iran. In Los Angeles, on the other hand, the TV and the newspapers had a completely different attitude: they even gave out information about the shah's crimes.

I am telling you all this because the behavior of the mass media, after all, reflects the great cultural diversity found in that country. In many universities, for example, there is very little information about musical developments in Italy. People have only very general knowledge of modern and contemporary European music culture. But there is also little information on developments in other fields, for example, on the advances made by electronic applications, with the computer. What surprised me at Juilliard, which is considered to be the premier music school in New York, was the stance that students and professors took against technological developments in the field of composition. At the end of one meeting I asked to have a discussion, and instead the professor closed the meeting saying it was late and telling me, with an obtuseness worthy of our worst teachers, to go to the Italian region the Marches where there is a firm that is testing pasta-making machines, a clear allusion to the electronic studios. Also among the students there was a kind of a priori thinking along the lines of, "How can we use these electronic machines without violating humanity?" It is a concept that rejects novelty and especially rejects the use of the means offered by technology to invent new musical languages.

The thing that really surprised me was instead something quite different. The level of accomplishment reached by musical ensembles formed within universities: technical preparation of the highest quality due to both an ultraspecialized training and also a tremendous ability to work collectively. Such is the talent of these student ensembles that they are able to perform (in an enviable way) works like *Moses und Aron* or others by Dallapiccola, Stockhausen, Berio, and so on. It is the students themselves who become the subjects of a production, a performance. I think this is very important, also bearing in mind that the American musical institutions are almost all private, with very high tuition fees and with a selective and consistently uniform population. In these schools, instead, it is the young people themselves through their own activities who are creating the foundations for a real musical life.

Did you also have meetings with musicians?

Yes. But not with those who are well known. I myself chose to be with the younger generation to understand what they are doing, what they are thinking, how they are going about things. In New York I met a young man, Carson Kievman, who has a specific interest in music theater. He has a group with which he can, in the space of two months and even amid great difficulties, stage some of his work in the theatrical spaces of Broadway. His is an original and advanced use of vocal and musical techniques, using mass media. But he is a complete outsider. In Pittsburgh, two young students impressed me very much with their creative abilities with new techniques for wind instruments.

So even with the restrictions of information that I was mentioning before, I think that there is a wealth of trends, of very pronounced personal creative inspiration. The extreme variety of American culture also requires these young people to undergo an experience that is not univocal: the choice of programs, places for performing, the audience, exchanges among themselves, relationships with other disciplines such as theater (stage design, directing), such as painting. The moment of individual creativity is enhanced precisely by a system which requires this kind of spontaneous organization. There are a lot of shows, concerts, and performances in a situation where there is a complete absence of state and public support, unlike what happens in Italy. In the United States, the majority of musical productions and university studies are all indebted to the support of private capital.

PART THREE

"Conscience, Feelings, Collective Reality"

I
Historical Presence of Music Today

1959

Today the governing tendency in both the creative and the critical-analytical spheres is an unwillingness to place an artistic-cultural phenomenon in its historical context. In other words, an unwillingness to consider it in relation to its origins and the elements that have formed it, not in relation to its role within the present reality and its effect on it, nor in relation to its ability to project into the future, but exclusively in and of itself, as an end in itself, and only in relation to that precise moment in which it occurs. Not only is it refused any integration in history, but, indeed, history itself is rejected, along with its evolutionary and constructive process.[1]

> moi Antonin Artaud je suis mon fils,
> mon père ma mère
> et moi;
> niveleur du périple imbécile où s'enferre
> l'engendrement,
> le périple papa-maman
> et l'enfant[i]

This is the manifesto of those who delude themselves that, in this way, they can inaugurate a new era *ex abrupto,* a program in which every-

---

This lecture was given in Darmstadt during the Internationale Ferienkurse für Neue Musik, 1959.

i. Georges Charbonnier, *Essai sur Antonin Artaud* (Paris: P. Seghers Editeur, 1959), [16].

thing should be new. They would like in this way to create a highly expedient way of establishing themselves automatically as both the beginning and the end, as a gospel.

This program is akin to the anarchic gesture of throwing a bomb, as if that were the one and ultimate way of bringing about a fictitious tabula rasa, an act of desperate reaction to a situation not yet been historically or subjectively overcome.

A program devoid of that constructive momentum that is truly revolutionary and which, in the clear awareness of a situation, causes the collapse of already existing structures to make way for new structures in development.

Not only does it reject history and its determining forces, but it goes so far as indicating within them constructive limits for a so-called "spontaneous freedom" of human creation.

Two formulations of this basic concept are found, different in their approach but similar in their consequences, in the work of two men from American culture: Joseph Schillinger (of Russian origin) and John Cage, who in recent years, whether directly or indirectly, have exerted an influence that has brought confusion to Europe.

At the beginning of the first chapter "Art and Nature" in *The Mathematical Basis of the Arts*,[ii] Joseph Schillinger proposes the following theory of the freedom and nonfreedom of the artist:[2]

> If art implies selectivity, skill, and organization, ascertainable principles must underlie it. Once such principles are discovered and formulated, works of art may be produced by scientific synthesis. There is a common misunderstanding about the freedom of an artist as it relates to self-expression. No artist is really free. He is subjected to the influences of his immediate surroundings in the manner of execution, and confined to the material media at his hand. If an artist were truly free, he would speak his own individual language. In reality, he speaks only the language of his immediate geographical and historical boundaries. There is no artist known who, being born in Paris, can express himself spontaneously in the medium of the Chinese in the fourth century A.D., nor is there any composer, born and reared in Vienna, who possesses an inborn mastery of the Javanese gamelan.
>
> The key to real freedom and emancipation from local dependence is through scientific method.

Schillinger thus notes man's ties to his historical and geographical location, but condemns this connection as an obstacle to spontaneity. If his statement were true that "no artist is really free," then throughout

---

ii. New York: Philosophical Library, 1948.

history art would never have existed because art and freedom are always synonymous when man expresses his conscience, his experience and his precise decision at a particular moment in the constructive and historical process, and when he intervenes consciously and decisively in the process of liberation that is realized in history.

The exhortation to scientific synthesis put forward by Schillinger as the only possible way to create works of art "freely" makes us think of the system of mass production based on a principle that is undeniably scientific, but completely eliminates the fundamental properties of a work of art: namely, its living force as an immutable and irreplaceable contribution of the times from which it emerges, as a testimony to its epoch.

The tendency to seek abstract refuge in a scientific principle or a mathematical relationship without regard for the when, the why, and the function of such principles, deprives any universal phenomenon of its basis for existence, by canceling its historical distinctiveness as a document typical of its era. One thus lapses back into the medievalism of dogmatic systems.

But creating a work of art never involves mere obedience to a schematic principle (whether scientific or mathematical), but rather only the synthesis—understood as the result of a dialectic—between a principle and its historical realization, that is, its identification at an absolutely determinate historical moment, neither earlier nor later.

As for John Cage, he has another way of giving an a priori account of his atemporal concept (and he does this apparently without having to sacrifice his indifference to the contemporary historical moment). He refers to the thoughts and maxims of certain wise men of the Chinese Celestial Empire.

These maxims can be used to wonderful effect as long as one keeps silent about the fact that, during the era of which they give a faithful testimony, the abolition of the historical process of evolution formed part of the religious and political program of the ruling dynasties, with the aim of avoiding the corrosive effect that the progress of time would have upon the tyrannical social structures of that era.

But the Chinese Celestial Empire collapsed, its spiritual structure has disappeared, and the historical process has refuted all of its foundational statements, unmasking them as a vain attempt to absolutize itself. Thus, the maxim of Daisetz Teitaro Suzuki, "He lived in the ninth or the tenth century ... or the eleventh century, or the twelfth or thirteenth century or the fourteenth,"[3] stated by John Cage at the beginning of his essay published in the recent *Darmstädter Beiträge*,[iii] has absolutely nothing to say regarding the current need for historical thought.

The ideal of an analogous static view of time was also found in the conception of the Holy Roman Empire, that is, in the ideal of a kingdom that, as the image of the kingdom of God on earth, awaited in an immutable hierarchical order the coming of the Last Judgment. Nevertheless, the Church has never been able to realize this ideal, since it had to be connected with an active mission. Phenomena such as the establishment of the Jesuit order in the sixteenth century and the worker priests in France to this day are the consequences which the Church was forced to accept by the inexorable advance of human evolution.

With naive innocence one would like to rush to the aid of the European mind, which is presumed to be in decline, by offering Europe's younger generation as a moral cure the resigned apathy of "it's all the same in any case," in the complacent form of "*I* am space, *I* am time." One thus seeks to relieve that generation of its own historical responsibility and toward its own era, a responsibility that, to the extent that it truly weighs upon us today, can be too great and too troublesome for some.

This is capitulation in the face of time, resigned flight from one's own responsibility. It can be understood only as an escape on the part of those who, with their more or less concealed ambitions to absolutize their own ego, find themselves out of breath from the various humiliations that history has inflicted upon them. It is the capitulation by those who, having become inwardly petty and narrow-minded, are capable outwardly of dealing with the absolutization of the "concept of time" in a most unprejudiced manner. They hope that this absolutization will be unable to harm their ego considered absolute and believe that in this way they can avoid looking ridiculous with the passage of time. This is the aspiration toward a state of ingenuous and indestructible innocence on the very part of those who feel guilty, yet would like to avoid true self-awareness. From that necessity they simply want to redeem themselves at any cost, even at the cost of that of their own intellectual vigor, especially since they evidently don't have much to lose.

It takes too much courage and too much strength to face up to their own time and to make decisions in it. It is much easier to bury one's head in the sand: "We are free because don't have a will; we are free, because we are dead; free like the stones; free like the one who was cas-

---

iii. *Darmstädter Beiträge zur Neuen Musik* (Mainz: B. Schott's Söhne, 1959), [46].

trated because he was a slave to his instincts; seriously, we are free because of the blindfold on our eyes, which we put there ourselves."

This is the calling card of this mentality. It is indeed new, but the mentality is very old, both in a historical and a biological sense. We are faced with a dry and deeply reactionary by-product of the failed enthronement of the ego characteristic of recent centuries, a by-product revealed as such no later than at the very moment we see the exhausted European spirit unsteadily walking toward it in order to be quickly "freed."

The cessation of all spiritual activity leads on the one hand to individual passivity, and on the other hand to activity involving material, the futile contemplation of which some seem to think the musical experience should settle for in the future. Even here, indeed, precisely here, the total lack of creative power possessed by this mentality is revealed, which is still unable to abandon the depressing spirit-matter dualism. On the one hand, there is that spirit toward which matter plays only the servile role of faithfully mirroring it (regardless of whether it is more or less suited to that role). On the other hand, there is that matter to which you attribute expressive possibilities in itself, while in the face of whose autonomous manifestations, the spirit remains passively in adoration. Of these two identically narrow options one naturally now chooses the latter, after seeing that the spirit has clearly demonstrated its bankruptcy.

In reality, this is not about choosing between these two options—a dualism typical of a conception of society that is now in decline—because there is only one possibility: conscious and responsible understanding of matter by means of the spirit, and a recognition of matter reached through an act of mutual interpenetration.

John Cage evidently has no inkling of this one single possibility, this necessity, and when he asks, "Are sounds sounds, or are they Webern?"[4] the question should immediately be turned around in this form, "Are men men or are they heads feet hands stomachs?"

Without that reciprocal interpenetration between concept and technique—which cannot be achieved if the spirit does not have a clear idea of itself—every expression of the material is limited to the decorative, the ornamental picturesque, and as such, it ends up being a frivolous entertainment for the ego, which both amuses itself royally and admires it with deadly seriousness. It is possible to reduce everything to its purely decorative element, and for this the simplest is taking some fragments from one civilization and then inserting them—deprived of their original meaning and function—into another civilization without any real connection.

This principle of collage is extremely ancient. In an work like Aachen Cathedral,[5] built around 800 A.D. in imitation of the Basilica of San Vitale in Ravenna (built two centuries earlier), it clearly involves the phenomenon of the transposition of a culture to a foreign land—a transposition which can have meaning as a document in the history of the human spirit only in so far as it testifies to the hegemonic principle, then in force, of an emperor, whose ideological aspirations—to impose his own culture on a foreign culture by force—required similar initiatives. The Venetians also favored collage when, during the period of their greatest expansion, they inserted victory trophies plundered from other peoples in their city's buildings. But this type of collage has the moral advantage of not denying its own nature. In St. Mark's, one stone or another that clearly comes from another civilization has the unequivocal function of bearing witness to a historic period characterized precisely by war trophies and plunder.

The collage method originates from a type of colonialist thinking, and there is no essential difference between a hollow drum which the Indians use for spells and which in a modern house functions as an ashtray, and the orientalisms that a certain Western culture employs to enhance the attractiveness of its aesthetic elaboration of material.

Instead of making a serious study of the spiritual substance of other civilizations, research that is unquestionably desirable and necessary, they seize their objects quickly, with heartless detachment and a kind of aesthetic thrill, in order to exploit the fascination emanating from their exoticism and in a belief this can be justified with philosophizing speculations borrowed from those lost civilizations.

But these justifications, as presented here in Darmstadt, derive most of their appeal from a phraseology crammed with such adjectives as "free" and "spontaneous." Actually, the technical concept that can justify this vocabulary is the ancient concept of "improvisation." In ancient Chinese music, improvisation was based on written texts in which there was one fixed parameter—the pitch of the sound—while the others were left free for improvisation. The performance of such improvisations was always reserved for particular castes, in which these methods were transmitted from generation to generation. Nor should we forget that these improvisations were always acts of worship, and, therefore, always referred to a higher being, a divinity.

A type of improvisation that is technically akin to it is found in the *commedia dell'arte*. At that time, the action of the plays was reduced to a few stage directions that referred to typical situations arising from the relationships between the characters. These directions determined the space within which the actor could freely improvise dialogue and action. But with the passage of time people no longer knew how to make use of this method, and under the influence of some actors who had excelled in all fields of acting, people then confined themselves to imitating such exalted models, profiting from them. In this way everything was reduced to a purely virtuoso act and a rigid ritual without any true creative force.

And today? Recent music now has two virtuosos of first-rate perfection, of which we will not see the like any time soon: flutist Severino Gazzelloni and pianist David Tudor. Even the worst music, when performed by them, always exerts a considerable musical fascination, due solely to the high technical level of their performance.

As a consequence scores for flute and piano are springing up like mushrooms, pieces in which the composers have not bothered to invent anything other than more or less ingenious methods of notation to spur the virtuosos Gazzelloni and Tudor on to improvisation. Such composers hope to increase their own prestige by taking advantage of the technical qualities of these virtuosos. These actions—and they are naturally mostly inexperienced beginners who hope in this way to quickly draw attention to themselves—these actions are not only a shameful abuse, but characterize the desperate situations of those who have confused composition with speculation.[6]

Moreover, even today improvisation takes place in the spirit of the cultural improvisation that was practiced in the East. If there they used it to appease a deity, today the deity they want to appease is the ego. This intention of their program is indeed explicitly declared by the way they strive confusedly to go back to a mysticism à la Meister Eckhart.[7]

Today someone wants improvisation to stand for liberation, as a guarantee for the freedom of the ego. And what, therefore, follows from this, of course, is a view of determinacy as a constriction of the ego, as fetters for it.[8] This alternative, which John Cage and his group have sought to establish here in Darmstadt,[9] is not only a confused juggling with concepts, but conceals within itself the temptation, especially for young beginners, to exchange *composition* for speculation.

The attempts, then, to compare so-called "totally determined" methods of composition (but do these muddle-headed people really know what *composition* is?) with a tendency toward totalitarian political systems past or present are, in their awkwardness, a pitiful attempt to influence the intellect which, by freedom, understands anything but the surrendering of one's will. The rhetorical insertion of such concepts as freedom and nonfreedom into a creative-artistic process is nothing more than yet the umpteenth propaganda device, and a very cheap one, to try to intimidate others.[10]

In this way distrust is bred toward concepts such as spiritual and artistic discipline, clarity of conscience, and frankness, a distrust explicable only by the hatred of those who cannot separate the concept of order from that of political and military oppression. By thus confusing those concepts, they once again reveal their inability to break away, either inwardly or outwardly, from the past.

Their "freedom" is the oppression exerted upon reason by instinct: their freedom is spiritual suicide. But, in fact, even the Inquisition in the Middle Ages believed itself able to "liberate" the man who had fallen prey to the devil by burning him at the stake.

Of the true concept of creative freedom, understood as the ability, arrived at consciously, to recognize and to take the necessary decisions in one's own time and for one's own time, our "aesthetes of freedom" know nothing. They are dead.

Their universal panacea, chance, can remain a subject for discussion among composers, provided it is understood and used only in the sense of an empirical moment within the process of study, a means of experimenting with various possibilities, including unprecedented ones. But the desire to posit chance and its acoustic effects automatically as *knowledge* in place of one's own decision can serve as a method only for those who are afraid of making decisions and who are afraid of the freedom expressed in so doing.

History does not need to make a judgment on these efforts because those fraudsters have already condemned themselves. They consider themselves free, and their drunkenness prevents them from noticing the prison bars that block out the sky of their freedom.[11]

Music will always remain a historical presence, a testimony of humans who consciously face up to the process of history, and who in every moment of that process decide, in the full light of their intuition and logical consciousness and act in a way that will open up new possibilities for the new structures that are vitally needed.

Art lives and will continue to fulfill its task. And there is still much wonderful work to be done.

2

Music and Resistance
1963

The Resistance occupies an important place in the musical work of Luigi Nono. . . . Twenty years after September 8, the beginning of the partisan war, we wanted to ask Nono four questions about his position and work as a composer. These are:
 1. What does the Resistance mean to you as a man and as a musician?
 2. How have you dealt with and how do you understand a constructive relationship between musical experience and the Resistance?
 3. In what way is Intolleranza 1960 *related to your previous compositional experiences?*
 4. In the theatrical, but also in the instrumental, realm, you reject the principles of the "open work" and aleatoricism. Why?
—Luigi Pestalozza[1]

1. The Resistance, as a genuinely revolutionary and fundamental act of our lives, requires, provokes and forms particular choices and an innovative consciousness. And it does so not only, and not once and for all, in the moment of armed struggle, but in its complex continuity, that is all the more essential and constructively determinate in light of the various efforts by the government parties, especially the Christian Democrats, to subject it to censorship, coercion, high-flown rhetoric and mystification, and the results that these efforts have obtained.

Resistance is not, then, in some limited sense a glorious banner of the past, but rather an unremitting struggle and a new consciousness in continuous development through subjective action, its aim being the objective process that leads to those ideals for which so many fell and continue even now to be murdered.

The musician too takes part in this fight.

On the contrary, he does so precisely to the extent that he contributes, not as a concave or convex mirror, but in an original and autonomous way with his studies, his research, his experiments, his inventive imagination. It is to the extent that he manages to bring into a dialectical relationship its two constitutive elements, the ideal on the one hand and the technical-linguistic on the other, with their particular requirements and properties, that the musician can attain full self-realization.

The theme of Resistance in music is, therefore, not to be associated only with the use of texts and situations of partisan struggle, in other words, frozen in time. Instead it is potentially present in those expressions where the truth and the novelty of research, inventiveness, and realization broaden and develop that imaginative ability, receptive intelligence, and human consciousness that strive for the elimination of the various *garrote* of neocapitalistic society and for socialist liberation.

Yesterday and today the theme of Resistance spreads to music as a fundamental cultural necessity, as recognized by Lenin, namely for the condition of "maximum freedom of personal initiative . . . maximum freedom of thought and imagination" (Vittorio Strada has lucidly explained the meaning of this in the July issue of *Il Contemporaneo*).[2]

2. In postwar Italy a kind of research and musical creativity is developing that clearly differentiates it from others.

Linked to the urgency of a new kind of ideal subject matter, caused by the Resistance is the search for adequate technical means, for new possibilities, including those of electronics.

The ideological commitment is accompanied by a commitment to language. Bruno Maderna, a pivotal figure on the new Italian musical scene, pointed the way. In 1951 he composed a chamber cantata, *Quattro lettere* [Four Letters]; the texts are taken from one of A. Gramsci's prison letters, from a letter to Milena by F. Kafka, from a letter of a Resistance fighter condemned to death, and from a letter of an industrialist.[3] In this composition, there is a reciprocal interaction between an idealistic subject matter that is new and complex and a musical conception and invention that aims to project itself in a new way. (Never performed in Italy.)

There were only a few of us then in Maderna's circle, talking about total commitment, both ideological as well as technical.

For years, many, especially abroad, shrugged their shoulders.

Now almost everyone is talking about commitment: moralistic, technical, metaphysical, existential, pragmatic, trying to smuggle it in as the only possible form of engagement available to the cultural left. And they amuse themselves with empty protests, with the exchange of skin-deep society chatter, with mechanistic copies of statistical formulas, with proclamations on indeterminacy and chance as the ultimate freedom, and more. Of course, they distinguish politics from art, and deny, within culture, the right to an ideology: note that they only and always deny the communist one.

Certainly this is the most Jesuitical kind of conformity to the ambiguousness of the times, becoming vehicles of the center-left, here by us, and of the *new frontier,* by others, succumbing, consciously or not, to the transformative power of neo-capitalist ideology.[4] Then as now there is a trend in Italian music, in practice, in theory, in criticism, that denounces on the one hand the limitation of a technological presence, which, nonetheless, results from an ideological choice, as well as, on the other hand, the limitation of a dogmatically schematic approach to the issue of content. Neither a vulgar obsession with content, nor formalism, therefore, but a responsible position by the musician toward the historical conflict of his time, expressed so as to fulfil and stimulate the process of developing linguistic methods, which in turn is objectively determined.

It is clear that the fundamental historical conflict of our age is characterized by the growing socialist revolution in the world. The historical choice of the totally committed musician is manifested only in the rich, diverse, multifaceted, and often contradictory struggle for socialism.

Also in this Italian musical trend the Resistance lives on and continues.

Not only protests, not only revolts, not only demolishing to a varying extent each other's language and ideals, but the overcoming of such still significant moments, through the involvement of musicians, with music, in the conscience and the conflicts of our time.

3. Maybe it is possible to see that, in *Intolleranza 1960*, all my experiences converge, projected into the sound-visual dimension of the theater. The ideal and technical themes of my music for Federico García Lorca, of *Il canto sospeso,* of *La terra e la compagna* (Pavese), of the *Cori di Didone* (Ungaretti—which I composed thinking of Mayakovsky,

Yesenin, Toller, De Staël, Arshile Gorky, not "suicides," but eliminated through "murder by society")[5]—and of *Diario polacco '58* (influenced by my contact with tragic reality, by the recent past, and the new impulse of life in Poland) developed into *Intolleranza 1960*, and with *Canti di vita e d'amore: Sul ponte di Hiroshima* (lyrics by Anders-Pacheco-Pavese) and *Canciones a Guiomar* (Machado) succeeded in provoking the imagination and invention in new and other ways. Their continuity is in the life that we live today: we shall see it in the new "opera" currently in progress.[6]

4. Because I believe in the composer's conscious control of the sound material. Heisenberg, questioned on the possible relationship between the uncertainty principle and a broader concept of freedom, denied it: noncontrol is still a negative motif, an ignorance of as yet undiscovered structural laws.[7]

For the interaction of compositional elements, there must be a new compositional organization corresponding to the current possibilities for the constitution and transformation of instrumental and electronic sound.

I also refute the equal-opposite reaction of aleatoricism: attempts to organize materials according to formal laws alleged to be *scientifically* deduced from them.

The form is the moment in which the composer's creative awareness of material as an expressive medium for content is revealed to the maximum degree of inventive freedom.

In this respect as well Arnold Schoenberg's teaching is fundamental.

3

Replies to Seven Questions by Martine Cadieu

1966

1. *What is the musician's place in contemporary society? To what extent can music contribute to the evolution of this society? What action do you expect from the modern composer?*
2. *What is the awareness or the inner journey that led you to differentiate yourself from some of your contemporaries and to adopt a clearly critical position toward form and content?*
3. *To what extent can the evolution of language and means of expression be understood by all and be placed at the service of every social or political manifestation?*
4. *Is there such a thing as a revolutionary art? What is it?*
5. *To what extent did tradition come to bear on your training as a musician?*
6. *Your links with recent Polish music. Your relationship with music of the East.*[1]
7. *Voice. Singing.*

—Martine Cadieu[2]

1. Neither total isolation, according to the cliché of those who, owing to their incapacity for analysis or their self-presumption, would like to subscribe to the notion of the "ivory tower." Nor any less, "above the fray," as a certain faction of the power structure established in the capitalist world presumes to demand, even in the name of "immutable" categories and relationships and in tribute to the spirituality of art—

with a capital *S* and a capital *A*. The more one talks about spirituality, beauty, or poetry—all categories with the initial capital—the more there is latent in them a precise ideological and practical interest in that social power that wants to present itself as the sole custodian and guarantor of those "immutable" values and principles of man and the universe, with the help of idealistic abstractions and of a class-based economic power structure, based precisely on violence toward humanity.

For the musician it is always and in every case a position of choice, active or passive, conscious or not, with respect to the constituent elements of contemporary society: that conservative one, established power, albeit obliged to use some new innovations, but not too much, and to quickly integrate them; then there is that of progress through innovative continuity, in which one also has to consider the purely technological moment, whether in its objective limits; or the decisive global challenge up to revolutionary, historical, and social rupture. Broadly speaking it is always possible, today as yesterday, also to trace the position of the musician back to these three moments, sometimes in their contradictory "confusion," sometimes in their distinct clarity.

Of course, it is well understood that all this must be analyzed and corroborated in the musician's work as a whole, in his position and his choice on the technical, linguistic, and expressive levels of communication, that is, in terms of his knowledge of the contemporary world, in the quality of his inventive, imaginative participation in the reality of his own time, and in the validity of his testimony.

Hence, along with and in relation to the economic and ideological conflict that marks the era.

Today, of course, peaceful competition, confrontation, and direct conflict between the capitalist and socialist systems are more intense than ever before.

Culture, and with it music, is by no means extraneous to all this.

I cannot see why music should not be more able to participate today in the discovery and affirmation of a new human dimension, a technical, imaginative, and real dimension that the current historical pivot—that is, the international workers' struggle for socialist freedom—indicates and discloses, even if various internal contradictions within it seem at times to repress it or otherwise put it into jeopardy.

In earlier epochs were there not connections between historical reasoning and creative imagination? Is there perhaps no link between the French Enlightenment and Mozart (a recent new and probing study on that connection came out in France)?[3] Between the achievements of bourgeois thought as a result of the French Revolution and Beethoven? Between the civil passion of the Risorgimento movement and Verdi? Up to the discovery of Russian populism and Mussorgsky, to Janáček to Bartók to Schoenberg—albeit to a limited extent, the tragedy of the Jewish people—up to Dallapiccola, whose choice of Catholic texts always falls on the great heretics or anyway not connected to orthodoxy.[4] Is this not also Dallapiccola's conscious choice and of great significance when compared to various composers whose choice was governed only by their deference to rigid orthodoxy?

Each musician chooses his own position in the contemporary world, and each choice is also a partisan *political* choice, that is, he does not act in an aristocratic or autonomous fashion but rather in a manner connected to the context of his current society, whether he is spiritualized in metaphysical abstractions, whether he is exalted by the beauty or purity of sounds, whether he considers having fulfilled his own commitment moralistically, whether he proclaims the uniqueness of the technological moment or process, or whether he identifies himself pragmatically within the musical act, whether he chooses Zen, cocaine, or irreverent anger.

Already implicit in this choice are the answers to the three questions that J.-P. Sartre poses regarding literature:

what is writing (music)?
why write (music)?
for whom does one write (music)?[5]

2. My new composition *A floresta é jovem e cheja de vida* premiered at the recent Biennale Festival in Venice—September—is dedicated to the Vietnamese FLN.[6]

Even dedications change throughout history, as do their motivation and inspiration. Popes, emperors, kings, princes, bourgeois, family, radio, foundations: always an act, sometimes formal, toward the established or recognized power, sometimes concerned with those who commission the works—princes or bourgeois or radio or foundations—sometimes purely sentimental.

What counts for me initially is the provocation to make music, the inspiration or the real, ideal motivation for "why and for whom does one write" (music).

Objective historical power today: in that great impulse currently in progress—the force of protest and transformation toward the prospect of world communism—I also recognize the truly decisive fulcrum of our epoch. (And this has been ever more clearly expressed in my work.) For this music of mine, the Vietnamese FLN is my ideal inspiration: the FLN is currently enduring perhaps the most intense moment in the direct struggle between capitalism and communism.

We are well aware of the political and strategic aims of American aggression: they tend to overwhelm political, economic, and cultural reasoning. Summed up in the Vietnamese FLN are all the various struggles sustained at various levels in the world today by the workers' movement, perhaps a moment, unfortunately exemplary for its harshness.

Otherwise it is as decisive as Stalingrad for the existence of all of us.

In an age when dedications are either self-interested or intimate or parochial, the internationalist opening up of the Bolshevik revolution, of the Chinese revolution, of the struggle in the Sierra Maestra and to varying degrees also those other struggles around the world, peaceful or not, legal or illegal, foster a much broader and more responsible consciousness in our actions, in our participation as men/musicians who have taken a stand.

The commitment does not exhaust or self-validate in this choice, of course: it is the motivating reason for my work.

The only thing that justifies it is the final result—in terms of music, skill, technical, and formal invention of communication, of expression—which should be analyzed and discussed, not subjected to a priori judgments.

3. For quite some time my comrade and friend Luigi Pestalozza, music critic of *Rinascita*,[7] and I have been experiencing something very significant. Invited by workers' cultural circles, we present some of my compositions, especially *La fabbrica illuminata* (for magnetic tape and voice, composed in the electronic Studio di Fonologia—Radio Milano [RAI]) and we discuss them together. For us it is a verification, a new test of the function, the reason for, and the consumption of music today. The subsequent discussions with the workers are extremely significant. The will and ability to understand why and how music can make the themes of the workers' life and struggle its own, the desire to gain technical understanding concerning the compositional process, concerning the formulation of the poetic text—based in this case on statements of the workers themselves, on fragments of union contracts, and on the poetic invention and montage of the young Venetian poet Giuliano Scabia.

The workers: they are often and almost completely devoid of academic cultural music "preparation." On the contrary they are subjected to the bombardment of escapist consumption through the radio and pop songs, but for their own lives and work they are required to be technically avant-garde: new technical means of production and labor. Fine: so it is specifically technical, rather than aesthetic analysis that is the vehicle for their comprehension. The process of work and composition in the electronic studio, and the phonetic and semantic analysis of the text in relation to its becoming music, is easily understood by them. The sound-noise relationship, that is, the particular sound structure of acoustic phenomenon, does not represent the same problem, real or artificial, for them as it might for the mainly middle-class audience that is normally in concert halls.

Here is a constant in their reactions: "Listening to this music composed with our sounds-noises and with our words, we become aware of our alienated state in the factory. We work like mechanized robots, almost no longer realizing the violence of the human sound situation. Now we are rediscovering it and recovering awareness of it even through music."

The workers. Not mythologized but present in the actual reality of their intelligence, their great openness to learning, their exemplary responsibility in life, in the struggle, and in contemporary culture.

They are those who inspire, commission, and are recipients of revolutionary culture who are often not given enough consideration, due to the passivity that sometimes occurs in our cultural initiatives.

But the encounter with them, in Genoa, Reggio Emilia, and Trieste, although limited in number, is an extremely important indication to me and likewise provides answers to the questions, "Why write? For whom does one write?" It is much more significant than encounters with the various usual audiences of concert halls or festivals from which it is the workers who are objectively and subjectively excluded.

4. At times a distinction has been made among art for the revolution, art of the revolution, and revolutionary art.

I refer especially to the great prerevolutionary Russian period and to the Soviet cultural explosion of the period of Lenin and Lunacharsky, the starting point for almost all subsequent European artistic experiences, and unfortunately still insufficiently known, studied, and made known.

Of course, as then, revolutionary art requires a truly revolutionary party, in a situation that is objectively and subjectively revolutionary. The choice, the decision, the cultural rigor, the expressive technique of the musician, painter, and poet, are necessary, like those of the politician.

5. Tradition is a blackmail argument used only by academics and bureaucrats. They use it against innovations that are sometimes initially not really popular, also for the lack of ability and organizational and political intelligence.

Mayakovsky teaches, "Art is not born art of the masses. It becomes that as a result of a sum of efforts:"[8] critical analysis to determine if its usefulness is permanent and effective; organized diffusion by the party and government apparatus in the event that this utility is demonstrated; rapid dissemination of the book among the masses; correspondence between the question raised in the book and its state of development among the masses; the better a book, the more it anticipates events.

Each of us discovers tradition, that is, points of reference, of learning, and of consideration that starting from today, from our problems in comparison with what has been, dialectically: from today to yesterday, from yesterday to today, in order to overcome our temporal condition.

Not only the Venetian school, above all Andrea and Giovanni Gabrieli, not only the Flemish musical civilization, Dufay, Josquin, and Ockeghem, not only the Squarcialupi codex nor just the great European musical history, but the study and comparative analysis of European, Asian, American, and African cultures. Japanese *noh, kabuki,* and *gagaku,* synagogue chants, Armstrong, Mingus, and Coltrane, Bantu songs, the gypsies of Andalusia, Gregorian chant, Mina and Rita Pavone, Landino, Indonesian and Javanese songs. From the highly varied Asian theater to the *happenings* of Kaprow, Oldenburg, and Dine (their function and character very different from those of their European imitators), Meyerhold, Mayakovsky, Tatlin, Piscator and Toller, Brecht, Schoenberg, and Dallapiccola. There is no end to the continual discovery of tradition, that is, from where and from whom we can learn, not scholastically in order to derive formulas or copy solutions from them, but to analyze and understand the mentality, the process of creative invention in various historical and exemplary moments.

6. In his Yalta memorandum about the problems of the socialist world, Comrade Togliatti writes, "The general impression is that of a slowness and resistance in returning to the Leninist norms that insured, within the Party and outside it, a wide liberty of expression and debate on cul-

ture, art and also on politics. This slowness and resistance is for us difficult to explain, above all in consideration of the present conditions when there is no longer capitalist encirclement and economic construction has had tremendous successes." And he adds, "A fact worrying us, and one we do not succeed in explaining fully, is the manifestation among the Socialist countries of a centrifugal tendency. In this lies an evident and serious danger with which the Soviet comrades should concern themselves. Without doubt there is a revival of nationalism."[9] Since 1958 I have had various regular meetings with young musicians of the Czechoslovak, Polish, Hungarian, Soviet, Romanian, Cuban, and Chinese popular republics. I could see the rightness of Togliatti's concerns in them. Difficulties of cultural development and bureaucratic delays on the one hand; delays of knowledge and information, substituted by improvised and superficial updating (sometimes compromises) that instead requires time for development in favor of an invention that is neither an imitation nor in some way "provocative."

And also in the art world I have noticed symptoms of those contradictions within socialist countries, concerning which Lenin, Stalin, and Mao Zedong rightly theorized about the continuity of the class struggle even after the conquest of power by the working class.

In the Soviet Union it seems that young musicians are much more rooted in social reality, that is, that the economic and political transformation that occurred there has been more noticeable and decisive in music as well than in other socialist countries.

Notwithstanding the persistence of bureaucratic difficulties that, even though they are declining, nevertheless tend to limit young composers' contact with the public—therefore mistakenly causing unnecessary resentment and confusion which naturally affects them in their work—as far as I know, it is possible to speak of four cities or the beginnings of schools with musical tendencies distinct from one another, even in the current overcoming of verifiably local characteristics: Moscow (Denisov, Shchedrin, Volkonsky, Karetnikov, Schnittke) with the decisive presence of Gennady Rozhdestvensky, the splendid new conductor, to whom young composers already owe a lot; Kiev (Silvestrov, Blazhkov); Leningrad (Tishchenko, Slonimsky, Salmanov); and Tallinn (Pärt, Rääts).[10]

These is all information that is limited to what I know so far. Certainly during my next trip to the USSR I will be able to meet other young composers and get a better idea of the new developments in the musical situation, both in terms of creativity and formal, aesthetic and technical analysis. Such developments were evident in the presentations and the discussions held at the Union of Composers in Moscow during the annual musicians' meeting—in February, if I remember correctly.

In the various meetings I was always struck by the limited information and the lack of relationships among the young composers of the various socialist countries: objective or subjective isolation? or bureaucratic, despite the various existing unions of composers and their official meetings?

Especially if one considers that the multiple initiatives by instrumental groups who would perform new music, particularly in Czechoslovakia, should facilitate, indeed foster, regular, wide-ranging, and direct contact with the musical situations in development today.

One brief opportunity for such a gathering is offered by the annual music festival in Warsaw, which could also be taken as a model for reinvention with other methods in other countries. I personally had the opportunity there to meet and strike up a friendship with Manuel Duchesne Cuzán, conductor of the National Symphony Orchestra of Havana, who told me about Cuban musical developments that are of great interest and of which too little is known. I also met with Huan Ho-Tang, deputy director of the Beijing conservatory: other information about a different musical life—teaching, courses, and experiences—of which we are almost completely ignorant. I met with the young Romanian composers Stroe, Olah, and Niculescu, still other musical situations that are in full development, and these also almost unknown.

It is to be hoped, and as far as possible encouraged, that the difficulties still in existence will be overcome and especially by virtue of the validity and quality of the new music and its dissemination in such a way that it will be possible to get to know about the fantastic human and technical development of the socialist countries also through the young composers. Another thing that struck me is a certain type of Catholic position emerging in Poland and to a limited extent in Czechoslovakia, one that involves strict orthodox and conformist observance, also conservative on a technical and musical level and strangely distant from positions that move with history and that also exist on the cultural left of Catholicism (I am thinking of Dallapiccola and P. Teilhard de Chardin), and that might be expected in socialist countries. Undoubtedly, the issue is more complex and involves other considerations.

In my opinion electronic studios, which represent a necessary and fundamental stage in experimental and creative preparatory musical study, should undergo greater development in socialist countries. From democratic [East] Berlin to Pilsen, Warsaw, Bratislava, and Moscow, they should receive greater impetus, overcoming the simplistic objections of those who see in them only a functional means of expressing catastrophes and disasters. The electronic studio greatly extends the knowledge, perception, and intelligence of acoustic phenomenon in a new creative, compositional, and human dimension, whether limited to materials of electronic origin or instrumental, vocal, or concrete materials.

7. For me, the freest and most powerful musical instrument is the human voice, free or freed from any a priori and artificial scale, extraordinary for its great technical, phonetic, and semantic richness, infinitely broader than the dichotomy between speech and song.

Even *bel canto* uses only part of the technical and acoustic possibilities of the voice, also as rhythmic speech and *Sprechgesang* do.

A comparative analytical study of the various conformations of the vocal apparatus in itself (for example, Japanese and Italian), in relation to the phonetics of the various languages spoken, in the various physical-acoustic techniques of voice emission would be very significant. What is also clearly fundamental is the comparative study of the use of the voice in different societies, cultures, and customs. For years I have been doing this, using texts on acoustical physics, written and live musical texts—Japanese, Indian, of Andalusian gypsies, of various synagogues, especially in the USSR and Poland, some African peoples, of the French *ars antiqua* and *nova,* and European vocal music up to the various ways of speaking today (Verdi, Mussorgsky, Bartók, Janáček, and Schoenberg teach us, naturally): for example, how the sound environment of work influences the speech of the workers even in their daily and family life.

A group of workers at the San Giorgio shipyard in Genoa gave me a demonstration of this that is proving very useful in my current preparation of a new music theater work.[11]

In the long period of experiments and research that preceded the composition of *A floresta é jovem e cheja de vida* at the Studio di Fonologia at Radio Milan, I was able to study certain technical procedures of processing and composition using the emission of phonemes and words by a number of actors and actresses: particular ways of using the microphone in recording, simultaneous intervention on the voice with the third-octave variable filter, the subsequent processing with a dynamic modulator, with variable speed control, with square-wave oscillators, and other means as well.

Starting live with phonemes or words or pure singing, my intention was to study the possibility of transformation and expansion of the simple raw material of the voice with immediate and mediated interventions, in sound structures that were made increasingly more complex until they became "noise." That is, to study the possibility of a wide technical and expressive arc of sound material based on one and the same material, specifically in order to realize the many gradations within both singing and speech, as well as the gradual autonomous stages between singing and speech, in order to overcome and broaden their schematic contrast.

For me it is a field still to be discovered and invented, in part already realized in *A floresta é jovem e cheja de vida,* but above all decisive for my next work, tempted as I am to base it all on the human voice.[12]

Venice, September 23, 1966[13]

4

Music and Power

1969

I

In 1959 in Darmstadt, during the Internationale Ferienkurse für Neue Musik, I gave a lecture entitled "Historical Presence of Music Today."[1] (And that was the beginning of a painful ostracism toward me on the part of young composers, with whom there had been until then a relationship of friendship, dialogue, and discussion.) It began like this:

> Today the governing tendency in both the creative and the critical-analytical spheres is an unwillingness to place an artistic-cultural phenomenon in its historical context. In other words, an unwillingness to consider it in relation to its origins and the elements that have formed it, not in relation to its role within the present reality and its effect on it, nor in relation to its ability to project into the future, but exclusively in and of itself, as an end in itself, and only in relation to that precise moment in which it occurs. Not only is it refused any integration in history, but, indeed, history itself is rejected, along with its evolutionary and constructive process.

And further on:

> those who delude themselves that, in this way, they can inaugurate a new era *ex abrupto*, a program in which everything should be new. They would like in this way to create a highly expedient way of establishing themselves automatically as both the beginning and the end, as a gospel.

It was the year in which the influence of John Cage had made itself felt in the Western European musical world in such an uncritical way (and not coincidentally in West Germany, politically and financially supported by the United States, which proposed its own model and guide for the development of industrial capitalism as an exemplar of its kind, corresponding fully to the interests and imperialist strategies of the Western world). Indeed, it was being praised as the road "of liberation."[2]

John Cage is an undoubtedly interesting expression of that specifically North American line that leads to him from Ives through Cowell, Ruggles, and the early Antheil. However, his demystification of "bourgeois" musical myths and rituals and his intuition concerning other acoustic materials were and are inhibited by a lack of a new perspective on the social function of music, by an absence of historical-scientific analysis of both material and compositional principles, and by an irresponsible neglect of a conscious relationship between artist and society (hence an active or passive, yet not disinterested, choice). These are further obstructed by the *objective* obstacles of a culture—the North American one—that imposes a pragmatic terroristic wall, all the more so if disguised as a so-called "Alliance for Progress,"[3] and the *subjective* obstacles for those who lack the eyes, the mind, or the energy to breach this wall, instead amusing themselves within own private safe havens which are vaguely anarchist or openly reactionary, even involving references to thoughts and observations of German medieval mystics or of certain wise men of the Chinese Celestial Empire (making them absolutely contrary to history itself, both those of the Chinese people and of humanity's revolutionary process),[4] using them to prop up ideas and practices of alleged liberation, of supposed knowledge, reduced to speculation; safe havens easily interchangeable and containable within the confines of "new frontiers."[5]

(Santo Domingo, Guatemala, the Playa Girón,[6] Vietnam, and the repression of blacks together testify to the actions of the various U.S. foundations, including USIS,[7] and to their all-pervasiveness, their corruption and cultural depredations based on the ability to blackmail with new and wide-ranging economic and technological opportunities that are totally subservient to particular imperialist interests. Recently, the latest—in 1969—the "Art and Technology Program" promoted by the Los Angeles County Museum, thanks to which, by means of the involvement of twenty-six major companies including American Cement [Corporation], Lockheed Aircraft Corporation, Bank of America, 20th Century Fox, IBM, Kaiser Steel Corp[oration], and the Jet Propulsion Laboratory—the structures of big capital and the concrete work of the artist are becoming ever more closely connected.[8] And Oldenburg will work for Walt Disney, Rauschenberg—friend and collaborator of John Cage—in the electronics industry, Vasarely at the research center of San José, Dubuffet at the American Cement Company—up to now there have been no invitations for musicians. This reveals how the more the number of commissions from big capital grows—and with it, the direct subordination of artists by means of the enormous quantity of the resources put at their disposal for use in the service of up-to-date techniques—the more we recognize the immaturity of the critical discourse on the actual relationship between artist and society. And this reveals how and where the proponents of this so-called "artistic freedom" *logically* stand, namely in a place where they can prop up those political and economic interests and forces.)

The assumption of Cagean models on the part of many young European composers began in 1959 in true neoclassical fashion. Rather than studying and analyzing them in order to understand *a moment* of a particular society (comparative study, critical knowledge should be extended as far as possible both to the past and the present in order to know and be able to intervene in history with an active critical conscience and a responsible decision-making choice) they took abstract schemes and processes divorced from their original context, from their determined meaning and function, and *pasted* them to mindsets and processes that were historically quite different, and with a subjection and a passive acquiescence of the cultural-imperialist type: just like new indigenous they submitted to and accepted the imposition of a "more civilized idea of freedom," that of the new Opus Dei, arrived in Western Europe with the domination, capital, and sphere of influence of North America.

In a society still dominated by the private ownership of the means and relations of production, where one still has to live (striving for any possible new perspective of meaning, application, and function), there is no critical assimilation or use of anything objectively positive contained within a phenomenon, a sign, a scientific-cultural study emerging in the society itself—but only a mere clothing, as in Aimé Césaire's *Roi Christophe*.[9]

(One thinks of the clothing that was applied, in a similar way, to the pedantic German thinking and mindset of Stockhausen: an extreme case.)

These are the real terms on which, in Darmstadt in 1959, I questioned the influence of John Cage on Western European music.

And I did not, as Mauricio Kagel incorrectly argues in his recent interview in the *Nuova Rivista Musicale Italiana* journal (no. 3, 1969),[10] presume to banish Cage and Kagel himself (!!!) from Darmstadt thanks to my alleged spirit of "intolerance" (and what powers would I have had then to do so???) and "because they didn't write twelve-tone or serial music." I always find it hard to understand why one should be saying to others things that were never said, unless for the sake of facile polemics or even misrepresentation. I remind Kagel that I have never "demanded" the exclusion of anyone from Darmstadt.[11] I had always advocated to my friend Steinecke, as far as I could, the need to invite young musicians and to have them perform at the Ferienkurse. Bussotti can testify, regarding himself, to the occasion of a meeting at my house in Venice, at which Metzger was present. That the paths and the positions between us have been clarified in different ways, that our discussions have become open controversies, that our controversies have caused enmity and hostility—this has affected each one of us, without exception, but any "intolerance" related to the interests and organizational power of various musicians connected to official musical organizations, especially in West Germany, is not my responsibility.[12]

One would have to analyze the role that this so-called advanced music criticism, both the German and that of the satellite nations, including Italy, has played and continues to play in this process of Cagean involution; the decisive influence of Adorno's thought in the void created particularly in West Germany through cultural misinformation brought about in the wake of the criminal void that the Nazis had caused, the various federal governments also being complicit in this. Suffice it to say that in West Germany the first complete reprints of Marxist texts, essential for the understanding and development of a new method of analysis, criticism, and contemporary thought, date back to 1961; that one has got no further than a kind of left Hegelianism (Adorno and Horkheimer keeping themselves up-to-date yet limiting themselves to a North American liberal sociology); that in the GDR, even with the happy results produced in the economy and in school, there has remained a lack of sources of information for the study of German culture before Nazism thanks to the ruling cultural bureaucracy. It likewise suffices to say that everything was and is exploited, in West Germany, in terms of liberal enlightenment at best, sharply anti-Marxist and anticommunist (from Bloch to the current rediscovery of Korsch), in order to understand how the so-called advanced German criticism, and its Italian adjuncts, was and is still oscillating, at best, among a neopositivism, a liberal sociologism, a statistical phenomenology, right up to "John Cage, or Liberated Music,"[13] displaying a direct communality of interests with the most advanced official bodies.

It must be said that only in Italy did a Marxian method of new musical study, analysis, and criticism was being developed, thanks to a composer, Giacomo Manzoni, and a critic, Luigi Pestalozza, who were both quickly isolated and all but ignored, deliberately, in the world of Western music.

But just such a situation would require a study of its own, which is not my purpose at this moment.

II

Ten years after my lecture in Darmstadt.

Today in the Western world the whole relationship between music, politics, and social commitment has been deliberately interrupted from various positions, each of which represents an active or passive, yet not disinterested, choice. Roughly, one can define five positions in the current debate, and one of them seeks to pose, though I would not say to resolve, the question.

The first position, which can be attributed to Pierre Boulez, declares that no relationship is possible between music and revolution. If the musician wishes to partake in revolution, then he should grab a rifle; when making music he should make music, according to the "objective" laws of his aesthetic. One can almost hear the "you are here to work and not do politics" of the Fascist era;[14] one can also almost hear the capitalist claim that the factory worker has to give his best, and shut up—strict observance of the capitalist division of labor typically imposed by special interests—and do it well. It is no coincidence that Boulez, even though he demonstrated social commitment especially at the time of the Algerian War, signing the Manifesto of the 121 along with Sartre,[15] went off to conduct the New York Philharmonic for three years, which is the most official of the official bodies of American culture.

The second position may be attributed to Mauricio Kagel: it takes account of 1968, but inverts the discussion. According to Kagel, only culture can cause revolution. This is because the working class is integrated, the peasants no longer exist, and it is pointless to engage with socially unproductive forces. It is rather the score, inasmuch as it constitutes an advanced technical product, which in itself plays out the explosive contradictions of mature capitalism. To break up the language means to put oneself as such in a revolutionary position. Which is another way to separate oneself from the struggle, to place oneself on an aesthetic testing ground that is perfectly acceptable to the most educated bourgeoisie. What is ultimately achieved, in the name of a badly—or all too well—interpreted Adornism, and an elementary conception of the working class and relationships of exploitation, is a reestablishment of the position of privilege and the practical isolation of the intellectual. Of Argentine origin, Kagel is now completely installed on the scene of official West German culture, whose Adornian "left" theorizes these very ideas. All this testifies to a very strange way of interpreting 1968, one that is closely conditioned by an outdated sociological analysis that is typically North American. First of all, it is not true that the working class is integrated everywhere. The tradition and the current reality of the struggles of workers and peasants in Italy and in France illustrate exactly the opposite. Even if they have been weakened and inactive, in Turin, in Milan, in Mestre-Marghera,[16] in Naples, in Genoa, in Pisa—to mention a few places where the workers' struggle continues—the spirit and the struggle of the working class is very much alive and, as in France, constitutes the true historical reality of the country. The progressive intellectual, if he wants to be progressive, will *participate*, and not simply associate himself with it. (I know from personal experience that this kind of participation is difficult to understand in West German cultural circles. Misinformation runs deep; the historical knowledge of the Italian tradition of antifascist and anticapitalist struggle in the unified action of workers and intellectuals—Gramsci—is minimal; the terms of the Italian class struggle are distorted by a mechanistic comparison with the dormant German working class. The relationship between the intellectual and the class struggle, active in Italy, is inconceivable or envisioned as a romantic-populist dream. The intellectual, rather than acting as a tool and an active voice for the political and cultural hegemony of the class struggle, makes at best populist claims to enlighten the people.)

Nineteen sixty-eight has shown that in countries such as the United States and West Germany, where the working class is integrated, except in rare cases, there are other social factors (economic and structural ones in the United States: the blacks, "Black Power," "Black Panthers"—cultural superstructures in Germany, students, the SDS, the ASTA, the APO),[17] who undertake to shake up and fight against the structures of the system, reviving the class struggle by other means.

It is no coincidence that Malcolm X was assassinated when he had understood—and begun acting accordingly—the close unity between the struggle of blacks in the United States and the liberation struggle of the peoples of Africa and Latin America. It is no coincidence that SDA students have formed groups to study and work within the German working class, convinced of the need that workers awake in order to complete the struggle against capitalist structures.

The working class may be integrated, but there are other social groups that will be or are replacing it, the blacks in the United States, or those who are fighting for its awakening.[18]

Of all this the composer Kagel has not the slightest idea, and he feels "necessary" to the German bourgeois world (his interview with the Italian magazine *Lo spettatore musicale*).[19]

A third position may be attributed to Stockhausen: technology as a value, a theory of painless technological-aesthetic evolution, a natural connection with the locations of the most advanced technical production, namely the United States and the West, an aristocratic contempt for all other cultures, and let's not even talk about the so-called Third World. (See his open letter to youth—published in the *Frankfurter Allgemeine* of August 22, 1968, in which he invites young people: "Let's stop thinking that it is a question of a French, Vietnamese, Czech, Russian, or African revolution.")[20]

It is perhaps the most consistent capitalist or neocapitalistic ideological position. I would call it even imperialist in its exaltation of scientific-technical evolution, seemingly abstract but instead claiming to represent a unique moment of truth closely connected with the development of the great technical power of the United States and West Germany, without the slightest critical consideration of the fact that "for every dollar that comes back to the USA there are four dead in Latin America," as the Second Declaration of Havana puts it.[21] In other words, there is no critical awareness of the possible cost of this technical development in terms of economic exploitation and plunder. This is a truly imperialist Eurocentric way of imposing a "superior" culture and civilization, especially in African and Latin American countries, thanks to the interests and actions of those complicit intellectuals. (The cultural congress in Havana, January 1968, clearly denounced this imperialist operation.)

What sense, then, can there be in speaking about new acoustic space, new environments, a new psychology of listening, of new techniques, of *höherer Mensch* [higher man] unless they are related to new human social structures no longer based on exploitation or neocapitalist or neocolonial domination, in a word socialist structures, or at least tending toward them? (in which socialism is to be created truly on the ground, and not by mechanically reproducing historically limited models, when what is needed is analytical-critical knowledge).

I remember, on my first trip to Latin America in 1967, a Bolivian music student of great intelligence, Florencio Posadas (who later died tragically). While objectively recognizing his need to gain knowledge and experience in an electronic studio, he refused the cultural imperialist blackmail of one of the many U.S. foundations. Instead he studied other original musical means and techniques that were possible in his social environment (including a phonetic-semantic use of the Quechua language of the Indians) and in this refusal and this choice he discovered how his own condition as a musician was necessarily linked to the armed struggle for the liberation of his country.[22]

The fourth position is that of certain leftist groups, who argue that, since each language is derived from the bourgeoisie, there is no possible art or cultural production that does not carry this cursed seal. Therefore, culture is not possible until after the revolution. This ends with offering yet another alibi to the musician. Since he is not able even to consider the problem of an intrinsic link with the revolution, he either continues to make music as before, or he stops, more or less undisturbed.

From this there also follows a deep distrust of culture, even one that claims to be leftist or revolutionary. What is more, this is especially true in West Germany, where the experience of the great cultural phase that preceded Hitlerism is probably a major factor. Before 1933, German revolutionary intellectuals enjoyed a season that was unparalleled in the rest of Europe. Yet it was of no use in the face of Nazism. This means that young people today do not believe in any possible role for the intellectuals other than a purely "technical" one in the service of the revolution. So they end up ignoring the fact that it was precisely the culture prior to Hitlerism which theorized and had a "social practice" of its own: the culture of *agit-prop,* the relationships with the workers' councils. These are all issues that we would do well to reexamine and in relation to which the GDR could and should make significant contributions. Right now, they seem only to have a negative effect or even to be at the root of the current impasse facing revolutionary culture in West Germany.

The fifth position, to which I myself subscribe, is that of attempting culture as a moment of awareness, of struggle, of provocation, of discussion, of participation. It involves the critical use of historical tools and languages, received or invented. It also involves a rejection of any Eurocentric conception through which Europe, in raising the flag of "superior" Western civilization, sees itself as a mandate from the God of Capital, or else an aristocratic conception of culture and language. Finally, it involves a working method based on verifying itself together with the social forces, before, during, and after.

Before, to understand who one is, where one is, what and how and why one chooses an area of work—namely, how one becomes a communist (Brecht used to say that one isn't one, one becomes one). *During,* to understand how and from which "point of view" one writes and is connected with whom and why and for whom. *After,* to verify the result by giving it a different form of dissemination, and a different form of consumption by a different audience, to whom one offers, and from whom one receives, provocation and participation. A culture no longer to be bestowed paternalistically, but to be tested out on a new social fabric. This is what I intend by making music: something to which I am committed in a way that is no different from participating in a demonstration or in a clash with the police, or as could be the case tomorrow, in the armed struggle.[23]

But this much is certain, that this isolates me from the music "power," more and more gridlocked on an international scale, ever more closely linked to the means of production of big capital; from whose attraction even musicians of the socialist countries cannot escape, such as a Penderecki, a Pole, who gets subsidized by American foundations in Berlin or who thinks nothing of working for a new organization of Latin American culture in Venezuela (a country which is a nerve center for the U.S. economy, heroically engaged in armed struggle for its liberation) on the initiative of the OAS which manages the cultural blackmail of big U.S. capital.[24]

III

But it is equally certain, that new subjective and objective horizons of responsibility, relationships, commitment, and work are opening up for me, so that even the maximum restrictions imposed by the institutionalized musical "powers" cause no recriminations in me whatsoever.

It is natural that each of the five positions described above involves different interests, criteria, judgments, and spaces. In fact, the first four can even mutually permeate one another, true alliances.

It is natural, therefore, that the various critical, polemical, or hostile positions taken toward me, repeatedly and variously expressed for example by Stockhausen, Kagel, Berio (and even Maderna), whenever they are in Italy and find a complacent and self-satisfied space for radio or official journal interviews, can be put into perspective again if traced back to their interests, to their criteria of judgment, and thus to their respective aesthetic-social base.

It is curious how a musician (Stockhausen), a publisher (Schott's Söhne), and almost the totality of German concert organizations all coincide in their judgment, in their interests, and in their rejection of my work, blocking it, more or less since 1958, a year before my lecture at Darmstadt. This was the period when my development of the relationship between technique and ideology was deepening, eluding ever more objectively the habit of understanding my musical presence at the Ferienkurse in a gratuitously partial way. This was shortly before the start of those compositions realized at the Studio di Fonologia in Milan, involving a different kind of electronic equipment and different aesthetic and social concerns, and the ever-growing conflict with my publisher up until the break in 1966, when it refused all my new electronic work.[25]

It is also curious how these new examples of a reversed Zhdanovism base their overall negative judgment toward me almost exclusively on the subject-matter of the works, on their texts (Nono is "political" and therefore: "bad music") ignoring or falsifying or being intolerant for their own convenience toward a different compositional practice. The use of voices is fundamental for me; for example the use of voices in themselves and in relation to the different texts in different languages in *A floresta é jovem e cheja de vida*. That is, voices not limited to phonetic games or psychic abstractions, which today appear vainly academic, but rather involved in the continuous practical research of new possibilities for the emission and articulation of sound, conducted for years with a group of young people with whom I work and with whom I create and perform my recent compositions—from *A floresta* to *Contrappunto dialettico alla mente* to *Musica-Manifesto n. 1: Un volto, e del mare—Non consumiamo Marx*, in a direct relationship with the particular characteristics of the individual phonetic-semantic-ideological components of the chosen texts: for the sixth episode of *A floresta*—last words exchanged between the South Vietnamese partisan Nguyen Van Troy—before his assassination in Saigon—to his companion Phan Thi Quyen,[26] first, we studied together the particular melodic and rhythmic inflections of the South Vietnamese language, then the individual phrases in light of their human and ideological significance, then various exercises involving the different appropriate musical qualities using the "voices" in my group (I remember the soprano Liliana Poli—actresses Kadigia Bove, Elena Vicini—and the actor Berto Troni), then together we found the technical approach and the right expression of meaning. For the seventh episode, we used a quotation from the Second Declaration of Havana. Together we studied particularly the inflections of the voice of Fidel Castro and the Cuban people, a study then carried further and directly verified on the ground during my two trips through Cuba, the first free territory in America. Simply comparing these two episodes is enough to understand and be able to analyze what I am attempting in my compositional practice as regards the relationship between voice and text: a text, however, that is not limited to a literal, naturalistic use, but is confronted in its internal linguistic structure in the living of its "life." Another example: my concept of time, no longer based on scansion or traditional metric subdivision or schematically played out with various serial parameters (as still happens in the majority of contemporary music practice), but in the continuous evolution of fluctuations (*panta rei*) of sound fields and sound bands, since *Incontri* for twenty-four instruments (1955). Example: *Per Bastiana—Tai-Yang Cheng* (1967): in its use of fluctuating harmonic structures (one instrumental group) based on chromatic intervals, taken from the Chinese folk song *The East is Red,* on subdivisions of the tone (from quarter tones onward) in two other instrumental groups, and the superimposition of various contiguous frequencies processed on magnetic tape.[27]

It is natural that if one does not study and analyze my compositional practice, including its relationship between technique and ideology, but remains conditioned by traditional and nowadays conservative beliefs concerning either technique or the ideological moment that *becomes music,* one falsifies and equivocates my active position as a musician who is totally engaged in the current political struggle.

5

In the Sierra and in the Parliament

1971[1]

To write about Cuba, of its continuous unstoppable revolutionary socialist process, of its continual continental militancy, means now more than ever to write about the *unarmed and armed* liberation struggle, the first of which does not exclude the second because the struggle can, out of necessity, become armed (as Chilean comrades affirm). This is what is taking place in Latin American countries in opposition to the imperialism and neocapitalism of the United States, the criminal presence of the CIA, and the national oligarchies closely associated with them. The fight for *socialism*, in an extremely arduous and bloody class struggle representing the political qualitative leap today, clearly significant for the struggle itself. The recent testimony of comrade Volodia Teitelboim,[2] of the Chilean Communist Party, illustrates this continental unity between socialist Cuba and other countries when he was speaking before Commander Fidel Castro on the tenth anniversary of the Cuban victory at Playa Girón,[3] celebrated in Havana on April 19, he declared, "We are aware that if Cuba had not begun the process of opening up to socialism in our countries, the revolutionary outcome for the people of Chile would not have been conceivable. Because without your triumph at Playa Girón, we would never have achieved the victories of September 4, 1970 and April 4, 1971"[4] (the two election victories through which the Unidad Popular were elected to government with President Salvador Allende and began the struggle for the conquest of power and the socialist transformation of Chile).[5]

Also, precisely, to write about the new Chilean revolutionary process does not mean that one should consider Chile as an island, or worse as a "peaceful model" that rejects armed struggle, but should understand it, again in the words of Volodia Teitelboim, "as inscribed in the context of the world revolutionary process. It is also a sign of how America is living through a moment, an explosive and volcanic period, which confirms the historical direction begun twelve years ago by glorious Cuba."[6] In this Latin America, the assassinations of "Che" Guevara, "Inti" Peredo, and Carlos Marighella,[7] while constituting a serious blow to the movement, have given rise in a positive way to a new consciousness of the struggle for *socialism,* for a new *socialist* organization, and for a new *socialist* strategy within individual countries and among them, as comrades in Chile, Peru, Venezuela, and Mexico, as well as in Cuba itself, confirmed to me during my recent trip. Let's consider: the extraordinary action of the Tupamaros in Uruguay and their support for the Frente Amplio (quite distinct from the Chilean Unidad Popular) formed for the upcoming November elections,[8] over which looms the possibility of interventions by a coup and the United States; in Argentina the spontaneous action of the workers in Cordoba and Rosario and that of the liberation movements (MRA, FAR, ERP);[9] in explosive Bolivia the ever more unified struggle of the miners, workers, peasants, and students; in Brazil the ongoing reorganization en masse of the various movements, up until now also isolated from one another; in Colombia the new organization of peasant and student armed struggle; in Venezuela the student militancy (in Caracas, the university was occupied and closed for months by the police, and in other university cities violent demonstrations and clashes with the police have occurred, with many dead, providing "impetus to the struggle that the Venezuelan people have decided is crucial: the battle and the victory against neocolonial dependency, against the antinational order imposed through the power of imperialist capital and the complicity of the 'national' capitalists"— as Alfredo Chacón, professor of sociology and anthropology at the University of Caracas, writes), and the continuous worker strikes and the new strategy—association with the masses—adopted by the armed movement of Douglas Bravo.[10] All this to name just a few new situations.

Today more than ever it is clear how, even in Latin America, U.S. imperialism finds itself in very serious difficulty (and the Chileans, Uruguayans, Bolivians, and the Cubans themselves are consciously concerned and anticipating new and more or less covert intervention by the

United States and the CIA—as was evident too in the latest provocation, the assassination of former Minister Zujovic,[11] meant to cause difficulties and worse for the Chilean government). There is a clear need for practical militant solidarity among the movements, country and country and continent and continent. Unity on the common basis of *class struggle* and not a generic "national and patriotic" anti-imperialism, which simply generates contradictions that are likely to be radicalized and explode, especially if the movement of popular struggle imposes class objectives beyond and contrary to the apparent "revolutionary" objective of capitalist restructuring sought even by groups of advanced neocapitalists.

In the case of Peru, contradictions are encountered mostly within capital: state control sought by the military government over domestic and international capital and the promotion of national investments to prevent their exportation, undermines the interests of the traditional capitalist groups. In fact, the departure, at the end of April, of the Peruvian government's Minister of Industry and Trade Dellepiane, a proponent of the new law for the industrial community—neither capitalist nor communist—and of state control, can be explained by the pressure of the SNI (National Industry Society), an organization linked to the U.S. opposition and the consequent limits it imposed on its investments: 80 percent of the capital of the Peruvian industrial bourgeoisie is North American. The attempt by the Peruvian military junta to numb the working class precisely by means of the industrial community law, even making it a partner through the acquisition of collective shares, has failed: strikes and the wage struggle and are increasing. Compared to the twenty miners' strikes in 1969, in 1970 there were seventy strikes. Next month in July there will be a wage dispute involving twenty-five thousand workers in the mines of central Morococho, owned by the Cerro de Pasco Corporation, supported by a common platform of fifteen trade unions. The company has already ruled out any negotiation. A political conscience is developing among the miners to expel the U.S. enterprise. This struggle will have the country's solidarity behind it. On May 5–6, the five thousand workers of the SIMA (an industrial maritime services firm for shipbuilding) went on strike in defense of their manager, who was fired. They staged a march to Lima, and there were clashes with the Civil Guard—the infamous instrument of repression—three hundred were arrested. The government intervened: whoever did not work during the strike was fired. (Another case of government repression accelerating the process of the politicization of the masses.) Between December 1970 and March 1971, the agricultural workers of the Huando company, with approximately five thousand hectares seventy kilometers from Lima with a very high index of fruit production and owned by the oligarchic Graña Elizalde family, organized a 110-day strike against the parceling out of land that occurred among family members and friends of the owners instead of the workers, in accordance with the land reforms. Together with the unions and with the support and participation of the students of the Department of Agriculture, they organized a march to Lima. Clashes occurred with the Civil Guard. The government intervened, declaring the land distribution void on the basis of "irregularities of formal procedure," but it did not redistribute the land to the workers, who were demanding the formation of cooperatives.

After 1968, the Civil Guard occupied the Faculty of Engineering in Lima (around five thousand students) and repeatedly with repressive interventions and confrontations. Students accused of being political agitators were expelled from the engineering faculty and also from the faculty of agriculture. The student reaction is not a mass one; its political consciousness is weak. During their vacations, the students organized voluntary work among the peasants, despite the opposition of the government. One now understands the need to unify the struggle among the students, workers, and peasants. These have been some recent episodes of contradictions manifested in the action of the military government, whose reformist policies conflict with certain U.S. interests, at the same time they are not based on the interests of the masses, and in their top-down authoritarianism and their proclamation of social choice, neither capitalist nor communist, are achieving just what they didn't want: an awakening of consciousness of the class struggle in the miners, peasants, workers, and students, precisely because of the obvious developing contradictions in the reality of Peru today. And Fidel, after recognizing that "in the Peruvian process the motives of the struggle against underdevelopment, against the external control of its economy, prevail along with its strongly patriotic and nationalist sentiments," adds, "We saw that the imperialists are worried, and when the imperialists are worried about something or are against something, even when it concerns contradictions not totally revolutionary, we will not do any favors for the imperialists."[12]

In Bolivia, the minimal relevance of the bourgeoisie, whether it be large, medium, or small, makes all the more evident the political conflict between the oligarchy on the one hand and the worker, peasant, and student classes on the other. In the middle is the army with its internal disputes and the current military government with all its contradictions. When General Torres offered the workers participation in his government—50 percent of the ministries—the workers refused and responded by asking for control and management of the mines and control of the economy.[13] On International Labor Day the worker-peasant assembly was officially established—all elected by the working and peasant classes—the first symbolic example for Latin America. Given the current government and the paralysis of the "bourgeois democratic" parliament, this assembly has considerable power over decision making, and not merely an advisory role. In this country—which has undergone 187 coup d'états in 126 years—the working class has a long history of hard and bloody battles, especially the much politicized miners with their strong unions, repeatedly subjected to massacres. The military government of General Torres (we should not forget that he was one of the three generals who collaborated directly with the CIA in the assassination of "Che" Guevara) is caught between the ultrareactionary forces within the army itself and the oligarchy, and the ever stronger and more unified impulse toward struggle by the workers, peasants, and students. But how long will the United States on one side, and the popular movement on the other, allow this to go on? Conflict is inevitable; no one denies this. Also because, as the Venezuelan Pedro Duno—a FALN guerrilla commander and now a university professor—writes, "No country (as Bolivia) has had as many revolutionary victims as a result of the guerrilla struggle. Undoubtedly in no other country is the revolutionaries' awareness of the guerrilla struggle more alive. Ñancahuazú, Teoponte are not names of defeats but of steps forward on the path of revolution. In Bolivia, there is the very real possibility of a workers' state in the hands of workers, administered by workers, and led by workers."[14]

And from revolutionary Cuba, in his address on the tenth anniversary of the victory of Playa Girón, Fidel exclaimed:

> Bolivia, where "Che" and his comrades set their epic in motion. "Che" died, but his feelings remained in the heart of the Bolivian people, his ideas remained, his example remained. As a result of the struggle of "Che" and his heroic sacrifice, one encounters a profound radicalization in the masses of workers, peasants, and students of Bolivia. In Bolivia, therefore, there is a revolutionary, agitated and radicalized people who do not want make-believe and demand a radical revolution, a profound revolution, a real revo-

lution. In Bolivia it is the people who go down to the streets to combat the threats of a fascist coup d'état. It is the people who require those fascist elements still dressed in military uniform to be deprived of their responsibilities. It is the people who demand the condemnation of the cops, those responsible for the murders of miners, workers, peasants, and students. It is the people who demand the accountability of those complicit with the CIA in the repression, in the assassination of guerrillas and "Che." . . . In Bolivia there is a revolutionary process fostering radicalization and a remarkable rise of consciousness among the masses.[15]

In Chile, with comrade Allende's Unidad Popular government, one can discern clearly the motive for the recent assassination of former Minister Zujovic and who was behind it. Its aim, to the sole advantage of a reactionary right linked to U.S. imperialism, was to create trouble verging on chaos in a country that, with great political astuteness, conscious solidarity, and the involvement of the people, is advancing toward the transformation of economic and political structures in a way that will make socialism a reality. Much that is totally false continues to be written and claimed about an alleged internal disorder and a climate of hatred caused by the new government (including the mystifying delirium of Forlani, the secretary of the Christian Democrats).[16] It is clear that this disorder is instigated exclusively by large landowners, industrialists, and financiers who are sabotaging production, hindering agriculture, and bombarding the country with actual incitements toward hatred, toward rebellion against the government, by means of newspaper, radio, and television, the vast majority of which are still in their hands. They continue arms trafficking, especially from Argentina (some of the landed estates are on the border of Chile and Argentina), to arm bands of killers targeted against peasants occupying lands mainly in the south, and who are bent on criminal repression. No great insight is required to reveal their backers, given their existing capitalist ties: the United States, the ubiquitous CIA, and the Pentagon itself.

Aligned against these forces is the revolutionary resolve and the strong historical consciousness of the Unidad Popular government, which, since the takeover of the government, has moved toward the difficult conquest of power on behalf of socialism. This is an irreversible process because it came about through Chilean constitutional legitimacy and the increasing support and participation of workers, miners, peasants, students, and technicians with a genuine mobilization of the class struggle. And again Fidel, the continent's continuous revolutionary example, states:

We are wholeheartedly united with the Chilean people and are willing to do whatever is necessary for the Chilean people and are ready to demonstrate our solidarity in any field. Not to help: to fulfill the elementary duty of brothers, to fulfill the elementary duty of cooperation with the revolutionary peoples of Latin America! Blood (he refers here to the a hundred thousand Cuban blood donations to the Peruvian people affected by the earthquake), sugar, whatever is needed! But this is very little! There is in the hearts of the Cuban people an even deeper, decisive, and more fraternal feeling. Just as, when Playa Girón was invaded by the mercenaries, thousands of Chileans wanted to sign up to come and fight in Cuba, the Chileans can be assured that if they face external, imperialist-sponsored aggression, millions of Cubans are ready to come to fight in Chile. In the face of external aggression you may consider, as of now, all Cuban revolutionaries to be signed up to the cause.[17]

(And in response to this declaration of internationalist solidarity, newspapers and radio and television stations in the hands of the Chilean reactionaries orchestrated a violent and ridiculous campaign against Cuba, "Cuba is preparing to invade Chile.") In Chile, where workers administer and manage industries, production has increased. In the coal mines of Lota (in municipal elections there were 82 percent of votes in support of the government: a true plebiscite!) whose general manager is now comrade Isidoro Carrillo, until recently a *barretero*, a simple miner and unionist,[18] production in 1971 increased to four thousand metric tons per day compared to thirty-four hundred in 1970. For May (I was in Lota at the end of April) expectations were for forty-four hundred tons per day. For November forty-seven hundred tons, coming ever closer to the necessary production target of five thousand tons daily. There are industries managed by workers, such as the textile factory in Tomé, near Concepción. It is the working class that invents, creates new forms of management, even in the absence of experts. The workers are now finally no longer an object, but a conscious and organizing subject. This is the result of the long, violent struggle of the Chilean working class from the end of the nineteenth century right up to today, of which little or nothing is known in Italy. From 1903 to 1969, there were riots and joint efforts by workers and peasants with demands such as "land to the peasants," "factories to the workers." Continuous insurrections, followed by appalling massacres: in Valparaiso, in 1903, thirty deaths and two hundred injured, in Santiago in 1905, two hundred assassinated, in Santa Maria in 1907, two thousand massacred, in 1925 in Coruña, three thousand massacred, to name only a few, up to those that occurred under the government of the Christian Democrat Frei, who, after going for talks with Franco in Spain, was accepted and welcomed in Italy as a paragon of bourgeois liberalism.[19] To these revolts must be added those of the army, like that of 1931. The sailors of the battleship *Almirante Latorre* rebelled, and in the pampas where they disembarked they set up "high councils of sailors and workers." The slogans were "land to the peasants," "nationalization of the banks," "solidarity with the workers." In addition to showing solidarity with the workers and peasants, in Concepción part of the army actually joined with them, but it was crushed by the use of air power. Following this, three hundred were condemned to death, but the sentences were later commuted to life. (The Chilean army is totally distinct from other torturer-armies like those of Brazil and Guatemala, for example, and in addition to its fidelity to the constitution, it has strong potential for the development of class consciousness, given its social composition.) In the history of the Chilean working class the figure of Luis Emilio Recabarrén emerges as someone with fundamental importance. He was a great union organizer and a founder of the Chilean Communist Party in 1922 (it is essential that the writings of this prestigious fighter for the working class get published in Italy!).[20] That party is, as one of the main leaders of the MIR affirms with great respect,[21] "the legitimate child of the struggle of the Chilean working class." The Chilean Communist Party, together with the Socialist Party (of which Salvador Allende was one of the founders) is still Chile's authentic historical cornerstone, especially after the election of the socialist Carlos Altamirano as its general secretary.

Class consciousness is developing more and more among the peasants, especially in the South, in the region around Temuco, where land occupations are taking place, and around Valdivia, the area of the timber industry. Peasants extraordinary for their centuries of struggles, first against the Spanish, then against the landowners, are now providing full support and impetus to the government. The Mapuches ("Men of the land")[22] are organized by the MIR and the MCR,[23] by the Communist Party and the Socialist Party. (After the election, the MIR, showing considerable political responsibility, has changed its tactics: it supports the government and the new organizational relationships with the Communist Party and the Socialist Party that have been in place for months. It is well known that most of the personal guard of comrade President Allende is made up of militants of the MIR.)

The peasants want: a) to recover the land that was stolen first by the Spanish, then by landowners, b) to farm those areas that were left uncultivated due to the negligence of the landowners, using cooperative production methods, c) socialism. They want to join with the peasants from other areas of the country, with workers, and with miners. Of course there are often serious difficulties both within industries (the presence of U.S. capital—technicians paid in dollars—therefore discrepancies in the [peasants'] actions—pricing policies, etc.) as well as regarding the landholdings. These were inherited in bad conditions of exploitation. There is the need for agricultural machinery, seeds, and fertilizers, which the government and CORA have not available in great measure.[24] There are continuous armed attacks by the landowners themselves. But in response to all of this is the new sense of responsibility and the capacity to organize and distribute labor and products, which occupy the peasants and workers, aware that the land, industries, and the government belong to them.

Students and professors, especially those of the university, are fully active participants in Chile's new situation. Universities are coming out from behind their traditional walls, holding courses in the field, participating in the life, in the work, and in the struggle of the peasants and the workers. A new technical university for workers appeared in May in the mining area of Lota [and] Coronel: The board of administration and planning directly elected by the workers consists of one engineer, two technical staff, three support staff and six workers.

The University of Concepción and the technical institute of Valdivia have proved exemplary in this new role. The professors and students of these institutions organize genuine periods of study and work in the regions occupied by the peasants, like Neltume—a site of the timber industry—bringing their contribution, practicing and learning while participating in the life of the peasants. Another element that characterizes the reality and outlook of Chile is the participation within the government of the Catholic left of the Christian Democrats, the MAPU headed by Radomiro Tomic.[25] It is a Latin American constant that Catholics recognize within socialism the only way forward for the liberation of man, for a new society.

It is obvious that the right and part of the center are not reconciled to this mobilization and popular initiative in support of the government. Anything but. And even less so are the United States, the CIA, and the Pentagon. But to every possible intervention, the answer will be unique, continental, and Chilean, as Carlos Altamirano, secretary general of the Socialist Party, affirmed in his speech on the thirty-eighth anniversary of the founding of the Socialist Party, "It will be that of Playa Girón."[26]

(I have limited myself to providing information indicative of the situation in Peru, Bolivia, and Chile, because the three are often confused, being mystified or distorted at whim. Their situations are totally different, despite their unity of their struggle to varying degrees for socialism.)

Cuba. Cuba continues, revolutionary and socialist, in constant unity between the people, the government, and the party, in a continuous deepening of *its* characteristics, demonstrating a continuous and exemplary common ground and responsiveness with the political and cultural struggles of Latin America. Cuba is developing socialism in living conditions that are as harsh and *heroic* as are those of a country ninety miles from the center of imperialist aggression, continually the object of sabotage and infiltration by the CIA, but with an ever more determined mobilization of conscious mass participation in its own confirmation of socialism.

One should study Fidel's recent speeches for the anniversary of Playa Girón, to the Conference of Education, for the International Workers' Day. They should be studied carefully along with the Law of April 1st concerning the *vagancia*,[27] the final resolution of the Conference of Education, the renewal of the workers' union and its purpose, the continued mass participation of the worker, peasant, student, and teacher groups, the discussions about the various problems, difficulties, and limits of functionality or organization, with guidelines that are always constructive, based on real-life experiences, and leading to changes and innovations in the administrative, political, and cultural management of the country.

Whoever has ears, eyes, intelligence, and a heart open to socialism, not in adherence to principle nor uncritically (and not with the mechanistic superimpositions of other historical experiences or not blocked by subjective intellectual or libertarian visions, by which one measures or lends one's support to an ongoing process towards socialism according to its degree of "artistic liberality" in relation to the nonliberality of bourgeois society, rather than according to the specifics of *socialist liberty itself;* in other words, a thinking not inflated by an academic and old-style Eurocentric authoritarian pretension of having power to give grades with a blue pencil and distribute them with five for excellence and zero for conduct), whoever, in short, is a militant cannot fail to recognize:

a) the need for information and continual knowledge, if possible on the ground, of the revolutionary development taking place in the country in question, such as Cuba, not deformed or distorted by binoculars of various kinds, but actually in the time frames, the objective conditions, the objective issues, and the continual subjective intervention aimed at modifying both time frames and conditions in their specific reality rather than according to abstract models;

b) if critical moments or mistakes occur—which is always possible during a revolutionary process—the militant will discuss them and clarify them directly within the group itself, if he wishes to continue to participate in the movement rather than to use these moments for some absurd ambition to prove arguments based on individual resentment or personal interests. The final resolution of the Havana conference on education rightly maintained that "the critical conscience of society is the people themselves and in first place the working class, prepared by its historical experience and by revolutionary ideology, to understand and judge the actions of the revolution with greater lucidity than any other social sector. The condition of the intellectual does not authorize any privilege. His responsibility is to take part in this critique with the people and among the people. But for him it is necessary to share the concerns, sacrifices, and dangers of this people." (And the Padilla question is viewed still more in its correct proportions, an ambiguous question to say the least, and "counterrevolutionary" as Padilla himself has declared. I also had initially been confused and I acceded to the first letter on the matter, but I must admit that it is Latin America itself that has been the principal factor in making me understand and correct my serious cultural and political mistake, specifically with my statement made in Santiago, Chile in early May.)[28]

a) and b) may be elementary considerations, but it is necessary to reassert them because for years and especially in recent months a campaign of "interpretive" falsifications of "zeros for conduct" has been unleashed against Cuba even by tourist-intellectuals fond of the *tumbadores—claves—guïro—quijada de burro* (musical instruments) that used to accompany the political songs and demonstrations in Cuba for a number of years. These were then replaced by a heavily equipped army prepared, as Fidel says, "not only for our own sake, not only to defend our territory, not only to defend our homeland, but also to express our solidarity when necessary with the peoples of Latin America," and again "with regard to Latin America at the moment and when other fraternal revolutionary peoples ask for it: technical assistance, like technicians and soldiers! As the most sacred of duties: as combatants".[29]

Insane falsifications and fabrications, among which the most ridiculous and irresponsible are: a dispute between Fidel and Raúl and the oversimplification:[30] domestic economic difficulties—aid from socialist countries—compromises and Cuba's renunciation of solidarity in the Latin American struggle (accusations in which a clear prejudice or generalized anti-Soviet feeling can be discerned).

A campaign unleashed against Cuba, with the dangerous tendency toward isolating it even more, and with the United States not simply "looking on."

Briefly: since July 26, 1970, to take a specific date, at all social levels, mass participation in discussions, debates, and socialist innovations has become very widespread.[31] On the peasants' recommendation, the method of sugar cane harvesting has been modified (now it is burned, using less manpower and time), 82 percent of workers have joined the union, if I am not mistaken, and participate in ongoing meetings and discussions on industrial management. All teachers have addressed the issue of education in its various aspects at the education conference in late April: schools, books, families, transportation, work, media, and artistic creation, "Revolution frees art and literature from the iron mechanisms of supply and demand prevailing in bourgeois society. Art and literature cease to be merchandise and create every possibility for expression and experimentation in their various manifestations based on ideological rigor and a high degree of technical qualification"; "that the masses be creators"; "that cultural creation be the work of the masses and enjoyed by the masses"; "our enhancement is political."[32]

In his speech of April 19th, which was of great international importance, Fidel continued, "Cuba maintains its same position, that of the Sierra Maestra, Playa Girón, that of all the moments. The first declaration of Havana and the second declaration of Havana. Cuba maintains its position of support for revolutionary governments as well as support for revolutionary movements in Latin America." And, citing the determination of the entire Cuban people, he focuses on Chile, Bolivia, Uruguay, Argentina, Brazil, Peru, Mexico, Santo Domingo, Guatemala, Arab and African countries, Korea, Vietnam, the Indochinese peoples on their revolutionary struggle, declaring, "Cuba will not give up—we repeat once again—will never renounce our solidarity with revolutionary governments, with revolutionary peoples, and with the revolutionary movement."³³ And in Chile, in Lima, in Caracas, in Mexico City, I could ascertain and experience the great interest and joyful responsiveness which greeted both this very harsh speech against the United States and those cultural ones about Cuba,³⁴ that continues to be revolutionary.

EXCURSUS IV

Technology to Discover a Universe of Sounds

Interview with Walter Prati and Roberto Masotti

1983[1]

Following your experiments while rehearsing at the SWR Experimental Studio in Freiburg we have recognized a distinctive change in your music.

Certainly, my current compositions are affected by the fact that I have worked for about two years in this studio. The procedure adopted is a very particular one. I begin with virtually no idea, at times not even a vague one. This is something really new dictated primarily by a need to study, to experiment, to validate perceptual capabilities and see how these things, with their particular responses, react to music. This process involves me as well as the two engineers, Professor Hans Peter Haller and Rudolf Strauss. Working like this is like being in the open sea, where from time to time you look to the stars to guide you. A star may lead you, through a special type of perception, to a musical element, one that is interpretable and resolvable each time in a different way. At other times, unexpectedly, we find ourselves facing real technical errors, which, as one would expect, are then of course analyzed and in some cases reused. Error, as Wittgenstein says, is sometimes much more important than the rule;[2] in error one can find a real way of breaking through to spaces that were hitherto unthinkable.

What I prepare as a musical outline is not a real score, but rather indications, musical thoughts that take shape and emerge by utilizing to the full the totally new kind of virtuosity displayed by the chosen performers. Scarponi, Fabbriciani, Schiaffini, Scodanibbio, and the two contraltos Manca di Nissa and Otto are asked to express themselves, not by means of a supposed academic virtuosity, but rather through the ability to produce and create interrelations among specific sound of very high quality: it's a problem of instrumental technique but is also related to the receptive capacity of the performers themselves: this applies to microintervals, to the control of breath and its emission. It is directly from this strict technical control that extraordinary timbral possibilities arise. For example, for wind instruments there is a continuous and imperceptible alternation between sound and breath. It is this idea of imperceptibility that fascinates me, not because of any unlikely "mystery" surrounding it, but for the sheer amount of material that it contains and develops within itself. Then, making manifest what is not directly perceptible through a technological "treatment," allows us to discover a universe of sounds to which we would not have access naturally.

In your music you have always given great importance to the text, either for structural reasons, or for reasons that were clearly ideological. On what basis do you work with it today?

For several years now, text and titles have arisen from my collaboration with Massimo Cacciari. We talk, we discuss, and then we proceed to develop our ideas. It is not a matter of a simple montage of texts; it is an original product which has at its core songs, poems, or something else, which have already been analyzed. *Guai ai gelidi mostri,* the title of my latest work, is a phrase taken from Nietzsche. The Cold Monster is the State. Other material used is from Lucretius, the description of the plague of Athens as a metaphor, then invectives against violence from Pound and, from Franz Rosenzweig, criticisms of the Hegelian conception of the State, as well as fragments from Michaelstaedter and Gottfried Benn. In the final part, meanwhile, there emerges a will to oppose the Cold Monster. In short, what is called for is the need for an active presence, following Rainer Maria Rilke's always valid injunction, "to be here in every moment," to be fully present, to face reality without fear.[3]

As a consequence of having worked extensively with many contemporary technical possibilities, and in particular with the soloists previously mentioned, have you also acquired a different way of using the voice, beyond a codified style?

It is a result that I certainly try to achieve. In *Diario polacco n. 2* the tendency toward vocal lyricism was still present, even though only to a very limited extent. Today I would do something completely different. Certainly, with respect to vocality and its technical possibilities, the studies I have made of instruments are at a more advanced level. As for singing, I'm looking for the answer through my experimental research right here at Freiburg. What is certain is that I no longer want operatic singing, rhythmic speaking, recitative, nor reading.

What relationship does the current electronic experience have with the electronic music of the 1950s and 1960s?
In the *musique concrète* of Pierre Schaeffer in Paris and in the electronic studios in Milan and Cologne (which, with different techniques, made use of electronically produced sounds that were recorded on tape and combined with live instruments), the predominant element was about capturing noise and then processing it, exploring especially the realm of urban sounds in all their violent expressiveness. There are still certain points of contact with the research of those years. The big difference, however, is that now this study of the imperceptible—demonstrated, for example, through techniques of slowing down the tape—does not then become fixed on tape as the final step [of the process]. This opens up many possibilities. We are not listening to a simple recording. The historical disconnect that occurs in performance between traditional instruments and tape is resolved. Each time we have the chance to work as required by the actual project, and, in particular, with regard to the space in which the performance will take place.

This avoids creating untenable listening situations, as often happens when the places are chosen more for scenographic requirements than for those that are strictly musical. For example churches, open spaces, or even worse, those set up for sporting events.

Let's return to the music of Guai ai gelidi mostri. *The parts that we have listened to these past days are based on the electronic development of sound bands* [fasce sonore] *within which a continuous microintervallic, dynamic and timbral variation appears. Going back in time, we might recall a different use of similar material, for example: the large bands in* Al gran sole carico d'amore, *or a piano cluster or the long strident sounds of beaten metal. Can one consider the music of this new work an expansion and a more profound analysis of previous material?*
The elements mentioned are certainly present. Indeed, ideas that have had their own particular genesis and development now resurface as memories associated with elements that are not new in the absolute

sense but that are, effectively, without precedent. From *Al gran sole* onward in my compositions I have always tried to limit as far as possible the number of instruments and the amount of sound material. After .....*sofferte onde serene*..., for piano and magnetic tape, I wrote a string quartet, wishing to verify certain ideas with a totally traditional ensemble.[4] Now I am working with six instruments and two voices, which, paradoxically, in relation to the available performance time, appear at times far too many. Too many because the manifestation of all the musical phenomena, of the infinite vibrations that are present, requires a fairly long time precisely because of the difficulties of perception. This is where the real difficulty lies given the miseducation of listening. In other words, we know that it would take only one instrument, one voice, to penetrate into a world virtually unexplored and rich with amazing surprises, all in real time, that is, at the very moment in which the musician plays. This feature is extremely important. The performer emits a sound, through a microphone its natural sound is introduced into the "machines" and, according to a previous programming, it undergoes various treatments. Through a set of speakers, adequately placed in the listening space, it is rendered audible. In a very few moments one is able to hear again the sound that has just been modified. At this point the musician intervenes again to superimpose other sounds, whether one wants to keep the same material or to completely change the type of sound. This requires great concentration and listening skills. Sometimes all this effort must take place in a few moments. This puts the experience of live electronics in a completely different domain from that of tape music and computer music.

Therefore, the same problem of real-time perception applies to the audience as well.

Certainly. I am fully aware that we are facing new problems, both for listening and for concert organization, for example, concerning the placement of musicians. This attention is always crucial in terms of the possibility of perceiving everything that occurs and therefore determining whether the concert is effective or not.

We must absolutely avoid present and past mistakes such as those that happened to Stravinsky in Venice. On that occasion the chorus and the orchestra were placed at the center of the Basilica of St. Mark's.[5] It was a "society" event: the occasion was not about being heard, but being seen. Given the tradition of the Venetian School of St. Mark's and the characteristics of that place, a solution of that kind seems quite unacceptable. Anyway, today I take a very negative view of any notion related to the vastness of either the space or the audience. The concept of "massive" should in my opinion be completely revised.

In what sense does it need to be revised?
It is the relationship between music and the masses that needs to be reanalyzed. I strongly disagree that the goal for today's composer is necessarily to compose for the masses. The notion that everyone should immediately understand something does not seem to me to be an absolutely positive idea. Here Nietzsche is right when he says that sometimes you write in such a way that not everyone will understand, to force those who do not understand to be interested in studying and deepening their knowledge.[6] The usual superficial reading of daily events, for example, very often discourages this search and is to be considered a negative factor in this sense. It is, ultimately, a question of power. The *media* focus on the "famous," it gives front-page coverage to singers and conductors, but technological research, new experiments and, still further, the serious problems of education: these are not even superficially touched upon. A country's musical state of affairs is not determined solely by the composer or his music, but from the totality of all these elements that then determine its progress or failure.

Speaking of experimentation, what happened to the RAI Studio di Fonologia in Milan?
The studio is now long dead and is an obvious example of the cultural ignorance of the management of that institution. The various directors have, over time, received proposals made by Berio, Maderna, and myself, proposals that involved part research and part teaching.[7] All this fell on deaf ears. The studio has stagnated with very old analog equipment from the 1960s. This is too bad because during those years it had taken on a role very distinct from that of the studios of Cologne, Utrecht, and that of Pierre Schaeffer. The situation is even more lamentable if we think of Maderna's great commitment and Marino Zuccheri's technical contribution. Today it is a closed chapter, but certainly not due to any lack of ideas.[8]

The concepts that you expressed on research, analysis, and listening, we think will lead, at first, to a phase of subjective internalization. The focus is no longer turned toward the outside but rather to within man himself. Is this a possible interpretation?

One of the great moments of Jewish thought, also taken up by Schoenberg, is the lack of distinction between the external and internal, the typical dualism of Western European society. The up, down, left and right, the outside and the inside, they are dynamic realities that form part of the same universe. I find that the concept of the intimate as a unique and definitive moment is a typical nineteenth-century idea. Today there is an absolute need to break with this demagogic form of socialization, the sharp contrast between external-social and internal-personal. It is beyond doubt that the need for this to be satisfied is greater than ever: to know the other, the different, to confront oneself with what is distinct. It is interesting to listen to what you do not usually listen to, to read what you do not normally read. I do not find these moments contradictory at all but, on the contrary, revitalizing because it is from them that a way emerges of listening to others and of being listened to. From this point of view one can also revisit the concept of solitude: no longer an illusory isolation, but a historical necessity of the individual. The value of the Benedictine way of life is undeniable in this regard; Hölderlin had his tower, Gramsci his cell. Solitude, when considered for its own sake, is an idiotic concept and even more idiotic when used in opposition to being together as an end in itself. Being alone allows us to reconnect with all those voices always inside of us which we must continually take into account.

Fundamentally, there appear to be many points of contact with certain concepts that Cage has put forward in past years. One of the mainstays of this concept was the consideration of silence as an autonomous entity.

Silence is also what you can listen to in Via Nazionale in Rome or in Via Manzoni in Milan during heavy traffic. Silence is our decision. What do we want to hear right at this moment?

Which is a Cageian concept: open the window and listen to what there is to hear.

Certainly. However, I would like to clarify a point referring to the Darmstadt period. What was then considered to be a dispute between Cage and me was, in fact, about my opposition to the "academic" application of Cageian conceptions. Therefore the more stubborn clash took place with Stockhausen, who had just finished writing his *Klavierstück XI*.[9] In this area there are truly so many possibilities, so many combinations that are sometimes unimaginable, instincts that are different and very remote and I believe that this is the mystique of our time. I feel a sense of urgency to discover whatever is different, new proposals and explorations that involve "hearings," being moved and touched in a new way. Bartók defined this as the anxiety of the unknown.

Hasn't this highly positive attitude on the part of composers and musicians perhaps come somewhat belatedly? Most of these concepts have always been part of the thinking and the forms of nonclassical music: why has their validity been denied until recently?

It was not denied but hidden, and still goes unmentioned. In Rome a Varèse festival has recently taken place.[10] This composer had an extraordinary relationship with African percussion, for example, through Amadeo Roldán. This is nowhere officially recognized. Varèse first told me about this composer whose music, whose persona I got to know later in Cuba. Roldán wrote pieces for percussion which involved an enormous number of indigenous instruments. It was not the composers who blocked the development of music in that sense, but the thought in vogue at that time, which wanted Varèse set in a very narrow context. The same thing happened for Schoenberg and Webern: they, too, were analyzed solely from a particular point of view, one that was true, certainly, but not the only one possible. Schoenberg's connection to Jewish thought has been consistently denied or considered insignificant. The same goes for Webern. You have to remove him from that one image that he has had over the years and to see him in the light of what was happening at that time in the cultural chaos that was Vienna (conservatism, cultural upheavals, and contacts with the East).

There has been talk of Luigi Nono's ideological, musical rupture. What has undergone; what is this rupture all about?

I am for many of these little ruptures, which are, therefore, many different moments of a single evolution. This very way of working today in Freiburg stems from one such rupture. There is a profound and intense collaboration among everyone. Whatever is accomplished I would define as a collective achievement, achieved with the indispensable contribution of every person, including the current technician Rudi Strauss. It is an interaction among several participants, and each one contributes with atypical instrumental practices related to his own instrument and adapted to the compositional purposes.

PART FOUR

Portraits and Dedications

1

Josef Svoboda

1968

Is music theater today breaking and overcoming all the a priori assumptions handed down to us in various ways by history (the stage area—the relationship of text, voices, sound, movement, singing, and action—the audience whose perspectives are limited by the closed form of a socially determined architecture—ritualistic staging in an economically and technically primitive revolutionary state) possible without breaking with and overcoming the social and economic structures that history has passed down to us?

Therefore, wait for this revolutionary break in blind faith, working on the superstructure while having a very clear picture of the necessary perspective of the fundamentals?

Or intervene to the extent that it is possible or not, working on the superstructure while having a very clear picture of the irrefutable base? In Havana, Cuba, nine years after the triumph of the revolution in January 1968, the exhibition of the "third world" took place,[1] not an exhibition, but true music theater of today, revolutionary. The mastership of contemporary visual, graphic, and acoustic techniques having a direct significance for a current issue—the struggle of the "third world," a true "libretto" that affects all of us—in which every historical, traditional, academic, and neoclassical prior assumption is categorically broken down and overcome, in (and by means of) the presence of the audience, which is no longer circumscribed and blocked, but free and constantly freeing itself.

This in Cuba, where years ago Josef Svoboda held courses on the new theater.[2]

Precisely Josef Svoboda.

A few months before this musical exhibition-theater, the Czechoslovak pavilion opened at the Montreal Expo,[3] invented by Svoboda with the most exciting technical expressive functional imagination.

Precisely Josef Svoboda, no longer bound by the limits of the *laterna magika,* no longer constrained by the difficult relationship between the work of the past and its contemporary realization. But freely moving in the present, mutual innovation of technique and thematics.

[In Cuba and Montreal:] Two exemplary moments of how and what and why the theater of today can exist. Two extremely reliable indications of how much dealing with theater today should mean, not just new technical and musical devices, obviously implicit, not only new physical and intellectual function, in the audience-theater relationship, but confronting, also in music theater, the issue of the social-cultural transformation of the socioeconomic context in which theater is developed. In other words, also to participate in the theater as musicians and, namely as musicians, in breaking down and overcoming all the historical prejudices I mentioned above.

This is why Josef Svoboda matters.

I met him in 1958 during my first visit to Prague.

Along with Alfréd Radok.

After seeing the *laterna magika,* which had just returned from the Brussels Expo,[4] we had long conversations and discussions.

Both in the booth of the *laterna magika* and in his workshop.

The encounter developed over the following years through continual exchanges of our ideas about experiences and projects.

And also about my project of a new "opera."[5]

His experiences, his studies, and his research influenced me and helped me in my studies, from Monteverdi to *kabuki* to Japanese *noh,* from Meyerhold to Flanagan's Federal Theatre Project, from Mussorgsky to the synagogue ritual, from Piscator to Balinese theater, from the stage techniques of the early nineteenth century to the Bolshevik mass theater from *Fidelio* and *Trovatore* to Weill and Schoenberg.

Studies, analyses on history, to overcome it.

And to overcome the limitations of Eurocentrism on European theater culture (even if it be the great Italian tradition).

The kinetic conception of the stage space, the overcoming of the single visual and acoustic dimension, of the unitary time perspective, wide-ranging correlations to continual cross-references, not exhausting their significance at the moment of the scenic event, but rendered dialectical in the multifacetedness not just of the formative elements of the theater itself, but also of the weight of their significance, rendered intelligible in various ways in their succession and simultaneity. Also my continual visits to Svoboda's workshop in Prague, the discussions of his projects, sketches, filming, about the development of his concept no longer limited to the stage, but naturally encompassing the totality of the theatrical realization, and thus in close collaborative contact with the musician (rather than his a posteriori involvement)—all these things contribute to a new understanding of our time, of our possibility of intervening as musicians as such in our lives and in the fight for our lives. *Intolleranza 1960* (in collaboration with Václav Kašlík) was a first achievement of this relationship, but limited by bureaucratic interference and by the fact that this composition was my first theatrical endeavor.

The realization of the projections already prepared in Prague had to be changed owing to the bureaucratic interference by the local Venetian Biennale. And so Emilio Vedova became involved in the total production. The "realistic" part prepared by Svoboda in Prague would have developed the physical stage action (characters-mimes-extras),[6] and the thematic meaning in a different way broadening it and making it more dynamic throughout the whole stage area, thus destroying the physical horizontality of the stage itself and intensifying its possibilities of meaning and visual "reading."

This part eliminated, Vedova's projections, some of them indeed very beautiful, acquired the significance of mobile scenery, a symbolic expansion through forms and colors and words. It resulted an almost a double parallel track between action and physical meaning (with regard to the characters, etc.) and the symbolic scenery. (In Arnold Schoenberg's *Die glückliche Hand,* a similar use is specified in the score by the composer himself: colors that intervene symbolically to "illuminate" particular moments of psychological action.) Given the schematic nature of this parallelism, at times the physical and visual presence of the characters, and so on irritated me.

That is, the scenic-visual spatiality of the action itself was lacking, in its immediacy and its correlation of possible meanings. In the production, again by Svoboda, in the theater in Boston—1965, the situation was infinitely worse due to the technical and economic limits of the theater: Svoboda was unable to realize even half of what he had invented and prepared.[7]

For many months Svoboda and I have been studying a new idea for a project together for a second theatrical musical endeavor.[8]

His collaboration is not limited to the stage space, but involves the stage in its entirety, including the action. The results will be different in terms of the unity of its conception, writing, and staging.

Because of this I believe that applying Svoboda's kinetic concept to a traditional work will only confront the problem of the scenery, in which an event based on other principles takes place. That is, I think a piece by Verdi, Weber, or Shakespeare, in one of Svoboda's scenic realizations, would need to undergo other transformations precisely in terms of the relationship between the action and the space of the stage.

I am thinking, in fact, of the need to overcome the naturalistic physicality of the character's singing voice with the use of some of today's methods: singing is heard but does not see it, action is seen but not naturalistic, in no way veering toward film or science fiction, but truly penetrating the visual acoustic aspect in a new functional unity of technique and expressive conception. Not merely experimental or "avant-garde," but addressing the issue of updated staging in its totality, considering the technical stylistic update that a work receives today in its performance, in relation to the original score, to its Time. Even in terms of this final consideration (the continuous stylistic and technical transformation of a work of the past in terms of performance) I am not a craftsman of historical reconstruction in the musical stage performance of a work, thus arriving at a result that is merely intellectually pleasing but objectively false.

September 1968

2

Remembering Two Musicians

1973

In November 1970 G. F. Malipiero gave me the first volume of the complete works of Giovanni Gabrieli, recently published by the Fondazione Cini on the San Giorgio Maggiore Island in Venice.[1] In a brief note the Maestro reminded me of our previous conversings [*conversari*] on the great importance of the Gabrielis and our shared love for them, and on the scarcity of existing studies, and of editions that were "original without distortions, or additions," like the one he was presenting to me.[2] (Of course, we were speaking of the edition by Denis Arnold of the American Institute of Musicology of Rome.)[3] This was a true gift of his sensitive intelligence, which was always ready to assist and develop musical knowledge, with suggestions, indications, and advice: for all this, too, G. F. Malipiero was a true Maestro.

He proved to be an affectionate Maestro to me, when in the years of brutal fascist rule, from 1943 to 1945, he accepted me as a student. And his lectures and talks opened me up to the study and knowledge of that music, which at the time had been decreed ostracized in Italy: Schoenberg and Webern, and Dallapiccola as well. And of course Monteverdi and Renaissance music.

And it was G. F. Malipiero himself who advised me to get to know Bruno Maderna, whom he at once held in high esteem, and with whom I then furthered my studies. And again at his instigation, Bruno, already very much the master, with a group of his students, including me, began to "rummage" in the Marciana Library among original manuscripts, including treatises on composition from Hucbald to Padre Martini, among the earliest printed music (published by Ottaviano Petrucci in Venice from 1501), in order to study, historically and on the basis of the original sources, the development of European music up to Schoenberg, Webern, and Berg. It was a very happy period of study, discovery, and discussions, into which Bruno drew us all with his maieutic enthusiasm. G. F. Malipiero followed our work with true delight when we informed him of the progress of our studies or when we brought him its concrete results (transcriptions in modern notation, instrumentation of pieces from *Odhecaton A*,[4] our studies in the various styles, or when we brought him the book of the masses by Jakobus de Kerle, a late Flemish composer, that we found uncataloged in the state archives in Venice).

At the time there was a truly lively rapport characteristic of a "workshop" of musical craftsmanship, wherein the undogmatic intelligence and cultured temperament of G. F. Malipiero was united with Bruno's tireless ability to continually discover with us music that was always new, to let us study it as always alive.

And yet again it was G. F. Malipiero who advised us all to take part in the international conducting course that Hermann Scherchen held in Venice in 1948.[5] It was the beginning of a long cultural companionship, intellectual and practical, between Scherchen and Bruno especially, and us as well.

These are quick mentions, of course, but even these are certainly evocative of G. F. Malipiero's true personality, which was not shut away exclusively in his scores, but like them was able to shed light on the way that the Maestro had come to be a strongly incisive symbol for the European revival of a part of Italian music.

Bruno Maderna is the epitome of human generosity. This is shown by his positive determination—always cheerful even through the various difficulties he suffered, the last being a serious illness—in his way of making music, of being music, of sharing music with everyone. And along with music, his lively intelligence, always dynamic in opening perspectives, where music interpenetrates with new technical-expressive means and new compositional methods. All this is resolved whenever man lives as a subject in our time, always reaching out toward mankind. Thus Bruno lived and continues to live.

This nature of his led him to elicit, cause, and determine major developments in today's music, with his always compelling and maieutic teaching for all the young people who encountered him, with his way of encouraging the study of music, with his ready capacity to always discover it anew in the company of others, and with his truly rare and unforgettable performer's art—for which Bruno Maderna continues to be admired and loved by orchestras and by thousands and thousands of people, who through him have been in direct communication with the living reality of music, lucid in its meanings, in its structure, in its function.

In London, in what was to be his last concert with the London Symphony, a week before his death, from one rehearsal to the next until the beautiful performance of Bartók's First Concerto for Piano and Orchestra and Schoenberg's Concerto for Piano and Orchestra,[6] Bruno had once again and with lucid serenity reasserted for himself his raison d'être, in spite of his illness.

And Bartók and Schoenberg were steadfastly, ideally, and humanly with him.

Now Bruno sleeps serenely next to his beloved Andrea and Giovanni Gabrieli, Claudio Monteverdi, and G. F. Malipiero.

3

Victor Jara's Song

1974

After having fought together with the students of the State Technical University against the Chilean military, the singer Victor Jara was arrested and detained in the national stadium in Santiago, Chile, which had been transformed into a concentration camp for thousands of patriots. Witnesses from those days tell of the heroic behavior of that communist intellectual: he endured torture without giving in to the request to betray others. In those grim days this song was born that brand *the terroristic mask of fascism* and sings of the President's blood that strikes just as *our fist will strike again.*[1] The text of this song remained unfinished. The beasts murdered the poet, conscious of the strength that emanated from his verses. Fascism slaughtered the creator, as it slaughters everything that inspires life and rebellion. Nevertheless, when that day comes, the justice of the people of Chile will make a clean sweep of the murderers of Victor Jara and will avenge the thousands of revolutionaries massacred by the junta.

This is the preface with which the *Verde Olivo,* the weekly magazine of the RAF (Revolutionary Armed Forces of Cuba), published the work of the comrade musician Victor Jara for the first time.[2]

Victor: one of the Chilean voices most charged with vehemence against those who violated the human and social rights of the workers, peasants, and miners; most tempered with cutting irony against the comfortable consumeristic life of the plunderers from the upper-class districts of Santiago (where subversive demonstrations by the wealthy middle class took place "con las cazuelas");[3] most vibrant in sharing the hopes, the achievements of the Unidad Popular government, in glorifying the struggle for common freedom in Latin America.

For Victor Jara, too, as for many Chilean intellectuals, cultural production, cultural action, and political struggle in their various manifestations were closely linked, operating in a dialectic. Thus, in his last days, he wrote his last song (the assassination of comrade Salvador Allende, the fascist terror unleashed, and the confidence "in our fist that will strike again"). And at the same time he was participating in the stiff resistance of the Chilean people. Once again he was expressing his creative imagination and at the same time putting into effect what he said in Havana in September 1972, referring to his own country: "One day we will have to exchange the guitar for the rifle."[4]

Victor Jara, whose voice is among the most popular and best loved in Chile and Latin America.

The long history of the struggles of the Chilean workers, miners, and peasants (massacres suffered, social achievements realized), a culture in itself, has given rise to a vast cultural production, which takes part in the history of the broader struggle of the peoples of Latin America: in Chile just as in Bolivia, Puerto Rico, Uruguay, Brazil, and in other harshly repressed and violently exploited countries continuously in revolt.

In the reality of their people's tough battle, for which socialist Cuba is a living indication, there are intellectuals, spokespersons, performers and creators working at different levels and in different fields. They develop their studies and their analyses (of their historical origins to be liberated from colonialist influence), together with research into new technical-expressive means that update their creative capacity.

From Martí, from Guillén to the new Cuban cinema, from Emilio Recabarrén to Violeta Parra to the new Chilean culture (I am restricting myself to only two Latin American countries as examples).[5] In Chile, especially during the years of the Unidad Popular, there was a burst of new culture: cinema (Miguel Littín), painting (up to the original experience of mural painting of the Ramona Parra Brigade and "Inti" Peredo), literature and music. In Chile, the new political song, namely those of Violeta Parra and onward.

Words of Victor Jara:

> The political song was always present in Chile, united to the peasant, the miner, the humiliated. Songs that were expressing their sufferings, their sorrows, their exploited condition. Violeta spent twenty years in the

countryside, in the mines, with the peoples of the South, she lived with the *mapuche*,[6] artisans, fishermen. This is the basis of the historical motivation that is so strong in her music. Violeta, with her profound knowledge of the people and its folklore, created a new song that was very poetic and above all genuinely of the people. Violeta pointed the way, and her song was definitive for the young. During the Unidad Popular campaign, this song gained its full expression. Her themes were those of the people: anti-imperialism, anti-oligarchy, against injustice and exploitation.[7]

And then a new song movement [Nueva Canción Chilena] was born in Chile in clear opposition to the so-called neofolklore, coming from the industrial record companies and used by the reactionary bourgeoisie. Songs were created through direct and live contact with the masses by singers like Isabel and Angel Parra (children of Violeta, the first now an exile in Cuba, the second, having been tortured and with his life in grave danger, is now confined in a concentration camp in the north); Gitano Rodríguez; Payo Grondona (union executive of MAPU,[8] now in Argentina); Luís Advis (author of, among others, that powerful popular cantata *Santa Maria de Iquique,* about the strike and the massacre of thirty-six hundred miners by the army that occurred in 1907 in the same city); Patricio Manns; Fernando Ugarte; and groups such as the Inti-Illimani (now in Italy) and Quilapayún (also now in Europe). All of them participated in the process of social transformation indicated by Salvador Allende's government and denounced the cultural penetration of imperialism, its cultural colonialism.

And Victor Jara, born in 1938 in Chillán in the south, was with all of them. From his peasant mother and her social background he received his first direct exposure to the local folklore. He graduated from the theater school of the University of Chile in Santiago. He was adviser and director of the Quilapayún group. His activities often took him outside his own country and even to Europe. He participated in various political song festivals. In 1969, Jara was in Helsinki for the world summit with Vietnam. Then in the USSR, in England, in the GDR, and in Cuba in March and September 1972.[9]

I first met Victor in Santiago in August 1967. And we immediately established a strong supportive friendship. Victor and other comrades we went on a long overnight bus trip to the south, to the Lota Schwager mine. We had conversations with miners, union members, and comrades for a whole day. They revealed the very harsh conditions of life and work, their bitter struggles (it was at the time of the Frei government). Miserable, one-room wooden houses for miners' families, without sanitary facilities, and with the highest infant mortality rate. And all this while private profits were very high, and the mine, among the richest in Latin America, was producing 85 percent of domestic coal production, with ninety-eight hundred miners. Conversations, discussions, political and economic data alternated with Victor's powerful songs, sung at the request of the miners themselves. (I returned to Lota in May 1972. The mine had been nationalized in January 1971, its production had increased, the management was in the hands of the miners themselves and government technicians. The managing director was Isidoro Carrillo, previously a simple *barretero,* working with a pickaxe in the mine, with the strong character of the unionist. He was among the first assassinated by the Chilean military.)

I met Victor again in Santiago at a extremely enthusiastic meeting in a cinema: he was singing with the Quilapayún group. The songs were all new, engaged in the common vision toward the socialism. Victor, as always, was cheerful, joyful, and vehement, a great interpreter of his own songs and of that same new Chilean reality.

Then I met him again at the meeting of Latin American music in Havana in September 1972.[10] Discussions, information, joint work took place with great political fervor in a climate of extraordinary and conscious joy of our Cuban comrades. The best proponents of Latin American political song were gathered there, from Daniel Viglietti (Uruguay) to Payo Grondona to Isabel Parra (Chile), to Los Olimareños to "Ducho" Gutiérrez (Uruguay), and the young creators of the new Cuban music, and together with the electronic composers. A meeting of great friendship and common interests, made even more committed by the intelligent humanity of comrade Haydée Santamaría,[11] present during the meeting.

They say that Victor Jara, a prisoner at the National Stadium of Santiago, began to sing. Immediately they severed his wrists, they hit him on the head, and left him bleeding for a long time. Then they murdered him.

But his songs go on, now more than ever true hymns of struggle for the saltpeter, coal, and copper workers; in short, for all those who are organizing the unified resistance to liberate Chile from the criminal usurpers of liberty—internal (military and civilian) and external (the United States, CIA, North American capital)—in order to take up the march toward socialism more decisively.

4

Preface to Arnold Schoenberg's *Harmonielehre*

1977

Given the various components of *Harmonielehre* (historical, methodological, theoretical, practical), there are various possibilities of reading, using, reflecting on, and studying it, even in its unity of conception and the proactive dialectic among its components. Schoenberg himself warned of its *complexity,* although oddly with a simplistic judgment on its "length." In fact, in the preface to *Praktischer Leitfaden* [Practical Guide], edited by Erwin Stein in 1923,[1] Schoenberg writes:

> My *Theory of Harmony* is obviously much too long. Once its author is out of the way—the living obstacle to judicious cutting—three quarters of the text must then surely go by the board.[2]

(But Stein's simplification was produced during Schoenberg's lifetime!) And yet:

> Constant revisions will be needed, so it can keep up with the always improving times, so that new generations can still make use of what little good can be found in an era which, for being earlier, is consequentially also worse.[3]

What are the reasons today for the musician, teacher and student for taking an interest in this textbook, surely of great historical importance and which forms an addition to the great practical and theoretical treatises of the past, ranging from that attributed to Hucbald of Saint-Amand (ninth-tenth centuries) to those of Gioseffo Zarlino (1558 and

1571), Jean-Philippe Rameau (1750), and Hugo Riemann (1880, 1887, 1905), to name but a few?

I will try here to propose some of them for consideration and discussion.

1. THE RELATIONSHIP BETWEEN TEACHER AND STUDENT

Schoenberg's various propositions in the textbook result in an extremely well-argued *ductus* with a great dialectical dynamism (and we are in 1911!). There is not the least trace in it of the habitual academicism used with coercive purpose, nor formulas for convenient and easy consumption which are enemies of analytical and historical knowledge and an ambitious instrument for those wishing to arrest the course of time with aesthetics or personal tastes (revealing wills that are closed and authoritarian). Such attitudes, in the period of study itself and, therefore, in the future as well, block rather than activate the student's imagination, research, and creativity. It is known that Schoenberg never made twelve-tone theory and practice the subject of his teaching. He never considered the student as a container to be filled up in order to propagate and affirm his own ideas.

Let's read carefully what Schoenberg himself writes:

This book I have learned from my pupils.

I never imposed those fixed rules with which a pupil's brain is so carefully tied up in knots.

But the teacher . . . does not have to pose as infallible, as one who knows all and never errs; he must rather be tireless, constantly searching, perhaps sometimes finding.

From the errors made by my pupils as a result of inadequate or wrong instructions I learned how to give the right instructions. (1911 Preface)[4]

And again:

Therefore, I do not exclude what I do not happen to mention.[5]

The teacher's task can only be to impart the technique of the masters to the pupil.[6]

One of the foremost tasks of instruction is to awaken in the pupil a sense of the past and at the same time to open up to him prospects for the future. Thus instruction may proceed historically, by making the connections

> between what was, what is, and what is likely to be. The historian can be productive if he . . . tries to read the future from the past.[7]
>
> Let the pupil . . . know that the conditions leading to the dissolution of the system are inherent in the conditions upon which it is established. Let him know that every living thing has within it that which changes, develops, and destroys it.[8]
>
> To represent life in art, life, with its flexibility, its possibilities for change, its necessities; to acknowledge as the sole eternal law evolution and change—this way has to be more fruitful than the other, where one assumes an end of evolution because one can thus round off the system.[9]

What emerges with great clarity from this is a concept that is not evolutionary, but dialectical. Today we are all the more able to recognize this as a clear pedagogical choice and a great historical example, considering the intellectual and practical consequences of anti-authoritarian democracy, for example, in Italian schools and universities (unfortunately the music conservatories, with few exceptions, remain like islands) by that strong wave of the 1968 student revolt. All the more so, the still stubborn and anachronistic methods oppose and set themselves against the new and necessary reforms. And it is no coincidence that *Harmonielehre* is the very text used by such democratic musicians as Giacomo Manzoni at the "G. Verdi" Conservatory of Milan—and he is not the only one—as a personal initiative from inside for a new basis of study.

2. ACOUSTIC MATERIAL

Schoenberg writes:

> The material of music is the tone; what it affects first, the ear. The sensory perception releases associations and connects tone, ear, and the world of feeling.[10]
>
> Perhaps it is indefensible to try to derive everything that constitutes the physics of harmony . . . just from the tone.[11]
>
> If the carpenter knows how to join pieces of wood securely, this knowledge is based no less on fruitful observation and experience than is the knowledge of the music theorist who understands how to join chords effectively.[12]

These are the subjects of careful reflection and study in music.

The material in itself.

And we know how today acoustical physics, electronics, and new methods of analysis are broadening the understanding of the acoustic phenomenon itself, how it is formed, how it varies, how it suggests alternative and substantially new principles of composition and the application of fundamental compositional formants, such as rhythm, duration, the harmonic spectrum and other elements of the musical language.

The ear and the physical, emotional, and rational perception, and their problems yesterday and today. Their continuous expansion, in study and practice as a consequence of expansion of register—at the higher and lower ends—whether of the orchestra or in the electronic studio.

Perceptual and semantic overcoming of the dichotomies consonance-dissonance and sound-noise for analysis and physical function, no longer based on the tonal or chromatic use of the physical scale, but enriched by a variety of microintervals (even less then the quarter-tone) and of harmonic fields, which are also studied and composed with the electronic frequency generator.

Implication of current analytical methods, even psychophysical ones, and active consideration of the acoustic and social environment in which we live and act, in its various and complex formants, and not a passive, a priori, aesthetic closed-mindedness resulting from attachment to a tradition both suffered and imposed, with all its superstructural implications, smuggled in and not modified in a necessary dialectical relationship with the transformation (or transformation in progress) of the social economic structure.

3. DIFFICULTIES AND OBSTACLES

Schoenberg writes:

> It is falsely concluded that these laws, since apparently correct with regard to the phenomena previously observed, must then surely hold for all future phenomena as well. And, what is most disastrous of all, it is then the belief that a *yardstick* has been found by which to measure artistic worth, even that of future works. As often as the theorists have been disavowed by reality, whenever they declared something to be inartistic "which did not with their rules agree," they still "cannot forsake their madness."[13]

Is this not also a clear and vibrant antidogmatic position for music, and does it not speak for itself?

> What today is remote can tomorrow be close at hand.[14]

And with regard to the dichotomy of consonance-dissonance:

> If I continue to use the expressions "consonance" and "dissonance," even though they are unwarranted, I do so because there are signs that the evolution of harmony will, in a short time, prove the inadequacy of this classification.[15]

And with regard to melody:

> It is hard to find a criterion; what was formerly unmelodic is today quite often felt to be melodic.[16]

It should be clear that these are not *ipse dixit* quotations, nor much less are they used in any way to justify the present of music, what is surely unnecessary, despite its problems. But they need to be treated as a particular interpretation, which reveals a position of openness to the continuing trend toward *new discoveries,* new practices, new creativity.

4. MUSICAL EXAMPLES

To be sure, Schoenberg limited himself to European classics or to examples that he formulated himself. Today the panorama has expanded considerably, as I said above. If again for pragmatic reasons, Schoenberg wrote *Structural Functions of Harmony* as late as 1948,[17] with many historical examples from Bach to himself, I believe today it is necessary to broaden our comparative studies to other non-European cultures, also in the field of ritual and folk song, along with new methods of scientific analytical knowledge.[18] Not for other "formulas," but to understand the various compositional mentalities with various musical materials, special processes, and social functions. Comparative studies among different civilizations and cultures, distant by history, customs, and economic development—are necessary today. Also to overcome Eurocentrism and study and better understand the processes of liberation and new development, cultural included, that in Asia, Africa, and Latin America are harshly but certainly being realized.

Schoenberg's musical development has been shown to be of historical significance, certainly contradictory, but worth having all its objective positivity drawn from it and worth being analyzed outside of any schematic and a priori system, both in itself and in the historical, musical, and social context of that era. And let me say immediately that Schoenberg should be studied, not as a musical phenomenon in his own right, but also in relation to his textbook, as someone determined by and determining of that broad innovative cultural ferment that characterized Vienna between the late nineteenth and early twentieth centuries, while the social, economic, and ideological structure of the Austro-Hungarian Empire was breaking up and dissolving. Thus the book should be studied with new methods of knowledge in relationship to literature, philosophy, architecture, painting, music, and to Austro-Marxism—also in its relationships with the Social Democrats David J. Bach, Ernst Mach, and Joseph Scheu. And its meaning should not be distorted, by stamping it as revolutionary according to our own understanding to justify its importance. Rather, it should be analyzed scientifically with the Marxist method, not a crude or vulgar Marxism, and not resolved with dogmatic quotations, phrases drawn, for example, from Hanns Eisler's writings and interviews, intelligent as they are.[19] There is a need for a development and real deepening of our analyses.

Harmonielehre is certainly stimulating both for the knowledge of the harmonic practice of a specific period as for its exhortations to study the past (one case among many being the controversy between Monteverdi and Artusi on dissonance), as well as other historical periods in their actual practice, and not by the sterility of academic textbooks. And for an openness toward the future.

Also for me, in other conditions and in other situations, Arnold Schoenberg's teaching has been an important lesson.[20] And it still is. The continuous study of his works, his thoughts and his theoretical writings with all their historical references and contradictions, help deepen the knowledge of his era—an era in which one of the greatest musical revolutions took place. Within this panorama, *Harmonielehre* continues to be valid even today.

Venice, Summer 1977

5

Bartók the Composer

1981

By deriving *anxiety for the unknown* from Bartók, Roberto Leydi gives me a fundamental initial stimulus.[1] That is, eagerness *for* the new, *for* the different, to get to know better what is already known, *for* the unknown. This is a starting point from which it is possible to consider how much Bartók was "constrained" by the known, how much Bartók was—above all as a composer, as an innovator—reduced to something that already existed, to schemas already familiar, already known. These are limits to which Bartók has been subjected, both through a lack of adequate analytical tools, and through what I think are cultural limitations (not only in terms of music, but of culture in general). This has occurred in Western countries; this has also constantly occurred in the so-called socialist countries.

Bartók—and I received confirmation of this in Budapest—lived in Hungary as an exile. Leydi spoke earlier of some rebellions against Hungarian institutions in Budapest. One of these rebellions involved not only Bartók, but the members of an entire cultural group that was started up in the early twentieth century by young Lukács. It was initiated by the intellectuals of the time—poets, writers, painters, architects—who wanted to differentiate themselves from the capital (or from Vienna) and try to regain and demonstrate their own originality.

Not only up to 1945, but I would say even up to 1956 there was a whole culture that was restricted, exiled. In fact, after his exile, Bartók chose exile from exile, and I would say that this form of his exile—not unlike the exile suffered by Webern, suffered by Varèse, suffered by Schoenberg and many others—continues today.

The will to overcome the already known, the will not to repeat what is already known, the will not to defend, not to preserve the already known, thus the will not to restore. Bartók the musician—whether in terms of his research on folklore or as a composer and teacher—forms part of a very original cultural environment. The exclusive emphasis on Bartók as musician and teacher, and without relating him to the great cultural currents of the era, demonstrates a typical corporate desire to make an abstraction of a musician. The same thing happens when one speaks of Schoenberg only as a musician, removing him from the great cultural life of innovation, ferment, restlessness: from the *anxiety for the unknown* that surrounded him. Those who fear the unknown because it calls their very selves into question are *against* it: this is not only a cultural fact but a political fact as well, and one that weighs heavily.

Bartók's relationship with the young Lukács in the years between the late nineteenth and early twentieth century. Relationships between Balázs and the Christian "Sunday Circle,"[2] attended by poets, in which relationships developed, especially with the philosophy that was coming from outside Hungary. The presence of the young Lukács in Heidelberg, the relationships of the young Lukács with Ernst Bloch, Max Weber, Simmel, Heidegger, and Martin Buber; relationships among writers and inventors and aesthetes—some known in Italy, such as Leo Popper—expanding also into the fields of architecture and graphic art. There was a whole cultural ferment involving a considerable *anxiety* for the unknown, for the unfamiliar. And along with this there were journals; *Nyugat* ["The West"], a journal founded in 1906 and unknown in Italy, had dedicated a lot of space to Bartók. Another important journal in 1919 devoted an entire issue to Bartók.[3] Other journals: *Logos,* created by philosophers of the time—from Husserl to others—in which the young Lukács also participated. This desire to overcome the limits of an era, an environment, a society, and a culture, was an intrinsic part of Bartók's knowledge, action, and thinking—his musical thinking included.

I would like to be extremely brief, limiting myself to touching on just a few points.

First point: micro-tempi. I refer—as in my lecture in Budapest last week—to a score from 1935, the *Rumänische Colinde.*[4] I believe that some of the analytical points made by Bartók regarding the pitches have not been read at all (even in scores, the eyes should be capable of reading what is written and of drawing practical consequences from it, as long as there is *anxiety for the unknown,* as long as there is respect, curiosity, and concern for those who are preoccupied with the unknown and who require it). *Rumänische Colinde,* from 1935: referring to the right tempo [*tempo giusto*], Bartók speaks about "parlando rubato."[5] When talking about music in a single tempo he speaks of "parlando rubato" in the sense of "tempo della voce," that is, "free tempo" of the voice, which in the field of academic music is designated by phrases like: "the music has to breathe" (therefore, breaths, *rallentandi, accelerandi*). This is an original practice that Bartók drew from his study of folklore, in this case from the Christmas carols sung by five-year-old children. Hungarian television has recently organized a series of broadcasts made by Professor Laszló Somfai (director of the Bartók archive) and the pianist Zoltán Kocsis (very good and very young, almost unknown in Italy). They had studied Bartók's original performances and developed this variety, these freedoms of tempo that can be traced back to "parlando rubato," that is, to the micro-tempi within the tempo. And this characteristic, this linguistic innovation (which, I repeat, is not the *accelerando* or the *rubato* or the *ritardando* that belongs to the tradition of classical or romantic music) is derived from observing the vocal practice of folk songs. Let's think of Mahler—a composer in whom you can rediscover a bridge with what Bartók had noted down and studied. Mahler sometimes undergoes falsifications of tempi (in the *rallentando,* in the *accelerando*) that do not depend on the musical structure but on habit, on "academic" schemas. Even for Mahler his relationships with the Bohemian world, with the music of those places, led him to use these "parlando rubati" in instrumental music, not just in vocal music.

Second point: microintervals (closely related to the issue of micro-tempi). In the same book Bartók not only describes and speaks of quarter-tones (which he indicates with a sharp divided by two [♯/2]) but adds another element which I think is of great importance: one arrow pointing upward and another pointing downward.[6] So we have two different indications: one—the sharp divided by two—which is clearly intended for the quarter-tone, the other—the arrow—used to make the sound mobile or to create a note that is, as they say in the conservatories, "out of tune." Both markings came from Bartók's study of folk songs, where sound is mobile, changing, going from "*vibrato* without *vibrato,*" to the slowest *vibrato,* to a faster *vibrato,* applying different shades to the same pitch (what in the electronic studio would be called different "amplitude modulations").

From micro-tempi and microintervals arise two considerations that involve both the study of folklore and the composer's teaching and linguistic innovation. Taking these innovations into consideration in the field of education, for example, would mean selecting (or proposing) in an "other" form, bimodal intonation alongside tonal technique. A teaching based on natural practice, then, and not on a bizarre insight. A practice that allows for a greater understanding of the material, of the vocal, instrumental, and musical possibilities in relation to the schemes of tonal music and which leads toward the *unknown* (I am placing great emphasis on this *anxiety for the unknown* that Bartók had—also in his studies of folklore—because I believe that, on the contrary, there has been against him a will to restore the known).

Another very interesting case concerning quarter-tones arises regarding the treatise on harmony by the Czechoslovak Alois Hába (in Russia as early as 1905 there were composers using quarter- and eighth-tones before Busoni wrote his *Sketch*).[7] There was a difference of opinion between Bartók and Schoenberg about this treatise.[8] There are two letters from Schoenberg to Bartók, one from 1912 and from 1919,[9] in which Schoenberg speaks of performances planned in the *Musikverein* (the solution invented by Schoenberg to be able to select and perform contemporary music for pure listening).[10] With respect to the Hába treatise on quarter-tones, Bartók praised above all else their use in the melodic line, while Schoenberg, on the other hand, was interested in the use of quarter-tones in the harmony. In the same period, in the same contemporaneity, two great composers faced similar problems, reacting to them in different ways. It is, I would say, the great strength of the creativity of the individual. And yet, and I say this to demonstrate cultural limitations, precisely in Budapest, at one of the round tables organized last week, it was Professor Dahlhaus—of the Berlin Faculty of Musicology, very well known in Germany—who stated simply that quarter-tones do not exist in practical terms, that they are unplayable.[11]

Amplitude modulation to the limit of the quarter-tone—namely what Bartók indicated with two arrows—is a differentiation that especially in recent times has been crucial in contemporary music to distinguish between the static, fixed, stationary sound (which derives, I think, from Gregorian chant) and the mobile sound we have in Hebrew songs, in synagogue chants, and that we have in Eastern chants: it is another kind of musical thinking.

[In the *Colinde* one recognizes how] the use of consonants and vowel structures also causes fluctuations of pitches that at times contrast with the sound determined by a vowel. Acoustically speaking, two consonants create many harmonics (that is, they create specific formants) that are totally distinct from the vowel, since the attack of the sound creates a formant that is highly complex compared to the attack of the sound produced solely by the vowel. This is also the fruit of direct experience, of the study that Bartók made of various folk songs, and other songs as well. Again in this book, Bartók designed certain precise markings above the note values, a simple little sign,[12] indicating a different type of note-value, a sign distinct from the fermata sign used in academic musical practice. Here he also uses what I would call a micro-elongation, in exactly the way that he uses micro-tempi, employed and put into practice in his own music, at the level of performance and of composition, and just as he used microintervals on the thematic and analytical, didactic and compositional level. Also within the durations—that is, with respect to a given tempo—he used extremely mobile varieties.

Bartók also arrives at the glissando in a structural way. It is not merely a mannerism, it is not the traditional *portamento* used in singing, nor is it the glissando à la Penderecki. It is an awareness of what is contained within the intervals, of the function of microintervals in relation to the harmonics. He uses first glissandi within a chromatic series (that is, use of the notes of the total chromatic), then of the "quasi glissando"—a term that is also used in an incredible number of ways. For example, if one has a minor third in relation to a minor second, the glissando is not a mechanical action, but rather is made up of the various microintervallic subdivisions that are possible within the minor third. Just as within the minor second, the microintervals that make it up are different in comparison with those of the minor third. At the same time he uses glissandi with different tempi. Thus, with other parameters that are not bound to the mechanics of the intervals based on the initial sound. It is possible to find this same phenomenon in certain composers of today, such as Xenakis, for example, whose use of the glissando is not the "vulgar" one. Let's think also of Cappelli and of the performance of his String Quartet,[13] of the glissandi in the cello part that, contrary to the notation, were played [here in Venice] in the traditional way. This is a falsification of the composer's idea, the very thing that remains characteristic of one of the moments of Bartók's "exile," who continues to be "exiled" precisely by the performer.

Third and last point: Bartók's slow tempi. In this score we have chords very similar to those used in another way by Schoenberg, Webern, and Varèse. It is a chord that suggests having been derived from an adaptable conception of musical space, understood as the combination of sounds deriving from various intervallic structures. The space is determined, is from time to time *revealed* by a composition based on intervals of the major second, minor second, minor third, and tritone. Many times, especially in *Music for Strings, Percussion, and Celesta* [1936] and in the First String Quartet [1908]—thus, works separated by a certain distance of time—Bartók forms spaces with intervals, then proceeds to fill them and transforms them, filling them in the sense that the notes of the total chromatic are produced in succession thanks to its exuberance. This happened at the same time that in Vienna a practice was being developed based on the ton row, which should not be considered in the way that it was by Leibowitz, Stockhausen, and others, but only as a space to be filled and unveiled, to be emptied out, to be made full or made empty, as if adopting the technique of a sculptor. In this, Bartók was an innovator to the fullest extent, on the same level as Webern, Schoenberg, and Varèse. And in the slow movements the harmonics remain, not wearing themselves out in the moment when the sound is emitted, but combine themselves with other harmonics, determining a harmonic structure for the sound in relation to complementary sounds. We see this in the slow movement of the Sonata for Two Pianos and Percussion [1937]. We see it in *Music for Strings, Percussion, and Celesta,* and in the First Quartet.

What does this mean on the level of performance?

If all these things are taken into account, it appears that Bartók was projected toward the unknown. Unless this is acknowledged, Bartók becomes completely castrated, in the true sense of the term, restricted, reduced to the routine of habit—not of tradition—the most reactionary one. This to me is indicative of the need for analytical tools. These exist in various forms, of course, but in highlighting Bartók's innovations one comes into conflict with those who want to maintain what is already known, already absorbed, already past. And this raises a very important issue concerning how one understands and how one wishes to relate to the audience. That is, whether one wants to keep the audience the way it is now, passive, or whether one wants to make it a more complex entity, extremely articulate, and participating in all that is new today.

Therefore: to introduce healthy and necessary anxiety.

Bartók's teaching cannot be passed on in an academic fashion. I believe that the problems of teaching composition exist (and are considerable) even at the Hungarian Academy of Budapest. I believe that there are conservative forces even there. It's the way one *thinks:* technique is not born of itself, but it comes from a musical way of thinking, from an evolution (this is one of Schoenberg's great truths and one of Bartók's great truths). There are composers—and Kurtág is among them—in whom one can see a way of inventing, a way of *finding* the unknown. It is not the sounds that are special, but rather the way they are invented, used, told, made to vibrate. It is this that demonstrates (in Kurtág, too) a capacity and an anxiety for the unknown.

The great teaching of Bartók, fundamental for young people (and I also speak for myself, who in 1947–48 studied Bartók's chromaticism together with that of Schoenberg, that of the Franco-Flemish contrapuntists, with Bruno Maderna) is the need for this *anxiety for the unknown*.

6

For Helmut

1983

"In philosophy one feels forced to look at a concept in a certain way. What I do is suggest, or even invent, other ways of looking at it. I suggest possibilities of which you had not previously thought. You thought there was one possibility, or only two at most. But I made you think of others.... Thus your mental cramp is relieved" (from *On Certainty* by L. Wittgenstein, Oxford 1969, Sec. 559).[1]

BUT how many mental cramps still "powerful or assumed to be so" tend to trivialize, ignore, hinder and condemn potential innovations that are new and diverse, which there are many of today in the various fields of culture, mental cramps that are hostile to the need and urgency of developing

    thoughts
    knowledges
    analyses
    feelings
    coexistences,

                                    to vivify, rather than
                                                  mortify

    life
    in its problematic complexity

culture
in its problematic multiplicity!

MUSIC INCLUDED, OF COURSE !!!

Helmut Lachenmann.
   exemplary example.
   is something else
   is different
   innovates.

and of course because of their mental cramps those young and suspicious EMPTY ARTUSI are incapable of listening, of reading.²
   even for the self-gratification of "repertoires of fictitious and ornamental images with respect to the actual mechanisms of the construction of our KNOWLEDGE and with respect to the SOCIAL and INTELLECTUAL energies that have not yet found the terrain of their own codification"
   (from *Il sapere senza fondamenti*, A. Gargani, Turin 1975)³

ALL THE MORE RIGOR   in thinking
                     in searching
                     in experimenting
                     in attempting
                     related to creative
                     innovative happiness

ALL THE MORE TO UNDERMINE   the rules of the game
                                  now obsolete

ALL THE MORE RECKLESS ADVENTUROUS ROUTES   in open oceans,
                                  among fantastic abysses
                                  stellar spaces to
                                  un-veil or re-veal

ALL THE MORE TO NURTURE   thought in
                          with language (K. Kraus)

ALL THE MORE TO ABANDON   the tiresome academic
                          presumption of repetitive craft

of a *können* at fixed schedules,
truly standardized by
the everyday marketplace

ALL THE MORE INSTEAD TO
SURRENDER ONESELF   to the urgency
of a *müssen* even in "creative idleness,"
for enlightenment
for experiments that are fascinating
    in themselves
and
for thinking "OTHER POSSIBILITIES"

ALL THE MORE INTELLIGENCE   of the most open kind
Giordano Bruno and the infinite worlds[4]

INNER SOUL the most Hölderlin-like
INTUITION the most surprising
GUT FEELING instinctive as well as unexpected

ALL OF THAT TOO AND ABOVE ALL IN THE LISTENING
to the many voices that live within us
(tradition—cultures—memories)
    who live with us
in the alas frenetic problems
of the current political and social reality
    (problems that demand and specify
    still and always OTHER WAYS OF THINKING
    OTHER FEELINGS OTHER KNOWLEDGE
    AND ROUTES AND STRUGGLES AND ANALYSES AND
    CHALLENGES—ALL INNOVATIVE
    against and beyond any kind of MODEL
    repeated, planned, pre-programmed
    suffocating to the point of total aphasia)

THEN
> WHAT BECOMES
>
> POSSIBLE ARE
>
> all the more new and different possibilities
> to truly take hold of in the hitherto impossible
> all the more new and different audibilities
> to truly perceive in the hitherto inaudible
> all the more new and different lights
> to truly read in the hitherto invisible
> > the hitherto unutterable.

THIS IS POSSIBLE.
> EVEN IF ONLY PERHAPS.

BUT IT IS CERTAIN: this weak messianic power
is given to us, it is in us.
let's not lose it,
Walter Benjamin tells us[5]

Helmut
> RUNS
> > STUMBLES
> > > FLIES EVER MORE TENSED UP
> > > > WITH ANXIETY FOR THE UNKNOWN

he notices   always something different, other
he listens   always to something different, other
he marks   always something different, other

throughout his authentic wanderings like an authentically modern musician, among the VERY RAREST that I know, and not only in West Germany.

and the various "ARTUSI" of today are not even distant descendants of the ANTI-MONTEVERDI Artusi, so formless or uniform are their face.

> Luigi Nono
> Venice, September 11, 1983

7

For Marino Zuccheri

1986

My first meeting with Marino Zuccheri was instantly a great lesson and an immediate personal connection.[1] His rigorous precision, his explosive laugh. In the Studio di Fonologia of RAI in Milan at that time, Bruno Maderna was there, as it was often the case, a brilliant teacher also in my initiation into this studio. Why is Bruno now almost or completely forgotten? A profound, *active* reflection and evaluation about Maderna needs to be done in current musical life.

For some hours we worked on the creation of an acoustic graph, "thoroughly" prepared by me in Venice. It involved several relationships between sinusoidal frequencies, with precise centimeter-duration measurements with varied attacks and intensities. The result was "something" almost insignificant and a tremendous *sganassada* [roaring laughter] for Marino and Bruno.

First immediate lesson: the electronic studio did not require projects "preplanned" on the desk, but rather study—experimentation—*always listening in real time* at every moment with a devoted patience extending beyond "time," with a continuous deepening of possible and impossible-utopian musical ways of thinking and knowing [*pensari e saperi*], to arrive at *other* theoretical-practical and musical ways of thinking, including the use of space.

And with Marino an extraordinary period of work (over fifteen years) and deep friendship began.

His intelligent theoretical lessons, explanatory graphs on the blackboard, his way of listening and using the tools of the studio, common researches into so many "different others": other composers, other existing electronic studios. At the Milan studio there was an aura both technical and human that vibrated vividly and in an *original* way: Maderna, Berio, and Zuccheri were part of all that.

With Marino we would study voices in terms of their particular characteristics, not using them abstractly, but analyzing them in order to understand and bring out their different qualities: Carla Henius, Liliana Poli, Elena Vicini, Franca Piacentini, Kadigia Bove, Berto Troni, Miriam Acevedo, Gabriella Ravazzi, the choruses of N. Antonellini at RAI-Rome and G. Bertola at RAI-Milan, the Living Theatre, and the clarinettist W. O. Smith, who had already been using the new technique of multiphonics before 1965, and so on.[2]

We were constantly trying to expand the various technical means of the Studio simultaneously (methods of recording—analysis—compositional testing and retesting—acoustic spectra up to microintervals), the possibilities of perception, different kinds of modulation, of spatial projection (increasingly more sound sources and loudspeakers, arranged until they formed a continuous circle around the audience: *Al gran sole carico d'amore*, Milan 1975).

A composition recorded on tape—*tape music*[3]—was not the *sole* "end" *in itself* (whether based on purely electronic materials or not) to be *repeated* in "performances," as some categorically maintained, but rather the innovations in electronics made the musical relationships arising from their use in *different spaces, with* live instruments or voices, whether amplified or not, more fascinating.

Already in 1952, Bruno Maderna had demonstrated this to everyone with the first version of *Musica su due dimensioni* for flute and tape, composed in Cologne and Bonn.[4]

When did a composition "begin" and when did it "end"?
And how?
We did not know.
The work began *ex nihilo* by revealing and unveiling compositional principles inherent in the material, principles which gradually "combined," elucidating the material itself.

Attempts—acoustic tests—that were always being called into question, provoking further tests.

Being extremely careful (practice-critique-practice) not to impose schemes, models, and precedents derived from other experiments, other materials.

And the material turned out to be already "imprinted," and it "imprinted" various compositional possibilities: to listen to them—arouse them—intuit them!

The "preparation" required a long time (had the composing already begun?), not only because of the technique of continually splicing the tape, a work of "embroidery" to produce the different sound attacks, but it was soon abandoned. The first artisan stage, rather boring, at times surprising because of a working method of quasi-"pulverization," almost like tesserae of a mosaic that could be assembled in various ways.

But because one proceeded by *initially adding together* the processed materials, to themselves and to each other, processing them again—so much testing and retesting, discarding, experiments redone. Not an arithmetical or mechanical sum.

And listening-analysis-listening, *continuous listening:* musical thoughts became clarified slowly and unexpectedly. Many successive moments of musical composition (sketches-preparatory studies).

Schematically:

Four 4-track tape recorders (two Studer and two assembled at the RAI);

Two 2-track tape recorders (Studer).

We recorded on one track (*various tapes—basic*) different processing of materials: filters—modulations of amplitude—of intensity—of attacks—of square-sinus-sawtooth waves. Harmonic spectra with different ratios—also time ratios—and other signals from instruments or voices.

We listened, we analyzed, we discussed, we chose.

We began to combine them onto four tracks: each track with other processing of recordings—of speeds.

We listened, we analyzed, we discussed, we chose in order to proceed.

We combined them again on the other 4-track tape, always continuing to vary, to modify on each track.

The result was the "sum" of sixteen tracks.

Then again on the other four tracks = sixty-four tracks *all variated.*

We tested other timings—synchronized or non-synchronized starts, other intensities, other pitch modulations (micro-macro intervals).

We used two 4-tracks with two 2-tracks simultaneously, and often *all* the tape recorders were turning. The studio became a fascinating "chaotic" vortex.

We preserved all the work tapes, including those for each combination, for every possible eventuality.

It was a procedure—"compositional"—preparatory: the varied variety of distinct sums of possible fragments-sections-blocks of musical experiments-studies.

In other words: material for *sixty-four voices "a sonar a cantar"* [to play and to sing].[5]

Everything was documented: graphics—notes—data—numbers in notebooks, to which we could refer in case other attempts were necessary.

Then we began a reverse procedure: *subtraction* also varied.

In other words: from sixty-four voices we subtracted, we reduced, and we chose one voice—five voices—twenty-seven voices—eleven voices—forty-three voices—seven voices, and so on. Often to a maximum confusion among ten voices (from one to ten).

We tried several times, we varied what was already varied, we modified by eliminating.

Harmonic spectra from the very complex to the simple, varied intensity (between *ffff* "no semo sordi" [we're not deaf][6] to *ppppp* "so' sordo devenuo" [I have become deaf]: our conversation would pass between Venice and Trieste dialects).

We threw away (erased) a lot ("nol creda" [don't believe it]).

We tested—and tested a lot again ("el se neta le reciasse" [clean out your ears]).

We cut out a lot ("tanto cavo tanto meto" [the more I take out the more I put in]).

Multiple subtractions were done from multiple tapes simultaneously.

Often it all came to nothing (the initial *ex nihilo!*).

Sometimes the blackboard—the album leaves—the command console filled up with graphics, projects, insights, questions, signs, times for continuing the composition.

Much of the combined, "composed," and discarded material remained.

We obtained lines—spectra—bands which were then "mixed up" among themselves.

Always *listening* intensely ("El 'scolta, sior Lu!" [Listen, Mister You!]).

And sometimes exhaustedly ("Molemo tuto, andemo a cior 'na sgnapa" [Let's leave everything, let's go have a grappa]).

Marino "dictated" the technical language for naming the various experiments, the various tapes.
In the studio he felt like being on his "island."
He was living it between the memory of Mali Lošinj in Yugoslavia and his eager desire to return there.[7]
Another "island" experienced during the summer, often there together with our families.
Fishing ("panolando") early in the morning,[8] *listening* to distant natural sounds—seagulls—*listening* to the sun that gave—gives rise to it all.
Making a fire to cook fish on those rocks that are reflected in the deep transparency of that sea of ecstasy. Marino on and in that sea *is* really happy. He himself is an infinite open "sea" in his amazing richness of natural human inventiveness.

Unexpected jokes, and games in the Milan studio happened by chance or we would invent them. Marino was inexhaustible. Moments of much-needed breaks—relaxation.

The School of Athens: a very funny tape-collage by Marino based on recordings of phrases of some musicians who had worked in the studio.[9] Marino cut, put together and reassembled them, making them say the opposite or something different from what someone had said, fragmenting them without any "logical" continuity.

"At the entrance there are some strange characters, about twenty. They claim to be working with you. But we have closed the gate and called the police," they phoned us from the concierge of the RAI in Corso Sempione, while Marino and I were expecting the Living Theatre and Giovanni Pirelli (friend and very dear colleague) to start rehearsals-recordings for *A floresta é jovem e cheja de vida* (1965–66). (It was the autumn of 1965 and various signs were already preparing for the 1968 explosion.)
We rushed to the concierge. Discussions between the serious and the ridiculous. Finally the director of RAI-Milan, who had been tracked down by phone, ordered to reopen the gate. The Living Theatre entered the RAI-Milan with its disruptive creative violence.

Every night for a week, the Living Theatre was unleashed.

Phonemes—screams—sounds—the famous collective reading of a dollar bill[10]—steps—fragments of a chorus. Actors and actresses approach and obstructed one another, ran along a real path of microphones, distributed by Marino in three recording studios, on multitracks. The dynamic was extremely mobile, improvised, unexpected, and varied like the signals, a masterful technique by Marino, who in turn was following, chasing, recording.

Each evening, then, *listening* to what had been recorded: astonishment and surprise even on the part of Julian Beck and Judith Malina—an extraordinary theatrical group very popular in Italy—when listening to themselves. Question-problem that is still topical: listening to themselves—in themselves, listening to *others, listening within listening*.

Analyses, processing, and choices were made later in the studio also with Giovanni Pirelli.

Carla Henius, an intelligent soprano, who improvises, often unpredictably, using her voice's wide range of articulation, was recorded onto herself and "composed" on four tracks: mixed sounds from the voice and from electronically processed materials—silences—surprise modulations. (For *La fabbrica illuminata*—1964—commissioned for the inaugural concert of the Prix Italia in Genoa and rejected because of Giuliano Scabia's text, which cited justifiably controversial statements by the workers of Italsider, Genoa. It was presented at the Venice Biennale in the same year.)[11]

Henius's voice wandering in space—four tracks—being connected—being interrupted—unifying the recorded and the live parts—mingling with fragments of workers' recorded voices—with fragments of the RAI-Milan chorus conducted by G. Bertola. Experiments to understand-intuit compositional possibilities.

Marino's special recording technique for avoiding differences between recorded tape and live voice (unamplified): there was neither *Dolby*—nor the *Digital System*.

Studies of space (the various spaces of different concert halls), an important musical component—a mobile variant.

Continual tests in order to experiment with and verify our capacity for perception using frequency generators (between one to eight generators simultaneously) with acoustic spectra underneath the difference of 1 Hz, with various modulators—using continuous, mixed, pure materials distributed among the four tracks.

Amusing searches through hardware stores to find bronze pipes of varying circumference—thickness—length—and copper plates of different thicknesses. Microphones placed inside the tubes. Pipes touched with fingers, almost caressed, barely touched at all, up to the point of a blow "col teston" [with the head]: very gentle vibrations without attack and strong hard attacks. Filtered, superimposed, and "composed" with different time relationships among themselves and with different materials. Composed, mixed with an operatic voice, the outstanding Liliana Poli, and nonoperatic voices, the excellent Kadigia Bove and Elena Vicini, with fragments-sections performed by RAI-Rome chorus conducted by N. Antonellini: always *adding-subtracting, composing-discomposing*. (1968, for *Il contrappunto dialettico alla mente,* commissioned for the Prix Italia and rejected for its "offense" to Italy's ally—the United States—because of the text edited by Nanni Balestrini: a poem about the assassination of Malcolm X, a flyer produced by a progressive women's movement of New York against the U.S. war in Vietnam.)[12]

The composition, the music, was being composed little by little. It was sudden, instinctive, reasoned, measured, and *heartfelt.* Often technical errors opened up new musical possibilities, in a mysterious inventive "game."

Marino: authentic musician—technician—theoretician—pragmatist—teacher—interpreter—performer of rare virtuosity—very human in his understanding, his engagement.

"His" Studio di Fonologia: an original musical world totally different from those of Paris, Cologne, Utrecht, and others.

A studio invented in 1954 by B. Maderna, L. Berio, M. Zuccheri, and the physicist Lietti that gradually, both for its new, innovative tools-possibilities, and for the creativity of composers very different from one another, *is* rightly "mythologized" within the music history-life of recent decades (and not just the Italian).

It has been closed for several years.[13]

The general management of RAI TV, in its various changes, in foolish ignorance, unable as it was to transform, innovate, *feel-anticipate* the times, devoted to the most consumerist consumption wanted to let this studio die. Now it wants to bury it by moving it to the museum (?) of the RAI.[14]

Attempts to intervene were to no avail—letters containing proposals by B. Maderna, L. Berio, me,[15] and Marino himself to the general management of Rome for adapting the Milan studio to new technology, to miniaturization, and to computerization.

IT IS SHAMEFUL IRRESPONSIBILITY!

Of course, thanks to some intelligent initiatives and extraordinary efforts, several educational, technological and operational studios have sprung up, in universities (in Padua, faculty of engineering, the Centro di Sonologia Computazionale, where Peppino di Giugno's famous $4x$ functions, "donated" by Pierre Boulez—IRCAM in Paris), in several conservatories (Pesaro—L'Aquila—Perugia, and so on). But they are necessarily limited by the restricted or nonexistent level of both interest and necessary subsidy from the state, from the management of the institutions themselves, and from sponsorship.

These studios are undoubtedly responding in some way (also with seminars and festivals) to the new urgent need for knowledge regarding musical experimentation.

Certain very passionate young people have been forced abroad for further studies and work. The sensational case of Marco Stroppa.[16]

Of course, these studios should be sustained, funded, subsidized.

Can they do it alone . . . ?

Where is it written that Italian musical instruction and creativity must be held back—obstructed—punished with respect to the third technological revolution with its disruptive effects on the current social and cultural transformation?

Why the self-defense from new knowledge, from new areas, from any anxiety for the unknown?

Concert, opera, and festival initiatives abound, institutionalized, subsidized, increasingly more conservative—the status quo!—insanely regressive, in which quantity distorts quality, mediocrity is the norm, programming falls into repetitive and banal resumptions of a past that contributes to reinforcing the status quo and to erecting other walls (involving value systems—markets—taste—consumption—habits with drastically levelling effects) against new, different and "disturbing" creative adventures, new dreams, new utopias.

May this exhibition on music technology,[17] strongly desired by Carlo Fontana and expertly realized by Alvise Vidolin, jolt and throw open new prospects for a different kind of musical culture, innovative, creative and wandering, dreaming in the unknown.

Luigi Nono—Berlin, August 1986

EXCURSUS V

Interview with Michelangelo Zurletti

1987[1]

Fragmente-Stille, an Diotima *(1979–80) is Nono's last work for traditional instruments. After this there is only one work (¿Donde estás, hermano?) written without live electronics: all others, from* Das atmende Klarsein *onwards, are written for various instruments, for various voices, but always processed with live electronics. Nono had worked previously with electroacoustic instruments: already* Omaggio a Emilio Vedova *from 1960 was directed toward the exploration of the electronic sound. That work was indeed the beginning of a series of works for magnetic tape and, though not always, live voices or instruments:* Intolleranza 1960, La fabbrica illuminata, A floresta é jovem e cheja de vida, Per Bastiana—Tai-Yang Cheng, Como una ola de fuerza y luz, ...sofferte onde serene. . ., *are numbered amongst the best known. Then came the frequency generators, namely electroacoustic sounds that were generated live (*Con Luigi Dallapiccola *is from 1979). But this was not enough for Nono. And finally, in 1980, the decisive encounter took place with the live electronics of the Experimental Studio of the Heinrich Strobel Foundation in Freiburg. Many important works arose from it, such as* Quando stanno morendo. Diario polacco n. 2; Guai ai gelidi mostri; Prometeo; A Pierre. Dell'azzurro silenzio, inquietum. *That discovery was decisive . . .*

I would say fundamental. Live electronics have liberated my sensibility to, if you will, a paroxysmal level. Today I have another ear. It has not been a "tragedy of listening," as the title of *Prometeo* puts it; it's

359

that I live—we live—in another moment, in another listening mode. And therefore in another mode of thinking about music.

It was an anticipated mode, however, prepared step by step. The list of your works is a testimony to this ongoing research.
Actually, it goes even further. And further back. It is not true that in Darmstadt, with Hermann Scherchen, we worked only with the twelve-tone row. Already at that time, with the great maestro, we would work, we would study on the basis of very little material: we would investigate even a single sound. To be sure, *Hommage à Edmond Jabès* is written with two notes, but this, too, came about from a very recondite study on one single note. It is this kind of study that I continue to do in Freiburg. Live electronics has accustomed me to working subtractively. A single sound can last ten, twenty minutes. Of course, I do not mean a precise, fixed sound: I mean, like those of the Western tradition, from the Gregorian onward. A mobile sound, able to be split into microintervals presenting itself always differently. The sound, so to speak, of Hebrew chant.

As a consequence, the approach to music changes, seeing that the materials change. Is this not traumatic?
The real trauma is the split that took place between music theory and practice. The unity of the two was always perfect, in Burgundy, France, Spain. Up until Maderna. Bruno knew the theory as much as the practice, just as the Gabrielis did. Then something reached a sticking-point, and the sticking-point originated with Maderna himself, who did not, in fact, create a school. We have learned how to define and we define more and more. But the Gabrielis did not define, they did not specify instruments or voices. And it was not difficult for their contemporaries to solve performance problems because they were so familiar with both theory and practice and knew how to assign the lines to voices and instruments. It is difficult for us today, seeing that this *seconda prattica* [second practice] has been lost. And it is difficult to find it again, maybe we'll never find it again.

But what does it mean for you, for your music, the loss of this unity of theory and practice?
It means, and it is my limitation, that I can no longer write a score. It is not by chance that *Prometeo* is in its fourth version. I am unable to

set the material down definitively. Perhaps it is no longer possible to define. We can only project, suggest, attempt, discuss.

Isn't that what the Gabrielis did?
Exactly, but we have to give up defining. And go back to studying. There is a huge contrast between commissions today, which are relatively easy to get, and what results from them. Today people would rather not seek out the results. But indeed, one should seek them out, and devote a lot of study to them. Personally, I think that I will come here to Paris to study the $4x$ system that Peppino Di Giugno created for Boulez. If I do so, then so should the young people, who do not study enough. Varèse studied all his life, Boulez continues to study. I spoke with him a few days ago of the need for study, and he agreed with me. At that time I have got to know him better, him, his music, his qualities, even the drama of his life of research.

Right at Boulez's side there is a young man who works and studies, Marco Stroppa. He is someone who studies.
Indeed, Stroppa is very good, but there are few like him. I must say that when I am talking about young people, I do not mean so much those of Stroppa's generation. They are indeed more attentive. I am speaking about the composers of the middle generation, aged between forty and fifty. It can be said that after the Darmstadt generation (Maderna, Feldman, Berio, Clementi),[2] composers have stopped studying. For the very young it is different. There is a good reason that they rebel against the patron. Some reject cultural corruption; they demand the necessary time to work, not simply the time offered by the patron. However, they are in the minority. Others find it hard to say no. They are more in favor of applied research and do not recognize the traps that have been set for them.

Could it be that the Italian conditions, the rare opportunities for work, force potential researchers to take what they can find? Or, if they really want to study, to pack their bags?
Sure, sure. And I do not know if the situation could be more dramatic or paradoxical. In an age as technological as ours, in Italy we don't have the tools. Berio cannot do anything. There are no studios, or institutions, or regional initiatives, or research centers. We cannot even come up with a plan to save Venice.

*There is that center in Padua.*³

That's right, but it is of very limited use. It is a center used by banks, the university, the tram company. You cannot work there for long. Also in Naples there is a center, but with the same problems. The CNR does nothing,⁴ and, on the other hand, it has no money. What we lack is a cultural project, a desire for analysis, for information. Even a political project, even in the PCI. Only by analyzing the information and addressing the real problems can a cultural-political project be initiated.

If everything you are saying was triggered by the discovery of live electronics, it must have been a huge discovery.

And very fascinating. Tape is no longer used, and, therefore, nothing is predetermined. The starting point is the study of sound in relation to the sound space, conducted analytically in Freiburg.⁵ The genuinely new factor is the musical component of the space. We work for days with the space to understand what can be done. No longer is there a predetermined distribution of the orchestral sound, but rather a sound that is newly created time after time.

And every time it gives different results. It is also a new form of creativity.

And this is what changes everything because it changes the relationship between theory and practice. This is why I can no longer write a score. The problem is that in writing, one would need to give at least six possible alternatives of dynamics, tempo, distribution. Just to set a limit.

It is a huge problem.

And I am in it up to my neck, and frankly I do not have any solutions. What remains is the enormous fascination. It is no longer electronic music, it is no longer computer music. It is about new discovery that is profoundly engaging, the cultural need to open people's ears more. The repetitiveness of a performance, the security of the outcome—all this is blown into the air. And this is not because myths have collapsed, but because there are new possibilities. At all levels. A new intelligence teaches us how to deal with things. Just take the case of Moscow. The new climate allows for open discussion. This is something we ignore because the great intellectual debates are left to the Craxis, the Martellis.⁶ I took part in a debate that lasted a week, with fifteen hundred people. Those who participated were people such as Wim Wenders, Hanna Schygulla, Alexander Kluge, Elem Klimov (the secretary of the Soviet filmmakers), Adamovich, Rasputin.⁷ I was surprised

Interview with Michelangelo Zurletti | 363

to see Soviet intellectuals openly discussing things. It is no coincidence that there is a new, interesting school of musicians, especially in the Baltic and in Georgia, a new generation of thirty-year-olds. They all admit to having Tarkovsky as a teacher; they continually watch, discuss, and analyze his films. This trend of young people is similar to that of the French youth or those in the GDR. In Berlin you can still find people dressed and wearing make-up like those of Brecht, Grosz. They come to meet you, but you can also find true intellectuals who are perhaps tempted toward the Kabbalah or alchemy but certainly not connected to the "Neue Wilde,"[8] who have gone back to expressionism.

Back to our main topic: it seems clear that with live electronics you have reached a turning point.
You hope to have accomplished many of them as transformations in different ways: instinctive, vital, rational. I believe that anyone emerging from the years of the Cold War has experienced turning points. It is impossible not to have had them. Gramsci's teaching (which we still are far from exhausting: we see how slowly his papers are coming to light) has led me to a turning point.[9] Mistakes, controversies (even very heated ones) I've made so many. Mila is right when he writes about me that the battle continues.[10] My hope is for continuous transformation.

Even in musical thought? Because it is one thing to transform the mode of communication; it is something else to transform thinking.
I reply yes and no at the same time. I say yes because the means have changed and, with these new means, I cannot think about things the way I used to. Today I feel the limitations of a work like *Ricorda cosa ti hanno fatto in Auschwitz*. And as the means have changed, so have the materials, which for me are very important. Something has changed, but I thrive on conflict. I say no when I think that works like *Polifonica-Monodia-Ritmica* included experiments, utopias, anticipations that I still believe in today. This is true of *La terra e la compagna* and of *Cori di Didone*. These were things that essentially followed the same path that I frequent today (and I hope it still is a utopian path).

In the program book, the "Festival d'Automne" publishes some of your letters to Scherchen, Hartmann, letters written between 1951 and 1962.[11] How do you feel seeing your friendship, devotion, and fraternity toward these two great protagonists of musical life of the midcentury brought back so publicly to light?

Letters should always be published because all too little is known about the authors. Through the letters one enters into direct contact with the author, his friends, his enemies, his tastes, his tics. Letters help to overcome the schematic form of the information. If we think of the prepared piano or clusters we immediately think of Cage. We never think of the person who invented them, Cowell, because nobody tells us about him. I like to write letters. Maybe because I need human relationships, to have a dialogue with people. I have excellent relationships with Sciarrino, Bussotti, Clementi, and with two young composers, Ambrosini and Cappelli. However, relationships are not necessarily musical. In Venice I frequently visit Cacciari, Tafuri, and Gregotti.[12] When I cannot visit them in person, then that's the time for letters. It's a correspondence that covers many countries and at least forty years of life.

PART FIVE

The "Possible Infinities"

I

Error as a Necessity

1983

Silence.
    It is very hard to listen.
    Very hard to listen, in the silence, *to others*.
    Other thoughts, other noises, other sonorities, other ideas. When we listen, we often try to find ourselves in others. Find our own mechanisms, system, rationalism, in the other.
    And this is a violence that is totally conservative.

Instead of listening to silence, instead of listening to others, we hope to listen to ourselves once more. It is a repetition that becomes academic, conservative, reactionary. It is a wall against ideas, against what is not possible to explain even today. It is the consequence of a systematic way of thinking based upon the a priori (internal or external, social or aesthetic). We love convenience, repetition, myths. We always like to listen to the same thing, with those small differences that allow us to show off our intelligence.

Listening to music.
    It is very difficult.
    I believe that, today, it is a rare phenomenon.
    We listen to literary things, we listen to what has been written, we listen to ourselves in a projection . . .

Space.
 The traditional concert hall is a horrible space.
 Because it does not offer *different* possibilities but only *a single* possibility.
 For every hall there is a specific task to do, just as once one used to write for one particular place or another, for one particular situation or another. The music I'm looking for is written with the space: it is never the same in every space, but instead works with it.

This allows for great diversity. In the spirit of Musil, if there is a sense of reality, there must also be a sense of possibility.[1] It is not quite true that whatever you choose is the one and only correct option; perhaps what you did not choose is more correct. In the work in the studio, in electronic music, this is what happens. There are many unforeseen events, issues, errors—errors that are of great importance, as Wittgenstein has theorized.[2]
 Because error is what happens and breaks the rules.
 Transgression.
 What goes against the established institution.
 What thrusts toward other spaces, other skies, other human feelings, internally and externally, with no dichotomy between the two, as the banal and the Manichaean way of thinking still maintains even now.

Diversity of musical thought.
 Not musical formulas, rules, or games.
 A musical thought which *transforms* the thinking of musicians, rather than providing them with a new skill that allows them to make the so-called music of today, a skill that can be applied like formulas.
 When Schoenberg founded his concert society,[3] always required many rehearsals. For example, for the *Kammersymphonie* op. 9,[4] he rehearsed some ten times. But he did not perform the concert.
 This gave me much to reflect upon.
 Research work is never-ending, in fact. The finality, the realization, involves another way of thinking. Perhaps Schoenberg's idea is not madness, but contains a great truth. Often, during research, or during rehearsals, conflicts break out. However, these are very emotional moments. Afterwards, there is the rituality of the concert.

Perhaps it is possible to change this rituality, perhaps it is possible to try and reawaken the ear.

Reawaken the ear, the eyes, the human mind, the intelligence, the utmost of externalized internalization.
    This is what is essential today.

2

Other Possibilities for Listening

1985

In order to give examples of the *other ways of listening* [*altri ascolti*] that I would like to discuss, I have prepared only a varied typology of fragments. My presentation will show no traces of continuity or coherence. Indeed, it aims at neither logic nor rationality. These fragments are above all theoretical examples of various, different *ways of thinking* [*pensari*]: ideas of physicists, philosophers, theologians, plus some sonic fragments from experiments in live electronics at the Studio of Freiburg im Breisgau (a place in which I have been working for more than five years). Naturally, I will choose among these fragments, knowing full well that any choice is never the best. Beyond any given choice there are always others, probably more interesting ones. Such is the poetics of someone whom—although he was no musician—I consider a master of musical composition: Robert Musil.[1] Any choice made is not unique, is not the sole and exclusive one, and not even the most perfect or perfectable; other choices are always possible which are omitted and which are often *superior*, in terms of importance and interest, than the choice actually made.

Through these fragments I will attempt to outline a trajectory useful in determining some ideas of relation, connections, and leaps. This serves also to describe the way in which I work and which other young colleagues have begun to experiment in the Freiburg Studio, at IRCAM in Paris, and in the studios at Stanford, Princeton, Harvard, and so on.

A short introductory statement: in the history of our *listening* experiences, we have already left behind the confines of an acoustic spectrum of *known* sounds, or at least, we are abandoning that spectrum. I am happy to note that my idea is shared by a young composer working and studying at Princeton,[2] Marco Stroppa (from Venice, where he studied with Vidolin and was then in Paris to study with Boulez, and is now working with extraordinary humanity and scholarly precision).

To shatter the broken. Today there is much that is *broken,* whether broken in itself or also broken *to be recomposed* (as in Massimo Cacciari's philosophy). The fragments I will play back are materials which, broken, are ready to be subjected to my attempt at *recomposition.*

I always enter the Freiburg Studio *without ideas.* Without plans. This is basic because it means the complete abandonment of the logocentric and the loss of the principle according to which an idea should always precede the music: the idea as something to be worked out or expressed in the music, or the story to be told in music. Naturally, what I say must be discussed, like anything, in terms of oppositions. These are all personal ideas. But I do know that many others think and work like this. As I said, one enters the studio. Musical instruments are available, and one can begin with one of two different methods, the first being that of acoustics pure and simple. In Freiburg, Hans Peter Haller, a physics professor at the University of Basel, designs physical-acoustic diagrams and graphs for what one can do in the studio with the available instruments, both analog and digital. We have many kinds of computers in Freiburg (a very specialized one has just arrived, we are not even acquainted with it yet). We work like gnostics in the studio: immediate and mediated intuition, instrumentation, research. My introduction to this was through the work of the Dutch philosopher Brouwer, the proponent of intuition in mathematics, the philosopher who affirms the need of the *perception of change.*[3] The perception of changes: we are living in an age of continual change, transformations, shatterings. We are continually moving towards the configuration of the microcosm and the miniaturization of all tools. With his particles, Rubbia has shown us the path of undelayable work on microstructures.[4] Thus I, as a musician, think about musical microintervals. All this leads to an infinite number of problems to be solved, to an almost infinite number of difficulties, even for us who work on perception and hearing. For, as I have said, we have left the acoustic field of those sounds that are already known and consumed. Others, young or old, agree with me on this, emphasizing that that world is over. Whoever works or researches today in computer science is doing so in a totally different field, one in which sound *is made with sound.* This may seem like a tautology, but it has a profound meaning waiting to be discovered, one which will eliminate any kind of immanent or de facto mechanistic consequences. Many things written about computers or computer-music relationships and vice versa, are journalistic banalities. Why? Perhaps to sell technology as if it were a commodity, like tomato sauce or household appliances? Let us not forget that, as I have said above, any computer-generated sound is made *with sound.* One begins with sound: what sound is, how one *qualifies* it, how sound reverberates, how space *composes* sound, how space intervenes in transforming sound, and how sound happens in space, namely in terms of combination of different sounds according to the different typology of the space.

New hearing has become *difficult* because it is complex and varied. It has been *difficult* in terms of selection, perception, and psychophysics. Sound *tires* because of its infinite tensions. This problem is totally open and reproduces itself continually.

TAPE: *Audio example 1.* This is a cello tuned initially with all four strings on G (i.e., not tuned in fifths, as is normal).[5] These four strings tuned to G are tuned to each other at microintervallic distances, and so there is not simply one G (as in the classical tonal or modal chromatic scale). The instrument is played by one person with two bows: one *underneath,* which, thus, touches the first and fourth strings; the other *above,* for the second and third strings. Thus, we obtain an audible microintervallic tuning among the four strings. This marked diversification is brought about by the use of the bow (the *two* bows) which is (are) *maneuvered*—literally [i.e., handled]—autonomously. The two bows do not generate sound in the same way (the bow hairs are both above and below the strings). Indeed, there are highly differentiated ways to play: the bow above "sul tasto"; the bow below (bow-hairs or wood!) "sul ponticello," and so on. The type of sound qualities changes completely, as well as the partials change, the composition changes, and the character changes: all change continually. It is possible to use one of the bows percussively on the strings while the other one continues to bow, thus, alternating and altering each other until reaching a *nonunitary sound.*

Besides this, we can employ the important technique of delay, which is frequently used by rock musicians. Sound is *recorded* and then made audible with a little delay. The difference in its use in the Freiburg electronic studio, compared to more common practice, lies in the fact that the delay can be prolonged up to half a second, and, thus, it can be manipulated from a minimum of hundredths of a second up to long intervals, almost a minute. In this procedure the intensity of the recorded material can be regulated almost infinitely. It is possible to make it *pause* or separate it. Its speed can be increased to a point at which the delay is no longer a *recording* in the classical sense. There is an incredible freedom in the essence of this technique: freedom both for the technician (i.e., the real performer) and for the performer (i.e., the real technician), both of whom can transform what comes to them already transformed. Thus, we have an opening of transformational possibilities on two fronts: one natural (the differentiated intonation of the cello's strings) and the other artificial—the delay—also including further possibilities of other computer transformations of the whole.

TAPE: *Audio example 2.* Questions and issues. What *time* is being heard? What is the sound being heard? What qualitative type of sound is being heard? What intervals, what ranges? All this not only makes the composer's work highly problematic, but also opens up a huge number of possibilities. I call these possibilities and not innovations, not *new materials.* I prefer to understand *possibility* in its subjective sense: other possibilities means for me a different hear for listening to the sounds emitted. Even if we can recognize them precisely using an available digital instrument, namely the Sonoscop. (This is an analyzer which uses three computers and which allows me to *see* on the screen what I hear, I see the sound for 0.25 second events; I see the sound as it is composed-colored, black and different grays, all the way to white sound—real sound, the fundamental, is black in its essence.) All this allows me to increase my auditory-perceptive capacities and recognize sound as a system made up of harmonics, partials, accidental and extraneous elements, and so on.

After some practice, it becomes possible and no longer difficult to discover, surprisingly, other partials in the sounds, other elements (e.g., very high-pitched ones) which are not normally heard, other *ways to make sound.* By means of these *ways* I can perceive what is really produced in the *resistance* of the bow and bridge material, of the fingerboard, bow-hairs or wood on the string. This is just a question of rediscovering the immediacy or precision in the experience of *what is normally heard,* also in concerts and recordings, and in the experience of *what is not heard,* but what is there and *must be heard.* Many times I ask myself what and how *one listens* in our world. I would also like to take a polemical tack. For instance, I hear that Rossini's *Maometto II* is an extraordinary work, and then I am told that the orchestra played badly, that the conductor was awful, worse than mediocre. So I ask myself, "What did you hear? How could you tell that the piece was good?" What kind of prejudices are in play here, and whose interests? Indeed, is one listening to *Maometto II* or are there categories, prejudices, or partial meanings which are being used in a random way? All these ways to hear what *there isn't* and vice versa?

The issue of *time*. There are many and varied kinds of time: those that correspond to the durations of the individual original or partial sounds, superimposed, brief, short, long, kept mobile, or transformed (because something also happens in time when one moves from fingerboard to bow to wood, since the durations of the various kinds of sound are different). There are many kinds of time. This is a current problem for which our aural capacity must become temporally more sensitive (and it can do so). Our ear should perceive the many different signals of sound-time. Clearly, the authoritarian and totalizing mode of listening to only one time, one privileged source, can thus be overcome or abandoned. Later in my presentation I will consider the issue of sound-space.

TAPE: *Audio example 3*. You are now hearing something like the song of a bird producing a very high E. Don't listen so much to the bird's E as to what follows, derived from it. Previously I had you hear the solo cello, played in an unusual way, but "naturally", real. Then I played these same sounds subject to delay. Now we are hearing another kind of transformation: namely, filters. The Vocoder analyzes the sound, then synthesizes it and passes it on to other instruments. Indeed, this signal, recognized and then synthesized, can be filtered. In this particular case of our example, the filters are "inverted." Thus, the filtered high segment of the sonic spectrum, rather than remaining high-pitched, seems low-pitched to the ear, or vice versa. This has taken place over time, *after* the production of the sound.

This transformation is neither simple nor mechanical. I would like to emphasize that never does anything *mechanical* take place here. The mechanistic revolution already happened in the past; now we are experiencing the computerized revolution, which is one of *transformation*. Everything happens because of transformation and the way it is transformed. Nothing occurs by virtue of a predetermined mechanism.

This synthesized sound is projected by different loudspeakers. Another filter (at the second or fifth) is then inserted. The filter works on the sonic spectrum: the filter at the second or the one at the fifth operate quite differently on the total range of the spectrum. What does it mean to invert the filter? Essentially, that anything passing through the high filter is transferred to the bass and anything passing through the low filter to the treble. For instance, you have almost always heard that any given high signal/sound which the treble filter transfers to the bass does *not contain* in itself the bass sound; the acoustic material to be processed does not exist after filtering—or, it is not supposed to exist. In the Freiburg Studio, we discovered that if one bows an already vibrating (or just vibrated) string (which happens often in orchestras where the strings are always played with some *vibrato*), then the filter restores various unheard bass frequencies of the sound: another signal, a kind of *spoken* one. In this case, filtering a cello's sound in the high frequencies, we can obtain residual signals from the missing sounds which give the idea of a *spoken sentence* of some sorts in an incomprehensible language. It is one thing, however, when a cello is played and then later one hears its sound, filtered high or low. It is another to follow these transformations according to different temporal functions, at different distances of time from the beginning of the transformation, all the way to zero distance, that is, in real time. What is happening in this case? What is being heard? The cello or the filter? The performer hears himself in the transformation of the sound taking place at that moment. And this means that the performer can react to himself, to his own already transformed sound. Thus, he is no longer a performer who simply performs a single given part. The given part will be written in a certain way, considering its possible transformation. When Flemish composers wrote enigmatic canons or masses on a fixed *tenor,* they used quite similar procedures. At that time the musician studied mathematics, physics, astronomy and logic. These long periods of study also expanded the dimensions of their musical thinking. Today, musical education is scandalous because its teaching consists only of imparting what is already known. (In the last few months, I was in Spain and discovered the conditions in Spanish conservatories: worse than our own.) I said that teaching and learning are stuck on the idea that teaching and learning mean teaching and learning what is already known. Schooling is repetitive, incapable of discovering the secrets of the past, and able only to block the curiosity and interest of young people for what different, *other,* and unknown exists in yesterday-today-tomorrow. In 1977, in his first lecture at the Collège de France, Roland Barthes attempted to shed light on this problem, speaking of one age being succeeded by another in which one would teach the unknown, seeking the moment in which one would discover by experimenting.[6] Perhaps ours is the age whose fundamental experience is that of *unlearning*, of *no-longer-knowing* what is known, to let forgetfulness do its job of unpredictably revising the sedimentation of cultures and beliefs that we have traversed.[7]

Here everything is turned upside-down. In a certain sense. Everything is upside-down—or is it that new possibilities of remembering the forgotten are being opened up everywhere? For me, the issue is not one of making ruptures, but rather of seeking other *continuities:* windows and doors that burst open unexpectedly. Massimo Cacciari's interpretation of Kafka's *Trial* is interesting in this regard:[8] the tragedy of that *trial* is that the doors and windows are open, the experience of the tragedy happens when aware of these possibilities, they are confronted. How to go beyond, how and what to do there, what to invent in that realm of possibilities? For us musicians today, the tragedy rests in passing to the effective use of the innovative and electronic devises at our disposal: how to work while freeing ourselves of all the models, freeing ourselves of what is already past and already known, imposed and maintained in life and art, defended like some fortress of who knows what. To open up to all the possibilities, with all the potential we have in ourselves, not only in our ears, not only in the wide field of perception, but in the life of our mind and our infinite *ways of thinking*.

Music is not only composition. It is neither handicraft nor a trade. Music is thought. All the great music theorists, from the ninth century onward, Italians, Venetians, Arabs, Jews, writers whom we unfortunately persist not to study, all of them supported and compared theories and visions of the different ways and worlds of conceiving music, precisely in Giordano Bruno's sense of the extreme variety of possible thinking: the fixed stars, the infinite *other* suns, the *other* planetary systems. Each of this worlds is and should be different. Let's say it with a very fashionable, journalistic name which we all use so much: each of these worlds is *plural* (or, it *exists in plurality*).

But now I think it would be a good idea to speak of diversity and conflict, of otherness, and of differences as principles capable of generating drama and tragedies (in a musical realm, *in* music itself and not *set to* music). In a time when everything is being "adjusted," when superpowers make agreements while open wars continue (massacres and human disasters which keep on perpetuating themselves), anyone who attempts to break this rule of the game, to violate it, and dissenting, attempts to discover other rules in other games, that person will be banned, as has always happened from antiquity to the present: banned and forgotten. This was the fate of Nicola Vincentino, who also studied the use of quarter-tones in composing. The same for Father Athanasius Kircher, who, in his enormous musical treatises left the idea of an infinitely chromatic music, with microintervals and open intervallic functions, which never came to pass. In these treatises and theories we find the sign of commitment to a true relationship between art and nature and with undefined matter. Reverberations; resonances; various ways of sound diffusion; sound transformations excluded from musical study and composition. These were ideas left behind in old books, among the proliferating theories of the learned. Or they were merely curiosities: consider the real influence on music of elements other than air, for example, water. I am thinking of Matthias Grünewald, the painter of the magnificent and striking Isenheim altarpiece.[9] He was a hydraulic engineer by trade. At that time, water was studied, not only in order to drill wells or to systematize hygiene, but also in relation to acoustic research. We know of hydraulic engineering projects used for the creation of musical events: statues and fountains were put in motion and transformed into sonic sources by solutions and inventions linked to the motion of the waters to which they were connected. The sun heated the water, which then moved statues which produced sounds automatically. So it was in Heidelberg, in the gardens of the Palatine palace. These were water arts, arts practiced by engineers, painters, and sculptors who lived in ideal contact with the elements of nature.

This is only a memory of a culture and knowledge which has now disappeared and which we would like to see return.

Other matters, other issues: piano and pianissimo. The difficulty that we are encountering today in making the four or five possible articulations of *p* performable and perceptible in a pianissimo sound or in making audible the minimal differences in the quantity of sound (*p, f, ff, fff, ffff*). All this is an issue linked to performance techniques and auditory dimensions which have almost disappeared. For me, only Carlos Kleiber, Claudio Abbado, the LaSalle and Arditti Quartets, Maurizio Pollini, Pierre Boulez know how to perform that difference in dynamics which has as an auditory consequence the sensation of the qualitative difference of sounds (a difference which, when performed, is heard and audible in different ways).

It was a great surprise for all of us when the flutist Roberto Fabbriciani—who has been working, studying, and collaborating with me for years—together with Ciro Scarponi, Giancarlo Schiaffini, and other very young students from the Freiburg Conservatory—managed to play a normal flute in the *bass* register at the *lowest level of piano*. It was there, in that experience that we discovered the infinite dynamic articulations of sound.

TAPE: *Audio example 4.* From a musical point of view, some extraordinary results come out of these listening sessions. *First:* when these friends play exchanging their parts, one can no longer discern which one of them is playing: flute, clarinet (Scarponi), or tuba (Schiaffini). Because none of these instruments preserves its own *partials* (that is, the harmonics which characterize the timbre specific to the instrument). As we found upon immediate sonographic analysis, these sounds have a pure wave form, sinusoidal. In other words, they completely lack timbre.

In other sonograms of these *sonic moments* we read a kind of barely recognizable thin line, made up of a few signs in the highest register. These small traces correspond to the minimal movements of the lips on the embouchure. So for the first time, contrary to what is usually taught, we can confirm that the wind instruments *can lack harmonics,* which destroys the entire idea of the *necessity of timbre.* This also really opens up the field of possibilities for new compositions, also opening up to different kinds of *new difficulties:* difficulty in hearing; difficulty in regulating loudspeakers; difficulty in the choice and setup of acoustic space. *Second:* to record this sound is difficult, but can be done (despite tape *hiss,* a kind of sound which is always audible no matter how much one tries to suppress it). *Third:* an aspect which eliminates this last problem. These quasi-sinusoidal sounds, especially in the tuba, do not begin *immediately* but rather with breathing-exhaling. Even if less evident, this occurs in the clarinet and flute too: the sound is still not produced immediately but rather is prepared by breathing-exhaling, little by little, until the desired sound is *found.* This is what I call the "new quality of sound," a sonic transformation which interacts with the very act of its formation. This is something which only a few rare performers know how to do. Some composers know how to rethink their work using this principle, verified in the analysis of the experience of performing, so as to conceive music which corresponds to these *new qualities.* Space participates in the compositional process by generating it. One need only study Andrea and Giovanni Gabrieli, Monteverdi, Bach, or the Spanish Renaissance polyphonic masters in order to discover how compositional techniques diversified according to the performance spaces used. One can check and understand whether a four-voice motet was to be sung with the sound emanating from a single source, or if a concerto of the Gabrielis for eight or more voices was to be diffused in an original, specific, appropriate space (whether St. Mark or a vast German, Spanish, English, or French cathedral). A tape recording, radio broadcast or CDs are all *falsifications:* space disappears completely in all of them. In these situations what one hears in the reproduction is only a kind of superimposition of musical parts, or a kind of *photograph* of a real event that is obviously not a real event. This is what was to be expected in Walter Benjamin's era of the first mechanical reproductions of artworks, that is, photographs. Today, in the computer age, we have at our disposal the possibility of taking advantage of many sonic sources, direct and indirect. Programmable ones. This means that if one hears from a source or sees a loudspeaker, if one can localize the spatial origins of sound in all its aspects, in the same way with a particular technique, sound can be diffused and transformed in other ways, being further transformed in space and time from its source to us.

Today's sound recording techniques are not capable of *fixing* or *archiving* this kind of event. And this means that contemporary technology, in the reproduction of the sonic event, has fallen behind programming and artistic creation. Perhaps this is a well-known goal, one which creates difficulties for the *how* and *why* multisource performances intentionally use certain spaces. Since space is a component and not a container, similar problems result for how *partial* recordings (one, two, three, even four tracks, or radio/video broadcasts, etc.) irremediably and unacceptably alter the *real* acoustic dimensions of compositions. This is one of the most serious problems for hearing and composing that must be addressed today.

Another example, another aspect: the voice.

TAPE: *Audio example 5.* There is a perceptible difference between whistling and singing. In this fragment, we hear whistling and singing treated by very special kinds of filters, those of second. It is clear that this happens in real time, that is, a soprano sings (or whistles), but the transformation (the filtering) happens at the same time as the performance. The singer hears herself *transformed* in such a way that, while listening, she can also modify her *natural* way of singing. It is a living form of improvisation. We use improvisation a lot, but not aleatory ones. Rather, we have taken on *real* improvisations and we choose in the realm of the most surprising possibilities.

What happens to space in this process? Here, too, something unprecedented takes place. In the Freiburg Studio there are six loudspeakers. The singer produces *her* sound, which is amplified and *circulated* in auditory space, continually or with some *interruptions.* The singing is filtered from time to time, from moment to moment, manipulated manually with filters. The same filtered sound circulates in various directions and can also move at different speeds, while its dynamics can be treated in different ways. This means that anyone singing or playing hears themselves *transformed,* both in the quality and the direction of the sound (depending on the use of the six loudspeakers, by leaps, diagonally, and so on). Space is *used* in two ways. This is the simplest: It is an action in regard to time. This continuously *rotating* sound has a time x; the same identical sound, filtered or not, disrupted by the various speakers has another time, let's call it time y. Thus, it is not only a matter of two different qualities of sound, not only two *tendencies* of sounds, but also of two or more *times* of sound. Today in the Freiburg Studio, there are six possible computer-programmed directional setups which we can take advantage of. This leads to technically new possibilities, which were, however, already intuited and otherwise sought out by those musicians who wrote polychoral music and whose compositional structures were conceived of with specific spatial setups in mind (in Venice, Spain, Germany). The only difference was, and is, that their sonic sources were fixed and static. Today, the Halaphon makes it possible to manipulate and modulate the intensity by modifying the *velocity,* regulating the entrances and exits of the sounds. Thus, a sound can *circulate* very quickly, slowing down, stopping, disappearing, fortissimo, pianissimo. It is possible to work on different materials with *fantastic* interventions never before conceivable. Any singer today must study *other* techniques, since a contemporary virtuoso is no longer the same as a traditional one.

Today technique really consists of the combination of control and study, for instance, of *breath,* which thus becomes "breath/sounding breath," the phonetic control of the emission of vowels and consonants, the control of the use of the instrument near and far. The performer must know how to distance himself from the microphone, move around it, and treat it like another instrument.

With these new techniques, the various instruments demand continuous applications of control and study: of the moving bow, no longer evenly bowed; control of a continually rotating bow (various times and qualities in the use of the strings); continually rotating bowing because even if the *fundamental* is the same—let's say a C—the produced sound continually becomes *an other* C. This is because it is impossible to maintain any given sound as fixed and stable insofar as its quality, its *partials,* the highest harmonics are continuous changing. Thus, ever new possibilities present themselves to the instrumentalist who must deal with them, possibilities which he must study as possible ways to control the transformation of the sound.

It is on this level that the conflict begins with concert institutions and artistic directors who continue to organize concerts with the same programs and music in the same halls. A conflict with institutions that spend their millions, of which a part, even a small part (I repeat, a fraction of the enormous public funds used for music) could fund new studios equipped with all of today's computerized instruments, suitable for programming and commissioning new music. Instead, the same historic spaces (halls of the eighteenth or nineteenth centuries) continue to be used, or the perpetual large-scale banality of stagings like Zeffirelli's (only one among many such cases) continue to be mounted. However, I do not wish here to attack history, historical music, or historical spaces. If I think of the construction of cathedrals, their builders and architects who, besides knowing everything about spatial acoustics, also knew how to combine that knowledge with ancient mystic lore, men who *interpreted* by constructing, then I am the first to be fascinated by such grand historical suggestions. In French and Spanish cathedrals, I have seen stained-glass windows with openings whose projections shone on a golden ring on the floor. I found out that these relations had been calculated in time so that the sun's rays would strike that circle on the floor, making it shine at precise dates and times. And then I remembered that something similar had been conceived by the architects of the pyramids, who had designed their buildings so that the pharaoh's head would be illuminated at the time of certain astronomic conjunctions, predicted quite precisely. This is an aspect of creativity no longer ours, but one which we should not think of as lost. For me, even in our time, there is the possibility of opening up art to the knowledge and study of past thought. These are possibilities that we should approach if we do not wish to remain blocked by the rules of the game in a stationary, repetitive, and *stabilizing* culture. Some encouraging signs come from certain daycare centers where some very young and intelligent teachers have invented educational games and systems which to make the children emit and *hear* sounds and music outside any convention or custom. This means that we begin to understand that *hearing* is not only hearing traditional music, but also *hearing the city,* hearing the acoustical environments in which we live. It means reacting to the presence or imposition of noises by also understanding the *other sounds* which exist or can be created.

Venice from the Giudecca, or from San Giorgio Maggiore, or from the water surface of the St. Mark Basin, around seven on a Friday evening is a beautiful sonic scene, truly magical. When the bells ring from the towers to announce some old religious signal (Vespers, or the Angelus), then reverberations and echoes layer themselves on top of these sounds, so that one can no longer tell from which tower the original sound comes, or how and where the exchange of sounds grow denser in all directions on the reflecting surface of the water. This is a happy natural and environmental *response* to the violence of sonic pollution. Among the current problems of ecology, sonic pollution is not the least important. Even at festivals (such as those of *l'Unità, Avanti!, Comunione e Liberazione*),[10] whether secular, Catholic, religious, political, the acoustic situation is always torture to the ear. Everywhere conversation and the sense of self are impeded; speech is impeded; *transformations* of speaking, hearing, conversing, are all impeded. Just as it is for the composer, this *transformation* of thinking and hearing ought to be a problem for everyone, a problem for the city official, the mayor, the head of government, for every individual. Whether desired or not—and two men of quite different cultural background, Berlinguer and Carlo De Benedetti, have both said it—we have entered into a completely new era: a computerized one. A world and way of living which transform our life, our hearing, and the composition of society itself. Work is being transformed; leisure is changing; and the new ability for rapidly supplying and obtaining information is active everywhere. If, in the face of this change, we remain closed (mentally, in our way of thinking, in our habits), we would have no choice but to live in a state of alarm, hostile to the *possible* and to the *unexpected*. Closure and hostility in facing the unexpected and surprising also means an inability to develop in other ways, that unexpected and surprising potential of abandoned traditions, including those dating back to the fifteenth, sixteenth, and seventeenth centuries—traditions that are anything but familiar and exhausted. I have just came back from Spain, and I remember Higinio Anglés,[11] a musicologist and friend of Schoenberg. Anglés also worked in Rome, at the Vatican, as a director of the Institute for Sacred Music (for Spain). I have personally experienced the fact that all the great Spanish repertory of the the fifteenth, sixteenth, and seventeenth centuries, masses, motets, secular and spiritual madrigals by great composers—all this music is very little known. Anglés attempted to have it printed and make editions of it in vain (his efforts were rapidly overcome by various difficulties). And yet I have come back from Spain with some important *historical* impressions. The large cathedrals have two organs in the middle and a third (as in Toledo) on the side. The choir is placed at the center of this acoustic architecture, and the congregation, the listeners, are (or *were*) placed at the different foci of these sonic geometries. This is how it is at the Escorial, since the disposition of the eight organs ordered by Philip II created an extraordinarily spatial listening situation. Nothing now supports such sonic splendor. The music is no longer available. A second volume of a series of Baroque polychoral music is in press. The first one was published in Barcelona in 1982.[12] I have found out that there are pieces for twenty-four voices, masses for nineteen (!) voices, psalms for sixteen voices. I have found out that there are so many compositions by great composers, like Victoria, that have survived and have never been studied. I have also found out that in that polyphonic tradition, ensembles of unusual numeric dimensions were tried out, for instance, odd-numbered ones. All this must be studied. In Spain, we are the middle of a cultural crossroads. Arab, Italian, Jewish influences come together even in the Spanish transformations of Gregorian chant.

Let me stop here. I simply wanted to call attention to the fact that now, even in this European Year of Music,[13] during which there are so many performances of overfamiliar music, sometimes in awful performances, there is neither the intelligence nor the culture to begin analyses, readings, discoveries of historical music which leads (or could lead) to the change and creation of new bases for European culture. This Spanish case is only one of many. It was not only at St. Mark or in Leipzig or other well-known places that the compositional work of musicians attempted to get around Counter-Reformation prohibitions. In Spain as well, this was done with a uniquely original creative and technical touch. But we knew nothing about all this. We knew nothing of the existence of an important center for the gathering of many traditions, a model of cultural combination. Venice, too, is a center *traversed* by different cultures. We need to do something to recover that sense and reconstruct those crossings, while also recovering the spirit and modernity of such diversity. I have spoken to Vittore Branca and Morelli about this.[14] Venetian musical culture has to be approached as a history of multiple and different cultural encounters, and something has to be produced in this vein. We must become aware of diversity in the historical experience of its encounters. Schoenberg also should be studied in light of "Jewish diversity." In Spain as well I found an anonymous fourteenth-century text, the *Sefer Yetzirah*,[15] containing the description of the ten divine Sefirot. To read this book and consider it as a component of Schoenberg's thought has helped me understand Schoenberg, and, through him, to think of musical ideas, which are not only technical ones, but formations of multicultural contributions. Today it is this necessity that drives me the hardest.

I would like to mention Claudio Ambrosini, a young Venetian composer whose search is for an unknown musical culture, without antecedents, that cannot be traced back to anything, but filled with distant relations and extreme diversities. And also Gilberto Cappelli,[16] a young composer who lives practically isolated in Romagna and who, when asked what his music is, says "I don't know." And if one insists "How did you make it?" says "I don't know." I think that Cappelli's answer is correct, because it is no longer possible to reply to certain questions today. Sometimes one cannot come up with the words because every mode of thought has been used up, just like the acoustic spectrum of music (finished, abandoned). For this reason one must wait. As I said at the beginning, one must proceed by intuition, gnostically. Today rationality illuminates and illustrates nothing. It is not capable of discovering what transformation or change really is. It doesn't knows what the *possible* is.

I think that the transformation taking place in our time is making intuition, intelligence, and the capacity of expressing such transformation into the new necessity of life: openness, studies, highly risky experiments, renouncing security and all guarantees, and even *purposes*. We have to know that we may fall at any moment, but we must always seek, nevertheless, seek the unknown.

3

Lecture at the Chartreuse in Villeneuve-les-Avignon

1989

Aristoxenus (300 B.C.) always spoke of how everything exists in contrast. Aristotle and Plato always spoke of the capacity of sound: quantitative sound and qualitative sound. Aristoxenus spoke about qualitative sound, not only as a predetermined, preordained, specified, sound for which it is necessary to follow a method. He also spoke about the possibility of quarter tones, the possibility of endlessly subdividing sound.[1] Of course, this had great value then as now. Consider, for example, the Council of Trent, which had rejected the musical intervals of the [chromatic] system.[2] Nicola Vicentino, in *Ancient Music Adapted to Modern Practice* (1555), says some extremely important things: perhaps you will be reading or listening to things that have no connection with rationality, just as it is possible that you might listen to things that have no connection with feelings, memory, or the psyche.[3] This is specifically a polemic against Plato's formulation in *The Republic,* where he states that gymnastics gives harmony to the human body and music gives harmony to the head.[4] This does not involve settled issues, but is disputed from year to year. Paul Klee, in the Bauhaus sketchbook,[5] pointed out that there is a direct relationship between two points. Later he questioned this. It is not true that the most direct connection between two points is the most correct, but there are also an infinite number of possible connections. Think of the extreme idea put forward by Aristoxenus, for whom everything is divisible, everything can be subdivided as long as the ear can perceive it. This leads directly to breaking the habit of considering sound or a signal as a fixed element. It leads to a different term for the interval.

The interval is the relationship. Things are related among four, five, or *x* relations of possibilities. In Paul Klee's book there is a succession of indications of possibilities. The signal does not remain fixed, that is, C is not C, minor or major, but a signal that has within itself particular features and qualities always to be reinvented, always to be activated with the capacities of criticism, knowledge, and memory. Now there are two points; afterward they become signals that enter into relationship with other relationships. Think about Aristoxenus's idea: one can subdivide up to the quarter tone. Think about Arabic music, on which there is a text in German by a young man who studied Arabic music until 1933,[6] confirming the thesis of Safi-ad-din's, the old fourteenth-century theorist, which is about the existence of a scale of thirty-two possibilities, not limited, but internally open to many other possibilities. Up to the technological possibilities of today, such as the Publison, the Halaphon, and the techniques that Professor Haller will show you, that is, the possibility of superimposing sounds that are completely specific.

Then comes the problem: listening. It is objectively true that listening is not as direct and as passive as listening was in past centuries, but it does not even have the capacity of direct listening as in Arabic music, Hebrew chants, or even in the rhythms produced by the *tambores* orchestras of the Pygmies and the Angolans, which have this relationship, which transmits this serenity. It is Fernando Ortiz, the Cuban musicologist, who has studied this formation of orchestras of *tambores*,[7] which are beaten on the drum skin with a variety of attacks and with different kinds of "legato."

The issues that arise today concern how to consider the field of sounds: not in relation to three or four sounds as Ligeti and Stockhausen or others do, but to maintain different subdivisions, different relationships, and the different capacity of the ear and especially of technique. From a pedagogical point of view it is an extraordinarily open and very difficult field, given the state of teaching in the conservatories. Almost everywhere in the world one can see that the conservatories are truly "conservative" environments and are not places that communicate information. Someone has to invent because there is no method to be applied. Such a method gives a false idea of music, which is truly demotivating and unthinkable. Music is similar to physics. Think of Max Planck,[8] think of all the new biology that today, especially in American universities, is being developed in connection with memory, criticism, imagination, and experimentation. The new thing is the experimentation that sets memory, rationality, and criticism in motion in a completely different way.

For example, take a sound, B♭. It is now possible with technology, with live electronics (or without), to use a part of the sound, a part of the air, or, suddenly, all of the sound, with a particular direction and a particular intensity, finally ending with nothing more than breath. So it is no longer a B♭, but the flutist is going to produce a breath of air closest to B♭, and live electronics make it possible to enhance it. All this is what today, can be achieved with technology, from a single sound, a sound that we used to consider to be very precise, uniform, and unitary. Think of the technique during the era of the woodwinds in Japan and the flutes in Korea, with which similar results could be achieved. Take Tarkovsky's film *The Sacrifice,*[9] for which Takemitsu wrote the flute part, using a flute from India without the aid of technology, but using only what the air can do, the mouth can do, and not only of the mouthpiece in its entirety.

Today this is possible: it is impossible to recognize the change from a bass clarinet to a six-valve tuba or a mezzo-soprano when they make an extremely soft sound. It is not possible for the reason that all instruments, all superimpositions of the harmonic elements of the sound disappear. I have used this expedient many times which leads to an extremely intense listening, to a listening extremely rare and to a listening in which there is almost *nothing to hear;* and above all, most importantly, it leads an inability to recognize what it is: whether it is a bass clarinet, a tuba, or a mezzo-soprano. One can then prove that there many possibilities of subdivision exist, in line with what Aristoxenus said, and what one can do today in an electronics studio with the help of computers. One can analyze a Gregorian chant or see and examine how a Hebrew chant contains thousandths of a tone. Of course one must educate the ear, get used to it, but I find that this is strongly connected to a part of cultural listening today.

One technique that you will analyze with Professor Haller involves the possibility of organizing a composition with a single pitch using the Halaphon, which is capable of creating various situations with the same pitch. The diversity of speed and direction make it possible to create, continual fragmentation of the selection of the interval from just one note, as I said before. By means of the filters one can use one part or another of a sound; the rest can be used later. We take a sound with a particular tempo (for example 60) and one direction through five loudspeakers. The same sound can go in the reverse direction, at the speed of 120. One can also break up the sound. In this way one does not have the sound in its continuity, but an entirely different element that is then superimposed, or better, is combined with the other, perhaps with a sound that exists in other directions with other speeds. In this way you have things extremely distinct, different in dynamics, direction, continuity, or discontinuity.

At this point it becomes necessary to begin talking about space, because of all the things I have said it is the important *element* that leads to innovating the continuous or noncontinuous transformation. Let's take a Mondrian painting: where is the center, the end, the limit, the beginning? There is a completely different concept in a picture, which for me is the same. There is the same thing in Magritte, with the red, the black, and the white: where is the limit of the white, the red, and the black, with all the internal variations for the disappearance of the colors and, also, with all the differences in the brushwork? As you can see, there are applications in painting that are more or less accepted. But in music it is not at that point of being natural or normal, integrated in life.

Another thing is the Gaudí Chapel in Spain, in Güell,[10] made with only three elements: stone, tin, ceramic, and nothing else. The entire construction, all the relationships, all conventions are completely broken with just *three* elements.

Having reached this point, I want you to listen to a part one of those things that Haller has already spoken to you about. It is *Diario polacco*.[11] *Diario polacco* is a composition that goes back to the technique of the Flemish enigmatic canon: to the fixed *tenor, recto modo,* or multiplied with dice in Josquin, or to the *tenor,* again in Josquin,[12] which provides other material. For a long time, as I will show you during my lectures on the music of *Con Luigi Dallapiccola,* I used a kind of monorhythm like in Dunstable, Tallis, and the Venetians. The difference regards abstraction, subtraction, and elimination. That is, I use different methods of live electronics: the material, the signal is the same, but the quality changes, the connection changes because there is a "linking" not only in the moment of the *legato,* but also among the sounds. It is the typical thing of which [?] speaks:[13] a principle A is equal to B. I work with A, and I start working a lot by subtraction. I take one element or the other—I delete everything—I join this and that—I break up the first element and use what I have not used . . . Schumann worked extensively with succession by subtraction in *Fantasy in C major* [op. 17 of 1836].

At the moment in which he repeats the motifs or cadences, he suppresses a part. And not only Schumann, but many others. In addition to this difference, there is another difference, other ways compared to those that I have just shown you, of transforming sound with live electronics. It is something that I call (but I don't know whether it is right) "isorhythm" because the model is repeated, changing continually. During Dunstable's era, the pitches, the syllables, and the pitches of speech were changed. I am really surprised when I find many things that remind me of those things of the past or the mentality of other composers, other cultures, other stories, and other eras. And here an extremely important issue takes over: the use or not of the capacity for critical analysis and to ask oneself "why yes" or "why no."

One important thing: up until now no one has noticed that at the beginning of *Diario polacco* there is an *A* mode and a *B* mode. Let's listen to the beginning, mode *A,* and then mode *B* with the various changes of the three cellos, the bass flute and the soprano voices.[14] Here, as Haller has demonstrated today, there is the possibility of using the Publison as a *reverser.*[15] At the same time in which one hears the voice, one can also hear "e" "tu" "cheich" "neim" "ac."[16] It is an extremely interesting instrument. It can destroy everything or it can be extremely constructive and open up other possibilities for singing and, also, for pedagogical problems.

[Listening: *Quando stanno morendo. Diario polacco n. 2*].

This was the beginning with two sopranos, in which one voice uses the other through the *gate* and the movement.[17] There are minimal alterations that the space renders extremely audible. The same problem arises in the realization of Gabrieli's music, including later for records and the radio. It is the same story even if the way of singing is different. It is a very long process in the studio, using minimum vibrato, not just for going together with the instruments—that are not there—but in order to use the human voice in another manner (and I am speaking mainly as an Italian!).

There are three cellos each time (here played by the cellist Frances-Marie Uitti). Each cello has the same string tuned to the same pitch but finely subdivided.[18]

Today I have addressed two points necessary for providing information and for achieving a purpose. At the same time I know that this is a kind of hard work on the music that involves a lot of difficulties, and not only in the live electronics studio—many difficulties because one needs special spaces, special seating arrangements of the audience, and all of these make a difference.

I want to end with *Spem in alium,* by Thomas Tallis,[19] which is an example of spatial music that can be performed even outdoors. There are eight choirs singing, which are positioned in relation to the space. The music itself is related to the space. With eight or more choirs, virtually only the tonic and dominant can be used. But the extraordinary thing is that with these so-called "minimal possibilities" you can explore the space and succeed in making the space come to life doing it so that the space itself begins to "sing." At the time of Tallis and at the time of Gabrieli, composers wrote either for a performance *en plein air* or for a special space—here, there was a forest, here, there were tapestries—or other features related to the Madonna dell'Orto Church.[20] There is, for example, a piece by Andrea Gabrieli in which there are Japanese elements because it was written for three Japanese princes who at that time had come to Venice.

Another concept: it is not only about the simple performance by some person. The elements involved in transforming the sound, the place of performance, the performer, and the audience must always be pushed to the limit. Something typical of Renaissance music: always high up. In St. Mark's and in all the other churches, the choir lofts are arranged up high, never down low, on high with two, four, or five possibilities. In the Granada Cathedral I counted up to eight possibilities for placing two or three voices, or in the huge Escorial cathedral the possibility of having up to eight organs. I believe that many of these transformations can help us change as musicians, as human beings, or to participate in the change that is necessary today. Maybe. Or maybe not. But I am an advocate of this need, which can be discussed or condemned. In all this I really feel, a "new" era (or an "other" era), even an "other" light, directly. And above all, on the educational level, the ability to communicate information (as I have now done).

I only give information. And I do not like—I say this frankly—the statement "Think of me tonight." These things are possibilities for me, but that is not why everyone should do them. I believe, on the contrary, that in the educational field one should study in a different way and each must find one's *own* specificity, one's *own* reason for living, one's *own* reason to speak with others.

EXCURSUS VI

"Proust" Questionnaire

1986

What for you is the greatest disaster?
The many wars today (Afghanistan, Iran, Iraq, San Salvador, Lebanon, Chile), the destruction of nature, the continuous development of nuclear and chemical weapons.

Where would you like to live?
Perhaps more within myself, that is, at the crossroads of many different cultures: more discoveries, more surprises as, for example, in a Venice to be newly rediscovered.

What is your idea of perfect happiness?
Very difficult to attain because it is constantly being destroyed; even though Cuba and Nicaragua live and love again.

What errors do you forgive most readily?
Jealousy, and the tendency to exclusive uniqueness.

Your favorite heroes in literature?
Those of Dostoyevsky, Franz K[afka], the Tanners.[1]

Your best-loved historical figure?
Ernesto "Che" Guevara, Giordano Bruno, St. Paul.

Your favorite heroines in real life?
Which real life? There are many of them and very different, thankfully.

Your most popular heroines in poetry?
Eurydice, Isolde, the beloved in *Caurapañcāśikā* ([The Love Thief] Sanskrit).[2]

Your favorite painters?
Rublev, Piero della Francesca, Grünewald, Pontormo, Tintoretto, Moreau, Pollock, Burri, Vedova, Boccioni, El Greco, Tápies, Pirosmani, Schiele, Fuseli, Turner, Klee, Kiefer: but always new surprises.

Your favorite composers?
From Machaut to the Hasidic songs, from Dufay, Tallis, from Victoria to Varèse, Feldman, Claudio Ambrosini, Miles Davis.

What qualities do you most value in men?
Continuous doubt, the awareness of problems even to the point of contradiction.

What qualities do you most value in women?
The ideal of sentiment and love, the continuity of the private into the public (Rosa Luxemburg, for example).

Your favorite virtue?
The willingness to stay and listen to the diversity of others.

Your favorite occupation?
Studying other cultures: for example, Arabic, Judaism, the Presocratics.

Who would you have liked to be?
The tower of Tübingen, to listen to Hölderlin.

The main trait of your character?
Nostalgia for the future.

What do you value most in your friends?
The continuous renewal of friendship through reciprocal criticism.

Your greatest mistake?
Maybe: falling into the trap of others' cunning.

Your dream of happiness?
The Promised Land: which one? The unsayable.

What would be the biggest disaster for you?
Opposition to the point of dogmatism against renewal, change, invention, risk.

What would you like to be?
I should answer: am I who I am? But: who am I or who would I like to be? Who knows.

Your favorite color?
It changes continuously just as the color changes in the *color-video-computer.*

Your favorite flower?
It changes continuously according to the changing of the woods and valleys, as for example in Sardinia or in Latin America.

Your favorite bird?
See above.

Your favorite writer?
Currently: Franz Rosenzweig, Massimo Cacciari, Gialâl ad-Dîn Rûmî, Bilhaṇa (Sanskrit).

Your favorite poet?
Ibn Zaydūn, Al Mu'tamid ibn Abbād, Halevi, Rilke, Jabès.

Your heroes in real life?
Savonarola, Antonio Gramsci, the unemployed, the heretics.

Your heroines in history?
Cassandra, Joan of Arc, the so-called witches in the Middle Ages. The mothers whose children have disappeared who protest in Argentina.

Your favorite names?
　Ariel, Fyodor, Tobias, Diotima, Lou, Silvia, Bastiana, Nuria, and the unsayable ones.

What abhors you the most?
　The different dictators: political, cultural, and economic.

What historical figure do you despise the most?
　I don't despise but hate: the different Hitlers from ancient times until today.

What military actions do you most admire?
　The Cuban Revolution of Fidel Castro.

What reform do you admire most?
　Decentralization, and cultural, economic, and political autonomy.

What natural gift would you wish to possess?
　To be able to fly, to wander in infinite space.

How would you like to die?
　Among the seven heavens.

Your current state of mind?
　Doubts, hopes, despair, serenity in each moment.

Your motto?
　And yet it moves (Galileo).

Notes

ABBREVIATIONS

Balázs 1985	Luigi Nono, *Írások—Interjúk—Elöadások*, ed. Balázs István. Budapest: Zenemukiadó, 1985.
De Assis 2014	Luigi Nono, *Escritos e entrevistas*, ed. Paulo de Assis. Lisbon: Casa da Musica, 2014.
De Benedictis-Rizzardi 2001	Luigi Nono, *Scritti e colloqui*, ed. Angela Ida De Benedictis and Veniero Rizzardi, 2 vols. Milan: Ricordi-LIM, 2001.
De Benedictis-Rizzardi 2007	Luigi Nono, *La nostalgia del futuro: Scritti scelti, 1948–1986*, ed. Angela Ida De Benedictis and Veniero Rizzardi. Milan: il Saggiatore, 2007.
Feneyrou 1993	Luigi Nono, *Écrits*, ed. Laurent Feneyrou. Paris: Christian Bourgois, 1993.
Feneyrou 2007	Luigi Nono, *Écrits: Nouvelle édition française de Laurent Feneyrou basée sur l'édition italienne d'Angela Ida De Benedictis et Veniero Rizzardi*. Geneva: Contrechamps, 2007.
Stenzl 1975	Luigi Nono, *Texte: Studien zu seiner Musik*, ed. Jürg Stenzl. Zurich: Atlantis, 1975.
ALN	Archivio Luigi Nono, Venice.
GDR	German Democratic Republic.

IMD	Internationales Musikinstitut (International Music Institute), Darmstadt.
NWDR	Nordwestdeutscher Rundfunk (Northwestern Germany Public Radio), Hamburg.
PCI	Partito Comunista Italiano (Italian Communist Party).
PSF	Paul Sacher Foundation, Basel.
PSI	Partito Socialista Italiano (Italian Socialist Party).
SWR	Südwestrundfunk (Southern Germany Public Radio), Baden Baden, Mainz, Stuttgart.
USSR	Union of Soviet Socialist Republics.
WDR	Westdeutscher Rundfunk (Western Germany Public Radio), Cologne.

INTRODUCTION

1. This expression, which appears in the title of the orchestral composition *A Carlo Scarpa, architetto, ai suoi infiniti possibili* (1984), is a hint to Giordano Bruno's philosophic dialogue *De l'infinito, universo et mondi* (1584) and can be translated as "possible infinities," implying also the notion of "infinite possibilities."

2. Rainer Maria Rilke, *Sonnets to Orpheus*, trans. and intro. David Young (Middletown, CT: Wesleyan University Press, 1987), 3.

3. For more information on Luigi Nono's life and works, see the biographical sketch, drawn up by Angela Ida De Benedictis, published on the official website of the Luigi Nono Archive (see www.luiginono.it/en/luigi-nono/biography [accessed November 21, 2017]).

4. Later, in 1961, Nono would recall giving up these lessons after two years on account of boredom; see "Duo con Luigi Nono," interview with Martine Cadieu, in De Benedictis-Rizzardi 2001: II: 3.

5. Nono speaks of this at length in the extensive autobiography published in this volume ("An Autobiography of the Author Recounted by Enzo Restagno"); see also part IV, chapter 2, "Remembering Two Musicians."

6. See in this volume "Interview with Renato Garavaglia."

7. See on this point "Remembering Two Musicians."

8. In that context, Nono rhetorically confuses the concepts of "indeterminacy" and "improvisation" (the latter extraneous to the poetics of Cage), to give greater vigor to his thesis.

9. See part III, chapter 4, "Music and Power."

10. On November 19, 1955, Schuller conducted *Polifonica-Monodia-Ritmica*, for seven instruments, at the Town Hall in New York City. The evening featured the Modern Jazz Quartet and other prominent jazz musicians such as

J.J. Johnson, Lucky Thompson, and Tony Scott. Among the performers of the Nono piece were Tony Scott and the pianist of the MJQ, John Lewis, who was also a friend of Nono. See www.jazzdiscography.com/Artists/Schuller/gas-disc.htm (accessed December 2017).

11. This comprised four pioneering multimedia pieces involving theater and electroacoustic music, live and on tape, conceived and performed by Robert Ashley, Harold Borkin, George Manupelli, and Gordon Mumma, directed by Milton Cohen, the creator of the Space Theater. The pieces were performed during September 11–13, 1964, at the Teatro La Fenice. See Michele Girardi and Franco Rossi, *Il teatro La Fenice: Cronologia degli spettacoli, 1938–1991* (Venice: Marsilio-Albrizzi, 1992), 192.

12. See in this regard the five texts anthologized in part II, "Music Onstage: from a 'Theater of Ideas' to the 'Tragedy of Listening.'"

13. Here represented by the texts collected in part III, "Conscience, Feelings, Collective Reality."

14. See Nono's touching recollection in "Interview with Renato Garavaglia."

15. See, for example, Massimo Mila, *Nono, la svolta* (1988), in Mila and Nono. *Nulla di oscuro tra noi: Lettere, 1952–1988*, ed. Angela Ida De Benedictis and Veniero Rizzardi (il Saggiatore: Milan, 2010), 324–33. The text had appeared for the first time in German (*Nono—die Wende*) in *Komponistenporträt Luigi Nono* (38. Berliner Festwochen), ed. Klaus Kropfinger (Berlin: Berliner Festspiele GmbH und Autoren, 1988), 70–77.

16. Among such studies, it suffices to mention here Carola Nielinger-Vakil's volume, *Luigi Nono: A Composer in Context* (Cambridge: Cambridge University Press, 2015). Among the most important initiatives, it is worth noting the recent international conference/workshop/concerts *Utopian Listening: The Late Electroacoustic Music of Luigi Nono: Technologies, Aesthetics, Histories, Futures,* held on March 23–26, 2016, at Tufts University, Medford, MA (in collaboration with Harvard University).

17. Chapter 3 of part I, "The Development of Serial Technique."

18. Stenzl 1975.

19. Letter of February 20, 1976, published in Mila and Nono, *Nulla di oscuro tra noi,* 147. Mila made the request on behalf of the Einaudi publishing house.

20. Letter of May 26, 1976, published entirely in ibid., 149.

21. Feneyrou 1993. Let us recall here that in 1985, before this first French translation, a collection of writings and some interviews was published in Hungary (Balázs 1985).

22. De Benedictis-Rizzardi 2001. For this edition, access was had to all the ALN resources and to the original typescripts and manuscripts of the composer's library. This is an invaluable collection of about ten thousand volumes, where it was possible to find printed sources for articles published in periodicals that are hard to access, as well as annotations that proved valuable in verifying citations, references, and circumstances; and further still correspondence, concert hall programs, Italian and international press reviews, and so on.

23. However, this was not a complete collection: texts were excluded that would have resulted in excessive redundancies without enhancing the philological quality of the edition.

24. De Benedictis-Rizzardi 2007.

25. See www.luiginono.it/en/works.

26. The number of the excluded writings—mostly shorter texts, often for journalistic or occasional use—was about twice that of those included.

27. These editions formed the basis of the new collection in French, Feneyrou 2007, and a more recent Portuguese edition, not annotated, which curiously reverts to the 2001 edition even for those texts subsequently revised or refined in the 2007 edition (De Assis 2014).

28. Angela Ida De Benedictis and Veniero Rizzardi, "On Some Difficulties in the Collection and Edition of the Writings of Luigi Nono," *Musica/Realtà* 115/1 (2018): 135–57. The article has originally appeared as "Intrigues philologiques dans la collecte et l'édition des écrits de Luigi Nono," in *Écrits de compositeurs: Une autorité en questions (XIXe et XXe siècles)*, ed. Michel Duchesneau et al. (Paris: Librairie Philosophique Vrin, 2013), 291–308.

29. De Benedictis-Rizzardi 2001: xv–xxviii and 559–606; and De Benedictis-Rizzardi 2007: 9–24 and 271–90.

30. Those who wish to explore further the extent of these differences, whether for study purposes or simply out of curiosity, are strongly advised to consult the 2001 and 2007 editions.

31. Often his use of the lower case did not even spare proper names or German nouns.

32. An eloquent *querelle* around the difficulty posed by Nono's writing style is the one that developed in 1956 with Luciano Berio regarding the publication of a text on serial technique; see in this regard the critical footnotes to chapter 3 of part I, "The Development of Serial Technique" (1957), and the details of the story given in De Benedictis and Rizzardi, "On Some Difficulties."

33. Other than in exceptional cases, all Nono's uses of the lower-case and long dashes in place of the period have therefore been normalized.

34. For this reason, at the first occurrence (112), the original term has also been included in square brackets. Another important word in Nono's vocabulary could also be cited as an example: *provocazione*, which is translated here in most cases with the cognate word in English, *provocation*, especially when Nono intends it to intensify the meaning of concepts such as "impulse" or "drive."

35. This was one of the arguments with which Nono rejected an editorial intervention by Berio; see above, note 32.

36. See, for example, certain terms related to South American social and political realities in chapter 5 of part III, "In the Sierra and in the Parliament."

37. In his preface to the first edition of the interview (*Nono* [Turin: EDT, 1987], ix, xi, esp. x), Restagno alerts the reader to the fact that he has accomplished a real work of "translation" on the assembled material, assuming the "responsibility for having taken such liberties."

OVERTURE. CLARIFICATIONS

1. Italics emphasize the added underlinings in the manuscript in red pencil.
2. "Uomo-sociale" in the original Italian, used in opposition to the next "uomo-poeta," here translated as "poet-man."
3. The quotation from Li Po found in Nono's note, marked with "i," is taken from the poem *A Tan Chiu;* see *Liriche cinesi (1753 A.C.–1278 D.C.),* ed. Giorgia Valensin and Eugenio Montale (Turin: Einaudi, 1943), 75–76, esp. 76 (book annotated in ALN); the English text that is closest to the quote is that of *To Tan Ch'iu,* in *The Poet Li-Po,* A.D. 701–762, by Arthur Waley (London: East and West, 1919), 27. For Mayakovsky's poem see Vladimir Mayakovsky, "150.000.000," in *Selected Poems,* trans. James H. McGavran III (Evanston, IL: Northwestern University Press, 2013), 199–247. The quote from Machado is taken from *Reflexiones sobre la lírica,* now in *Poesía y prosa,* ed. O. Macrí (Madrid: Espasa Calpe / Fundación Antonio Machado, 1989), 1653.

EXCURSUS I. AN AUTOBIOGRAPHY RECOUNTED BY ENZO RESTAGNO

1. The treatise by Paul Hindemith has an English translation by Arthur Mendel and Otto Ortmann with the title *The Craft of Musical Composition* (New York: Associated Music Publishers, 1942–70).
2. The concert, entitled "Concerto della giovane scuola italiana" (Concert of the Young Italian School), took place on September 21, 1946, at the Teatro La Fenice in Venice. The program consisted of the *Serenata per undici strumenti* by Maderna and also: Riccardo Malipiero, *Piccolo concerto,* for piano and chamber orchestra; Valentino Bucchi, *La dolce pena;* Guido Turchi, *Trio,* for flute, clarinet, and viola; and Camillo Togni, *Variazioni,* for piano and orchestra.
3. Considered to have been lost until a few years ago, Maderna's *Requiem* was found in 2006 by Veniero Rizzardi, who in 2012 edited the publication for Suvini Zerboni (Milan). See also Veniero Rizzardi, *Esumazione di un Requiem: Edizione anastatica della partitura e note informative sul ritrovamento del giovanile "Requiem" di Maderna* (Florence: Olschki, 2007).
4. The former was translated into English in 2008 by Lucille Corwin ("*Le Istitutioni Harmoniche* of Gioseffo Zarlino, Part 1: A Translation with Introduction," Ph.D. diss., City University of New York). For the latter see Gioseffo Zarlino, *Dimostrationi harmoniche,* facsimile of the 1571 edition (New York: Broude Brothers, 1965).
5. See Robert Schumann, *Advice to Young Musicians,* trans. Henry Hugo Pierson (Leipzig and New York: [J. Schuberth], 2009), e-book. In the original text, Nono read from an Italian version (the copy is still present in the library at the ALN) bought in 1944 (Robert Schumann, *Precetti ai giovani studiosi di musica,* trans. Carlo Schmidl [Trieste: Schmidl, n.d.]).
6. Here Nono refers probably to Luigi Vio, a priest who was at that time choir director of the Basilica.
7. With "black shirt" (*camicia nera* in the original Italian), Nono is openly referring to fascism and, more precisely, to the voluntary militia of the members

of the National Fascist Party, the uniform of which was characterized by the black shirt.

8. See Gian Francesco Malipiero, *Igor Stravinskij*, presentation by Gianandrea Gavazzeni (Pordenone: Thesis, 1982; 1st ed., Venice: Il Cavallino, 1945).

9. A Soviet literary group founded in 1921 at St. Petersburg (then Petrograd) and disbanded at the beginning of the 1930s. Among the Serapion Brothers are remembered: Lunts, Kaverin, Slonimsky, Tikhonov, and Shklovsky.

10. *Il Politecnico* was a magazine first published in Milan in 1945 by Giulio Einaudi and edited by Elio Vittorini. It had a pioneering role in introducing for the first time a lot of contemporary foreign writers in Italy, among them Hemingway, Eliot, Kafka, Joyce. *Il Politecnico* ceased its activity at the end of 1947.

11. At the ALN there is a copy of the *Trattato pratico d'armonia* [Practical Manual of Harmony], by Nicolai Rimsky-Korsakov, trans. G. F. Bucchi and A. Zamorski (Milan: Sonzogno, 1932) that reveals visible traces of study.

12. Nono is here referring to the triptych *L'Orfeide* by Malipiero, assembled in 1922 and made up of *La morte delle maschere, Orfeo,* and *Sette canzoni.*

13. In Italy, in the State Conservatories of Music, the traditional course of composition lasted ten years and was split up into the final examinations for the "lower course" (fourth year), the "intermediate course" (seventh year), and the "advanced course" (tenth year). Only by passing the last examination can one receive the final diploma, something that Nono never achieved.

14. See Herbert Fleischer, *La musica contemporanea,* trans. Augusto Hermet in collaboration with the author (Milan: Hoepli, 1938).

15. In Venice, in the district of Dorsoduro.

16. Nono's memory here requires correction: in reality he graduated on November 15, 1947, with a thesis in criminal law entitled *L'exceptio veritatis;* see also Alessandra Carlotta Pellegrini, "Musica o diritto? La nascita di un compositore," in *Gli anni giovanili di Luigi Nono,* proceedings from the conference "Luigi Nono: Musica e impegno politico nel secondo Novecento," Venice, Fondazione Giorgio Cini, December 3–4, 2004, published online: http://static.luiginono.it/atti-convegno-2004/acp_testo.html (accessed December 28, 2017).

17. The title "Poema della solitudine" (Poem of Solitude) does not appear in the catalog of Ungaretti's works. One can suppose that Nono is referring to the poem "Solitudine," taken from *L'allegria* (in Giuseppe Ungaretti, *Vita d'un uomo: Tutte le poesie,* ed. Leone Piccioni [Milan: Mondadori, 1969]). This hypothesis is supported by the presence, among the handwritten material kept in the ALN, of some sketches connected to this project. For a thorough examination of their relationship see Luigi Nono and Giuseppe Ungaretti, *Per un sospeso fuoco: Lettere, 1950–1969,* ed. Paolo Dal Molin and Maria Carla Papini (Milan: il Saggiatore 2016).

18. Nono is referring to the International Forum "For a Nuclear-Free World, for the Survival of Humanity," which took place in Moscow on February 16, 1987.

19. See Nicola Vicentino, *Ancient Music Adapted to Modern Practice,* trans. with introduction and notes, by Maria Rika Maniates, ed. Claude V. Palisca (New Haven, CT: Yale University Press, 1996), 6 ("Book on Music Theory," chap. 1 proem).

20. With this formula Nono summarizes a set of concepts that return insistently in the poetry of Hölderlin. See Friedrich Hölderlin, *Sämtliche Werke und Briefe,* vol. I, ed. Michael Knaupp (Munich: Hanser 1992), in particular: "Der Weingott," ll. 120ff. (318), l. 147 (319); "Brod und Wein" (first version), ll. 109ff. (378); "Heimkunft," ll. 103–4 (322). Poems translated into English in *Selected Poems and Fragments,* trans. Michael Hamburger (London: Penguin Books, 1998).

21. See also Michael Long, "Symbol and Ritual in Josquin's *Missa Di Dadi," Journal of the American Musicological Society* 42/1 (Spring 1989): 1–22.

22. More about this in "Toward *Prometeo*: Journal Fragments," in chapter 5 of part II in this volume.

23. "Consider what moderation is required to express oneself so briefly. Every glance can be extended into a poem, every sigh into a novel. But to express a novel in a single gesture, joy in a single indrawn breath—such concentration can only be present when there is a corresponding absence of self-indulgence"; Schoenberg, in Anton Webern, *Sechs Bagatellen für Streichquartett op. 9,* pocket score (Vienna: Universal Edition, 1924), 2. Original in German.

24. Nono is probably referring to opus 28.

25. The purpose of the recollection is to connect it with the monographic concert and the public debate dedicated to Webern on July 23, 1953, at Darmstadt, on the occasion of the composer's seventieth anniversary. On this occasion, Nono gave a short talk, which was later also read on an NWDR radio program; the original typescript, in German, is held at the IMD archives. See critical notes to the Italian translation published in De Benedictis-Rizzardi 2001: I: 559–60, esp. 560.

26. See chapter 1 of part III in this volume "Historical Presence of Music Today."

27. In the letters that Nono and Steinecke exchanged between February and August 1958 (held in original and in copy at the ALN), one can read about the development of the idea of entrusting to Nono (at first in collaboration with Karl-Heinz Wörner) an issue of the journal, on a collection of subjects that are nonetheless not precisely identified until the Ferienkurse of the following September, when John Cage and David Tudor held their performance with music by Earle Brown, Morton Feldman, Christian Wolff, and by Cage himself. On October 28, Nono writes to Steinecke: "I wrote already to Cage-Brown for the next issue-Cage-January. Also Ligeti-Stockhausen to write. Also Tudor. Me, too. What do you think? . . . at the end I would like to include in facsimile a piece by Cage" (original in German). In a letter of November 12, 1958, from Milan, Cage thanks Nono for the initiative: "In short. Of the 3 (Brown, Feldman and Wolff) only Wolff, in reality, studied with me. He also wrote an article on new and electronic music that I have here with me. Further, Schillinger has nothing to do with the development of my concepts and actions. Therefore I suggest Wolff's article with or without one of Brown's./David [Tudor] prefers not to write an article. I suggest to ask one from Heinz-Klaus Metzger, who of all the critics has been the single one to have a conception of my work. . . . I am pleased that you have managed to do this issue of the journal and I hope that we will have some time together to talk about this and in general while I am in

Italy" (original in English). In a subsequent undated letter Nono wrote to Steinecke: "Now: I wrote to Cage a long time ago about a Cage volume with him, with Brown, with Stock[hausen], with me, with Ligeti: he answered totally differently, he wants it to be totally different, with Metzger etc. and I don't want to go this way: the Cage volume is canceled. Because: my idea was: a sort of discussion about Cage and his mentality, in order to clarify [his position] here—if possible—and also a discussion about chance, indeterminacy etc. thus the compositional problem—as in no. 11 by Stock[hausen]/as with Pousseur/and Boulez/and Cage—should be confronted and discussed" (original in German). It is to be noted here how Nono had asked Cage to clarify his relationship with Joseph Schillinger. However, both Cage and Schillinger were to become the objects of controversy in the lecture that Nono would give at Darmstadt in 1959 (here published with the title "Historical Presence of Music Today"). For more detail of these events, see Martin Iddon, *New Music at Darmstadt: Nono, Stockhausen, Cage, and Boulez* (Cambridge: Cambridge University Press, 2013), 229–31, esp. 230 (from which is taken, with some alterations, the translation of the undated last letter of Nono to Steinecke).

28. See Arthur Schopenhauer, "On the Aesthetics of Poetry," in *The World as Will and Representation*, trans. Eric F. J. Payne (New York: Dover, 1969), II: 435–36 ("Supplements to the Third Book," n. 37).

29. See Giorgio Agamben, *Stanzas: Word and Phantasm in Western Cultures*, trans. Ronald L. Martinez (Minneapolis: University of Minnesota Press, 1993), 26. In the passage cited by Nono, Agamben is commenting on the concept of melancholy in relation to the meaning of the term *nigredo* in alchemy.

30. Henri Corbin, *Spiritual Body and Celestial Earth: From Mazdean Iran to Shi'ite Iran,* trans. Nancy Pearson (Princeton, NJ: Princeton University Press, 1977), 88. The part in parentheses contains a passage present in the Italian edition, quoted by Nono in the interview, which is not present in the English version.

31. In the volumes of Scriabin's writings that were consulted, it was not possible to recover this quote. In Anatole Leikin, *The Performing Style of Alexander Scriabin* (Burlington: Ashgate, 2011) a similar quote refers to a saying of the music critic Leonid Sabaneev: "[Scriabin] often said that silence also resounds, that there is sound in silence. . . . Once, he told Sabaneev, well in advance of John Cage's 4'33", that there might be a musical composition consisting of only silence" (41).

32. Edgard Varèse in Gunther Schuller, "Conversation with Varèse," *Perspectives of New Music* 3/2 (1965): 32–37, esp. 34.

33. It was not possible to find in Wittgenstein's theoretical work any precise reference to the concept of *Unklangbar* (translated as "Unsoundable"). Presumably here Nono is using his own personal "translation" of the concept of *Unsagbar* ("Unspeakable") expressed by Wittgenstein, among other things, in proposition 4.115 of *Tractatus Logico-Philosophicus*: "It will mean the unspeakable by clearly displaying the speakable"; see English edition, trans. Charles Kay Ogden (London: Routledge & Kegan Paul, 1922).

34. Nono refers to the *Fantasia e fuga per due pianoforti* of 1949 (known in some sources also as *Bach-Variationen für zwei Klaviere* or *Fantasia e Fuga su*

BACH). The manuscript of the work, long given up for lost, was found in 1987 in the archives of the International Summer Course in Darmstadt by Raymond Fearn (see Fearn, "At the Doors of Kranichstein: Maderna's 'Fantasia for two pianos,'" *Tempo* 163 (1987): 14–20; see also Susanna Pasticci, "Vers la pensée serielle: La 'Fantasia e fuga per due pianoforti,'" in *À Bruno Maderna,* ed. sous la direction de Geneviève Mathon et al. (Paris: Basalte 2009), II: 285–309.

35. The "instrumental group" remembered by Nono is the Internationales Kranichsteiner Kammer-Ensemble.

36. This is referring to no. 8 of *Il canto sospeso.*

37. See in this regard the interesting video document of the rehearsals of *Déserts* conducted by Maderna in *Les grandes répétitions,* five films by Gérard Patris and Luc Ferrari (1965–67) (Paris: ORTF—K-films, 2010). See also Gianmario Borio, "'A Strange Phenomenon': Varèse's Influence on the European Avant-Garde," in *Edgard Varèse: Composer, Sound Sculptor, Visionary,* ed. Felix Meyer and Heidy Zimmermann (Woodbridge, England: Boydell Press, 2006), 361–70, esp. 366–68.

38. See Athanasii Kircher, *Neue Hall- und Thon- Kunst,* facsimile of the 1684 original (Hannover: Libri Rari Th. Schäfer, 1983).

39. More likely it was the Pan American Association of Composers, of which, however, neither Roldán nor Malipiero were members.

40. The meeting remembered by Nono took place in 1965; see also "Excursus III" in this book "Interview with Renato Garavaglia" (ca. 1979–80), esp. 253.

41. The reference is to a chapter of the volume Marius Schneider, *Il significato della musica,* intro. Elémire Zolla (Milan: Rusconi, 1979), 231–43 (§ "The Drum").

42. Nono refers properly to the conducting score, reconstructed by Scherchen on the basis of the microfilm provided by Gertrud Schoenberg; see also Monika Lichtenfeld, "Über Schönbergs 'Moses und Aron,'" in *Arnold Schönberg: Gedenkausstellung, 1974,* ed. Ernst Hilmar (Vienna: Universal Edition, 1974), 125–34, esp. 134. In ALN is preserved a cablegram by Hübner to Nono of April 25, 1953, where he asks advice about an expert of Schoenberg's handwriting, in order to realize a "Dirigentenpartitur."

43. In fact, it was in 1965. The trip to America was made on the occasion of the staging of *Intolleranza 1960* in Boston, which opened on February 21, 1965. See also "Excursus II" in this volume, "A Letter from Los Angeles," and "Interview with Renato Garavaglia," esp. 247.

44. See Ferruccio Busoni, *Entwurf einer neuen Ästhetik der Tonkunst,* facsimile of the 1916 edition with handwritten notes by Arnold Schoenberg (Frankfurt am Main: Insel, 1974).

45. Nono's recollections of Schoenberg's library and of the visits of the FBI would appear not to be reliable and, given the vicissitudes of the interview (see introduction), cannot be verified with the original audio source. According to Nuria Schoenberg Nono (in a personal communication to the editors), the library seen by the composer during his visit to Los Angeles was limited to a part of the volumes in Schoenberg's possession during his lifetime (many of which had been previously destroyed). Among these were certainly classics of philosophy and volumes by Adorno. Probably also the facts related to the

"extremely frequent" visits of the FBI to the Schoenberg household should be put into perspective, attributable to an information-gathering inspection on the composer Hanns Eisler.

46. Nono is referring to Erwin Stein, *Arnold Schönberg: Briefe* (Mainz: Schott, 1958); English edition, *Arnold Schoenberg Letters,* selected and ed. Erwin Stein, trans. Eithne Wilkins (London: Faber and Faber, 1964).

47. In ALN is preserved an annotated Italian version of the *Sefer Yetzirah* (*Il libro della creazione*: Rome: Beniamino Carucci, 1979). The book is translated in English as *Book of Formation* or *Book of Creation.*

48. From Catunda's more detailed testimony, it emerges that not only Maderna but also Nono and Catunda herself each composed a short cycle of Greek lyrics (using the translations by Salvatore Quasimodo published in 1941 in issues of the journal *Corrente*). Together, these works constituted the tribute that the three composers offered to Scherchen during a visit they made to Florence in the spring of 1949. While there, Scherchen conducted a concert with music by Dallapiccola. See Eunice Katunda, "A minha viagem para Europa," in Carlos Kater, ed., *Eunice Katunda: Musicista brasileira* (São Paulo: Fapesp, 2001) 57–62 (Eunice Catunda, in 1964, changed to K the initial of her name, following the divorce from her husband, Omar Catunda).

49. In fact, only from the point of view of rhythm; an analysis of the composition process does not reveal any evidence of the use of this song from the intervallic point of view.

50. This is about *Epitaffio per Federico García Lorca III: Memento. Romance de la Guardia civil española.*

51. The reference is to the *Studi per "Il Processo" di Franz Kafka,* which was actually written in 1950 and which followed a theatrical project that was never realized, dateable to 1949.

52. Nono refers to the Groupe de Recherche sur la Musique Concrète (GRMC), founded by Schaeffer in 1951 (formerly Studio d'Essai).

53. Nono is referring to his "meeting" with Russian culture and not to his relationship with Ripellino, to whom he wrote for the first time only on January 4, 1960. The complete correspondence between Nono and the writer is published in Angela Ida De Benedictis, "L'opera si racconta . . . *Intolleranza 1960* nelle voci epistolari dei protagonisti," in *"Intolleranza 1960" a cinquant'anni dalla prima assoluta,* ed. Angela Ida De Benedictis and Giorgio Mastinu (Venice: Marsilio, 2011), 59–111.

54. See Angelo Maria Ripellino, *Majakovskij e il teatro russo d'avanguardia* (Turin: Einaudi, 1959; repr. 1982).

55. "Language is the mother of thought, not its handmaiden" (quotation from a 1912 issue of *Die Fackel,* his newspaper).

56. See René Leibowitz, *Introduction à la musique de douze sons: Les "Variations pour orchestre" op. 31 d'Arnold Schoenberg* (Paris: L'Arche, 1949); in English translation, see *Schoenberg and His School: The Contemporary Stage in the Language of Music,* trans. Dika Newlin (New York: Philosophical Library, 1949).

57. Nono reconstructs in his own words the meaning of the famous letter of July 27, 1932, with which Schoenberg responds to the point raised by Rudolf

Kolisch about a note in a place that was incongruous with respect to the order of the series in a passage of the Third String Quartet; see *Arnold Schoenberg Letters*, ed. Stein, trans. Wilkins, 164–65.

58. See the enthusiastic letter written by Ravel to Stravinsky on June 26, 1923, after listening to *Les noces* in Paris and the words written, on the same day, to Roland-Manuel ("[*Les noces*] is a splendid work. I even believe that it's Stravinsky's masterpiece to date"); see *A Ravel Reader: Correspondence, Articles, Interviews*, compiled and ed. Arbie Orenstein (New York: Columbia University Press, 1990), 244.

59. See György Lukács, *Diario (1910–1911)*, ed. Gabriella Caramore, with an essay by Massimo Cacciari (Milan: Adelphi, 1983). Cacciari, contrary to what Nono says, had not edited the volume but had instead written an introductory essay. Italian edition translated from *Napló-Tagebuch* (Budapest: Akadémia, 1981). Although there is no English translation, the reader is referred for further details to Mary Gluck, *Georg Lukács and His Generation* (Cambridge, MA: Harvard University Press, 1991), where the diaries are quoted extensively.

60. In Venice, Igor Stravinsky conducted the premiere of *Canticum sacrum in honorem Sancti Marci nominis* on September 13, 1956. *Monumentum pro Gesualdo da Venosa ad CD annum* was instead composed four years later, in 1960.

61. See *Testimony: The Memoirs of Dmitri Shostakovich, as Related to and Ed. by Solomon Volkov*, trans. Antonina W. Bouis (London: Hamilton, 1979). Nono had read the Italian edition of the volume (*Testimonianza: Le memorie di Dmitrij Šostakovič* [Milan: Mondadori, 1979]).

62. See Karlheinz Stockhausen, "Sprache und Musik II," *Darmstädter Beiträge zur Neuen Musik* 1 (1958): 66ff., now in Stockhausen, *Texte zu eigenen Werken, zur Kunst Anderer, Aktuelles, Band II (1952–1962)* (Cologne: DuMont Schauberg, 1964), 157–66; and Massimo Mila, "La linea Nono (A proposito de *Il Canto sospeso*)," *La Rassegna Musicale* 30/4 (1960): 297–311, now in Massimo Mila and Luigi Nono, *Nulla di oscuro tra noi: Lettere, 1952–1988*, ed. Angela Ida De Benedictis and Veniero Rizzardi (Milan: il Saggiatore, 2010), 257–74.

63. For the aforementioned essay by Mila ("La linea Nono") and for insights on the "profound friendship" that united the composer and the music critic, see Mila and Nono, *Nulla di oscuro tra noi*.

64. The first issue on disc of *Il canto sospeso* followed just one year after the interview, in 1988 (CD Stradivarius, a recording of the concert conducted by Bruno Maderna in Venice, September 17, 1960, with the WDR Symphony Orchestra and Chorus of Cologne). Since then, four other commercial recordings have followed: in 1993 (CD Sony SK 53360) and 2004 (DVD EU, Berlin), both conducted by Claudio Abbado); in 2005 (CD Studio Wolfgang Feder, recording of a concert conducted by Hermann Scherchen in Cologne in 1958), and in 2011 (CD Polmic 075, Polish Composer's Union, conducted by Lucas Vis).

65. Regarding this extraordinary figure and his work at the Studio di Fonologia of the Italian Broadcasting Corporation (RAI) of Milan see chapter 7 of part IV in this volume "For Marino Zuccheri."

66. They are actually two completely different compositions, which have in common only the title and the designated instrument.

67. Contrary to what is usually reported, even in catalogs and work lists, no text by Aimé Césaire appears in *Intolleranza 1960*.

68. In fact, the invitation arrived about a year ahead of the target date for the premiere. The three months mentioned by Nono correspond to the time actually spent on the task of composition, which in itself shows the divergence between his dramaturgical views and those of Ripellino. The phrase "on an idea of Ripellino," to which Nono alludes further on in his response, were actually proposed by Ripellino himself. For further reading on the genesis of *Intolleranza 1960* see Angela Ida De Benedictis, "The Dramaturgical and Compositional Genesis of Luigi Nono's Intolleranza 1960," *Twentieth-Century Music* 9/1–2 (2012): 101–41.

69. According to the correspondence preserved in ALN, the trip to Prague and the knowledge of *laterna magika* should almost certainly be dated to 1959. It was also only in that year that the *laterna magika,* after its international success at the Universal Exhibition in Brussels in 1958 (where it was presented for the first time), was taken to the theater in Prague.

70. The communication also came in writing, with a letter sent by the Czech Ministry of Culture, January 15, 1961. Only later on, on January 30, Nono wrote to Togliatti; letters reproduced in De Benedictis, "L'opera si racconta . . . Intolleranza 1960 nelle voci epistolari dei protagonisti."

71. *Ricorda cosa ti hanno fatto in Auschwitz* is actually an autonomous composition, not in a functional relationship to the stage, created in 1966 from the choral materials present on tape of the real incidental music for *Die Ermittlung,* of 1965.

72. The meeting actually took place in 1952. The concert to which Nono refers took place on February 18 of that year at the NWDR within the cycle "Das neue Werk," with the title *Das Junge Italie.* On that occasion, Maderna conducted his *Improvvisazione n. 1* and *Composizione per orchestra* by Nono, both as premieres, in addition to: Guido Turchi, *Cinque commenti alle "Baccanti" di Euripide;* Luigi Dallapiccola, *Tre poemi;* Goffredo Petrassi, *Coro di morti.*

73. Here Nono makes a sudden slip forward, to 1965, the year he met Weiss, who had recently written *Die Ermittlung* [The Investigation], and in which he finally firmed up the collaboration with Piscator.

74. Short title of *The Persecution and Assassination of Marat, as Performed by the Inmates of the Asylum of Charenton, under the Direction of the Marquis of Sade* (London: John Calder, 1964). The English translation was published in the same year of the first German edition.

75. Allusion to the incipit ("Ich fühle Luft von anderem Planeten") from Stefan George's poem "Entrückung," the text of which is used by Schoenberg in the final movement of the Second String Quartet op. 10.

76. See "Excursus VI" in this volume, "'Proust' Questionnaire" (1986), and the bibliographic references to the first edition here on p. 468.

77. Second part of the diptych *Musica-Manifesto n. 1,* preceded by *Un volto, e del mare,* cited by Nono further on.

78. *Daß Narrenschyff ad Narrgoniam* was the original title of the book of satire published by the theologian Sebastian Brant in Basel in 1494. The first edition, or adaptation, in English dates from 1509 and was made by Alexander Barclay. Historical edition of reference: Sebastian Brant, *The Ship of Fools*, trans., intro., and commentary by Edwin Hermann Zeydel (New York: Columbia University Press, 1944).

79. The two compositions, clearly distinct from each other, form an inseparable diptych (see note 77).

80. Reference to the poem by Cesare Pavese, "Terra rossa terra nera," published in the collection *Verrà la morte e avrà i tuoi occhi* (Turin: Einaudi, 1951), 11—which, with "Tu sei come una terra" (ibid., 12) constitutes the verbal material of *La terra e la compagna*. Both poems ("Red earth black earth" and "You are like a land") are in Cesare Pavese, *Disaffections: Complete Poems*, ed. Geoffrey Brock (Seattle: Copper Canyon Press, 2002).

81. The incipit and refrain of "Romance sonambulo," fourth poem of the cycle *Romancero gitano* (1924–27); see *Somnambule Ballad: The Selected Poems of Federico García Lorca*, intro. William Stanley Merwin, trans. Roy Campbell et al. (New York: New Directions, 2005), 71.

82. See in this regard "Victor Jara's Song" (chapter 3, part IV in this volume) and "In the Sierra and in the Parliament" (chapter 5, part III).

83. Actually, according to various sources, Marquez had declared to have been listening to Bartók's Third Piano Concerto while writing the *Autumn of the Patriarch*.

84. See Carlos Franqui, *El circulo de piedra: Litografías de Adami, Calder, Camacho, Cardenas, César, Corneille, Erró, Jorn, Kowalski, Lam, Miró, Pignon, Rebeyrolle, Tápies, Vedova, música de Nono* (Milan: Grafica Uno Giorgio Upiglio, [1969]).

85. Deutsche Grammophon 2530 436, released in 1974.

86. Stockhausen expresses in different places, and always in a different manner, this idea, bound to the "transistor metaphor" cited later by Restagno and Nono. Consider, for example, the same words that form the "musical" text of "Intensity" in *From the Seven Days* ("play single sounds/with such dedication/until you feel the warmth/that radiates from you"), or the introductory notes to the score of *Hymnen* or even to what the composer affirms in the interview with Jonathan Cott in 1973: "We are all transistors in the literal sense." Now in *Composers on Music: Eight Centuries of Writings*, ed. Josiah Fisk (Boston: Northeastern University Press, 1997), 450–53, esp. 450.

87. See Alexander Kluge, *Schlachtbeschreibung* (Olten-Freiburg im Breisgau: Walter, 1964); 1st English ed.: *The Battle*, trans. Leila Vennewitz (Columbus, OH: McGraw-Hill, 1967).

88. The recollection must be dated a year prior to the interview, to 1986.

89. See Abraham Zvi Idelsohn, *Hebräisch-orientalischer Melodienschatz*, 10 vols. (Leipzig: Breitkopf & Härtel-Friedrich Hofmeister-Benjamin Harz, 1914–32).

90. See Martin Buber, *Tales of the Hasidim: The Early Masters/The Later Masters*, trans. Olga Marx (New York: Schocken, 1991).

91. See, in this regard, the testimony of Lyubimov and Nono on the early stages of their collaboration in *Intervista di Solomon Volkov e M. Rachmanova*, in De Benedictis-Rizzardi 2001: II: 143–51, esp. 149–50.

92. Some letters between Nono and members of the PCI concerning this issue are published in *Luigi Nono: Carteggi concernenti politica, cultura e Partito Comunista Italiano*, ed. Antonio Trudu (Florence: Olschki, 2008), esp. 206–11.

93. The concert Nono refers to was held at the ninth International Festival of Contemporary Music of the Venice Biennale, September 17, 1946 (in addition to Dallapiccola, the program included the *Symphony* op. 21 by Webern, the *Sonata da camera* for cello and small orchestra by Martinů, and the *Concerto spirituale "De la incarnatione del Verbo Divino"* by Ghedini).

94. See chapter 1 of part I in this volume, "Dallapiccola and the *Sex Carmina Alcaei*."

95. For more interesting details on these meetings with Dallapiccola see also "Interview with Renato Garavaglia."

96. This refers to *Congedo di Girolamo Savonarola* (1941), for chorus and percussion.

97. The correspondence of Luigi Nono—today part of which is already the subject of publications that summarize individual branches of letters (such as those with Massimo Mila, Helmut Lachenmann, or Giuseppe Ungaretti) or mixed ones—has been sorted and is today held in the ALN in Venice. The correspondence of Pierre Boulez is held at the PSF in Basel.

98. In the original Italian, Restagno uses the word *svolta* ("turning point"), a clear allusion to an essay by Heinz-Klaus Metzger, dedicated to *Fragmente-Stille, an Diotima*, where the expression *turning point* appears even in the title: "Wendepunkt Quartett?" *Musik-Konzepte Luigi Nono* 20 (1981): 93–112. Some years later, in 1988, Massimo Mila too used the same word in the title of an essay dedicated to the works that followed *Fragmente-Stille, an Diotima;* see "Nono, la svolta," now in Mila and Nono, *Nulla di oscuro tra noi*, 324–33.

99. Nono refers to the historical-critical edition in eighteen volumes edited by Sattler, which reproduces in facsimile all the poet's manuscripts side by side with diplomatic transcriptions; see Friedrich Hölderlin, *Sämtliche Werke—Frankfurter Ausgabe*, 18 vols., historical-critical edition, ed. Dietrich E. Sattler (Frankfurt am Main: Roter Stern, 1979–95).

100. The concept of "evening theophany" (*teofania vespertina*) is not by Hölderlin himself, it has indeed been introduced by the Italian Germanist Ladislao Mittner in his history of German literature: *Storia della letteratura tedesca*, vol. II, tome 3 (Turin: Einaudi, 1977), 713.

101. Since 1987 several essays have been devoted to the musical reception of Hölderlin; among these, and with reference to some compositions by Luigi Nono, see Ute Schomerus, "'Chanté au pied des Alpes': La poésie de Friedrich Hölderlin dans les oeuvres des compositeurs italiens," in *Musique vocales en Italie depuis 1945*, ed. Pierre Michel and Gianmario Borio (Paris: Millénaire III, 2005), 135–76. See also the recent book by Carolin Abeln, *Sprache und Neue Musik: Hölderlin-Rezeption bei Wilhelm Killmayer, Heinz Holliger, Wolfgang Rihm und Luigi Nono* (Freiburg: Rombach Verlag, 2017).

102. Edmond Jabès, *Le livre des questions* (Paris: Gallimard, 1963); 1st English ed.: *The Book of Questions*, trans. Rosmarie Waldrop (Middletown, CT: Wesleyan University Press, 1976).

103. "We met Luigi Nono for the first time in the mid-1950s at the Ferienkurse in Darmstadt and that was when he promised to write us a quartet. He thought about it for a long time ... twenty-five years!"; see "*Fragmente-Stille, an Diotima* nella testimonianza di Walter Levin," transcription and notes ed. Angela Ida De Benedictis, in *Luigi Nono e il suono elettronico*, Milano Musica 2000, catalog ed. Francesco Degrada (Milan: Edition of the Teatro alla Scala, 2000), 93–96, esp. 93. The recording of the *workshop*—held in Berlin on September 4, 1983—is currently kept at ALN.

104. The Milan studio, already obsolete in the 1970s, was accordingly decommissioned permanently and closed in 1983. See for the story of this electronic laboratory *The Studio di Fonologia: A Musical Journey, 1954–1983*, ed. Maria Maddalena Novati and John Dack (Milan: Ricordi, 2009); and *New Music on the Radio: Experiences at the Studio di Fonologia of the RAI*, ed. Veniero Rizzardi and Angela Ida De Benedictis (Rome: RAI-ERI, 2000), esp. 177–213.

105. This is the historic "Die Halde Hotel" (www.halde.com).

106. This concept is central in the last years of Nono, who developed it in the lecture "Other Possibilities for Listening" (1985), chapter 2 of part V in this volume.

107. The workshops and the series of concerts took place in 1981 and 1982.

108. To be read as "to interpret Prokofiev as if it were the music of Gian Carlo Menotti," a composer whom Nono held in quite poor regard.

109. In 1986, a year before the interview with Restagno, Nono had written a short and intense text dedicated to the cited piece by Gubaidulina; see "[Su Stimmen ... verstummen ... di Sofija Gubajdulina]," in De Benedictis-Rizzardi 2001: I: 414.

110. In the original, Nono erroneously says: "the Lithuanian Artemyev."

111. *Guai ai gelidi mostri* (translatable as "Woe to the Cold Monsters") takes a passage from "The New Idol", chapter 11 of *Thus Spake Zarathustra* ("A state, is called the coldest of all cold monsters").

112. Nono here uses the term *mono-livellatrice* ("mono-leveling"), which doesn't exist in Italian as such and can't be properly translated in this context.

113. Here as above in the text Nono refers to a more general and psychological, than musical, concept of time.

114. Nono refers almost certainly to the *Requiem* (also mentioned above), in which Verdi uses such extreme dynamics for the choir (for example, "*pppppp* estremamente piano con voce cupa e tristissima" in the *Liber scriptus*). Nono knew these indications from the facsimile autograph score (copy held in the ALN).

115. On the genesis of the text and, more generally, on analytical aspects related to *Prometeo*, see, among others, Carola Nieliger-Vakil, *Luigi Nono: A Composer in Context* (Cambridge: Cambridge University Press, 2015), esp. 191–316.

116. Held twenty years before the date of the interview, in 1967.

117. The sentence clearly refers to the poem *Caminante* by Antonio Machado (a poet loved by Luigi Nono and set in *"Ha venido": Canciones para Silvia* of 1960): "Caminante, no hay camino,/se hace camino al andar./[. . .] Caminante, no hay camino,/sino estelas en la mar." See Antonio Machado, *Border of a Dream: Selected Poems,* trans. Willis Barnstone (Port Townsend, WA: Copper Canyon Press, 2004), 280.

118. This work plan was later modified. The first composition of the cycle, entitled 1°) *Caminantes . . . Ayacucho,* is followed, later in 1987 2°) *"No hay caminos, hay que caminar" . . . Andrej Tarkowskij* (for seven orchestral groups). Subsequently Nono only composed *La lontananza nostalgica utopica futura: Madrigale per più "caminantes" con Gidon Kremer* (1988, for violin and magnetic tape), in the subtitle of which appears the word *caminantes,* and finally *"Hay que caminar" sognando* (1989, for two violins), derived from the same musical materials used in *La lontananza nostalgica utopica futura.*

119. Giordano Bruno, *To the Principles of the Universe,* in *Cause, Principle, and Unity, and Essays on Magic,* ed. Richard J. Blackwell and Robert de Lucca, intro. Alfonso Ingegno (Cambridge: Cambridge University Press, 1998), 12. In the original interview, Nono specified to be reading this passage "in the Italian translation"; the passage is therefore modified according to the aforementioned English edition.

120. Various sources report that the words of St. Augustine placed at the end of the score of *Ulisse* ("Fecisti nos ad te et inquietum est cor nostrum, donec requiescat in te") had been found by Dallapiccola in an inscription found at a train station in Westport, Connecticut.

PART ONE. MUSICAL ANALYSIS AND COMPOSITION

1. LUIGI DALLAPICCOLA AND THE *SEX CARMINA ALCAEI*

1. In the score we read: "This work, dedicated to ANTON WEBERN on day of his sixtieth birthday (December 3, 1943), I offer today to his memory, with humility and devotion./September 15, 1945. L.D." See *Sex carmina Alcaei, una voce canenda, nonnullis comitantibus musicis:* "Canones diversi, motu recto contrarioque, simplices ac duplices, cancrizantes, etc., super seriem unam tonorum duodecim" (Milan: Suvini Zerboni, 1946), 5.

2. In a first draft manuscript (ALN), Nono inserts the transcription of the tone row after the colon, interspersing among the various pitches the interval's amplitude (indicated with the same system constantly employed in his sketches):

"C♯ $\overset{3-}{—}$ E $\overset{2+}{—}$ F♯ $\overset{2-}{-}$ G $\overset{3+}{—}$ E♭ $\overset{5}{—}$ B♭ $\overset{2-}{—}$ A $\overset{2-}{—}$ A♭ $\overset{3+}{—}$ F $\overset{6+}{—}$ D $\overset{3-}{—}$ B $\overset{2-}{—}$ C."

3. Bars. 1–4.
4. Bars. 5–7; in the retrograde the row is transposed up by a minor second.
5. *Canones diversi,* bars. 23 ff.
6. *Canon perpetuus,* bars. 9–20; the row is transposed up by a minor third.
7. *Vago e leggero,* bars. 63–64.
8. *Mosso, ma non tanto; ritmato con grazia* and *Conclusio.*

2. ON THE DEVELOPMENT OF SERIAL TECHNIQUE

1. In the first published version in *Gravesaner Blätter* (see this chapter's entry in "Bibliographic Notes and Comments to the Text"), this sentence erroneously precedes the example from the Variations op. 31.

2. In the *Gravesaner Blätter* version this reads *"Klavierstücke (Nr. 2),"* the original title which grouped together the *Klavierstücke* I–IV.

3. Here both the original German version and the subsequent Italian translation (see "Bibliographic Notes and Comments to the Text") were somehow cumbersome. In substance, Nono limits himself here to illustrating with a quick synthesis how the choice of the *Allintervallreihe,* insofar as it is the basic series of the entire composition, has been made taking into account a coordination that simultaneously governs the different parameters: pitches, durations, intensities, and the fixation of the registers.

3. THE DEVELOPMENT OF SERIAL TECHNIQUE

1. In this text Nono uses the term *serial* in a seemingly inconsistent way. He begins his essay using the term within quotation marks, while dealing with Schoenberg's twelve-tone conception, but stops using the quotes in the course of his argument, and resumes them later. This use has been maintained in the translation. For this and other peculiarities of Nono's lexicon, see the introduction to this volume.

2. Nono seems here to allude to the concept of "time-measures" and "time spectra" elaborated by Stockhausen in his essay " . . . wie die Zeit vergeht . . .," (1957, now in *Texte zur elektronischen und instrumentalen Musik, Band I, 1952–1962* [Cologne: DuMont Schauberg, 1963], 99–139), and applied to some of his compositions of the years 1956–57, such as *Zeitmasse,* which indeed Nono discusses further in this article.

3. See Arnold Schoenberg, "Composition with Twelve Tones," in *Style and Idea* (New York: Philosophical Library, 1950), 103 and 107. What Nono quotes is the result of a montage of three passages somewhat removed from one another, which slightly alters Schoenberg's original wording. All quotations from Schoenberg, Webern, and Rufer are in German in Nono's original typescript.

4. See Josef Rufer, *Die Komposition mit zwölf Tönen* (Berlin: Max Hesses, 1952), 86; in English: *Composition with Twelve Notes Related Only to One Another,* trans. Humphrey Searle (New York: Macmillan, 1954), 92.

5. See ibid., 89; 94–95.

6. See Anton Webern, *The Path to the New Music,* ed. Willi Reich, trans. Leo Black (Bryn Mawr, PA, and Vienna: Theodor Presser and Universal Edition, 1963), 62. Nono quotes from the original German *Der Weg zur neuen Musik,* ed. Willi Reich (Vienna: Universal Edition, 1960), 68. In fact the text of Webern's lecture was still unpublished in 1957; Nono probably had the opportunity to consult a copy of Webern's book thanks to its future editor, Willi Reich, with whom he was in contact for the German translation of this essay.

7. In the typescript the name "Berio" is mentioned here in the first place, but no work of Luciano Berio is later taken into consideration.

8. To indicate the forms of the tone row Nono uses the German words *Krebs* ("retrograde"), *Umkehrung* ("inversion"), *Krebs-Umkehrung* ("retrograde inversion"), and also *Spiegel* ("mirror"). They are left here untranslated in accordance with the wishes of the author (see the letter of Nono to Berio of October 11, 1956: "My analysis is to be published *as I wrote it, exactly in every word* and intention and scheme (thus also with the German words = Krebs/Spiegel)," preserved in the Luciano Berio Collection, PSF; see also "Bibliographic Notes and Comments on the Texts").

9. Nono refers here, of course, to the German musical nomenclature in which "B" corresponds to B-flat and "H" to B-natural.

10. With this qualification, absent in all the texts published until De Benedictis-Rizzardi 2001, Nono clarifies what would otherwise seem inconsistent or tendentious: Nono in fact takes a vertical aggregate (in the woodwinds) as a central motif ("b") of the "melodic projection" to demonstrate the symmetrical superimposition of the two series, leaving out a melodic motif (B♭ B D C♯, motif "a" transposed by a semitone) that appears in the violins at bars 24–26.

11. Clarification absent in all publications previous to De Benedictis-Rizzardi 2001.

12. Ibid.

13. Nono is referring here—if somehow cryptically—to the system of permutation and proliferation of series by means of the technique of "magic squares" employed by Maderna and by Nono himself between 1951 and 1958–59. See Gianmario Borio, "Sull'interazione tra studio degli schizzi e analisi dell'opera," in *La nuova ricerca sulla musica di Luigi Nono* (Florence: Olschki, 1998), 15–17. See also Veniero Rizzardi, "The Tone Row, Squared: Bruno Maderna and the Birth of Serial Music in Italy," in *Rewriting Recent Music History: The Development of Early Serialism, 1947–1957*, ed. Mark Delaere (Leuven: Peeters, 2011), 45–66.

14. As is made clear by a letter of Luciano Berio held at the ALN—undated, written probably between March 25 and 31, 1957—Nono had requested some information ahead of this conference. In his reply Berio, among other things, observed: "I think that if you have to talk about the 'latest developments in serial music' you have to establish the fact that the series, as such, is dead and buried: it only serves to prepare material on the basis of which music is *invented*."

15. More correctly *Studi per "Il processo" di Franz Kafka*; the composition is in a single movement.

16. Composed in 1951.

17. Or rather *Studie I* (not *Studie II*, as indicated at Stenzl 1975: 32). The title quoted by Nono is the one by which the composition was known at the time this text was written. Nono gathered information about the composition from Karlheinz Stockhausen, "*Komposition 1953 n. 2, Studie I, Analyse*," in *Technische Hausmitteilungen des Nordwestdeutschen Rundfunk* 6/1–2 (1954)—text subsequently published in Stockhausen, *Texte zu eigenen Werken, zur Kunst Anderer, Aktuelles, Band II (1952–1962)* (Cologne: DuMont Schauberg, 1964), 23–36.

18. Reprinted with some changes in Stockhausen, *Texte zu eigenen Werken*, II: 47. The translation given here is taken from the text prepared in 1992 for the

booklet that accompanies the CD no. 4 (*Kontra-Punkte, Zeitmasze, Stop, Adieu*) of Stockhausen's "complete editon." The translation, approved by the composer, was made by Suzanne Stephens and Richard Toop.

4. TEXT—MUSIC—SONG

1. Here Nono erroneously combines the liberal arts of the trivium (grammar and rhetoric, along with logic or dialectic) with music, when in fact it was part of the quadrivium, along with arithmetic, geometry, and astronomy.

2. Joachim Burmeister's three theoretical texts (ca. 1566–1629) were published respectively in 1599, in 1601 and in 1606. The third volume mentioned is available in a modern edition: *Musical Poetics,* trans. Benito V. Rivera (New Haven, CT: Yale University Press, 1993).

3. Having referred to the "final volumes" of Monteverdi's madrigals, Nono cites by reason of obvious stylistic analogy *La lettera amorosa,* which is in fact included in *Concerto: Settimo libro de madrigali, a 1 2 3 4 & 6 voci, con altri generi de canti* (1619).

4. This text corresponds indeed to a lecture in two parts that Nono gave in Darmstadt on July 7 and 8, 1960. The parts are marked here as sections I and II.

5. The reference to Merleau-Ponty an his *Phénoménologie de la perception* (Paris: Gallimard, 1945) is drawn from the formulation provided by Jean-Paul Sartre, "Qu'est-ce que la litterature?" in *Situations II* (Paris, Gallimard, 1948); in English: *What Is Literature?* trans. Bernard Frechtman (New York: Philosophical Library, 1949), now in *What Is Literature? and Other Essays,* intro. Steven Ungar (Cambridge, MA: Harvard University Press, 1988), 25. Nono's source is the Italian trans., *Che cos'è la letteratura?* (Milan: il Saggiatore, 1960), 118 (annotated copy at the ALN).

6. See Joseph Müller-Blattau, *Das Verhältnis von Wort und Ton in der Geschichte der Musik,* 31.

7. The miniature score held at the ALN, Ludwig van Beethoven, *9. Symphonie Opus 125 mit Schlusschor über Schillers Ode "And die Freude,"* rev. Max Unger, intro. Wilhelm Altmann (Leipzig: CF Peters, s.d.) contains several annotations by Nono relating to the examples mentioned.

8. Arnold Schoenberg, preface to the score of *Pierrot lunaire* (Vienna: Universal Edition, 1914), in *Schoenberg: "Pierrot lunaire" companion,* ed. Christian Meyer (Vienna: Arnold Schoenberg Center–Universal Edition, 2012), 6.

9. *Moses und Aron,* opera, ed. Christian Martin Schmidt (Mainz: Ernst Eulenburg, 1984), x–xi. Nono quotes from the ed. Mainz: Schott, 1958, 3 (annotated copy at the ALN).

10. The following quotation from Sartre is taken up by Nono in other written texts up until 1963, "Appunti per un teatro musicale attuale" (1961; see De Benedictis-Rizzardi 2001: I: 86–93); "Possibility and Necessity of a New Music Theater" (see chapter 2 of part II in this volume), and again in "*Simplicius Simplicissimus e Concerto funebre*" (1962–63; see De Benedictis-Rizzardi 2001: I: 148).

11. Quote from *Lettere di condannati a morte della Resistenza europea,* ed. Piero Malvezzi and Giovanni Pirelli (Turin: Einaudi, 1963), 539.

12. In the lecture recording (tape held at the IMD) Nono interrupts here and announces, "Listen now to *La terra e la compagna*."

13. The following example shows the intertwining of the "two texts" mentioned just above by Nono: *Terra rossa terra nera* ("Red earth black earth"): ("Red earth black earth/You come from the sea,/from the arid green,/place of ancient words/bloodred weariness/geranium and among stones—/you bear opinions more than you know/of sea and words and toil,/you, rich [. . .]/as the barren countryside,/you, hard and honeyed/word"); and in italics *Tu sei come una terra* ("You are like a land") ("You wait for nothing/if not for the word/That will burst from the deep"); Cesare Pavese, *Disaffections: Complete Poems, 1930–1950*, trans. Geoffrey Brock (Port Townsend, WA: Copper Canyon Press, 2002), 309 and 311.

14. Nono draws this and subsequent examples from a piano reduction—see Johann Sebastian Bach, *H-moll-Messe*, piano score with text (Leipzig: Peters, s.d., ed. N. 4397), 5, 4, 6 (annotated copy at the ALN).

15. See above, note 4.

16. The text selected by Nono for no. 3 of *Il canto sospeso* states: " . . . they are taking me to Kessariani to be executed together with seven other prisoners. I am dying for freedom and for my country . . . today they will shoot us. We are dying like men for our country. Be worthy of us . . . they will hang me in the square because I am a patriot. Your son is leaving, he will not hear the bells of freedom . . . " The source in each case is *Lettere di condannati a morte della Resistenza europea*, ed. Malvezzi and Pirelli.

17. In Karl Friedrich von Weizsäcker, *Die Sprache* (Munich: Vortragsreihe, 1959), ed. Bayerische Akademie der schönen Künste (Munich: R. Oldenbourg, 1959), 36.

18. Nono refers to "Tu non sai le colline" ("You do not know the hills"), poetry selected for *La terra e la compagna* together with two other poems from the collection *La terra e la morte* (Earth and Death) ("Terra rossa terra nera" and "Tu sei come una terra"); see above, note 13.

19. Here Nono announces in the lecture: "We will listen to this work at the end."

20. The example in question (verbally in the passage that follows) was written during the lecture on the blackboard.

21. This point in the text was the subject of discussion in correspondence between Nono and Massimo Mila, who had requested the German typescript of the lecture to gather information with a view to writing an article—what became "La linea Nono: A proposito de *Il canto sospeso*," in *Rassegna Musicale* 30 (1960): 297–311, now in Massimo Mila and Luigi Nono, *Nulla di oscuro tra noi: Lettere, 1952–1988*, ed. Angela Ida De Benedictis and Veniero Rizzardi (Milan: il Saggiatore, 2010), 257–74. Mila noted an apparent inconsistency in Nono's use of the concept of "immediacy" (*Unmittelbarkeit*) to refer both to the immediacy of the "word" and that of "music." In a letter dated October 31, 1960, Nono clarified: "It is precisely *Unmittelbarkeit*, which here also carries the sense of immediacy [*immediatezza*]. That is: 'in the composition it is transposed from the immediacy of the word as understood to the noncon-

ceptual immediacy of the music as heard'" (see ibid., 45). But see also a letter of Nono of November 1, 1960 (ibid., 49–50).

22. Nono is referring here to the analysis undertaken by Karlheinz Stockhausen, "Musik und Sprache," cited explicitly in footnote xv in this chapter.

23. Nono concludes the lecture by announcing, "Listen now to *Cori di Didone.*"

5. [ABOUT *IL CANTO SOSPESO*]

1. This refers to *Quattro lettere (Kranichsteiner Kammerkantate),* for soprano, bass, and chamber orchestra. Kranichstein is a district of the city of Darmstadt, where stands the eponymous castle, and where the piece was performed for the first time, at the summer courses in 1953. At the time this text was written the cantata had not yet been performed in Italy. See also in chapter 2 of part 3 in this volume "Music and Resistance," note 3.

2. In the "small book" (Turin: Einaudi, 1976; new edition, ed. Ulrich Mosch, 1999), Mila committed to print the texts of his twelve radio talks on the music of Bruno Maderna, broadcast on the Third Program of RAI between November 1974 and February 1975.

3. This refers to Mario Lizzero, former partisan and then, in the 1960s, elected to the Italian Parliament. According to another testimony, the secretary of the regional federation (constituency) of the Communist Party would have spoken these words on the occasion of the interview, which, like any aspiring member, Nono would have had to undergo to be accepted as a new member. By exposing on that occasion his motivation and his beliefs, Nono would have openly declared himself to be, as a musician, in disagreement with the official positions of the party on the matter of artistic expression, then aligned to the principles of social realism. See Várnai Péter, *Beszélgetések Luigi Nonóval* (Conversations with Luigi Nono) (Budapest: Zenemükiadó, 1978), 37–38. With "Scelba's repression," Nono is referring to Mario Scelba, member of the Italian Parliament for the Christian Democrats who, maintaining a stance of rigid anti-Communism, was minister of the interior between 1947 and 1953. In those early years of the Cold War he had the responsibility for the bloody repression of the strikes and demonstrations organized by the unions of workers and the parties of the left.

4. Markos Vafiadis, leader of the KKE (Communist Party of Greece) at the time of the resistance against the German occupation (1941–44).

5. The work was actually composed between 1953 and 1954.

6. *Canticum sacrum ad honorem Sancti Marci nominis* was in fact already composed in 1955 on texts taken from the Gospel of Mark; all three of the other compositions cited in this last paragraph were composed between 1955 and 1956. The text of the electroacoustic composition of Karlheinz Stockhausen, *Gesang der Jünglinge,* was taken from the deuterocanonical fragment of the Book of Daniel.

7. With "antifascist front" Nono is referring to the Popular Front, a temporary and unsuccessful electoral alliance between the Socialist Party and the

Communist Party which was formed in anticipation of the general elections of 1948, the outcome of which was suspected of having been rigged, as well as indubitably influenced by the intervention of the CIA.

8. Turin: Einaudi, 1954.

9. Nono foreshadows here the difficulties that he himself encountered at the time, in Germany, with musical organizations (radio, festival, and publishing organizations) that had supported and promoted him in the past, but which seemed not to welcome the increasing explicitness of his political choices in the texts of his compositions. See also chapter 4 of part III in this volume "Music and Power;" also note 25 of that chapter.

10. Nono is probably alluding to Karlheinz Stockhausen, "Situation des Handwerks (Kriterien der 'punktuellen Musik')," in *Texte zur elektronischen und instrumentalen Musik, Band I: 1952–1962* (Cologne: DuMont Schauberg, 1963), 17–23; and Herbert Eimert, who was among the first to introduce in music criticism the term "punktuell," with reference to the music of Anton Webern. See Herbert Eimert, *Lehrbuch der Zwölftontechnik* (Wiesbaden: Breitkopf & Härtel, 1952).

11. See Karlheinz Stockhausen, "Sprache und Musik," in *Darmstädter Beiträge zur Neuen Musik,* no. 1 (1958): 66 ff., now in Stockhausen, *Texte zu eigenen Werken, zur Kunst Anderer, Aktuelles, Band II (1952–1962)* (Cologne: DuMont Schauberg, 1964), 157–66.

12. The dispute took place between 1959 and 1960; see, in this volume, "Text—Music—Song," esp. 176–77.

13. Different materials held at the ALN testify to Nono's study of Arab-Andalusian music—mainly its rhythmic aspect—which is at the basis of the cycle of the *Epitaffi per Federico García Lorca* of the years 1952–53.

14. See Julius Stockhausen, *Gesangsmethode* (Leipzig: Peters, s.d. [ed. no. 2190]). The publication of this method dates back in fact to 1884. There are, however, two volumes of *Gesangs-Technik und Stimmbildung* that date from 1886–87.

15. See, chapter 7 of part IV in this volume, "For Marino Zuccheri."

EXCURSUS II. A LETTER FROM LOS ANGELES

1. The meeting with the students took place on February 20, 1965; see Claudia Vincis, "To Nono: A No": Luigi Nono and His *Intolleranza 1965* in the U.S.," in *Crosscurrents: American and European Music in Interaction, 1900–2000,* ed. Felix Meyer, Carol J. Oja, Wolfgang Rathert, and Anne Shreffler (Woodbridge, England: Boydell Press, 2014), 320–31, esp. 329.

2. A million lire was then equivalent to five hundred U.S. dollars. It should be noted that in Italy in 1965 the average weekly salary of a worker would amount to around eight-six thousand lire (forty dollars).

3. On all these issues, as well as what is later described by Nono, see Vincis, "To Nono: A No," *passim.*

4. In *Intolleranza 1960* in the third scene of the first act there is a "Grande dimostrazione di popolo" ("Great mass dimostration") where the people chant

five slogans: "Nie wieder Krieg!" (by the German Spartacists after the First World War); "No pasaran" (by the freedom fighters of the Spanish Civil War); "Morte al fascismo—Libertà ai popoli" (by the communist partisans during the struggle against the Nazis); "La sale guerre" (against the French colonialists' Indochina war); "Down with discrimination" (against racial discrimination in the United States). The composer intended the scene to be a kind of synthesis of the struggles for freedom in the twentieth century. For further information, see also chapter 1 of part II in this volume "Some Clarifications on *Intolleranza 1960.*"

5. The premiere of *Intolleranza 1960*, staged at the Teatro La Fenice in Venice on April 13, 1961, was interrupted by violent protests in the concert hall, previously organized by supporters of the right.

6. See Albert Goldberg, "Experimental Sound of Nono Music," *Los Angeles Times,* March 21, 1965; and "Nono? Yes and No," *Newsweek* (March 8, 1965), 65.

7. Sidney Finkelstein, American Marxist musical critic.

PART TWO. MUSIC ONSTAGE

1. SOME CLARIFICATIONS ON *INTOLLERANZA 1960*

1. It was in fact in May 1960 that the invitation was extended by Labroca (then director of the International Festival of Contemporary Music of the Venice Biennale); see Angela Ida De Benedictis, "The Dramaturgical and Compositional Genesis of Luigi Nono's Intolleranza 1960," *Twentieth-Century Music* 9/1–2 (2012): 101–41. See also "Excursus I" in this volume "An Autobiography of the Author Recounted by Enzo Restagno" (esp. note 68).

2. This refers to the ballet *Il mantello rosso* [The Red Mantel]—for soprano, baritone, mixed chorus, and orchestra; choreography by Tatjana Gsovsky—based on an abridged version of *Don Perlimplín* by Federico García Lorca in Heinrich Beck's translation.

3. Svoboda and Kašlík collaborated on the staging of *Intolleranza 1960* respectively as director and scenographer.

4. Quotation drawn from Jean-Paul Sartre, "Beyond Bourgeois Theater" (1960), *Tulane Drama Review* 5/3 (March 1961): 3–11, esp. 5.

5. The reference is to the French journalist Henri Alleg, director of the *Alger Républicain,* an opposition newspaper, who was arrested and tortured in 1957 by the French army. At that time Nono had read Alleg's book documenting his experiences, *La tortura* (see below, note 18). In English: *The Question,* trans. John Calder, pref. Jean-Paul Sartre (London: John Calder, 1958).

6. Julius Fučík, journalist and a leader of the Czechoslovak Resistance, hanged by the Nazis in Berlin on September 8, 1943 (see below, note 16).

7. Sentence taken from the introductory text to *Composizione per orchestra n. 2—Diario polacco '58* (see De Benedictis-Rizzardi 2001: I: 433–36, esp. 433).

8. On August 8, 1956, 253 miners died in Marcinelle of whom 136 were Italians.

9. Reference to the popular demonstrations against the government headed by Ferdinando Tambroni, supported by the Italian neofascist party, MSI (Movimento Sociale Italiano).

10. Regarding the tragic flood of 1951, see *I giorni del grande fiume: il Polesine e l'alluvione del Po, Novembre 1951*, ed. Franca Varignana, photographs Walter Breveglieri (Bologna: Minerva, 2001).

11. "To Live is to be Awake;" in Angelo Maria Ripellino, *Non un giorno ma adesso* (Rome: Grafica, 1960), 62. Here and subsequently, reference is made to the source texts of the composer, held in the ALN.

12. Paul Éluard, "Liberté" [Freedom], in *Choix de poemes* (Paris: Gallimard, 1951), 277–80. The selection of the text was made using the French edition; only later did Nono opt for the Italian translation *La libertà*, ed. Franco Fortini (Turin: Einaudi, 1955), 290–95.

13. "Our March"; see Vladimir Maiakovski, *Opere*, ed. Ignazio Ambrogio, vol. I, 1912–21 (Cassino: Editori Riuniti, 1958), 143; and *Poesia russa del 900*, ed. Angelo M. Ripellino (Parma: Guanda, 1954), 284. The fragments used by Nono are the result of a mixture of the two translations.

14. "To Those Born After"; in Bertolt Brecht, *Poesie e canzoni*, ed. Ruth Leiser and Franco Fortini (Turin: Einaudi, 1958), 215–19.

15. "Nie wieder Krieg!": no more war; "No pasaran": they shall not pass; "Morte al fascismo—Libertà ai popoli": death to fascism, freedom to the people; "La sale guerre": the dirty war.

16. See Julius Fučík, *Scritto sotto la forca*, ed. Franco Calamandrei (Milan: Universale Economica, 1951); the parts used are taken from pp. 16, 25, and 51 (a very similar selection of texts had been used by Nono in 1951 in view of a composition dedicated to Fučík, for two speakers and orchestra, of which he completed only one episode; materials held in the ALN). Eng. trans.: *Notes from the Gallows* (New York: New Century Publishers, 1948).

17. The book *La cancrena* collected several testimonies of Algerians about French police questionings. The edition used by Nono was that translated by Raniero Panzieri for Einaudi of Turin in 1959. The book was translated into English under the title *The Gangrene* in 1960 and issued anonymously by the publisher Lyle Stuart.

18. For this and the next reference see Henri Alleg, *La tortura*, with an essay by Jean-Paul Sartre (Turin: Einaudi, 1958), 26 (for the "voice of Alleg") and 18 (for the "voice of Sartre"). Eng. trans.: *The Question* (London: John Calder, 1958).

19. This poster is reproduced in Gerhard Strauss, *Käthe Kollwitz* (Dresden: Sachsenverlag, 1950), 123.

20. Now collected in *Heart of Spain: Robert Capa's Photographs of the Spanish Civil War*, from the collection of the Museo Nacional Centro de Arte Reina Sofia (New York: Aperture, 2005).

21. For the first of the quoted texts, "Appunti per un teatro musicale attuale"—published in *Rassegna Musicale* 30/4 (1961): 418–24—see De Benedictis-Rizzardi 2001: I: 86–95. The second essay, reproduced in the next chapter of this collection, is, in its substance, an in-depth and expanded elaboration of this 1961 article written in reaction to the controversy unleashed in the aftermath of the first staging of *Intolleranza 1960* (April 13 and 15, 1961).

22. It should be noted that for the drafting of the essay Nono had transcribed all the musical examples afresh, sometimes making slight modifications to the score of *Intolleranza 1960* used for the premiere (published in 1962, with only the German text, by Schott, AV 75). It is here restored the correct numeration of bars in Part 1 (which in both Nono's original text and in AV 75 fails to take account of the twelve-bar cut made by the author in the orchestral prelude just before the premiere) and the definitive version of the score, with text in Italian, as provided in the new edition of *Intolleranza 1960*, revised and corrected by Angela Ida De Benedictis (Mainz: Schott, 2013).

23. For the premiere, the choruses were recorded in Milan at the Studio di Fonologia of the Italian Radio (RAI) with the chorus of RAI-Milan conducted by Nino Antonellini.

24. See note 13. Verses of the poem "Our March."

25. In the score published by Schott in 1962 (AV 75), the work is given on the cover and the title page simply as *Intolleranza*. In the new 2013 edition (see above, note 22), the year (*1960*) has been restored.

26. In the first edition of the text, what follows is the signature and, at the bottom, the bibliographic references: "A.M. RIPELLINO, *Non un giorno ma adesso,* Ed. Grafica, Roma./J. FUCIK, *Scritto sotto la forca,* Ed. Universale economica./H. ALLEG, *La cancrena,* Einaudi, Torino./—*La tortura,* Einaudi, Torino./P. ELUARD, *Poesie,* Einaudi, Torino./B. BRECHT, *Poesie e canzoni,* Einaudi, Torino./W. MAJAKOWSKIJ, *La nostra marcia,* Turin./J.-P. SARTRE, *Oltre il teatro borghese,* Ed. del teatro stabile della città di Genova."

2. POSSIBILITY AND NECESSITY OF A NEW MUSIC THEATER

1. In Nono's last typewritten draft the following can be read after this last sentence: "musical theater is reemerging then not as a *dernier cri* in accordance with the remarks made by Niccolò Castiglioni in his investigation into the problems of today's music in issue n. 4 of la Rassegna Musicale—remarks which make one suspect this composer of a 'Dior mentality' somewhat far removed from a critical-creative consciousness." The reference is to a brief contribution by Castiglioni published in the same issue of *La Rassegna Musicale* that contained another text by Nono on theater, not included in this volume: "Appunti per un teatro musicale attuale" ("Notes toward a Current Music Theater"; for the complete text, De Benedictis-Rizzardi 2001: I: 86–93), then revised and incorporated by the author into this essay. See Niccolò Castiglioni, "Eteronomia dell'esperienza musicale," in *La Rassegna Musicale* 31/4, 1961: 457–58.

2. Again during the proceedings of the "IV Corso internazionale di alta cultura contemporanea: Aspetti e problemi" (Fourth International Course of Contemporary High Culture: Aspects and Problems), at which Nono read this text (see "Bibliographic Notes and Comments to the Text"), the art critic Umbro Apollonio had made a contribution on new trends in contemporary expression. The positions expressed by Apollonio can be read in "Ipotesi su nuove modalità creative" (1962), in *Quadrum* 14 (1963): 5–34; now in *Occasioni del tempo: Riflessioni, ipotesi* (Turin: Studio Forma, 1979), 122–29.

3. With these definitions, Nono is presumably alluding to contemporary stage productions respectively by Karlheinz Stockhausen, Mauricio Kagel, and John Cage (see also chapter 3 of part II in this volume, "Play and Truth in the New Music Theater," note 2).

4. Nono is here referring to the Calvino's essay "La 'belle époque' inattesa" (in *Tempi Moderni* 4/6 [1961]: 24–29), republished with the title "La 'belle époque' inaspettata," in Italo Calvino, *Una pietra sopra: Discorsi di letteratura e società* (Turin: Einaudi, 1980), 70–74 (hence Milan: Mondadori, 1995).

5. Milan: Feltrinelli, 1960.

6. In Italian "modo di formare." Nono takes here a polemical stance on Umberto Eco with an ironic quote of the title of his essay "Del modo di formare come impegno sulla realtà" (Of the Way of Forming as a Commitment to Reality), first published in 1962 in *Il Menabò* 5: 235–90, and subsequently included in the second edition of his *Opera aperta*. The essay appeared in English as "Form and Social Commitment," in Umberto Eco, *The Open Work*, trans. Anna Cancogni (Cambridge, MA: Harvard University Press, 1989), 123–57.

7. See Galvano Della Volpe, *Crisi dell'estetica romantica* (Rome: Samonà & Savelli, 1963). Despite the date of its first publication, Della Volpe's essay mostly dates back to 1941.

8. The last typewritten draft continues at this point: "(N.B.: we have spoken here of 'ideas objectively expressed' in the work, not of 'ideologies' consciously assumed by the author. Ideologies which, as evidenced by the famous case of Balzac, can be in contradiction with the 'ideas objectively expressed')."

9. In his original formulation, Nono takes up here almost verbatim the point made in Francis Jeanson, *Sartre*, trans. Augusta Mattioli (Milan: Mondadori, 1961), 11 ("In contrast to tragedy or the psychological theater Sartre himself described the *theater of situations* as the only form of theater he considers possible in our time"; annotated copy held at the ALN). In the last typewritten draft, this phrase follows: "(and Squarzina told you about it)." The director Luigi Squarzina also participated in the "Fourth International Course of Contemporary High Culture: Aspects and Problems" (see above, note 2) with the lecture "Il palcoscenico ideologico degli anni '60." This contribution was then widely quoted by Nono in a text devoted to the staging of Italo Svevo's *Zeno's Conscience*, realized by Tullio Kezich (see De Benedictis-Rizzardi 2001: I: 171–73, esp. 171).

10. This engraving can be seen in *Pieter Bruegel the Elder and Lucas van Leyden: The Complete Engravings, Etchings, and Woodcuts*, ed. Jacques Lavalleye (London: Thames and Hudson, 1967).

11. Ferruccio Busoni, *The Score of "Doktor Faust,"* in Ferruccio Busoni, *The Essence of Music: And Other Papers*, trans. Rosamond Ley (New York: Philosophical Library 1957), 70–76; 74.

12. In the last typewritten draft this paragraph reads: "We have lost sight here of certain objective structural elements, not determined exclusively by a particular aesthetic, but by the modern necessities of staging."

13. See "*The Yellow Sound:* A Stage Composition," in *The Blaue Reiter Almanac*, ed. Wassily Kandinsky and Franz Marc, trans. Henning Falkenstein, new documentary edition, ed. and with an intro. Klaus Lankheit (New York:

Viking Press, 1974), 207–25. In fact, it is not a ballet but an abstract dramatic action.

14. Following on from this in the last typewritten draft is the sentence: "Today, with contemporary techniques of staging, it would be possible to give this ingenious score the fully realization it still awaits."

15. See Arnold Schönberg, *Moses und Aron* (Mainz: Schott, 1958), I: 3.

16. Quotation from Willi Reich, *Schoenberg: A Critical Biography*, trans. Leo Black (New York: Praeger, 1971), 103–4; original German ed.: *Schönberg oder Der konservative Revolutionär* (Vienna: Fritz Molden, 1968), 139.

17. After "research" in the final typescript comes: "of the State Archives at the Frari. Maybe, a theme to be proposed to the Fondazione Cini."

18. Works written respectively between 1929 and 1935 and between 1944 and 1948.

19. For this and the following quotation see Angelo Maria Ripellino, *Majakovskij e il teatro russo d'avanguardia* (Turin: Einaudi, 1982), 126.

20. Instead of this phrase—incorporated later by means of a handwritten note—the final typewritten draft reads, "and here it must be said—adds Ripellino—that in Meyerhold the political tendency never stifles the autonomy of form."

21. In his original text Nono cites and translates the quotation from Joseph Gregor and René Fülöp-Miller, *Das russische Theater: Sein Wesen und seine Geschichte mit besonderer Berücksichtigung der Revolutionsperiode* (Zurich: Amalthea, 1927), 49 (copy held at the ALN). The translation here is from Nono's original and the reader is referred, for possible comparisons with the official English version, to Joseph Gregor and René Fülöp-Miller, *The Russian Theatre: Its Character and History with Especial Reference to the Revolutionary Period*, trans. Paul England (London: George G. Harrap, 1930; new ed., 1968).

22. Under this title, on the occasion of the third anniversary of the Soviet Revolution, November 7, 1920, a reconstruction of the events preceding the revolution was staged in St. Petersburg (then Petrograd). With the help of directors Petrov, Kugel, and Annenkov, the principal director Nikolai Evreinov coordinated the movements of a battalion of the army and eight thousand citizens. This event is mentioned, formulated almost identically, in "Play and Truth in the New Music Theater."

23. Giulio Carlo Argan, "*Intolleranza 1960* e il teatro d'avanguardia," *Avanti!* (May 18, 1961) (see above in the text).

24. In the penultimate typewritten draft comes the following: "(standing as a rare example of the documentation of the fundamental experiences of modern theatre by an Italian publisher is the translation of *Das politische Theater* by Piscator, published by Einaudi, the reading of which I recommend to any who wish to deepen their knowledge of that moment)." Nono is referring here to the Italian translation of Piscator's text (titled *Il teatro politico*) made by Alberto Spaini in 1960. English ed.: *The Political Theatre: A History, 1914–1929*, trans. Hugh Rorrison (New York: Avon, 1978).

25. The comedy *Puss in Boots* was actually written between 1795 and 1797 and its first performance took place in 1797. The same erroneous date had

appeared in "Notes toward a Current Music Theater," of 1961 (see above, note 1, and De Benedictis-Rizzardi 2001: I: 86–92, esp. 91), and returns in "Play and Truth in the New Music Theater."

26. In addition to Nono himself (the "composer" mentioned in the text), the others who took part in the collective were Emilio Vedova ("painter"), Luca Ronconi ("director"), and Giuliano Scabia ("writer-actor").

27. The latter two authors were also chosen by Nono while selecting the texts for two contemporaneous works, *Djamila Boupachá*, second part of *Canti di vita e d'amore. Sul ponte di Hiroshima* (1962), and *Canciones a Guiomar* (1962–63).

28. Walter Gropius (1883–69), Farkas Molnár (1897–1945), and Andor Weininger (1899–1985), architects united by their experience of the Bauhaus, founders respectively of "total theater," "U-Theater," and "spherical theater."

29. Jean-Paul Sartre, *What Is Literature?* trans. Bernard Frechtman (New York: Philosophical Library, 1949), 62–63; new ed.: "*What Is Literature?" and Other Essays* (Cambridge, MA: Harvard University Press, 1988), 67. See also in this volume, note 10 to "Text—Music—Song."

3. PLAY AND TRUTH IN THE NEW MUSIC THEATER

1. The phrase, which translates as "Attention: bandits!," appeared on signboards put out by the Nazis to refer disparagingly to Italian partisans during the occupation of 1943–45.

2. The last two works mentioned by Nono present certain ambiguities in their titles. By *Ich: Musikalisches Theater; Karlheinz Stockhausen* he presumably meant *Originale: Musikalisches Theater* of 1961. *Instrumentales Theater* of Kagel does not refer to a precise work but to a concept (that of instrumental theater) developed especially from *Sur scène* (1959–60) onward and expressed theoretically in the book of the same name published by Kagel in Bonn in 1976. See also the previous chapter in this volume, "Possibility and Necessity of a New Music Theater," note 3.

3. Original edition: Marc Saporta, *Composition No. 1* (Paris: Seuil, 1962); first English ed.: trans. Richard Howard (New York, Simon and Schuster, 1963).

4. The largest Italian automobile manufacturer, based in Turin, now part of Fiat Chrysler Automobiles. FIAT was originally an acronym for Fabbrica Italiana Automobili Torino.

5. Lelio Basso (1903–78), lawyer, former active member of the Resistance, and founder of the Italian Socialist Party of Proletarian Unity (PSIUP) in 1945, addressed the illusions of the policy directives of the new American President Kennedy in different editorials of the journal *Problemi del Socialismo*, which he founded in 1958. Nono's reference in this case corresponds to the editorial published in May 1961, no. 5, pp. 487–89 ("For a few months Kennedy was the great hope of the Italian 'center-leftists' . . . : everyone was talking then of 'new frontiers,' everyone was ready to join the Kennedy party. We took a position also against this latest illusion, always in the name of the class logic that does not allow a U.S. president, today, to stand against the imperialist interests that supported him in the struggle for power").

6. At that time, and still, *Corriere della Sera,* based in Milan, is the main and most authoritative Italian national newspaper, of famously moderate political orientation, almost always, in its history, close to the government in charge.

7. The words quoted—echoing a similar sentence found in Antonin Artaud, *The Theatre and Its Double*—had indeed appeared in the program notes of *Theater of Chance,* a dyptich premiered on June 22, 1960, composed of *The Marrying Maiden* by Jackson McLow (with music by John Cage) and *Women of Trachis* by Sophocles in a version by Ezra Pound. Some years later the actors of the Living Theatre had a collaboration with Nono: they performed extended vocal actions which were collected and elaborated on the tape part of *A floresta é jovem e cheja de vida* (1965–66), for soloists, percussion, and two four-track tapes (see chapter 7 of part IV in this volume "For Marino Zuccheri").

8. The idea for a further text was never actually realized in the pages of *Il filo rosso,* the journal that printed this text.

9. Theater company directed by Grotowski, 1959–63.

10. See the previous chapter in this volume, "Possibility and Necessity of a New Music Theater," note 25.

11. See Jack Gelber, *The Apple* (New York: Grove Press, 1961). Nono had read the Italian translation (*La mela*) published in *Nuovo teatro americano,* ed. Furio Colombo (Milan: Bompiani, 1963), 233–86.

12. See "Possibility and Necessity of a New Music Theater," note 22.

13. See, in this regard, Robert Russell, *Russian Drama of the Revolutionary Period* (Totowa, NJ: Barnes & Noble Books, 1988), 32.

14. In the course of *Originale,* "Dogs or monkeys were brought on the stage and fed and members of the audience received fruits as well (both only 'if they ask');" see Eric Salzman and Thomas Desi, *The New Music Theater: Seeing the Voice, Hearing the Body* (Oxford: Oxford University Press, 2008), 145–46.

15. Started in Osaka in 1954 by Jiro Yoshihara, the artistic movement, and group, Gutai often proposed radical multidisciplinary actions, thus stimulating the active involvement of the audience.

16. Jim Dine realized a happening in 1960 entitled *Car Crash,* inspired by his personal experience of a car accident.

17. *Nuovo teatro americano* (see note 11), 31.

18. Nono is probably referring to Pietilä's first important project, the modular pavilion of Finland at the 1958 Expo in Brussels.

19. See chapter 1 in the current part of this volume. This essay had been published for a few months at the time of the first edition of this text.

4. *DIE ERMITTLUNG*: A MUSICAL AND THEATRICAL EXPERIENCE WITH WEISS AND PISCATOR [MUSIC AND THEATER]

1. The music for *Die Ermittlung,* for magnetic tape alone, was composed in 1965 at the Studio di Fonologia of RAI in Milan (ed. Ricordi 132668). The first English translation of Weiss's text was published by Calder & Boyars, London, in 1966 (*The Investigation: Oratorio in 11 Cantos,* trans. Alexander Gross).

2. On Josef Svoboda see in this volume the portrait traced by Nono in chapter 1 of part IV.

3. *Hamlet* was not put on "also" in Brussels but rather premiered there; see Denis Bablet, *Josef Svoboda* (Lausanne, Switzerland: Éditions L'Age d'Homme, 1970 [2004]), 91.

4. Nono refers to the trial of a group of officials of the Auschwitz extermination camp, held in Frankfurt from December 12, 1963, to August 20, 1965. It is on the evidence put to this trial that the book-document *The Investigation* by Peter Weiss is based.

5. Square brackets by Nono (this part was omitted in the first edition of the text; see the entry for this chapter in "Bibliographic Notes and Comments to the Text"). The route mentioned by the composer does not follow Weiss's original, which includes, besides the songs mentioned in the text (in the order nos. 2, 4, 5, 7, 8 and 10), "The Song of the Platform" (1), "The Song of the Swing" (3), "The Song of S.S. Corporal Stark" (6), "The Song of the Bunker Block" (9), and "The Song of the Fire Ovens" (11).

6. This refers to *Jeanne d'Arc*, a film by Carl Theodor Dreyer in 1928.

7. It was actually Erwin Piscator who proposed to Nono the collaboration on *Die Ermittlung;* see Angela Ida De Benedictis and Ute Schomerus, "La lotta 'con le armi dell'arte': Erwin Piscator e Luigi Nono; Riflessioni e documenti," in *Musica/Realtà* 21, no. 61 (2000): 151–84, esp. 161, and 178–79.

8. The Brechtian adaptation of Shakespeare's play was first performed in 1964, with choreography by Ruth Berghaus and music by Paul Dessau.

9. From 1964, for female voice and magnetic tape (documentary texts assembled by Giuliano Scabia with a fragment by Cesare Pavese).

5. TOWARD *PROMETEO*: JOURNAL FRAGMENTS

1. After his electronic phase pursued at the Studio di Fonologia of RAI in Milan, which lasted from 1960 until the late 1970s, Nono began work in 1980 with the new technology of live electronics at the Experimental Studio of the Heinrich Strobel Foundation of South-West German Radio in Freiburg im Breisgau. In this studio Nono would create all the works of the 1980s that used electronic means (live or prerecorded), from *Das atmende Klarsein* (1981) to *La lontananza nostalgica utopica futura* (1988–89).

2. Published in Hamburg (annotated copy held at the ALN). See chapters 10, "Die Kapitel der Lehre Israel (Thora) als Text für eine akustische Analyse im Sonograph" (92–112), and 11, "Sonographische Analyse von 14 Proben verschiedener israelitischer Stämme" (113–68).

3. With "eolien" Nono means Aeolian sounds, the airy pitched resonances which are produced on the flute by blowing across the embouchure, a technique frequently used in his late pieces.

4. The title quoted by Nono refers to the entire *opus* edited by Abraham Zvi Idelsohn, published between 1914 and 1932 (copublished by Breitkopf & Härtel, Leipzig, Friedrich Hofmeister, Leipzig; Benjamin Harz, Jerusalem-Berlin-Vienna). The volume to which reference is made in the text is the fourth (*Gesänge der Orientalischen Sefardim*). The whole collection is held at the

ALN. It is published only partially in English under the title *Thesaurus of Hebrew Oriental Melodies.*

5. Centro di Sonologia Computazionale of the University of Padua, formally established in 1979 although operating since 1974. Among its founders was Alvise Vidolin, mentioned by Nono later in the text.

6. Nono draws these references from the previously mentioned Joel Walbe, *Der Gesang Israels und seine Quellen* (see 76–78 n. 2).

7. See Gioseffo Zarlino, *Dimostrationi harmoniche,* facsimile edition of 1571 (New York: Broude Brothers, 1965), 237.

8. Nicola Vicentino, *Ancient Music Adapted to Modern Practice,* trans. and intro. Maria Rika Maniates, ed. Claude V. Palisca (New Haven, CT: Yale University Press, 1996), 195. "Demonstration and Example of a Completely Chromatic Composition for Four Voices" is chap. 44 of book III ("On Music Practice").

9. See ibid., 196–97 (*Alleluia-exultemus*) and 223–25 (*Hierusalem, convertere ad Dominum Deum tuum*).

10. See Gian Francesco Malipiero, *L'armonioso labirinto: Da Zarlino a Padre Martini (1558–1774)* (Milan: Rosa and Ballo, 1946), 4. "Scudo" is the name for different coins used in Italy until the nineteenth century.

11. Nono refers to the twenty-second Council session (September 17, 1562), dedicated specifically to deliberations concerning problems of a musical character; see in this regard Craig A. Monson, "The Council of Trent Revisited," *Journal of the American Musicological Society* 55/1 (Spring 2002): 1–37.

12. The years of birth (1571) and death (1638) of the British composer John Ward, were uncertain at the time this text was written.

13. Published by Kistner & Siegel. Hába's volume (*New Harmony-Textbook of the Diatonic, Chromatic, Quarter-, Third-, Sixth-, and Twelfth-tone Systems*) is not translated into English.

14. See also chapter 5 of part IV in this volume, "Bartók the Composer."

15. Nono's remarks on peculiar pianissimo dynamics by Verdi are also found in "An Autobiography of the Author Recounted by Enzo Restagno," in this volume.

16. Nono refers here to the interpreters (sound engineers and performers) associated with the genesis and the first performances of almost all his works in the 1980s.

17. Text in the example reads: "VLE" ("violas"), "arco in su" ("up bow"), "NORMALE" ("normal"), "arco in giù" ("down bow"), "GIÙ" ("downwards"), "SUL PONTE" ("close to the bridge").

18. Text in the example reads: "FLAUTATO", "LEGNO" ("bow"), "TASTO" ("fingerboard"), "PONTE" ("bridge"), "CRINI" ("bow hair"), "arco battuto al ponte" ("on the hair near the tip, close to the bridge").

19. See chapter 7 of part IV in this volume for the text dedicated by Nono to Marino Zuccheri.

20. On this electronic devices see *The Studio di Fonologia: A Musical Journey,* ed. Maria Maddalena Novati and John Dack (Milan: Ricordi, 2009), 61–67.

21. Reference to certain pages of Goethe's *Italian Journey* (English trans.: W. H. Auden and Elizabeth Mayer [London: Penguin Books, 1970]).

22. Works on the Philharmonie in Berlin, designed by Hans Scharoun, began in 1956—the date specified by Nono—and ended in 1963.

23. The quote is literally taken from the textual material of *Prometeo* ("Il Maestro del gioco," section 8), developed by Massimo Cacciari freely from various sources, including W. Benjamin.

24. It is likely that Nono refers in particular to the 1960 performance with the New York Philharmonic, a live recording that was released in the early 1980s by Fonit Cetra (14834–49—copy held at the ALN).

25. Nono resumes here almost verbatim the theme of "listening to silence" already developed in the opening of "Error as a Necessity" (see chapter 1 of part V in this volume).

26. Nono refers to the so-called Arca (Ark), an architectural structure built by Renzo Piano entirely of wood, installed in the space of the church of St. Lorenzo for the world premiere of *Prometeo*.

EXCURSUS III. INTERVIEW WITH RENATO GARAVAGLIA

1. See "Excursus II" in this volume, "A Letter from Los Angeles."

2. In fact, as is apparent from the letters exchanged with Gunther Schuller in June 1965 (ALN) on his return from the United States, Nono also stopped in New York where he met Schuller, who had been his friend for several years, and with him Charles Mingus.

3. Fritz Winckel in fact collaborated on *Gravesaner Blätter,* a journal founded and directed by Hermann Scherchen from 1955 to 1966. Winckel's name does not appear in the Darmstadt yearbooks between 1946 and 1966. In ALN one can find four letters from Winckel to Nono that bear evidence that the two had met in Venice in 1955, and subsequently corresponded until 1964.

4. This refers to *Quattro lettere* (*Kranichsteiner Kammerkantate*), for soprano, bass, and chamber orchestra. See also chapter 2 of part III (note 3) in this volume, "Music and Resistance."

5. I.e., the International Festival of Contemporary Music of the Venice Biennale.

6. Nono alludes here to a movement originated by a group of young German composers who in those years, under such names as "Neue Einfachkeit" placed themselves controversially outside the avant-garde. In general, they did not recognize either the criteria or the problems of composition as presented and dealt with in the courses at Darmstadt. "Fare il '68" is an Italian expression that means having taken an active part in the anti-authoritarian movement first developed among university students in 1968 and later expanded to the rest of society. It had converged notably with workers' struggles, from 1969 especially and continuing during the following years.

7. Associate professor at Stanford University since 1964, Chowning was then director of the university's Center for Computer Research and Musical Acoustics (CCRMA).

8. In 1978 Charles Dodge became director of the Brooklyn College Center for Computer Music (BC-CCM) at the Brooklyn College of City University of New York, where he was already teaching.

9. Nono is referring to Karlheinz Stockhausen, "Struktur und Erlebniszeit," *Die Reihe* 2 (1955): 69–79; English trans.: "Structure and Experiential Time," *Die Reihe* 2 (1958): 64–74. Nono's personal copy (in German—ALN) contains several marginalia that reflect his lively dissent from the content of the article, dedicated to an analysis of Webern's Quartet op. 28.

10. "East" is here for Nono a comprehensive term, more spiritually than geographically connotated.

11. Reference to the analytical method used by René Leibowitz in *Introduction à la musique de douze sons: Les "Variations pour orchestre" op. 31 d'Arnold Schoenberg* (Paris: L'Arche, 1949).

12. Nono is probably referring to *Tres toques* of 1931. The instrument of "animal bones" is probably the *quijada de burro* (donkey's jawbone), a traditional Afro-Cuban instrument that Roldán uses among the percussion instruments in the orchestral pieces *The Rebambaramba* (1928) and *Ritmicas V and VI* (1930). Varèse's *Ionisation* dates from 1931. See also Carola Nielinger-Vakil, *Luigi Nono: A Composer in Context* (Cambridge: Cambridge University Press 2015), 156–57 n. 21.

13. See Fernando Ortiz, *Africanía de la música folklórica de Cuba* (Havana: Editora Universitaria, 1965).

14. This refers to *Con Luigi Dallapiccola*—for six percussionists and ring modulators—whose title at the time of the interview was still uncertain.

15. Giovanni Gabrieli composed indeed *canzonas, sonatas,* and *sacrae symphoniae* in five, six, seven, eight, ten, twelve, fourteen, fifteen, sixteen, seventeen, nineteen, up to twenty-two parts.

16. This means the Italian section of the International Society of Contemporary Music (ISCM).

17. Nono refers here to the concert that took place on September 15, 1964, at the twenty-seventh International Festival of Contemporary Music of the Venice Biennale. On this occasion *La fabbrica illuminata* was premiered along with *Sequenza II* for harp by Berio, *Musica stricta* op. 11 by Volkonsky, and *Pierrot lunaire* op. 21 by Schoenberg (conducted by Bruno Maderna).

18. The quartet *Fragmente-Stille, an Diotima* was completed in 1980. The genesis of *Prometeo* lasted from 1978 until 1984, the year of the Venice premiere.

19. On the experience with Luca Ronconi, see the interview with Gerhard Müller, "Nuovi progetti—lavori collettivi" (De Benedictis-Rizzardi 2001: II: 220–23).

20. With this formula Nono summarizes a set of concepts that return insistently in the work of Hölderlin. See Friedrich Hölderlin, *Sämtliche Werke und Briefe*, vol. I, ed. Michael Knaupp (Munich: Hanser,1992), esp.: "Der Weingott," ll. 120 ff. (318), l. 147 (319); "Brod und Wein" (first version), ll. 109 ff. (378); "Heimkunft," ll. 103–4 (322). English trans. in *Poems and Fragments*, trans. Michael Hamburger (Cambridge: Cambridge University Press, 1980).

21. See in this respect *Incontro alla Columbia University (New York)* (De Benedictis-Rizzardi 2001: II: 227–34).

22. Nono refers to the so called "1979 Revolution," which led to the establishment of the Islamic republic.

PART THREE. "CONSCIENCE, FEELINGS, COLLECTIVE REALITY"

I. HISTORICAL PRESENCE OF MUSIC TODAY

1. The following quotation is taken from the opening words of the poem "Here Lies" ("I, Antonin Artaud, am my son,/my father, my mother,/my self;/leveller of the imbecile periplum rooted/to the family tree:/the periplum papamummy/and infant wee"); in Antonin Artaud, *Selected Writings*, ed. Susan Sontag (Berkeley: University of California Press, 1988), 537.

2. The long quotation cited later in Nono's text is taken from Joseph Schillinger, *The Mathematical Basis of the Arts* (New York: Philosophical Library, 1948), 3 (annotated copy held at ALN).

3. John Cage, "History of Experimental Music in the United States," in *Silence. Lectures and Writings* (Middletown CT: Wesleyan University Press, 1961), 67. As Cage himself explains in his introduction, the text was requested by Wolfgang Steinecke, director of the Darmstadt summer courses, for the *Darmstädter Beiträge zur Neue Musik*.

4. The Cage citation, as it appears in "Composition as Process, III: Communication," in *Silence*, 41, is actually: "Are sounds just sounds or are they Beethoven?" This text had been prepared for the occasion of the lecture-performance that Cage held at Darmstadt on September 9, 1958; see *Im Zenit der Moderne: Die Internationale Ferienkurse für Neue Musik Darmstadt, 1946–1966*, ed. Gianmario Borio and Hermann Danuser (Freiburg im Breisgau: Rombach, 1997), III: 592. Nono's quotation comes from a typescript copy of the German translation which was distributed in the hall during the lecture, itself given by Cage in English. The translation—edited by Heinz-Klaus Metzger, Hans G. Helms, and Wolf Rosenberg, and approved by Cage himself—introduced significant variants to the English text with the deliberate aim of exacerbating its already provocative nature. These included the substitution of "Beethoven" with "Webern." This translation, with the title "Komposition als Prozess (1958): Drei Studios. III: Kommunikation," is published in *Musik-Konzepte* 1 (1999, *Darmstadt-Dokumente I*): 137–74 (passage quoted on 161). See also Christopher Shultis, "Cage and Europe," in *The Cambridge Companion to John Cage*, ed. David Nicholls (Cambridge: Cambridge University Press, 2002), 36–38: and Martin Iddon, *New Music at Darmstadt: Nono, Stockhausen, Cage, and Boulez* (Cambridge: Cambridge University Press, 2013), 202–28.

5. More properly the Palatine Chapel, which is the original core of the cathedral.

6. The meaning of this passage can be better understood in the light of an unusual circumstance: Nono had wanted his lecture to be preceded, and followed, by the performance of a new work that he had specifically requested from Earle Brown, without him being aware of the use Nono intended to make of it. *Hodograph (I)*, this work of Brown, included improvised sections, and was to have been performed by Severino Gazzelloni and David Tudor themselves along with Christoph Caskel on percussion. See also below, note 9. Nono was also aware of the fact that Brown had studied composition according to Schillinger's method, which might explain the way Nono aligns Schillinger with

Cage as the target of his polemic. It should be noted once more that, on a previous occasion, Nono had specifically asked Cage if his work had any relation to Schillinger, receiving a negative reply (see Cage's letter to Nono of November 11, 1958, ALN).

7. See John Cage, "Composition as Process, III: Communication," 47: "'Not wondering,' to quote Meister Eckhart, 'am I right or doing something wrong?'"

8. Echoed here are the words of the physicist Werner Heisenberg: "I do not think that the uncertainty principle has a direct relationship with the concept of freedom," which Nono takes from Werner Heisenberg and Erwin Schrödinger, *Discussione sulla fisica moderna,* trans. Adolfo Verson (Turin: Einaudi, 1959), 23. In the margin near this passage, underlined in Nono's personal copy (ALN) is the annotation "for Darmstadt." Other markings and marginalia present in that copy relate several of Nono's references to the then current musical situation.

9. The Cage "group" referred to by Nono is that formed by Earle Brown, Morton Feldman, and Christian Wolff, whose music had been presented by Cage and David Tudor in Darmstadt the previous year (1958), in a concert for two pianos designed to demonstrate different compositional procedures based on indeterminacy.

10. Nono seems to allude here to the positions of Heinz-Klaus Metzger in support of Cage; see Heinz-Klaus Metzger, "John Cage o della liberazione" (trans. Sylvano Bussotti), in *Incontri Musicali* 3 (August 1959): 16–31; English trans.: "John Cage, or Liberated Music" (trans. Ian Pepper), in *October* 82 (Fall 1997): 49–61. Metzger will later take issue with Nono, specifically on the content of this text, in "Das Altern der jüngsten Musik" (1964), now collected in Metzger, *Musik Wozu: Literatur zu Noten,* ed. Rainer Riehn (Frankfurt: Suhrkamp, 1980), 117–18.

11. This expression forms the title of the first publication of this text in German: "Gitterstäbe am Himmel der Freiheit."

2. MUSIC AND RESISTANCE

1. Chief music critic of the press linked to the PCI (the newspaper *l'Unità,* the monthly *Rinascita*) and also head of the Party music policy during the years 1960–70, Pestalozza (1928–2017) was the critic and music organizer publicly closest to Nono during this time. His inquiry was occasioned by the twentieth anniversary of the Resistance, which is conventionally represented as beginning from September 8, 1943. After the war, the forces of the left especially would often appeal to the "spirit of the Resistance" as a model of democratic and antifascist political action.

2. The quotation is from Lenin's "Party Organization and Party Literature," a text of 1906 mentioned extensively by the literary critic Vittorio Strada in "Problemi del rapporto direzione-libertà nella cultura dell'Urss"—in *Il Contemporaneo* 6/62 (July 1963): 4–29, esp. 7–10—in support of the view that in those theses of Lenin is "already foreshadowed the subsequent criticism of certain positions of Soviet cultural policy." Founded in 1954, *Il Contemporaneo* was a periodical of the PCI that dealt with literature, art, film, and theater from

a Marxist point of view. The canons of realism and the primacy of the national and popular characteristics of the artwork had been established in Soviet cultural policy and, consequently, in the Western communist parties especially since 1948. At the time this article was written, they had very recently been under discussion by artists and intellectuals who did not subscribe to them, even within the Party. The quoted article by Strada refers to this kind of "problem," which was addressed on the pages of the same newspaper by Luigi Pestalozza with his "Problemi della musica sovietica"—in *Il Contemporaneo* 6/65 (October 1963): 3–26—an article written at the end of a journey made in the USSR along with Nono (who instead reported the experience in the pages of *l'Unità* (December 12, 1963). See also "Viaggio attraverso la musica nell'Urss," now in De Benedictis-Rizzardi 2001: I: 150–57.

3. *Quattro lettere (Kranichsteiner Kammerkantate)* for soprano, bass, and chamber orchestra, actually composed in 1953. Note that Nono dates Maderna's composition before his own cycle of compositions, the *Epitaffi a Federico García Lorca* (1952–53), in which the choice of texts has clear political resonances, with reference to the Spanish Civil War of 1936. The idea of setting to music a letter from a partisan sentenced to death is subsequently taken up again and extended by Nono in *Il canto sospeso,* in 1955–56.

4. Nono here takes a stand against various forms of "moderate left." "New Frontier" is an allusion to the slogan coined by John F. Kennedy in 1960 to the Democratic Convention in Los Angeles. "Center-left" [*centro sinistra*] in Italian political jargon of the time, had a precise meaning in relation to the recent entry of the Socialist Party into the coalition government, which since 1948 had been almost exclusively occupied by the centrist party of the Christian Democrats. The operation, which began in 1962, had resulted in some significant social reforms, which had also had the political function of decreasing the strong pressure of the communist opposition.

5. In the text drafted in 1960 for *Cori di Didone* (see De Benedictis-Rizzardi 2001: I: 432 and 590) Nono uses for the first time the same formulation "murder by society" attributing it to Camus, although it actually paraphrases the title of a text by Antonin Artaud, "Van Gogh, the Man Suicided by Society," in *Selected Writings,* ed. Susan Sontag (Berkeley: University of California Press, 1988), 483.

6. This probably refers to the unfinished theater project *Technically Sweet,* inspired by the figure of the scientist Robert Oppenheimer, on which Nono was working in 1963 with texts supplied to him by the writer Emilio Jona.

7. See the previous chapter in this volume, "Historical Presence of Music Today," note 8.

3. REPLIES TO SEVEN QUESTIONS BY MARTINE CADIEU

1. "East" is here short for "Eastern European Countries," i.e., the Soviet Union and the countries of the Warsaw Pact.

2. Martine Cadieu (1924–2008), journalist, active as a music critic especially at Radio France, published novels, collections of poetry, and, among other books, *Présence de Luigi Nono* (Paris: Pro Musica, 1995).

3. The topic is covered in Jacques Duron, "Mozart et le mythe de Don Juan"—in *La Revue Musicale* 256 (1965), special issue—the text to which Nono is presumably referring. 1964 was the date of *Mozart* by Jean Barraqué (Paris: Hachette), a volume in which there are occasional references to the link between Mozart and the European Enlightenment.

4. Nono is probably referring to the *Canti di Prigionia* of 1938–41, and in particular to *Congedo di Girolamo Savonarola*, setting a text of the Dominican preacher excommunicated in 1497 and soon afterward sentenced to death as a heretic and burned at the stake.

5. The questions raised in quotation marks correspond to the titles of the first three paragraphs of Jean-Paul Sartre, "What Is Literature?" trans. Bernard Frechtman (New York: Philosophical Library, 1949), now in *What Is Literature? and Other Essays,* intro. Steven Ungar (Cambridge, MA: Harvard University Press, 1988), 25, 48, 70.

6. National Liberation Front of Vietnam, the organization which brought together several political parties and was the main component in the resistance for the liberation of South Vietnam from the dictatorship backed by the US government. *A floresta é jovem e cheja de vida* was performed for the first time at the International Festival of Contemporary Music of the Venice Biennale, September 7, 1966.

7. See in this volume the previous chapter, "Music and Resistance," note 1.

8. See Vladimir Mayakovsky, "The Workers and Peasants Don't Understand You," in *Selected Works in Three Volumes,* ed. Alexander Ushakov, trans. Dorian Rottenberg (Moscow: Raduga 1985), 215.

9. See Palmiro Togliatti, *Promemoria sulle questioni del movimento operaio internazionale [Il memoriale di Yalta]* (1964), in *Opere,* ed. Luciano Gruppi, vol. VI, 1956–64 (Rome: Editori Riuniti, 1984), 823–33, esp. 832 (for both quotations). An English trans. (*The "Togliatti Memorandum"*) is available at the site www.marxists.org/archive/togliatti/1964/memorandum.htm (accessed January 2018).

10. Nono dwells considerably on these composers in the account of his journey made to the USSR in 1963, published in the pages of *l'Unità* December 15, 1963; see "Viaggio attraverso la musica nell'Urss," De Benedictis-Rizzardi 2001: I: 150–57.

11. This is probably one of theater projects developed with Giovanni Pirelli during the years 1966–68 that did not, however, come to full realization.

12. Indeed some of the later works of Nono are based exclusively on vocal material (*Un volto, e del mare* from 1969, and *Y entonces comprendió* from 1970).

13. Nono prefaces the date with his initials and the words: "for Lettres Françaises and Martine Cadieu."

4. MUSIC AND POWER

1. See chapter 1 in this section of the book.

2. See note 10 of the chapter cited above. Here too the text being referenced is Heinz-Klaus Metzger, "John Cage, or Liberated Music" (trans. Ian Pepper), in *October* 82 (Fall 1997): 49–61.

3. *Alianza para el progreso,* an (essentially failed) funding program of twenty billion dollars to the countries of the OAS (see below, note 24), launched by John F. Kennedy in 1961 to prevent the spread of the example of the Cuban Revolution of 1959.

4. Nono alludes here to quotations of Daisetz Suzuki and Meister Eckhart used by John Cage and criticized in "Historical Presence of Music Today."

5. Nono is again playing here with Kennedy's "new frontier" slogan (see in this regard, in this volume, "Music and Resistance," note 4, and "Play and Truth in the New Music Theater," note 5).

6. Playa Girón is the beach that was the theater of the failed military invasion of Cuba undertaken on April 17, 1961, by a paramilitary group of Cuban exiles backed by the CIA. While in English the incident is commonly referred to as the "Bay of Pigs Invasion"—and such remains in literal translation in most other languages—Nono always prefers the name used in Cuba (whereas Cuban exiles usually call it "Bahía de los Cochinos").

7. United States Information Service: this was the overseas name of the USIA (U.S. Information Agency), a government agency established in 1953 with functions of "public diplomacy" and, ultimately, of propaganda. It ceased operations in 1999.

8. The "Art and Technology Program," curated by Maurice Tuchman, ran between 1967 and 1971. The artists invited used to be required to develop creative projects with the support of an industrial partner. A total of forty large corporations took part in the program and seventy-six artists were invited. Among those mentioned below by Nono, Victor Vasarely worked with IBM and Robert Rauschenberg with Teledyne. In addition to the Fluxus artist and musician George Brecht, the only composer invited was Karlheinz Stockhausen, but his project proved unfeasible. See the catalog *A Report on the Art and Technology Program* (Los Angeles: County Museum, 1971).

9. The reference is to *La tragédie du Roi Christophe* (Paris: Présence Africaine, 1963); English trans.: *The Tragedy of King Christophe: A Play,* trans. and intro. Paul Breslin and Rachel Ney (Evanston, IL: Northwestern University Press, 2015).

10. See Leonardo Pinzauti, "A colloquio con Mauricio Kagel," in *Nuova Rivista Musicale Italiana* 3/3 (1969): 486–95; also in *Musicisti d'oggi: Venti colloqui* (Turin: Eri, 1978), 109–18, esp. 116.

11. Deleted after "I remind Kagel" on the typescript are the words "our meeting in 1958 in Cologne, our discussion on the performance of his Sextet for strings [*Sexteto de cuerdas,* 1953, rev. 1957] and the trip together to Darmstadt, on my part as a pleasant memory and that I had never 'demanded.'"

12. The entire passage between "I always find it hard" and "is not my responsibility" does not appear in the first edition of the Italian text; it was, however, present in the first German edition (see this chapter in "Bibliographic Notes and Comments to the Texts").

13. Here Nono refers again to the title of Metzger's essay, mentioned above in note 2.

14. During the fascist period in Italy signs were indeed exhibited in public places that prohibited "talking about politics."

15. In support of the national liberation struggle of Algeria, 1961.

16. The towns of Mestre and Marghera formed at the time one of the most important Italian industrial districts, located on the edge of the Venetian lagoon.

17. SDS, Sozialistischer Deutscher Studentenbund (League of German Socialist Students); ASTA, Allgemeiner Studentenausschuss (General Organization of Students); APO, Ausserparlamentarische Opposition (Extraparliamentary Opposition).

18. This last sentence does not appear in the first edition of the Italian text; it was, however, present in the first German edition (see this chapter's entry in "Bibliographic Notes and Comments to the Texts").

19. Kagel's first interview in the pages of *Lo spettatore musicale* was published shortly after the appearance of the present text (see Mauricio Kagel, "A proposito di *Ludwig Van*," interview with Karl Faust, in *Lo spettatore musicale* [March–April 1970]: 22–24). In the former text, devoted exclusively to the aesthetic-creative aspects of the composition *Ludwig Van* on the occasion of its recording for Deutsche Grammophon (December 1969), there is no reference to the discursive context cited by Nono. In all likelihood, Nono is here mixed up over the title of the periodical: these topics, along with Kagel's strong stand against Nono's antibourgeois opinions, are indeed expressed in the aforementioned interview with Pinzauti which appeared in spring 1969 in the *Nuova Rivista Musicale Italiana* (see above, note 10, esp. 115–17).

20. See Karlheinz Stockhausen, *Freibrief an die Jugend* (Open Letter to Youth), first published in the *Journal Musical Français,* in May 1968, and later collected in *Texte zur Musik, 1963–1970* (Cologne: Du Mont Schauberg, 1971), III: 295. In the first Italian publication of the text, the whole section between the brackets does not appear. In the first German published version of this text (see this chapter's entry in "Bibliographic Notes and Comments to the Texts"), on the other hand, the passage quoted from Stockhausen is much more extensive.

21. "Manifesto for the Liberation of the Americas": *"The Second Declaration of Havana,"* Havana, February 4, 1962, now in *The Fidel Castro Reader,* ed. David Deutschmann and Deborah Shnookal (Melbourne: Ocean Press, 2008), 241–68. In it, he proclaimed the establishment of a socialist revolutionary movement among the peoples of Latin America. Nono also used one of the passages of the Declaration in two different compositions: as sung text in *A floresta é jovem e cheja de vida* of 1965–66 (see below in the text), and using the recorded voice of Fidel Castro in *Für Paul Dessau* (1974). The sound document was published as *The Historic Second Declaration of Havana,* Paredon Records P-1013, 1973 (LP), now available as a digital download from the Smithsonian/Folkways catalog (www.folkways.si.edu).

22. In the first published version in Italian and German: "of Bolivia."

23. In the first published version in Italian and German: "that is, to the class struggle."

24. The OAS, Organization of American States, founded in 1948, is a cooperative body that currently brings together all thirty-five independent states of the American continents (excluded were only Cuba, from 1962 to 2009, and Honduras from 2009 to 2011).

25. "I remember phone calls and letters from the publisher Schott; they would tell me 'if you continue with electronic music, we shall no longer have any interest in publishing you';" Luigi Nono, "Intervista di Philippe Albèra" (1987), in De Benedictis-Rizzardi 2001: II: 421. The last part of the sentence from "and the ever-growing," does not appear in the first edition of the Italian text.

26. This episode is also discussed by Nono in another text, ["Against the War in Vietnam"] (1966), not included here (but see De Benedictis-Rizzardi 2001: I: 216–20). Part of its content is shared with different texts used in the composition A floresta é jovem e cheja de vida of 1966.

27. Nono later added here: "In each of these four bands a special time is constructed; from the simultaneity of those same bands arises a temporal relationship that is varied in yet a further different way."

5. IN THE SIERRA AND IN THE PARLIAMENT

1. In its first publication in the journal *Astrolabio* Nono's text was preceded by the following editorial preface: "Back from a long journey to the Latin American subcontinent and Cuba, Maestro Nono discusses in this article the difficulties and the progress of the struggle for socialism, documenting the victories won by the popular masses and their vanguards in the various countries and emphasizing the uniqueness of the revolutionary process, notwithstanding the diversity of their particular experiences (armed struggle—parliamentary elections). On the issue of the relationship between intellectuals and the revolutionary struggle, especially relevant today in Cuba after the "Padilla case," the Italian artist admits with frank self-criticism his Eurocentric distortions, but condemns the bureaucratic excesses." *Astrolabio* was a weekly journal of the independent left, founded and directed by Ferruccio Parri, a partisan leader who had taken part in the Resistance in the ranks of the radical "Partito d'Azione" (Action Party) and was the first president of the Council of Ministers of the newly formed Italian republic. It is significant that Nono chose (or was advised) to publish his report about Latin America in an organ of this kind, since the article shows opinions on the armed struggle that would not have been appreciated in the official press of the PCI, for which Nono regularly wrote. The composer made his trip in early 1971 through Chile, Peru, Venezuela, and Cuba. Regarding the "Padilla case," see below, note 28.

2. Valentín Teitelboim Volosky, aka Volodia, Chilean writer, journalist, and literary critic, was the active leader of the Chilean Communist Party since 1945 and was subsequently its secretary general between 1989 and 1994.

3. See in this regard, chapter 4 of part III in this volume "Music and Power," note 6.

4. The quotation is taken from Volodia Teitelboim's opening speech commemorating the Tenth anniversary of the Battle of Playa Girón, made by Fidel Castro on April 19, 1971. It is not clear what source Nono used here. Teitelboim's speech was not included in the official transcript published later (see below, note 12).

5. Salvador Allende was cofounder and leader of the Socialist Party of Chile. Elected president of the Republic of Chile in 1970 at the head of the Unidad

Popular coalition, he was deposed by the violent coup d'état of September 11, 1973.

6. See above, note 4.

7. Three Hispanic militants who supported the underground armed struggle and were killed in ambushes by the police or army are mentioned here: Ernesto "Che" Guevara; "Inti" Peredo, who used to be part of the guerrilla group close to Guevara in Bolivia; Carlos Marighella, a communist militant since the 1930s, distanced himself from the Communist Party of Brazil to form, in 1967, the Ação Libertadora Nacional (Action for National Liberation) group.

8. The Frente Amplio, a left-wing political coalition, was formed during the Uruguayan presidential elections of 1971. The Movimiento de Liberación Nacional—Tupamaros (MLN-T), formed during the 1960s and responsible for many guerrilla actions, used to support the Frente Amplio indirectly through the Movimiento 26 de Marzo.

9. MRA, Movimiento Revolucionario Argentino (Argentine Revolutionary Movement): FAR, Fuerzas Armadas Revolucionarias (Revolutionary Armed Forces); ERP, Ejército Revolucionario del Pueblo (Revolutionary Army of the People).

10. Douglas Bravo, political leader and Venezuelan guerrilla, was the head of the movement Frente de Liberación Nacional (FLN, National Liberation Front), whose armed wing was the Fuerzas Armadas de Liberación Nacional (FALN, National Liberation Armed Forces). In 1968 Nono dedicated the electroacoustic composition *Contrappunto dialettico alla mente* to Douglas Bravo and the FLN-FALN movement, and in 1969 curated an album of songs and spoken texts, *Venezuela: In questo momento guerriglia; FLN-FALN*, LP (Milan: Edizioni del Gallo, 1969). The album is accompanied by a forty-three-page booklet of documents prefaced and edited by Nono himself.

11. Edmundo Pérez Zujovic was minister of the interior, public works, and the economy in the government of Christian Democrat Eduardo Frei Montalva. He was killed in an attack on June 8, 1971, responsibility for which was attributed to the terrorist group of the Vanguardia Organizada del Pueblo (VOP, Organized Vanguard of the People).

12. Fidel Castro, *Discurso pronunciado por el Comandante Fidel Castro Ruz, Primer Secretario del Comité Central del Partido Comunista de Cuba y Primer Ministro del Gobierno Revolucionario, en el acto central en conmemoración del X aniversario de la victoria de Playa Girón, efectuado en el teatro de la Ctc el 19 de Abril de 1971*, in www.cuba.cu/gobierno/discursos/1971/esp /f190471e.html (government website that collects the official transcripts of the speeches of Fidel Castro–accessed January 2018). Nono's source was not found.

13. During the years 1970–71, General Juan José Torres formed a military junta of the left whose political program was centered on nationalization and the opening of a constituent assembly. In August 1971 he was deposed by a coup d'état led by Colonel Hugo Banzer Suárez.

14. The Ejercito de Liberación Nacional (ELN, National Liberation Army), founded by "Che" Guevara at Ñancahuazú, carried out the first guerrilla actions. In 1970, three years after the capture and death of Guevara, the ELN conducted a guerrilla war in the mountains of Teoponte that lasted for several

months. The source of the quotation cannot be traced. Words of Pedro Duno, commander of the FALN, appear among the texts of *A floresta é jovem e cheja de vida*, composed by Nono in 1965–66.

15. See above, note 12.

16. Arnaldo Forlani, political secretary of the Italian Christian Democrat party in the years 1969–73 and again in 1989–92.

17. See above, note 12.

18. Isidoro Carrillo, communist trade unionist, was appointed general director of the Empresa Nacional del Carbón by the Unidad Popular government; following the military coup d'état he was arrested and shot in October 1973.

19. Eduardo Frei Montalva, founder of the Falange Nacional Party and later president of the Partido Demócrata Cristiano, was president of Chile from 1964 to 1970. Francisco Franco, following the civil war of 1936, remained at the head of the authoritarian government that ruled Spain until his death in 1975.

20. Luis Emilio Recabarrén, founder in 1918 of the Partido Obrero Socialista of Chile and, after its affiliation to the International in 1922, of the Communist Party.

21. MIR, Movimiento de Izquierda Revolucionaria (Movement of the Revolutionary Left).

22. Indigenous population of the southern part of the South American continent (Araucanía and Patagonia). The Mapuche were the only group to successfully resist the invasions of the Spanish in the sixteenth century and those of the Indians two centuries earlier. After they lost control of their land in 1885, they settled in the south of Chile and Argentina, in rural communities and in the city.

23. MCR, Movimiento Campesino Revolucionario (Revolutionary Peasant Movement).

24. The CORA, Corporación de la Reforma Agraria (Agrarian Reform Corporation) was created in 1962, originating in the transformation of the Caja de Colonización Agrícola; under the Unidad Popular government it became the instrument for implementing the nationalization of large estates and land redistribution as part of a program of "transition to socialism."

25. The MAPU, Movimiento de Acción Popular Unitaria (Popular Unitary Action Movement) was formed in 1968 and caused a split in the Christian Democrat left. In 1970 it then joined the Unidad Popular coalition which, together with socialists, communists, and radicals, supported Salvador Allende's candidacy in the presidential elections. Radomiro Tomic (1914–92), former cofounder of the Falange Nacional, stayed at the head of what remained of the progressive wing of the Partido Demócrata Cristiano after the MAPU split, and he ran in the presidential elections of 1970, won by Allende. These elections did not result in an absolute majority of votes; the Chilean constitution allowed for a parliamentary verification in this case, and Tomic voted for Allende's confirmation as president.

26. Carlos Altamirano Orrego, secretary general of the Socialist Party since 1971, fled to Cuba and then to West Germany after the coup d'état of 1973. He retained his position in exile until 1979 and returned to his homeland in 1993.

27. The law against "vagrancy" in 1971 was aimed primarily at subordinating labor relations to state control, making no exceptions. The state used the penalty of forced "rehabilitation" against self-employed workers or those peasants who refused to follow the production planning established by the government, after the revolutionary redistribution of land.

28. The Cuban poet Herberto Padilla was arrested in 1971 on charges of counterrevolutionary propaganda. Having initially joined an appeal made by European intellectuals in support of Padilla, Nono then dissociated himself publicly in an article published in a newspaper based in Santiago, Chile. See Luigi Nono, "Cuando se comete un error, no hay error más grave que el no admitirlo," *El Siglo* (September 9, 1971): 12 (see De Benedictis-Rizzardi 2001: II: 612).

29. See above, note 12.

30. Raúl Castro Ruz, Fidel's brother, participated in the Cuban Revolution and, having always occupied second place in the hierarchy of official positions of the Republic of Cuba, became president of the Council of State in 2008 after the resignation of Fidel, who died in 2016.

31. July 26 is celebrated in Cuba as the anniversary of the assault on the Moncada barracks, which in 1953 marked the beginning of the revolution. Fidel Castro's speech on the anniversary in 1970 was highly self-critical in light of the difficult economic conditions besetting the country. After publicly raising the issue of his resignation, he won a plebiscite in his favor. See *Discurso pronunciado por el Comandante Fidel Castro Ruz,* in www.cuba.cu/gobierno/discursos/1970/esp/f260770e.html.

32. Ibid.

33. See above, note 12.

34. The concluding sentence, evidently hasty and elliptical, does not appear in the published text. Presumably Nono is referring to the various speeches of Castro quoted in the course of the article and in particular the speech cited above.

EXCURSUS IV. INTERVIEW WITH WALTER PRATI AND ROBERTO MASOTTI

1. The interview was accompanied by the following abstract: "The interview was conducted on September 28 and 29 in Freiburg Experimental Studio, where Luigi Nono has been working for about two years. Created by the Heinrich Strobel Foundation in 1971 to develop research in the field of music, this studio has equipment that is quite special because it consists of a combination of analogue devices controlled by computer, a characteristic that makes it unique in Europe. The current director is Professor Haller, aided by Rudolf Strauss, who assisted Nono through all the experiments leading toward *Guai ai gelidi mostri,* his latest work performed in late October in Cologne. Participating in these rehearsals were Roberto Fabbriciani (flute), Ciro Scarponi (clarinet), Giancarlo Schiaffini (tuba, piccolo trumpet), Stefano Scodanibbio (bass), the contraltos Susanne Otto and Bernadette Manca di Nissa, Charlotte Geselbracht (viola) and Christine Theus (cello)."

2. Nono refers to the thoughts expressed by Wittgenstein in "Remarks on Frazer's 'Golden Bough,'" in *Wittgenstein: Sources and Perspectives*, ed. C. G. Luckhardt (Bristol: Thoemmes Press 1996), esp. 28 ("we must uncover the source of the error. . . . We must find the *road* from error to truth"), and 29.

3. This is probably an allusion to the ninth of the *Duineser Elegien* "Because we ourselves seem to be needed/by all things present; by the here and the now;/by this fleeting World, for it touches us nearly;/touches us, the most fleeting, once only./Only once for each and for all; once and no more./Ourselves one time only and never again." See Rainer Maria Rilke, *Duino Elegies: A Bilingual Edition,* trans. Stephen Cohn, pref. Peter Porter (Evanston, IL: Northwestern University Press, 1989), 71

4. The reference is to *Fragmente-Stille, an Diotima,* of 1979–80.

5. Nono seems to be referring here to the premiere of *Canticum sacrum in honorem Sancti Marci nominis* (Venice, September 13, 1956).

6. Nono's paraphrase refers to a concept found in various of Nietzsche's writings, particularly *Aphorisms.*

7. See in this respect *Lettera a Leone Piccioni* (De Benedictis-Rizzardi 2001: I: 221–23).

8. The date of Marino Zuccheri's retirement, February 1983, can be treated also as that of the definitive closure of the Studio di Fonologia.

9. See chapter 1 of part III in this volume "Historical Presence of Music Today."

10. Nineteen eighty-three was the centenary of Edgard Varèse's birth and several concerts were organized in Italy in his honor.

PART FOUR. PORTRAITS AND DEDICATIONS

1. JOSEF SVOBODA

1. Nono is probably referring to the Congreso Cultural de la Habana, a large demonstration organized by the Cuban government in January 1968, to which four hundred artists and intellectuals were invited from all over the world and during which numerous shows, concerts, and sound installations were organized as fringe events.

2. Svoboda's presence in Havana in 1964 is documented, the year when he set up at the local Teatro Mella *Romeo and Juliet* of Shakespeare; see Denis Bablet, *Josef Svoboda* (Lausanne, Switzerland: Éditions L'Age d'Homme, 1970, repr. 2004), 205.

3. This refers to the 1967 International and Universal Exposition in Montreal (Expo 67), for which Svoboda created *Polyvision,* "a spatial installation comprising three-dimensional mobile objects onto which slides and film images were projected with music, forming different audio-visual compositions" (see www.svoboda-scenograf.cz/en/polyekran-polyvision).

4. Nono refers to the 1958 International and Universal Exposition (Expo 58), where Svoboda presented, along with Emil and Alfréd Radok, the *laterna magika* and a system with eight screens called *Polyekran.* After the worldwide

success of the Expo the *laterna magika* was transferred to the National Theatre in Prague in 1959, where Nono had his first encounter with Svoboda (see "Excursus I" in this volume, "An Autobiography of the Author Recounted by Enzo Restagno," note 69).

5. *Intolleranza 1960*, produced in Venice on February 13, 1961, with sets by Svoboda and directed by Václav Kašlík.

6. Nono refers here to pictures of naturalistic character that Svoboda had prepared on transparencies for the premiere of *Intolleranza 1960* and which Nono, subsequently, decided to substitute with abstract images painted by Emilio Vedova.

7. See in this regard the report of the 1965 performance in "A Letter from Los Angeles," in this volume. Despite the limitations highlighted by Nono, Svoboda was still able to present in Boston certain solutions that were technically much more advanced than those of the Venetian staging in 1961, and in effect produced the first scenography ever realized by means of TV images transmitted in real time on the big screen (*Eidophor*). See Josef Svoboda, *The Secrets of Theatrical Space: The Memoirs of Josef Svoboda*, trans. and ed. Jarka M. Buria (New York, Applause, 1993).

8. To date no other evidence has been found for this planned collaboration with Svoboda. Nono was at that time currently working on the idea of a new theatrical work provisionally entitled *L'immaginazione prende il potere* (The Imagination Takes Over). The project came to nothing.

2. REMEMBERING TWO MUSICIANS

1. Giovanni Gabrieli, *Opera omnia*, vol. I, *Sacrae symphoniae* (Venice: Fondazione Giorgio Cini—Universal Edition, 1969).

2. "Dear Nono, during one of your last visits you told me that you wanted to study the Gabrielis. This is why I asked the Fondazione Giorgio Cini to send you the first volume of the works of Giovanni Gabrieli. The edition reproduces the original, without distortions, or additions. It is useful./With best regards./G. Francesco Malipiero./Asolo (Treviso) 8.XI.1970" (letter preserved in ALN).

3. See Giovanni Gabrieli, *Opera omnia*, 11 vols., ed. Denis Arnold (Rome: American Institute of Musicology, 1956–69).

4. *Harmonice musices odhecaton* (RISM 1504^2). Facsimile ed.: Ottaviano dei Petrucci, *Harmonice musices odhecaton A* (Sala Bolognese: A. Forni, 2003). The instrumentation referred to by Nono was accomplished between 1949 and 1950 and edited by Bruno Maderna: *Odhecaton (1501): Werke von Josquin, Compere, Ockeghem und anderen Meistern des 15. Jahrhunderts, für kleines Orchester* (Zurich: Ars Viva, 1951; new ed., Milan: Suvini Zerboni, 1977).

5. See also "Excursus I" in this volume, "An Autobiography of the Author Recounted by Enzo Restagno."

6. The concert was held November 5, 1973, at the Royal Festival Hall in London with the London Symphony Orchestra; the pianist was Alfred Brendel (see *Bruno Maderna's Last Concert*, CD Stradivarius STR 10071, 1993; this edition erroneously gives the name of the BBC Symphony Orchestra).

3. VICTOR JARA'S SONG

1. This is a quotation of two lines from *Estadio Chile* by Jara: "¡Qué espanto produce el rostro del fascismo! [What horror the face of fascism creates!]/Así golpeará nuestro puño nuevamente. [So will our fist strike again!]." Jara wrote the poem in the stadium in Santiago, where he was detained along with thousands of other militants and sympathizers of the Unidad Popular, in the aftermath of the military coup of September 11, 1973. It is said that the text was delivered, incomplete, to a comrade just before Jara, already exhausted by prior torture, was taken to be tortured again and finally killed. The text appears in *Twentieth-Century Latin American Poetry: A Bilingual Anthology*, ed. Stephen Tapscott (Austin: University of Texas Press, 1996), 337–38.

2. This refers again to *Estadio Chile*.

3. "With the pots," which were beaten in demonstrations against the Unidad Popular government.

4. Nono cites here a phrase uttered by Jara at the "Encuentro de Musica Latinoamericana," Casa de las Americas, Havana, Cuba 1972 (see below, note 10).

5. José Martí, Cuban poet of Spanish origin, committed to the anticolonialist political struggle, repeatedly exiled, died in one of the first battles of the Cuban war of independence in 1895; Nicolás Guillén, also a scholar and combatant, gave poetic expression especially to the Afro-Cuban culture, and returned to Cuba from exile in North America only after the Castro revolution of 1959; Violeta Parra, singer, poet, and painter, she devoted herself to the collection and dissemination of Chile's traditional music, which paved the way for the Nueva Canción Chilena movement; with regard to Luis Emilio Recabarrén, see chapter 5 of part III in this volume, "In the Sierra and in the Parliament" (note 20).

6. Indigenous population of the southern part of the South American continent (Araucanía and Patagonia; see ibid., note 22).

7. Nono's source is the Italian volume Victor Jara, *Canto libre*, ed. Michele L. Straniero (Florence: Vallecchi, 1976), 49–50 (copy at the ALN).

8. Movimiento de Acción Popular Unitaria (Popular Unitary Action Movement); see "In the Sierra and in the Parliament" (note 25).

9. For further information on the biography of Victor Jara, see Joan Jara, *Victor: An Unfinished Song* (London: Bloomsbury, 1998).

10. This refers to the "Encuentro de Musica Latinoamericana," Casa de las Americas, Havana, Cuba, 1972; it should be noted that the ALN holds about fifty sheets of notes taken by Nono at this event.

11. Haydée Santamaría Cuadrado (1923–80) was part of the original group of Cuban revolutionaries, led by Fidel Castro, that assaulted the Moncada barracks in Santiago de Cuba on July 26, 1953, an action regarded as the beginning of the Cuban Revolution. Nono set words by Santamaría in three of his compositions, *Voci destroying muros* (1970, withdrawn), *Ein Gespenst geht um in der Welt* (1971), and the stage work *Al gran sole carico d'amore* (1972–74).

4. PREFACE TO ARNOLD SCHOENBERG'S *HARMONIELEHRE*

1. Erwin Stein, *Praktischer Leitfaden zu Schönbergs Harmonielehre: Ein Hilfbuch für Lehrer und Schüler* (Vienna: Universal Edition, 1923).

2. Ibid., 1, here in the English translation published in Arnold Schoenberg, *Theory of Harmony*, trans. Roy E. Carter (Berkeley: University of California Press, 1983 [1st ed., 1978]), xiii ("Translator's Preface"). In a review to Carter's edition, Claudio Spies points out Schoenberg's "characteristically sardonic" nuances of this sentence; see *Journal of the Arnold Schoenberg Institute* 3/1 (1979): 179–86, esp. 185.

3. Schoenberg, in Stein, *Praktischer Leitfaden zu Schönbergs Harmonielehre*, 1, here translated from the Italian quotation in Nono's original text (see for more details the "Bibliographic Notes and Comments to the Texts"). A totally different translation, from Schoenberg's original German, is suggested by Spies in the review quoted above (see note 2): "As it is, that part would have to be newly revised and constantly brought into conformity with ever increasing and expanding knowledge, if the good features left over from previous times are to continue to be palatable" (ibid.).

4. Arnold Schönberg, *Harmonielehre* (Vienna: Universal Edition, 1911 [3rd ed., 1922]), here in the English translation by Roy E. Carter published in *Theory of Harmony*, 1.

5. Ibid., 417.
6. Ibid., 15.
7. Ibid., 29.
8. Ibid.
9. Ibid., 31.
10. Ibid., 19.
11. Ibid.
12. Ibid., 7.

13. Ibid., 8. Schoenberg refers here to the words sung by Hans Sachs in the third scene of the first act of Wagner's *Meistersinger* ("If ye by rules would measure/What doth with your rules agree,/Forgetting all your learning,/Seek ye first what its rules may be." Trans. Frederick Jameson: *The Mastersingers of Nuremberg*, complete vocal score in a facilitated arrangement by Karl Klindworth [New York: G. Schirmer, 1903]).

14. Ibid., 21.
15. Ibid.
16. Ibid., 43.

17. See Arnold Schoenberg, *Structural Functions of Harmony*, ed. Leonard Stein (London: Benn, 1969).

18. In the Italian typescript and in the first draft in German (see this chapter's entry in "Bibliographic Notes and Comments to the Texts"), this is followed by: "the continued Marxist creativity."

19. Nono probably is referring to the collection of interviews by Hanns Eisler, *Gespräche mit Hans Bunge* (Leipzig: VEB Deutscher Verlag für Musik, 1975) (*Gesammelte Werke*, series III, vol. VII). To understand the reasons for the critical reference to Eisler and for the observations contained in the whole paragraph in general, it should be noted here that the edition of *Harmonielehre* prefaced by Nono was published by the publishing house of the GDR. Eisler, a former pupil of Schoenberg in Vienna, had moved to the United States because of Nazi persecution but, for his notorious communist sympathies, he ended up

targeted by the House Committee on Un-American Activities, which forced him, in 1948, to leave the country. Eisler finally found refuge in the GDR, where he was able to enjoy great prestige (he composed, among other things, its national anthem).

20. In the first printed edition (see the entry for this chapter in "Bibliographic Notes and Comments to the Texts"), this sentence is preceded by: "Although I belong to another generation and my development has other presuppositions."

5. BARTÓK THE COMPOSER

1. The ethnomusicologist Roberto Leydi was among the speakers at the international conference "The Contemporaneity of Bartók," organized in Venice (Teatro La Fenice, October 14 to 17, 1981; see "Bibliographic Notes and Comments to the Texts," 466).

2. The "Sunday Circle" (or "Sunday Society") founded during the First World War, between 1915 and 1916, by a circle of friends—including philosophers, historians, and art historians—and formed around Béla Balázs and György Lukács (Anna Leszai, Emma Ritoók, Béla Fogarasi, Lajos Fülep, Karl Mannheim, Antal Frigyes, Arnold Hauser, Károl Tolnay, and so on). For an account of the orientations and positions of its members, see György Lukács, *Record of a Life: An Autobiographical Sketch,* ed. István Eörsi, trans. Rodney Livingstone (London: Verso, 1983), 49–51 and 54–55.

3. It is impossible to deduce a title from the information Nono provides here; the date he gives, however, might indicate the German *Rheinische Musik- und Theater Zeitung,* whose issue no. 5/6 of February 8, 1919, carried an autobiographical text by Bartók in its introduction.

4. See Bela Bartók, *Melodien der Rumänischen Colinde (Weihnachtslieder),* 484 melodies, with an introductory essay (Vienna: Universal Edition, 1935), no. 10259; the annotated score is held at the ALN. As Nono himself recalls here, the same point had already been the object of discussion in Budapest on October 2, 1981, during a lecture he held as part of a conference organized and sponsored by UNESCO.

5. Ibid., xii and xxxiv.

6. Ibid., xviii and xxxiii.

7. See "Sketch of a New Aesthetic of Music," in *Three Classics in the Aesthetic of Music* (New York: Dover, 1962); 1st ed., *Entwurf einer neuen Ästhetik der Tonkunst* (Trieste: Schmidl, 1907).

8. In the correspondence kept up between the two composers (see below), Hába's name does not in fact appear, nor would a comparison with the treatise on quarter-tones have been possible at that time. Hába's first essay, "Harmonic Foundations of Quarter-Tone System" ("Harmonické základy čtvrttónové soustavy," in *Hudební Matice Umělecké Besedy,* Prague) dates in fact from 1922, and the second—and most famous—*Neue Harmonielehre des Diatonischen, Chromatischen Viertel-, Drittel-, Sechstel- und Zwölftel- Tonsystems* (Lipsia: Kistner & Siegel) from 1927; both therefore belong to a period subsequent to the correspondence between Schoenberg and Bartók. The parallel

developed by Nono later in the text should be understood more as an opposition of principles (made from his own personal perspective) than as the account of an actual dispute.

9. These letters can be read in Denijs Dille, "Die Beziehungen zwischen Bartók und Schönberg," in *Documenta Bartókiana: Beiträge über Bartóks Tätigkeiten und seine Selbstbiographien,* no. 2 (Mainz: Schott, 1965), 53–61.

10. What is meant is the *Verein für musikalische Privataufführungen,* founded by Schoenberg in 1918.

11. Given the absence of audio recordings of the Budapest proceedings, Nono's affirmation is unfortunately not verifiable.

12. See Bartók, *Melodien der Rumänischen Colinde (Weihnachtslieder),* xxii.

13. Gilberto Cappelli's String Quartet was composed in 1981 and premiered in Venice at the Music Biennale on the October 9 of the same year, a few days before this lecture. See also chapter 2 of part V in this volume, "Other Possibilities of Listening."

6. FOR HELMUT

1. The quotation is not, in fact, drawn from *On Certainty*—where it does not appear—but rather from an unreferenced lecture quoted by Norman Malcolm in his *Ludwig Wittgenstein: A Memoir* (Oxford: Oxford University Press, 1958–2001), 43. The sentence was quoted by Aldo Gargani in his *Wittgenstein tra Austria e Inghilterra* (Turin: Stampatori, 1979), 15, which is the actual source for Nono (annotated copy in the ALN).

2. The reference to Giovanni Maria Artusi, taken up again even more explicitly in the last lines of the text, is to the famous controversy between the Bolognese canon and Claudio Monteverdi, which began following the publication in 1600 of the dialogue *L'Artusi; overo, Delle imperfettioni della moderna musica,* a libel in which Artusi railed against certain innovations in madrigal writing introduced by Monteverdi. The controversy lasted for several years and was sealed by the lapidary statement made by Monteverdi in the preface to his fifth book of madrigals (1605): "Io non faccio le mie cose a caso" ("I do not write things by accident"); see *Composers on Music: Eight Centuries of Writings,* ed. Josiah Fisk (Boston: Northeastern University Press, 1997), 15.

3. In this case too, Nono's bibliographic reference is revealed to be inaccurate; the quote is in fact taken from Aldo Gargani, introduction to *Crisi della ragione: Nuovi modelli nel rapporto tra sapere e attività umane,* ed. Aldo Gargani (Turin: Einaudi, 1979), 5.

4. The reference is to the treatise *De l'infinito, universo e mondi* (Venice, 1584). The preceding expressions *können* and *müssen* refer to a well-known aphorism by Schoenberg, "Kunst kommt nicht von Können, sondern von Müssen" ("Art doesn't come from being able to do something, but from having to do it").

5. "The past carries with it a secret index by which it is referred to redemption. . . . If so, then there is a secret agreement between past generations and the present one. Then our coming was expected on earth. In that case we are anticipated on earth. Then, like every generation that preceded us, we have been

endowed with a *weak* messianic power, a power on which the past has a claim"; Walter Benjamin, "On the Concept of History," in *Selected Writings,* vol. IV, 1938–40, ed. Howard Eiland and Michael W. Jennings (Cambridge, MA: Belknap Press of Harvard University Press, 2003), 390.

7. FOR MARINO ZUCCHERI

1. Marino Zuccheri (1923–2005) has been the main technician of the Studio di Fonologia at RAI-Milan, since its inception in 1955 until his retirement in 1983, which practically marked the closure of the studio itself. The meeting, and the incident referred to later, could be dated around 1956, when Nono produced a first attempt at serial electroacoustic composition, as is documented by jottings found in a notebook (ALN) containing several sketches for *Il canto sospeso*. The first real collaboration with Zuccheri was in October 1960, during the creation of Nono's first electronic work, *Omaggio a Emilio Vedova*. It is from this point that the "over 15 years" mentioned later on should be dated. Subsequent memories of this first meeting were later joyfully confirmed by Marino Zuccheri in Angela Ida De Benedictis, ". . . at the Times of the Tubes . . . : A Conversation with Marino Zuccheri," in *New Music on the Radio: Experiences at the Studio di Fonologia of the Rai, Milan 1954–1959,* ed. Angela Ida De Benedictis and Veniero Rizzardi (Rome: Cidim-Eri, 2000), 176–212.

2. Here, and elsewhere in the text, Nono lists several performers (singers, actors, instrumentalists and choir conductors) who contributed in different ways and different times to the realization of certain of his electroacoustic works produced between 1964 and 1972 at the Studio di Fonologia of the Milan RAI.

3. "Tape music" English in original.

4. It is not really a "first version," but a quite different piece, and independent of the electroacoustic composition of the same title created by Maderna in 1958 at the Studio di Fonologia. The 1952 piece—which, contrary what Nono says, is unrelated to the Cologne Studio—was created at the Institut für Phonetik und Kommunikationsforschung of the University of Bonn with the help of Werner Meyer-Eppler.

5. "A sonar e a cantar" is the subtitle of the tenth part (*Stasimo secondo*) of *Prometeo* (1978–85), a clear reference to the indication "per cantar e sonar"—"to sing and to play," meaning an equally possible vocal and/or instrumental realization of the parts—introduced in 1587 by Giovanni Gabrieli in his first madrigal (*Lieto godea*) composed with the technique of *cori spezzati*.

6. In the original, this and the expressions that follow in inverted commas alternate between Venetian dialect (Nono) and Triestine dialect (Zuccheri).

7. Mali Lošinj, an island now part of Croatia, had been a territory of the Venetian republic since the thirteenth century until 1797 and was subsequently part of Italy in the years 1918–47. Nono here calls it with the Italian name "Lussinpiccolo."

8. The Triestine expression *panolar* means angling so that the fishing line moves with the motion of the boat.

9. The tape is currently held in the "Marino Zuccheri Collection" at the NoMus Association (Milan), with other, similar humorous collages made of outtakes from the studio sessions.

10. This refers to the "Dollar Poem" by John Harriman—part of the Living Theatre's collective show *Mysteries and Smaller Pieces*—based on the expressive reading of texts and numbers printed on a dollar bill, used among other things by Nono in the tapes of *A floresta é jovem e cheja de vida*.

11. The concert took place on September 15, 1964, during the twenty-seventh International Festival of Contemporary Music of the Biennale of Venice. *La fabbrica illuminata* was played along with *Sequenza II* by Berio, *Musica stricta* op. 11 by Volkonsky, and *Pierrot lunaire* op. 21 by Schoenberg (conductor: Bruno Maderna).

12. Regarding this episode, on Aug. 31, 1968, Nono wrote a controversial article for the PCI newspapers *Paese Sera* and *l'Unità*, re-released as "Declaration of Luigi Nono" in De Benedictis-Rizzardi 2001: I: 243–44. The poem mentioned is "Malcolm," by Sonia Sánchez, and the "flyer" is the appeal of Black Women Enraged against the drafting of American blacks into the army units that were fighting in Vietnam.

13. See above, note 1.

14. In the printed text: "Now there is a move to bury it in the Museum of the RAI [in Turin] but this has been held back by ridiculous caution." The proposal to "reconstruct" the Studio di Fonologia in a museum was implemented only in 2008 with the setting up of a special section in the Musical Instrument Museum of the City of Milan, at Castello Sforzesco.

15. Already in 1967 Nono had proposed in a letter to the then general director of RAI, Leone Piccioni, a plan for a possible update of the studio, see the "Letter to Leone Piccioni," in De Benedictis-Rizzardi 2001: I: 221–23.

16. The composer Marco Stroppa had moved to the Media Laboratory of the Massachusetts Institute of Technology (Cambridge, MA) in 1984 with a Fulbright scholarship and was then invited by Pierre Boulez to collaborate with the research staff at IRCAM in Paris, where between 1987 and 1990, he held the post of director of the Department of Musical Research.

17. Nono's text had been written for the catalog of the exhibition *Nuova Atlantide. Il continente della musica elettronica, 1900–1986* [New Atlantis: The Continent of Electronic Music, 1900–1986], ed. Alvise Vidolin and Roberto Doati, which took place in Venice, under the auspices of the Music Biennale (October–November 1986), then directed by Carlo Fontana.

EXCURSUS V. INTERVIEW WITH MICHELANGELO ZURLETTI

1. In the printed text, which was first published in a volume in honor of the critic Leonardo Pinzauti (see "Bibliographic Notes and Comments to the Texts"), Zurletti wrote this introductory note: "The following interview evidences my last meeting with Luigi Nono. The meeting took place in Paris, in a small, comfortable hotel on Boulevard St. Michel. Nono had come there for a personal festival [Luigi Nono: Festival d'Automne à Paris, in 1987]; I attended

the concerts for the newspaper *La Repubblica*. The interview had been arranged as part of a series of meetings with Italian intellectuals, but the series was nipped in the bud and the interview was not published. And when Nono died I tried in vain to find among my papers this evidence of our last meeting: . . . the interview could not be found. I found it a few years later. Certainly, time had changed many things. Nono still speaks of the GDR, of Khrennikov as president of the Soviet composers, he speaks of the PCI, of Craxi. But his definition of his relationship with the world, with study, with music, with live electronics is still a useful one. To remind us once again of what a unique character has disappeared with him. I have tried to preserve, in Nono's fluent speech, the informality of the live conversation, including moments where it leaps forward and goes back to things that have already been mentioned. Including even the syntactical play that is given free rein in the conversation."

2. Morton Feldman did not attend the Darmstadt Ferienkurse personally until 1984. Assuming the fidelity of the spoken transcription, Nono's statement marks a significant change in perspective regarding the new music; see also "Excursus VI" in this volume, "'Proust' Questionnaire."

3. The CSC (Centro di Sonologia Computazionale), a research center of the University of Padua, founded in 1979 and directed, at the time of the interview, by Graziano Tisato. The first version of *Prometeo* (Venice, 1984) made use of synthesized sounds of the *4i* computer supplied and operated by the CSC of Padua and its staff.

4. Consiglio Nazionale delle Ricerche (National Research Council), the largest public research institution in Italy, responsible for promoting and developing research in different fields of knowledge.

5. Namely at the Experimental Studio of the Heinrich Strobel Foundation in Freiburg im Breisgau, Germany, with which Nono worked from 1980.

6. Nono's irony refers to Bettino Craxi and Claudio Martelli, respectively secretary and deputy secretary of the PSI, then in government.

7. Nono refers to the forum "For a Nuclear-Free World, for the Survival of Humanity," held in Moscow in February 1987. See also "Excursus I" in this volume, "An Autobiography of the Author Recounted by Enzo Restagno."

8. The painting movement of the "Neue Wilde," which developed in Germany in the early 1980s.

9. Initiated from the critical edition of the *Prison Notebooks* edited by Valentino Gerratana in 1975, there had been indeed in Italy an editorial resurgence of Gramsci, notably, at the time of this interview, an edition of the articles originally appeared on *l'Ordine Nuovo* and another new (partial) edition of the *Notebooks*.

10. A paraphrase of what Massimo Mila wrote both in *Dove vai, Gigi?* in *Nono*, ed. Enzo Restagno (Turin: EDT, 1987), 281–82, and in "Nono: La svolta," *Musica/Realtà* 12/34 (1991): 119–27, esp. 125–26, now in Massimo Mila and Luigi Nono, *Nulla oscuro tra noi: Lettere, 1952–1988*, ed. Angela Ida De Benedictis and Veniero Rizzardi (Milan: il Saggiatore, 2010), 324–33.

11. See Luigi Nono, *Festival d'Automne à Paris, 1987: Contrechamps* (exhibition catalog), 35–53.

12. Besides Cacciari, with whom he worked especially between 1978 and 1987, Nono mentions here two figures then also linked to the University of Architecture of Venice (IUAV), the historian Manfredo Tafuri and the architect and writer Vittorio Gregotti.

PART FIVE. THE "POSSIBLE INFINITIES"

1. ERROR AS A NECESSITY

1. See Robert Musil, *The Man without Qualities*, trans. Sophie Wilkins and Burton Pike, rev. ed. (New York: Picador, 2011), chapter title, § 4, "If there is a sense of reality, there must be a sense of possibility." In 1981, Nono had quoted a passage from this same paragraph of *The Man without Qualities* in a text written on the occasion of the premiere of *Das atmende Klarsein* (see De Benedictis-Rizzardi 2001: I: 487). See also in this section, "Other Possibilities for Listening," note 1.

2. Nono refers to the thoughts expressed by Ludwig Wittgenstein in "Remarks on Frazer's 'Golden Bough'" (in *Wittgenstein: Sources and Perspectives*, ed. C. Grant Luckhardt [Bristol: Thoemmes Press, 1996]); esp. 28 ("We must uncover the source of the error.... We must find the *road* from error to truth") and 29.

3. This is the *Verein für Musikalische Privataufführungen*, founded by Schoenberg in 1918.

4. Composed in 1906.

2. OTHER POSSIBILITIES FOR LISTENING

1. Evidence for this "poetics" can be found in Musil's novel *The Man without Qualities*, which Nono frequently cited in various writings from the 1980s (cf. *Das atmende Klarsein*, De Benedictis-Rizzardi 2001: I: 487, or chapter 1 of part V in this volume, "Error as a Necessity"). It could summed up by the protagonist's (Ulrich) conviction that "*God* creates the *world* and thinks while He is at it that it could just as well be done *differently*"; Robert Musil, *The Man without Qualities*, trans. Sophie Wilkins and Burton Pike, rev. ed. (New York: Picador, 2011), 14.

2. Marco Stroppa was actually studying at that time in Cambridge, Massachusetts, at the Media Laboratory of the Massachusetts Institute of Technology. See also chapter 7 of part IV, "For Marino Zuccheri," note 16.

3. See the three essays of Luitzen Egbertus Jan Brouwer published in *Mathematische Annalen* between 1925 and 1927 with the same title: "Zur Begründung der intuitionistischen Mathematik," no. 93 (1925): 244–57; no. 94 (1926): 453–72; no. 95 (1927): 451–88. In the notes to the premiere of *Caminantes ... Ayacucho* (1986–87), Nono would again cite Brouwer's "perception of change and of transformations" (cf. De Benedictis-Rizzardi 2001: I: 499). It should be noted that Brouwer's theories were studied by Nono's oldest child, Silvia, in her graduate work, "Un nodo fondamentale della filosofia intuizionistica della

matematica: Il teorema dello sbarramento" (A Fundamental Issue of the Mathematical Intuition Philosophy: The Bar Theorem), discussed in 1984 (copy in ALN).

4. A year before this talk, in 1984, Carlo Rubbia had been awarded the Nobel Prize in physics for his contributions to the discovery of elementary particles.

5. For this and the following techniques for cello see the "Notes" in *Quando stanno morendo. Diario polacco n. 2*, score (Milan: Ricordi, 1999, c1982), xix–xxix.

6. Nono source was Roland Barthes, *Lezione: Il punto sulla semiotica letteraria*, trans. R. Guidieri (Turin: Einaudi, 1981) (an annotated copy is in ALN); an English translation (by Richard Howard) is published with the title *Lecture in Inauguration of the Chair of Literary Semiology, Collège de France, January 7, 1977*, in *October* 8 (Spring 1979): 3–16; reprinted in *Oxford Literary Review* 4/1 (February 2012): 31–44.

7. See ibid.

8. See Massimo Cacciari, "La porta aperta," in *Icone della legge* (Milan: Adelphi, 1985), 56–137.

9. I. e., the *Crucifixion*, now at the Musée de Unterlinden, Colmar (France).

10. Nono refers here to three popular conventions-festivals promoted in Italy at that time by *l'Unità* (the official newspaper of the PCI—now of the Democratic Party), *Avanti!* (official newspaper of the PSI), and *Comunione e Liberazione*, a lay movement of the Catholic Church. Organized at a local as well as at national levels, they used to be important social events, attended by large audiences.

11. Director of the Music Department of the Biblioteca de Catalunya, died in 1969. For the reference cited below in the text see Higinio Anglés, *La música de las Cantigas de Santa María del Rey Alfonso el Sabio* (Barcelona: Diputacíon Provincial Biblioteca Central, 1964).

12. Cf. Miquel Querol Gavaldá, *Música barroca española: Polifonía policoral litúrgica* (Barcelona: Climent, 1982).

13. Following a proposal put forward by sixty-two members of the European Parliament, the European Community, and the Council of Europe decided to celebrate in 1985 the "European Year of Music." Every country of the network was then encouraged to develop extraordinary initiatives in order to support and promote music through festivals, concert series, and different initiatives.

14. Giovanni Morelli (1942–2011) had been appointed in 1985 as director of the Music Institute of the Fondazione Giorgio Cini in Venice. In the same year he invited Nono to give this lecture at the foundation, which he subsequently transcribed, edited, and published. See "Bibliographic Notes and Comments to the Texts," 468.

15. *Sefer Yetzirah, o Libro de la formacíon*, trans. and ed. J. M. Rotger (Barcelona: Obelisco, 1982). In ALN is preserved an annotated Italian version of the *Sefer Yetzirah* (*Il libro della creazione*) [Rome: Beniamino Carucci, 1979]). See also "Excursus I" in this volume, "An Autobiography of the Author Recounted by Enzo Restagno," note 47.

16. About Nono's appreciation of Ambrosini and Cappelli see ibid., 111. Romagna is a historical region of Italy now comprised in the larger Emilia-Romagna.

3. LECTURE AT THE CHARTREUSE IN VILLENEUVE-LES-AVIGNON

1. In *Elementa harmonica* (also *Harmonics*), the oldest treatise of the genre that has survived intact, Aristoxenus considers the practice of subdivision of the interval down to the quarter tone and, theoretically, down to the twelfth.

2. The word spoken by Nono here is incomprehensible. The editorial insertion is justified by the context and the presence of a similar reference in chapter 5 of part II, "Toward *Prometeo:* Journal Fragments" (note 11). It should be remembered that the Council of Trent did not actually take any special action regarding the use of specific intervals of any system or genre (in a theoretical or traditional sense), let alone with respect to the theoretical-musical or technical-compositional aspects. In reality it limited itself to giving general directives on liturgical music, supplementing a tradition of reform that had already emerged over the previous years and that mostly addressed the intelligibility of the text and the purging of the secular component; see on this the study by Craig A. Monson, "The Council of Trent Revisited," *Journal of the American Musicological Society* 55/1 (Spring 2002): 1–37. Nono's idea presumably has to do with the directive of the twenty-second session of the Council of September 17, 1562, directed against the use of "lascivious or impure" melodies (see p. 11).

3. "You will recognize many cases in which reason is not a friend to sense, and sense is not receptive to reason;" see *Ancient Music Adapted to Modern Practice,* trans. Maria Rika Maniates, ed. Claude V. Palisca (New Haven, CT: Yale University Press, 1996), 6. The same line, with the original wording of Vicentino, had already been quoted by Nono in his text written 1986–87 for *Caminantes . . . Ayacucho* (see De Benedictis-Rizzardi 2001: I: 499), and in the interview with Restagno at the beginning of this volume (see note 19).

4. See especially books III and VII. In *The Republic,* book 3 (1175) it is stated: "There complexity engendered license, and here disease; whereas simplicity in music was the parent of temperance in the soul; and simplicity in gymnastic of health in the body."

5. Nono is referring here to *Pädagogisches Skizzenbuchs,* ed. Hans M. Wingler (Mainz: Florian Kupferberg, 1965); annotated copy at the ALN. English ed.: *Pedagogical Sketchbook,* intro. and trans. Sibyl Moholy-Nagy (London: Faber and Faber, 1968).

6. This refers to Habib Hassan Touma, *Die Musik der Araber* (Wilhelmshaven: Heinrichshofen, 1975); English ed.: *The Music of the Arabs,* new expanded ed., trans. Laurie Schwartz and Reinhard G. Pauly (Portland, OR: Amadeus Press, 2002).

7. See Fernando Ortiz, *La Africanía de la música floklórica de Cuba* (Havana: Editora Universitaria, 1965); annotated copy at the ALN.

8. Max Planck (1858–1947), considered to be the founder of quantum mechanics.

9. *Offret* (Sweden, 1986), the last film by Andrei Tarkovsky. The music for bamboo flute (*hocchiku*) was actually written and performed by the Rinzai Zen *roshi* Watazumi Doso (1911–92).

10. What is meant is the crypt of the temple, never finished, of the industrial colony Güell in Santa Coloma de Cervelló, near Barcelona.

11. Here and elsewhere in the text, Nono refers to the second of the compositions that have this name, *Quando stanno morendo. Diario polacco n. 2*, of 1982, for two sopranos, mezzo-soprano, contralto, bass flute, cello, and live electronics (texts assembled and elaborated by Massimo Cacciari).

12. Reference to *Missa Di dadi* by Josquin, where the duration values of the *tenor* may vary according to a numerical factor determined by the roll of a dice.

13. Incomprehensible name.

14. In *Quando stanno morendo. Diario polacco n. 2*, the cellist must have three instruments, one for each section of the piece, and with a particular detuning applied to each (see below, note 18).

15. Publison, actually the name of the manufacturer, designates in essence the first digital multifunction audio processor, the Infernal Machine (1985), often used in Nono's compositions during the later years. The *reverser* function allows for the sequential sampling of brief sound fragments to then play them back immediately in retrograde motion. It is used especially in the second part of the composition mentioned ("Mosca—chi sei? Mosca—vetusto cranio" ["Moscow—who are you? Moscow—ancient skull"]).

16. Nono is giving here an approximate imitation of the effect produced by the reverser on the part of *Diario polacco n. 2* at the words cited above, note 15 (*ay—too—kheekh—naym—akh*).

17. The *gate,* or dynamic modulator, is a voltage control amplifier by which it is possible to control the dynamic level of a signal B using the envelope of a signal A. See in this regard the "Notes" about the sound projection in *Quando stanno morendo. Diario polacco n. 2*, score (Milan: Ricordi, 1999—c1982), xix–xxix.

18. The first cello has four A strings tuned to four different intonations of the note F; the second has four G strings tuned around F#; the third uses four C strings tuned around the same pitch.

19. *Spem in alium nunquam habui,* a motet for eight choirs of five voices (forty parts), composed ca. 1570–71; see score ed. P. Brett (London: Oxford University Press, 1966; annotated copy at the ALN).

20. Church of Venice, in the Cannaregio district, where Tintoretto is buried.

EXCURSUS VI. "PROUST" QUESTIONNAIRE

1. Novel by Robert Walser (*The Tanners,* trans. Susan Bernofsky [New York: New Directions, 2009]).

2. See *Phantasies of a Love-Thief: The Caurapañcāśikā Attributed to Bilhaṇa,* ed. and trans. Barbara Stoler Miller (New York: Columbia University Press, 1971). Bilhaṇa is quoted by Nono even further in the text.

Bibliographic Notes and Comments to the Texts

These notes give an account of the history of the texts anthologized in this volume and of the main publications and reprints. Unless explicitly indicated, the reference source (SOURCE TEXT) for the English translation is drawn from De Benedictis–Rizzardi 2007. Also specified in the list are the first publications of each text (FE = first edition) and subsequent reprints (OE = other editions). For the bibliographic references see the list of abbreviations for this book on p. 395.

OVERTURE. CLARIFICATIONS (1956)
    FE: "Precisazioni," De Benedictis–Rizzardi 2007: 29–31.

This text was sent on January 10, 1956, to Luciano Berio in response to a request for an article for the first issue of the journal *Incontri Musicali,* in which, however, it was never published. Nono reused it in 1958, adding a brief postscript on Cesare Pavese, under the guise of a written presentation to *La terra e la compagna,* and as such it appears in De Benedictis–Rizzardi: I: 429–30 (see also the related endnotes, ibid., 589).

The original typescript is held at the PSF in the Luciano Berio Collection. Two German translations of the text are held at the ALN: the first does not contain the final postscript on Pavese; the second, made by Hans Werner Henze and written on the stationery of the WDR radio station of Cologne, contains the additional text about the Italian poet.

An additional and different German version is included in the presentation of Nono's biography in a brochure issued by the publisher Schott, with a catalog of Nono's works, whose compilation dates back to June 1966.

EXCURSUS I. AN AUTOBIOGRAPHY OF THE AUTHOR RECOUNTED BY ENZO RESTAGNO (1987)

FE: "Un'autobiografia dell'autore raccontata da Enzo Restagno," in *Nono*, ed. Enzo Restagno (Turin: EDT, 1987), 3–73.

OE: Feneyrou 1993: 23–129.

De Benedictis–Rizzardi 2001: II: 477–568 (SOURCE TEXT).

Luigi Nono: Dokumente, Materialien, ed. Andreas Wagner for Netzwerk Musik Saar, trans. Andreas Wagner and Sigrid Konrad (Saarbrücken: PFAU, 2003), 34–138.

Incontri: Luigi Nono im Gespräch mit Enzo Restagno; Berlin, März 1987, ed. Matteo Nanni and Rainer Schmusch (Hofheim: Wolke, 2004).

The interview took place at Nono's apartment in Berlin in March 1987. By Restagno's own admission (see FE, ix–x), Nono's words, recorded during a week, have then been the subject of intensive editing. Regarding Nono's authorship, the peculiarities of the interview, and the caution necessary in determining its interpretation, please refer to introduction of the editors in this volume (20).

PART ONE. MUSICAL ANALYSIS AND COMPOSITION
1. LUIGI DALLAPICCOLA AND THE *SEX CARMINA ALCAEI* (ca. 1948)

FE: "Luigi Dallapiccola e i *Sex Carmina Alcæi*," De Benedictis–Rizzardi 2001: I: 3–5.

OE: De Benedictis–Rizzardi 2007: 35–36.

Feneyrou 2007: 29–31.

De Assis 2014: 20–21.

The date of this short text discovered by the editors among the papers belonging to the period of Nono's studies with Hermann Scherchen and Bruno Maderna (1948–49), cannot be prior to the end of 1947. This is because in a letter dated November 16, 1947, Luigi Dallapiccola provides Nono with instructions on how to obtain the scores commented upon in the text. The care taken by Nono in the preparation of his paper (in addition to the typescript on which the FE is based, a further, rather troubled, draft is held at the ALN) suggests that it was destined to be published, even though no confirmation of that has yet been found.

2. ON THE DEVELOPMENT OF SERIAL TECHNIQUE (1956)

FE: "Zur Entwicklung der Serientechnik," *Gravesaner Blätter* 2/4 (May 1956): 14–18.

OE: Stenzl 1975: 16–20.

Feneyrou 1993: 133–38.

De Benedictis–Rizzardi 2001: I: 9–14.

De Benedictis–Rizzardi 2007: 37–42.

Feneyrou 2007: 38–43.

De Assis 2014: 24–29.

The typescript chosen by the editors as the base text for the 2001 (and subsequently the 2007) Italian edition is a translation of the FE made by Luca Lombardi between 1975 and 1976. It is part of a set of translations that Nono assembled in those same years with a view toward producing an Italian edition of his writings, a project that was not followed through (see the Introduction to this book). This source has many handwritten corrections and clarifications by Nono, which are often decisive for clarifying particular lexical ambiguities in the FE.

In the FE, where the text appeared along with other contributions of Hermann Scherchen and Hans Werner Henze in a section titled "Manipulation und Konzeption" (Manipulation and Concept), the numbering of music examples follows an order different from that shown here. All the examples that appear in the FE were prepared by Scherchen himself.

3. THE DEVELOPMENT OF SERIAL TECHNIQUE (1957)

FE: "Die Entwicklung der Reihentechnik," *Darmstädter Beiträge zur Neuen Musik* 1 (1958): 25–37.

OE: Stenzl 1975: 21–33.

Feneyrou 1993: 139–57.

De Benedictis–Rizzardi 2001: I: 19–42.

De Benedictis–Rizzardi 2007: 37–42.

Feneyrou 2007: 49–67.

Arnold Schönberg, "*Variationen für Orchester op. 31:*" *Partitura analizzata da Luigi Nono* (Belluno–Venice: Fondazione Archivio Luigi Nono ONLUS–Colophon Edition, 2011), 43–54 (partial).

In the Italian version of 2001, subsequently revised in the 2007 collection, the editors reconstructed this text from two basic sources: one typewritten in Italian, incomplete, found in the ALN, that allows the reinstatement of the author's original terminology in one of his most important theoretical writings, and the FE for the missing parts.

The text published in the FE is the result of the author's reelaboration of a work from the lecture given in Darmstadt on July 23, 1957; see *Im Zenit der Moderne: Die Internationale Ferienkurse für Neue Musik Darmstadt, 1946–1966*, ed. Gianmario Borio and Hermann Danuser (Freiburg im Breisgau: Rombach, 1997), III: 586. In fact, as is clear from the correspondence with Luciano Berio (ALN-PSF), the part about the "Thema" of the Variations op. 31

by Schoenberg (here on pp. 135–41) was already completed in 1956. Berio intended to publish it in the journal *Incontri Musicali*, but, during the editing process, Nono rejected Berio's attempt to alter his distinctive tone and forbade its publication (see for further reading Angela Ida De Benedictis and Veniero Rizzardi, "On Some Difficulties in the Collection and Edition of the Writings of Luigi Nono," *Musica/Realtà*, 115/1 (2018): 135–57). Both Nono's original and Berio's reformulation are held in ALN and PSF (Cathy Berberian Collection).

An attempt has been made here to maintain the utmost fidelity to the original version, simply spelling out a few abbreviations and translating into English the quotations, musical note names and names of instruments that Nono wrote in German. Conversely, those German expressions that Nono intended not to be translated in the Italian publication are left unaltered.

The original Italian typescript lacks the final page dedicated to Schoenberg's Variations op. 31; on the other hand, the last two sections—relating to recent music developments—appear in draft manuscript form (ALN, 5 ff.). With the exception of this last part, the editing of the typescript is relatively accurate and conforms to the German translation of Willi Reich published in the FE. The missing sections—the conclusion of the analysis of the Variations op. 31 and the part dedicated to recent music—have been integrated using either an earlier typewritten draft (ALN; being the original Italian text intended for *Incontri Musicali*) or a translation from German of the FE. Integrations from either text are placed in angle brackets.

A draft manuscript exists of the last two sections of the text—from "Some of the current methods of serial composition . . . " (see 148) to the end—that follows the initial typed formulation. It shows significant variants such as the different order of the musical examples, and the idea of discussing briefly *Modes de valeurs et d'intensités*, by Messiaen, subsequently replaced by the *Premier livre* of Boulez's *Structures*. It is reproduced in the original Italian as an appendix to the final version in De Benedictis–Rizzardi 2001: I: 38–41, and De Benedictis–Rizzardi 2007: 61–63.

4. TEXT—MUSIC—SONG (1960)

FE: "Text—Musik—Gesang," Stenzl 1975: 41–60.

OE: *Al gran sole carico d'amore*, ed. Francesco Degrada (Milan: Ricordi, 1977), 15–24.

Balázs 1985: 26–52.

Feneyrou 1993: 166–88.

Helmut Lachenmann, *Musik als existentielle Erfahrung: Schriften, 1966–1995*, ed. Josef Häusler (Wiesbaden: Breitkopf & Härtel, 1996), 317–28 (only the second conference).

De Benedictis–Rizzardi 2001: I: 57–83.

De Benedictis–Rizzardi 2007: 64–87.

Feneyrou 2007: 80–95.

De Assis 2014: 40–62.

The text refers to the two lectures held on July 7 and 8, 1960, at Darmstadt. The FE was transcribed from recordings of the lectures held at the IMD archives (see Stenzl 1975: 460). The text of the second lecture was formulated in German by Helmut Lachenmann, while only for the first lecture the Italian typescript is preserved. The latter corresponds to Nono's original version, and appears to have been used as the basis for the first Italian publication of the full text (1977), translated here. According to a personal communication from Francesco Degrada to the editors (2001), this publication was overseen and approved by Nono himself.

5. [ABOUT *IL CANTO SOSPESO*] (1976)

FE: "Testimonianza di Luigi Nono," program notes for the concerts of Mestre, Padua, and Venice on November 12/14 (Venice: Teatro La Fenice, 1976), [5–9].

OE: *Vi insegnerò differenze*, ed. Angela Ida De Benedictis (Milan: Banca Popolare di Milan–Luigi Nono Archive, 2000), 101–13.

De Benedictis–Rizzardi 2001: I: 331–35.

De Benedictis–Rizzardi 2007: 198–201.

Feneyrou 2007: 602–6.

The text was included in the program notes of a series of concerts organized by La Fenice in Venice, with the title "A Testimony by Luigi Nono." The carbon copy of the text sent for publication—the typescript being signed at the bottom—is held at the ALN and corresponds fully to the first printed version of 1976.

EXCURSUS II. A LETTER FROM LOS ANGELES (1965)

FE: "Lettera da Los Angeles," *Rinascita* 22/16 (April 17, 1965): 32 (Italian).

Boston Globe (May 26, 1965): 13 (English, SOURCE TEXT).

OE: Stenzl 1975: 150–54.

Feneyrou 1993: 359–64.

De Benedictis–Rizzardi 2001: I: 177–81.

Feneyrou 2007: 209–12.

De Assis 2014: 106–10.

Letter sent to the editorial staff of the Italian journal *Rinascita* following the American premiere of *Intolleranza 1960*. The work was produced and staged by Sarah Caldwell of the Back Bay Theater, Boston, on February 21, 1965 (conductor: Bruno Maderna, set and lighting: Josef Svoboda; wardrobe: Jan Skalicky). The notes at the foot of the page correspond to the original editorial notes in the Italian FE. After its publication in *Rinascita,* the letter was translated into English by the FBI and later published in various Boston newspapers, including the *Boston Globe,* May 26, 1965, as part of Michael Steinberg's article, "Red Composer

Nono Bites Hub Hospitality." For all these aspects and for the controversies, mostly of a political character, that followed Nono's stay in the United States, see Claudia Vincis, "To Nono: A No": Luigi Nono and His *Intolleranza 1965* in the U.S.," in *Crosscurrents: American and European Music in Interaction, 1900–2000*, ed. Felix Meyer, Carol J. Oja, Wolfgang Rathert, and Anne Shreffler (Woodbridge, England: Boydell Press, 2014), 328–29.

The text reproduced here is in fact based on this first translation by the FBI (copy at the ALN), which was very faithful to Nono's text, edited and integrated with two short missing parts from the Italian FE.

PART TWO. MUSIC ONSTAGE: FROM A "THEATER OF IDEAS" TO THE "TRAGEDY OF LISTENING"

1. SOME CLARIFICATIONS ON *INTOLLERANZA 1960* (1962)

    FE: "Alcune precisazioni su *Intolleranza 1960*," *La Rassegna Musicale* 32/2–4 (1962): 277–89.

    OE: Stenzl 1975: 68–81.

    Balázs 1985: 53–69.

    Luigi Nono: Intolleranza 1960 (Stuttgart: Staatsoper Stuttgart, 1992), 25–39.

    Feneyrou 1993: 198–212.

    Luigi Nono, *Intolleranza 1960*, booklet accompanying the CD, Teldec 4509-97304-2, 1995: 89–102.

    De Benedictis-Rizzardi 2001: I: 100–114.

    Luigi Nono "Intolleranza 1960": Materialien, Skizzen, Hintergründe zur Inszenierung des Saarländischen Staatstheaters, ed. Alexander Jansen and Andreas Wagner (Saarbrücken: Pfau 2004), 21–37.

    De Benedictis-Rizzardi 2007: 97–110.

    Feneyrou 2007: 123–38.

    Intolleranza 1960, Teatro La Fenice, Season 2011, ed. Angela Ida De Benedictis (Venice: Marsilio, 2011), 8–19.

    De Assis 2014: 70–84.

Various typewritten drafts of the text are held at the ALN, the latest of which conforms fully to the FE. The music examples published here have been amended on the basis of the new edition of *Intolleranza 1960*, revised and corrected by Angela Ida De Benedictis (Mainz: Schott, 2013).

2. POSSIBILITY AND NECESSITY OF A NEW MUSIC THEATER (1962)

    FE: *Nutida Musik*, November 1962 (in Swedish).

           "Possibilità e necessità di un nuovo teatro musicale," *Il Verri* 9 (1963): 59–70.

Oe: Stenzl 1975: 87–99.

Arte e cultura contemporanea, ed. Piero Nardi (Florence: Sansoni, 1966), 265–83.

Al gran sole carico d'amore, ed. Francesco Degrada (Milan: Ricordi, 1974), 11–16.

Al gran sole carico d'amore, ed. Francesco Degrada (Milan: Ricordi, 1977), 9–14.

Aspetti del teatro musicale del Novecento: Saggi, documenti e testimonianze, ed. Armando Gentilucci (Milan: Assessorato alla Cultura della Provincia, 1980), 33–44.

Balázs 1985: 77–96.

Contrechamps 4 (1985): 55–67, from which: Feneyrou 1993: 219–33.

Con Luigi Nono, (Rome: Cemat, 2000), 31–39.

De Benedictis–Rizzardi 2001: I: 118–32.

De Benedictis–Rizzardi 2007: 111–23.

Feneyrou 2007: 139–53.

De Assis 2014: 85–97.

Lecture held on September 27, 1962, at San Giorgio Maggiore Island, Venice, for the "Fourth International Course of Contemporary High Culture: Aspects and Problems," organized by the Fondazione Giorgio Cini.

Nono based the wording of the text on an earlier essay, "Appunti per un teatro musicale attuale" [Notes toward a Current Music Theater] published the previous year in *La Rassegna Musicale*, 31/4, (1961): 418–24; now in De Benedictis–Rizzardi 2001: I: 86–92), extending and developing certain sections. Besides a copy of *La Rassegna Musicale* of 1961, which contains the composer's handwritten notes that refer back to the first additions and changes to the text, the ALN holds five other different drafts, the last of which (incomplete and ostensibly conforming to the version read at the Fondazione Giorgio Cini) is fairly similar to the version published in *Il Verri*. Some particularly significant variants between this version and the Fe are here mentioned in the editing notes to the text.

The last part of the essay (section 4, from "In May this year [1962], a group of Venetian friends ... ") was also published under the title *Un'indicazione di oggi per una esperienza teatrale* [A Direction for Today toward a New Theatrical Experience], in the exhibition catalog *Parole e immagini*, with writings by Umberto Eco, Enrico Filippini, Luigi Nono, Luigi Pestalozza; Dipinti di Vittorio Basaglia, Giordano Castagna, Vincenzo Eulisse, Paolo Giordani, Andrea Pagnacco, Petrus, Giorgio Rizzardi (Venice: Opera Bevilacqua La Masa, 1963), [11–13].

3. PLAY AND TRUTH IN THE NEW MUSIC THEATER (1962)

Fe: "Gioco e verità nel nuovo teatro musicale," *Il filo rosso* 1 (1963): 86–89.

Oe: Stenzl 1975: 82–86.

Balázs 1985: 70–76.

Feneyrou 1993: 213–18.

De Benedictis–Rizzardi 2001: I: 136–40.

De Benedictis–Rizzardi 2007: 124–28.

Feneyrou 2007: 158–62.

The first publication of the text and all subsequent publications up to De Benedictis–Rizzardi 2001, vol. I, transmit a version that is very different from Nono's original (discovered by Angela Ida De Benedictis in the ALN in 2004). During editing in 1963, the text underwent a near total revision, especially in formal terms, with changes that were so extensive as to sometimes seriously affect the content and change the sequential order of points in the argument. In 1975, in view of the publication of his writings (see the introduction), Nono therefore rejected the version published in the FE, in favor of the original, which however was first published only in the second Italian edition of 2007 (the basis for the present translation).

4. *DIE ERMITTLUNG*: A MUSICAL AND THEATRICAL EXPERIENCE WITH WEISS AND PISCATOR [MUSIC AND THEATER] (1966)

FE: "*Die Ermittlung*: un'esperienza musicale teatrale con Weiss e Piscator," *La Città Futura: Mensile dei Giovani Comunisti* 16 (March 1966): 14–16.

OE: "Musique et théâtre," *Cité-Panorama* [journal of Théâtre de la Cité Villeurbanne] 9 (September–November 1966): 13 (partial).

"Über die Musik [zu P. Weiss's *Die Ermittlung*]," in *Erwin Piscator: Eine Arbeitsbiographie in 2 Bänden,* ed. Knut Boeser and Renata Vatková (Berlin: Edition Hentrich, 1986): II: 260–61 (partial).

"Musique et théâtre," Feneyrou 1993: 366–69 (partial).

"Musica e Teatro," De Benedictis–Rizzardi 2001: I: 210–15.

De Benedictis–Rizzardi 2007: 129–33.

Feneyrou 2007: 241–46.

De Assis 2014: 98–102.

FE was discovered after the publication of De Benedictis–Rizzardi 2001. This was possible thanks to the recovery in the ALN, in 2004, of the last two pages of the final typescript, found by Angela Ida De Benedictis in a volume from Luigi Nono's personal library while cataloging the collection of his writings (see, in this regard, De Benedictis–Rizzardi 2007: 278). The text published here therefore restores the final version written by Nono, already reproduced fairly faithfully in the FE.

The French version published in *Cité-Panorama* (and presented unchanged in the 1986 German publication and in Feneyrou 1993) was subjected to copious cuts and omissions, significant enough to alter the flow of Nono's discourse.

Nono's typescript does not have a title. Therefore, both the title in the FE, as well as the one chosen for the first French translation (and resumed in all subsequent OE) could be regarded as spurious and the result of editorial choices. However, the decision has been made here to reinstate the title of the first publication of the Italian text, and to leave in square brackets the title under which the text has been transmitted hitherto.

5. TOWARD *PROMETEO*: JOURNAL FRAGMENTS (1984)

FE: "Verso *Prometeo*: Frammenti di diari," in *Luigi Nono, Verso Prometeo*, ed. Massimo Cacciari (Milan: Ricordi, 1984), 7–16.

OE: Feneyrou 1993: 258–69.

Brennpunkt Nono, ed. Josef Häusler (Zurich: Palladion, 1993), 87–89 (partial translation, with no signs of *omissis*).

De Benedictis–Rizzardi 2001: I: 385–96.

Nono-Vedova: Diario di bordo: Da "Intolleranza '60" a "Prometeo," ed. Stefano Cecchetto and Giorgio Mastinu (Turin: Umberto Allemandi, 2005), 109–23.

De Benedictis–Rizzardi 2007: 134–43.

Feneyrou 2007: 517–29.

EXCURSUS III. INTERVIEW WITH RENATO GARAVAGLIA (CA. 1979–80)

FE: De Benedictis–Rizzardi, 2001: II: 235–48 (SOURCE TEXT).

The typescript taken as the basis for the 2001 publication bears a few corrections in the composer's own hand; attached to it is Garavaglia's handwritten letter in which he specifies that the interview is transcribed "exactly as it was on tape." In a personal communication to the editors, Garavaglia said the interview was destined for the Italian journal *Discoteca Hi-Fi*, in which, however, it was not published. The dating of the interview is conjectural, and has been derived from the content of Nono's answers regarding his then recent compositions.

PART THREE. "CONSCIENCE, FEELINGS, COLLECTIVE REALITY"

1. HISTORICAL PRESENCE OF MUSIC TODAY (1959)

FE: "Gitterstäbe am Himmel der Freiheit," *Melos* 27 (1960): 69–75.

"Geschichte und Gegenwart in der Musik von heute," *Darmstädter Beiträge zur Neuen Musik* 3 (1960): 41–47.

"The Historical Reality of Music Today," *The Score* 27 (1960): 41–45.

"Realtà storica nella musica d'oggi," *Il Verri* 2 (1960): 96–103.

"Presenza storica nella musica d'oggi," *La Rassegna Musicale* 30/1 (1960): 1–8.

OE: *Slovenská Hudba* 12 (1968): 174–77 (in Czech).

Horyzonti Muzyki (1970): text no. 12 (in Polish).

Al gran sole carico d'amore, ed. Francesco Degrada (Milan: Ricordi, 1974), 7–9.

Stenzl 1975: 34–40.

Al gran sole carico d'amore, ed. Francesco Degrada (Milan: Ricordi, 1977), 5–7.

Balázs 1985: 15–25.

Nono, ed. Enzo Restagno (Turin: EDT, 1987): 239–45.

Creación 4 (1992): 63–70 (in Castilian).

Feneyrou 1993: 158–64.

Helmut Lachenmann, *Musik als existentielle Erfahrung: Schriften, 1966–1995*, ed. Josef Häusler (Wiesbaden: Breitkopf & Härtel, 1996): 311–16.

De Benedictis–Rizzardi 2001: I: 46–54.

Glissando 6 (2005): 88–90 (in Polish).

De Benedictis–Rizzardi 2007: 147–57.

Feneyrou 2007: 71–79.

De Assis 2014: 30–37.

The text was originally written for a lecture given in Darmstadt on September 1, 1959 (the recording is held at the IMD), and was formulated in German by Helmut Lachenmann on the basis of notes supplied to him by Nono. During 1960, the text was published in three languages in five periodicals with four different titles. The contiguity of these publications makes it difficult to establish a reliable chronological priority (hence the multiplicity of sources referred to as FE).

The Italian publication took place simultaneously in *La Rassegna Musicale* and in *Il Verri* with no variants (other than the title) and is the basis of all subsequent publications in Italian. The translation from German was made by Giacomo Manzoni, revised by Massimo Mila and approved by Nono (see Massimo Mila and Luigi Nono, *Nulla di oscuro tra noi: Lettere, 1952–1988*, ed. Angela Ida De Benedictis and Veniero Rizzardi [Milan: il Saggiatore, 2010, 41–46]). Manzoni's translation is the result of a cross-fertilization between the German version of *Melos*, which is closer to the text of the lecture, and the stylistic revision made by the editors of the *Darmstädter Beiträge* (edited by Wolfgang Steinecke and Karlheinz Stockhausen). In the latter, the three paragraphs that follow on from "And today?" up to "mysticism à la Meister Eckhart" (see in this volume, 271) are omitted entirely, presumably at the behest of Nono himself. The same happens in the version published by *The Score*, which also lacks the first paragraph, and takes perhaps too much liberties with respect to the original text. The editors therefore opted for an entirely new translation.

It should be noted that Stenzl published a text that blends several German sources (oral and written, some of them unpublished; see Stenzl 1975: 459) in which are indicated the places where the Darmstadt audience applauded the oral presentation.

The fact that the final wording of the text was developed by Lachenmann has generated a persistent misconception about the true authorship of the text, even to the point of speaking of "coauthorship" of the content itself. For example, this view was expressed by Heinz-Klaus Metzger in a public commemoration of Luigi Nono held at La Fenice in Venice on May 8, 1992. Years later, however, he retracted these allegations: this is evidenced by private correspondence, unpublished, between Metzger and Lachenmann himself (PSF, Helmut Lachemann Collection). Certain of Nono's manuscripts and typescripts held at the ALN and the PSF evidence a first draft that is in large measure very close to the approved text (see facsimiles in De Benedictis–Rizzardi 2001: I: 55–56). Of particular note are six handwritten sheets and three additional typescripts and manuscripts sent by Nono to Lachenmann attached to an undated letter (PSF, Lachenmann Collection, and now in Helmut Lachenmann—Luigi Nono, *Alla ricerca di luce e chiarezza: L'epistolario Helmut Lachenmann–Luigi Nono (1957–1990)*, ed. Angela Ida De Benedictis and Ulrich Mosch [Florence: Olschki, 2012, 44–47]). See also the facsimile reproduction in De Benedictis–Rizzardi 2001: I: 55–56.

2. MUSIC AND RESISTANCE (1963)

FE: "Musica e Resistenza," *Rinascita* 20/34 (September 7, 1963): 27.

OE: Stenzl 1975: 101–3.

Balázs 1985: 97–101.

Feneyrou 1993: 236–39.

De Benedictis–Rizzardi 2001: I: 144–47.

De Benedictis–Rizzardi 2007: 158–61.

Feneyrou 2007: 166–70.

In the FE, the text is normalized and sometimes distorted in its contents. The version presented here is based on the author's final typescript, which was found by the editors and published for the first time in the 2001 edition.

3. REPLIES TO SEVEN QUESTIONS BY MARTINE CADIEU (1966)

FE (partial): "Entretien avec Luigi Nono," *Les Lettres Françaises* (September 29, 1966): 18–19.

OE: Stenzl 1975: 187–91 (from FE).

Martine Cadieu, "Luigi Nono: Tout choix est politique," in Cadieu, *A l'écoute des compositeurs* (Paris: Minerve, 1992), 113–18 (from FE).

"Risposte a sette domande di Martine Cadieu," De Benedictis–Rizzardi 2001: I: 196–205.

De Benedictis–Rizzardi 2007: 162–70.

Feneyrou 2007: 224–32.

The questionnaire was sent by Martine Cadieu on January 12, 1965, but Nono's responses arrived, after several reminders, only on September 23, 1966, as attested by the signature and handwritten date appended by Nono to his final typescript, and Cadieu's letter of September 26, 1966 (all documents in ALN).

The version published in the FE reflects the order of the answers provided by Nono, but sometimes it changes the wording or expunges whole passages. The composer did not agree with the final state of the FE. He sent Cadieu a letter of strong protest (see her reply of October 11, 1966, ALN).

Many parts of this interview of 1966—already published or omitted in the FE—were then reused freely by Cadieu in "Entretien avec Luigi Nono" (*Panorama instrumental* 18 [October 1970]: 19–23; then in Stenzl 1975: 234–38), a kind of pastiche in which she also incorporated whole passages from "Duo avec Luigi Nono," an interview that took place in 1961 for *Les Nouvelles Littéraires* (no. 1754, April 13, 1961: 1 and 9; now in De Benedictis–Rizzardi 2001: II: 3–6). Nono, for his part, reused in 1966 some of his replies (nos. 1, 3, and 2) in "Il musicista nella fabbrica" [The Musician in the Factory], not included in this collection (see De Benedictis–Rizzardi 2001: I: 206–9).

To ensure a smooth readability, no account is given here of the many variations with respect to the FE and to the interview published in 1970. In this way it thereby restores the original configuration of the text, the drafting of which was particularly challenging for Nono (numerous handwritten and typewritten drafts, preliminary to the final version, are preserved).

Cadieu's questions (originally nineteen, assembled and reduced by the composer into seven distinct nuclei) are here reproduced and numbered in the order of the answers provided by Nono.

4. MUSIC AND POWER (1969)

FE: "Musik und Revolution," *Spandauer Volksblatt* 24/7080 (September 14, 1969): 31–35 (I); and 24/7086 (September 21, 1969): 31 and 35 (II).

"Il potere musicale," *Compagni* 1/1 (April 1970): 43–45.

OE: Stenzl 1975: 107–15.

Balázs 1985: 102–16.

Feneyrou 1993: 244–55.

De Benedictis–Rizzardi 2001: I: 261–71.

De Benedictis–Rizzardi 2007: 171–80.

Feneyrou 2007: 312–23.

De Assis 2014: 128–37.

The drafting of the text can be dated to the first half of 1969. The original wording in Nono's Italian text (the basis for this translation) is evidenced by a typescript held in ALN (antigraph of the two FE with handwritten corrections).

In a round table published in 1969 under the title "Dopo la contestazione: Conversazione sul rapporto intellettuale—produzione culturale—politica, condotta da R. Rossanda" (*il Manifesto* 1/2–3 [July–August 1969: 50–55, esp. 54–55]; see De Benedictis–Rizzardi 2001: II: 34–46, esp. 43–45), there appears a long response by Nono which is a kind of synthesis of part II of "Music and Power," identical both in wording as well as in its sequence of points. It is difficult to establish a line of derivation or chronology between the two texts. Regarding the conversation published in 1969, it could be that Nono used the material already drafted for "Music and Power." On the other hand, it could be that part II of the latter was developed from an expansion of positions previously expressed. This second hypothesis would render more plausible the reference to the interview with Kagel, which appeared only in 1970 (note 19). Certain substantial variants (cuts) distinguish the first Italian publication from the composer's final typescript, which nonetheless conforms more or less to the first German publication. These variants are highlighted here in the editorial notes to the text.

The only verified Italian title for the text is "Il potere musicale," seen not only in the FE (*Compagni*) but also in a letter written by the composer himself to the editorial staff of *Mondo Nuovo* on April 26, 1970—see "Una lettera di Luigi Nono," De Benedictis–Rizzardi 2001: I: 284. This title had therefore been reinstated in the Italian editions of 2001 and 2007 instead of the more common "Musica e rivoluzione" [Music and Revolution] of German derivation. "Music and Power" translates better, even if not literally, the concept elaborated by Nono in his article.

Parts of this paper drawn from part II later appear in an article published in Portugal (see "Luigi Nono: Una visita de esclarecimento," in *O Seculo Ilustrado* [February 1, 1975]: 58–59).

5. IN THE SIERRA AND IN THE PARLIAMENT (1971)

FE: "Nella Sierra e in Parlamento," *Astrolabio* 9/13 (June 20, 1971): 33–37.

OE: De Benedictis–Rizzardi 2001: I: 290–301.

De Benedictis–Rizzardi 2007: 181–91.

Feneyrou 2007: 349–61.

De Assis 2014: 111–22.

The discovery of the carbon copy of the final version sent by Nono to *Astrolabio* (typescript ALN, first published in De Benedictis–Rizzardi 2007) is subsequent to the 2001 publication, in which the FE was reproduced (which is fairly faithful to Nono's wording except for some minor editorial cuts, not reported here). In the ALN, a typescript is also held that contains a rather orderly set of notes organized by Nono connected to his reporting. From this document one can deduce that much of the information provided in the article was obtained from local publications and personal contacts, a fact that has made it very difficult to clarify certain data (references and/or quotations).

EXCURSUS IV. TECHNOLOGY TO DISCOVER A UNIVERSE OF SOUNDS: INTERVIEW WITH WALTER PRATI AND ROBERTO MASOTTI (1983)

    FE: "La tecnologia per scoprire un universo di suoni," *Musica Viva* 7/12 (December 1983): 50–53.

    OE   De Benedictis Rizzardi 2001: II: 309–15 (SOURCE TEXT).

    De Assis 2014: 302–8.

The interview took place on September 28 and 29 at the Experimental Studio of the Heinrich Strobel Foundation in Freiburg im Breisgau, Germany.

PART FOUR. PORTRAITS AND DEDICATIONS

1. JOSEF SVOBODA (1968)

    FE: "Josef Svoboda," in Denis Bablet, *La scena e l'immagine: Saggio su Josef Svoboda* (Turin: Einaudi, 1970), 191–94.

    OE: Denis Bablet, *Svoboda* (Lausanne: La Cité–L'Age d'Homme, 1970), 245–48.

    Feneyrou 1993: 381–84.

    De Benedictis–Rizzardi 2001: I: 245–48.

    Svoboda Magika, ed. Alessandro Forlani and Massimo Puliani (Matelica: Halley Editrice, 2006), 81–86.

    De Benedictis–Rizzardi 2007: 225–28.

    Feneyrou 2007: 283–86.

Regarding the chronology of the two 1970 publications, note the information next to the copyright in the Italian text (FE): "This *Essay* was written specifically for Einaudi publications."

2. REMEMBERING TWO MUSICIANS (1973)

    FE: "Ricordo di due musicisti," *Cronache musicali Ricordi*, 3 (December 1973): 1–3.

    OE: Stenzl 1975: 175–76.

    Luigi Nono, *Festival d'Automne à Paris, 1987: Contrechamps* (exhibition catalog), 54–55.

    Feneyrou 1993: 412–14.

    De Benedictis–Rizzardi 2001: I: 307–9.

    De Benedictis–Rizzardi 2007: 195–97.

Feneyrou 2007: 376–78.

De Assis 2014: 140–42.

The text—without the first two paragraphs, which are exclusively dedicated to Malipiero—was later republished as "Ricordo di Bruno Maderna," in *La Biennale di Venezia* 25 (1975): 836–37.

3. VICTOR JARA'S SONG (1974)

F<small>E</small>: "Il canto di Victor Jara," *l'Unità* (January 12, 1974).

O<small>E</small>: De Benedictis–Rizzardi 2001: I: 310–13.

De Benedictis–Rizzardi 2007: 229–32.

Feneyrou 2007: 379–82.

4. PREFACE TO ARNOLD SCHOENBERG'S *HARMONIELEHRE* (1977)

F<small>E</small>: "Preface," in Arnold Schönberg, *Harmonielehre*, ed. Eberhardt Klemm (Leipzig: Peters, 1977), v–xi.

O<small>E</small>: *Musica/Realtà* 1/1 (1980): 37–42.

Feneyrou 1993: 444–50.

De Benedictis–Rizzardi 2001: I: 336–42.

De Benedictis–Rizzardi 2007: 202–7.

Feneyrou 2007: 428–34.

Arnold Schoenberg, *Manuale di armonia*, ed. Luigi Rognoni (Milan: il Saggiatore, 2008), xi–xvi.

De Assis 2014: 144–49.

Arnold Schoenberg, *Trattato di armonia*, ed. Anna Maria Morazzoni (Milan: il Saggiatore, 2014), 581–87.

The drawing up of this text—the preface to a fascimile reprint of *Harmonielehre* (Vienna: Universal Edition, 1922) published in the GDR—is documented by three successive typewritten drafts, all preserved in ALN: *a*) the original Italian; *b*) a first German translation, assisted—as evidenced by the handwriting of some corrections in the typescript—by Nuria Schoenberg Nono; and *c*) a subsequent final editing in German, carbon copy with a signature at the bottom, in which there are certain changes already present in *b* and, at the end of the paper, an addition written directly in German (i.e., the last sentences that goes from "And it still is," until the end). Compared to the latest of these drafts, however, the text published in the F<small>E</small> appears further altered. The first Italian publication of 1980 was based, considering that the original Italian was lost, on a translation of the F<small>E</small> by Luca Lombardi, part of the incomplete publishing project of 1975–76 (see the introduction).

Reproduced here, starting out from the Italian version of typescript *a*, is the text structured as it finally appeared in the German typescript *c*, the major deviations with respect to the FE being indicated in the editorial notes.

5. BARTÓK THE COMPOSER (1981)

FE: "Bartók compositore," De Benedictis–Rizzardi 2001: I: 515–21.

OE: De Benedictis–Rizzardi 2007: 208–13.

Feneyrou 2007: 484–90.

Lecture given at the international conference "Contemporaneità di Bartók," organized in Venice (Teatro La Fenice, October 14–17, 1981) as part of a series of events in celebration of Bartok's centennial; see *Béla Bartók: Il musicista, il didatta, il ricercatore,* ed. Laboratorio Musica (Milan: Ricordi, 1981), a volume published on the occasion of the festival. Access to the recording of Nono's speech was kindly granted to the editors by Flavio Spano; it was transcribed by Angela Ida De Benedictis. Given the erratic and improvisatory character of Nono's contribution, the transcription required substantial editorial intervention.

6. FOR HELMUT (1983)

FE: "Per Helmut," *Schweizerische Musikzeitung/Revue Musicale Suisse* 123/6 (November–December 1983): 334–36 (reproduction of Nono's original manuscript, in Italian).

OE: Feneyrou 1993: 451–54.

Helmut Lachenmann, *Musik als existentielle Erfahrung: Schriften, 1966–1995,* ed. Josef Häusler (Wiesbaden: Breitkopf & Härtel, 1996), ix–xii (facsimile of the manuscript reproduced in the FE) and xii–xv (German translation).

De Benedictis–Rizzardi 2001: I: 376–79.

De Benedictis–Rizzardi 2007: 233–36.

Feneyrou 2007: 503–6.

Alla ricerca di luce e chiarezza: L'epistolario Helmut Lachenmann–Luigi Nono (1957–1990), ed. Angela Ida De Benedictis and Ulrich Mosch (Florence: Olschki, 2012), 139–42.

De Assis 2014: 150–53.

The various publications of this text, even in translation, are faithful to the original graphic layout of Nono's manuscript, published in the FE.

7. FOR MARINO ZUCCHERI (1986)

FE: "Per Marino Zuccheri," in *Nuova Atlantide: Il continente della musica elettronica, 1900–1986,* ed. Roberto Doati and Alvise Vidolin (Venice: ERI–RAI–Biennale di Venezia, 1986), 174–76.

OE: Feneyrou 1993: 467–75.

De Benedictis–Rizzardi 2001: I: 406–13.

De Benedictis–Rizzardi 2007: 214–21.

Feneyrou 2007: 560–67.

Luigi Nono's manuscript is held in the private archive of Alvise Vidolin (who is thanked for kindly granting access to the original).

EXCURSUS V. INTERVIEW WITH MICHELANGELO
ZURLETTI (1987)

FE: "Colloquio con Luigi Nono," in *Studi e fantasie, saggi, versi, musica e testimonianze in onore di Leonardo Pinzauti*, ed. Daniele Spini (Florence: Passigli, 1996), 417–22.

OE: De Benedictis–Rizzardi 2001: II: 446–50.

The interview was conducted in Paris in 1987 at the Festival d'Automne, dedicated that year to Nono (see note 1 in the text).

PART FIVE. THE "POSSIBLE INFINITIES"
1. ERROR AS A NECESSITY (1983)

FE: "L'erreur comme nécessité," *Révolution* 169 (May 27–June 2, 1983): 50–51.

OE: *Schweizerische Musikzeitung/Revue Musicale Suisse* 123/5 (September–October 1983): 270–71.

Feneyrou 1993: 256–57.

Voci enigmatiche, ed. Francesca Gentile Camerana (Turin: De Sono, 1990), 109–11.

Quaderni di Octandre 1 (1993): 35.

Tage für Neue Musik Zürich (program notes for the concerts on November 11–13), Zurich, 1994: n.n.

Jürg Stenzl, *Luigi Nono* (Reinbeck bei Hamburg: Rowohlt, 1998), 105–6.

Vi insegnerò differenze, ed. Angela Ida De Benedictis (Milan: Banca Popolare di Milano-Archivio Luigi Nono, 2000), 71–75.

De Benedictis–Rizzardi 2001: I: 522–24.

De Benedictis–Rizzardi 2007: 243–44.

Feneyrou 2007: 495–97.

De Assis 2014: 156–57.

Speech made in French on March 17, 1983, at the Salle Patino, Geneva, at a *Contrechamps* concert dedicated to Nono. The FE and the first French reprint of the same year are preceded by an introductory page by Philippe Albèra (not reproduced here), who edited the transcription of Nono's speech. The original audio recording of Nono's lecture was issued on the CD attached to Feneyrou 2007.

2. OTHER POSSIBILITIES FOR LISTENING (1985)

FE: "Altre possibilità di ascolto," *L'Europa musicale. Un nuovo rinascimento: la civiltà dell'ascolto,* ed. Anna Laura Bellina and Giovanni Morelli (Florence: Vallecchi, 1988): 107–24.

OE: De Benedictis–Rizzardi 2001: I: 525–39.

De Benedictis–Rizzardi 2007: 245–59.

Feneyrou 2007: 544–59.

De Assis 2014: 158–71.

Lecture held as part of the 27th "Corso di alta cultura" [Course of High Culture] of the Fondazione Giorgio Cini in Venice (August 30–31, 1985), transcribed ed edited by Giovanni Morelli. Most expressions put between commas in FE have been rendered here with italics, corresponding to emphases used by Nono in his spoken style.

The present translation is largely based on a first draft made by Robert L. Kendrick.

3. LECTURE AT THE CHARTREUSE IN VILLENEUVE-LES-AVIGNON (1989)

FE (French): Feneyrou 1993: 270–76.

FE (Italian): De Benedictis–Rizzardi 2001: I: 540–46.

OE: De Benedictis–Rizzardi 2007: 260–65.

Feneyrou 2007: 585–91.

De Assis 2014: 172–77.

Opening lecture given on July 16, 1989, during the courses of the "Centre Acanthes" within the Festival d'Avignon" (July 15–30), devoted entirely to Luigi Nono. The version published in De Benedictis–Rizzardi 2001 and 2007 is based on a new transcription of the tapes kindly made available by the "Centre Acanthes" Archive; it therefore differs considerably from the one published in Feneyrou 1993.

EXCURSUS VI. "PROUST" QUESTIONNAIRE (1986)

FE: *Frankfurter Allgemeine Zeitung-Magazin* (October 3, 1986): 50.

OE: *Brennpunkt Nono,* ed. Josef Häusler (Zurich: Palladion, 1993), 144 (photographic reproduction of the FE).

De Benedictis–Rizzardi 2001: I: 415–18.

De Benedictis–Rizzardi 2007: 267–70.

Feneyrou 2007: 569–73.

Held in the ALN are two distinct versions of the questionnaire in Italian (with questions typewritten and answers handwritten), incomplete and largely dissimilar from the wording released in the FE. The translation presented here is founded on the version developed by the editors on the basis of Nono's original wording (for the answers that are unchanged in the FE).

Chronology of Nono's Works

This chronological list includes, in addition to all Nono's works that can be considered complete—published, unpublished, unacknowledged, withdrawn—other works ranging from scores that were left unfinished but nearly completed (*Due liriche greche; Julius Fučík*) to compositions that were actually performed but for which there remain neither scores nor other documentary or recorded traces that might confer upon them the definite status of a "work" (*Découvrir la subversion. Hommage à Edmond Jabès; Post-Prae-Ludium BAAB-ARR*).

Since a definitive catalog of Luigi Nono's works has not yet been established, this list should be considered as reflecting the current state of research (January 2018). Some lingering uncertainties about titles have been resolved by recourse to various archival sources in which the use of sufficiently clear or consistent forms can be found. Of particular importance, in this sense, is a brochure discovered in the ALN containing the catalog of Nono's works published by B. Schott's Söhne, Mainz (printed in 1966)—to whom Nono was contractually bound until 1964—in which the composer corrects certain titles, giving them the Italian form instead of the German, and supplies others not listed and/or subsequent to the publication of the booklet.

At the end of the chronology is added, for guidance, a partial list of projects that did not materialize in any form, but for which there remain drafts substantial enough to allow the identification of at least a clearly authorial intention. These mainly involve ideas for musical theater—formal sketches, literary and/or musical materials—developed, sometimes at length, in collaboration with other parties.

This chronology is intended to provide the reader with an overall orientation regarding Nono's creative history and, ultimately, a point of reference with respect to the works quoted in this volume.

1945   La discesa di Cristo agli inferi. Lost.[i]

1948   Movement of Trio, for Strings. Unpublished.

1948–49 [Due liriche greche]: La stella mattutina, for chorus (four contraltos) and seven instruments (text of Ion of Chios, trans. Salvatore Quasimodo); and Ai Dioscuri, for mixed chorus, piano, timpani and percussion (text of Alcaeus, trans. Salvatore Quasimodo). Unpublished.

1949–50 Variazioni canoniche sulla serie dell'op. 41 di Arnold Schönberg (reconstruction by the composer, 1985). Ricordi 133874.

1951   [Julius Fučík] (First episode), for two narrators and orchestra (text by Julius Fučík). Incomplete (reconstruction by Peter Hirsch, 2005). Unpublished.

Polifonica-Monodia-Ritmica, for six instruments and percussion. Ars Viva AV 76.[ii]

Polifonica-Monodia-Ritmica, for six instruments and percussion (first version). Schott (posthumous edition).

Composizione [n. 1] per orchestra. Ars Viva.

1951–52 Epitaffio per Federico García Lorca I: España en el corazón, three studies for soprano, baritone, speaking chorus, and instruments (texts by Federico García Lorca and Pablo Neruda). Ars Viva AV 42.

1952   Epitaffio per Federico García Lorca II: Y su sangre ya viene cantando, for flute and small orchestra. Ars Viva AV 55.

1952–53 Epitaffio per Federico García Lorca III: Memento. Romance de la Guardia civil española, for narrator, speaking chorus and orchestra (text by Federico García Lorca). Ars Viva AV 49.

1953   Due espressioni per orchestra. Ars Viva.

1954   La victoire de Guernica, for mixed chorus and orchestra (text by Paul Éluard). Ars Viva AV 69.

Il mantello rosso (Der rote Mantel), ballet in three scenes by Tatjana Gsovsky from Don Perlimplín, by Federico García Lorca, for

---

i. Information about this composition—finished, but lost—is obtained from two interviews with Nono: Péter Várnai, Beszélgetések Luigi Nonóval (Budapest: Zeneműkiadó, 1978), 22, and Renato Garavaglia (1979–80, in this vol., 255). The first interview reveals its year of composition, the second reveals its title.

ii. The first published score of Polifonica-Monodia-Ritmica is the result of substantial cuts (about 2/3 of the piece) on the original manuscript, that were made by Hermann Scherchen in view of the first Darmstadt performance (July 10, 1951), which he was to conduct. While initially disappointed, Nono finally consented to publish this shortened version in the Ars Viva Editions (then owned by Scherchen himself, subsequently incorporated into Schott Editions). The original, uncut version was found in 1993 among Nono's papers and is the base for the new edition.

soprano, baritone, mixed chorus, and orchestra (trans. Heinrich Beck). Ars Viva.

Il mantello rosso, concert suite (A) for soprano, baritone, mixed chorus, and orchestra. Ars Viva.

Il mantello rosso, concert suite (B) for orchestra. Ars Viva.

Incidental music for *Was ihr wollt (As You Like It)*, by William Shakespeare, for five instrumentalists. Unpublished.

Liebeslied, for mixed chorus and instruments (text by Luigi Nono). Ars Viva AV 60.

1955　*Canti per 13.* Ars Viva.

Incontri, for twenty-four instruments. Ars Viva AV 52.

1955–56　*Il canto sospeso*, for soprano, alto, tenor, mixed chorus, and orchestra (texts: letters of the Resistance fighters condemned to death, collected by Giovanni Pirelli). Ars Viva AV 50.

1957　*Varianti*, music for solo violin, strings, and woodwinds. Ars Viva AV 51.

La terra e la compagna, songs by Cesare Pavese for soprano, tenor, chorus, and instruments. Ars Viva AV 56.

1958　*Piccola gala notturna veneziana in onore dei sessanta anni di Heinrich Strobel*, for fourteen instruments.[iii]

Cori di Didone, from *La terra promessa*, by Giuseppe Ungaretti, for chorus and percussion. Ars Viva AV 54.

1959　*Composizione per orchestra n. 2–Diario polacco '58.* Ars Viva AV 66.

1960　*Sarà dolce tacere*, song for eight soloists from *La terra e la morte*, by Cesare Pavese. Ars Viva AV 5.

"Ha venido." Canciones para Silvia, for soprano and chorus of six sopranos (text by Antonio Machado). Ars Viva AV 6.

Omaggio a Emilio Vedova, for magnetic tape. Ricordi 131271.

1960–61　*Intolleranza 1960*, scenic action in two parts based on an idea of Angelo Maria Ripellino, for soloists, chorus, orchestra, and magnetic tape (texts by Henri Alleg, Bertolt Brecht, Paul Éluard, Julius Fučík, Vladimir Mayakovsky, Angelo Maria Ripellino, Jean-Paul Sartre). Ars Viva AV 75.

1962　*Canti di vita e d'amore. Sul ponte di Hiroshima*, for soprano, tenor, and orchestra (texts by Günther Anders, Jesus Lopez Pacheco, Cesare Pavese). Ars Viva AV 78.

---

iii. With regard to this short occasional piece, nothing is known about either the publication or its possible performance. The score, consisting in five bars only, is held at the *ALN* and dated "4-29-58."

1962–63   *Canciones a Guiomar,* for soprano, chorus of six female voices, and instruments (text by Antonio Machado). Ars Viva AV 284.

1964   *Da un diario italiano,* for two choruses (texts by Giuliano Scabia). Schott.

La fabbrica illuminata, for female voice and magnetic tape (documentary texts elaborated by Giuliano Scabia with a fragment from Cesare Pavese). Ricordi 131242.

1965   *Composizione per orchestra n. 2—Diario polacco '58,* new version with magnetic tape. Ars Viva.

Music for *Die Ermittlung* of Peter Weiss, for magnetic tape. Ricordi 132668.

1965–66   *A floresta é jovem e cheja de vida,* for soprano, clarinet, three actors' voices, bronze plates, and magnetic tape (documentary texts collected by Giovanni Pirelli). Ricordi 131241.

1966   *Ricorda cosa ti hanno fatto in Auschwitz,* for magnetic tape. Ricordi 131244.

1967   *Per Bastiana—Tai-Yang Cheng,* for orchestra and magnetic tape. Ricordi 131289.

1968   *Contrappunto dialettico alla mente,* for magnetic tape (texts by Nanni Balestrini and Sonia Sánchez, documentary texts). Ricordi 131457.

1969   *Suite da concerto da "Intolleranza 1960,"* for soprano, chorus, and orchestra. Ars Viva AV 78.

Musica-Manifesto n. 1: (a) *Un volto, e del mare,* for two female voices and magnetic tape (text: Cesare Pavese); (b) *Non consumiamo Marx,* for magnetic tape (documentary texts). Ricordi 131528/9.

Musiche per Manzù, for magnetic tape (music for the film *Pace e guerra* produced on behalf of the "Raccolta Amici di Manzù"). Ricordi 131244.

1969–70   *Y entonces comprendió,* for three sopranos, three actresses' voices, chorus, and magnetic tape (texts by Carlos Franqui and Ernesto "Che" Guevara). Ricordi 131647.

San Vittore 1969 (electroacoustic composition on the songs of Mario Buffa Moncalvo). Ricordi.

1970   *Intolleranza 1970* (see *Intolleranza 1960*).[iv]

Voci destroying muros, for two sopranos, two reciting female voices, female chorus, and orchestra (texts by Rosa Luxemburg,

---

iv. This involves a production of *Intolleranza 1960* staged in Nurenberg on May 10, 1970, which differs from the first version only with regard to the magnetic tape part and also because of a reworking of the text by Yaak Karsunke.

Hannie Schaft, Riek Snel, Haydée Santamaría, Celia Sánchez, Cesare Pavese, documentary texts). Ricordi, withdrawn.

1971   *Ein Gespenst geht um in der Welt,* for soprano, mixed chorus, and orchestra (texts by Karl Marx, Celia Sánchez, and Haydée Santamaría). Ricordi 131806.

1971–72   *Como una ola de fuerza y luz,* for soprano, piano, orchestra, and magnetic tape (text by Julio Huasi). Ricordi 131983.

1972–74   *Al gran sole carico d'amore,* scenic action in two parts for soloists, small and large chorus, orchestra, and magnetic tape (texts by Bertolt Brecht, Tania Bunke, Fidel Castro, Ernesto "Che" Guevara, Dimitrov, Maxim Gorky, Antonio Gramsci, Lenin, Karl Marx, Louise Michel, Cesare Pavese, Arthur Rimbaud, Celia Sánchez, and Haydée Santamaría). Ricordi 132262.

1973   *Siamo la gioventù del Vietnam,* for unison chorus (texts: Girolamo Federici, and Declaration of Independence of the Democratic Republic of Vietnam). Unpublished.[v]

1974   *Für Paul Dessau,* for magnetic tape. Ricordi 132670.

1976   *Frammenti da "Al gran sole carico d'amore,"* for soloists, chorus, orchestra, and magnetic tape. Ricordi 134420.

. . . . . *sofferte onde serene. . .,* for piano and magnetic tape. Ricordi 132564.

Incidental music for *I turcs tal Friûl,* by Pier Paolo Pasolini, for voices and instruments. Unpublished.

1977   *Al gran sole carico d'amore* (new version). Ricordi 132625.

1979   *Con Luigi Dallapiccola,* for six percussionists and ring modulators. Ricordi 132945.

1979–80   *Fragmente-Stille, an Diotima,* for string quartet. Ricordi 133049.

1981   *Das atmende Klarsein,* for bass flute, small chorus, live electronics, and magnetic tape (texts by Rainer Maria Rilke and the Orphic hymns collected and adapted by Massimo Cacciari). Ricordi 133476.

Io, frammento dal Prometeo, for three sopranos, small chorus, bass flute, bass clarinet, and live electronics (texts by Aeschylus and Friedrich Hölderlin collected and adapted by Massimo Cacciari). Ricordi 133368.

1982   *Quando stanno morendo. Diario polacco n. 2,* for two sopranos, mezzo-soprano, contralto, bass flute, cello, and live electronics (texts by Endre Ady, Alexander Blok, Velimir Khlebnikov, Czeslaw

---

v. A reproduction of the manuscript can be found in Jürg Stenzl, *Luigi Nono* (Reinbek bei Hamburg: Rowohlt, 1998), 82.

Milosz, Boris Pasternak, collected and adapted by Massimo Cacciari). Ricordi 133462.

¿*Donde estás, hermano?* for four female voices (Text: "¿Donde estás, hermano?"). Ricordi 133477.

1983   *Omaggio a György Kurtág* (first version), for contralto, flute, clarinet, tuba, and live electronics (text: "György Kurtág"). Ricordi.[vi]

Guai ai gelidi mostri, for two contraltos, viola, cello, double bass, flute, clarinet, tuba, and live electronics (texts by Gottfried Benn, Lucretius, Friedrich Nietzsche, Edgar Allan Poe, Rainer Maria Rilke, collected and adapted by Massimo Cacciari). Ricordi 133783.

1984   *Prometeo, tragedia dell'ascolto,* for vocal and instrumental soloists, chorus, orchestra, and live electronics (texts by Walter Benjamin, Aeschylus, Euripides, Johann Wolfgang von Goethe, Herodotus, Hesiod, Friedrich Hölderlin, Pindar, Arnold Schoenberg, and Sophocles, collected and adapted by Massimo Cacciari). Ricordi 133786.

A Carlo Scarpa, architetto, ai suoi infiniti possibili, for microintervals orchestra. Ricordi 133838.

1985   *Prometeo, tragedia dell'ascolto* (new version). Ricordi 133786.

A Pierre. Dell'azzurro silenzio, inquietum, "a più cori," for contrabass flute, contrabass clarinet, and live electronics. Ricordi 133943.

1986   *Omaggio a György Kurtág* (final version). Ricordi 133784.

Risonanze erranti. Liederzyklus a Massimo Cacciari, for mezzo-soprano, flute, tuba, six percussionists, and live electronics (texts by Ingeborg Bachmann and Herman Melville). Ricordi 134201.

1986–87   *1°) Caminantes . . . Ayacucho,* for contralto, flute, small and large chorus, organ, three choruses [orchestral groups], and live electronics (text by Giordano Bruno). Ricordi 134351.

1987   *Découvrir la subversion. Hommage à Edmond Jabès,* for contralto, narrator, flute, tuba, horn, and live electronics (text by Edmond Jabès). Ricordi, posthumously withdrawn.[vii]

---

vi. The first version of *Omaggio a György Kurtág* was basically a conducted improvisation over some materials that Nono had sketched in view of the first performance. No score of this version has ever existed. Three years later, Nono prepared a final, notated version of the piece.

vii. The composition, as well as the subsequent *Post-Prae-Ludium n. 3 BAAB-ARR,* were withdrawn by the Editorial Committee for the Works of Luigi Nono in 1993, after the author's death. See *Remarks on "Découvrir la subversion. Hommage à Edmond Jabès" and "Post-Prae-Ludium n. 3 Baab-arr" by Luigi Nono: Essays by Jürg Stenzl and Hans Peter Haller with a Statement by the Editorial Committee for the Works of Luigi Nono* (Milan: Ricordi, 1993).

Post-Prae-Ludium per Donau, for tuba and live electronics. Ricordi 134668.

2°) "*No hay caminos, hay que caminar*" . . . *Andrej Tarkowskij*, for seven choruses [orchestral groups]. Ricordi 134518.

1988   *Post-Prae-Ludium n. 3 BAAB-ARR*, for piccolo. Ricordi 134800, posthumously withdrawn.

1988–89   *La lontananza nostalgica utopica futura. Madrigale per più "caminantes" con Gidon Kremer*, for violin and magnetic tapes. Ricordi 134798.[viii]

1989   "*Hay que caminar*" *sognando*, for two violins. Ricordi 134955.

UNFINISHED PROJECTS (PARTIAL LIST)

1963   *Technically Sweet*, music theater on texts by Emilio Jona.
1963–64   *Un diario italiano*, music theater on texts by Giuliano Scabia.
1964–65   *Deola e Masino*, music theater.
1965–68   *L'immaginazione prende il potere*, music theater in collaboration with Giovanni Pirelli.

viii. A first version (1988) was entitled *La lontananza nostalgica futura*.

General Index

Abbado, Claudio, 93, 95, 97, 98, 107, 110, 377, 405
Acevedo, Miriam, 350
Achilles, 258
Adamovich, Ludwig jr., 362
Adorno, Theodor Wiesengrund, 48, 52, 62, 248, 290, 403
Advis, Luís, 330; *Santa Maria de Iquique*, 330
Ady, Endre, 113, 475
Aeschylus, 117, 258, 475–76
Agamben, Giorgio, 45, 402
Aldini, Edmonda, 81
Alessandri, Ms, 3
Al Mu'tamid ibn' Abbād, Muhammad, 393
Al-Waleed Ahmad ibn Zaydún al-Makhzumi, Abu, 393
Albèra, Philippe, 434, 467
Alcaeus, 472
Alleg, Henri, 195, 196, 417, 418, 473
Allende, Salvador, 93, 298, 303, 305, 329, 330, 434, 436
Altamirano Orrego, Carlos, 305, 306, 436
Ambrosini, Claudio, 92, 111, 364, 384, 392, 449
Anders, Günther, 75, 276, 474
Andersch, Alfred, 193
Anglés, Higinio, 382, 448
Annenkov, Jurij, 421
Antal, Frigyes, 442
Antheil, George, 50, 103, 288

Antonellini, Nino, 83, 350, 355, 419
Apollinaire, Guillaume, 56, 86
Apollonio, Umbro, 210, 419
Argan, Giulio Carlo, 211, 421
Aristoxenus, 385, 387, 449
Aristotle, 385
Armstrong, Louis, 282
Arnold, Denis, 325
Arom, Simha, 50
Artaud, Antonin, 81, 265, 423, 428, 430
Artemyev, Eduard Nikolaevich, 112, 409
Artusi, Giovanni Maria, 337, 346, 348, 443
Ashley, Robert, 397

Bach, Johann Sebastian, 63, 81, 82, 107, 125, 156, 161, 164, 165, 167, 238, 243, 336, 337, 378; Mass in B minor, 165, 167; *The Art of Fugue*, 125
Bach, David J., 337
Bachmann, Ingeborg, 476
Balázs, Béla, 339, 442
Balázs, István, 397
Balestrini, Nanni, 355, 474
Balzac, Honoré de, 420
Banchieri, Adriano, 83; *Contrappunto bestiale alla mente*, 83
Banzer Suárez, Hugo, 435
Baratto, Mario, 180
Barchin, Michael Grigorevich, 244
Barthes, Roland, 375

480 | General Index

Bartók, Béla, 4, 34, 48, 61, 62, 66, 86, 103, 113, 114, 238, 239, 279, 285, 317, 327, 338–44, 407, 442, 466; First Concerto for Piano and Orchestra, 327; First String Quartet, 343; *Melodien der Rumänischen Colinde*, 340, 341; *Music for String, Percussion and Celesta*, 343; *Sonata for two Pianos and Percussion*, 343; Third Concerto for Piano and Orchestra, 407
Basso, Lelio, 226, 422
Beck, Heinrich, 417, 473
Beck, Julian, 226, 354
Beethoven, Ludwig van, 31, 40, 52, 115, 157–59, 168, 186, 254, 279, 428; *Fidelio* op. 72, 322; Ninth Simphony in D min. op. 125, 115, 157–58
Belaúnde Terry, Fernando, 85
Bellini, Vincenzo, 45–47, 53, 75, 107, 111; *Norma*, 45, 46, 75; *Il pirata*, 47, 75
Benjamin, Walter, 9, 50, 82, 117, 244, 258, 348, 379, 426, 444, 476
Benn, Gottfried, 312, 476
Berdyaev, Nikolai Alexandrovich, 36
Berg, Alban, 35, 43, 52, 64, 103, 159–60, 217, 248–49, 326; *Lulu*, 43, 215; *Lyrische Suite*, 64; *Three Pieces for Orchestra*, op. 6, 43; *Wozzeck*, 43
Berghaus, Ruth, 424
Berio, Luciano, 2, 7, 25, 48, 249, 259, 261, 297, 315, 350, 355, 356, 361, 398, 411, 412, 427, 445, 451, 453–54; *Sequenza II for harp*, 427, 445
Berlinguer, Enrico, 96, 97, 382
Bertola, Giulio, 350, 354
Bilhaṇa, Kavi, 393, 450
Blazhkov, Igor, 283
Bloch, Ernst, 290, 339
Blok, Aleksander Alexandrovich, 57, 475
Bobbio, Norberto, 36
Boccioni, Umberto, 392
Bollati, Giulio, 59
Bolzoni, Giovanni, 70
Bontempelli, Massimo, 27, 33
Borkin, Harold, 397
Borovsky, David, 97–98, 107
Bortolotto, Mario, 66
Boulez, Pierre, 2, 6, 11, 48, 56, 60, 62, 64, 71, 86, 92, 103, 106, 110, 130, 135, 149, 248, 291, 356, 361, 371, 377, 402, 408, 445, 454; *Structures pour deux pianos*, 56, 130, 149, 454
Bove, Kadigia, 83, 297, 350, 355
Brahms, Johannes, 40, 52, 107, 183, 238
Branca, Vittore, 383
Brandt, Willy, 96

Brant, Sebastian, 407
Bravo, Douglas, 299, 435
Brecht, Bertolt, 52, 71, 98, 182, 186, 196, 211, 217, 227, 229, 232, 282, 295, 363, 424, 473, 475
Brecht, George, 432
Brendel, Alfred, 439
Brouwer, Luitzen Egbertus Jan, 371, 447
Brown, Earle, 7, 401–2, 428–29; *Hodograph I*, 428
Bruckner, Anton Joseph, 111, 115
Bruno, Giordano, 10, 38, 39, 50, 81, 120–21, 238, 347, 376, 391, 396, 476
Buber, Martin, 50, 95, 339
Bucchi, Valentino, 28, 399; *La dolce pena*, 399
Buffa Moncalvo, Mario, 474
Bunke, Tamara (or Tania; Laura Gutiérrez Bauer), 475
Buñuel, Luis, 220, 221
Burmeister, Joachim, 155, 413
Burri, Alberto, 57, 65, 392
Busoni, Ferruccio, 52, 215, 237, 249, 341
Bussotti, Sylvano, 102, 106, 110, 259, 290, 364, 429
Bustini, Alessandro, 28

Cacciari, Massimo, 9, 62, 114, 117–18, 120, 242–43, 245, 252, 258–59, 312, 364, 371, 376, 393, 405, 426, 447, 450, 475, 476
Cadieu, Martine, 277, 430, 431, 462
Cage, John; Cageian, 6, 7, 44, 45, 64, 105, 189, 237, 266–69, 271, 287, 288–91, 316, 364, 396, 401, 403, 420, 423, 428–29, 432; *4'33"*, 105, 402
Caldwell, Sara, 187, 455
Calvino, Italo, 59, 193, 211
Campigli, Massimo, 34
Camus, Albert, 430
Canetti, Elias, 79, 94, 95, 114
Capa, Robert, 198, 220
Cappelli, Gilberto, 111, 342, 364, 384, 443, 449; String Quartet (1981), 342, 443
Cardazzo, Carlo, 33–35
Carluccio, Francesco, 259
Carpentier, Alejo, 85–86
Carrillo Torneria, Isidoro Del Carmen, 84, 304, 331, 436
Carucci, Jacopo (Pontormo), 81, 392
Caskel, Christoph, 48, 428
Castiglioni, Niccolò, 419
Castro Ruz, Fidel, 79, 82, 87, 297, 298, 301–3, 307–9, 394, 433–35, 437, 440, 475

Castro Ruz, Raúl, 309, 437
Catunda, Eunice, 53–55, 404
Catunda, Omar, 404
Caturla, Alejandro García, 86
Celibidache, Sergiu, 121
Césaire, Aimé, 71, 289, 406
Chacón, Alfredo, 299
Char, René, 86
Chowning, John, 108, 251, 426
Ciardi, Guglielmo, 30
Čiurlionis, Mikalojus Konstantinas, 112
Clementi, Aldo, 42, 48, 110, 224, 259, 361, 364; *Collage*, 224
Cochin, Charles Nicolas II, 244
Cocteau, Jean, 33
Cohen, Milton, 397
Colombo, Furio, 228
Coltrane, John, 282
Corbin, Henri, 45
Cott, Jonathan, 407
Cowell, Henry, 50, 288, 364
Craxi, Bettino, 362, 446
Cruz, Luciano, 93–94
Cumar, Raffaele, 35

Dahlhaus, Carl, 341
Dal Co, Francesco, 258
Dallapiccola, Luigi, 4, 34–35, 41, 62, 101–3, 122, 125–26, 179–80, 217, 254, 255, 261, 279, 282, 284, 325, 404, 406, 408, 410, 452; *Canti di liberazione*, 101, 180; *Canti di prigionia*, 101, 125, 431; *Congedo di Girolamo Savonarola*, 125–26, 408, 431; *Il prigioniero*, 101–2, 179, 217; *Liriche greche*, 101, 125; *Sex Carmina Alcæi*, 125–26; *Tre Poemi*, 406; *Ulisse*, 410
Dall'Oglio, Renzo, 39
Davis, Miles, 392
Dazzi, Manlio, 180
De Benedetti, Carlo, 382
De Benedictis, Angela Ida, 396, 458, 466
Debussy, Claude, 46, 76, 77, 106, 110; *La mer*, 76
De Falla, Manuel, 114
Degrada, Francesco, 455
Della Volpe, Galvano, 213, 420
Denisov, Edison (Eddy), 111–12, 283
De Pablo, Luis, 113
De Sabata, Victor, 110
Desprez, Josquin, 40, 56, 156, 282, 388, 450; *Missa Di dadi*, 40, 450
Dessau, Paul, 103, 148, 217, 424; *Das Verhör des Lukullus*, 217; *Die Ausnahme und die Regel*, 217; *Herr Puntila und sein Knecht Matti*, 217
De Staël, Nicholas, 276
Di Giugno, Giuseppe (Peppino), 236, 356, 361
Dimitrov, Georgi, 475
Dine, Jim, 189, 228, 282, 423
Dior, Christian, 419
Dobrovolskaya, Yulia, 64
Dodge, Charles, 251, 426
Donatoni, Franco, 109–10
Doni, Giovanni Battista, 27
Donizetti, Gaetano, 46
Dorigo, Wladimiro, 95
Doso, Watazumi, 450
Dostoyevsky, Fyodor Mikhailovich, 38, 391
Dreyer, Carl Theodor, 231, 424
Duchamp, Marcel, 26
Dubuffet, Jean, 289
Duchesne Cuzán, Manuel, 284
Dufay, Guillaume, 156, 282, 392
Dufourt, Hugues, 92
Duno, Pedro, 302, 436
Dunstable, John, 40, 388–89
Dutschke, Rudi, 81

Eckhart, Johannes, 271, 429, 432, 460
Eco, Umberto, 420
Eimert, Herbert, 416
Einaudi, Giulio, 59, 60, 400
Einstein, Albert; Einstenian, 49, 53, 217
Eisenstein, Sergei Mikhailovich, 57
Eisler, Hanns, 52, 217, 337, 404, 441, 442; *Die Massnahme*, 217
Éluard, Paul, 7, 56, 59, 71, 79, 86, 196–97, 472, 473
Evangelisti, Franco, 48, 248
Evreinov, Nikolai, 421

Fabbriciani, Roberto, 89, 90, 116, 119, 121, 239, 244, 311, 377, 437
Fabris, Gastone, 39
Favretto, Giacomo, 30
Federici, Girolamo, 475
Feldman, Morton, 361, 392, 401, 429, 446
Feltrinelli, Giangiacomo, 60
Feuchtwanger, Lion, 52
Finkelstein, Sidney, 188, 417
Flanagan, Hallie, 322
Flimm, Jürg, 99
Florensky, Pavel, 112
Fogarasi, Béla, 442
Fontana, Carlo, 357, 445
Forlani, Arnaldo, 303, 436
Fortner, Wolfgang, 48
Franco, Francisco, 114, 196, 219, 305, 436

Franqui, Carlos, 87, 474
Frei Montalva, Eduardo, 304, 330, 435–36
Frescobaldi, Girolamo, 42
Fučík, Julius, 195–97, 417, 418, 472, 473
Fülep, Lajos, 442
Furtseva, Yekaterina, 96
Furtwängler, Wilhelm, 110

Gabrieli, Andrea, 34, 68, 253, 360–61, 378, 389–90, 439
Gabrieli, Giovanni, 34, 60, 68, 169, 253–54, 282, 325, 327, 360–61, 378, 389–90, 427, 439, 444; *O magnum Mysterium*, 169
Gaffurio, Franchino, 4, 27
Galilei, Galileo, 29, 156, 394
Garavaglia, Renato, 459
Gargani, Aldo, 252, 443
Gaudí y Cornet, Antoni, 388
Gazzelloni, Severino, 48, 54, 71, 271, 428
Gelber, Jack, 227
George, Stefan, 406
Geselbracht, Charlotte, 437
Gesualdo, Carlo, Prince of Venosa, 63, 156, 164, 172, 238; *Il sol, qual or più splende*, 173–75; *Madrigali* [libri I-VI], 172, 238; *Responsoria*, 238
Geymonat, Ludovico, 212
Ghedini, Giorgio Federico, 408; *Concerto spirituale "De la incarnatione del Verbo Divino,"* 408
Gielen, Michael, 91, 99
Giotto (Angiolo da Bondone), 36
Giulini, Carlo Maria, 110
Gobetti, Piero, 59
Goethe, Johann Wolfgang, 118, 157, 242, 476
Goeyvaerts, Karel, 248
Gogol, Nikolai Vasilievich, 33
Gomez, Italo, 109–10
Gomułka, Władysław, 69
Gorbachev, Mikhail Sergeyevich, 37, 38
Gorky, Arshile, 67, 276
Gorky, Maxim, 98, 475
Gramsci, Antonio, 7, 59, 60, 81, 180–81, 249, 255, 274, 292, 316, 363, 393, 446, 475
Grassi, Paolo, 95–98
Gregotti, Vittorio, 364, 447
Grisey, Gérard, 92
Grondona, Payo, 330–31
Gropius, Walter, 57, 222, 244, 422
Grosz, George, 363
Grotowski, Jerzy, 227, 423
Grünewald, Matthias, 50, 108, 377, 392

Gsovsky, Tatjana, 55, 417, 472
Gubaidulina, Sofia, 111–12, 409; *Stimmen ... verstummen*, 112, 409
Guevara, Ernesto "Che," 82, 299, 302, 391, 435, 474, 475
Guillén, Nicolás, 329, 440
Gutierrez, "Ducho," 331

Hába, Alois, 238, 249, 341, 425, 442
Handel, Georg Frideric, 156
Halevi, Yehudah, 50, 393
Halffter, Cristóbal, 113
Haller, Hans Peter, 83, 108, 109, 239, 311, 371, 386–89, 437
Hartmann, Karl Amadeus, 48, 103, 249, 363
Hauser, Arnold, 442
Haydn, Franz Joseph, 44
Hegel, Georg Wilhelm Friedrich; Hegelianism; Hegelian, 290, 312
Heidegger, Martin, 339
Heisenberg, Werner, 276, 429
Helms, Hans G., 428
Henius, Carla, 350, 354
Henze, Hans Werner, 6, 48, 224, 248, 451, 453; *Elegie für junge Liebende*, 224
Hindemith, Paul, 27, 54, 217, 249, 399; *Das badener Lehrstück vom Einverständnis*, 217
Hirsch, Peter, 472
Hitler, Adolf; Hitlerims, 294, 394
Hölderlin, Friedrich, 9, 38, 43, 80, 81, 104–7, 206, 316, 347, 392, 401, 408, 427, 475, 476
Horkheimer, Max, 48, 248, 290
Ho-Tang, Huan, 284
Huasi, Julio, 93, 475
Hübner, Herbert, 51, 403
Hucbald of Saint-Amand, 28, 326, 332
Husserl, Edmund, 339

Ibn Zaydūn. *See* Al-Waleed Ahmad *ibn Zaydún* al-Makhzumi, Abu
Idelsohn, Abraham Zvi, 94, 236, 424
Incardona, Federico, 111
Ion of Chios, 472
Ionesco, Eugène, 211
Isaac, Heinrich, 42
Ives, Charles Edward, 288

Jabès, Edmond, 9, 43, 94–95, 104–5, 107, 393, 476
Janáček, Leoš, 106, 154, 279, 285
Jara, Victor, 84, 328–31, 440
Jesenská, Milena, 180, 249, 274

Joachim, Joseph, 107, 183, 238
Joan of Arc, 231, 393
Johnson, James Louis ("J.J."), 397
Jona, Emilio, 430, 477

Kafka, Franz, 113, 180, 249, 274, 376, 400
Kagel, Mauricio, 224, 289–90, 291–93, 296, 420, 422, 432, 433, 463; *Instrumentales Theater. See Sur Scène*; *Ludwig van*, 433; Sextet for String (*Sexteto de cuerdas*), 432; *Sur Scène*, 224, 422
Kakhidze, Jansug Ivanes, 121
Kandinsky, Wassily, 52, 86, 118, 215; *Der gelbe Klang*, 215
Kaprow, Allan, 228, 282
Karajan, Herbert von, 120
Karetnikov, Nikolai Nikolayevich, 283
Karsunke, Yaak, 474
Kašlík, Václav, 72, 194, 323, 417, 439
Kassák, Lajos, 113
Kennedy, John Fitzgerald; Kennedyism, 188, 226, 422, 430, 432
Kerle, Jakobus de, 326
Khlebnikov, Velimir, 57, 118, 475
Khrennikov, Tikhon Nikolayevich, 446
Kiefer, Anselm, 58, 392
Kievman, Carson, 261
Kircher, Athanasius, 50, 377
Kirchner, Leon, 188
Klebe, Giselher, 48
Klee, Paul, 385, 386, 392
Kleiber, Carlos, 110, 377
Kleiber, Erich, 110
Klemperer, Otto Nossan, 52, 110
Klimov, Elem Germanovich, 112, 362
Kluge, Alexander, 91, 362
Kocsis, Zoltán, 340
Koellreuter, Hans-Joachim, 53
Kolisch Schoenberg, Gertrud, 52, 185, 403
Kolisch, Rudolf, 48, 52, 61, 250, 405
Kollwitz, Käthe, 198
Kontarsky, Alfons, 48
Kontarsky, Aloys, 48
Korsch, Karl, 290
Kraus, Karl, 59, 106, 346
Kremer, Gidon, 37
Kugel, Aleksàndr, 421
Kurtág, György, 77, 113, 115, 344

Labroca, Mario, 71, 72, 193, 417
Lachenmann, Helmut, 77, 112, 346, 408, 455, 460, 461
Lam, Wifredo, 87
Landini, Francesco, 41

Lasso, Orlando di, 156
Leibowitz, René, 48, 61, 252, 343
Lenin; Leninist. *See* Ulyanov, Vladimir Ilich
Leszai, Anna, 442
Lévy, Roland Alexis Manuel, 405
Levin, Walter, 107
Leyden, Lucas van, 214
Leydi, Roberto, 338, 442
Lietti, Alfredo, 355
Ligeti, György, 65, 386, 401, 402
Li Po, 399
Littín, Miguel, 329
Lizzero, Mario, 180, 415
Llorens i Cisteró, Josep Maria, 113
Lombardi, Luca, 453, 465
Lorca, Federico García, 7, 53–55, 58–60, 69, 82, 94, 114, 275, 417, 472
Lucretius Carus Titus, 312, 476
Lukács, György, 62, 113, 338, 339, 405, 442
Lunacharsky, Anatoly Vasilyevich, 281
Lunts, Lev Natanovich, 33
Lutosławski, Witold, 69
Luxemburg, Rosa, 81, 392, 474
Lyubimov, Yuri, 64, 95–98, 107, 118, 408

Macchi, Egisto, 224; *Anno Domini*, 224
Mach, Ernst, 337
Machado, Antonio, 24, 67, 75–76, 78, 221, 276, 399, 410, 473, 474
Machaut, Guillaume de, 40, 254, 392
Maderna, Bruno, 1, 4, 5, 7, 27–30, 39, 40–45, 47–49, 51, 54–58, 60, 61, 67, 68, 70–73, 85, 101, 103, 135, 149, 150, 179, 180, 182, 185, 187, 188, 248, 249, 254, 255, 274, 275, 296, 315, 325, 326–27, 344, 349, 350, 355, 356, 360, 361, 399, 403–6, 412, 415, 427, 430, 444, 445, 452, 455, 465; *Fantasia e fuga per due pianoforti (Bach-Variationen für zwei Klaviere)*, 48, 402; *Improvvisazione n. 1*, 406; *Musica su due dimensioni* (1952), 71, 350; *Musica su due dimensioni* (1958), 71; *Quattro lettere (Kranichsteiner Kammerkantate)*, 179–80, 249, 274, 415, 426, 430; *Requiem*, 28, 399; *Serenata per undici strumenti*, 399; *Studi per "Il Processo" di Kafka*, 55, 149, 404; String Quartet in two movements, 150
Magris, Claudio, 252
Magritte, René, 388
Mahler, Gustav, 31, 43–44, 49, 111, 115, 245, 340; First Symphony in D Major, 49, 245; Fifth Symphony, *Adagietto* from the, 31; Ninth Symphony, 43–44

484 | General Index

Malcolm X, 292, 355
Malevich, Kazimir Severinovich, 57, 118
Malina, Judith, 226, 354
Malipiero, Gian Francesco, 1, 3, 4, 27–29,
    33–35, 47, 50, 101, 103, 114, 237, 255,
    325–26, 327, 400, 403, 439, 465;
    Orfeide, 400
Malipiero, Riccardo, 399; *Piccolo concerto*,
    399
Mallarmé, Stéphane, 106–7, 118
Malvezzi, Piero, 181
Manca di Nissa, Bernadette, 239, 312, 437
Mann, Thomas, 52
Mannheim, Karl, 442
Manns, Patricio, 330
Manupelli, George, 397
Manzoni, Giacomo, 110, 224, 248, 259,
    291, 334, 460; *La sentenza*, 224
Marighella, Carlos, 299, 435
Markos. *See* Vafiadis, Markos
Marquez, Gabriel García, 82, 86, 407
Martelli, Claudio, 362, 446
Martí, José, 329, 440
Martini, Arturo, 27, 33
Martini, Giovanni Battista, 327
Martinů, Bohuslav Jan, 408; *Sonata da
    camera*, 408
Marx, Karl; Marxism; Marxian; Marxist, 8,
    52, 185, 226, 290, 291, 337, 430, 441,
    475
Mascagni, Andrea, 111
Mayakovsky, Vladimir Vladimirovich, 7,
    24, 57, 67, 71, 186, 196, 275, 282, 399,
    473
Mazzini, Benedetta (Mina), 282
McCarthy, Joseph, 52, 188
McLow, Jackson, 423
McLuhan, Marshall, 106
Mehta, Zubin, 247
Meinhof, Ulrike, 81
Meister Eckhart. *See* Eckhart, Johannes
Mengelberg, Misha, 31
Menotti, Gian Carlo; "Menotticizing," 111,
    409
Melville, Herman, 476
Merleau-Ponty, Maurice, 158, 171, 413
Merulo, Claudio, 29
Messiaen, Olivier, 62, 180, 454; *Modes de
    valeurs et d'intensités*, 454; *Oiseaux
    exotiques*, 180
Metzger, Heinz-Klaus, 290, 401, 402, 408,
    428, 429, 431, 432, 461
Metzger, Mayor Ludwig, 48
Meyer-Eppler, Werner, 71, 248, 444

Meyerhold, Vsevolod Emilevich, 7, 57,
    71–73, 218, 227, 282, 322, 421
Michaelstaedter, Carlo Raimondo, 312
Michel, Louise, 98, 475
Mila, Massimo, 12, 59, 65, 66, 77, 180,
    256, 363, 397, 405, 408, 414, 415, 446,
    460
Milosz, Czeslaw, 476
Milyutin, Nikolay Alexeyevich, 118
Mina. *See* Mazzini, Benedetta
Mingus, Charles, 282, 426
Miró, Joan, 86, 87
Mitropoulos, Dimitri, 245
Mittner, Ladislao, 408
Moholy-Nagy, László, 113
Molnár, Farkas, 222, 422
Mondrian, Piet, 388
Monteverdi, Claudio, 4, 27, 34, 107, 156,
    255, 322, 325, 327, 337, 348, 378, 413,
    443; *Concerto: Settimo Libro de
    Madrigali*, 413; *Lettera amorosa*, 156,
    413; *Orfeo*, 34; *Quinto libro de
    Madrigali*, 443; *Madrigali Guerrieri et
    Amorosi*, 156
Morandi, Giorgio, 34
Moreau, Gustave, 392
Morelli, Giovanni, 383, 448, 468
Motz, Wolfgang, 113
Mozart, Wolfgang Amadeus, 167, 168, 186,
    278, 431; *Requiem* KV 626, 167
Müller, Heiner, 113
Müller-Blattau, Joseph, 155, 157
Mumma, Gordon, 397
Musil, Robert, 9, 42, 238, 368, 370, 447
Mussorgsky, Modest Petrovich, 3, 31, 75,
    154, 239, 279, 285, 322; *Boris
    Godunov*, 3, 31

Neruda, Pablo, 7, 472
Newton, Isaac, 217
Niculescu, Stefan, 284
Nietzsche, Friedrich Wilhelm, 10, 91, 114,
    117, 120, 312, 315, 438, 476
Noland, Kenneth, 189
Noll, Bernd, 109
Nono, Serena Bastiana, 77, 79, 85, 189
Nono, Luigi, Sr., 3, 30
Nono, Silvia, 67, 79, 85, 189, 447

Ockeghem, Johannes, 41, 282
Ogolovets, Alexej Stepanovich, 112, 237
Olah, Tiberiu, 284
Oldenburg, Claes, 189, 282, 288
Olimareños (Los), 331

Ortiz, Fernando, 50, 253, 386
Otto, Susanne, 119, 121, 312, 437

Pacheco, Jesus López, 221, 276, 473
Padilla, Herberto, 308, 434, 437
Pajetta, Giancarlo, 96
Palestrina, Giovanni Pierluigi da, 31; *Missa Papae Marcelli*, 31
Palmastierna, Gunilla, 74
Parra, Angel, 330
Parra, Isabel, 330, 331
Parra, Ramona, 329
Parra, Violeta, 329, 330, 440
Pärt, Arvo, 283
Pasolini, Pier Paolo, 475
Pasternak, Boris Leonidovich, 476
Patkowski, Josef, 69
Paul (the Apostle), 391
Pavese, Cesare, 7, 33, 59, 67–68, 75, 82, 98, 171, 275, 276, 407, 424, 451, 473, 474, 475
Pavone, Rita, 282
Pekarsky, Mark, 112
Penderecki, Krzysztof, 295, 342
Peredo, 'Inti', 299, 329, 435
Perten, Hanns Anselm, 230
Pestalozza, Luigi, 111, 187, 273, 280, 291, 429–30, 457
Petrassi, Goffredo, 28, 406; *Coro di morti*, 406
Petrov, Nikolai, 421
Petrucci, Ottaviano, 29, 326; *Odhecaton*, 29
Philip II, King of Spain, 89, 383
Piacentini, Franca, 350
Piano, Renzo, 10, 117–19, 246, 426
Picasso, Pablo, 56, 59, 86, 220, 221
Piero della Francesca, 77, 392
Pietilä, Reima, 228, 423
Pinochet Ugarte, Augusto José Ramón, 84
Pirandello, Luigi, 218, 227
Pirelli, Giovanni, 84, 181, 353, 354, 431, 473, 474, 477
Pirosmani, Niko, 392
Piscator, Erwin, 7, 57, 71–74, 218, 227, 229–33, 282, 322, 406, 421, 424
Pizzetti, Ildebrando, 111
Planck, Max, 386, 449
Plato; Platonic, 29, 385
Poe, Edgar Allan, 476
Poli, Liliana, 83, 297, 350, 355
Pollini, Maurizio, 93, 99, 100, 377
Pollock, Jackson, 65, 67, 392
Pontormo. *See* Carucci, Jacopo

Popper, Leo, 339
Posadas, Florencio, 294
Pound, Ezra Weston Loomis, 312, 423
Pousseur, Henri, 6, 44, 248, 402
Priuli Bon [family], 3, 30
Prokofiev, Sergei Sergejewitsch, 111–12, 409
Proust Marcel, 77
Puccini, Giacomo, 110
Purcell, Henry, 115

Quasimodo, Salvatore, 54, 404, 472
Quyen, Phan Thi, 296

Rääts, Jaan, 283
Radok, Alfréd, 72, 194, 322, 438
Radok, Emil, 438
Rameau Jean-Philippe, 333
Rasputin, Grigori Yefimovich, 362
Rauschenberg, Robert Milton Ernest, 289, 432
Ravazzi, Gabriella, 350
Ravel, Maurice, 62, 66, 106, 110, 405; *Pavane pour une infante défunte*, 66
Recabarrén, Luis Emilio, 305, 329, 436, 440
Reich, Willi, 134, 411, 454
Restagno, Enzo, 14, 20, 398, 407–49, 452
Riemann, Hugo, 333
Rihm, Wolfgang, 112; *Hamletmaschine*, 112
Rilke, Rainer Maria; Rilkean, 3, 9, 33, 36, 61, 105, 312, 393, 475, 476
Rimbaud, Arthur, 475
Rimsky-Korsakov, Nikolai Andreyevich, 34
Ripellino, Angelo Maria, 57, 71–73, 196, 218, 404, 406, 419, 421, 473
Ritoók, Emma, 442
Rizzardi, Veniero, 399
Rodríguez, Gitano, 330
Roland-Manuel. *See* Lévy, Roland Alexis Manuel
Roldán, Amadeo, 50, 86, 252, 253, 317, 403, 427; *The Rebambaramba*, 427; *Ritmicas*, 427; *Tres toques*, 253, 427
Ronconi, Luca, 258, 422, 427
Rosbaud, Hans, 52
Rosenberg, Wolf, 428
Rosenzweig, Franz, 50, 114, 312, 393
Rossanda, Rossana, 256, 463
Rosselli brothers, 59
Rossi, Francesco, 32
Rossini, Gioachino Antonio, 46, 373; *Maometto II*, 373–74

Rothko, Mark, 45
Rozanov, Vasily Vasilievich, 112
Rozhdestvensky, Gennady, 283
Rudolf II, King of Hungary and Bohemia, 50, 92
Rubbia, Carlo, 371, 448
Rublev, Andrey, 77, 392
Rufer, Josef, 133-34, 411
Ruggles, Carl, 50, 288
Rûmî, Gialâl ad-Dîn, 393
Runge, Philipp Otto, 118

Sacchini, Antonio, 3, 30; *Montezuma*, 3, 30
Safi-ad-din (Safiy-yüd-Din), 50, 386
Salmanov, Vadim Nikolaevich, 283
Sánchez, Celia, 98, 475
Sánchez, Sonia, 445, 474
Sandberg, Mordecai, 237
Santamaría Cuadrado, Haydée, 98, 331, 440, 475
Saporta, Marc, 225
Sartre, Jean-Paul, 7, 8, 15, 71, 161, 195, 196, 213, 223, 256, 279, 291, 413, 417, 418, 420, 431, 473
Savonarola, Girolamo, 102, 393
Scabia, Giuliano, 257, 280, 354, 422, 424, 474, 477
Scarponi, Ciro, 116, 119, 239, 244, 311, 377, 378, 437
Scelba, Mario, 180-81, 415
Schaeffer, Pierre, 56, 68, 313, 315, 404
Schaft, Hannie, 475
Scharoun, Hans, 119, 243, 426
Schelling, Friedrich Wilhelm Joseph von, 258
Scherchen, Hermann, 5, 34, 47-49, 51-58, 61, 70, 74, 101, 103, 110, 157, 247, 249, 326, 360, 363, 403-5, 426, 452, 453, 472
Scheu, Joseph, 337
Schiaffini, Giancarlo, 119, 239, 244, 311, 377, 378, 437
Schiele, Egon, 392
Schiller, Johann Christoph Friedrich von, 158, 258
Schillinger, Joseph, 7, 266-67, 401-2, 428-29
Schlegel, August Wilhelm von, 157
Schmitz, Arnold, 155, 156, 161
Schneider Marius, 51
Schnittke, Alfred, 77, 111, 112, 283
Schoenberg Nono, Nuria, 5, 13, 51-53, 59, 63, 71, 79, 85, 185, 189, 394, 403, 405, 465
Schoenberg, Randol, 53

Schoenberg Arnold, ix, 2, 4, 5, 19, 34-35, 40, 43, 48-53, 56, 58, 61, 63, 74, 75, 82, 101, 103, 114, 118, 126, 127-29, 133-35, 153-54, 157-62, 179, 185, 208, 215-16, 218, 236, 239, 248-49, 252, 254-55, 276, 279, 282, 285, 316-17, 322-23, 325-27, 332-37, 339, 341-44, 368, 382-84, 403, 404, 406, 411, 441, 442, 443, 445, 447, 454, 476; *A Survivor from Warsaw* op. 46, 55, 161-62, 179, 216; Concerto for Piano and Orchestra op. 42, 327; *De Profundis* (Psalm 130) op. 50b, 53; *Die glückliche Hand* op. 18, 118, 215, 218, 323; *Die Jakobsleiter*, 216; Kammersymphonie n. 1 op. 9, 368; *Ode to Napoleon* op. 41, 5, 42, 255; *Pierrot lunaire* op. 21, 160, 427, 445; *Moses und Aron*, 51, 160, 216, 252, 261; Second String Quartet op. 10, 406; Serenade op. 24, 127-28; Third String Quartet op. 30, 405; Variations for Orchestra op. 31, 128-29, 134, 135-41, 411, 453-54
Schopenhauer, Arthur, 45
Schnittke, Alfred, 77, 111-12, 283
Schubert, Franz, 41-43, 153-54, 158, 186
Schuller, Gunther, 7, 396, 426
Schulz, Johann Abraham Peter, 157-58
Schumann, Robert, 31, 40-43, 81, 388; Fantasy in C op. 17, 40, 43, 388-89
Schygulla, Hanna, 362
Sciarrino, Salvatore, 46, 110, 259, 364
Scodanibbio, Stefano, 119, 239, 311, 437
Scott, Tony, 397
Scriabin, Alexander, 46, 47, 49, 112, 118, 402; *The Poem of Ecstasy*, 118; *Prometheus*, 118
Selvatico, Lino, 30
Shakespeare, William, 28, 232, 324, 424, 438, 473
Shchedrin, Rodion Konstantinovich, 283
Shostakovich, Dmitri Dmitriyevich, 64, 112, 179
Sinfonia n. 10, 179
Sonata for Viola and Piano, op. 147, 64
Siciliani, Francesco, 72
Silvestrov, Valentin Vassilievich, 283
Simmel, Georg, 339
Sironi, Mario, 34
Slonimsky, Sergei Mikhailovich, 283, 400
Smith, William Overton (Bill), 350
Snel, Riek, 475
Solovyov, Vladimir Sergeyevich, 112
Somfai, Laszló, 340

General Index | 487

Sophocles, 423
Spahlinger, Mathias, 113
Spano, Flavio, 466
Squarzina, Luigi, 420
St. Francis of Assisi, 36
Stalin, Joseph (Dzhugashvili, Iosif Vissarionovich); Stalinist, 57, 64, 69, 96, 110, 283
Stein, Erwin, 52, 332
Steinecke, Hella, 67
Steinecke, Wolfgang, 44, 48, 67, 103, 248–49, 290, 401, 402, 428, 460
Stenzl, Jürg, 461
Steuermann, Edward, 48, 61, 250
Stockhausen, Doris, 71
Stockhausen, Karlheinz, 2, 6, 11, 44–45, 48, 63–65, 68, 71, 90, 103, 120, 131, 135, 150–51, 176–77, 180, 182, 219, 248, 250, 252, 261, 289, 293, 296, 316, 343, 386, 401, 407, 411, 413, 415, 416, 420, 432, 433, 460; *Gesang der Jünglinge* [The Song of the Youths], 71, 120, 180, 415; *Klavierstück I*, 131–32; *Klavierstücke I–IV*, 411; *Klavierstück XI*, 316; *Komposition 1953 Nr. 2 für Sinustöne* [*Studie I*], 150; *Momente*, 219; *Originale*, 224, 227, 422; *Zeitmaße*, 151, 411, 413
Stockhausen, Julius, 182
Strada, Vittorio, 274, 429–30
Strauss, Richard, 46, 116
Strauss, Rudolf (Rudi), 83, 109, 239, 311, 317, 437
Stravinsky Igor Fyodorovich, 4, 33, 48, 61–63, 86, 114, 180, 249, 255, 314, 405; *Canticum Sacrum ad honorem Sancti Marci nominis*, 63, 180, 405, 415, 438; *Les noces*, 62, 63, 405; *Monumentum pro Gesualdo da Venosa ad CD annum*, 63, 405; *The Rite of Spring*, 62
Striggio, Alessandro, 76
Strobel, Heinrich, 48, 54
Stroe, Aurel, 284
Stroppa, Marco, 92, 111, 356, 361, 371, 445, 447
Stuckenschmidt, Hans-Heinz, 48
Suzuki, Daisetz Teitaro, 267, 432
Svoboda, Josef, 72, 73, 186–87, 194, 229–30, 321–24, 417, 424, 438–39, 455
Syrkus, Szymon, 244

Tafuri, Manfredo, 364, 447
Tairov Alexander Yakovlevich, 218

Takemitsu, Toru, 387
Tallis, Thomas, 76, 388, 390, 392
Spem in alium nunquam habui, 390, 450
Tambroni, Ferdinando, 418
Tápies, Antoni, 392
Tarkovsky, Andrei Arsenyevich, 81, 363, 387, 450
Tatlin, Vladimir Yevgraphovich, 57, 282
Teilhard de Chardin, Pierre, 284
Teitelboim Volosky, Valentín (Volodia), 298–99, 434
Thcavar, Vaffarti, 20
Theotokopulos, Domenico (El Greco), 392
Theus, Christine, 437
Thompson, Eli "Lucky," 397
Tieck, Ludwig, 218–19, 227
Tiepolo, Giovanni Battista, 77
Timotheus of Miletus, 237
Tintoretto, Jacopo, 57, 65, 77, 392, 450
Tishchenko, Boris Iwanowitsch, 283
Tobey, Mark, 45
Tofler, Lili, 230
Togliatti, Palmiro, 72, 96, 282–83, 406
Togni, Camillo, 399; *Variazioni* for piano and orchestra, 399
Toller, Ernst, 57, 195, 276, 282
Tolnay, Károl, 442
Tomic, Radomiro, 306, 436
Torres, Juan José, 302, 435
Toscanini, Arturo, 31
Troni, Umberto (Berto), 297, 350
Trotskyists, 188
Tudor, David, 271, 401, 428, 429
Turchi, Guido, 28, 399, 406; *Cinque commenti alle "Baccanti" di Euripide*, 406; *Trio*, 399
Turner, Joseph Mallord William, 77–78, 392

Ugarte, Fernando, 330
Uitti, Frances-Marie, 389
Ulivi, Giacomo, 162
Ulyanov, Vladimir Ilich (Lenin), 274, 281–83, 429, 475
Ungaretti, Giuseppe, 7, 36, 58, 67–68, 76, 103, 275, 400, 408, 473

Vacchi, Fabio, 111
Vakhtàngov, Sergei Evgenevich, 244
Vafiadis, Markos, 180, 415
Van Gogh, Vincent, 77
Van Troy, Nguyen, 296
Varèse, Edgar, 5, 7, 46–51, 54–56, 61, 66, 70–71, 76, 85–86, 103, 179, 247–48,

Varèse, Edgar *(continued)*
  252–53, 317, 339, 342–43, 361, 392, 402, 403, 427, 438; *Arcana*, 76, 179, 403; *Déserts*, 71; *Ionisation*, 51, 253, 427; *Poème électronique*, 70–71
Vasarely, Victor, 289, 432
Vedova, Emilio, 35, 57, 65, 69, 72–73, 87, 118–19, 198, 245, 323, 359, 392, 422, 439
Verdi, Giuseppe, 47, 75, 107, 110, 116, 154, 230, 239, 279, 285, 324, 409, 425; *Il trovatore*, 230, 322; *Otello*, 47; *Requiem*, 75, 409
Verlaine, Paul, 33
Vertov, Dziga, 57
Vespignani, Arcangelo, 27, 32–35
Vespignani, Giovanni, 32
Vespignani, Luigi, 32
Vicente, Lusitano, 237
Vicentino, Nicola, 4, 27, 38, 237, 385, 449
Vicini, Elena, 297, 350, 355
Victoria, Tomás Luis de, 76, 383, 392
Vidolin, Alvise, 92, 240, 357, 371, 425, 467
Viglietti, Daniel, 331
Vio, Luigi, 399
Viola, Francesco della, 29
Vishnegradsky, Ivan Alexandrovich, 112, 237
Vittorini, Elio, 60, 400
Vlad, Roman, 28
Volkonsky, Andrei Mikhaylovich (André), 283, 427, 445; *Musica stricta*, 427, 445
Volkov, Solomon, 64
Vysotsky, Volodya, 96

Wagner, Richard, 31, 45–47, 75, 91–92, 107, 157, 441; *Meistersinger*, 441; *Tristan*, 46, 76; *Siegfried*, 91
Walbe, Joel, 235
Walser, Robert, 41
Walter, Bruno, 110
Ward, John, 238, 425
Weber, Max, 339
Webern, Anton, 4–5, 19, 34–35, 41–44, 47–49, 51–52, 54, 60, 64, 75, 101, 125–26, 129, 134, 142, 147–49, 155, 248–49, 252, 255, 269, 317, 324–26, 339, 342–43, 401, 408, 410, 411, 416, 427, 428; *Concerto for Nine Instruments*, op. 24, 44; *Quartet* op. 28, 427; *Symphony* op. 21, 129, 408; *Variations* op. 30, 134, 142–48
Weill, Kurt, 217, 249, 322; *Aufstieg und Fall der Stadt Mahagonny*, 217
Weininger, Andor, 222, 422
Weiss, Peter, 73–74, 78, 229–30, 232, 406, 423, 424
Weizsäcker, Karl Friedrich von, 171
Wenders, Wim, 362
Wilbye, John, 238
Willaert, Adrian, 29, 107
Winckel, Fritz, 249, 426
Wittgenstein, Ludwig, 38, 47, 89, 109, 311, 345, 368, 402, 438, 447
Wolf, Hugo, 3, 30, 41–43; *Italienische Lieder*, 3, 30; *Montezuma*, 30
Wolff, Christian, 401, 429
Wörner, Karl-Heinz, 44
Woytowicz, Stefania, 233

Xenakis, Iannis, 40, 49, 70, 180, 342; *Metastasis*, 180

Yesenin, Sergei Alexandrovich, 33, 67, 276
Yoshihara, Jiro, 423

Zafred, Mario, 28
Zandonai, Riccardo, 111
Zarlino, Gioseffo, 4, 27–29, 50, 237, 332
Zedong (Tse-Tung), Mao, 283
Zeffirelli, Franco, 381
Zelter, Carl Friedrich, 157
Zhdanov, Andrei Alexandrovich; Zhdanovism, 64, 80, 110, 211, 296
Zuccheri, Marino, 70, 73, 82–83, 93, 98, 100, 182–83, 241, 315, 349–57, 405, 425, 438, 444–45
Zujovic, Edmundo Pérez, 300, 303, 435

Index of Luigi Nono's Works

1°) *Caminantes . . . Ayacucho*, 66, 120–21, 410, 447, 449, 476
2°) *"No hay caminos, hay que caminar" . . . Andrej Tarkowskij*, 120, 410, 477

A Carlo Scarpa, architetto, ai suoi infiniti possibili, 396, 476
A floresta é jovem e cheja de vida, 7, 78, 81, 83–84, 279, 285–86, 296, 353, 359, 423, 431, 433, 434, 436, 445, 474
Al gran sole carico d'amore, 8, 9, 64, 74, 95–96, 98–100, 257–59, 313–14, 350, 440, 475
A Pierre. Dell'azzurro silenzio, inquietum, 359, 476

Canciones a Guiomar, 74, 78, 276, 422, 474
Canti di vita e d'amore. Sul ponte di Hiroshima, 74, 78, 276, 422, 473
Canti per 13, 59, 60, 64, 473
Como una ola de fuerza y luz, 93–94, 100, 359, 475
Composizione per orchestra [n. 1], 406, 472
Composizione per orchestra n. 2—Diario polacco '58, 6, 68–69, 276, 417, 473
Composizione per orchestra n. 2—Diario polacco '58 (vers. 1965), 474
Con Luigi Dallapiccola, 101–2, 253, 359, 388, 427, 475

Contrappunto dialettico alla mente, 78, 82–83, 296, 355, 435, 474
Cori di Didone, 6, 9, 67–68, 76, 94, 171, 178, 183, 275, 363, 415, 430, 473

Da un diario italiano, 474
Das atmende Klarsein, 10, 242, 359, 424, 447, 475
Découvrir la subversion. Hommage à Edmond Jabès, 360, 471, 476
Deola e Masino (music theater project), 477
Die Ermittlung, 73, 229–34, 406, 423–24, 458, 474
¿Donde estás, hermano?, 359, 476
Due espressioni per orchestra, 9, 472
Due liriche greche, 101, 125, 471, 472

Ein Gespenst geht um in der Welt, 440, 475
Epitaffio a Federico García Lorca, 53, 55, 69, 94, 426, 430; I: *España en el corazón*, 6, 54, 75, 472; II: *Y su sangre ya viene cantando*, 54–55, 472; III: *Memento. Romance de la Guardia civil española*, 404, 472

Fragmente-Stille, an Diotima, 9, 69, 75, 103–8, 240–41, 257, 314, 359, 408, 409, 427, 438, 475
Frammenti da "Al gran sole carico d'amore," 475
Für Paul Dessau, 433, 475, 473

489

Index of Luigi Nono's Works

Guai ai gelidi mostri, 10, 114–15, 243, 312–13, 359, 409, 437, 476

"Ha venido." Canciones para Silvia, 67–68, 183, 410, 473
"Hay que caminar" sognando, 120, 410, 477

I Turcs tal Friûl, 475
Il canto sospeso, 7, 9, 15, 49, 63–67, 75, 94, 105, 132, 168, 176, 179–83, 275, 403, 405, 414, 415, 430, 444, 455, 473
Il mantello rosso (Der rote Mantel), 55, 193, 417, 472
Il mantello rosso, suite da concerto (A and B), 473
Incontri, 6, 25, 64–65, 150, 205, 297, 473
Intolleranza 1960, 8, 10–11, 15, 71–75, 78, 95–97, 185–88, 193–208, 211, 222, 224, 228, 247, 273, 275–26, 323, 359, 403, 404, 406, 416, 417–19, 421, 439, 455, 456, 473
Intolleranza 1970 (vers. Nurenberg), 474
Io, frammento dal Prometeo, 10, 475

Julius Fučík (incomplete), 418, 471, 472

La discesa di Cristo agli inferi, 4, 255, 472
La fabbrica illuminata, 78, 81–82, 234, 255–56, 280, 354, 359, 427, 445, 474
La lontananza nostalgica utopica futura. Madrigale per più "caminantes" con Gidon Kremer, 410, 424, 477
La terra e la compagna, 9, 67, 162–63, 168, 171, 183, 275, 363, 407, 414, 451, 473
La victoire de Guernica, 6, 55–56, 58–60, 69, 79, 472
Liebeslied, 59, 473
L'immaginazione prende il potere (music theater project), 439, 477

Musica-Manifesto n. 1: Un volto, e del mare—Non consumiamo Marx, 78–82, 296, 406, 431, 474
Musiche per Manzù, 474

Omaggio a Emilio Vedova, 69, 71, 359, 444, 473
Omaggio a György Kurtág, 115, 476

Per Bastiana—Tai-Yang Cheng, 78, 247, 297, 359, 473
Piccola gala notturna veneziana in onore dei sessanta anni di Heinrich Strobel, 473
Polifonica-Monodia-Ritmica, 6, 9, 54–55, 58, 75, 363, 396, 472
Post-Prae-Ludium per Donau, 477
Post-Prae-Ludium n. 3 BAAB-ARR, 471, 476, 477
Prometeo, 10, 66, 88, 115, 117–20, 235–46, 257–58, 359–60, 409, 424, 426, 427, 444, 446, 476

Quando stanno morendo. Diario polacco n. 2, 10, 66, 115, 312, 388–89, 359, 448, 450, 475

Ricorda cosa ti hanno fatto in Auschwitz, 73, 78, 363, 406, 474
Risonanze erranti. Liederzyklus a Massimo Cacciari, 66, 476

San Vittore 1969, 474
Sarà dolce tacere, 67–68, 473
Siamo la gioventù del Vietnam, 475
. . . . .sofferte onde serene . . . , 75, 99, 102, 258, 314, 359, 475
Suite da concerto da "Intolleranza 1960," 474

Technically Sweet (music theater project), 430, 477
Trio (movement of), 472

Un diario italiano (music theater project), 477

Varianti, 240, 473
Variazioni canoniche sulla serie dell'op. 41 di Arnold Schönberg, 5, 6, 42, 47–48, 55, 58, 247, 255, 472
Voci destroying muros, 440, 474

Was ihr wollt (incidental music), 473
Y entonces comprendió, 78, 81, 86–87, 241, 431, 474